DEPOSITION

Marissa Lee Benedict,
Daniel de Paula, and David Rueter

**Mousse
Publishing**

CONTENTS

Preface 7

I. ABSTRACTION

Diagrams 14

Manifesto 29

II. LATENCY

Storage (2018–21) 34

III. SPECULATION

Historical Images: Chicago Board of Trade 48

IV. EXCAVATION

Remnants 82

What State Are Things In? 98

Conversation with Dan Peterman

V. DISPLACEMENT

Interim 116

Chicago Loading 128

Tracking 134

São Paulo Unloading 142

VI. DEPOSITION

Installation 160

Property Lease Agreement (Template) 172

Contrato de Locação de Bem (Executado) 173

An Object Displaced, A Place to Gather Different Bodies 206
Conversation with Paulo Miyada and Jacopo Crivelli Visconti

VII. CIRCUMSCRIPTION
Levitators 226
Cameron Hu

About Wheels, Mills, Gears, and the Circle of Life 238
Yamila Goldfarb

Taking Stock 246
Ana Teixeira Pinto

VIII. REACTIVATION
Dimension of Art, Dimension of Life 256
Conversation with Beatriz Cruz and Vânia Medeiros

Bienal Programming 270

Texts in Portuguese 318
Biographies 338
Image Credits 343
Acknowledgments 344

PREFACE

i. Karsten Lund Chicago (USA)

It is a striking image: a huge octagonal structure planted at the heart of the Pavilhão Ciccillo Matarazzo, the iconic pavilion, designed by Oscar Niemeyer, which has been the setting for the Bienal de São Paulo since 1957. Hard geometry rises like a dark crystal among the smooth white curves of the building. Participating in the 34th edition of the Bienal, artists Marissa Lee Benedict, Daniel de Paula, and David Rueter staged this unlikely meeting of forms in the pavilion's central atrium. This moment, it's worth saying, is neither the beginning nor the end.

This enigmatic platform is worn by use; it looks like a place for gathering, an amphitheater in miniature. For most observers, though, its origins are probably hard to guess. This immense tangible shape becomes an abstraction of sorts, inviting speculation. In fact, it harkens to another setting where these same two functions—abstraction and speculation—were key, albeit in very different ways. This structure is, or rather was, a trading pit. For decades, professional traders in color-coded jackets packed themselves onto its seven tiered steps to buy and sell commodity futures—and specifically, on this one, to speculate on the future prices of corn. Benedict, de Paula, and Rueter acquired this trading pit, the thing itself, the last of its kind, from the Chicago Board of Trade (CBOT) after it was slated to be removed. New technology has changed the game, and the physical landscape of finance has changed with it.

One might describe *deposition* as an artist project, although its continuing evolution and its many phases—not to mention the artists' interests in both public display and hidden processes—all pose a challenge for any efforts to describe where the project begins and ends. On its surface, this volume follows the salvage, displacement, and exhibition of the trading pit, as the artists break apart its thirty-two substantial fragments and drag them from Chicago to São Paulo. Along with a large collection of images, this book includes essays and interviews that provide various perspectives from which to view the work. They move in range between intimate and distant, and in style from personal to scholarly to conversational. Gradually, these diverse contributions scan over the object, the many actors involved, the art institution, and the geopolitical landscape in which these elements operate.

The first half of the book begins with documents amassed by the artists and a descriptive account of the floor's salvage by artist and educator Dan Peterman. In this section, a series of archival photographs also excavate the history of financial trading in Chicago and the historical importance of the futures trading practices that developed in the city in the mid-nineteenth century and were carried into the twentieth century. In the second half of the book, the corn futures trading floor reappears, as it is reinstalled in one of the most iconic modernist pavilions in the world. Amid this architecture—haunted by the agro-industrial modernization of Brazil, its colonial histories, and the current volatility of the nation's political climate—the trading pit is repurposed by the artists within a tradition of institutional critique.

The presentation of *deposition* in São Paulo was not exactly a straightforward exhibition, at least not under the usual terms. This comes to light in the interview with two of the curators of the Bienal, Paulo Miyada and Jacopo Crivelli Visconti, as they discuss the artists' contract, their own interest in dialogue as a guiding practice, and the various negotiations involved in exhibiting *deposition*, which yielded a dynamic that is irreducible to the decisions of any one party. The curators' desire to use the platform as a stage for discourse and dissonance further shaped what unfolded in São Paulo, and for four months, the trading pit became the setting for a variety of assemblies and gatherings. An interview with the artists and programmers Vânia Medeiros and Beatriz Cruz, who organized one series of public programs at the Bienal, delves into this process wherein the octagon became a new staging ground or forum.

The trading floor's tiered octagonal form looks a bit like a vortex, as if it might pull everything into its center. But the movements of capitalism, ever-evolving, are more often centrifugal—spreading outward relentlessly. Global connections proliferate, in this case from the United States to Brazil and far beyond. In a series of new essays, cultural anthropologist Cameron Hu, geographer Yamila Goldfarb, and writer and theorist Ana Teixeira Pinto consider the outlines of *deposition* while introducing a much larger context and beginning to suggest what's at stake. In their contributions, they speak lucidly to countless interweaving forces: agribusiness, colonialism, technology, financialization, deregulation, patents, and geopolitical flows, to name just a few. They also touch on the history of art and literature, from which such things can hardly be disentangled.

In this book, and in *deposition* more broadly, it might at first seem like everything builds toward the moment of exhibition in Brazil, when the trading pit reappears on the world stage, exchanging the private halls of the CBOT for the public venue of a major international art exhibition. Ultimately, however, the Bienal is just one moment among others. Benedict, de Paula, and Rueter's work is not solely focused on the trading pit itself; it is also concerned with its movement and circulation, all the complex logistics and occasional friction that entails, and what this reveals about the world and its operational systems.

The trading pit was once a site of abstraction and speculation—qualities that still haunt it in its afterlife. As the chapter headings in this volume suggest, the artists also start to propose an expanding set of functions: excavation, displacement, circumscription, and reactivation. There is one other word that hovers over the book: "deposition," the project's title. "Deposition" has different meanings in different contexts: in a legal setting, it refers to evidentiary testimony gathered outside of court; in geology, it describes a process where sediments accumulate in a landform; in the histories of art and religion, it implies a burial and describes scenes of taking Jesus down from the cross; and in the political realm, it refers to the overthrowing of a monarch or another power. Section by section, this publication evokes many of these various meanings. Within the layers of images and texts here, Benedict, de Paula, and Rueter are engaged in their own acts of evidence gathering, excavation, removal, and slow accumulation.

In the end, their project is an open proposition more than a closed loop. *deposition* is invested in the trading pit's past and its present, but also its futures, most of which remain to be seen. As you reach the end of the book, it is not the end of the line. In the simplest sense, the trading floor has other destinations on the horizon already, places where it will be redeployed and reimagined. The deposits will continue to accumulate. The evidence will grow. For now, you can read what's been assembled in these pages; then, follow the shipping manifests and the data flows, and go ahead and bet on the future.

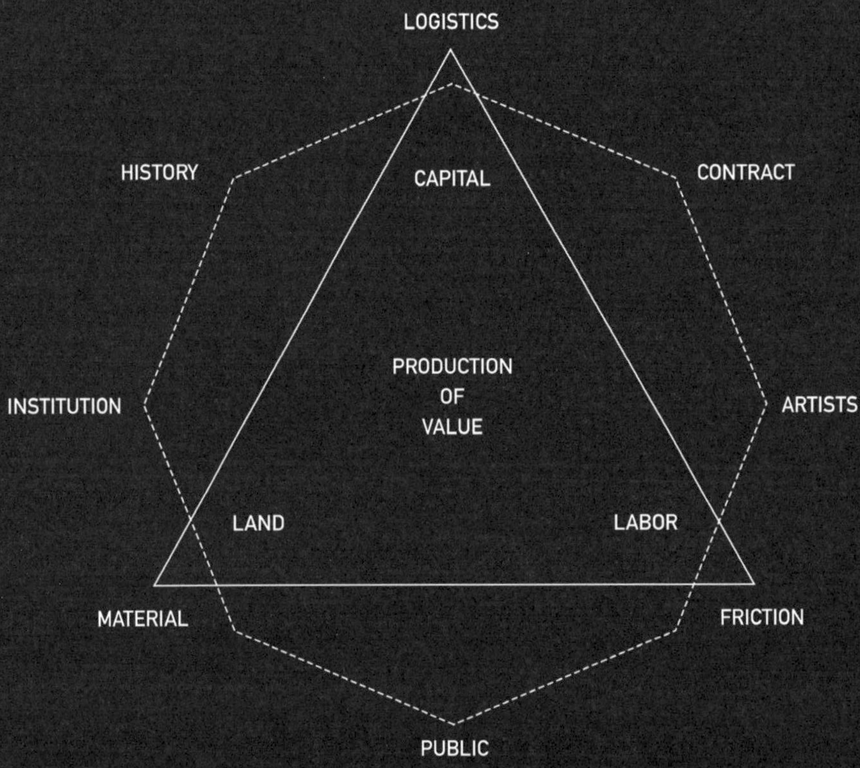
LOGISTICS
HISTORY
CAPITAL
CONTRACT
PRODUCTION
OF
VALUE
INSTITUTION
ARTISTS
LAND
LABOR
MATERIAL
FRICTION
PUBLIC

AB STRAC TION I

14

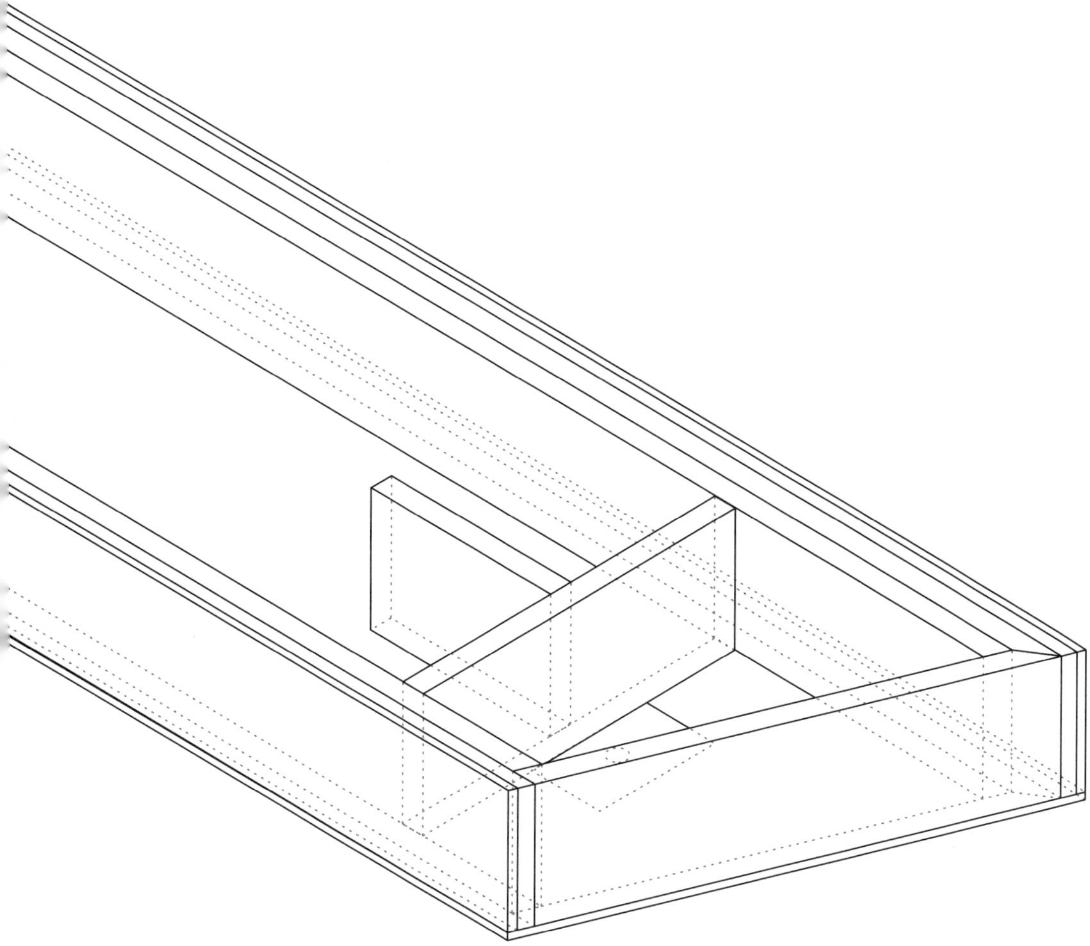

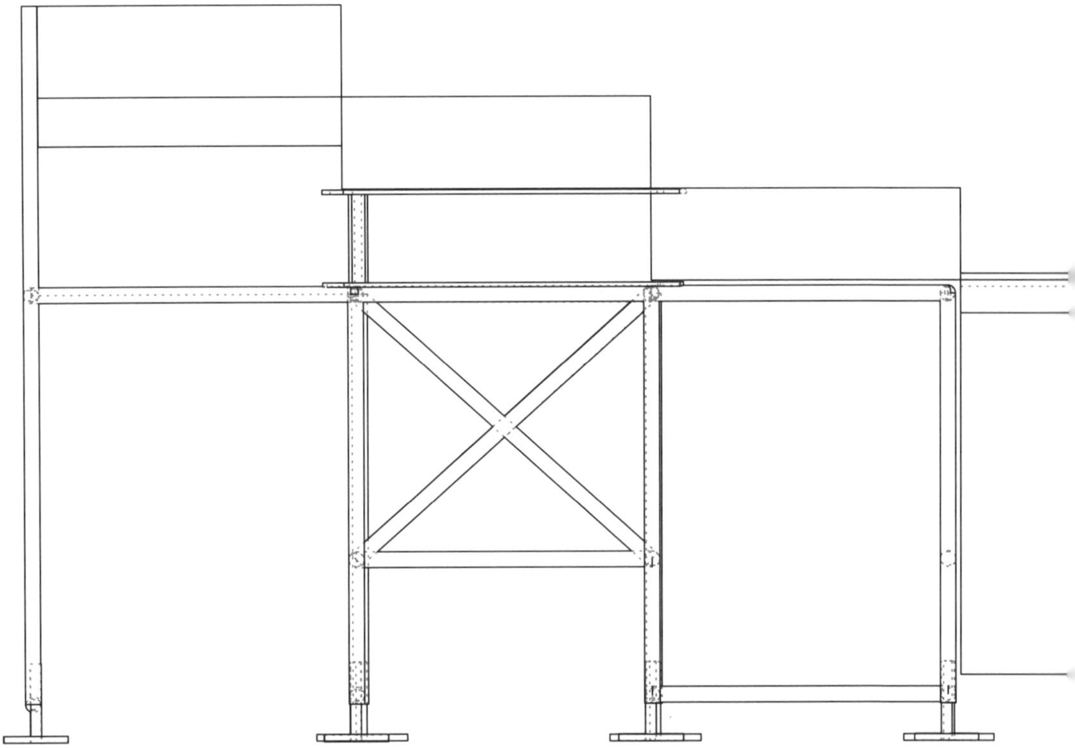

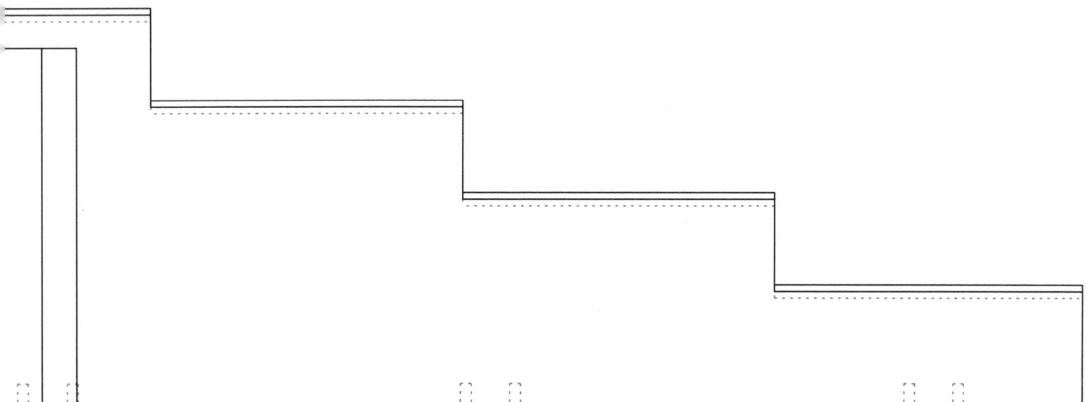

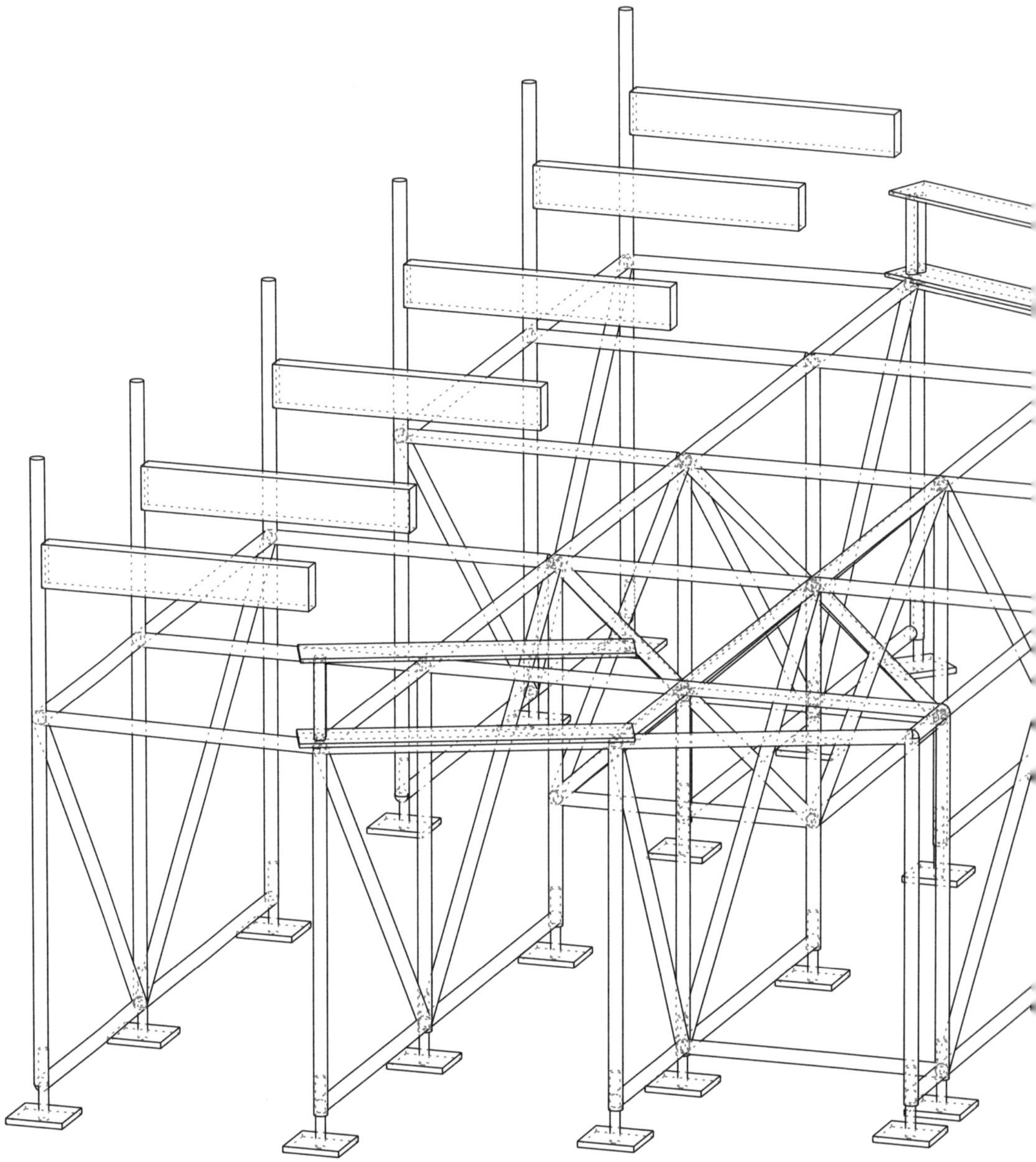

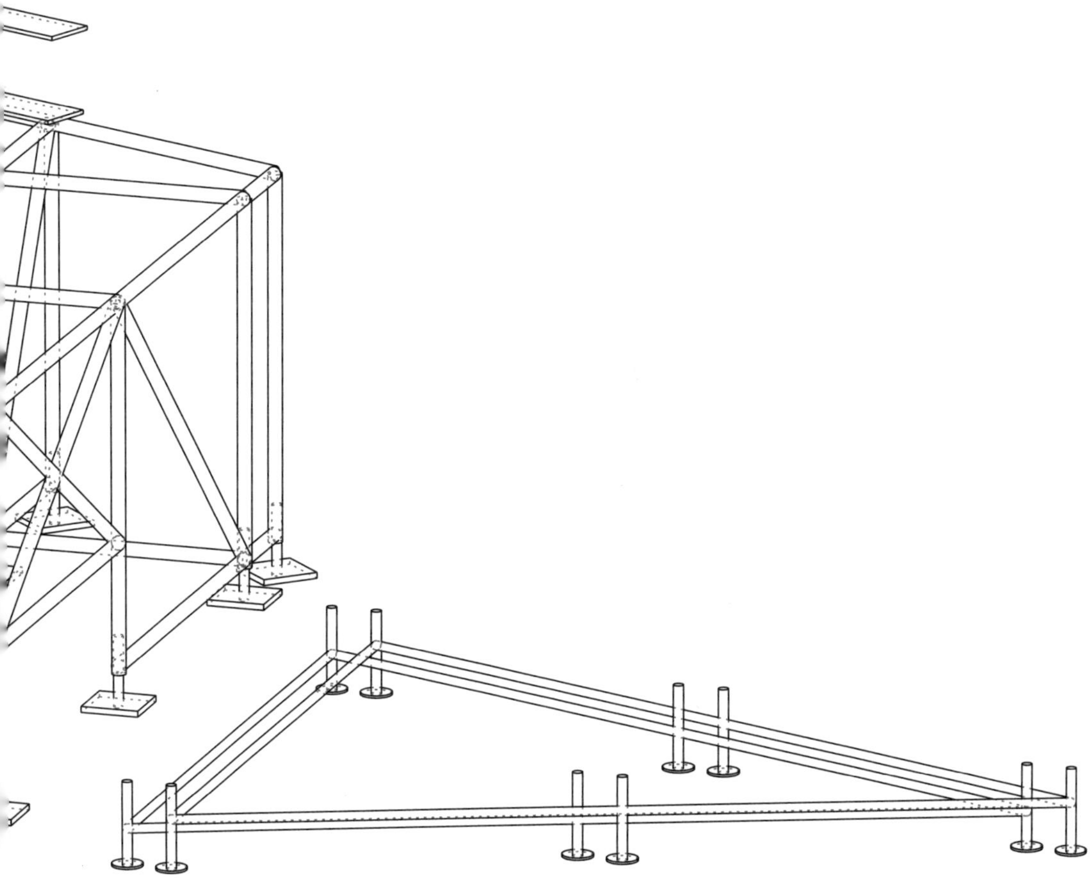

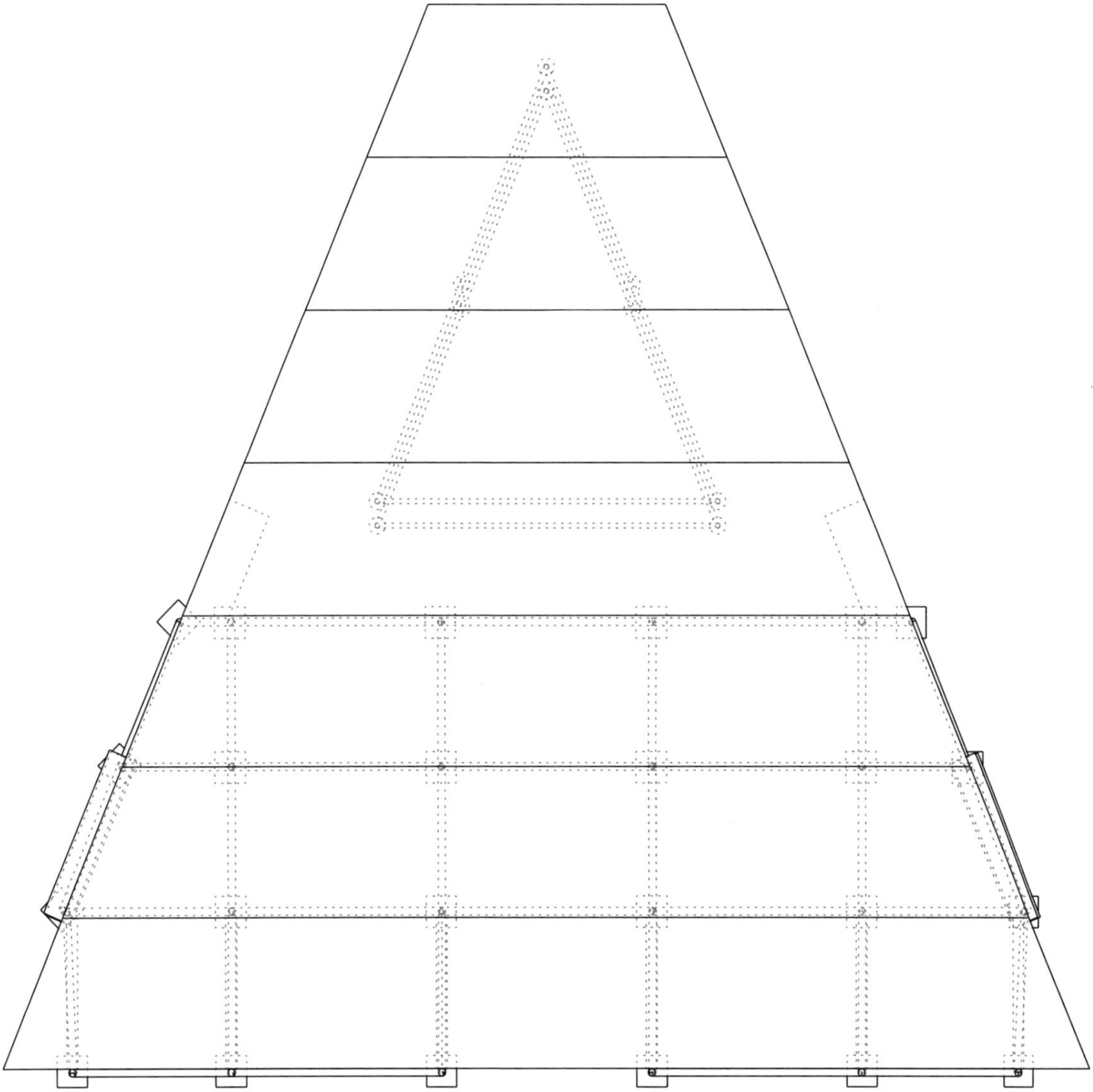

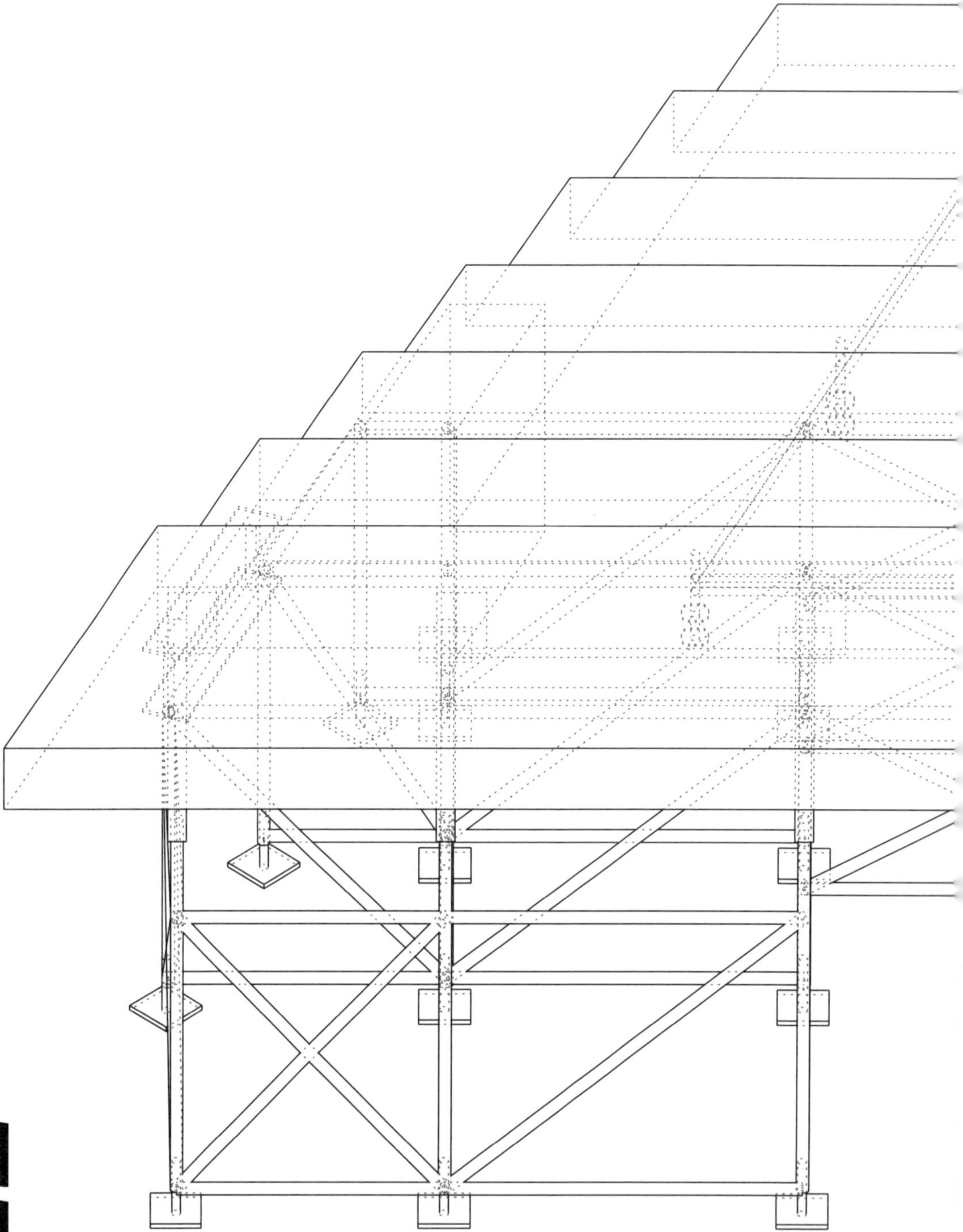

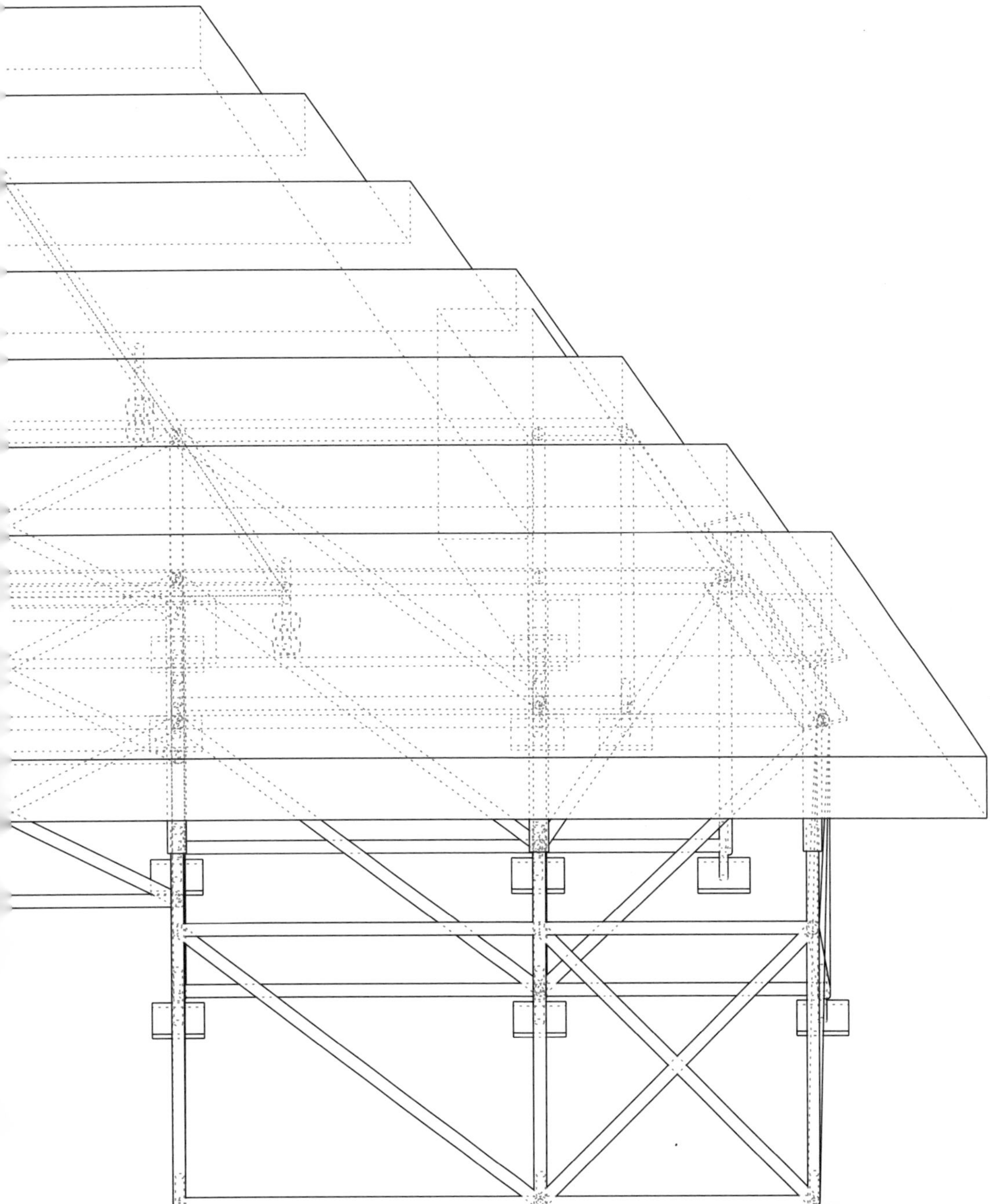

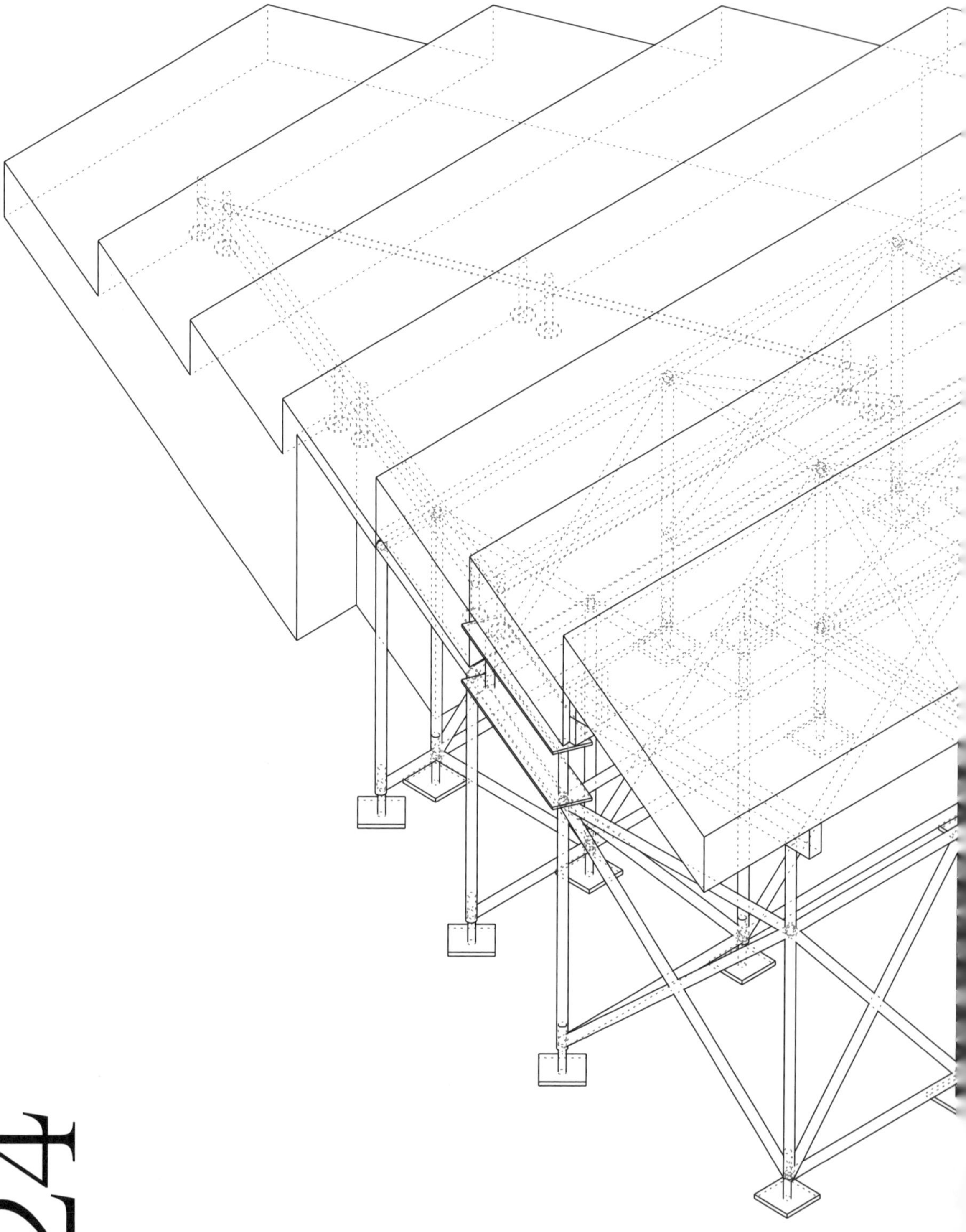

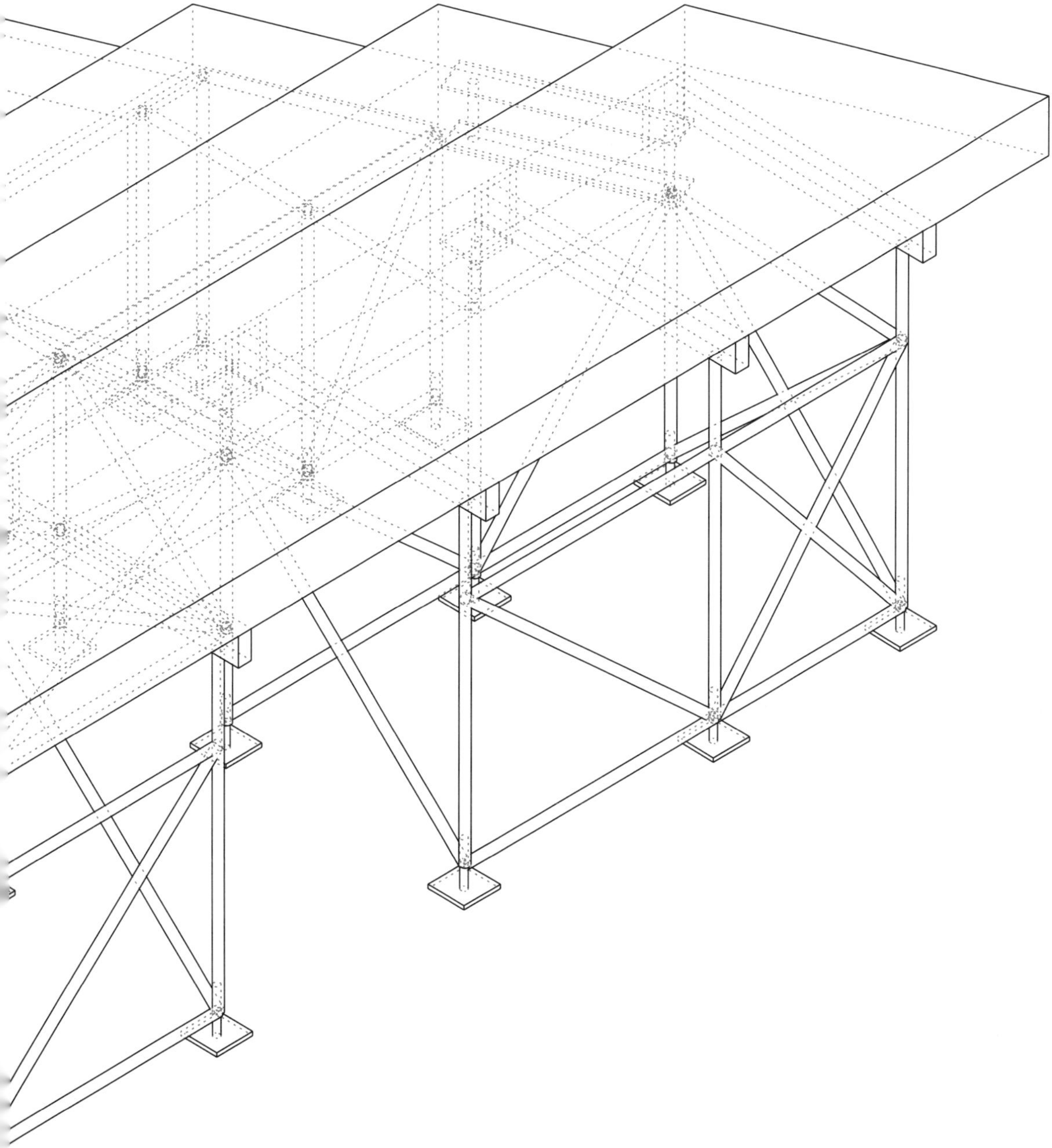

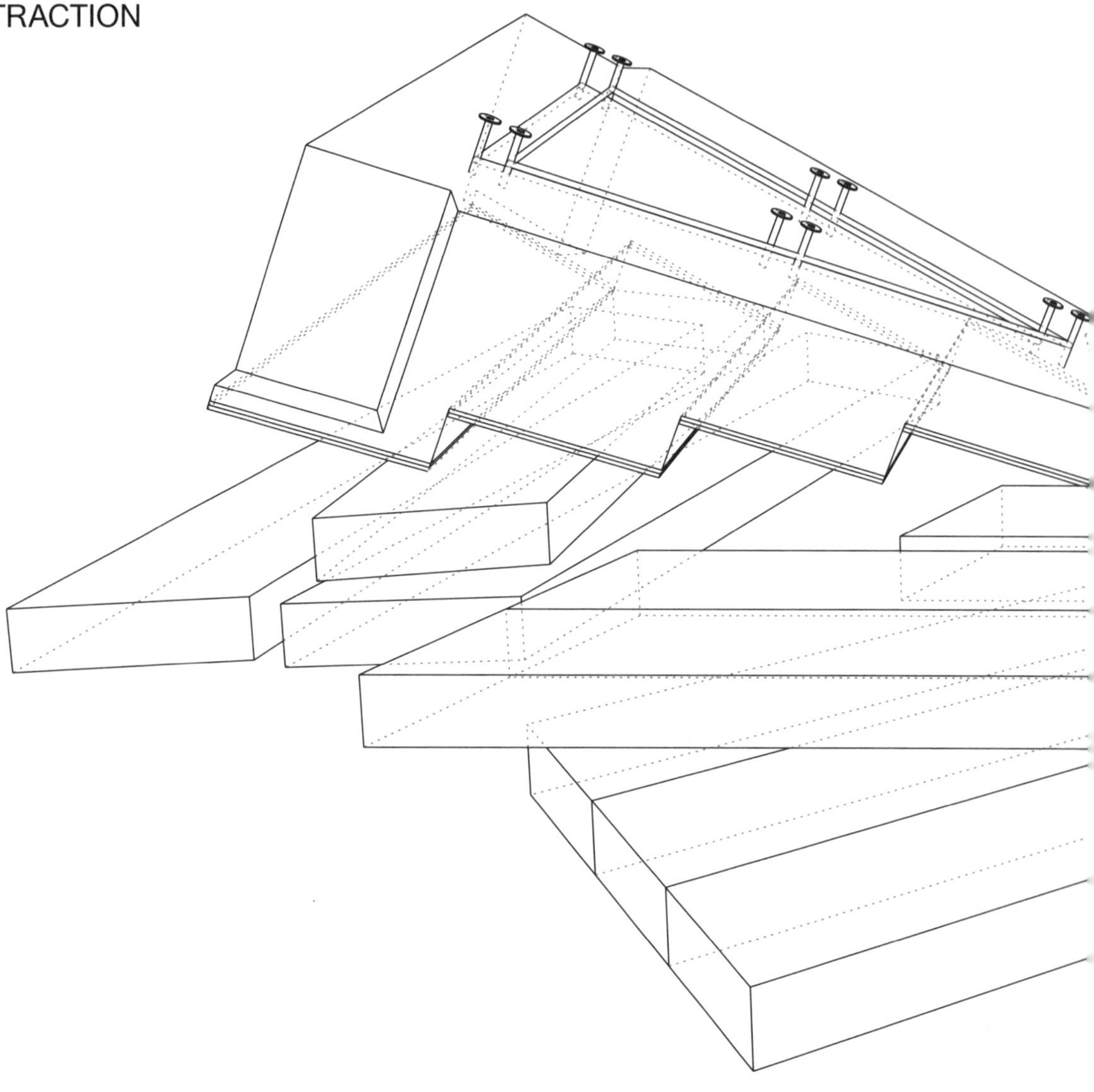

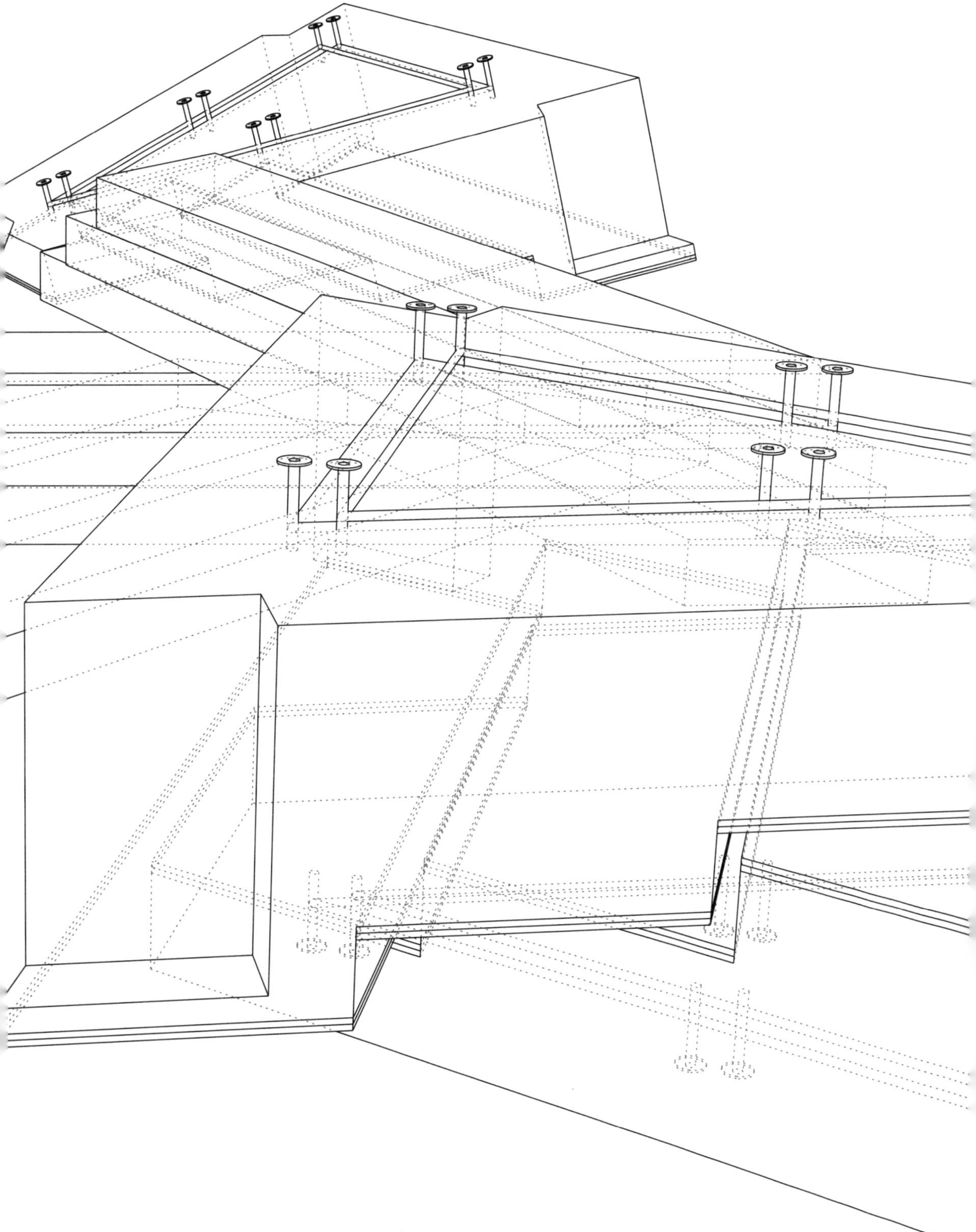

UNITED STATES PATENT OFFICE.

DANIEL DE PAULA OF BRAZIL
MARISSA LEE BENEDICT AND DAVID RUETER OF THE USA

IMPROVEMENT IN TRADING-PITS.

Specification forming part of Letters Patent No. **203,837,** dated May 21, 1878; application filed December 19, 1877.

To all whom it may concern:

WE[1] HAVE A TRADING PIT.[2]

IT IS SIGNIFICANT BECAUSE IT WAS USED IN THE 19TH, 20TH & 21ST CENTURIES,[3] BUT NOW IT IS OBSOLETE. IT IS OBSOLETE BECAUSE COMPUTER TECHNOLOGY AUTOMATED THE PRACTICES IT WAS DESIGNED FOR.[4]

WE GOT IT FOR FREE WHEN THEY THREW IT AWAY.[5] IT IS VERY HEAVY AND VERY BIG. IT IS BOTH MATERIAL AND IMAGE. IT HOLDS THE WEIGHT OF LAND, LABOR, AND CAPITAL.[6]

MANY HEAVY, MOSTLY LARGE, MOSTLY MALE BODIES FOUGHT AND YELLED AT EACH OTHER IN THE PIT.[7]

WE WANT TO PUT THE PIT IN A GALLERY. OR A PUBLIC SQUARE. OR A WAREHOUSE OR STORAGE FACILITY. OR A UNIVERSITY. FIRST IN PIECES. THEN AS A WHOLE THING AGAIN. WE ARE AWARE IT IS NEVER GOING BACK TOGETHER THE WAY IT WAS BEFORE.

WE WANT TO TALK ABOUT IT, WE WANT TO LISTEN TO IT, WE WANT TO TALK TO IT. WE WANT TO DISSECT IT, TEAR IT APART, WEAR IT DOWN.

WE WANT IT TO HOST CONTEXTUAL PUBLIC PROGRAMS.[8] IT IS TOO HEAVY FOR JUST US. IT CONTAINS THE POSSIBILITY OF A PUBLIC. THIS PUBLIC MIGHT NOT GET ALONG WELL BUT WE THINK IT NEEDS TO GET TOGETHER AND FIGURE SOME THINGS OUT.

WE WANT TO MOVE IT AROUND. IT MAY KEEP MOVING, MAYBE FOR YEARS. WE THINK IT SHOULD MOVE SOUTH. ITS WEIGHT WILL GOUGE HOLES AS IT IS DRAGGED. IT WILL GENERATE FRICTION.

WE WANT IT TO SPEAK WITH PEOPLE AND PLACES WHO HAVE BEEN AFFECTED BY IT. IT IS PART OF COMPLEX STORIES OF VIOLENCE AND EXPLOITATION.[9]

WE WANT IT TO HOUSE A DEBATE ABOUT WHAT IT DISPLACES, AND WHAT DISPLACES IT. WE WANT TO PUT IT ON TRIAL. WE WANT TO EXTRADITE IT. WE WANT TO EXPOSE IT TO POTENTIAL EXPULSION.

THE PIT CANNOT BE SOLD. THIS IS A TEMPORARY INSTALLATION.[10]

Fig. 1.

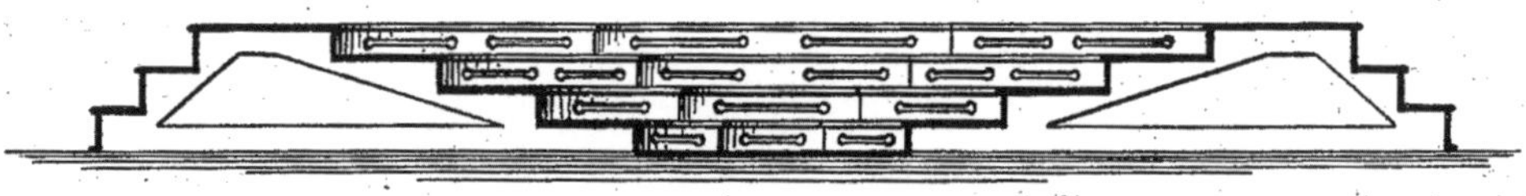

Fig. 2.

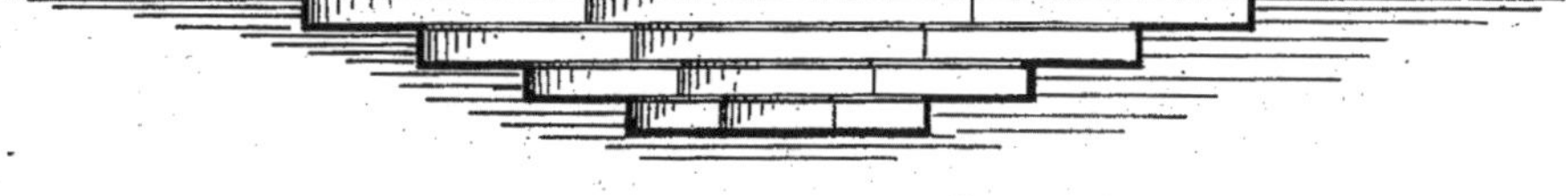

N. PETERS, PHOTO-LITHOGRAPHER, WASHINGTON. D. C.

D. DE PAULA, M. BENEDICT, D. RUETER.
Trading-Pit

N°. 203,837 Patented May 21, 1878.

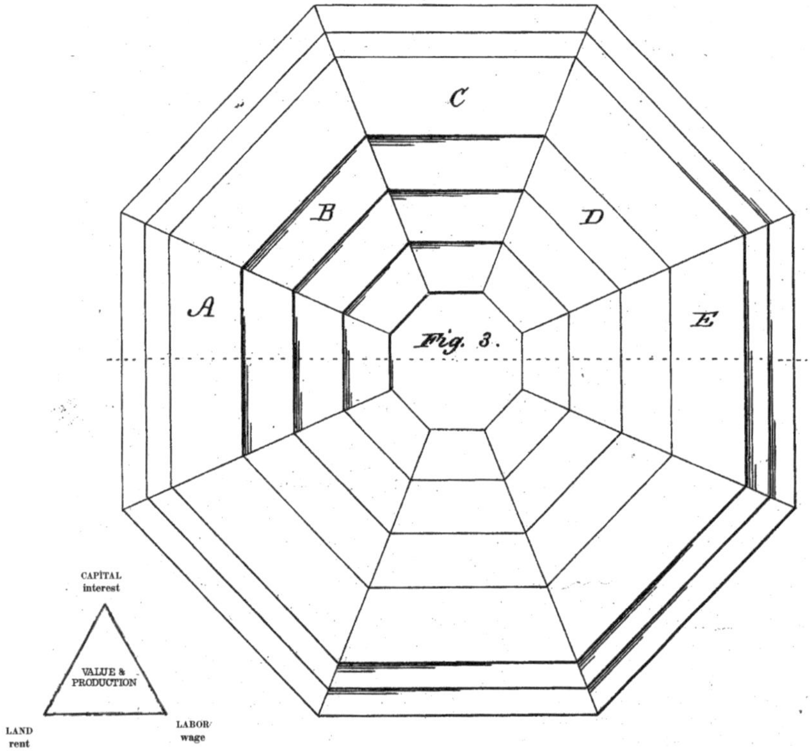

1. We, henceforth, refers to the three artists involved in the project: Daniel de Paula, Marissa Lee Benedict, and David Rueter.
2. The project began with the last-minute salvage of a 12-meter in diameter octagonal trading pit from the grain room trading floor of the Chicago Board of Trade (CBOT). Consisting of a series of stepped platforms, facing each other, and descending to a center space, the structure was designed to optimize peer-to-peer communication for commodities trading. Verbal signals and hand gestures were used by trading professionals in the pit to buy and sell a particular asset: in this case corn futures contracts- legal agreements or obligations to deliver a quantity of a particular grade of corn at a specified future date.
3. In 1878, Ruben S. Jennings of Chicago attempted but failed to enforce a patent for "a new and Improved Trading Pit or Platform." In active use at the CBOT since 1870, the trading pit design borrows from classical Western architectures of social representation, exchange, and spectacle: from the agora of Greece and the Roman Forum, to amphitheaters and parliaments across the globe. Similarly designed trading floors were later replicated throughout financial markets worldwide due to their capacity to optimize trade.
4. The CBOT's grain trading room, responsible for determining prices of grains such as corn, soya, and wheat for the global markets, ceased operation in 2015 after years of decreasing physical use driven by the proliferation of electronic trading. The once tangible and visible architecture of the trading pit is sinking into the obscurity of the black box server racks of the contemporary world interior of capital.
5. On August 6th 2018, artist Daniel de Paula contacted K.L., real-estate manager at the Chicago Mercantile Exchange Group (CME, owner of the CBOT), to request, for research purposes, detailed plans or 3D architectural models of the grain room trading floor. In their exchanges, K.L. informed de Paula that the CME Group was currently in the process of disposing of the corn pit. All of the other grain trading pits had already been dismantled and removed from the commodities trading floor. Realizing there was a short time window for possible salvage, de Paula began a series of email exchanges and negotiations. In the process, a collaboration with artists David Rueter and Marissa Lee Benedict was initiated. de Paula, Rueter and Benedict jointly financed the salvage through personal loans and revolving credit, and, finally, with on-site assistance and in-kind contributions from artist Dan Peterman and contractor G. Lane, the corn pit was brought in six dump truck loads to a warehouse managed by Ken Dunn's Resource Center located on the South Side of Chicago.
6. The pit bears a double weight: the weight of its thick layers of rubber, wood, and honeycomb aluminum, and the weight of the millions of transactions transporting masses of corn from one piece of land to another, enriching certain bodies and territories, and extracting from others.
7. A visit to a trading pit in action would yield a bodily metaphor for the gendered and racial violence endemic to the financial system, while electronic price feeds appear more innocent of such implications.
8. Any exhibiting institution will agree to enter into negotiations with the artists (de Paula, Rueter, and Benedict) to generate a contract specifying a framework for contextual programming that activates the pit and its history by staging various forms of adversarial investigation and exchange. The contract will provide guidelines for positioning the pit and the bodies that occupy it.
9. The expansion of the global production of grain commodities, especially soya and corn, conceals an interest in rural real estate as a financial asset. Consequently, in countries such as Brazil, the accelerated territorial occupation of agribusiness, stimulated by financial agents, electronic trading, and international investment and pension funds, leads to recurring violent practices such as land grabbing and deforestation, along with violence committed towards local peasant and indigenous communities, revealing inextricable colonial-era holdovers that continually organize space.
10. The pit is not to be owned by any single institution or individual, although a multitude of institutions may play a key role in its logistical transportation, maintenance, rental, installation, programming, and public exhibition. The continued displacement of the pit will necessarily wear it down, rendering it finite and unmonumental.

Fig. 6

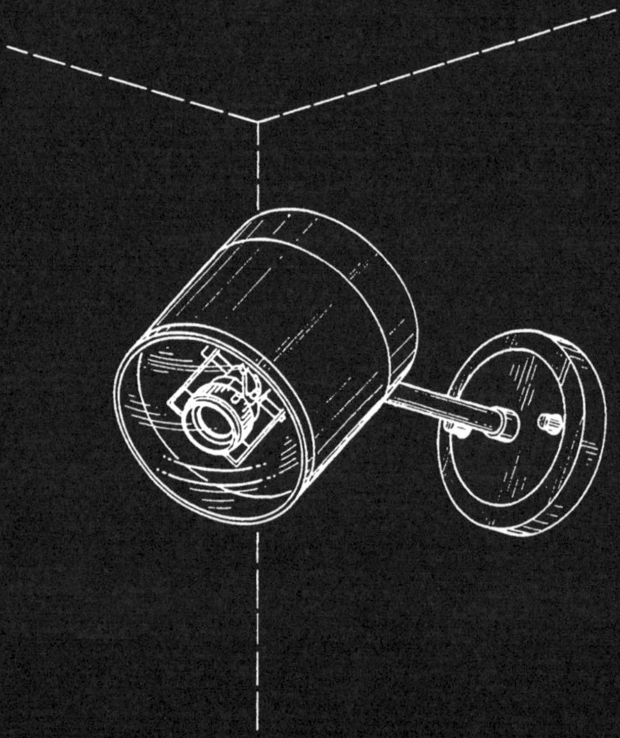

LA TENCY II

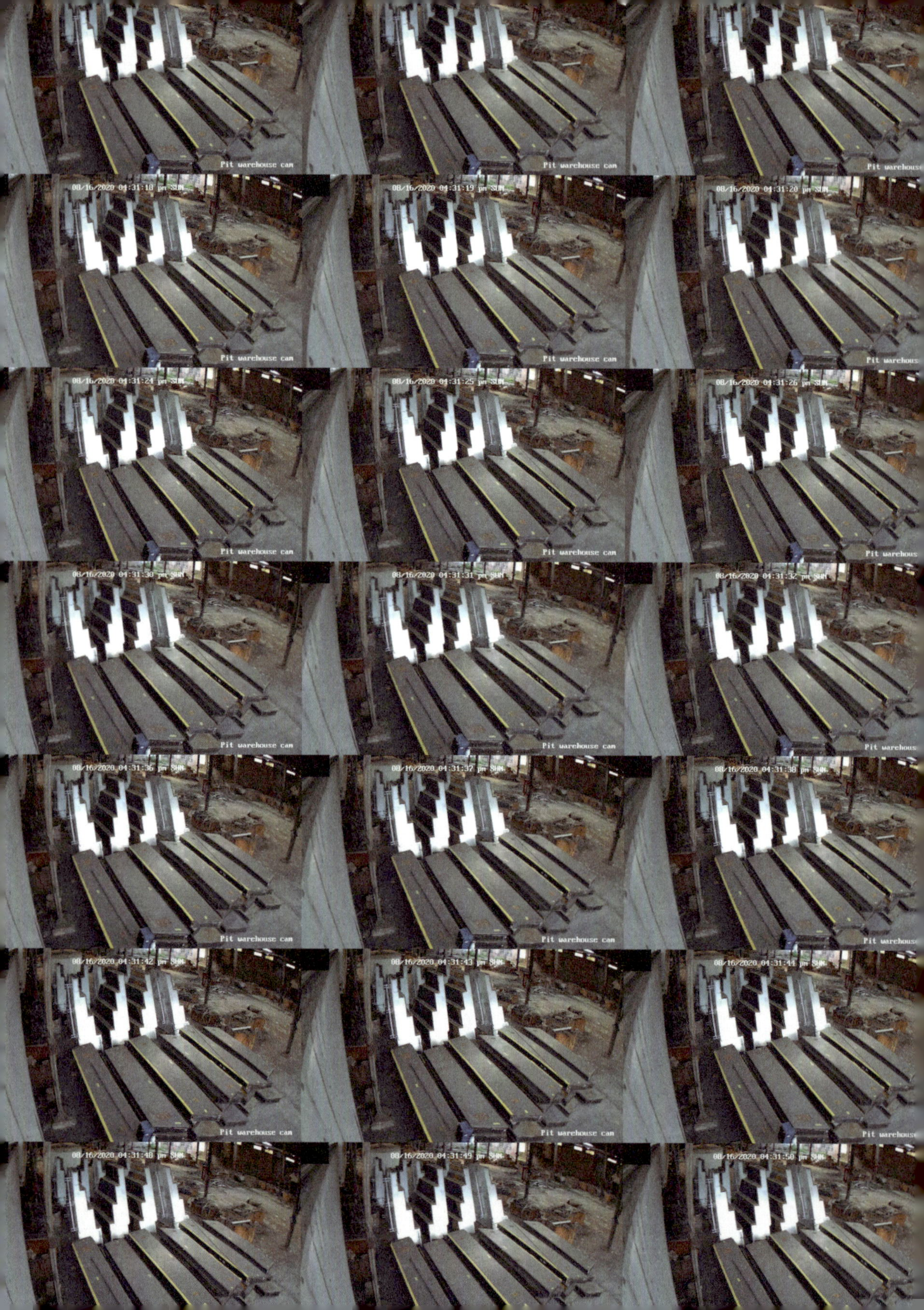

Pit warehouse cam
Pit warehouse cam
08/16/2020 04:31:18 pm SUN
08/16/2020 04:31:19 pm SUN
08/16/2020 04:31:20 pm SUN
Pit warehouse cam
Pit warehouse cam
08/16/2020 04:31:24 pm SUN
08/16/2020 04:31:25 pm SUN
08/16/2020 04:31:26 pm SUN
Pit warehouse cam
Pit warehouse cam
08/16/2020 04:31:30 pm SUN
08/16/2020 04:31:31 pm SUN
08/16/2020 04:31:32 pm SUN
Pit warehouse cam
Pit warehouse cam
08/16/2020 04:31:36 pm SUN
08/16/2020 04:31:37 pm SUN
08/16/2020 04:31:38 pm SUN
Pit warehouse cam
Pit warehouse cam
08/16/2020 04:31:42 pm SUN
08/16/2020 04:31:43 pm SUN
08/16/2020 04:31:44 pm SUN
Pit warehouse cam
Pit warehouse cam
08/16/2020 04:31:48 pm SUN
08/16/2020 04:31:49 pm SUN
08/16/2020 04:31:50 pm SUN

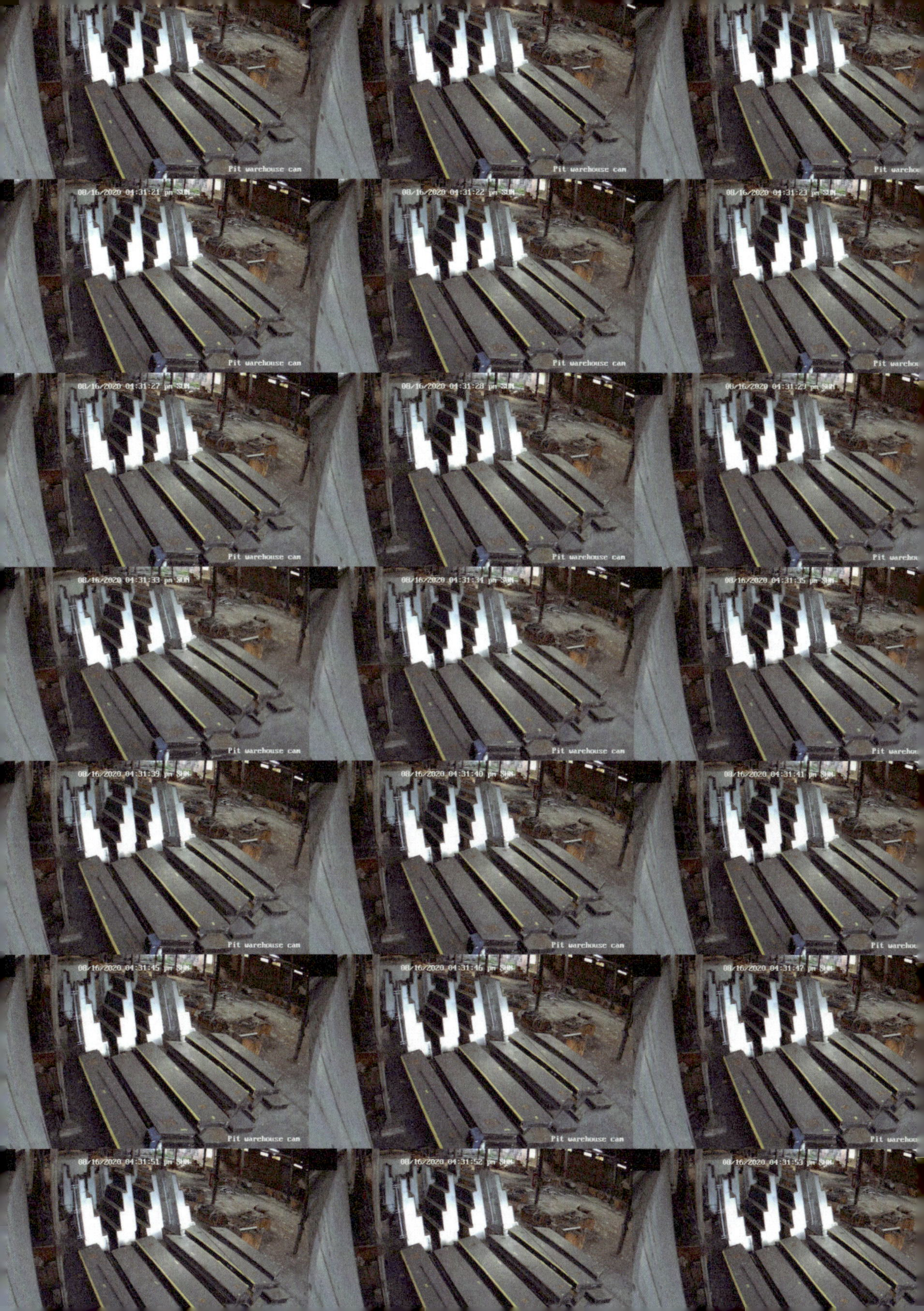
Pit warehouse cam
Pit warehouse cam
Pit warehou
08/16/2020 04:31:21 pm SUN
Pit warehouse cam
08/16/2020 04:31:22 pm SUN
Pit warehouse cam
08/16/2020 04:31:23 pm SUN
Pit warehou
08/16/2020 04:31:27 pm SUN
Pit warehouse cam
08/16/2020 04:31:28 pm SUN
Pit warehouse cam
08/16/2020 04:31:29 pm SUN
Pit warehou
08/16/2020 04:31:33 pm SUN
Pit warehouse cam
08/16/2020 04:31:34 pm SUN
Pit warehouse cam
08/16/2020 04:31:35 pm SUN
Pit warehou
08/16/2020 04:31:39 pm SUN
Pit warehouse cam
08/16/2020 04:31:40 pm SUN
Pit warehouse cam
08/16/2020 04:31:41 pm SUN
Pit warehou
08/16/2020 04:31:45 pm SUN
Pit warehouse cam
08/16/2020 04:31:46 pm SUN
Pit warehouse cam
08/16/2020 04:31:47 pm SUN
Pit warehou
08/16/2020 04:31:51 pm SUN
08/16/2020 04:31:52 pm SUN
08/16/2020 04:31:53 pm SUN

Corn cam
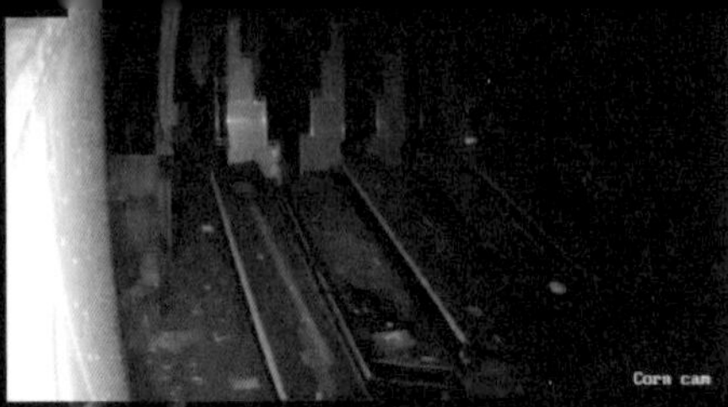
Corn cam
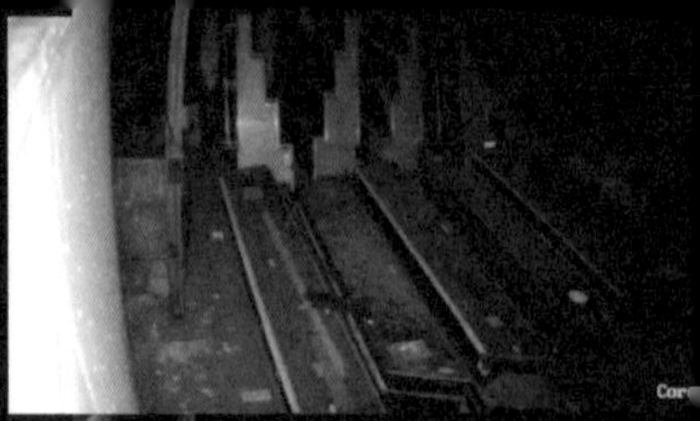
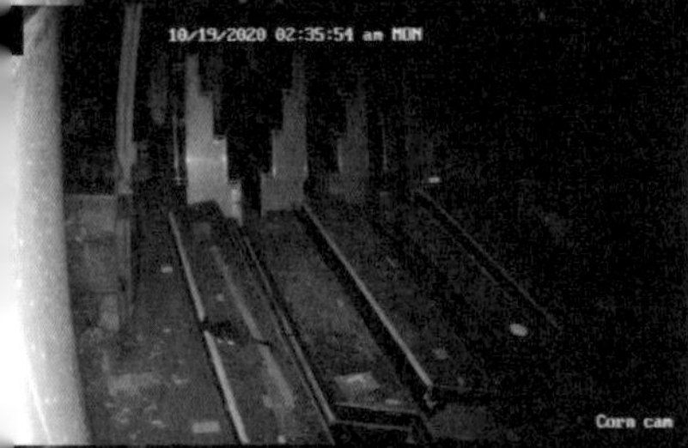
10/19/2020 02:35:54 am MON
Corn cam
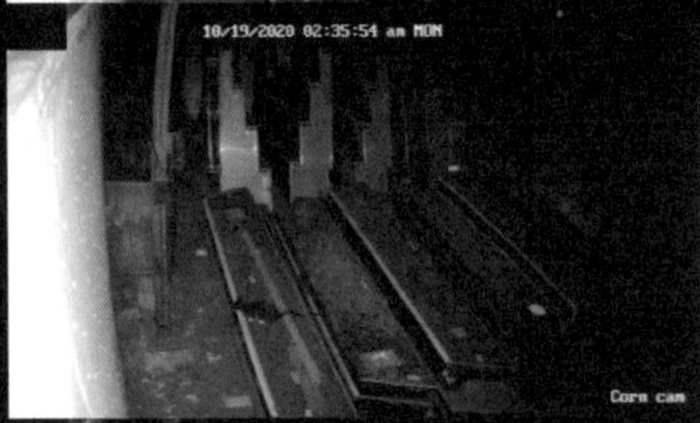
10/19/2020 02:35:54 am MON
Corn cam
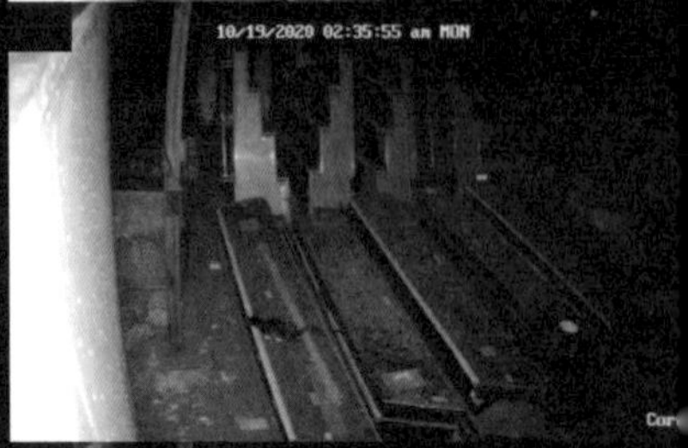
10/19/2020 02:35:55 am MON
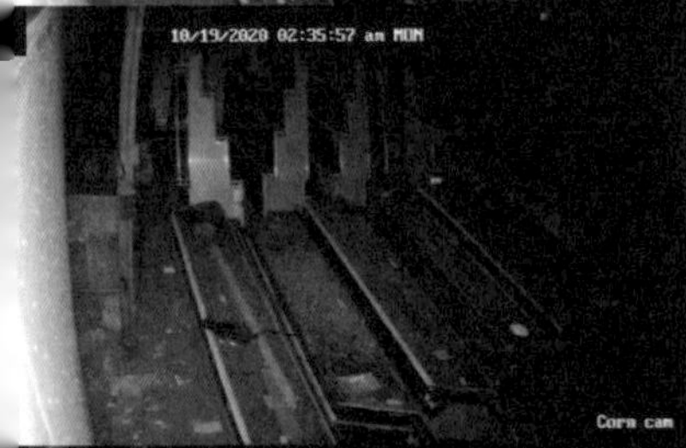
10/19/2020 02:35:57 am MON
Corn cam
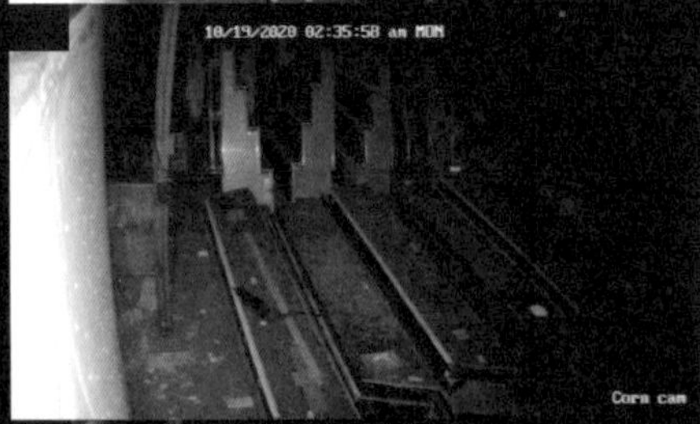
10/19/2020 02:35:58 am MON
Corn cam
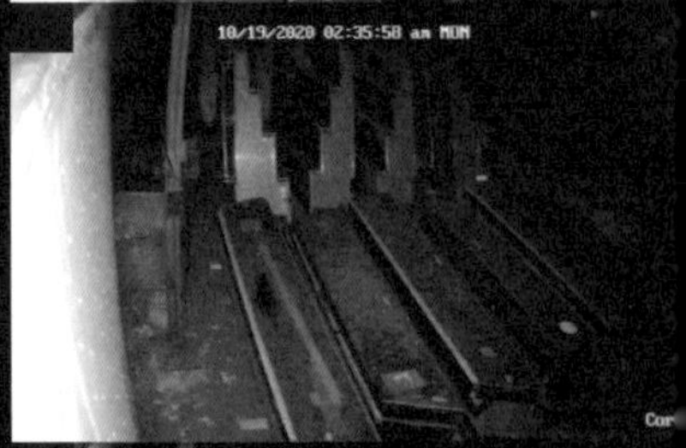
10/19/2020 02:35:58 am MON
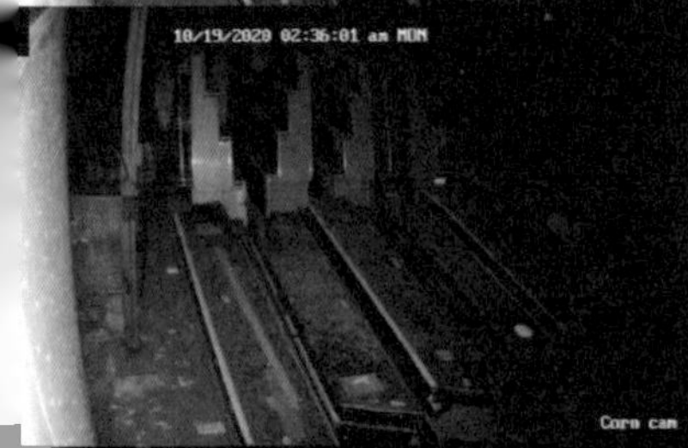
10/19/2020 02:36:01 am MON
Corn cam
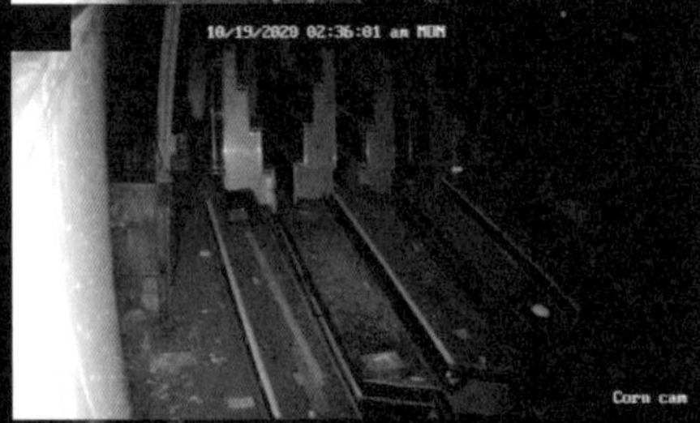
10/19/2020 02:36:01 am MON
Corn cam
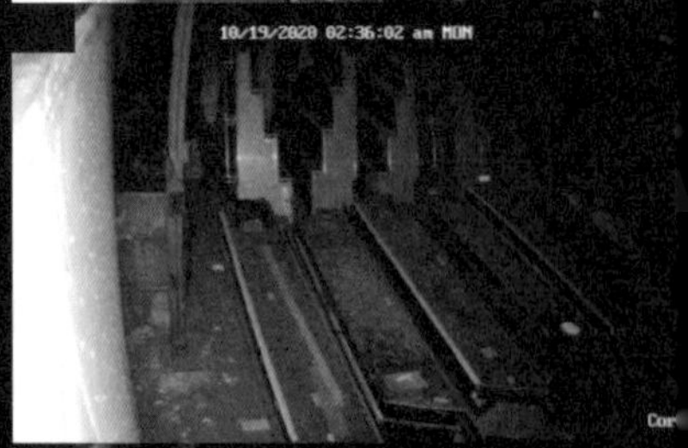
10/19/2020 02:36:02 am MON
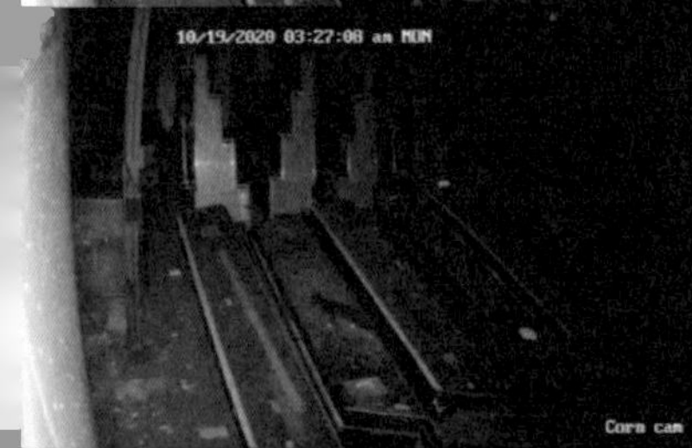
10/19/2020 03:27:08 am MON
Corn cam
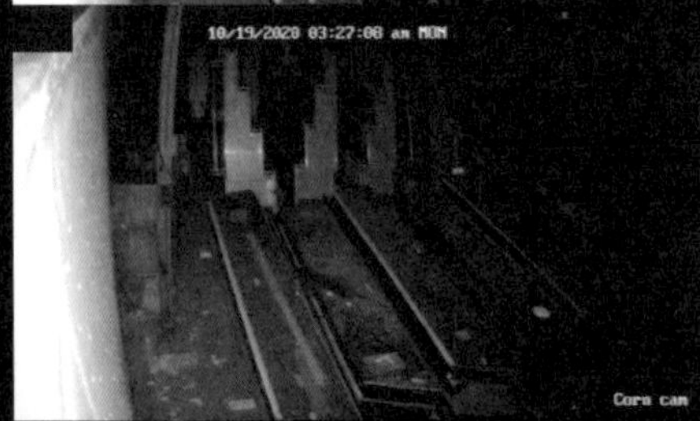
10/19/2020 03:27:08 am MON
Corn cam
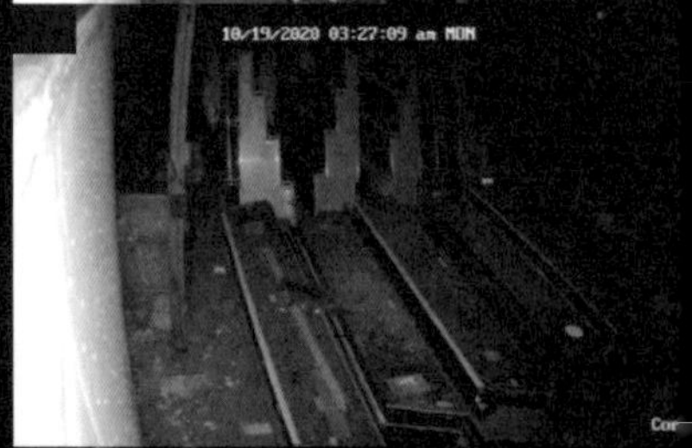
10/19/2020 03:27:09 am MON
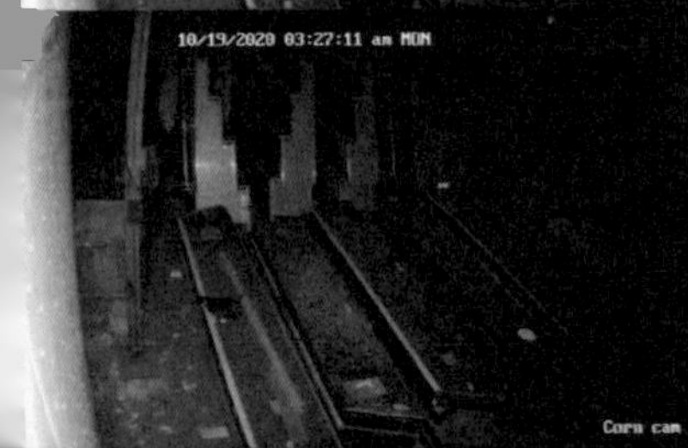
10/19/2020 03:27:11 am MON
Corn cam
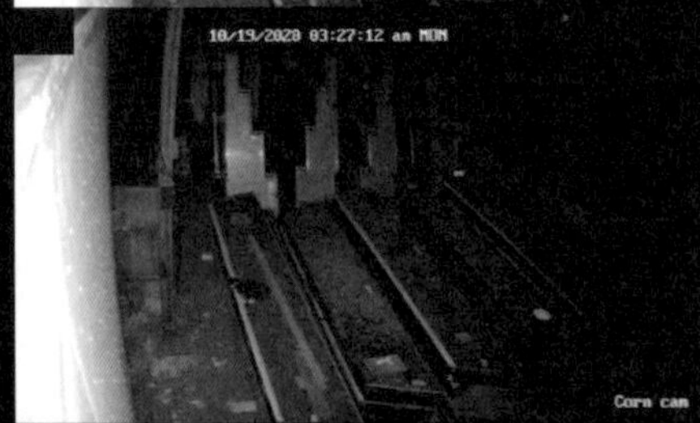
10/19/2020 03:27:12 am MON
Corn cam
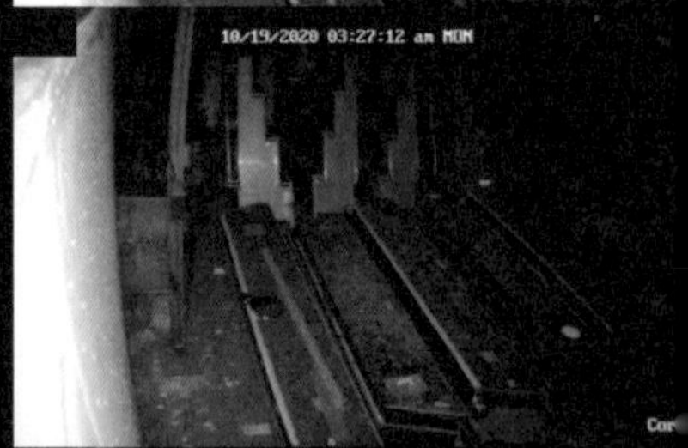
10/19/2020 03:27:12 am MON
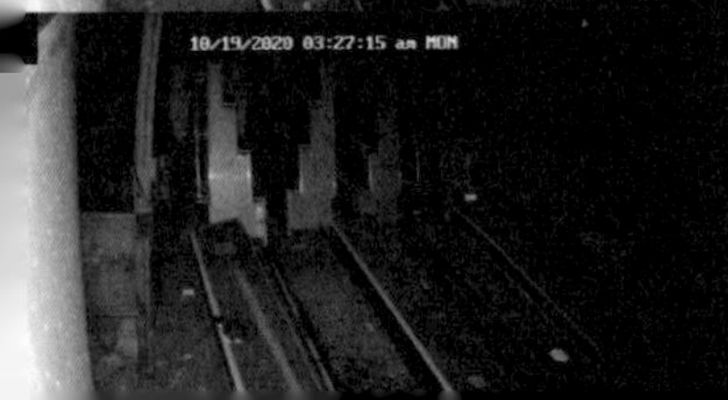
10/19/2020 03:27:15 am MON
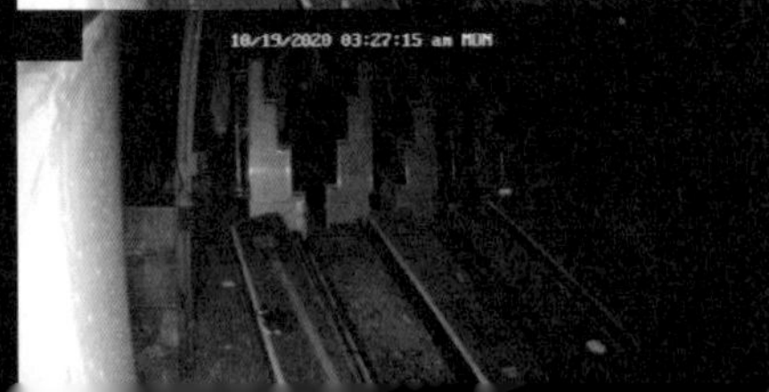
10/19/2020 03:27:15 am MON
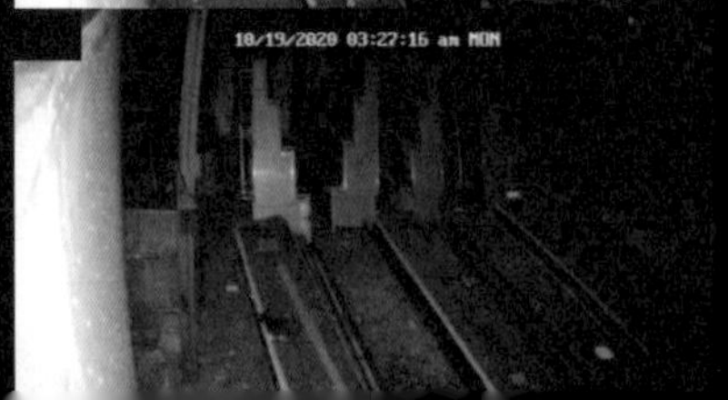
10/19/2020 03:27:16 am MON

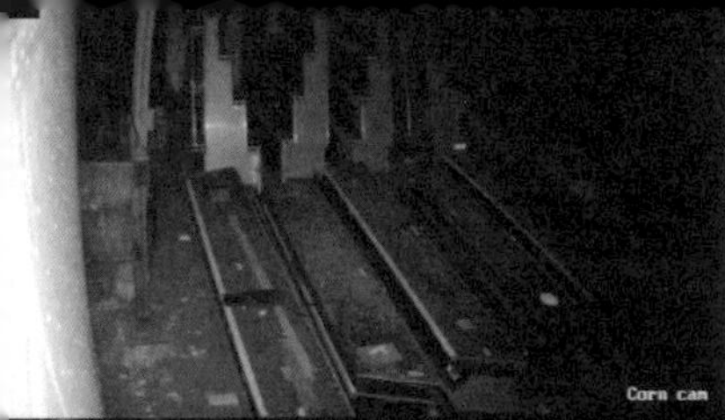
Corn cam
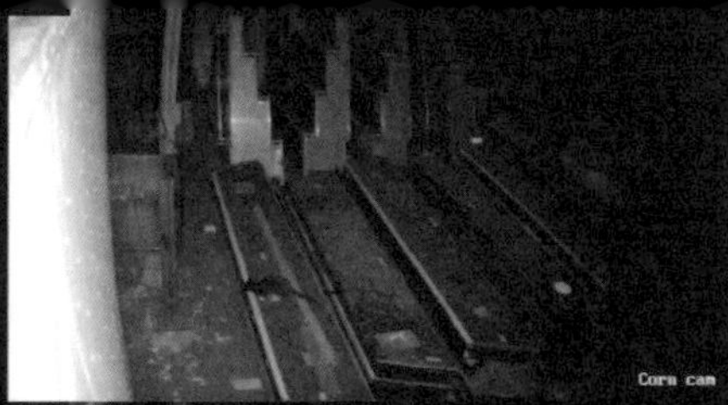
Corn cam
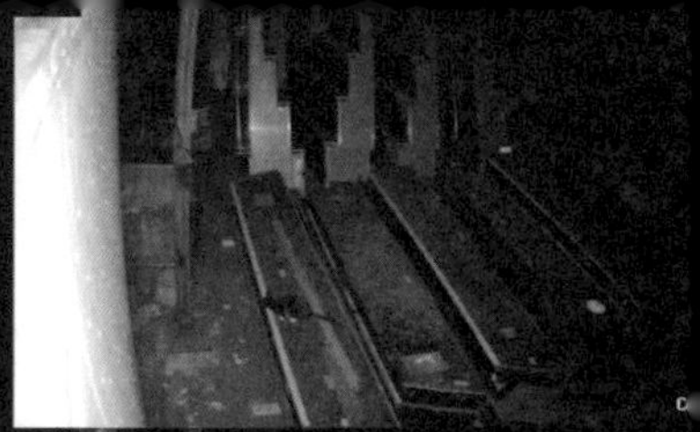
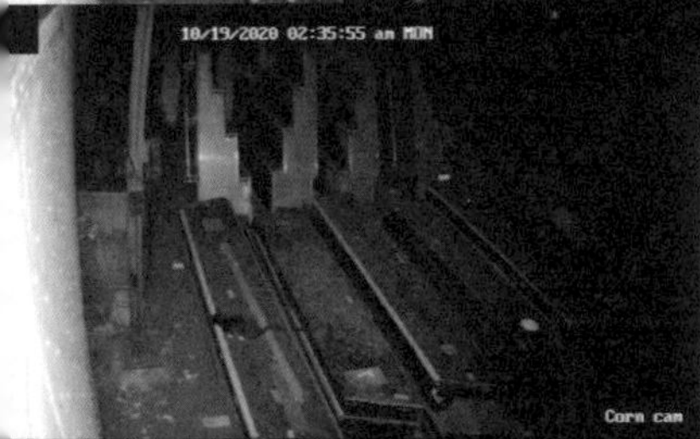
10/19/2020 02:35:55 am MON
Corn cam
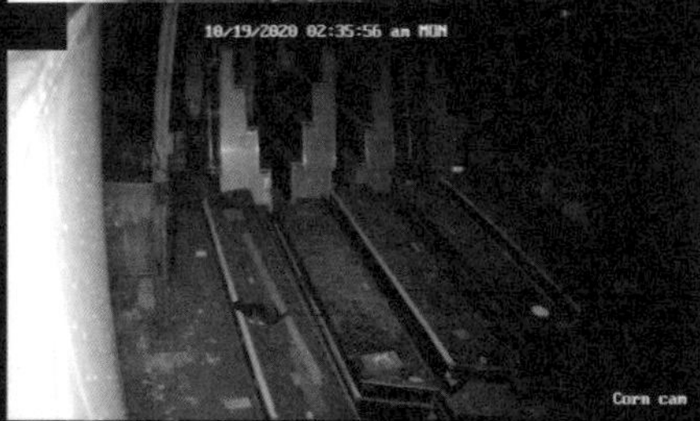
10/19/2020 02:35:56 am MON
Corn cam
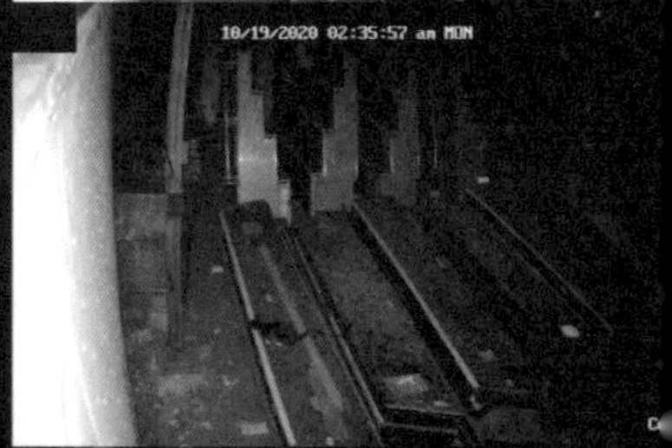
10/19/2020 02:35:57 am MON
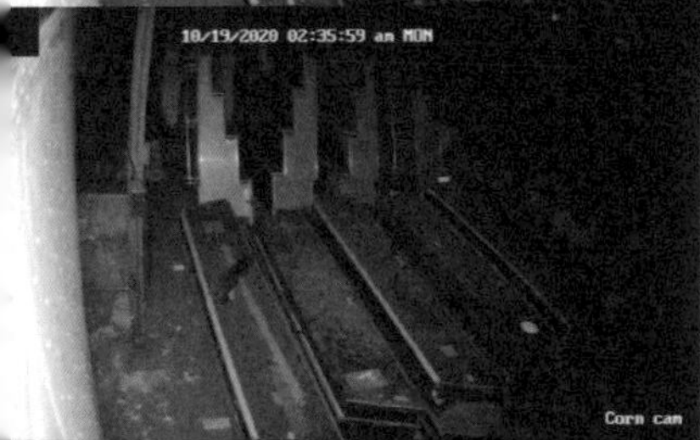
10/19/2020 02:35:59 am MON
Corn cam
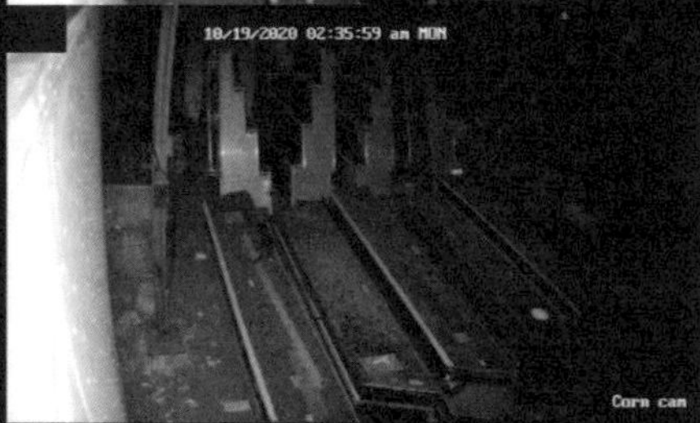
10/19/2020 02:35:59 am MON
Corn cam
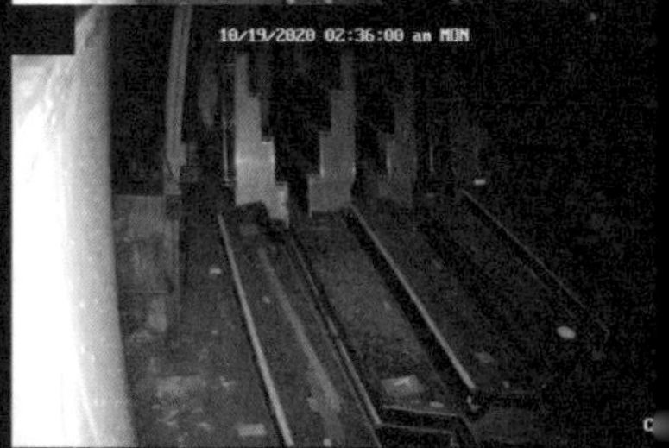
10/19/2020 02:36:00 am MON
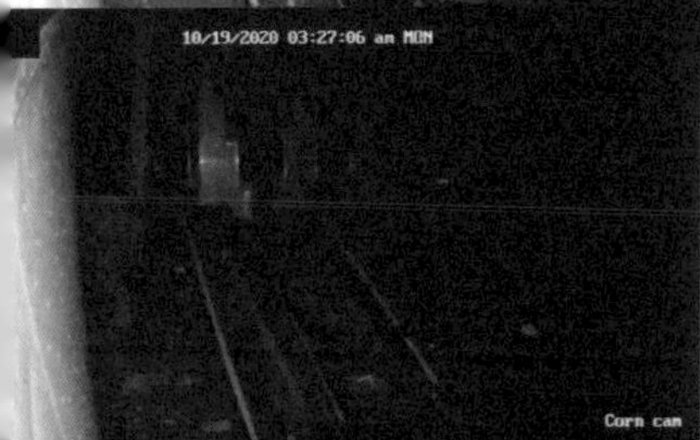
10/19/2020 03:27:06 am MON
Corn cam
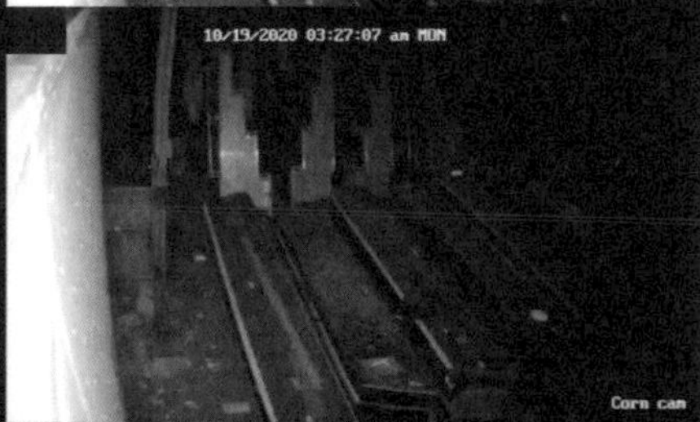
10/19/2020 03:27:07 am MON
Corn cam
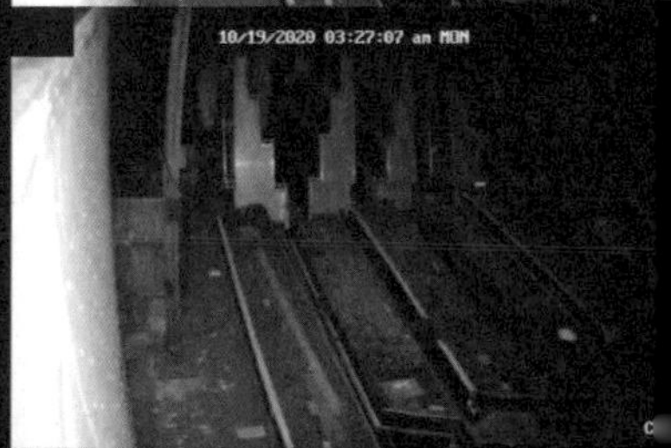
10/19/2020 03:27:07 am MON
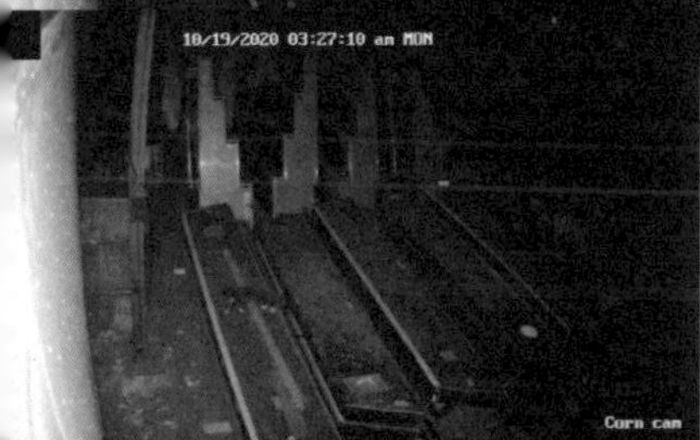
10/19/2020 03:27:10 am MON
Corn cam
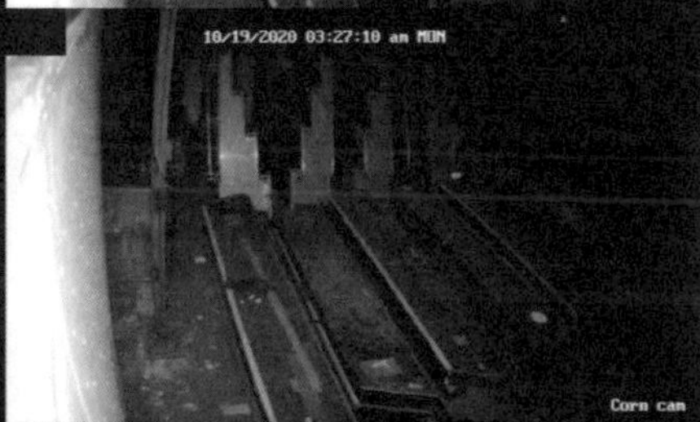
10/19/2020 03:27:10 am MON
Corn cam
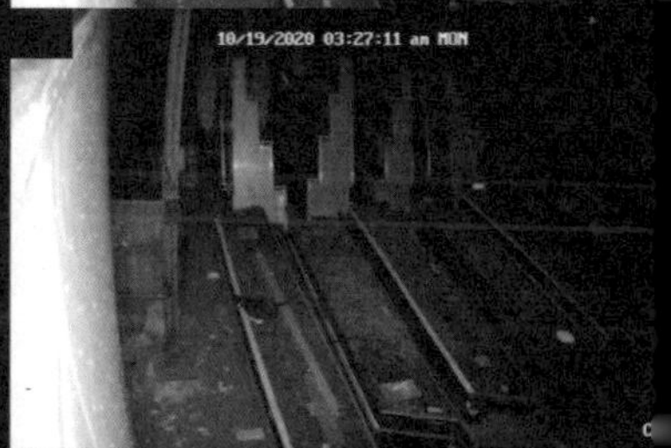
10/19/2020 03:27:11 am MON
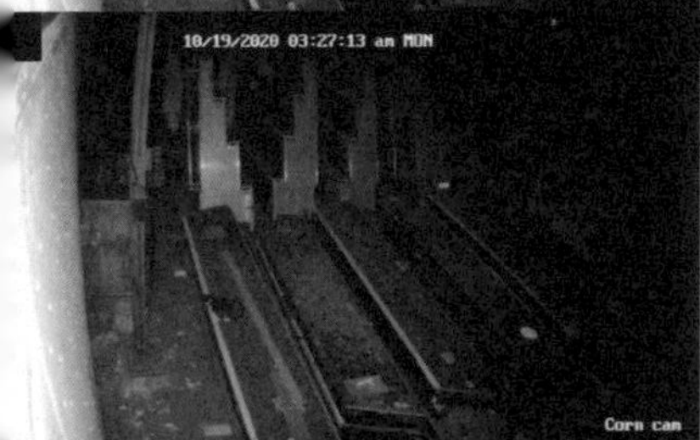
10/19/2020 03:27:13 am MON
Corn cam
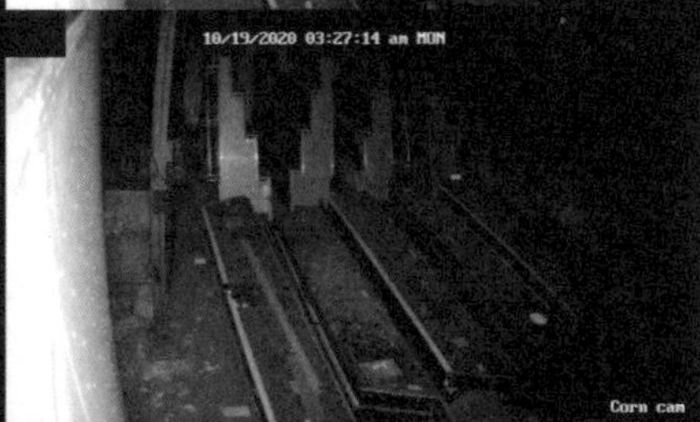
10/19/2020 03:27:14 am MON
Corn cam
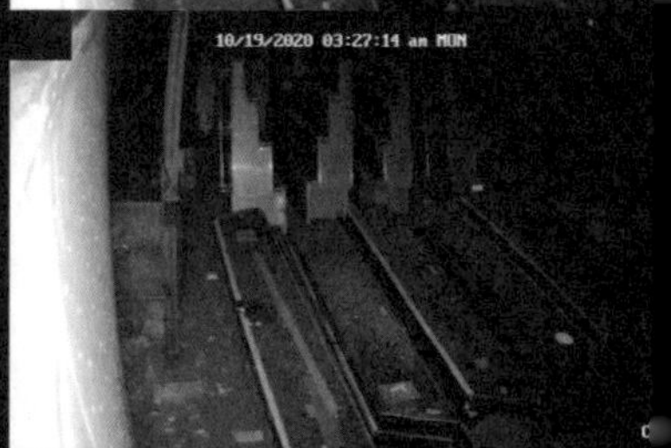
10/19/2020 03:27:14 am MON
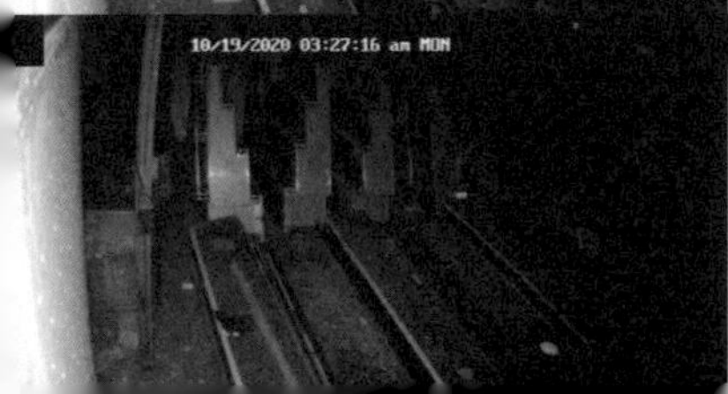
10/19/2020 03:27:16 am MON
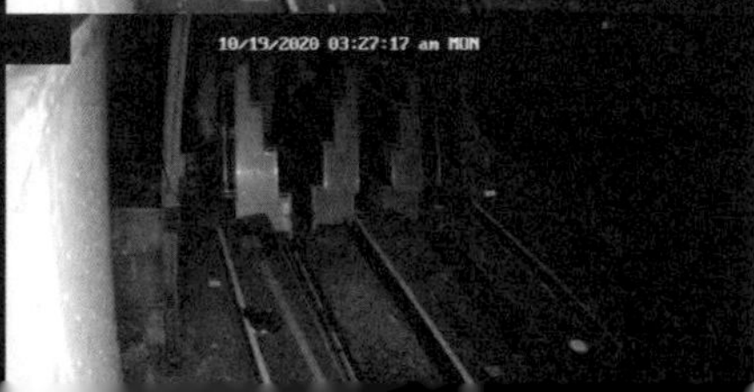
10/19/2020 03:27:17 am MON
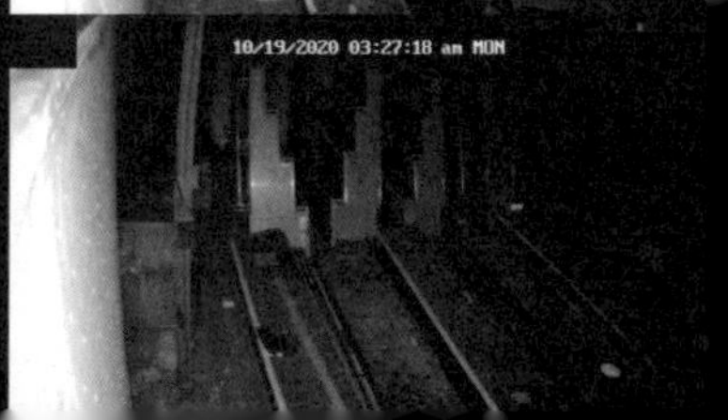
10/19/2020 03:27:18 am MON

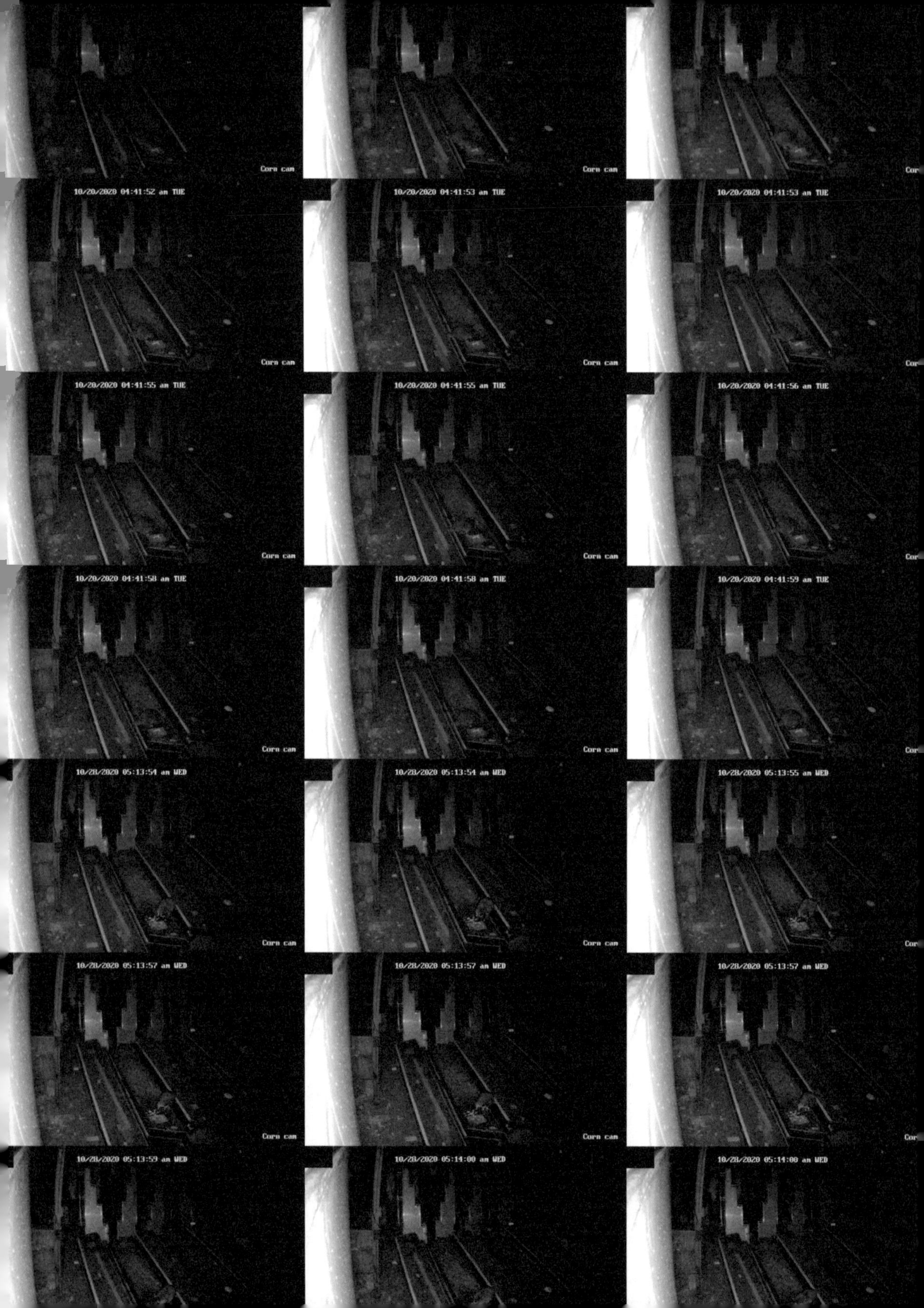
Corn cam
Corn cam
10/20/2020 04:41:52 am TUE
Corn cam
10/20/2020 04:41:53 am TUE
Corn cam
10/20/2020 04:41:53 am TUE
10/20/2020 04:41:55 am TUE
Corn cam
10/20/2020 04:41:55 am TUE
Corn cam
10/20/2020 04:41:56 am TUE
10/20/2020 04:41:58 am TUE
Corn cam
10/20/2020 04:41:58 am TUE
Corn cam
10/20/2020 04:41:59 am TUE
10/28/2020 05:13:54 am WED
Corn cam
10/28/2020 05:13:54 am WED
Corn cam
10/28/2020 05:13:55 am WED
10/28/2020 05:13:57 am WED
Corn cam
10/28/2020 05:13:57 am WED
Corn cam
10/28/2020 05:13:57 am WED
10/28/2020 05:13:59 am WED
10/28/2020 05:14:00 am WED
10/28/2020 05:14:00 am WED

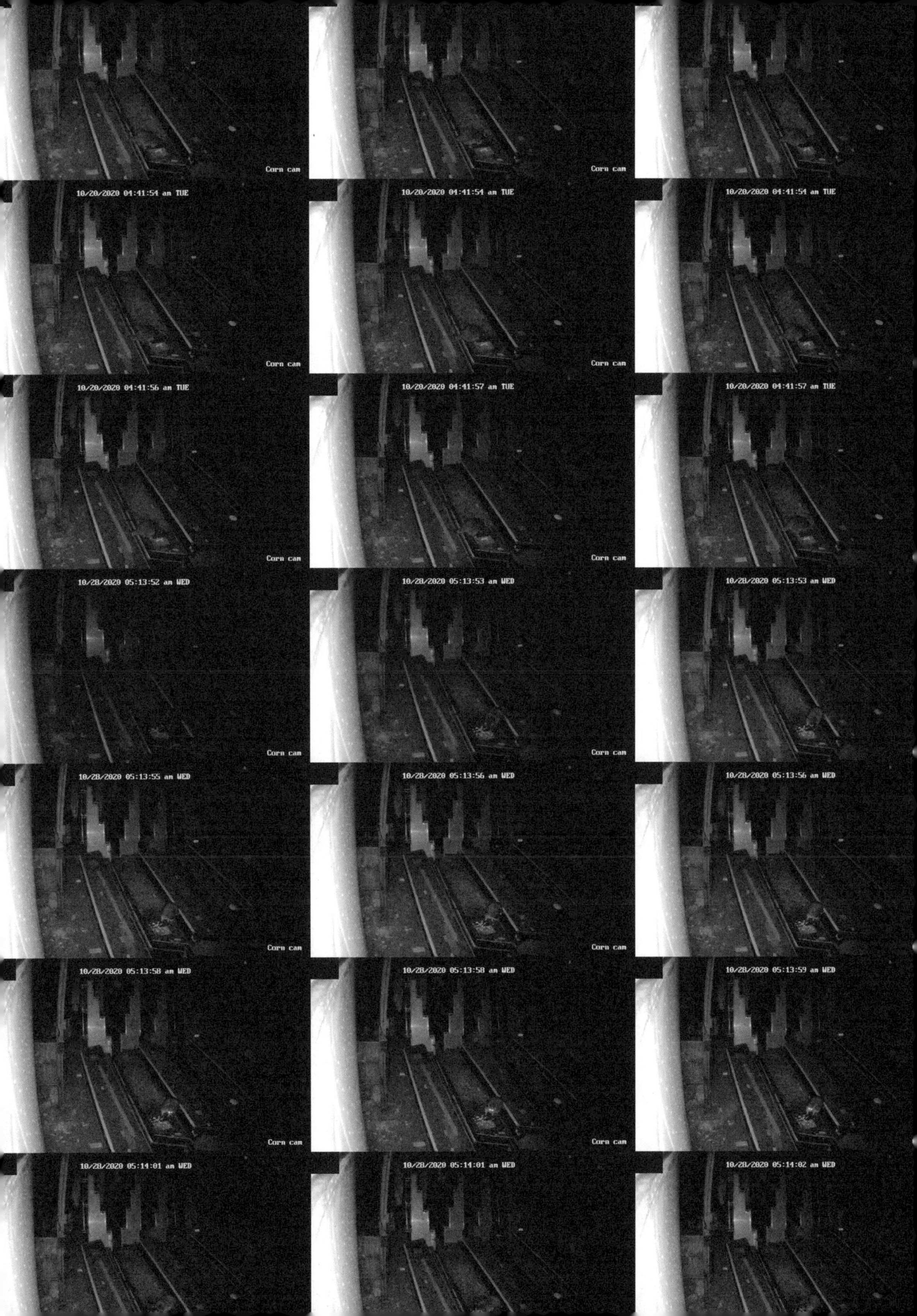
Corn cam
Corn cam
Corn cam
10/20/2020 04:41:54 am TUE
10/20/2020 04:41:54 am TUE
10/20/2020 04:41:54 am TUE
Corn cam
Corn cam
Corn cam
10/20/2020 04:41:56 am TUE
10/20/2020 04:41:57 am TUE
10/20/2020 04:41:57 am TUE
Corn cam
Corn cam
Corn cam
10/28/2020 05:13:52 am WED
10/28/2020 05:13:53 am WED
10/28/2020 05:13:53 am WED
Corn cam
Corn cam
Corn cam
10/28/2020 05:13:55 am WED
10/28/2020 05:13:56 am WED
10/28/2020 05:13:56 am WED
Corn cam
Corn cam
Corn cam
10/28/2020 05:13:58 am WED
10/28/2020 05:13:58 am WED
10/28/2020 05:13:59 am WED
Corn cam
Corn cam
10/28/2020 05:14:01 am WED
10/28/2020 05:14:01 am WED
10/28/2020 05:14:02 am WED

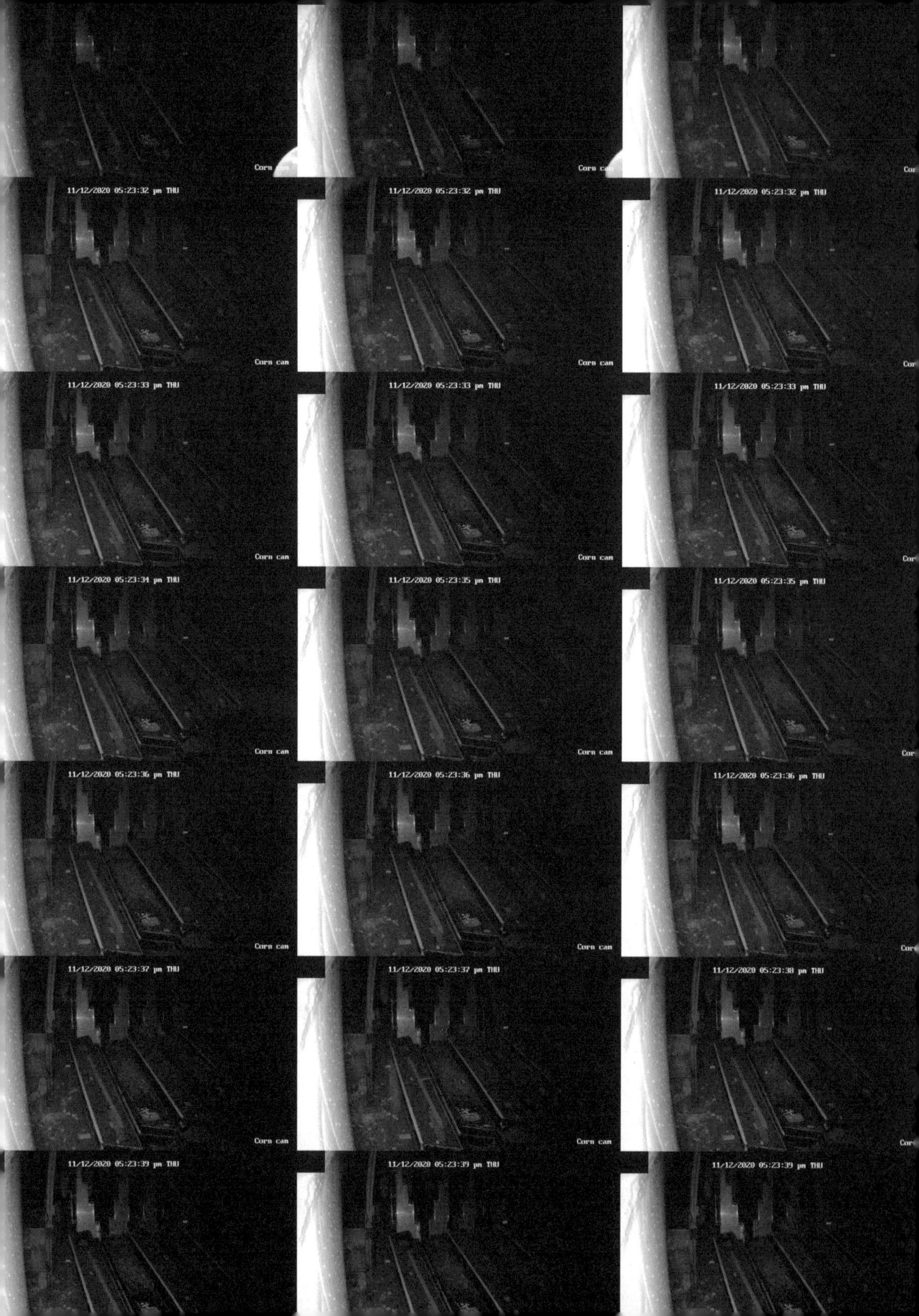
11/12/2020 05:23:32 pm THU
11/12/2020 05:23:32 pm THU
11/12/2020 05:23:32 pm THU
Corn cam
Corn cam
11/12/2020 05:23:33 pm THU
11/12/2020 05:23:33 pm THU
11/12/2020 05:23:33 pm THU
Corn cam
Corn cam
11/12/2020 05:23:34 pm THU
11/12/2020 05:23:35 pm THU
11/12/2020 05:23:35 pm THU
Corn cam
Corn cam
11/12/2020 05:23:36 pm THU
11/12/2020 05:23:36 pm THU
11/12/2020 05:23:36 pm THU
Corn cam
Corn cam
11/12/2020 05:23:37 pm THU
11/12/2020 05:23:37 pm THU
11/12/2020 05:23:38 pm THU
Corn cam
Corn cam
11/12/2020 05:23:39 pm THU
11/12/2020 05:23:39 pm THU
11/12/2020 05:23:39 pm THU

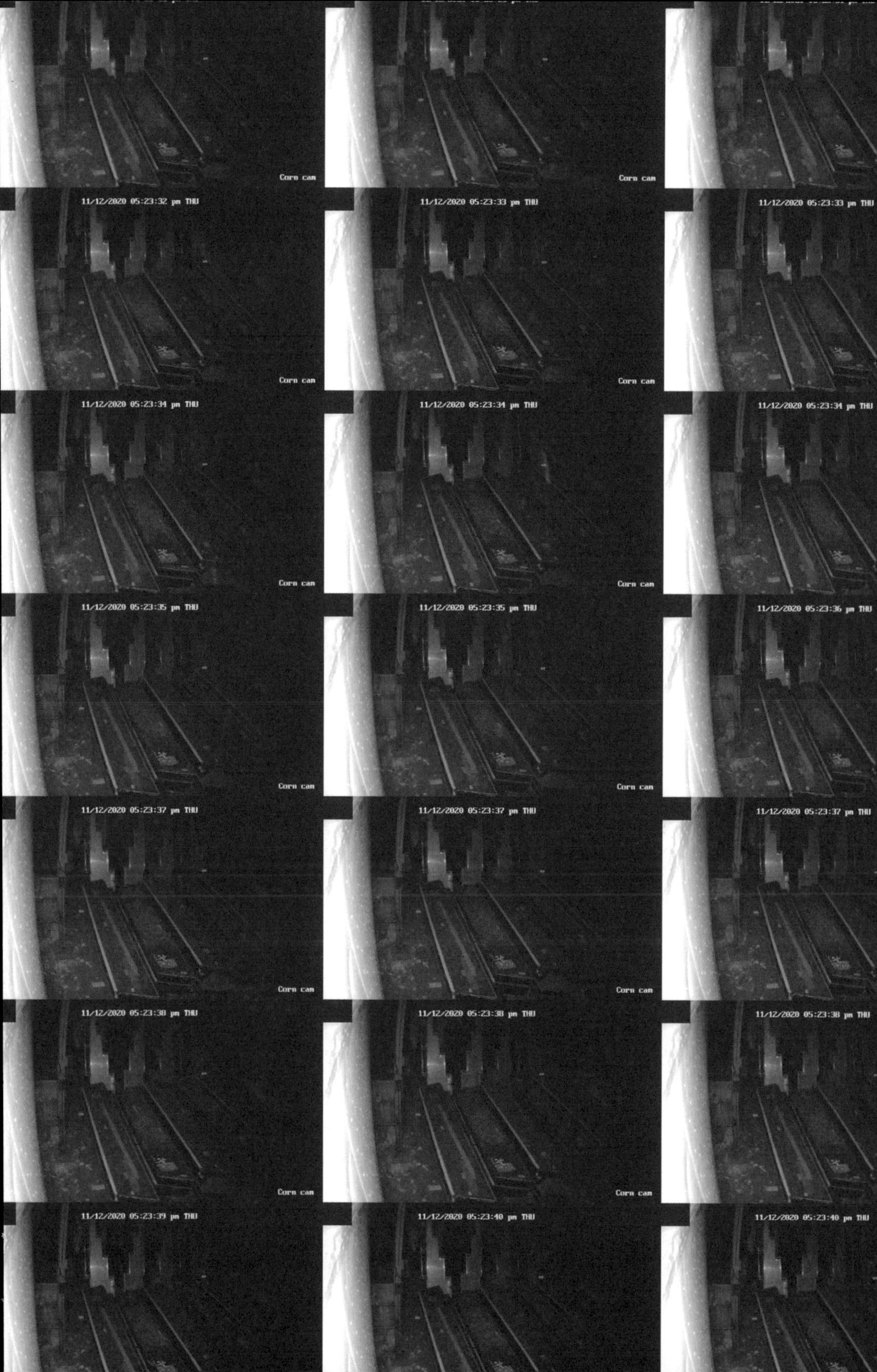
Corn cam
Corn cam
11/12/2020 05:23:32 pm THU
Corn cam
11/12/2020 05:23:33 pm THU
Corn cam
11/12/2020 05:23:33 pm THU
11/12/2020 05:23:34 pm THU
Corn cam
11/12/2020 05:23:34 pm THU
Corn cam
11/12/2020 05:23:34 pm THU
11/12/2020 05:23:35 pm THU
Corn cam
11/12/2020 05:23:35 pm THU
Corn cam
11/12/2020 05:23:36 pm THU
11/12/2020 05:23:37 pm THU
Corn cam
11/12/2020 05:23:37 pm THU
Corn cam
11/12/2020 05:23:37 pm THU
11/12/2020 05:23:38 pm THU
Corn cam
11/12/2020 05:23:38 pm THU
Corn cam
11/12/2020 05:23:38 pm THU
11/12/2020 05:23:39 pm THU
11/12/2020 05:23:40 pm THU
11/12/2020 05:23:40 pm THU

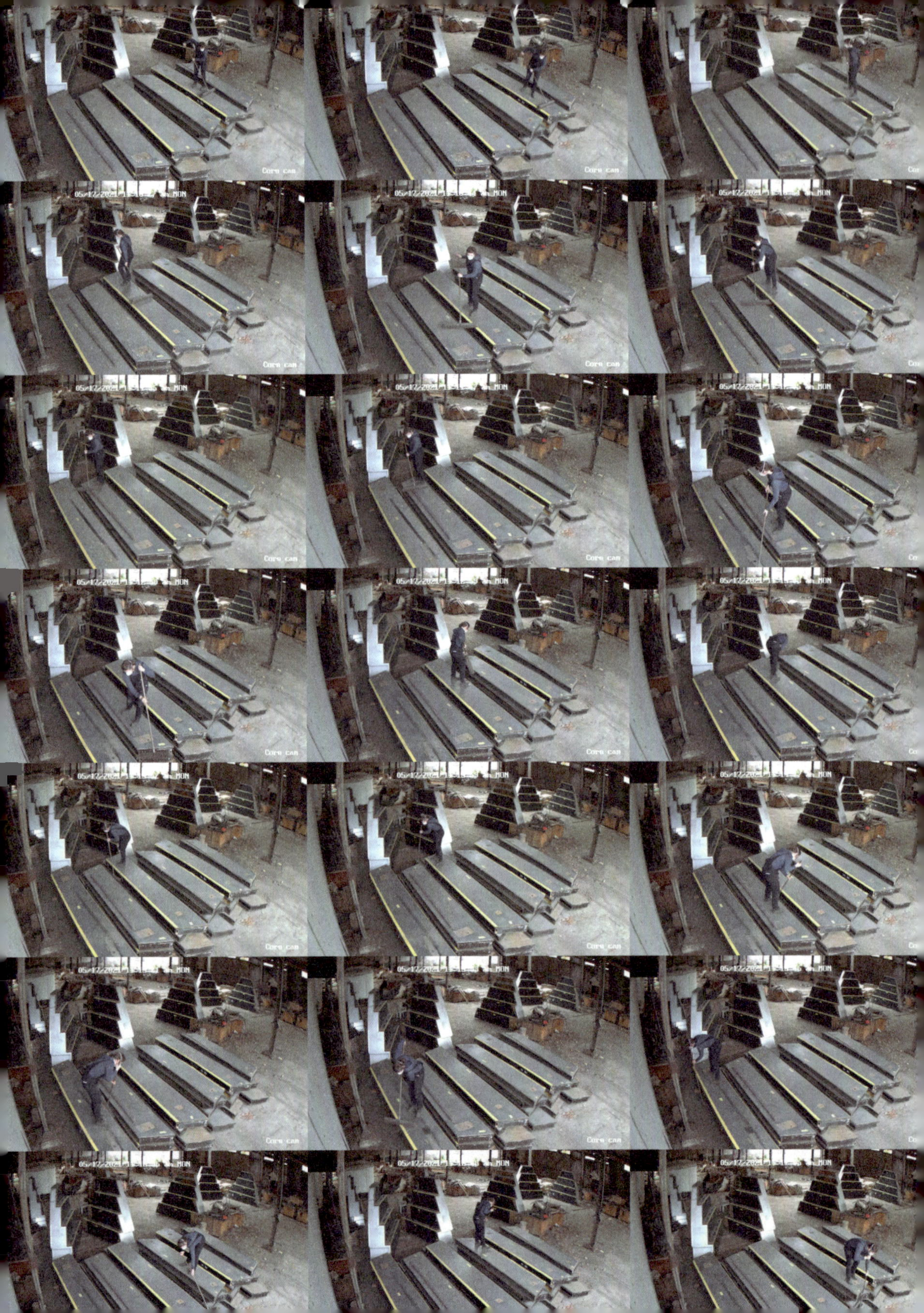
Core cam

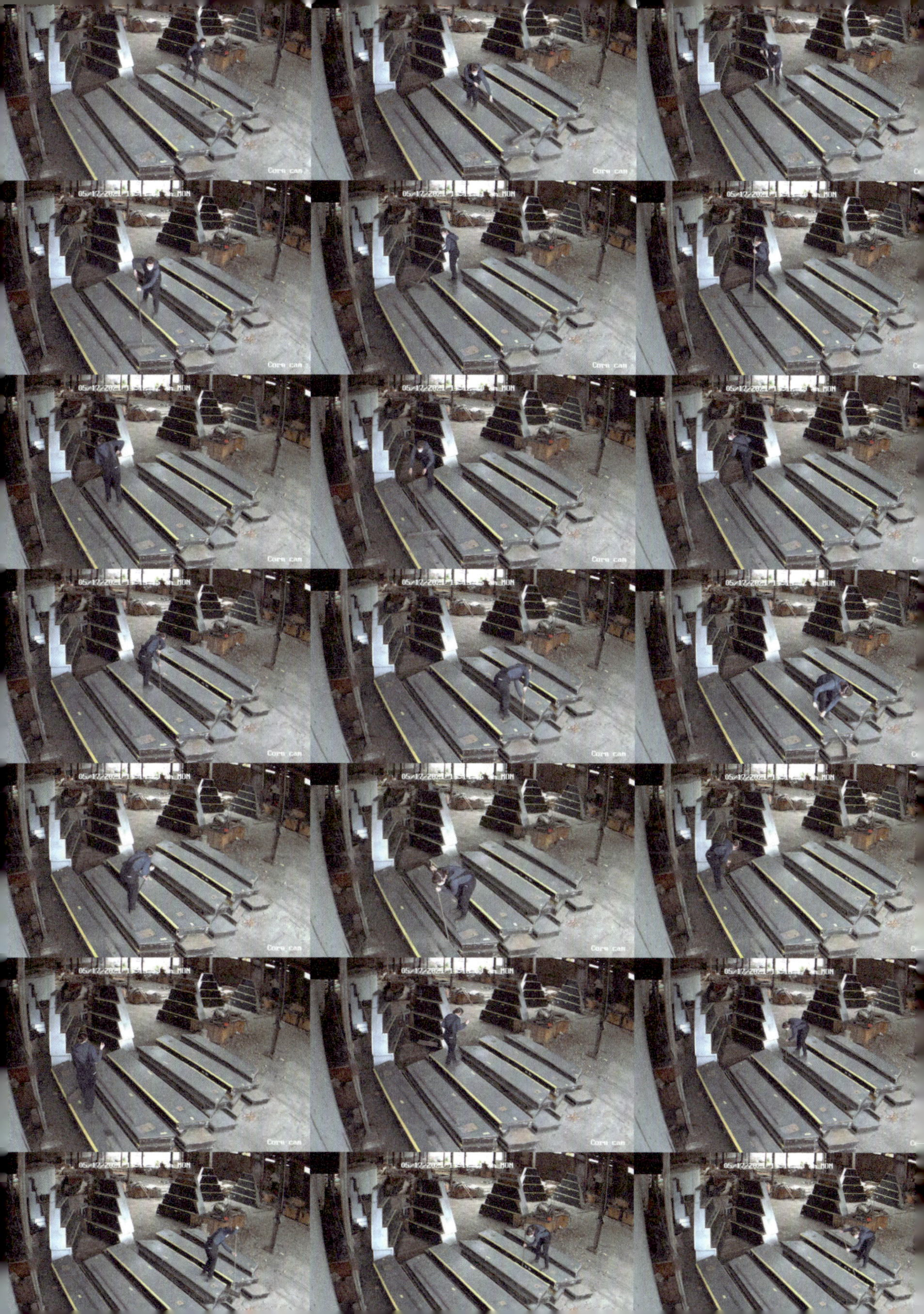
Core cam

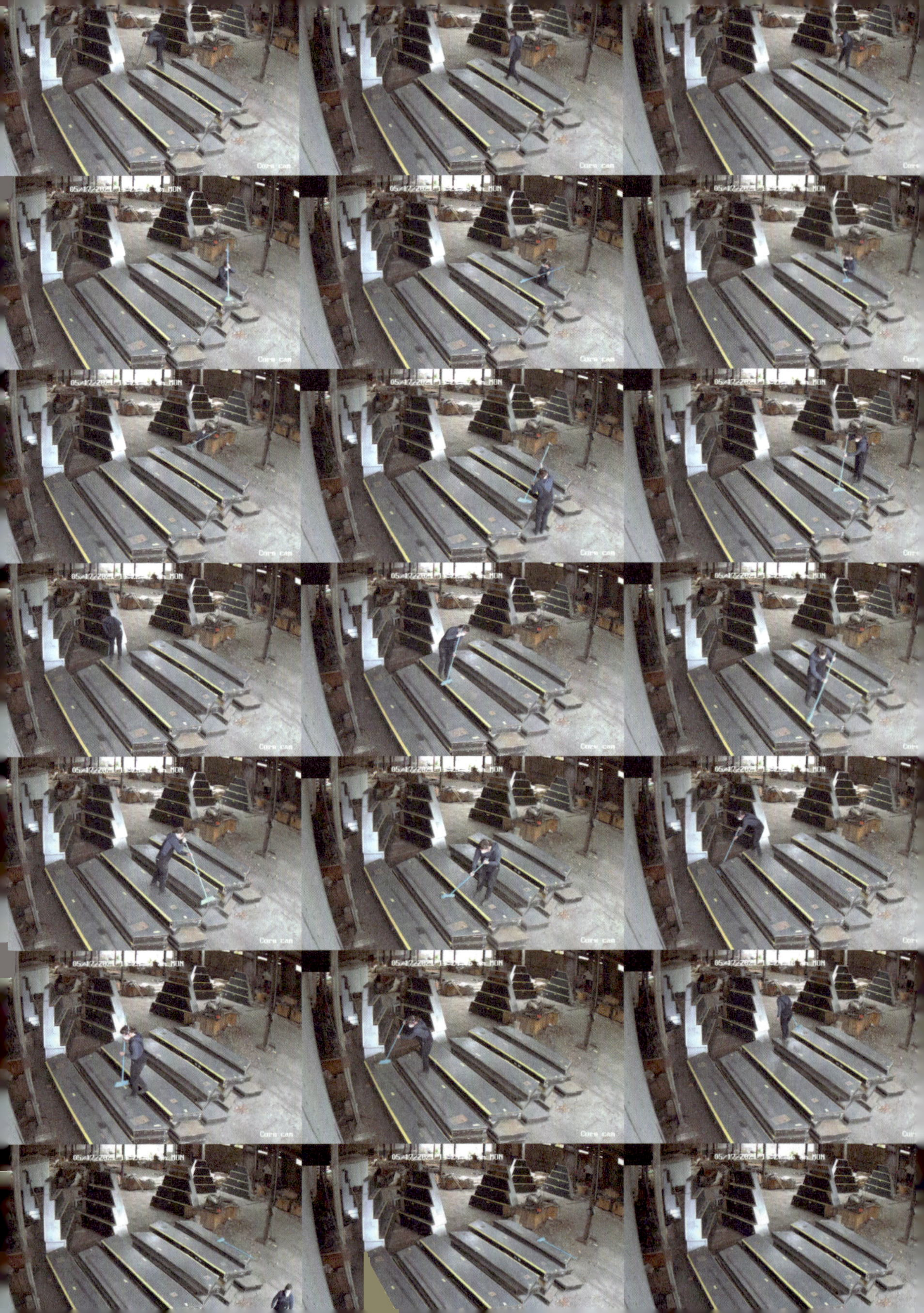

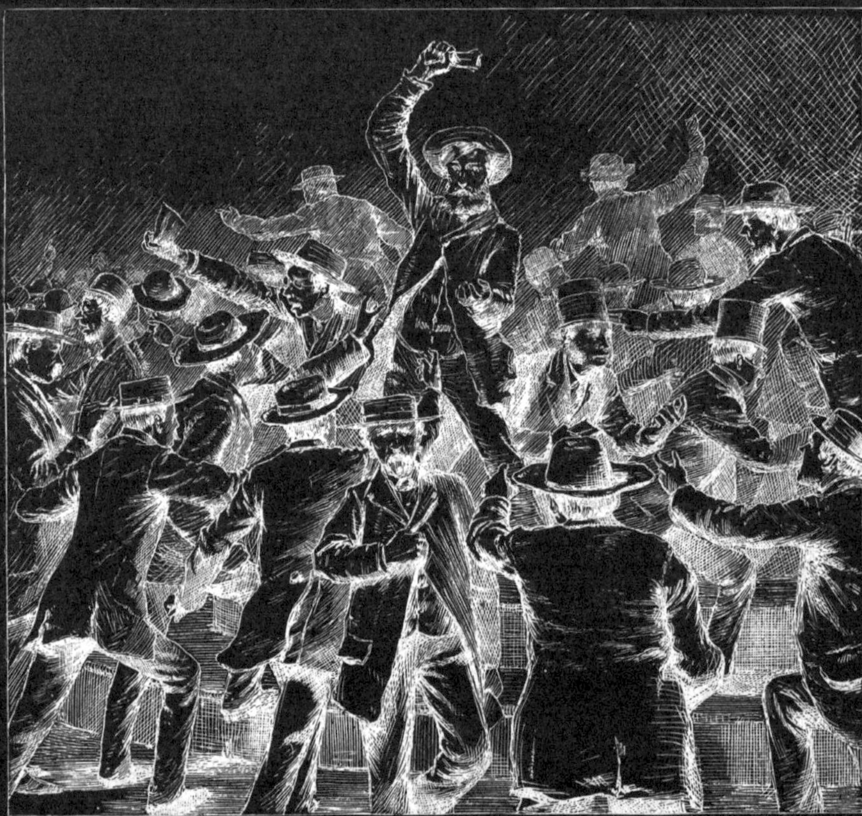

A FLURRY IN WHEAT.

SPEC ULA TION III

1

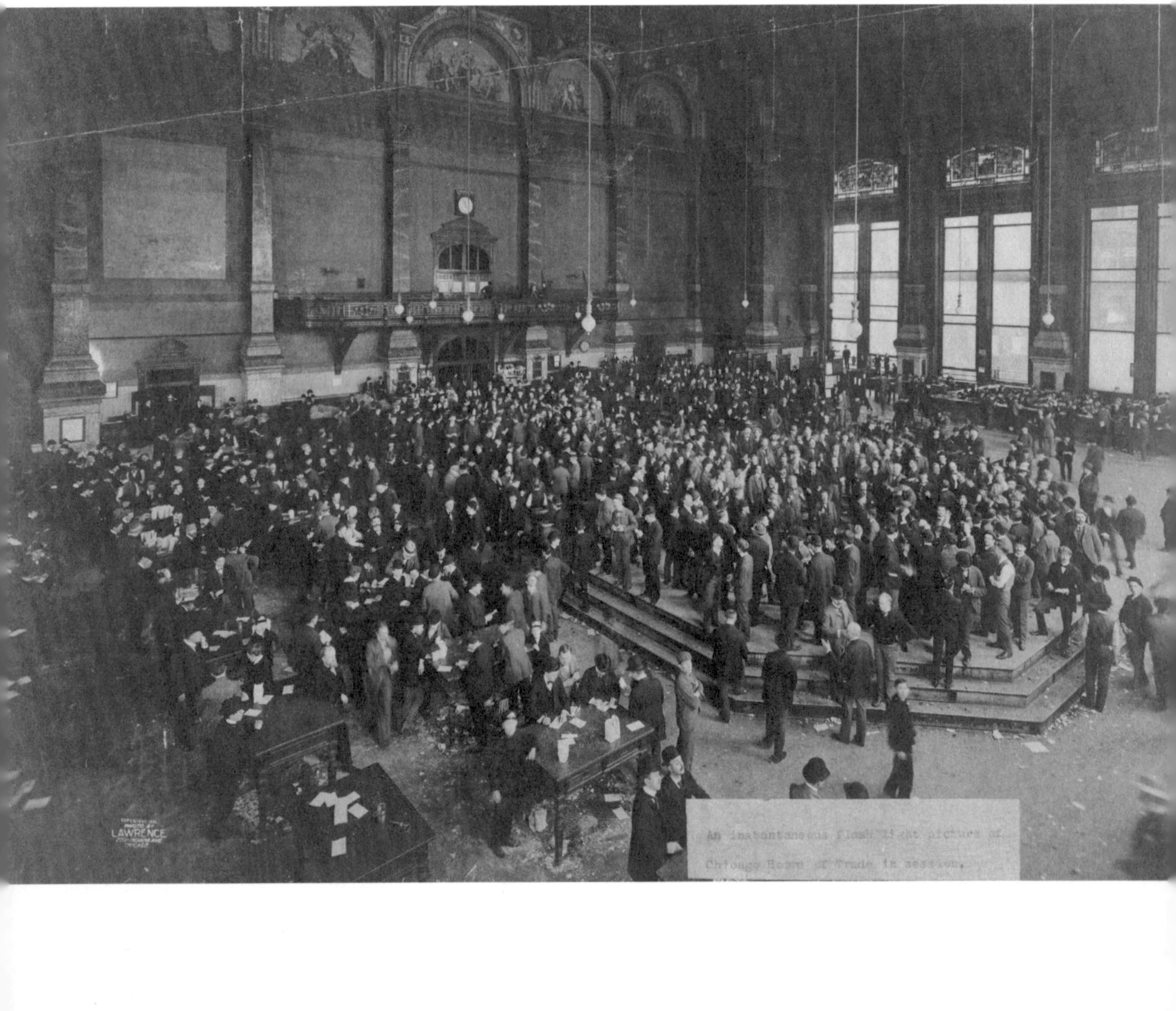
LAWRENCE
An instantaneous flash light picture of
Chicago Board of Trade in session.

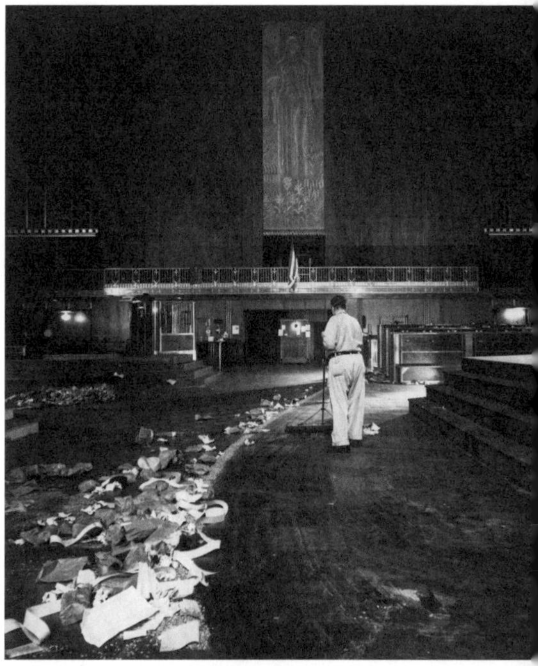

2

3

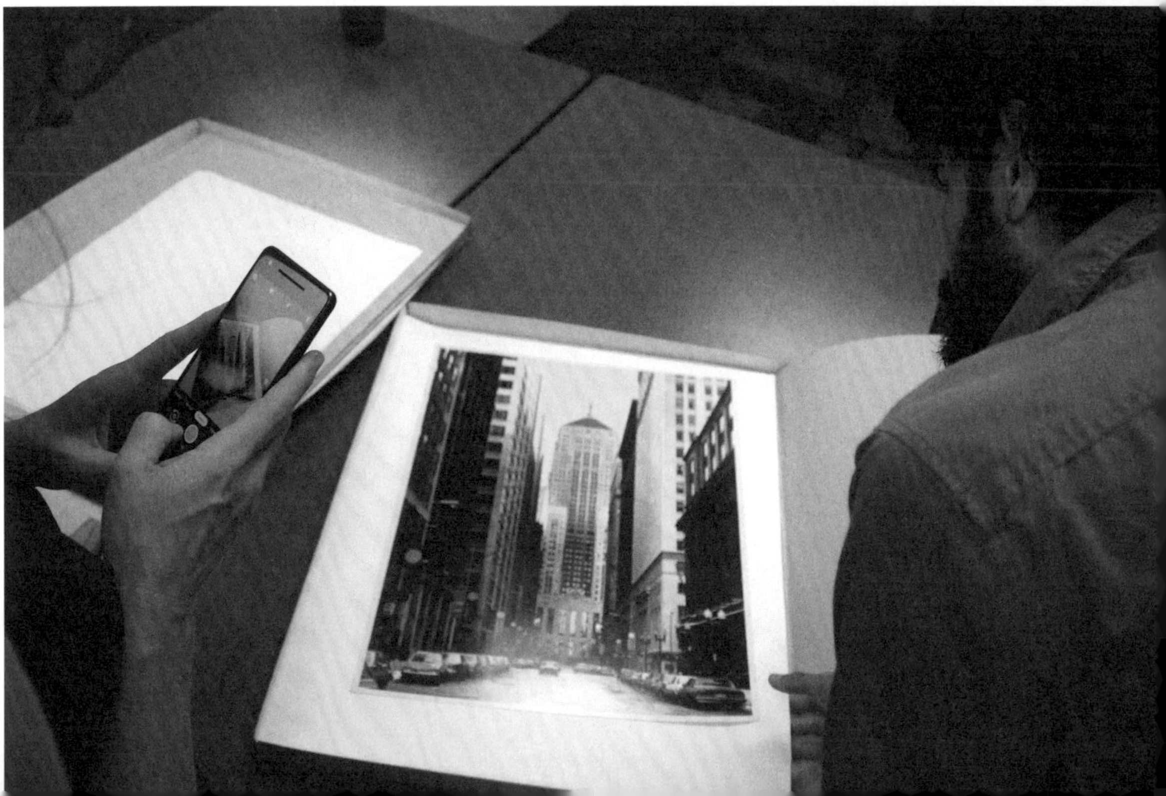

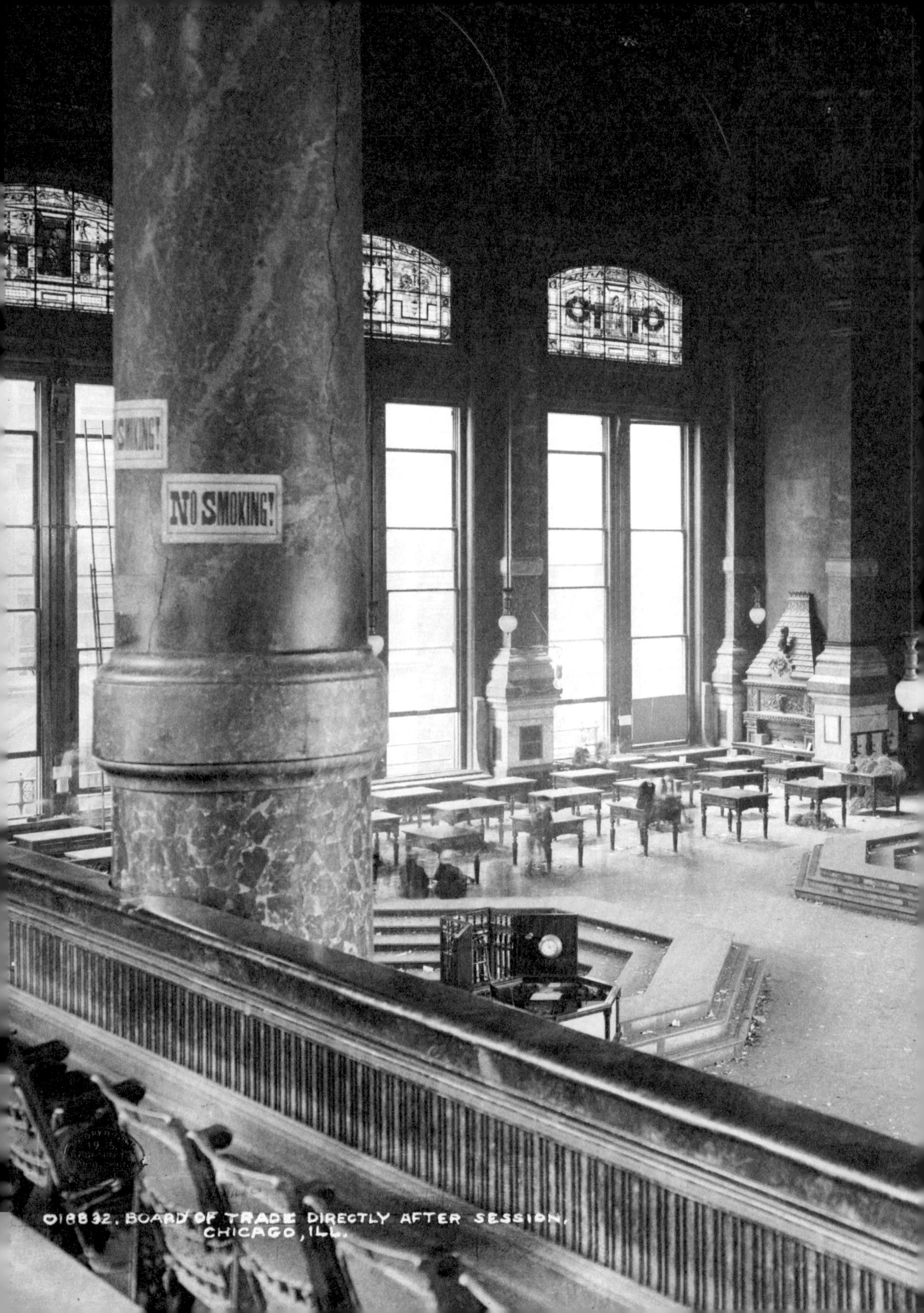

018832. BOARD OF TRADE DIRECTLY AFTER SESSION, CHICAGO, ILL.

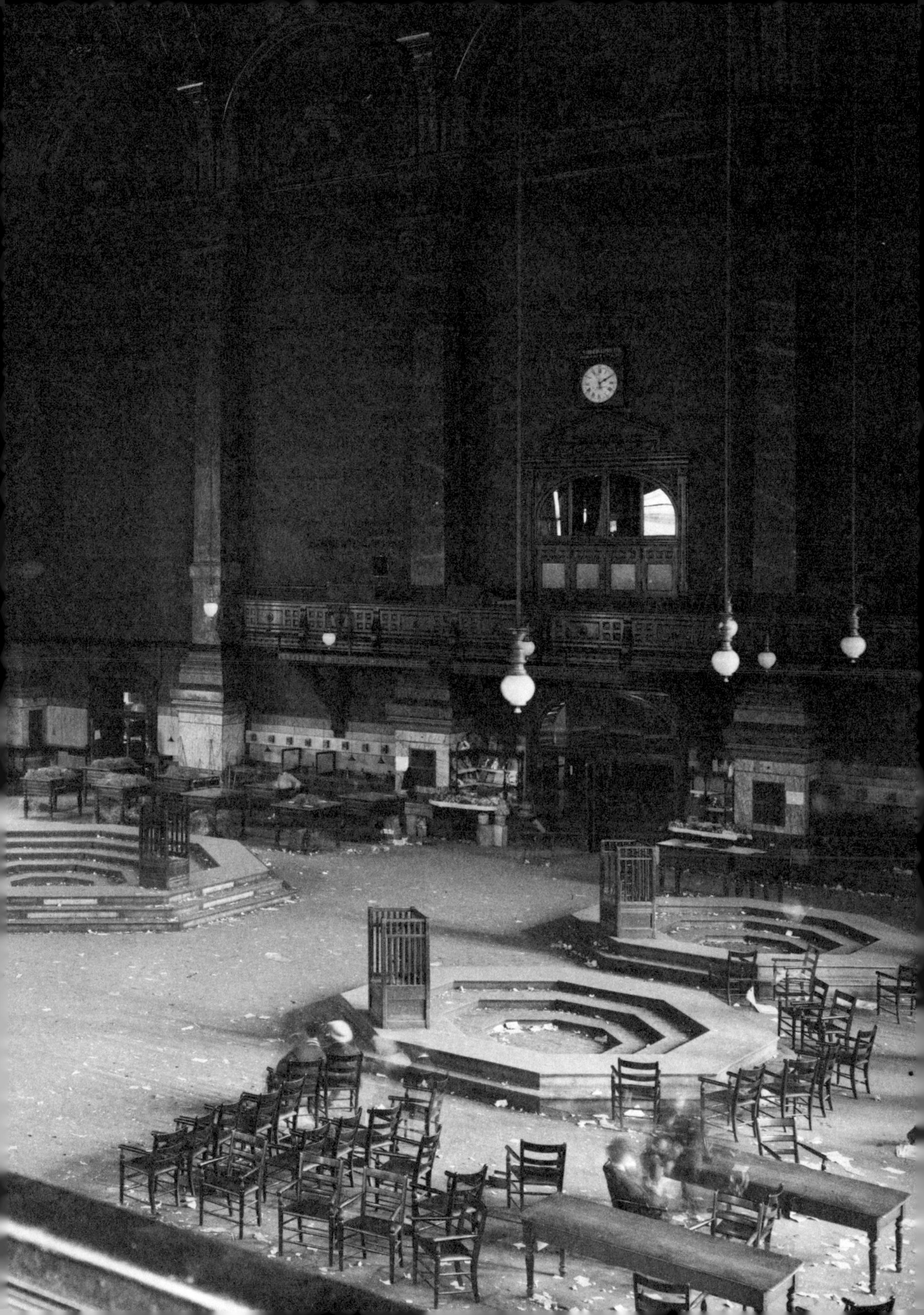

5

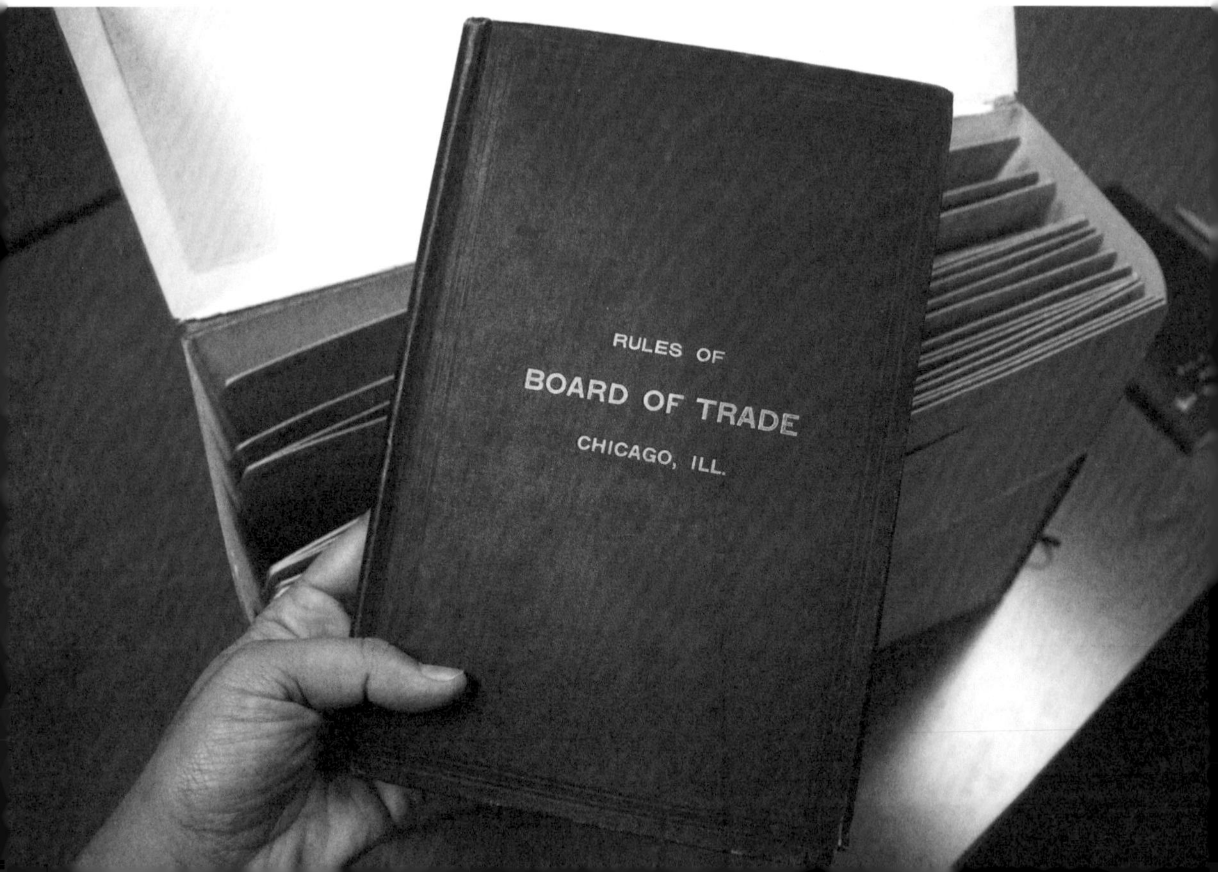

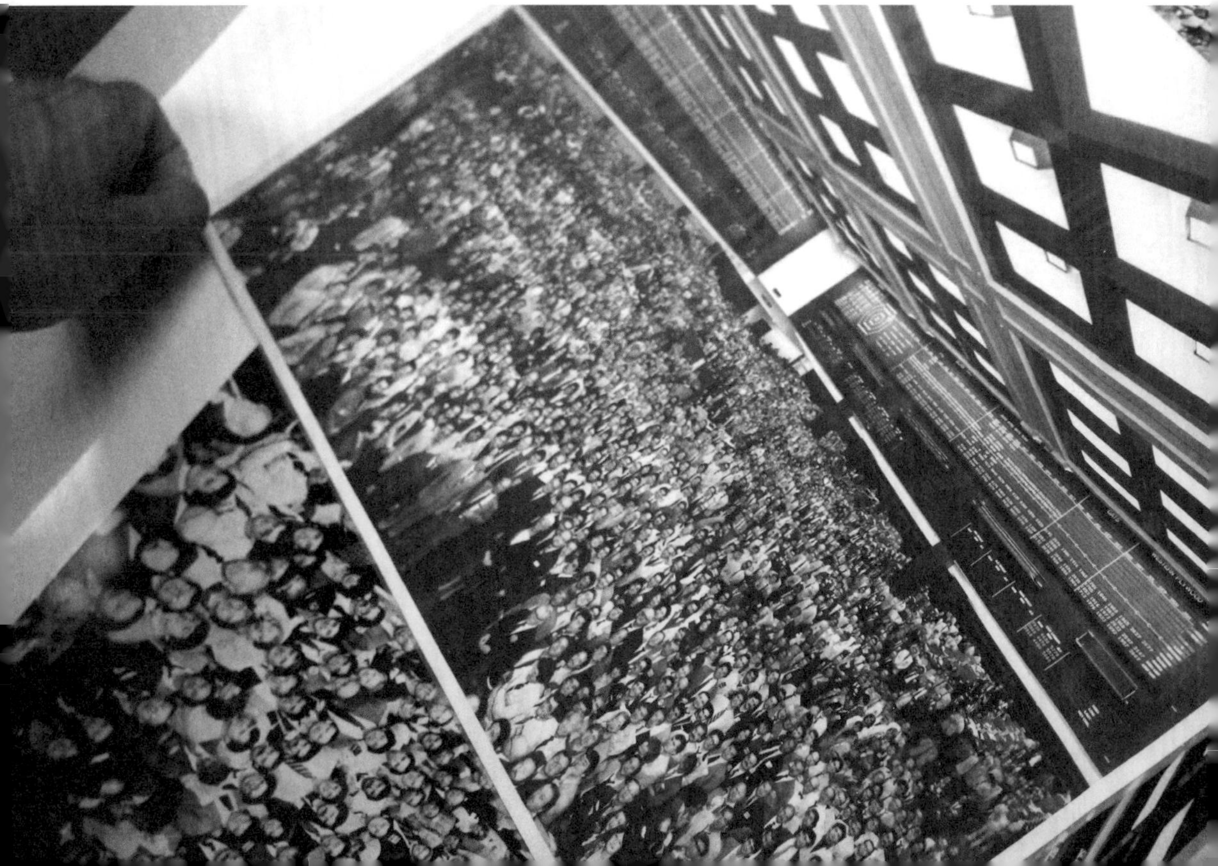

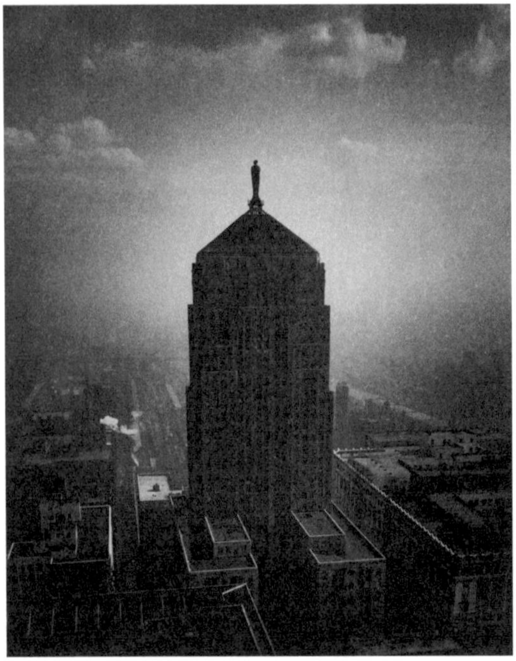

7

8

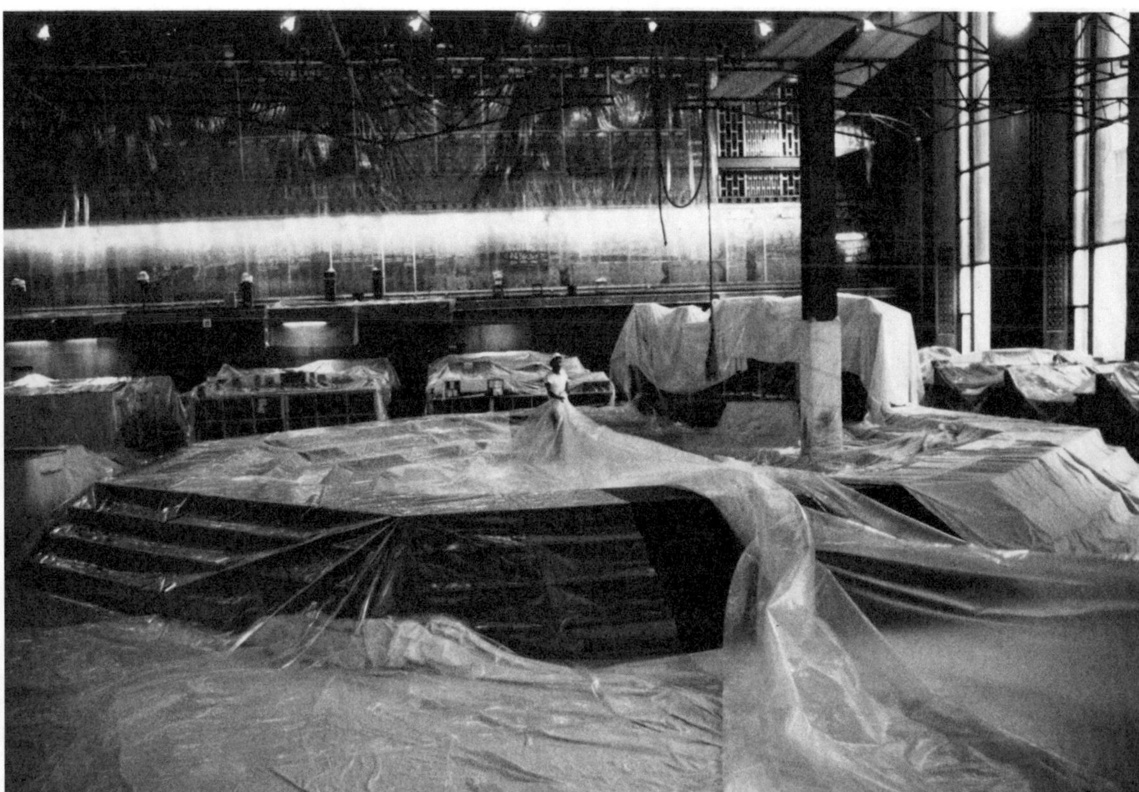

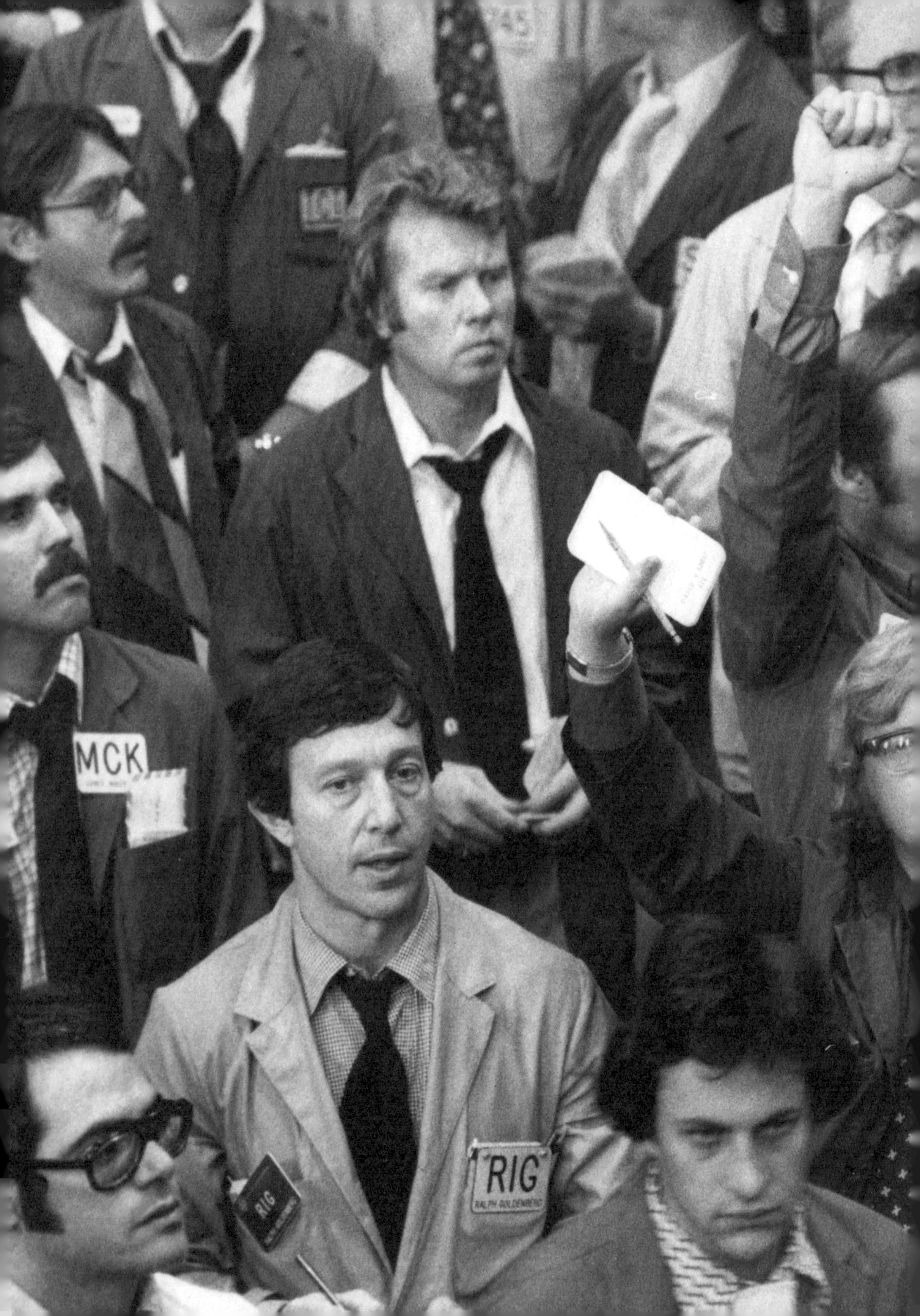
MCK
RIG
RIG

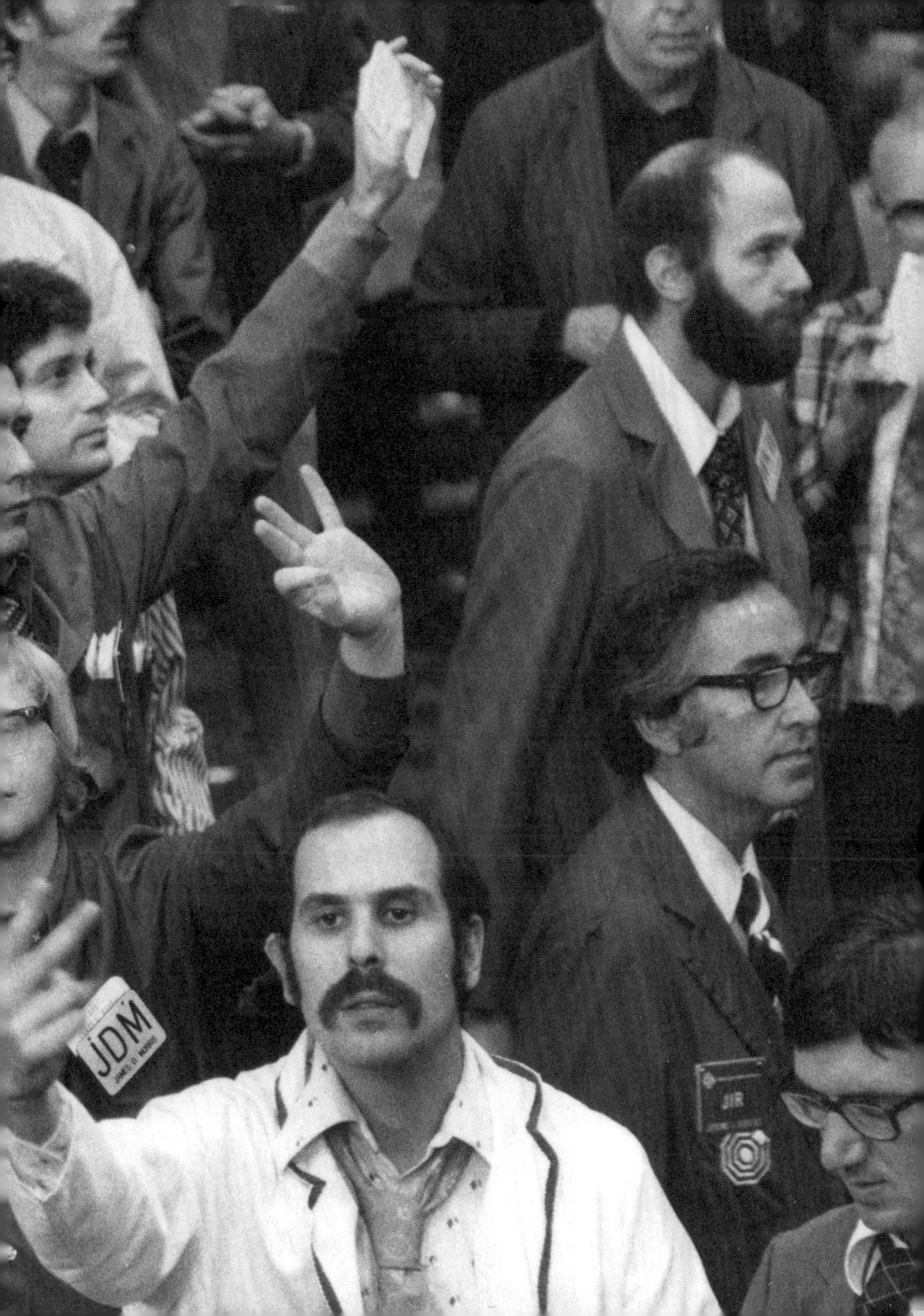
JDM
JIR

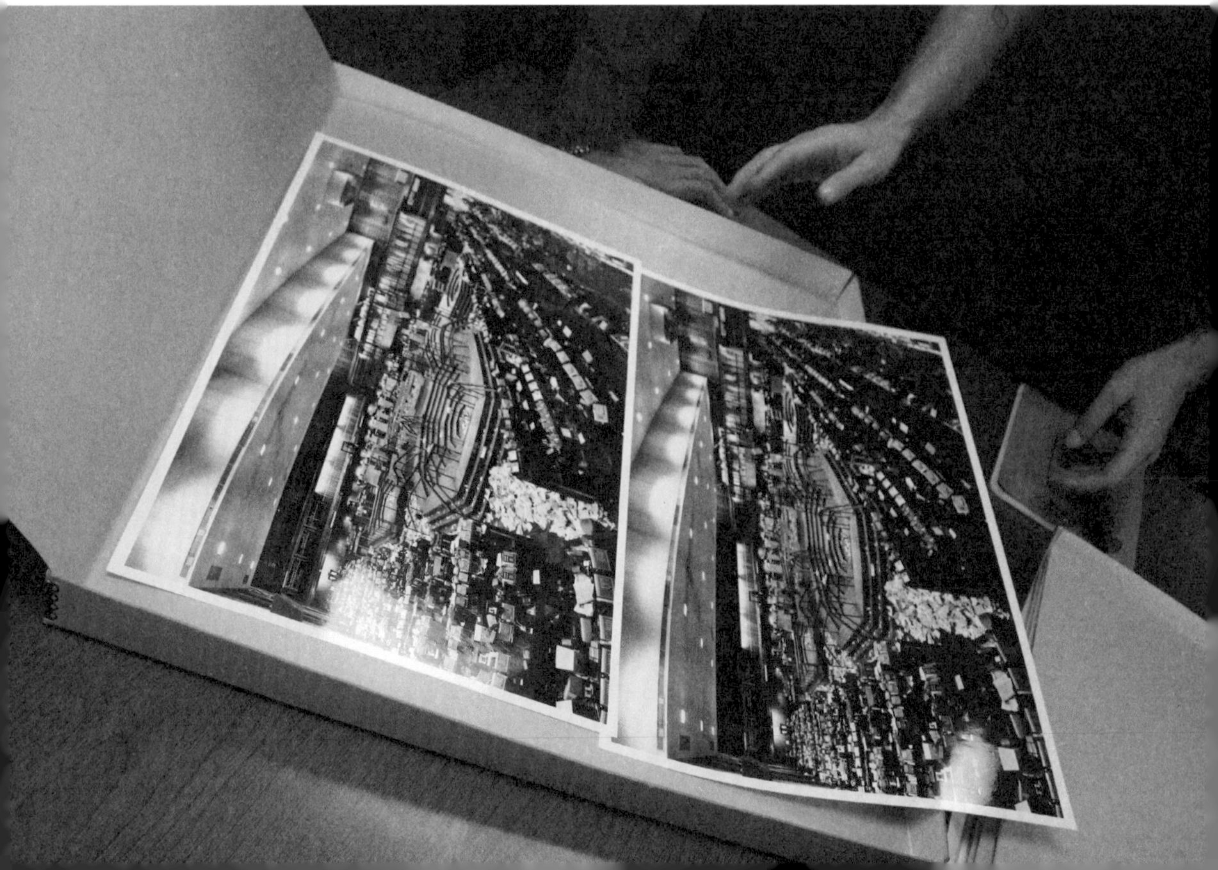

11

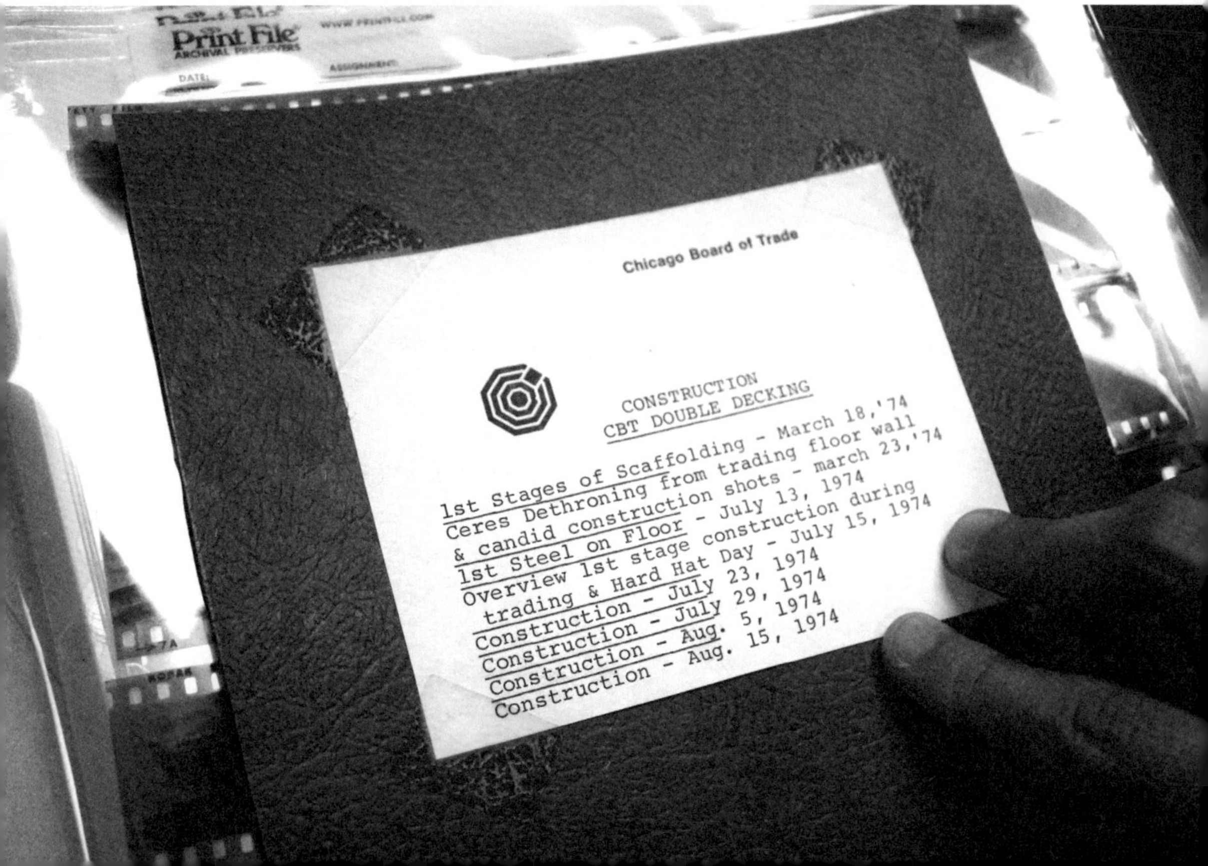
Print File
Chicago Board of Trade
CONSTRUCTION
CBT DOUBLE DECKING
1st Stages of Scaffolding - March 18,'74
Ceres Dethroning from trading floor wall
& candid construction shots - march 23,'74
1st Steel on Floor - July 13, 1974
Overview 1st stage construction during
trading & Hard Hat Day - July 15, 1974
Construction - July 23, 1974
Construction - July 29, 1974
Construction - Aug. 5, 1974
Construction - Aug. 15, 1974

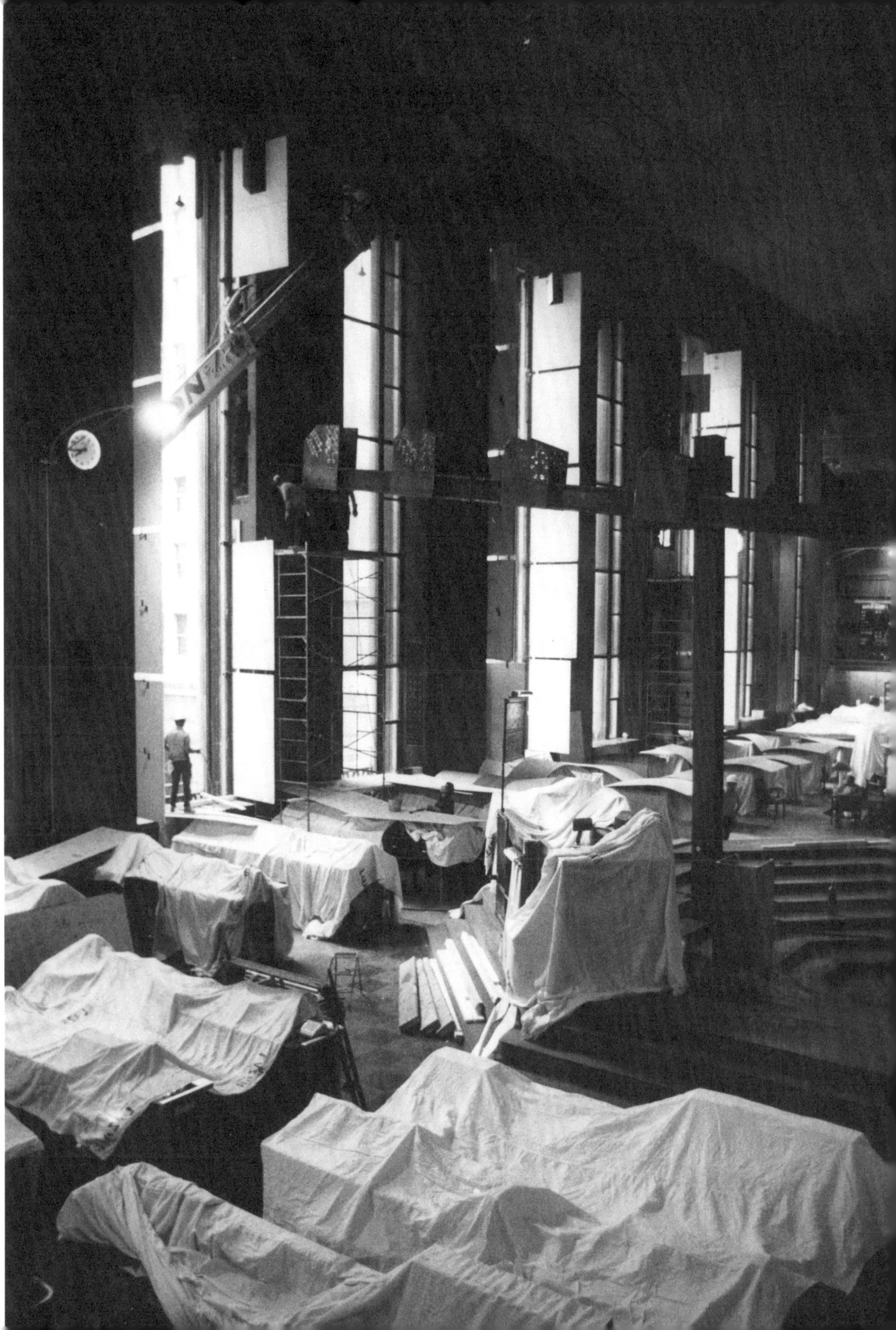

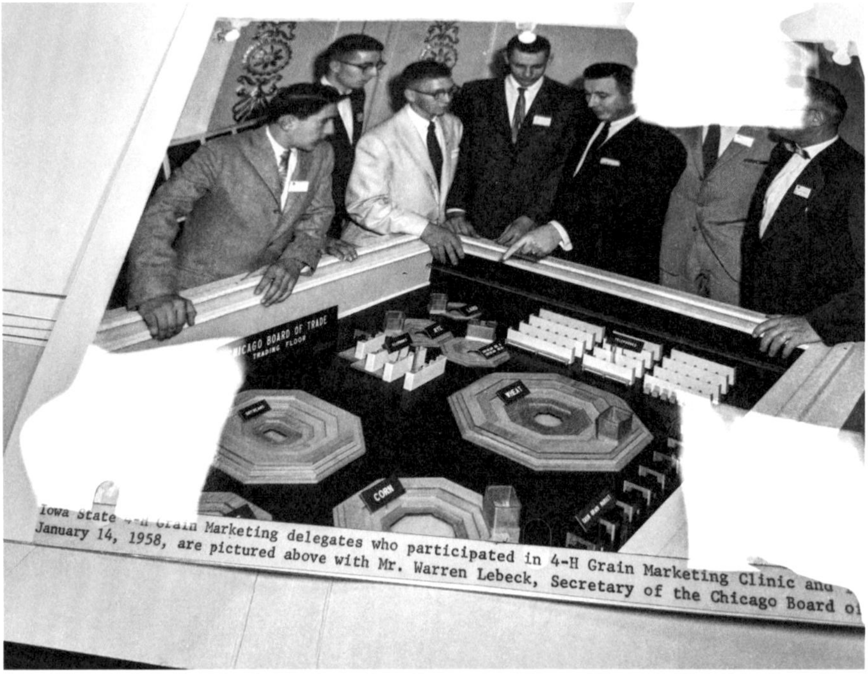
CHICAGO BOARD OF TRADE
TRADING FLOOR
RYE
WHEAT
CORN
Iowa State 4-H Grain Marketing delegates who participated in 4-H Grain Marketing Clinic and
January 14, 1958, are pictured above with Mr. Warren Lebeck, Secretary of the Chicago Board of

13

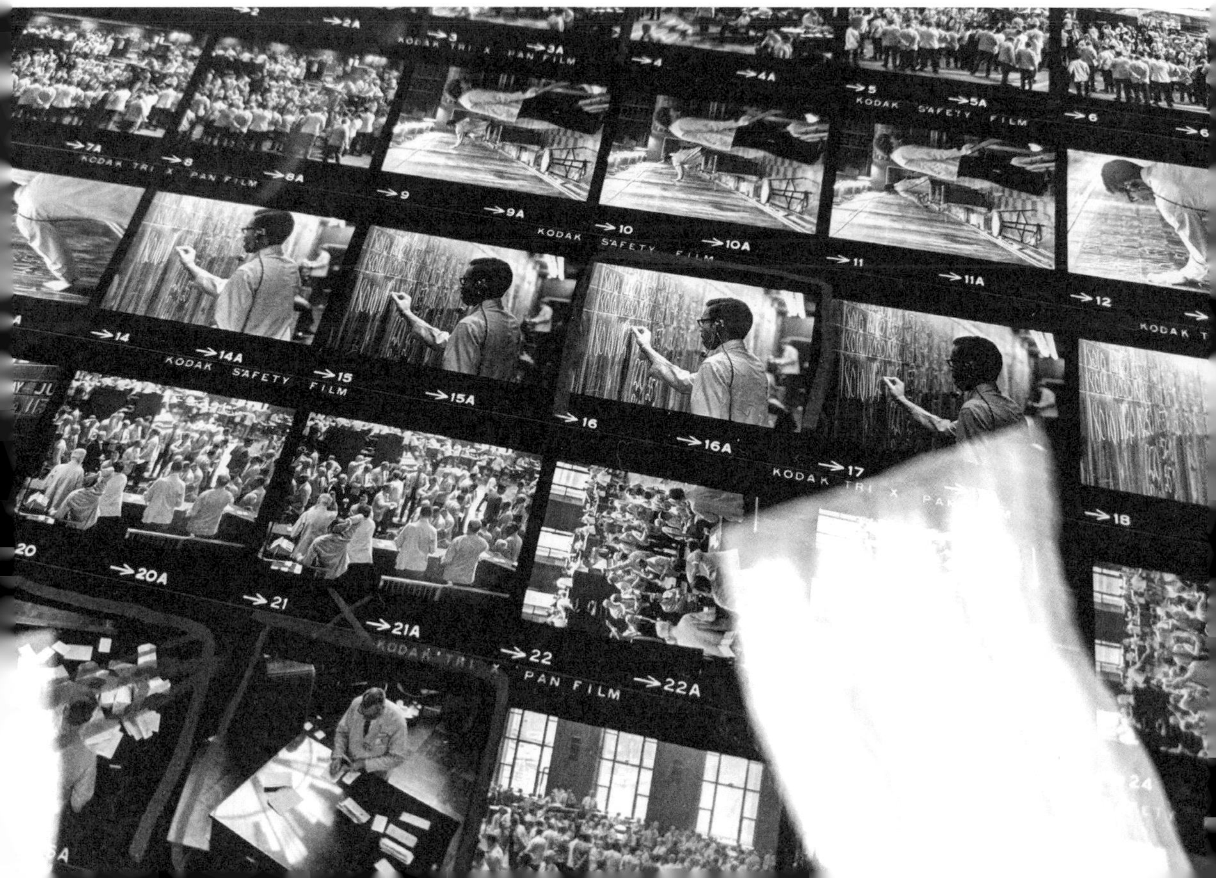
KODAK TRI X PAN FILM
KODAK SAFETY FILM

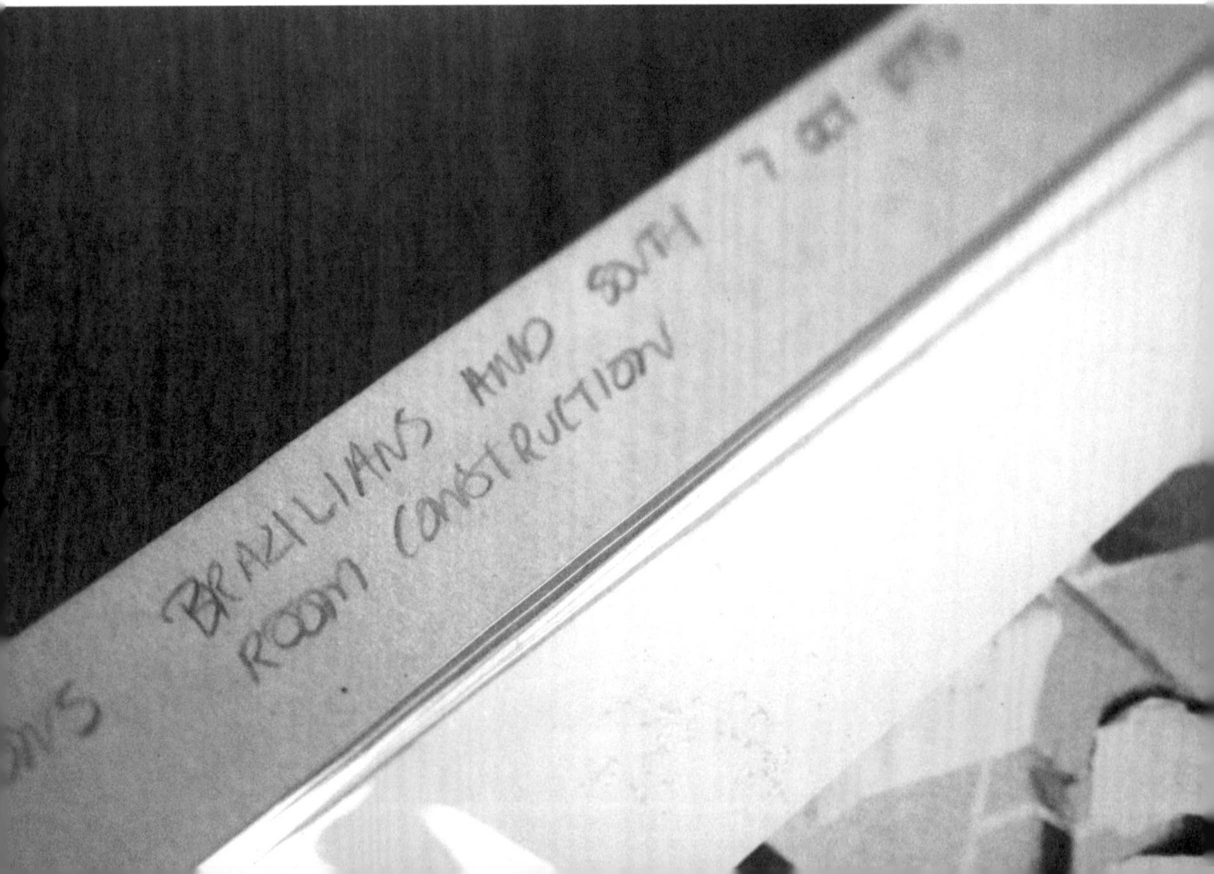
BRAZILIANS AND SOUTH
ROOM CONSTRUCTION

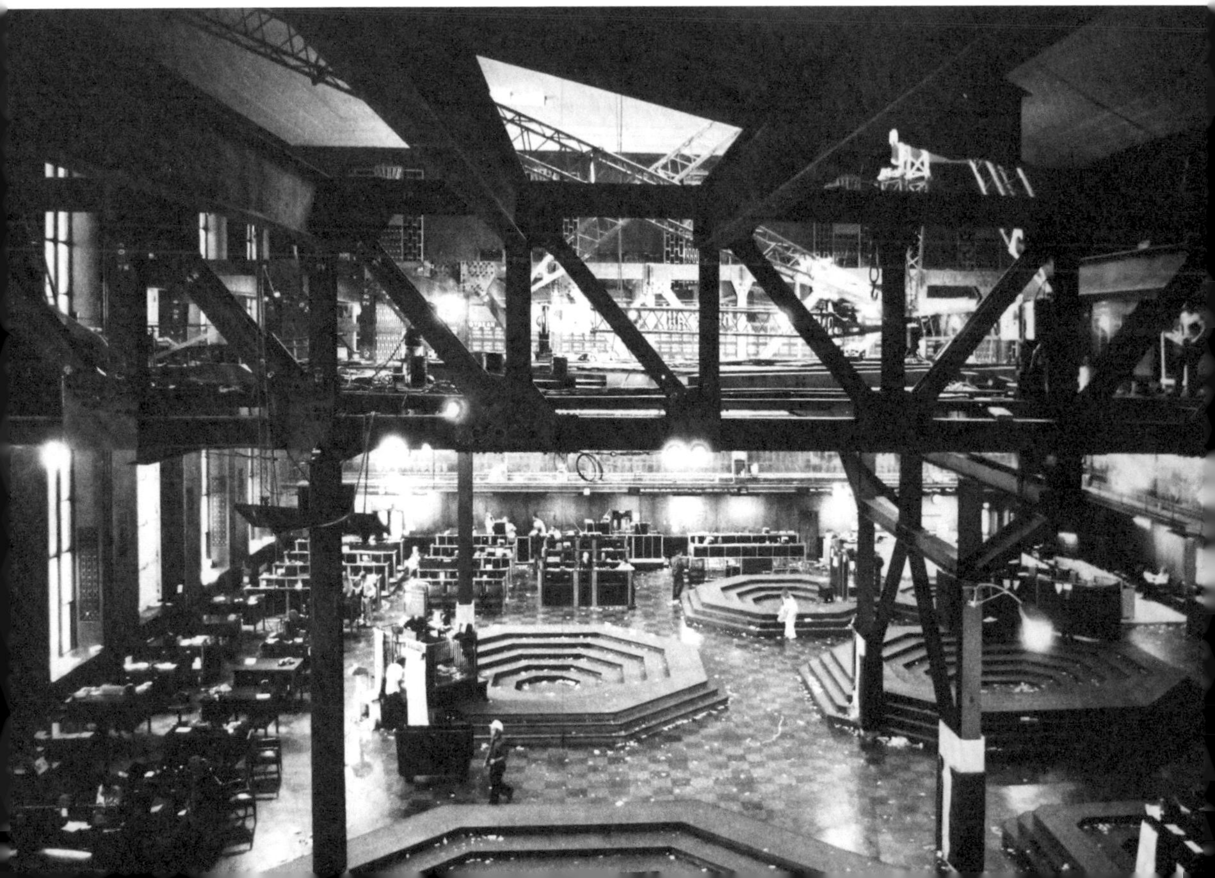

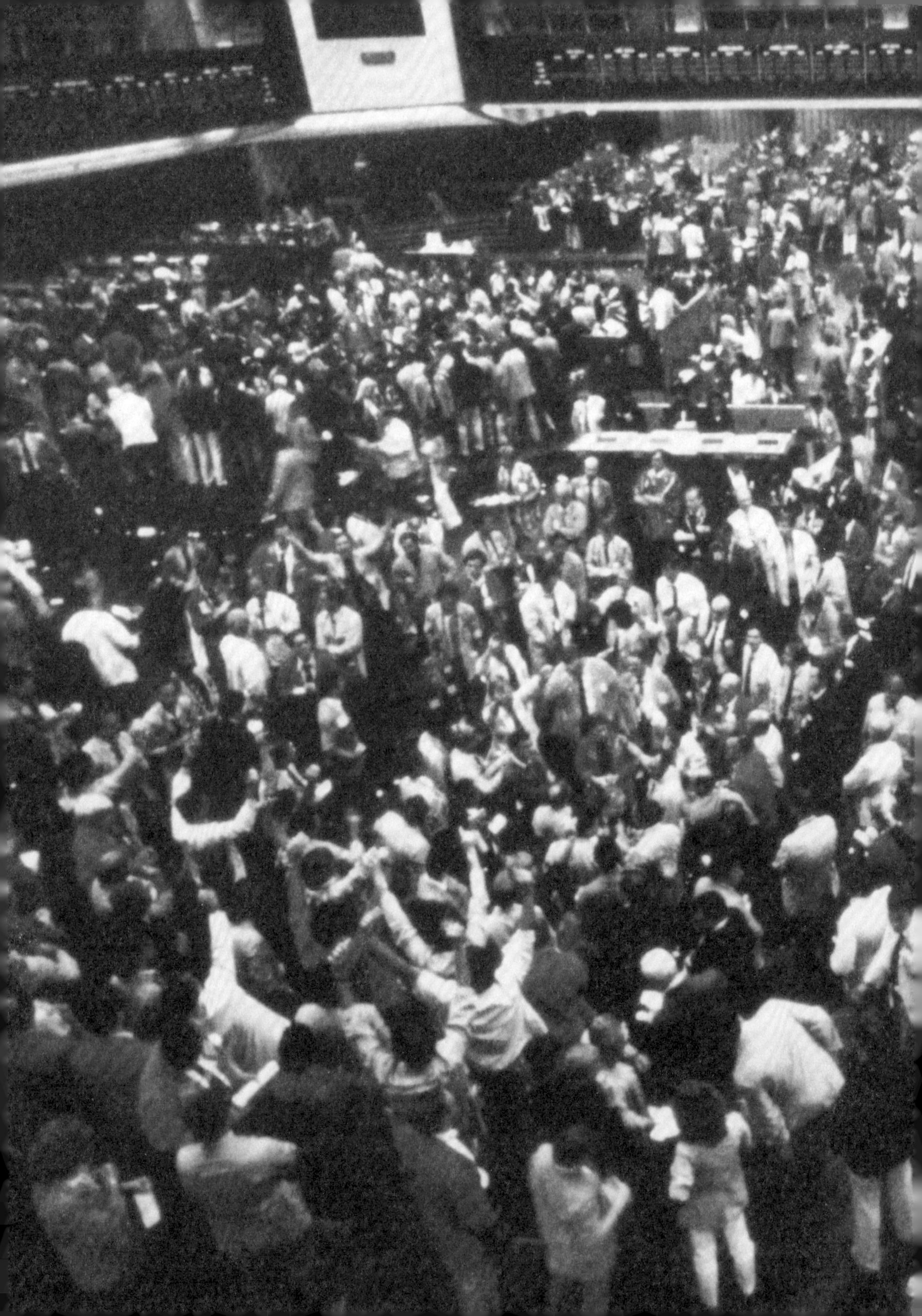

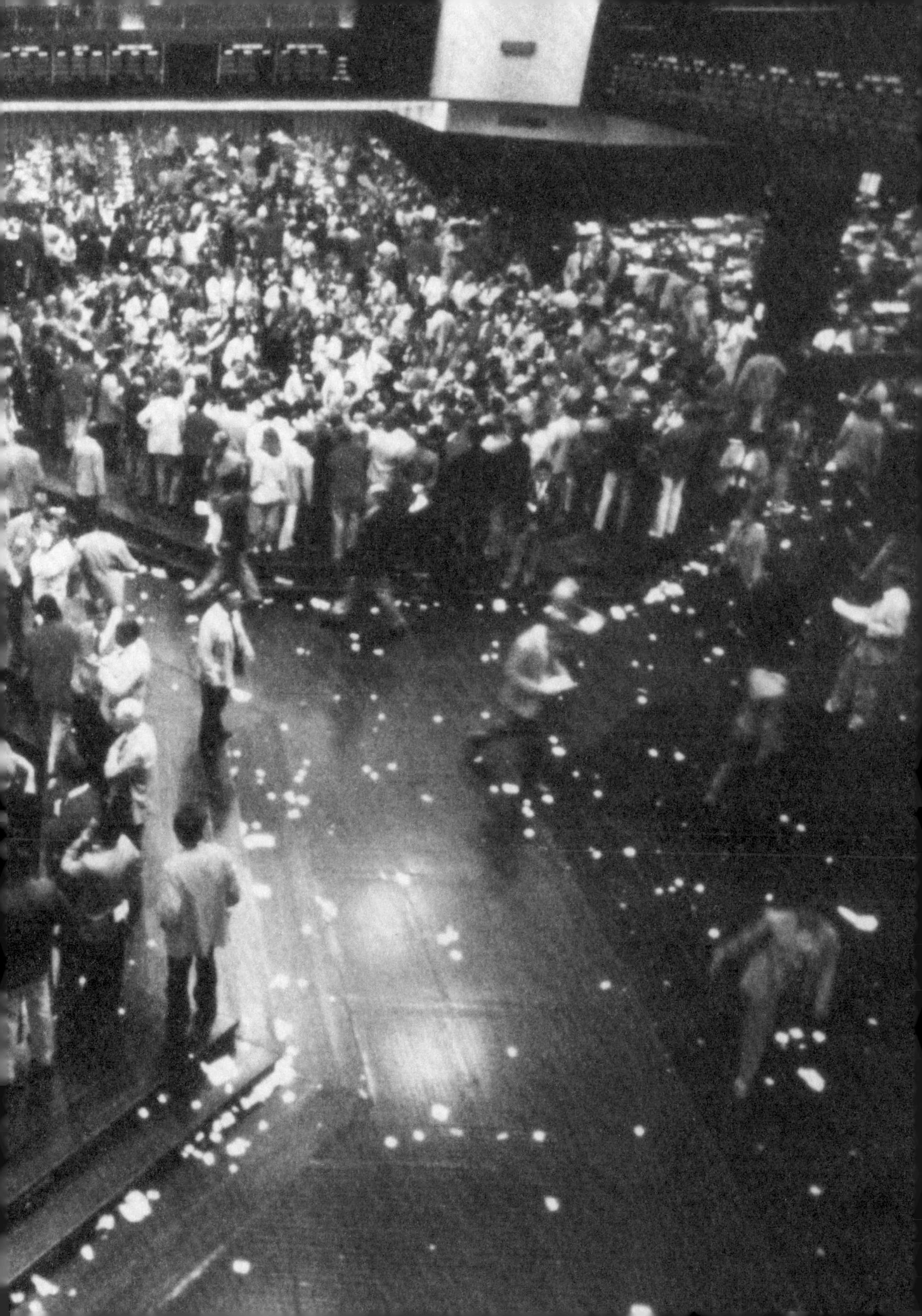

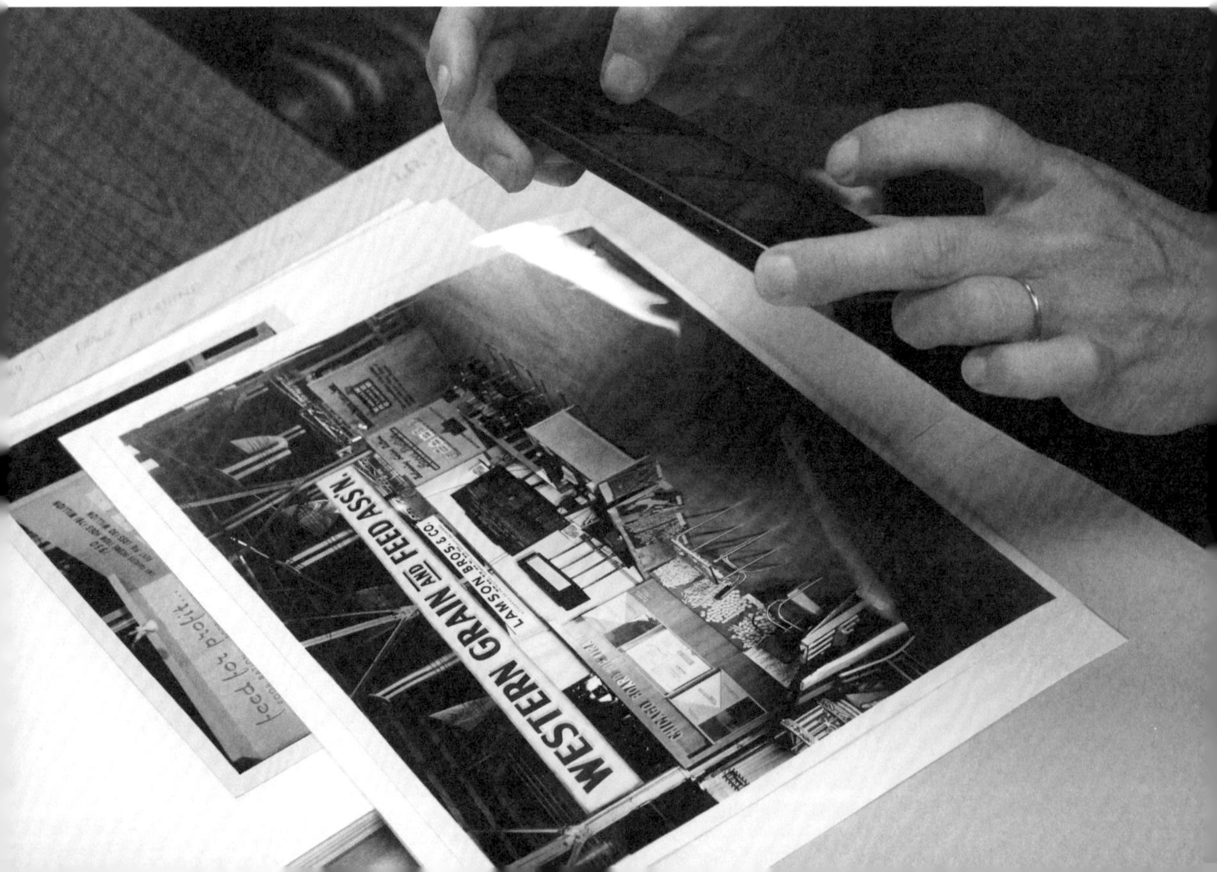
WESTERN GRAIN AND FEED ASS'N.
LAMSON BROS. & CO.
feed for profit

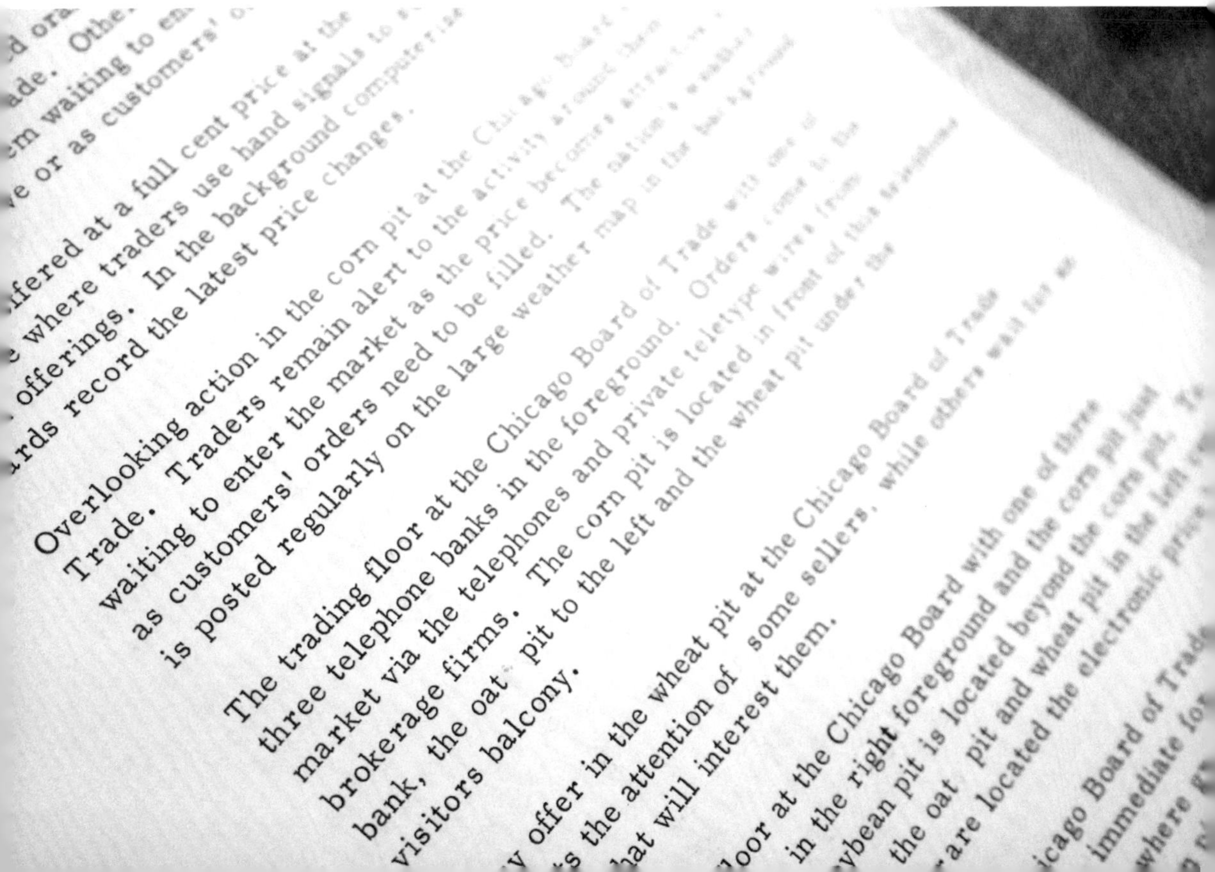
Overlooking action in the corn pit at the Chicago Board
Trade. Traders remain alert to the activity around them
waiting to enter the market as the price becomes
as customers' orders need to be filled. The nation's
is posted regularly on the large weather map in the
The trading floor at the Chicago Board of Trade with one of
three telephone banks in the foreground. Orders come to the
market via the telephones and private teletype wires from
brokerage firms. The corn pit is located in front of this
bank, the oat pit to the left and the wheat pit under the
visitors balcony.

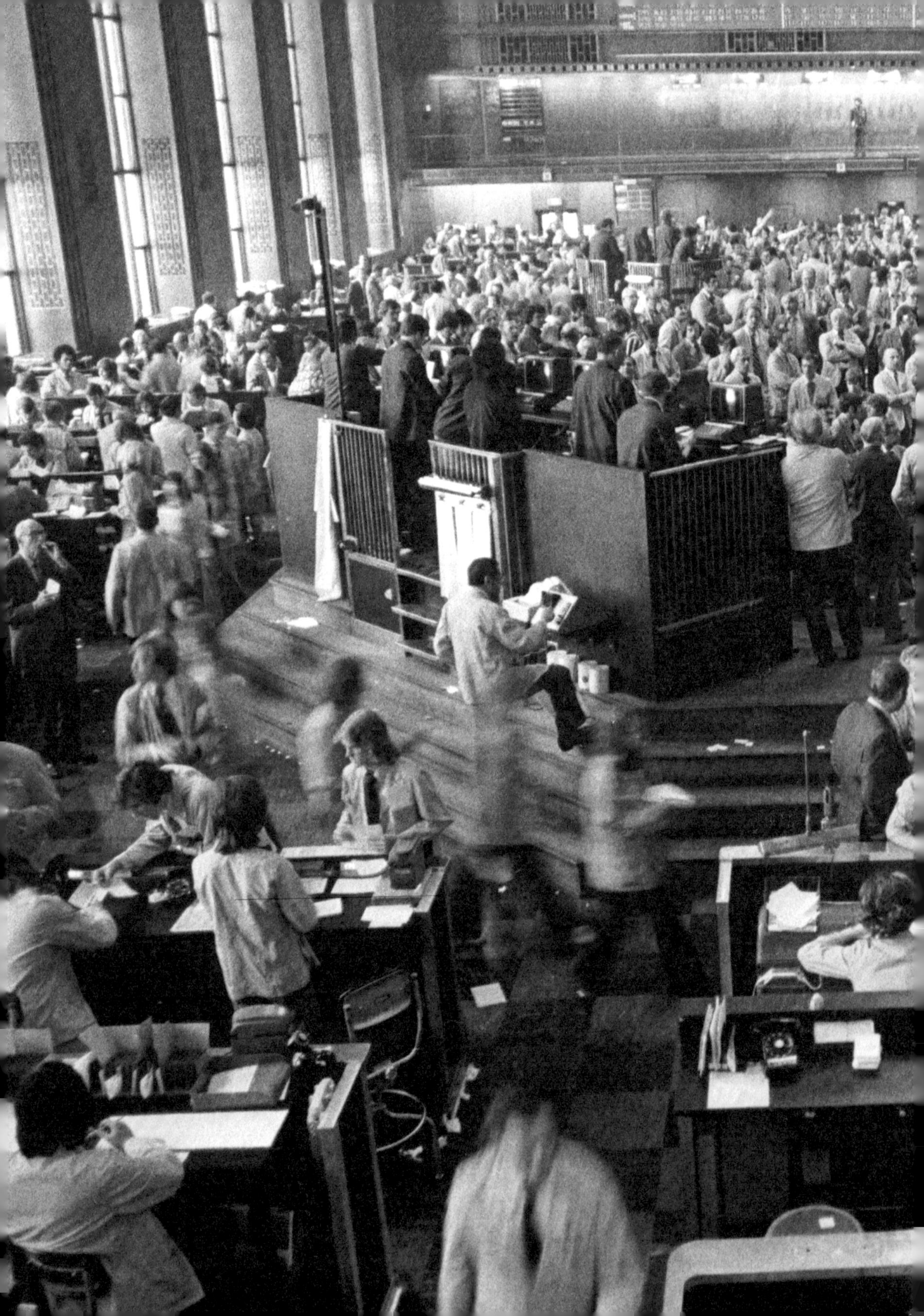

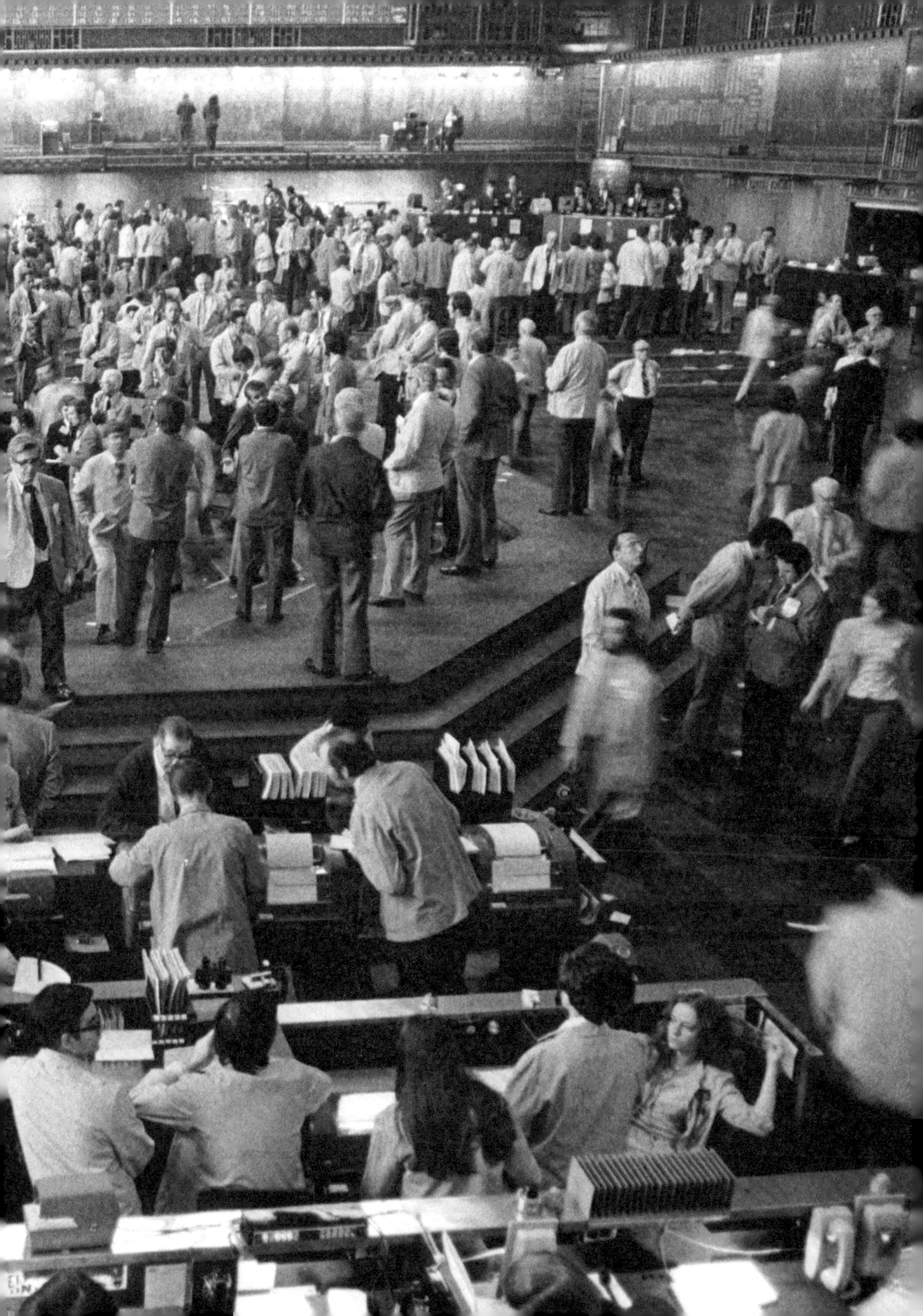

21

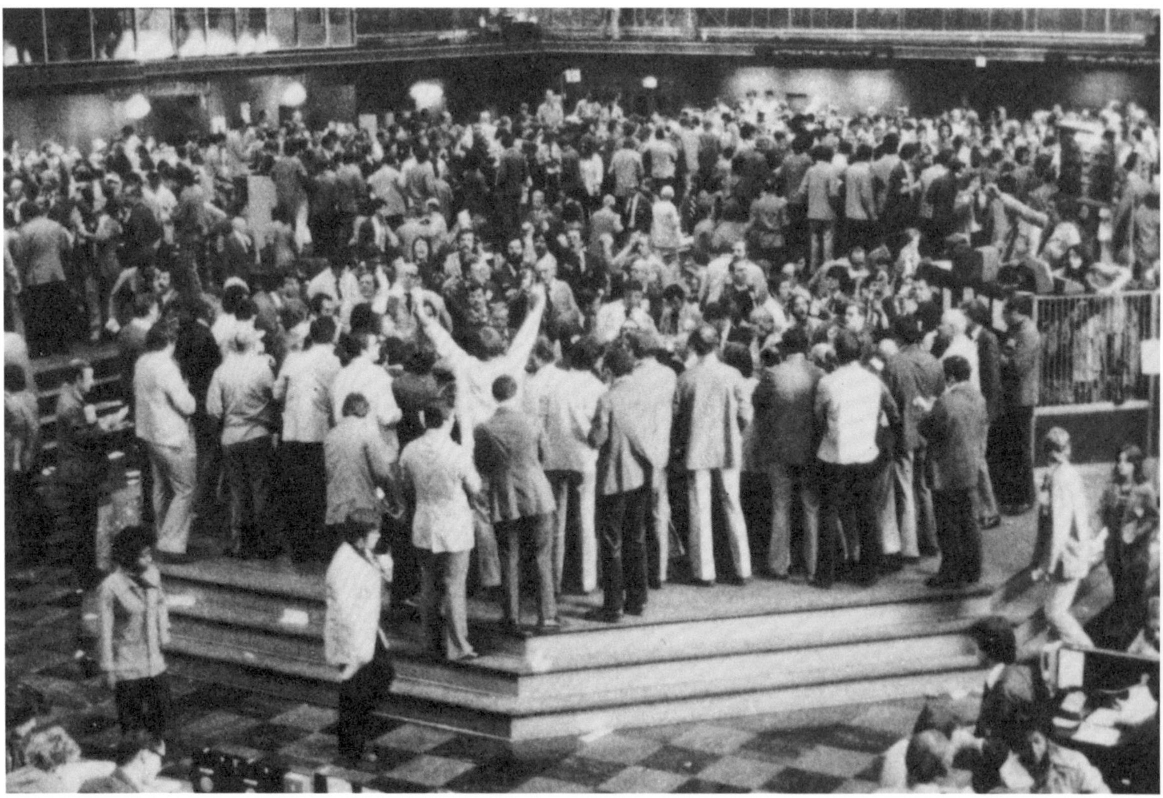

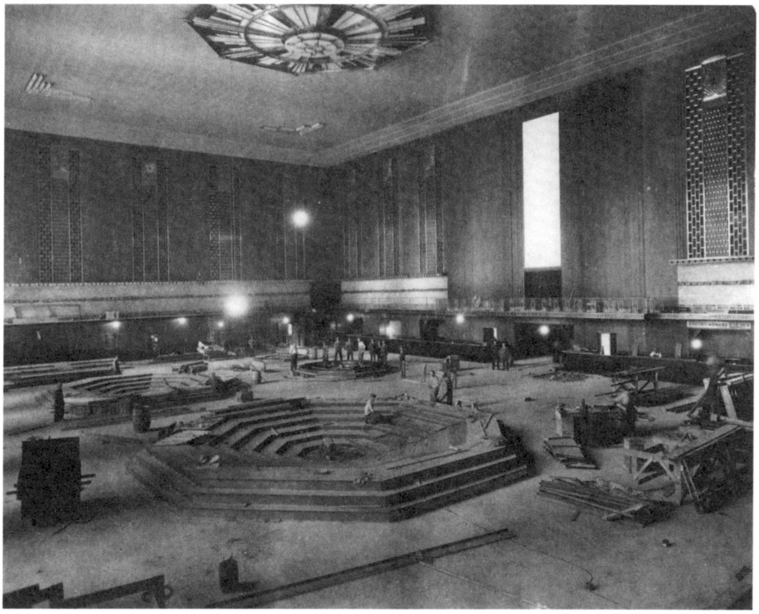

22

23

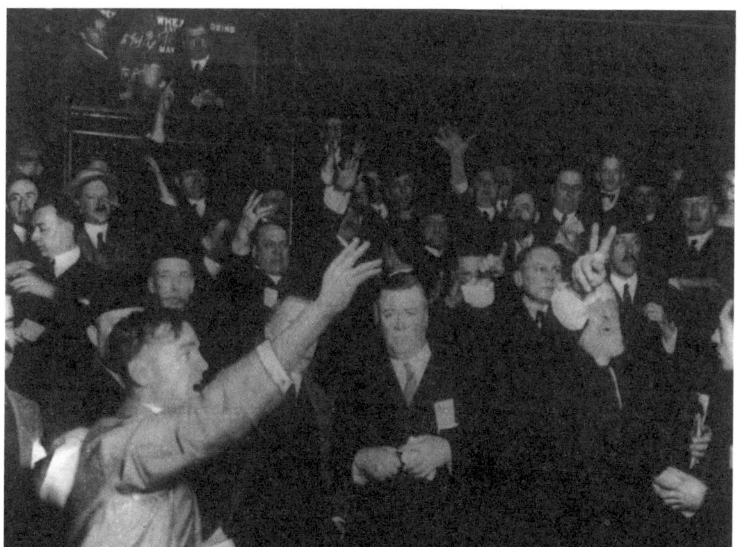

24

KEY T

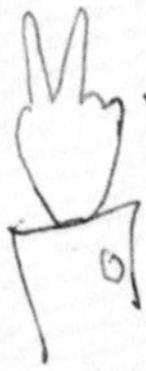

THE PITS: Contracts to buy or sell commodities for delivery in a future month are made here, the unit of trade in grain being 5,000 bushels, indicated by each finger held vertically. Two fingers, for example, mean 10,000 bushels; four fingers, 20,000 bushels, and so on. Palm outward is an offer to sell; toward the trader signifies a bid. Price signals, for which the code is given here, are indicated by the fingers held horizontally. Under normal conditions wide public interest is attracted to these markets since it is here that world opinion on grain, provisions and cotton supply and demand is registered. Country shippers, processors and manufacturers find in the futures markets hedging facilities, or insurance against wide price changes. Hedges made against the purchase of cash commodities enable these factors in the industry to move crops to market at a narrow cost spread between producer and consumer. A wide investment and speculative trade builds up the volume necessary to create a broad, liquid market in which hedges may be executed at all times. By reason of the Board of Trade employment is directly given to 30,000 persons, and indirectly to 100,000.

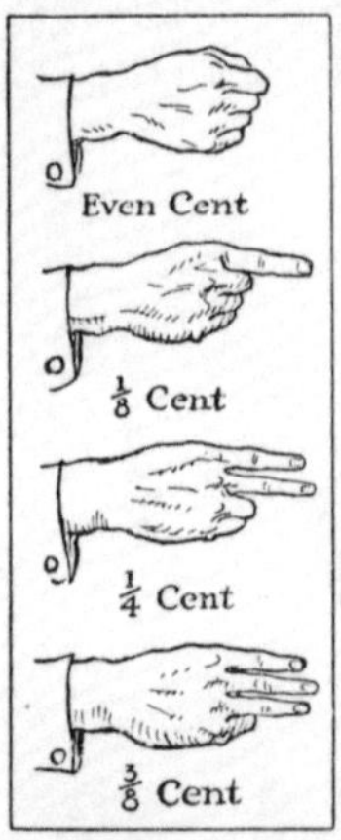

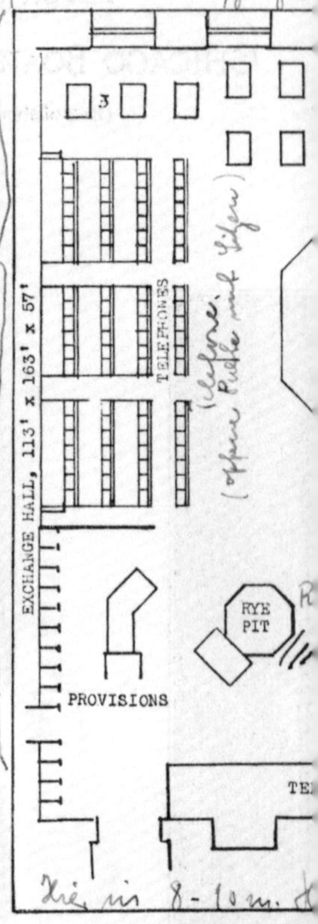

TELEPHONES: Telephone brokers are stationed at both ends of the exchange floor and directly in front of the Visitors' Gallery. Their work is an important link in the lightning-like speed of Board of Trade quotations and the sales services of its members. Orders from world points arriving at office headquarters of member firms are 'phoned directly to the exchange floor and transmitted by messenger or signal to pit brokers for execution in the open market. When an order is executed, confirmation flashes back over the same quick route. So highly geared is the service over these privately leased wires that it is possible for an order to leave Kansas City, Minneapolis or another pivotal point, be

executed by a Boa
and confirmed bac
within 15 seconds.
floor is numbered.
automatically if a
has left his post is

PIT REPORTERS:
in stands above th
reporters recording
made by the trade
trained, competent
most active marke
only the month of
the price changes
mated. The slip of
automatic time stam
to a teletype operat
a few keys which
typed message in
another operator
taps out a price cha

PLAN and PRICE CODE

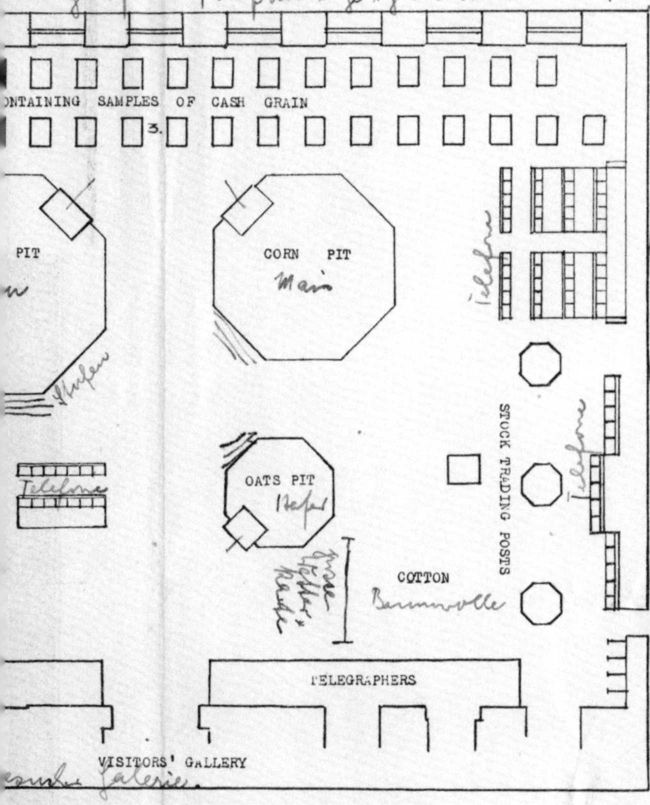

rade member,
nt of origin
phone on the
mber flashes
broker who

ned employes
re quotations
ange in price
y are highly
breast of the
write down
e traded and
are consum-
s fed into an
e and handed
operator taps
y produce a
room. Here
ecial machine
ed simultane-

ously by tickers and private wires to more than six hundred American cities. At the same time a Morse code operator in the control room flashes the price to blackboard markers on the exchange floor.

CASH GRAIN TABLES: Each of the small paper bags on these tables represents a carload of grain arrived in the Chicago district which has been properly inspected, graded and certified by inspectors of the State of Illinois. Board of Trade members in this department must be shrewd bargainers and keen judges of grain qualities. They must compete continually with others and so their firms maintain constant touch with country shippers and strive for the highest possible price for the farmer's grain. Commission men hedge purchases of grain by selling a like amount in the nearby pit, thus insuring against price swings. The combination of cash and futures trading enables Board of Trade members to market the farmer's grain at a lower cost than that of any other staple commodity.

STOCK TRADING POSTS: The huge wire and quotations service of Board of Trade houses is available for the trade in stocks and bonds. Tapping new investment territory, this wire system gives weight to the belief that this department of the Board of Trade will become one of the leading securities markets of the world. Sales on other leading stock exchanges are shown by news projectors and blackboards.

COTTON: This was the first Cotton Futures market to designate the Galveston - Houston basin as delivery point on cotton contracts. The Cotton Futures market has won high commercial praise as a progressive unit of the exchange. Growers, spinners and shippers approve its contract as basically sound and commercially attractive.

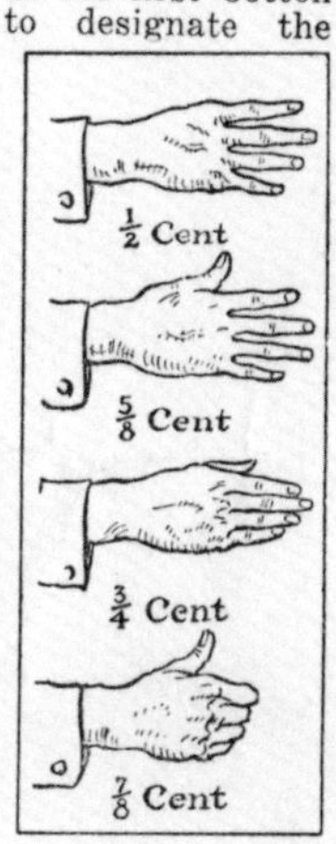

PROVISIONS: Lard and Dry Salted Bellies are the commodities marketed here. This is the largest market of its kind in the world and its quotations have an important bearing on American and European prices for pork products.

Trading Hours—Grain and Provisions

Daily...............9:30 a.m. to 1:15 p.m.
Saturdays ....9:30 a.m. to 12:00 noon
Cotton and Securities hours conform to other exchanges

BUILDING FEATURES

Basement, Safety Deposit Vaults; Fifth Floor, Executive Offices; Seventh Floor, Weighmaster's Dep't., and Electric Miniature Grain Elevator; Eleventh Floor, Sampling Dep't.
OBSERVATION TOWER: (Admission 25c) Forty-fourth Floor.

Published by National Syndicate Service

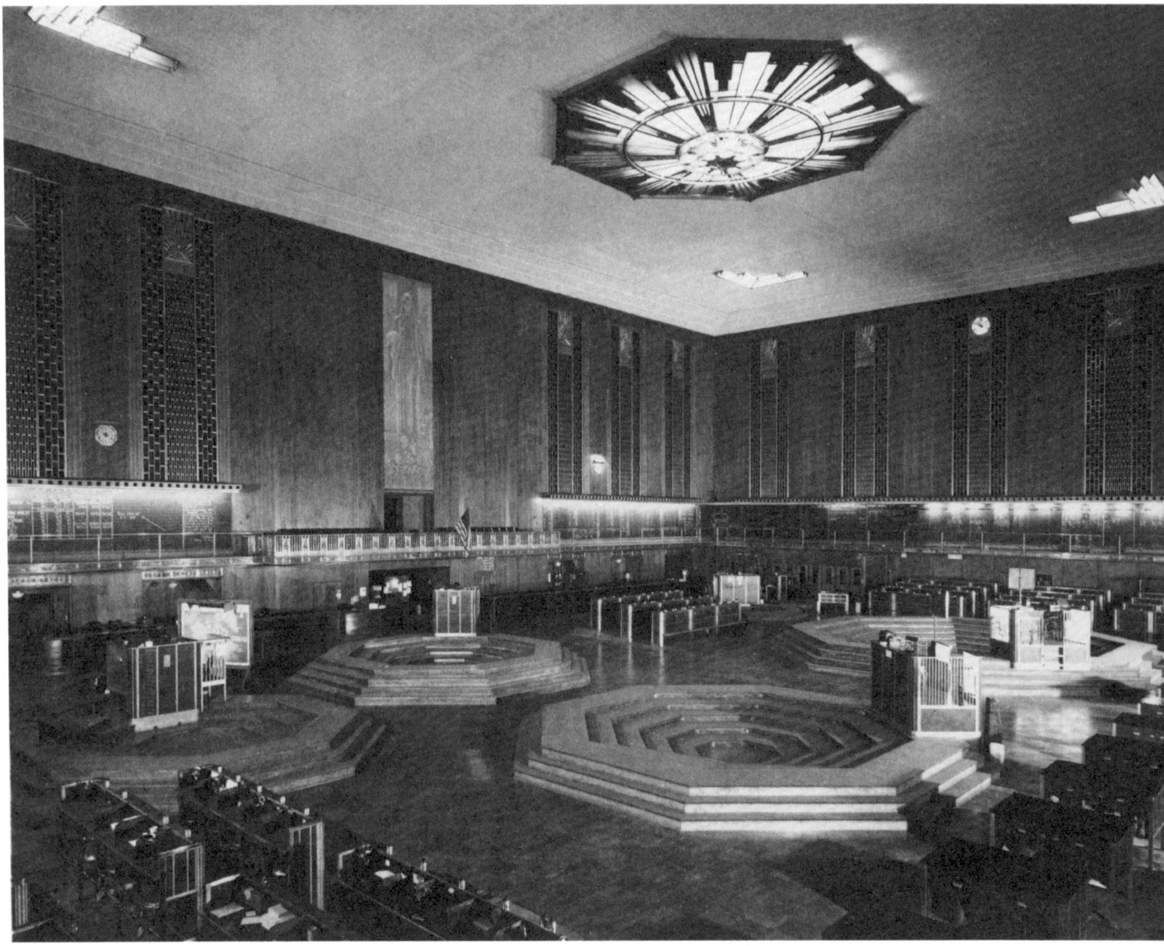

25

1. *An Instantaneous flash picture of the Chicago Board of Trade in session.* Photograph by Geo. R. Lawrence, circa 1900. Library of Congress Prints and Photographs Division Washington, D.C. 20540 USA.
2. *Interior of the Chicago Board of Trade after closing.* A janitor sweeps up papers after closing at the Chicago Board of Trade, Chicago, Illinois. Photograph by Gordon H. Coster, circa 1948. Chicago History Museum, ICHi-074237.
3. The artists conducting research in the Chicago Board of Trade (CBOT) records at the University of Illinois at Chicago (UIC) Special Collections (Richard J. Daley Library). Pictured is the CBOT Building, built and occupied by the CBOT since 1930, photographed looking south down the LaSalle Street "canyon." Photograph by Renata de Bonis, 2019. Reproduced with permission. © 1998 CME Group Inc.
4. (full page spread) *Board of Trade directly after session, Chicago, Ill.* Image taken from a gallery looking at the trading floor and pits in the first building designed in 1881 by William W. Boyington for the CBOT, which opened in 1885 at 141 West Jackson Boulevard. This building was torn down to make way for the current CBOT Building designed by Holabird & Root in 1925 and opened in 1930. Published by the Detroit Publishing Co., circa 1905. Library of Congress Prints and Photographs Division Washington, D.C. 20540 USA.
5. The artists conducting research in the CBOT records at the UIC Special Collections (Richard J. Daley Library). Pictured is a book that details the rules, regulations, and bylaws of the CBOT, updated and published yearly by the CBOT, from a collection of such manuals from 1865 to 1895. Photograph by Renata de Bonis, 2019. Reproduced with permission. © 1998 CME Group Inc.
6. The artists conducting research in the CBOT records at the UIC Special Collections (Richard J. Daley Library). Group photographs of CBOT traders for the opening of a new 32,000-square-foot trading floor in 1982. The CBOT introduced new options trading that year and began to trade options on Treasury bond futures, later adding soybean futures in 1984, and futures on heating oil and crude oil (https://www.referenceforbusiness.com/history2/25/Chicago-Board-of-Trade.html). Photograph by Renata de Bonis, 2019. Reproduced with permission. © 1998 CME Group Inc.
7. *Chicago Board of Trade.* Exterior aerial view of the CBOT Building, Chicago, Illinois. Photograph by Gordon H. Coster, undated. Chicago History Museum, ICHi-076713.
8. Photograph taken during a 1974 trading floor construction project at the CBOT as part of a series of expansions of its trading floors at the time. Starting in 1968 the CBOT added pits for non-grain commodities (plywood, silver, gold); began trading in financial instruments; began to introduce computer systems to its floors; and in 1973 founded an off-site sister entity, the Chicago Board Options Exchange (CBOE) to trade in the option to buy a futures contract (securities options). Image held in the CBOT Records at the UIC Special Collections (Richard J. Daley Library). Reproduced with permission. © 1998 CME Group Inc.
9. (full page spread) "Tight shots" of images of floor traders in action on the floors using hand signals, from 1976 public relations materials produced for the CBOT. Image held in the CBOT Records at the UIC Special Collections (Richard J. Daley Library). Reproduced with permission. © 1998 CME Group Inc.
10. The artists conducting research in the CBOT records at the UIC Special Collections (Richard J. Daley Library). Empty trading pits, likely the bond trading room or "The South Room" (built in 1975) based on an inscription on the top step of the pit in the foreground reading "JUN 1 BONDS." Photograph by Renata de Bonis, 2019. Reproduced with permission. © 1998 CME Group Inc.
11. The artists conducting research in the CBOT records at the UIC Special Collections (Richard J. Daley Library). Archival material detailing the various stages of a renovation project in 1974 for "double decking" the main trading floor, which seems to include the addition of a larger viewing gallery, electronic boards, and a drop ceiling with lighting and possibly HVAC. Reproduced with permission. © 1998 CME Group Inc.
12. (full page) 1974 "double decking" construction project for the main trading floor, part of a series of renovations and expansions in the CBOT Building in the 1970s. Image held in the CBOT Records at the UIC Special Collections (Richard J. Daley Library). Reproduced with permission. © 1998 CME Group Inc.
13. Delegates from Iowa State 4-H Grain Marketing Program and CBOT Secretary with a model of the agricultural trading pits of the CBOT (1958). Based on archival public relations and education materials found by the artists, the CBOT was actively involved in 4-H programs through targeted involvement with land-grant universities in the Midwest. The 4-H is a US program founded at the turn of the twentieth century focused on instructing rural youth in farming practices, which later included introducing youth to new agricultural technologies. Photograph by Renata de Bonis, 2019. Image held in the CBOT Records at the UIC Special Collections (Richard J. Daley Library). Reproduced with permission. © 1998 CME Group Inc.
14. The artists conducting research in the CBOT records at the UIC Special Collections (Richard J. Daley Library). Contact sheet of activity on the CBOT grain trading room floor taken for public relations purposes in 1970. Images include chalkboards that were used until the 1970s to report recent trades; these were gradually replaced by electronic boards. Photograph by Renata

de Bonis, 2019. Reproduced with permission. © 1998 CME Group Inc.

15. The artists conducting research in the CBOT records at the UIC Special Collections (Richard J. Daley Library). Folder of public relations and diplomatic visits to the CBOT, including a visit by Brazilian delegates to The South Room trading floor while it was under construction in 1975. Photograph by Renata de Bonis, 2019. Reproduced with permission. © 1998 CME Group Inc.

16. Steel scaffolding installed over the CBOT's main trading pits in 1974 for "double decking" additions and renovations. Image held in the CBOT Records at the UIC Special Collections (Richard J. Daley Library). Reproduced with permission. © 1998 CME Group Inc.

17. (full page spread) CBOT trading floor in action circa 1980. Image held in the CBOT Records at the UIC Special Collections (Richard J. Daley Library). Reproduced with permission. © 1998 CME Group Inc.

18. The artists conducting research in the CBOT records at the UIC Special Collections (Richard J. Daley Library). Pictured is a CBOT booth at a trade show from a folder of public relations materials from 1950 to 1951. Photograph by Renata de Bonis, 2019. Reproduced with permission. © 1998 CME Group Inc.

19. The artists conducting research in the CBOT records at the UIC Special Collections (Richard J. Daley Library). Pictured are captions for public relations images taken for the CBOT during the 1960s, 1970s, and early 1980s. Photograph by Renata de Bonis, 2019. Reproduced with permission. © 1998 CME Group Inc.

20. (full page spread) "Traders are hard at work at the Chicago Board of Trade in Chicago, Illinois on May 31, 1973." US Department of Agriculture, 20120105-OC-AMW-0425.

21. Open outcry trading pits in action circa 1975, captioned "N-3 Trading Floor." Image held in the CBOT Records at the UIC Special Collections (Richard J. Daley Library). Reproduced with permission. © 1998 CME Group Inc.

22. Construction of the main commodities trading floor and pits at 141 West Jackson Boulevard. This picture was published in the Chicago Tribune on Sunday, 18 May 1930 under the headline "First Photograph of World Wheat Mart." The caption goes on to describe the trading floor room: "Here's a first photograph of one of the world's greatest trading floors, that of the new Chicago Board of Trade. This huge vaulted chamber is 57 ½ feet high and is 111x167. It will house facilities for trading in wheat, corn, oats, rye, barley, provisions, and cotton. The floors of the trading pits are to be of teakwood. The walls are paneled in wood. A second room, 51x72, is connected by a passageway and will be used for the board's securities market." Photographer unknown.

23. *In the wheat pit of the Board of Trade of the city of Chicago.* Photographer unknown, circa 1920. Library of Congress Prints and Photographs Division Washington, D.C. 20540 USA.

24. Floor plan and description of the grain exchange room, with handwritten annotations and notes by Elisabeth Hauptmann. Sent to Bertolt Brecht in Denmark by Hauptmann from America in the 1930s. Akademie der Künste, Berlin, Bertolt-Brecht-Archiv 894/103-106.

25. *Chicago Board of Trade Pit Room.* "Interior view of the Pit Room of Chicago Board of Trade, 141 West Jackson Boulevard, Chicago, Illinois." Photograph by Hubert Henry for Hedrich-Blessing, 20 June 1947. Chicago History Museum, Hedrich-Blessing Collection HB-10297.

MEMORANDUM

Of Fee Paid at U. S. Patent Office.

9220 N

Inventor,

Reuben S. Jennings

Patent to be issued to

Invention,

Trading pit

Date of Payment,

May 13th 78

Fee,

$ 20

Solicitor,

E. E. Masson

EXCA VA TION IV

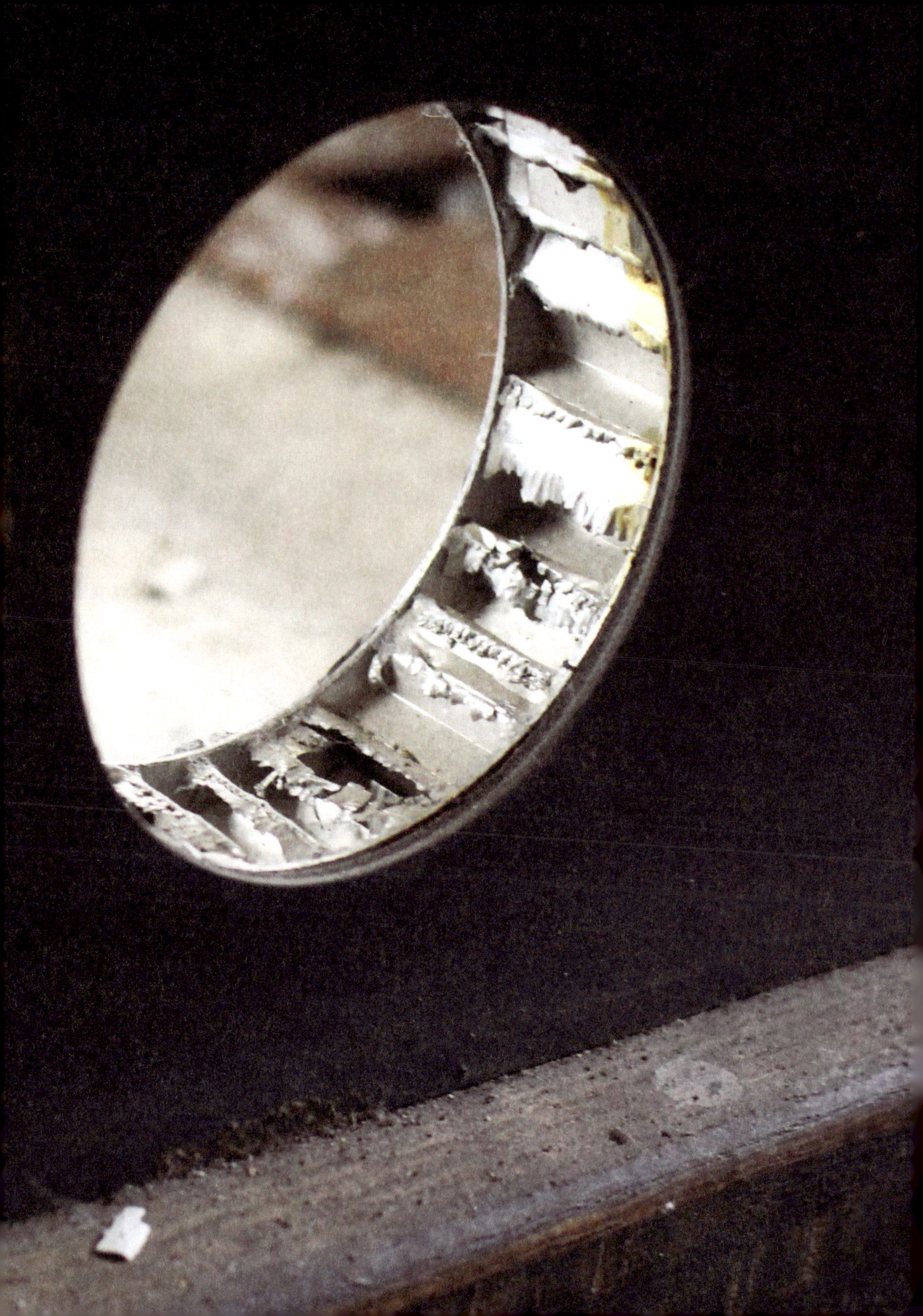

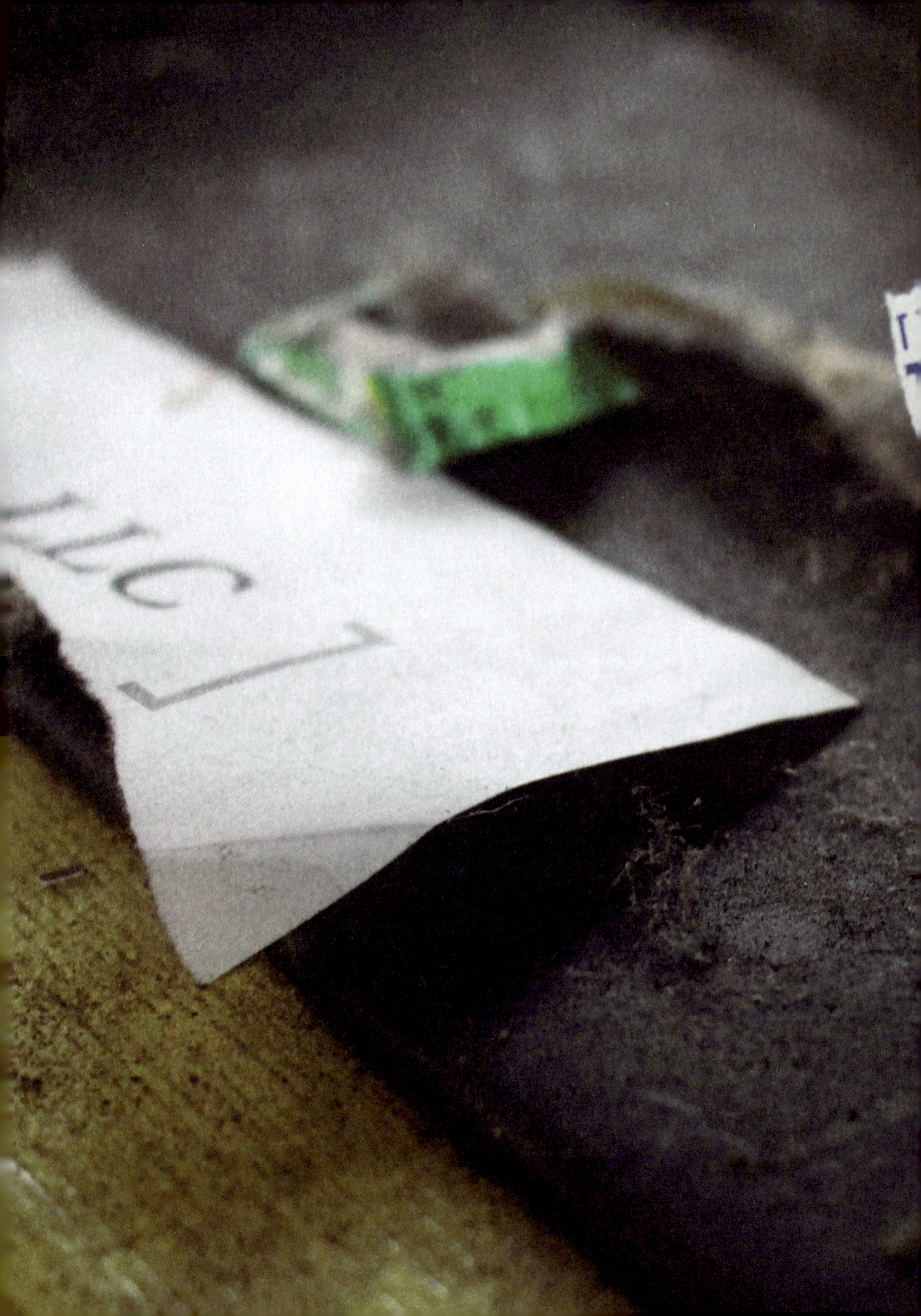

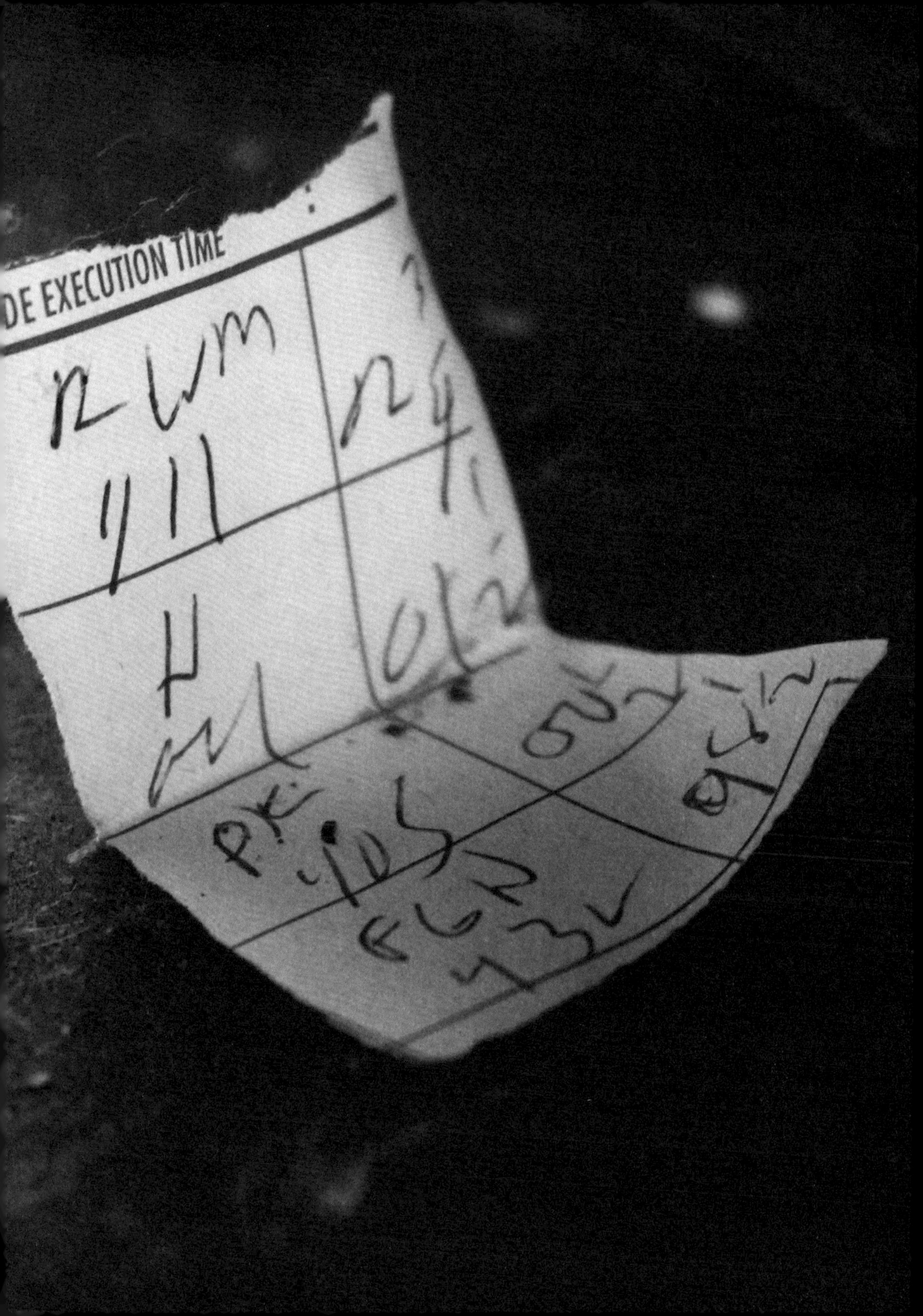
DE EXECUTION TIME

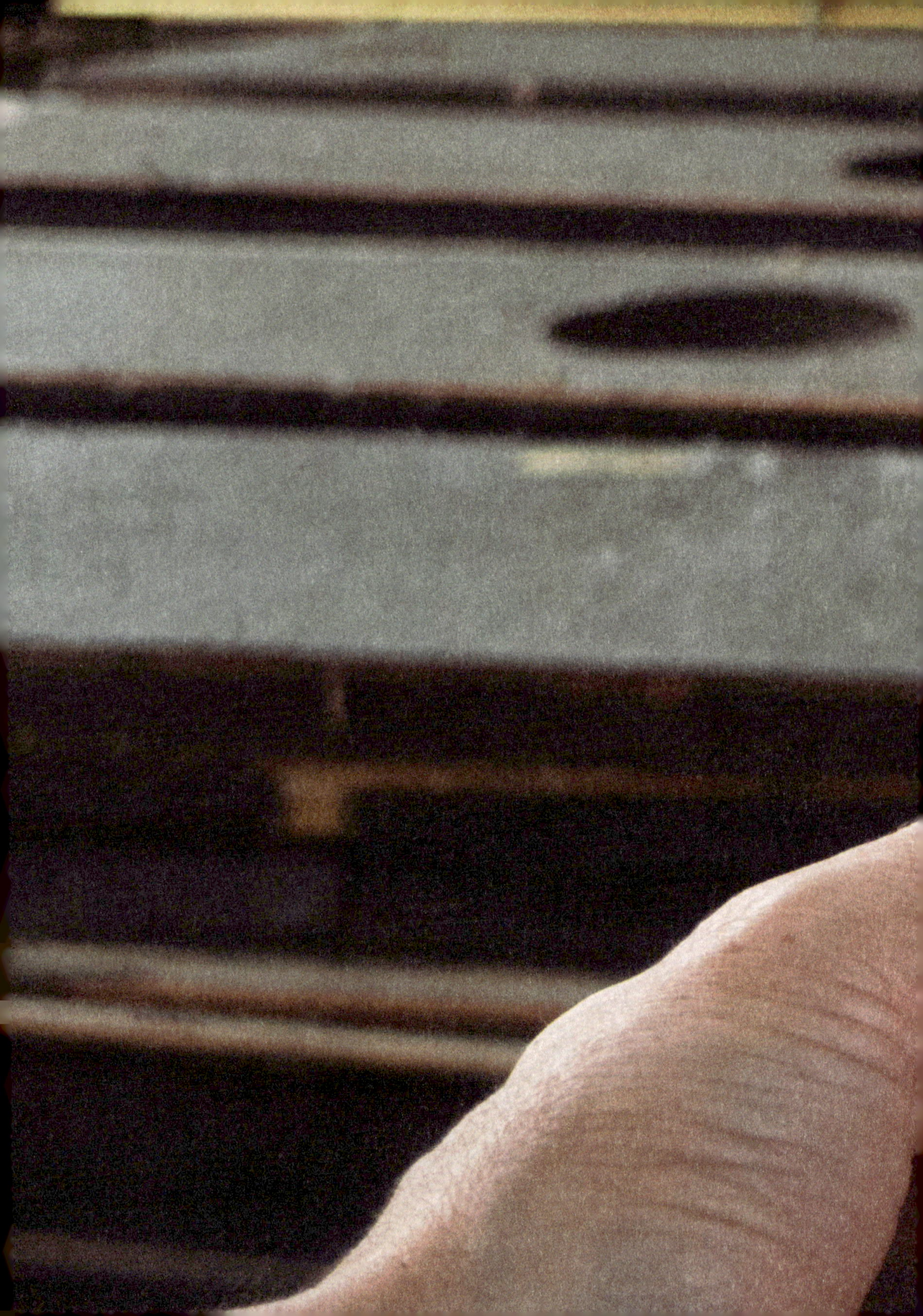

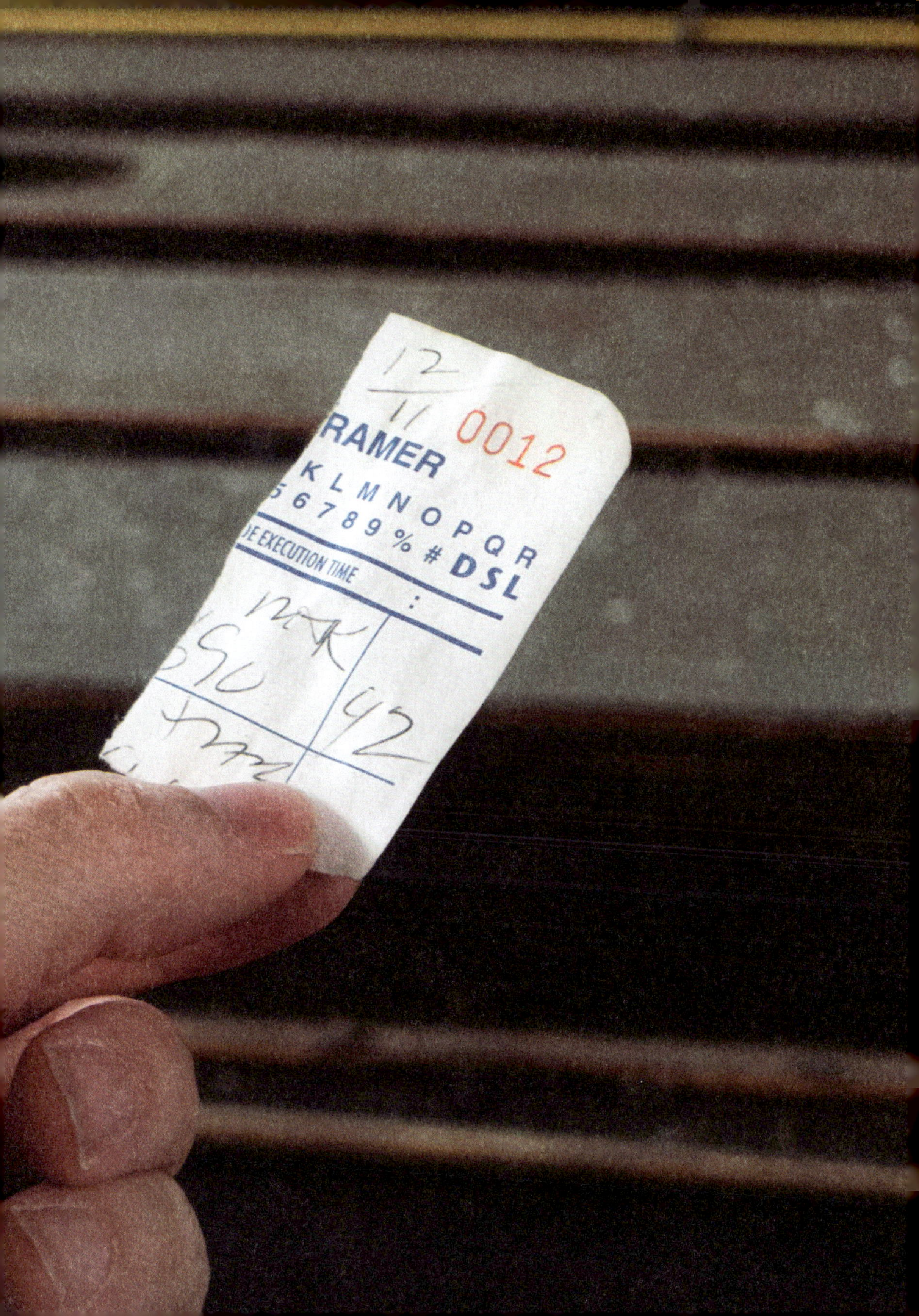

RAMER
0012
K L M N O P Q R
6 7 8 9 % # DSL
EXECUTION TIME

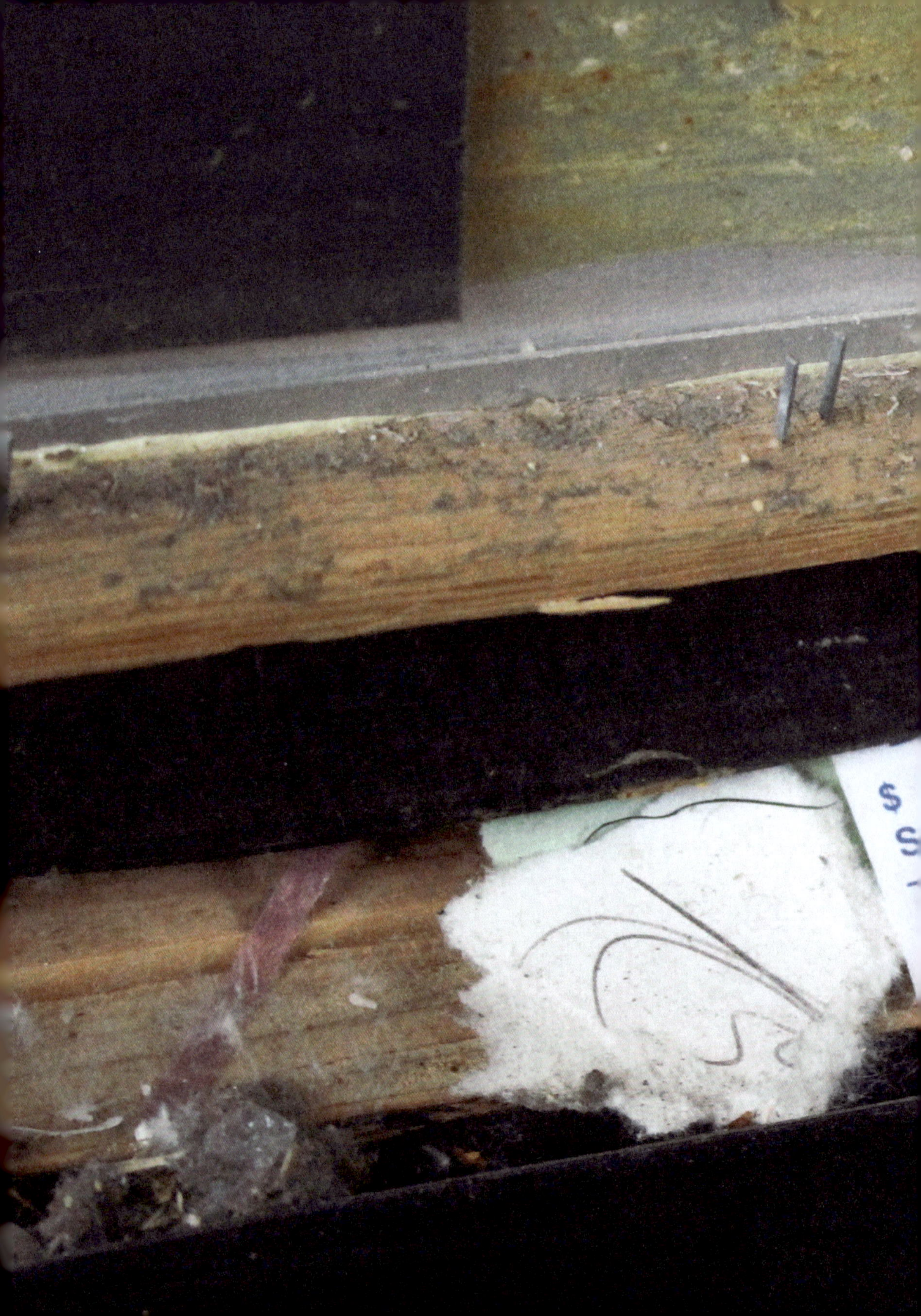

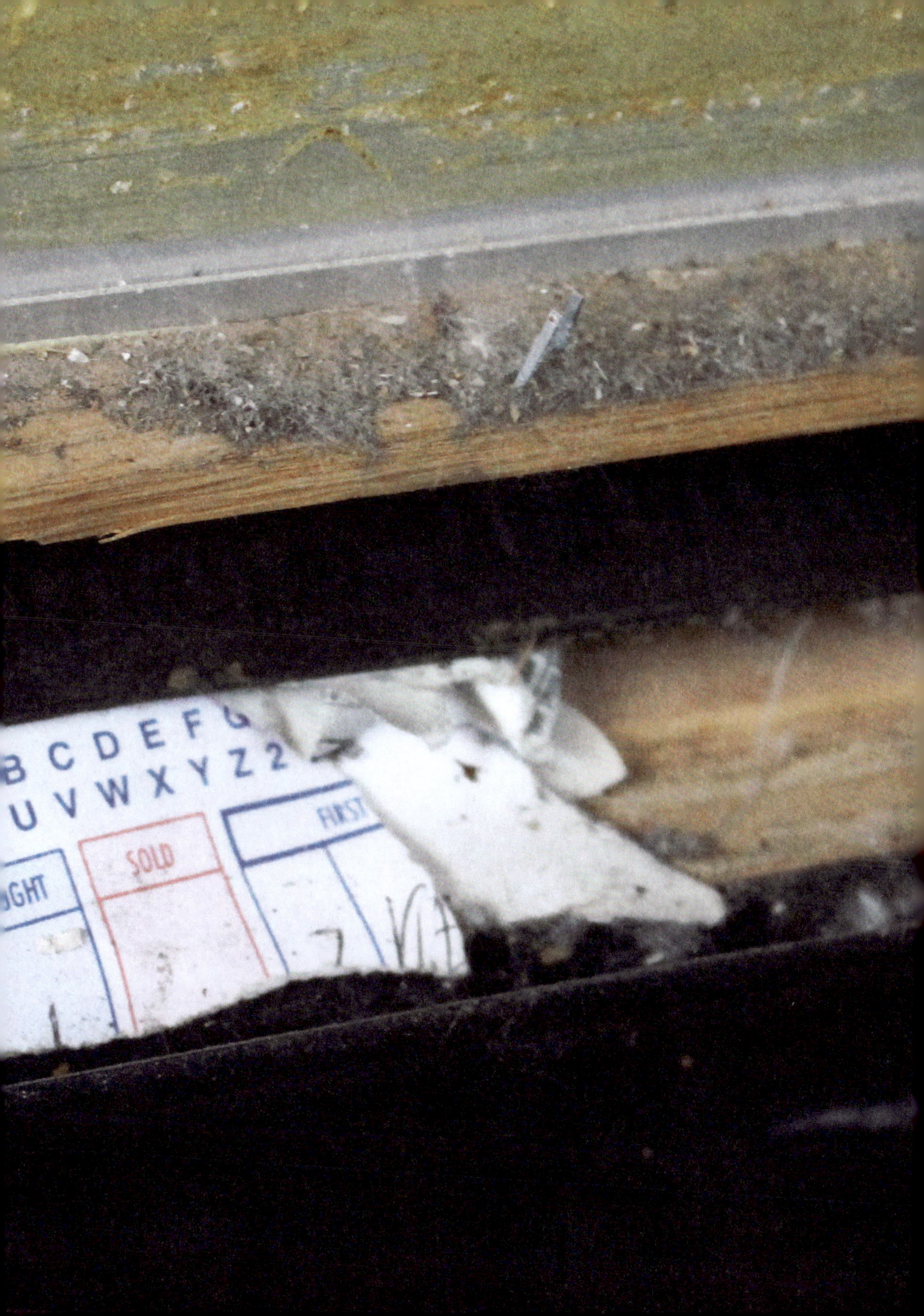
B C D E F
U V W X Y Z 2
SOLD
FIRST

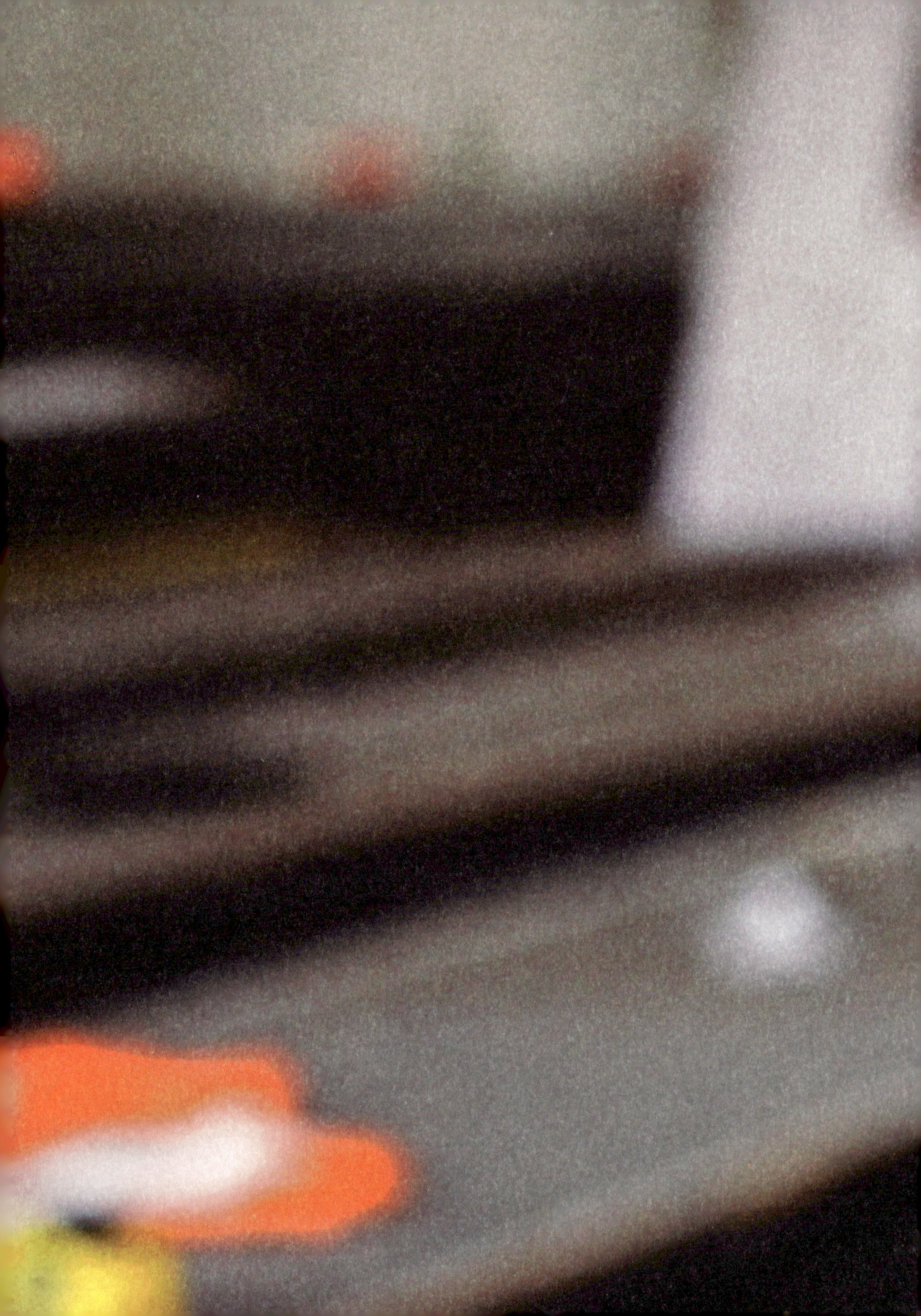

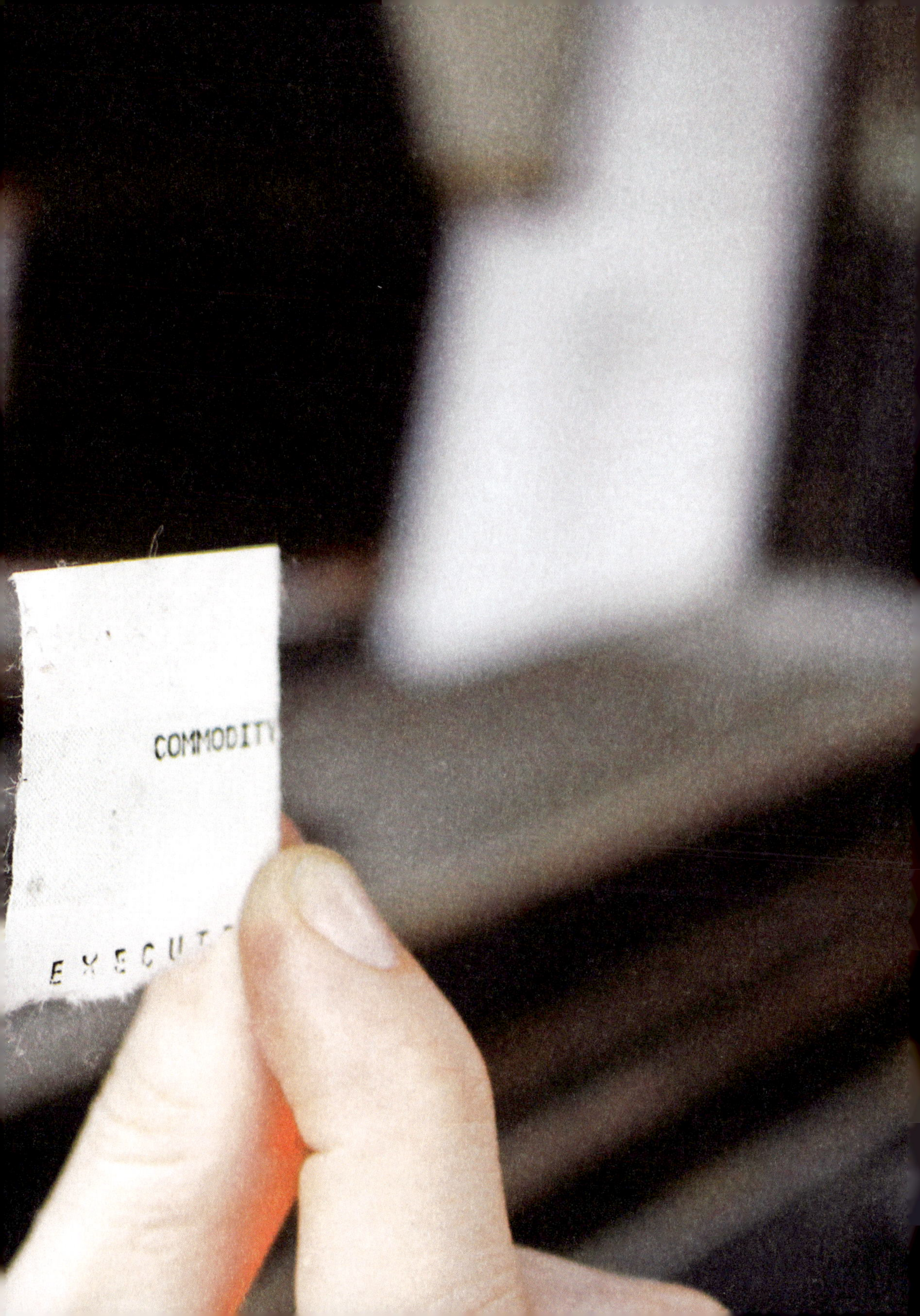
COMMODITY

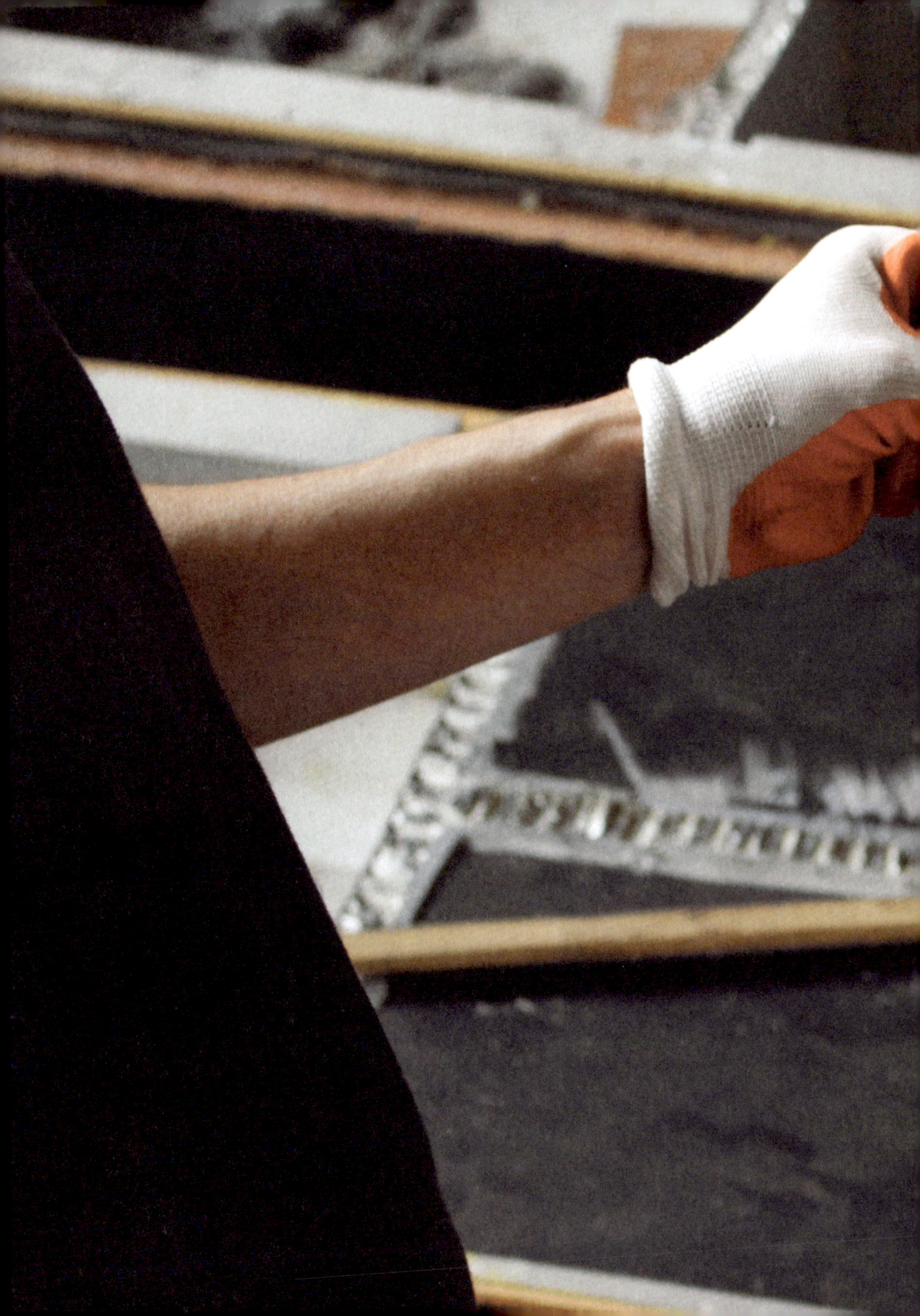

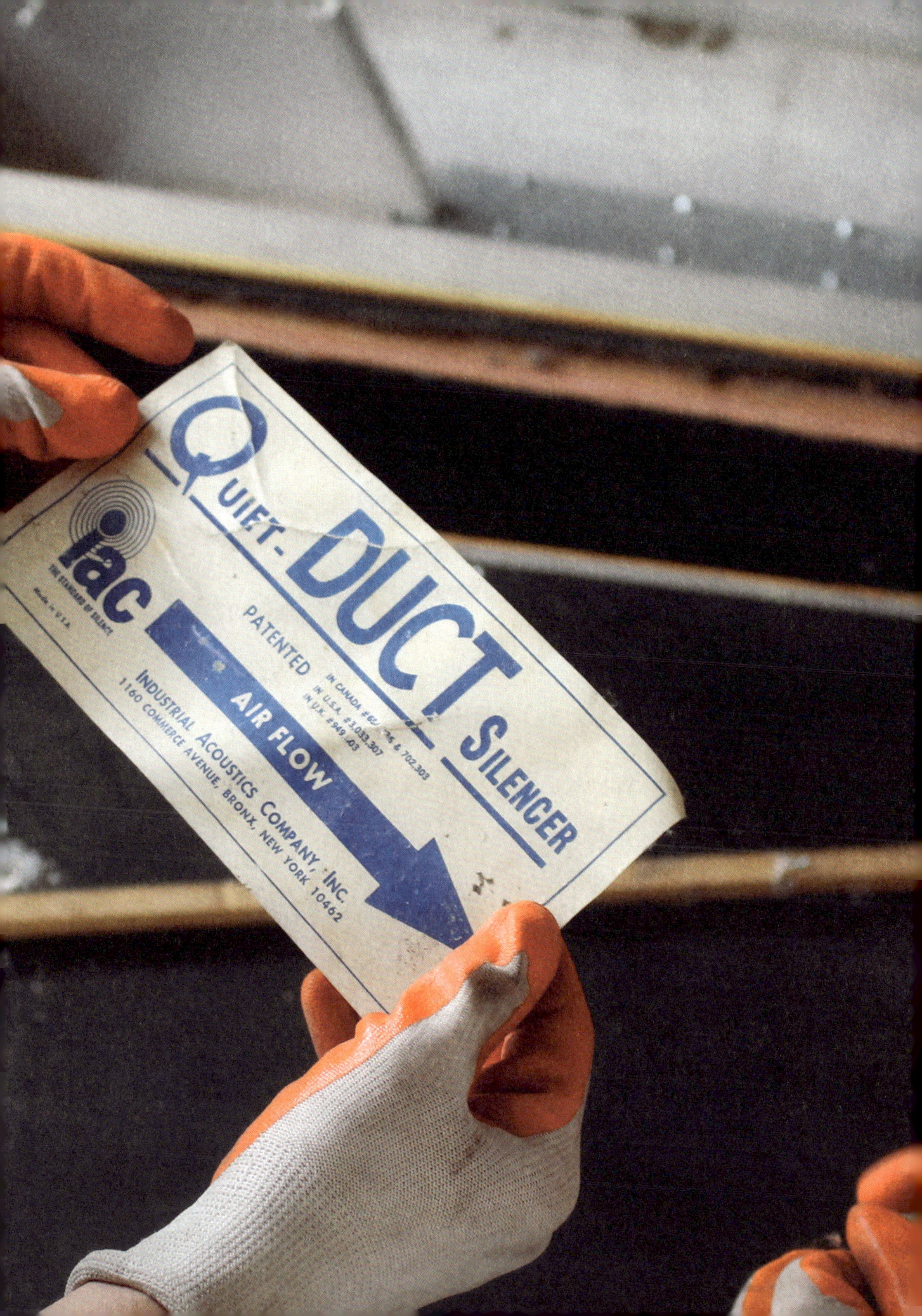
iac
THE STANDARD OF SILENCE
QUIET-DUCT
SILENCER
PATENTED
AIR FLOW
INDUSTRIAL ACOUSTICS COMPANY, INC.
1160 COMMERCE AVENUE, BRONX, NEW YORK 10462

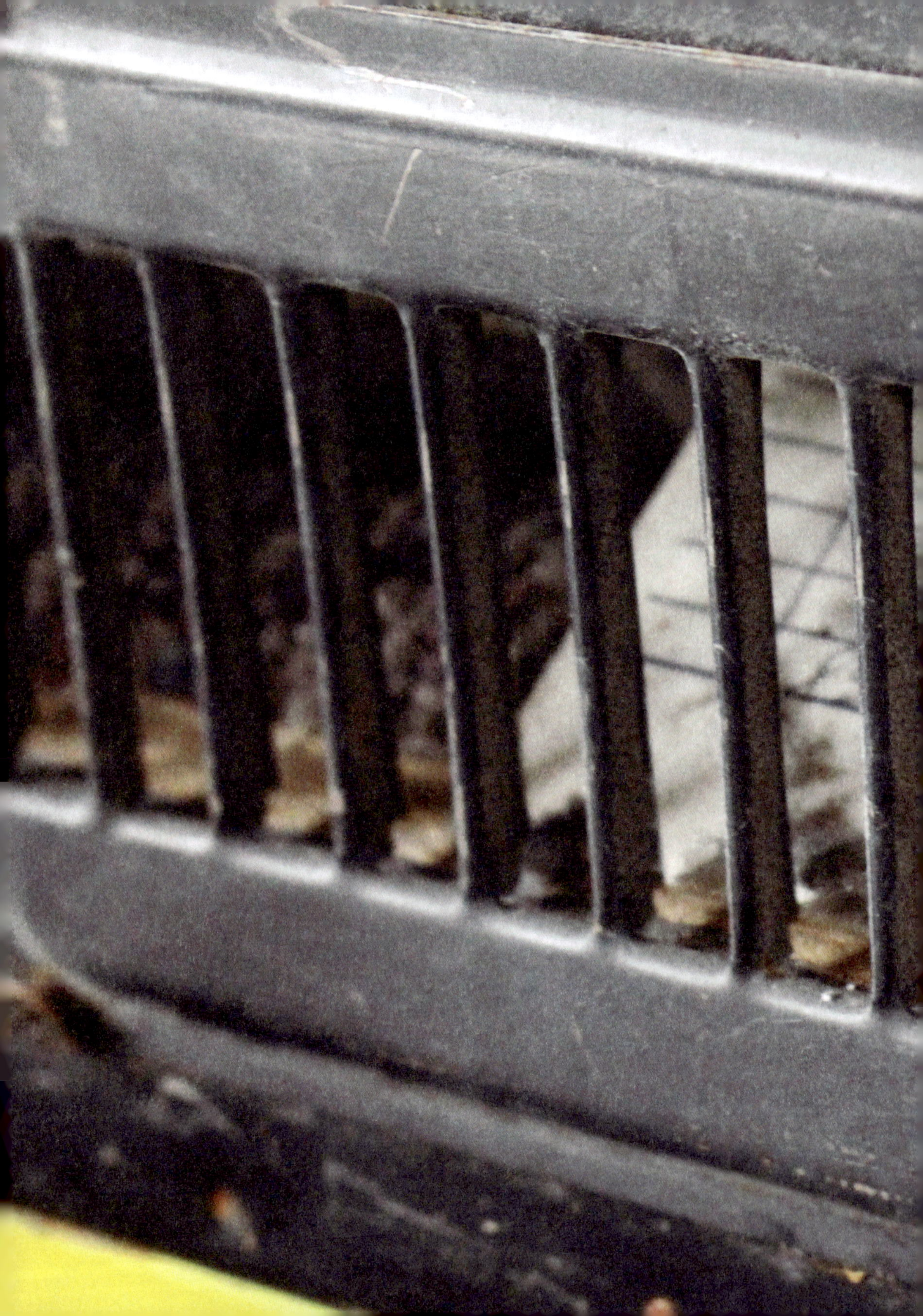

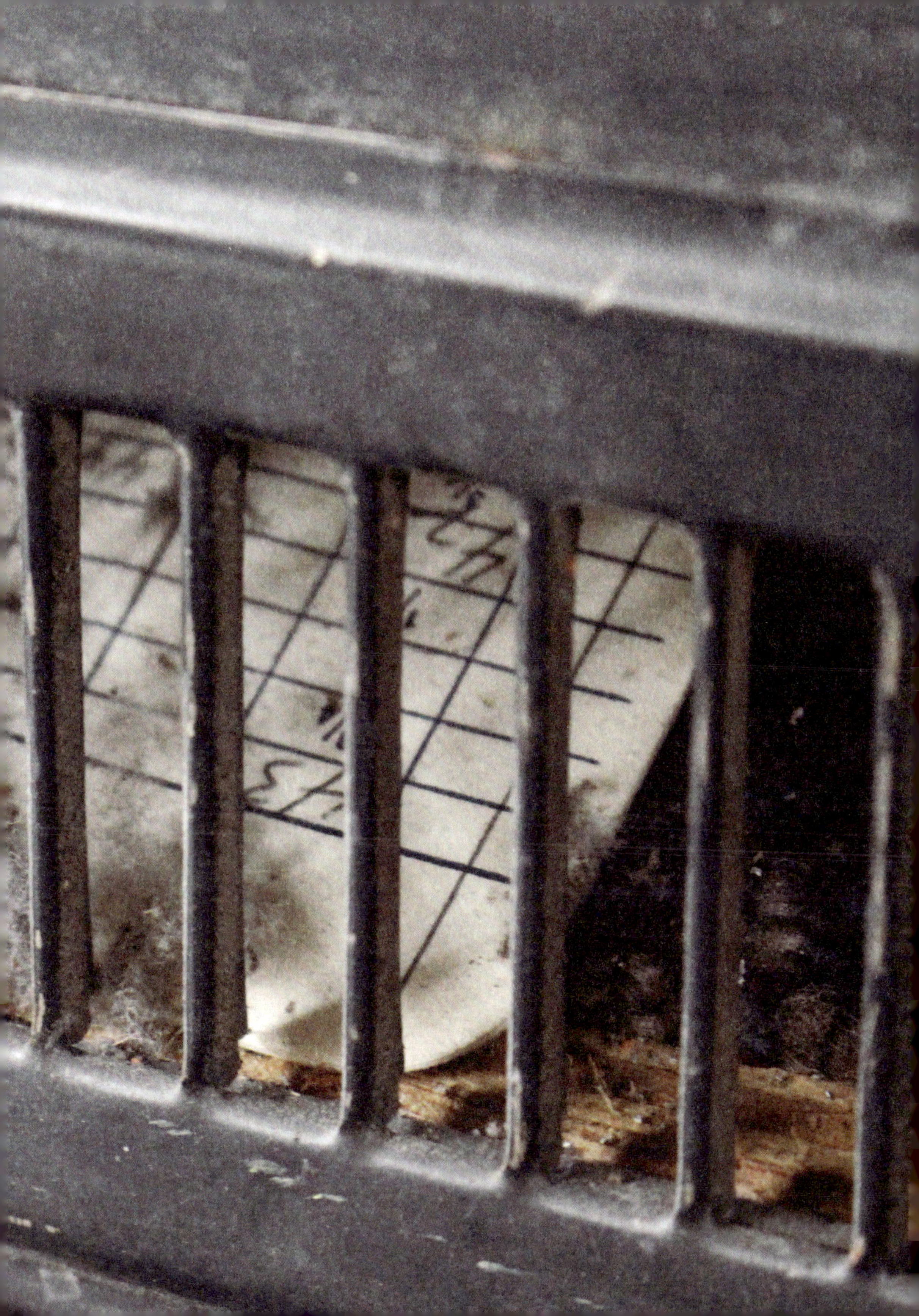

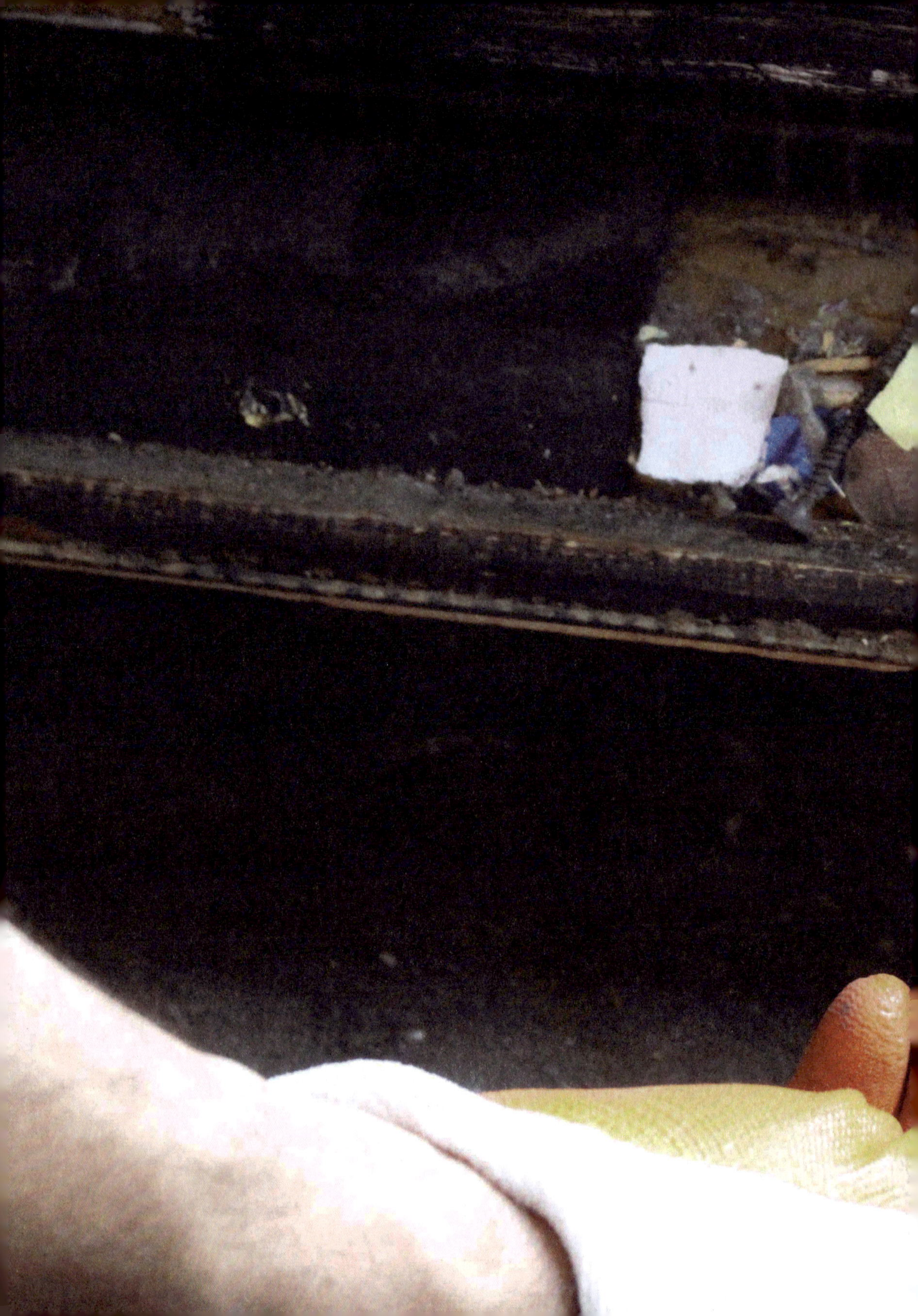

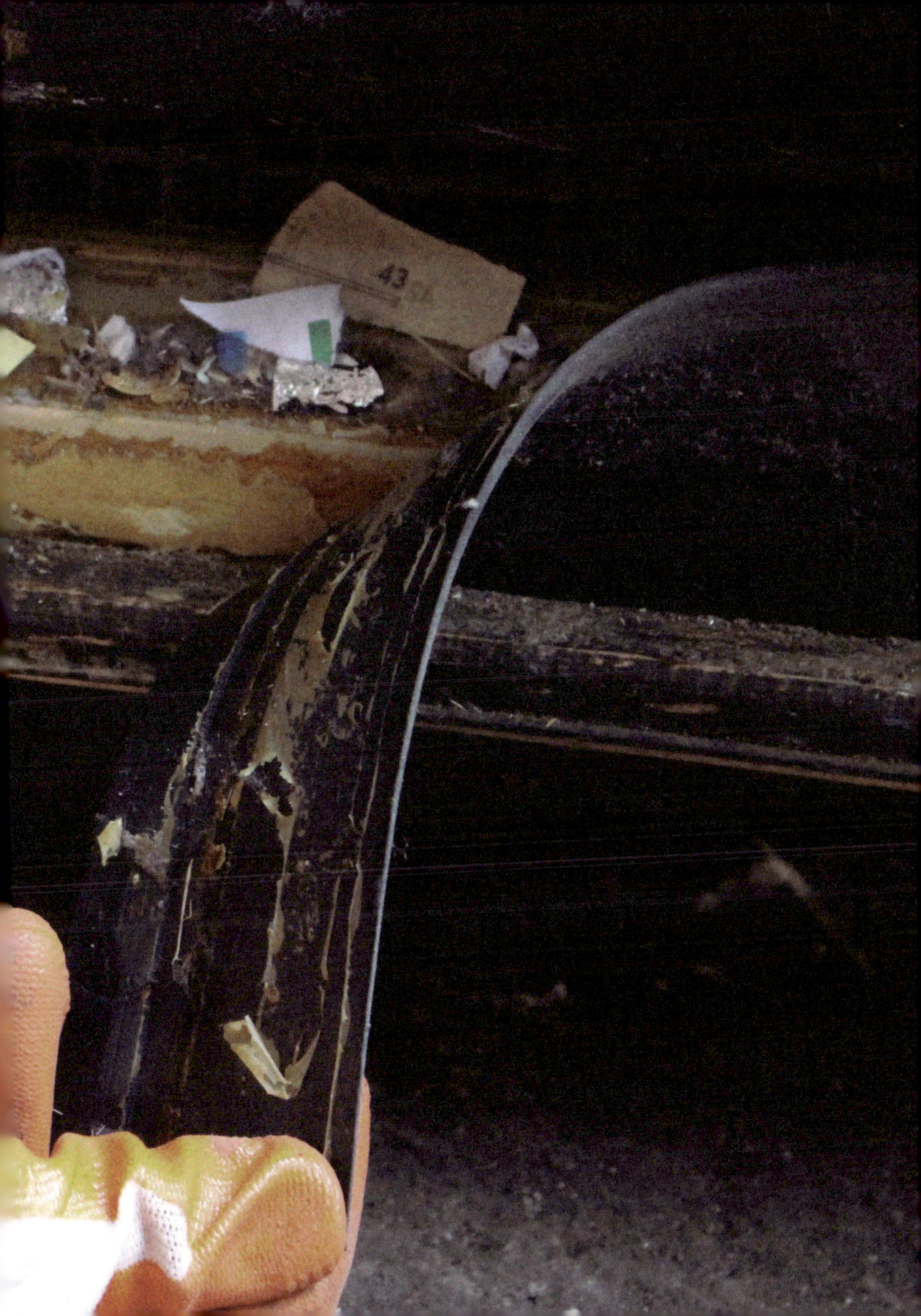

WHAT STATE ARE THINGS IN?

ii. Dan Peterman with Marissa Lee Benedict and David Rueter

Chicago (USA)
Amsterdam (NL)

Marissa Lee Benedict Thank you, Dan, for sitting down with us to discuss the history of this project, *deposition*, which began in 2018. I wanted to start off by talking a bit about your work in relation to the project. I've known you to be an artist and an organizer, for many decades, and we share an interest in salvaged or repurposed architectural materials as part of long-term investigations into the deep intertwining of material and social forms. I've also seen your work, over many years, speaking to relations between heavy industry and prairie ecology.

Dan Peterman I wouldn't say my work is specifically prairie related, in the sense of being limited to Midwestern ecologies, but rather it speaks to a general sense of ecological thinking. It's a pretty sprawling approach, with everything that entails, so in a way the works expand beyond what's practical, and maybe don't cohere to a certain region or topic. I'm following networks of ideas: moving in and out of ecosystems and natural environments, but also in and out of man-made environments, urban settings, and industrial settings; seeing how, and sometimes why, those pathways lead where they lead. This offers multiple connections to place: a wide-angle vision is always happening, even as something starts to come into more detailed focus. I'm often questioning where things belong—or how they're encountered—and identifying landscapes that are undergoing change. It's a kind of vision that asks: "What are the pathways, the systems, the industries, the economies in play?" Then I work to find a way to build the coherence of a particular project. But that coherence might have very different terms from project to project. There's always an intuitive driving force that needs to be fully operative. It's not that a project needs to be clear at the beginning, and it's not about an absolute clarity at the end either, but rather it's about entering into an investigatory process that brings about a kind of questioning that isn't just about any one place or approach to that place; any one system or approach to that system. It's an approach that requires intuition to operate in parallel to what we might call the structure of an ecosystem.

MLB I think in mine and David's and Daniel de Paula's work we've also considered the ways in which networks sprawl and expand, and how we might engage such diffuse conditions through momentarily capturing an instance of them. It's a way of working that sees a material or an object or a form as an instance pulled from a greater network or system. The whole thing—the network or system—may be too large to fully conceive, but we might encounter a fragment of it through this act of selecting an instance.

DP I think using that word, "instance," starts to open up to a consideration of temporal frames. Things are changing over time, and one way a thing gets imbued with meaning is through a historical understanding or reading of it. We're constantly moving through time ourselves, which changes our experience of encountering a thing, and the thing itself is also changing over time. I enjoy encountering objects in relation to a complex sense of time. Take, for instance, the scavenging of the corn pit: from that moment in which you first encountered it to the present, that object evolved, and is evolving, along with the project itself. With the trading floor, of course, the heavier historical weight of the thing resides in the preceding century, within the geometries of its form, and in the way its design helped structure the marketplace itself—in the 1800s—perhaps even more than in this physical version of the floor.[1] Within the concentrated idea of what a trading pit is, and in what the development of futures markets meant, there are significant temporal forces at play.[2]

MLB ______ For you, is there anything particular about Chicago that speaks specifically to the relations between physical and temporal networks?

DP ______ Doors opened for me in Chicago as a young artist through recycling systems. Many modes of operating came into play for me, in part because of the nature of the city. Chicago is, as you know, an industrial city, or post-industrial city, shaped by constant rehabilitation and reinvention. The recycling industry invites assessing things, as they are, in the present, but also recognizes that they may need a new system to operate in, or a new pathway forward. You might need to reinvent the way things are currently moving in order to bring them into alignment with a vision of what would, or could, be a better system. And within that, you need to contend with what it means to propose a better or worse way of doing things. Understanding this comes down to how one unpacks these systems and how they carry meaning in the present. The nature of this complexity holds its own mysteries and ambiguities. I've realized that, for me, there was a starting point in fairly concrete systems and in some efforts to modify these systems—in initiating projects to alter the flows of recycled materials to create a complex understanding of these networks, moving over time. I have an equal interest in the way things might be stuck—stagnant and fixed—and the way things are in motion—constantly evolving and changing. I've developed a sensibility for both of these kinds of things. In Chicago, having access to all kinds of industries was something I was very aware of as an artist. I had many points of access. And I've taken this sensibility, or this way of working, from Chicago into other parts of the world, and into other situations that are beyond what I might touch or see more locally.

MLB ______ This sense of Chicago as a place that hosts these flows of circulating and stagnated materials makes me think of environmental historian William Cronon's *Nature's Metropolis: Chicago and the Great West* (1991), and the way he narrates complex relationships between concrete, or physical, forces and more abstract ones.

David Rueter That's actually a part of the story of *deposition*—of how Daniel was led to us through our previous residency in Chicago.[3] When we met in the Netherlands, Daniel was researching the Chicago Board of Trade (CBOT) trading pit histories, and, more specifically, the soy futures trading pit, at the time.[4]

DP That connection was really meaningful to me—that this interest in the corn pit was initiated by Daniel, who brought an outside perspective into something that is Chicago-centric.[5] I think this immediately starts to impact the way that you read the thing. This outside perspective allows for a reentering of the infrastructure through an unexpected or oblique angle—because in the end, there's going to have to be a reframing of the thing. When you guys contacted me, as a Chicago connection, I was curious about what the thing was and what it would look like, but I was fundamentally aware of the fact that it was interesting that the road had led from Brazil back to Chicago, through questions of land use and agribusiness, as asked by an artist.

DR I remember it was in September 2018 that I came back from the Netherlands and saw the trading pit floor for the first time. I visited you and the pit in storage in Chicago, and I remember that you described the salvage operation as something like a string of minor miracles.

DP I knew when the initial request involved help accessing the salvage operation at the CME Group Inc. (CME Group)[6] that the demolition was not going to be a "grab what you can," or a "pulling things from a dumpster" situation.[7] I mean, this is a Chicago Loop location, in a famous building, in a high-security financial zone. Part of the process was just figuring out: what does the flow look like in this demolition process? What state are things in? I thought that the situation would be interesting, no matter what. There were clearly limits to what you guys—Daniel, David, and Marissa—could do remotely. At that time, when you contacted me, the project was derailed. Daniel had begun to enter into conversations, and processes of questioning the trading floor, that were legible and interesting to me as an artist—and I think for you, David and Marissa, as well—but at the end of the day it was necessary for a walking and talking person to be there to meet with the building managers, the property managers, and the demolition team. There was a lot of goodwill, which I give the CME Group credit for, in recognizing their own history and appreciating this interest from an outside perspective. But this process had led, for them, to frustration, and that's where it felt like there was a new level of negotiation needed, immediately, to try and make something work. Things needed some way to move from A to B, and the CBOT demolition crew was willing to help, but decisions had to be made on the spot. At that point, bringing in Greg Lane to manage the salvage and transfer to a warehouse storage site was key.[8] He's a very insightful person and was able to read into the context, as an intellectual enterprise as much as a jobsite, and we managed to gain access through the back door amidst this demolition process. I give credit to Greg, and Ken Dunn as well,[9] and some of the other people in the recycling network that I also reached out to.

DR And we give significant credit to you, Dan, and your expertise and understanding of how to navigate this complex situation so successfully. I think this comes from many years of experience—but more than that, it comes from the ways in which your work interrogates the kinds of forces that were at play.

MLB Also, I remember, at the time we were trying to find a shared language to communicate with the CBOT about what we wanted, and we found using language around architectural salvage and preservation was a way to communicate why this object would be of value for the CBOT to go to this extra length to preserve and extract.

DP There's that conversation that was happening, but then there were also all the forces of the real estate industry at work in this central, prime, downtown location. Their demolition calendars were already fixed, the space was going to be empty at a certain fixed point in time, and then the former CME Group grain trading room at the CBOT would be scheduled to move into the hands of a different agency. There were all of these things that close down how much flexibility anybody might have to do something out of the ordinary, because there are deadlines and economic constraints that are placed on this kind of building operation that deals in the extensive renovation of a space. A jobsite like that, it's just pushing material through. It's got to move. The floor had to move.

MLB Maybe it was you, Dan, or someone else who narrated it to me, but the way the demolition crew cut apart and freed the pieces of the corn pit was very carefully done—the way they'd sliced the sections apart, the whole thing seems to have come out much the same way it went in.

DP I think that was just the nature of the demolition of this really large set of constructions, this modular raised flooring system—when a demolition like this happens, it's not chaotic. People have to get in and figure out what would be a good system for moving this stuff through the building, and for moving it out through the city. But the first step is to figure out how to dismantle the structure and get it out the first door and down the hall. The CBOT is not an industrial site that's designed for hauling things in and out on that scale, so a lot of energy goes into the logistics of that kind of demolition. A lot of energy has to go into handling things efficiently. I think that meant there was some care in the dismantling so that it didn't just turn into a wrecking-ball style demolition, with debris all over the place. It was systematic. And the floor itself also seems to have come in that way: in these built-in sections that would fit into the building systematically, which makes sense. They needed to think in terms of modular structures and how they can get in efficiently and build out quickly.

MLB We've been trying to find more photos of the CBOT in the public archive of images donated by the CME Group to the Richard J. Daley Library Special Collections at the University of Illinois at Chicago (UIC), specifically from the grain room's remodel and reinstallation over the decades. The floor we have is such an interesting object of accumulation and accretion, with these layers of oak and rubber and panels of honeycomb aluminum as a substructure to the whole thing.

DP When I think about it, I think about the space program in the 1970s, and the way space capsules were built. Imagining that the CME Group had a big budget—and you get things done the way you want with that—they would have been looking at building a high-tech unique, customized HVAC system that people could stand on.[10] The Chicago commodities trading floors presented an intense set of demands for packing people together in that particular way. It really was a unique thing, and I think that carries over into the fundamental nature of the artifact: as a space designed around human occupancy, with this intense programming set to occur within it. You used to be able to go in and take an overlook of the CBOT grain commodities trading floor and it was like looking into a beehive. There was this intensity—a kind of humming, vibrating intensity. And then you would see some of that geometry, like those concentric octagons. You would see the pits, and would get a sense of this motion and energy. There is something, on an intuitive level, relating to that condition of occupancy, that's just remarkable. And I think that's part of what informed this work, *deposition*, from the beginning—these fragments carry meaning that links back to that energy of the trading floor. Images are intense and so memorable—those images of the CBOT, and of traders, and of the signaling and split-second timing that was running through their bodies are palpable. Now, I think this energy is only intensified through memories, documentation, and historical narratives of something we can no longer witness.

DR Now, it's almost impossible to get a tour of one of these data centers where the trading activity is actually taking place. Not only that, those sites aren't recognizable spaces for people to see, let alone acquire a piece of. To salvage a server rack is not as meaningful, perhaps.

MLB Financialization has removed the bodies—not the activity, just the bodies. However, in this absence, there's no fundamental transformation of the forces at play. We've been talking a lot about this—that the obsolescence of in-person commodities trading floors doesn't present a rupture. The system of finance—and all it links to—hasn't changed; if anything, it's dug deeper. The removal of this floor doesn't speak to the absence of the system that created it; it may, actually, just speak to an intensification of this system.

DR But it does perhaps tell us something about the nature of the power situated within it—that we can now have access to the floor in this way, and that we can possess it. We've used the metaphor of a snake shedding its skin—of something that remains while the expanding creature moves on. We can never quite get a hold on it.

DP Well, I think this is such a multifaceted kind of artifact, a kind of social space, and we can now know what it feels like to stand on it, sit on it, and gather people within it. There's something that's contiguous in this reinhabitation: it's fascinating to provide greater opportunities to access or experience or witness it. Of course, the trading pit has been shed in terms of its capacity for data to flow through it. Human bodies are in the way as digital pathways open up and speed ahead, so the floor became obsolete. But I think this object is still essentially tethered to functioning economies—to futures trading, to Wall Street, and to the business of the CME Group—things that people completely identify as charging ahead, even accelerating. The trading pit floor is a link to a whole constellation of things: from free enterprise to economist Milton Friedman and "The Chicago Boys."[11] It's not a story about just looking back at what was put in play. It's a remnant linked very concretely to active forces, and you are picking up on threads of those histories. I think what's fundamentally exciting here is that, again, it's not just an artifact coming out of the CBOT's history that is staying in Chicago, but rather the project is now fueled by this encounter with what is now a significant global artifact. There's no way to escape into the charm—the nostalgia—of it as a Chicago artifact, or to use it for a friendly approach to local history. I think, instead, it opens up to something that is much more complex and interesting and impactful—something that really speaks to the scale of what these markets do, and what they have meant over time. Of course none of this is really my expertise, but I immediately start to hunger for the ideas of people who *do* have this expertise. The collaborative nature of the way all three of you have been framing this thing, I think, is so appropriate, and exciting, and it brings different voices into this fragment of such a powerful infrastructure, opening it up from oblique angles.

MLB Yes, I see the CBOT trading floors as being created for this very select public, let's say, and so the salvage and displacement and circulation of the floor is a kind of opening. It's been ripped out, forced to leave, and is now circulating through global channels in fragmented pieces—and those pieces are, literally, shedding and falling apart and being worn down by this transit. This object, the trading pit floor, seems to be almost unwinding itself as it physically transits. And what's left is now forced to host this new cacophony of voices—and some voices unlike those that created the cacophony before. I've, myself, felt a desire to suggest potential ideas for performances or other activities to be hosted in the trading pit, but it's been a big movement for us—Daniel, David, and myself—to come to the thought that perhaps the most important question is: how do we situate this floor? The work seems to draw out institutional desires wherever it goes, and *deposition*'s ability to be situated, and to understand itself, in relation to these institutional desires seems to be a vital thing. I might go so far as to say the work only exists in relation to institutional desires. And no two institutions, contexts, or moments are the same.

DP Well, I think this is what it means to have an artist-led research project, one that is not trying to steer toward a certain agenda, nor trying to unpack the thing from one place or end up in one place. Such work begins in an intuitive way, and may somehow end up in that intuitive place again—but in between there are all kinds of ways of encountering it, playing with it, modifying it, activating it, and reasoning with it—never in the same way twice. I think this way of working speaks to complexity and the potential richness of artist-led research. It's not a single-channel approach to how something should be read, as an artifact.

DR It occurred to me that we had written a question earlier for you about your work, *Sulfur Cycle* (1994),[12] and I was thinking about this as you were talking about the temporal aspects of the trading pit and *deposition*. I'm not sure that I want to directly draw a connection between the two projects, but I think I'm interested in your experience with the *Sulfur Cycle* project, having executed it over a space of twenty years or so, and what it meant for you to redo this project recently, considering how times have, or haven't, changed?

DP In approaching the stewardship of a project that's fundamentally informed by how it already exists in the world, the task becomes to unpack that project—to find the ways in which it already carries meaning. It's a really different artistic gesture than saying, "I'm going to transform this thing into the artwork that now sits statically resolved from this moment forward." *Sulfur Cycle* was a project founded on a particular set of conditions that mostly occur in industrial networks, but lack useful narratives or perspectives—the general public, the art museum, and the building industry each held important threads of connection for the work. The project asks questions, and those questions are the things that I'm trying to locate, manage, and bring forth. Time, as an element of the project, is active: that twenty-year period of time has a presence because there is an ecological reality embedded in the piece. When you go back to the work you can see how it's been constantly changing, or how certain critical perspectives, over time, have changed the ways it might be read, for example: author Naomi Klein's writings about the free market and disaster capitalism; working with a different curator in 2021 than in 1994, which brings a different generational perspective; or thinking about philosopher Timothy Morton and his concept of "hyperobjects," which helps identify the sprawling ways things operate in the world. Again, I'm not in control of any of these things, but I can be part of a process that brings them into a new perspective. But the work has a temporal element, especially in its attempt at storytelling, and trying to manage the complex narratives and material events in and around it. In that sense I think there are a lot of parallels with *deposition*. It's important to fundamentally respect the things you are working with and in the beginning of a project to recognize the complexity of an object, or process, or situation in the world. We, as art makers—or me, in my projects, I won't speak for you guys—recognize the importance of being a bit humbled by one's role in this. These kinds of things are so complex, engaging, and poetic, and we get to follow their lead.

MLB For me, your mention of stewardship also brings up certain questions—what seem very practical questions—about our ownership of the trading pit. The necessity of taking ownership of this object became a requirement due to the systemic forces of liability, transportation, shipping, and circulation; this is aside from the fact that even considering a de-installed floor as part-object part-infrastructural form is a unique challenge to ideas of bounded property. There are, I think, some very interesting, complex questions about transference and transmutation when property, such as the floor, leaves its corporate context and becomes subject to a different form of collective ownership in the midst of a salvage operation. *deposition* encounters some core issues within the complex nature of power dynamics within these materials and systems, especially as they begin to move or dislocate, and this is where things can get really interesting, and maybe troubling, in relation to the way that things are, or are going.

DP Yes, and I'm really satisfied that there isn't any one particular pathway that you guys are choosing around these questions of ownership, and that you're opening up the complexity of those decisions. The work isn't just falling into one kind of practice, whether defined by the commercial art world—as in, the way artists with their galleries want to own or manage their output as commodities—or one kind of art institution. You've been shaping a kind of open-source approach to something that is public in nature. I'm happy that you guys are really wrestling with this, more than looking for any one outcome for where it ends up. By whatever means, it will end up somewhere—and that may be a place that's really satisfying, or it may get derailed—but again, I'm happy that there are artists who are really wrestling with the complexity of it and that are in charge of it right now, and I'm happy we all get to watch.

DR Beside the ethical political questions that one might have about ownership, there's also a formal, aesthetic set of questions too about whether ownership, or claimed ownership, actually just centers the material too much—when one actually wants to focus on those things that it intersects with, and that can't perhaps be "owned" as such. I think this is something that's really interesting, and that gets at a part of your work, Dan. I know that your work primarily deals with objects and materials, but that the works also extend far beyond the site of exhibition, in the ways that we've been talking about. And I'm interested in this idea that ownership possibly limits how we understand what an object could be, and what kind of stories it could be involved in.

DP It obviously makes so much sense—since it's framed fundamentally within a kind of economic infrastructure that has been so impactful globally—that the trading floor can be seen in relation to that. That question needs to be opened, for instance: what kind of a system should the floor now operate in? What does it mean to be on the other side of its useful life—by one set of definitions—when there's a whole other useful life that's opening up with a different set of questions around permanence, economy, reuse, and repurposing?

MLB These are at once functional and symbolic questions. It will be interesting to see how this plays out in multiple situations. I also have an interest, in a different register, in these infrastructural *and* architectural objects—and I go back and forth on those words—and the way a project, like your *Sulfur Cycle,* sits into the walls of the institution and asks really particular, key questions about institutional dynamics and the continuities between these dynamics and those of free market economies.

DP Yes, I enjoy unpacking some of the mythologies of how an art space operates. Sometimes it's useful to disrupt art as usual, just as it's useful, in another way, to disrupt standard encounters with all kinds of situations. And, again, that's the potential that I see in what you are doing with *deposition*. It is a radical repurposing, and an invitation for somebody who encounters the trading floor to think about the futures markets and consider what it all means, and where an extended chain of cause and effect might lead. I doubt there is a clear answer to these questions. But for somebody to realize that a futures market is even a thing to question—that's an invitation that I think is powerful. This project has such a real-time, "figuring it out," "in the moment" energy to it.

DR We've been giving several talks on the work, *deposition*, the three of us, and there's a sense of different orbits—of people who are brought along with it. It doesn't all cohere, but these stories and perspectives do start to conglomerate. We're always interested in expanding that orbit, thinking about how these things are recorded or fade away, and figuring out who else could be brought into this orbit—this center of gravity that this hulking mass of an object exerts.

DP There's something that happens as it's being activated, as you're figuring it out, as you're having these kinds of discussions, and that's the most lively and engaging part of the project—that's really where it's most exciting for me. The object will end up somewhere—either in storage, or torn apart, or in a museum. But again I'm not so invested in how you control that outcome; right now it's in a living phase, and that's important.

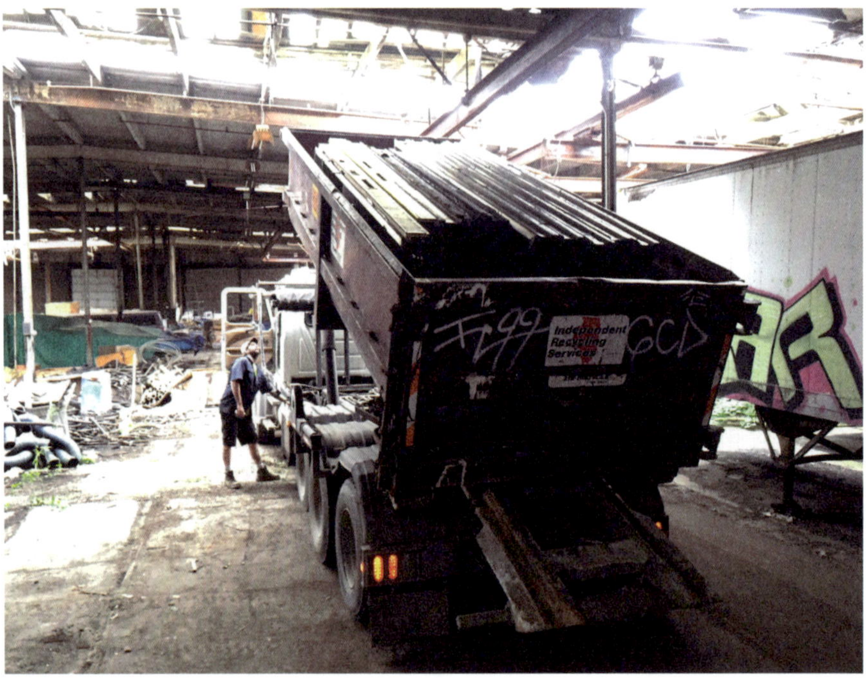

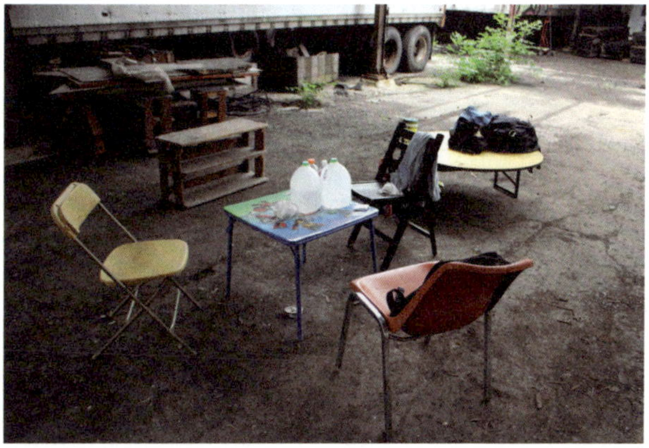

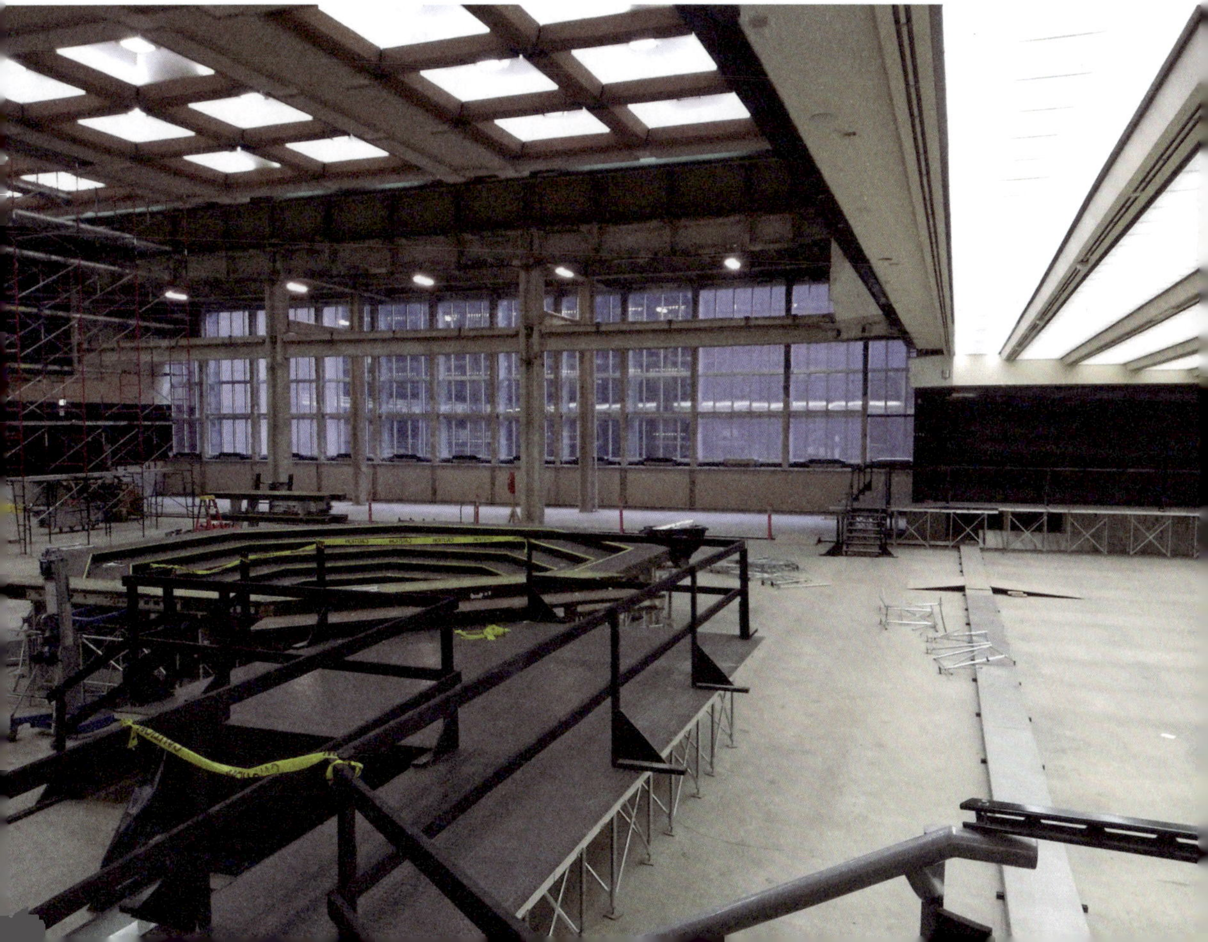

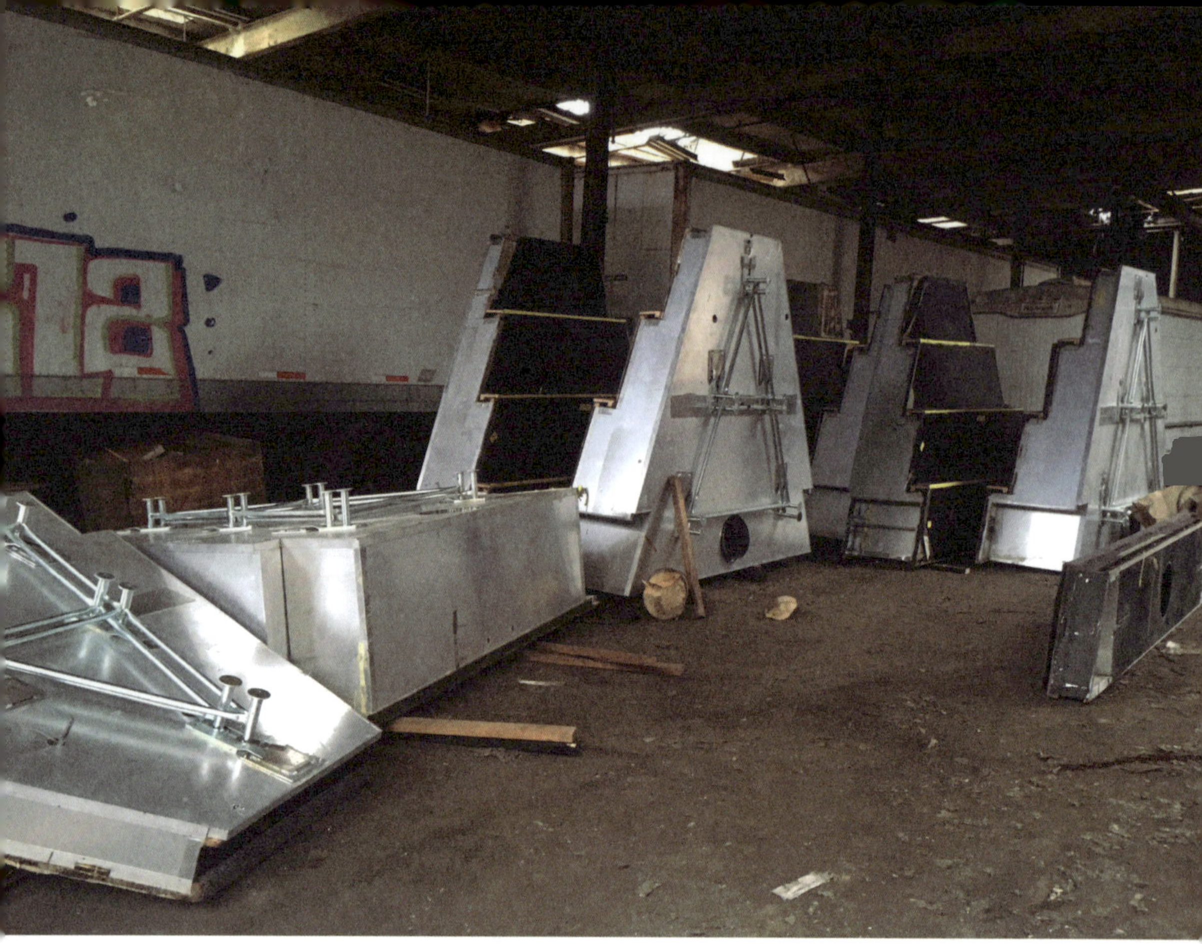

1. In 1848 the Chicago Board of Trade (CBOT) founded the first officially regulated futures exchange (see: https://www.cmegroup.com/company/history/timeline-of-achievements.html). The physical location of the CBOT has changed numerous times since 1848, requiring the trading pits to be built and rebuilt. According to a document submitted to the National Historic Register of Places: "During its early years, the Board seemed constantly on the move in a search for more floor space for its rapidly expanding operations. In 1852 the Board relocated in a building on the corner of Clark and South Water Streets; in 1853 on 8 Dearborn Street; in 1854 on the corner of Wells and South Water Streets; in 1856 on the corner of South Water and LaSalle Streets; and in 1860 on South Water between Wells and LaSalle Streets. In 1865 the Board moved to its first really [sic] permanent home in the Chamber of Commerce Building located at the southwest corner of LaSalle and Washington Streets. In 1871, the Chicago fires destroyed this structure, and for several months, the Board conducted business in a 90-foot-square wigwam near the corner of Washington and Market Streets. By the end of the year, however, the Chamber of Commerce Building had been rebuilt, and the Board had returned to its old location. In 1881 the Board decided to construct its own building, purchased property at what is now 141 West Jackson Boulevard . . . By the mid-1920s, however, it had become too small for the Board's needs and increasingly uneconomical to operate, and in 1927, the members voted to demolish it and construct a new building designed by Holabird & Root on the site. While the new edifice was under construction in 1928–30, the Board established temporary headquarters in a building at 447–511 South Clark Street. The Chicago Board of Trade Building, one of Holabird & Root's first major projects, is a prime example of a new type of skyscraper architecture which appeared in the late 1920s . . .'" (see: https://npgallery.nps.gov/GetAsset/8cebb2f5-271f-4332-ba3d-5c3689b00158/). Once established in their permanent home in the Chicago Board of Trade Building, the CBOT built and renovated the grain trading room floor in the 1970s, the 1980s, and the 1990s to accommodate new and emerging markets, and new information technologies. A major renovation of the grain room took place from 1972 to 1974, and is documented in the CBOT materials donated to the Richard J. Daley Library, Special Collections and University Archives at the University of Illinois at Chicago (UIC). For related images, see pages 55, 59, 61, and 65.

2. Futures are a form of commodities contract traded on the CBOT floors. "A major difference between futures and stocks is that stocks represent ownership in a corporation whereas futures contracts represent a future obligation to receive or deliver a commodity at a future date." CME Market Education Department, *An Introduction to Futures and Options: Student Manual* (2006), https://www.cmegroup.com/files/intro_fut_opt.pdf.

3. Benedict and Rueter both lived and worked in Chicago after completing Master of Fine Arts degrees (at different times) at the School of the Art Institute of Chicago (SAIC). Benedict lived in Chicago from 2009 to 2016, and Rueter from 2011 to 2016.

4. In 2018, when de Paula was researching the pits, he, Benedict, and Rueter met at the Jan van Eyck Academie, Maastricht, where he and Benedict were participants from 2018 to 2019.

5. de Paula's research draws on his personal experience as an artist living and working in São Paulo, Brazil, for more than two decades.

6. The Chicago Mercantile Exchange (CME) and the CBOT both emerged as two distinct markets for the buying and selling of agricultural commodities—and the options, futures, and derivatives of these commodities—beginning in Chicago in the nineteenth century. In 2006 the companies managing these exchanges merged to form the CME Group Inc. (CME Group), which continued to acquire and merge with numerous national and international exchanges and indexes from 2006 to 2018. In 2018 the CME Group managed the real estate of the CBOT Building on LaSalle and Jackson. See: http://investor.cmegroup.com/news-releases/news-release-details/cme-and-cbot-merge-creating-25-billion-premier-global.

7. Closure of open outcry futures trading at CME Group properties began in 2015, and included closure and initial demolition of the south trading floor, also know as the grain commodities trading room, in the CBOT Building (see: http://investor.cmegroup.com/news-releases/news-release-details/cme-group-close-most-open-outcry-futures-trading-chicago-and-new). According to an on-site source that was exchanging emails with de Paula at the time, by 2018 all but the corn futures pit had been demolished and removed from the grain room in anticipation of subleasing the space. The execution of an agreement with the CME Group in 2018 to sublease the former south trading floor put into motion the final stage of demolition, which was to remove the corn futures trading pit and its substructures.

8. Greg Lane is a Chicago-based community activist, former publisher of *The Baffler* journal, and carpenter. Lane has worked closely with Peterman on various projects.

9. Ken Dunn has lived and worked in Chicago since the 1970s, originally arriving in the city to attend a PhD program in Philosophy at the University of Chicago. Dunn left the program to found The Resource Center in 1975, and for more than forty years Dunn and the nonprofit have been devoted to "the economic and educational revitalization of city neighborhoods through recycling, composting, urban

farming, creative reuse initiatives, and other programs that reclaim and reuse resources" (see: https://theresourcecenterchicago.org/about-us). Benedict, de Paula, and Rueter worked with Peterman, Lane, Dunn, and The Resource Center in 2018 to facilitate the removal, storage, and transport of the salvaged corn futures trading pit floor.

10. Reuben S. Jennings's 1878 US patent for "Improvement in Trading-Pits" (No. 203,837) specifically mentions the installation of an HVAC system below the trading floor as a technologic innovation of the trading pits. Jennings cites this as one of three arguments he makes for the patentability of the floor: "What I claim as my invention is . . . 3. A trading-pit formed in removable sections, heated and ventilated by hot or cold air admitted through the risers of the steps from the closed space or air-chamber under said steps, said air-chamber being supplied by pipes, substantially as described."

11. "The Chicago Boys" were a school of economic technocrats, including at least 150 Chilean post-graduates who were awarded US government-sponsored fellowships to study economics at the University of Chicago in the 1950s and 1960s, under the tutelage of neoclassical economists Milton Friedman and Arnold Harberger. "Beyond their antagonism to socialist policies, The Chicago Boys were convinced Chile's economy had been smothered for decades by an overblown welfare state, and they dreamed of replacing it with a pure free-market model." (Pamela Constable and Arturo Valenzuela, *A Nation of Enemies*, W. W. Norton & Company, 1991). In Chile, these technocrats served as top-level economic advisors to General Augusto Pinochet's military dictatorship, where they "conducted a kind of revolution 'from above,' transforming the social, economic, political, and even cultural bases of Chilean society." (Patricio Silva, *In the Name of Reason: Technocrats and Politics in Chile*, Penn State University Press, 2008). In more recent history, the current Minister of Economy in Brazil, Paulo Guedes—appointed in 2018 by Jair Bolsonaro—is identified with The Chicago Boys: not only did he graduate from the University of Chicago but he also was invited to work as a researcher at the University of Chile in the 1980s by Jorge Selume Zaror, Pinochet's former director of the budget. Guedes' plan for economic reform in Brazil included widespread privatization of industry among other neoliberal reforms aligned with The Chicago Boys ideology. See: https://www.telesurenglish.net/news/Brazil-Bolsonaros-Economy-Minister-Inspired-by-Pinochet-20181102-0015.html.

12. "*Sulfur Cycle* [1994] was realized as a solo project, *Options: 48*, at the [Museum of Contemporary Art Chicago] in 1994 and was among the last exhibitions at the museum's former site on Ontario Avenue. The exhibition consisted of seven one-ton stacks of gypsum wallboard that collectively contained one ton of sulfur captured in a pollution control process related to burning coal for electrical production. Sulfur diverted from the atmosphere is thereby chemically bonded in a form of synthetic gypsum. A six page brochure . . . accompanied the exhibition along with a certificate confirming a 'transaction' from the SO_2 sulfur emission rights trading market at the Chicago Board of Trade that authorized the museum to emit one ton of sulfur into the atmosphere. This one-ton emission right expired in 2001–meaning that this sulfur was 'prevented' from being emitted into the atmosphere. This dynamic interconnection of industry, ecological interests, pollution trading markets innovation and end use as a building material are reflections of Chicago's bioregional complexity and interconnectedness. The current status of the *Sulfur Cycle* project is that the single ton of sulfur that was exhibited in the former museum, now resides in the walls of the current museum. Although never formally acquired by the museum as an artwork the ton of sulfur is permanently, yet invisibly, on display" (see: http://www.danpeterman.com/2015/04/sulfur-cycle.html). In 2021 Peterman was asked to reexamine this work and produced *Sulfur Cycle 2.0* (2021) more than twenty years after the original work's conception and execution. *Sulfur Cycle 2.0* involved, among other gestures: cutting hundreds of rectangular holes into the walls of the museum, searching for the original gypsum boards, and working with the museum registrar to address the latent conditions of the work, which was integrated into the museum but never properly "owned," or collected, by the institution.

ING CARRIER		15. PORT OF LOADING / EXPORT	10. LOADING PIER / TERMINAL	
KARACHI V 122S		NEW YORK		
N PORT OF UNLOADING		17. PLACE OF DELIVERY BY PRE-CARRIER	11. TYPE OF MOVE	PREPAID/COLLECT
, BRASIL				PREPAID

AND NUMBERS (18)	NUMBER OF PACKAGES (19)	DESCRIPTION OF COMMODITIES *in Schedule B detail* (20)	GROSS WEIGHT (*Kilos*) (21)	MEASUREMENTS (22)
H.C.	1	40 FT. H.C. CONT# SEAL# (SLAC 48 PIECES) OF A TRADING PIT FOR TEMPORARY EXHIBITION AT "34". BIENAL DE SAO PAULO" PRIORITY CARGO - CULTUTAL HARACTER GOODS -IN.1600/15 " BELOW DECK STOWAGE REQUIRED" NRA# 027010-001-00340-000 AES ITN: X20210518969813	10,000.00 Lbs 4,535.97 Kgs	
TOTALS:	1	Number of Pieces: 37 Container Number: CAIU 942557 4561 Seal Number: 0574420, 0574439 Weight: ≈ 5,825 lbs	**10,000.00 Lbs** **4,535.97 Kgs**	**0.00 Cft** **Cbm**

…ncy payment, solicitation, or receipt of any rebate, directly or indirectly, which would be unlawful under the United State Shipping Act, 1984 as amended

…LUE READ CLAUSE 29 HEREOF CONCERNING EXTRA FREIGHT AND CARRIER'S LIMITATIONS OF LIABILITY

…BY:

RECEIVED THE ABOVE DESCRIBED GOODS OR PACKAGES

INTERIM 116
CHICAGO LOADING 128
TRACKING 134
SÃO PAULO UNLOADING 142

DIS PLACE MENT V

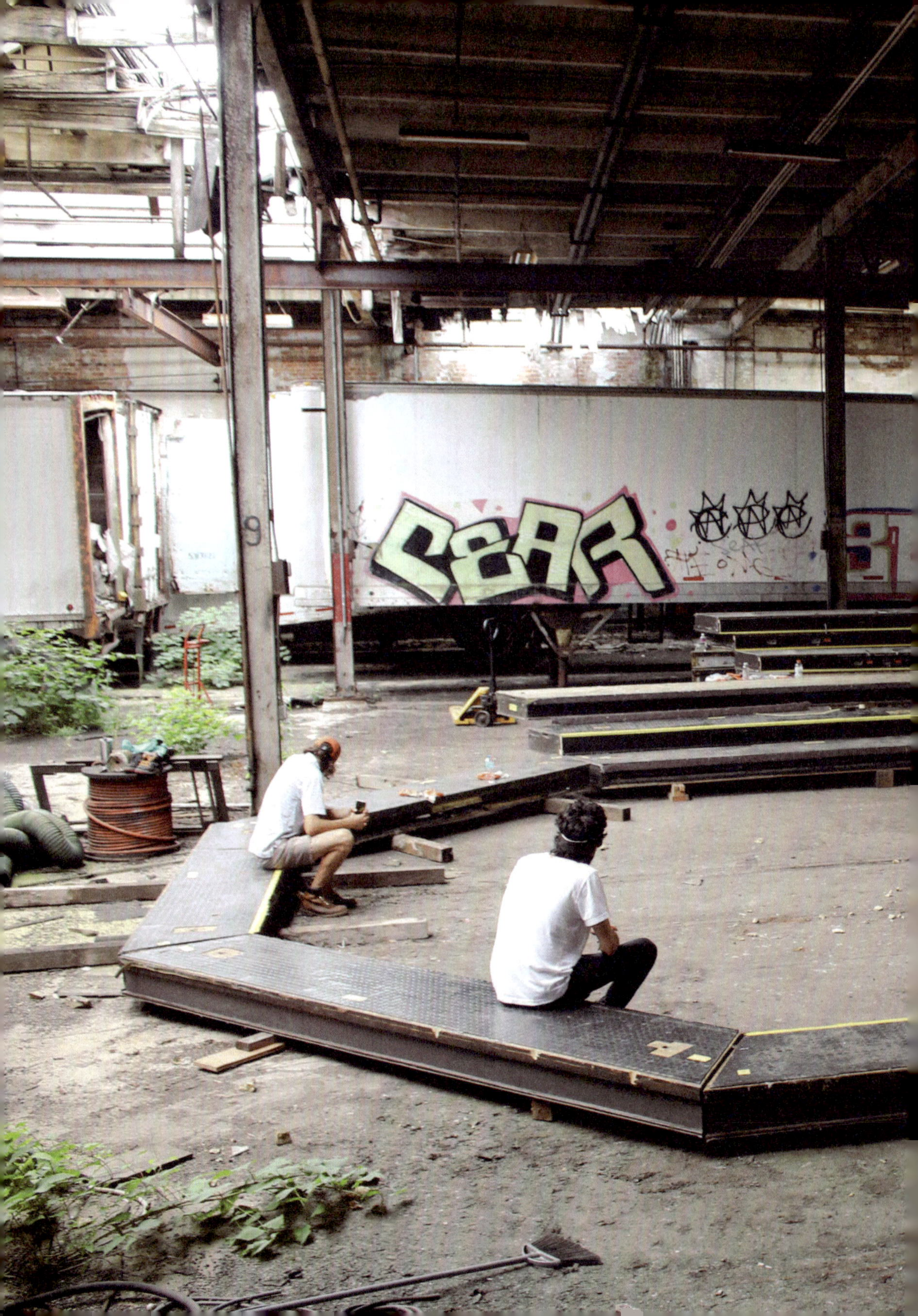

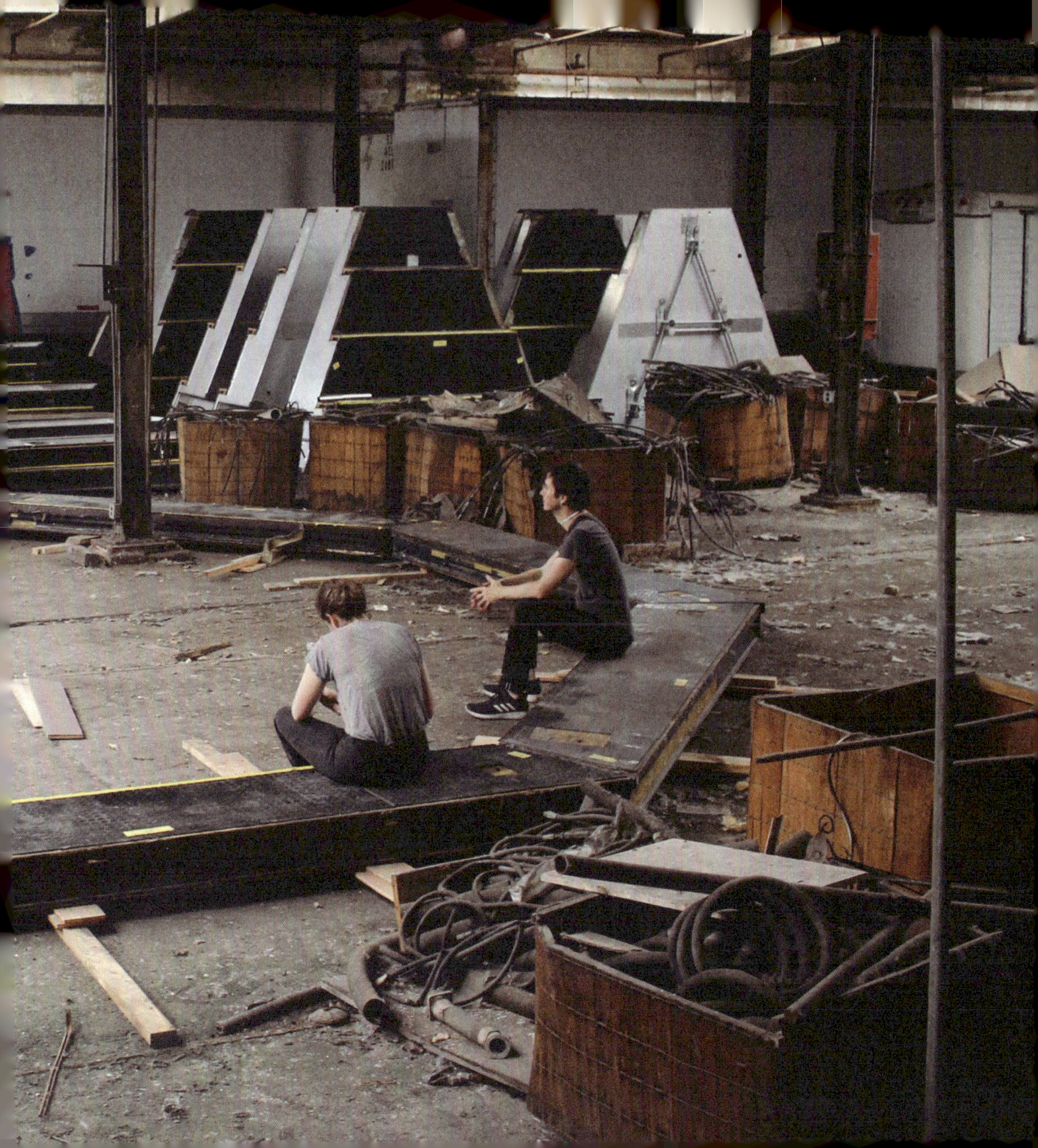

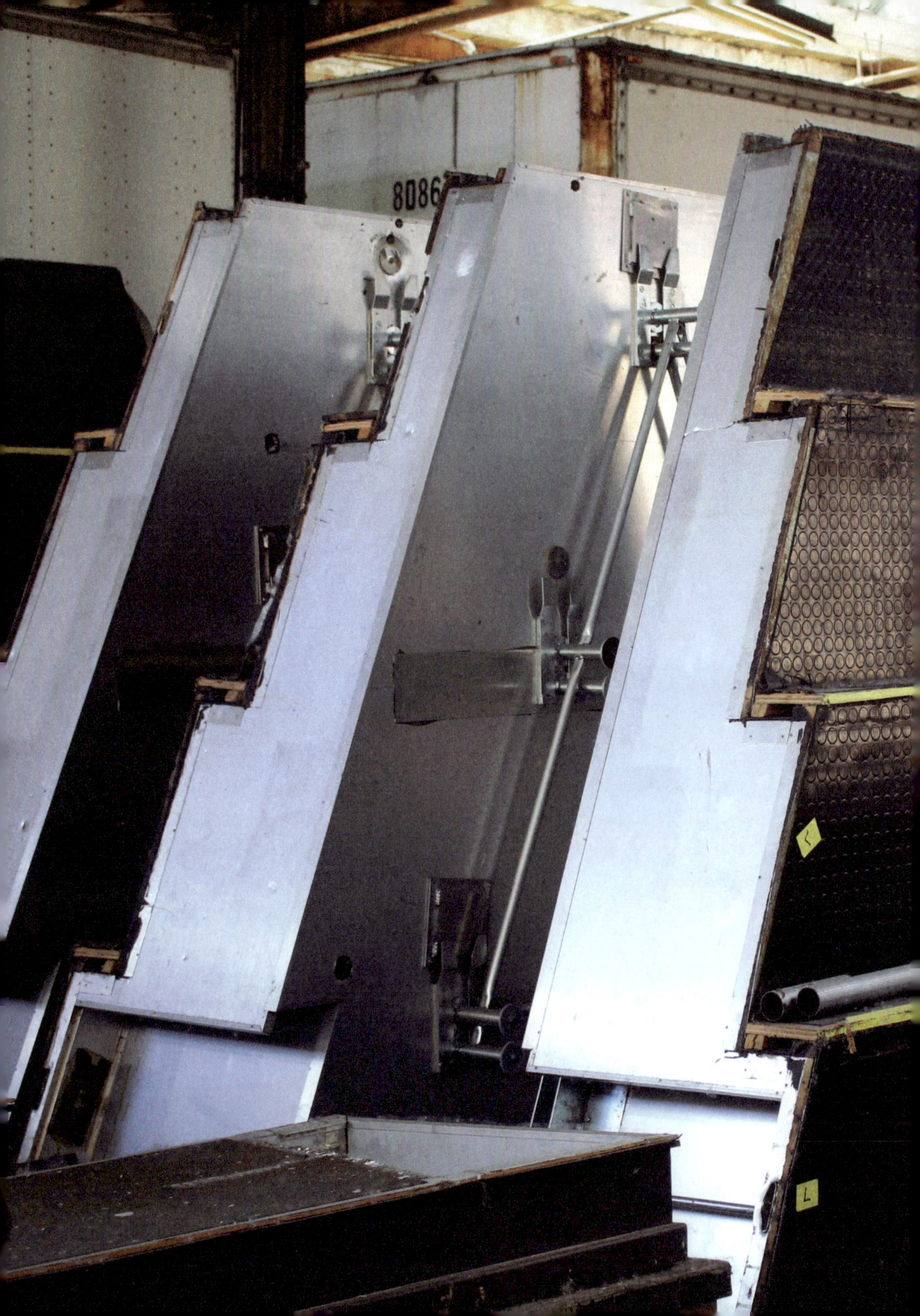

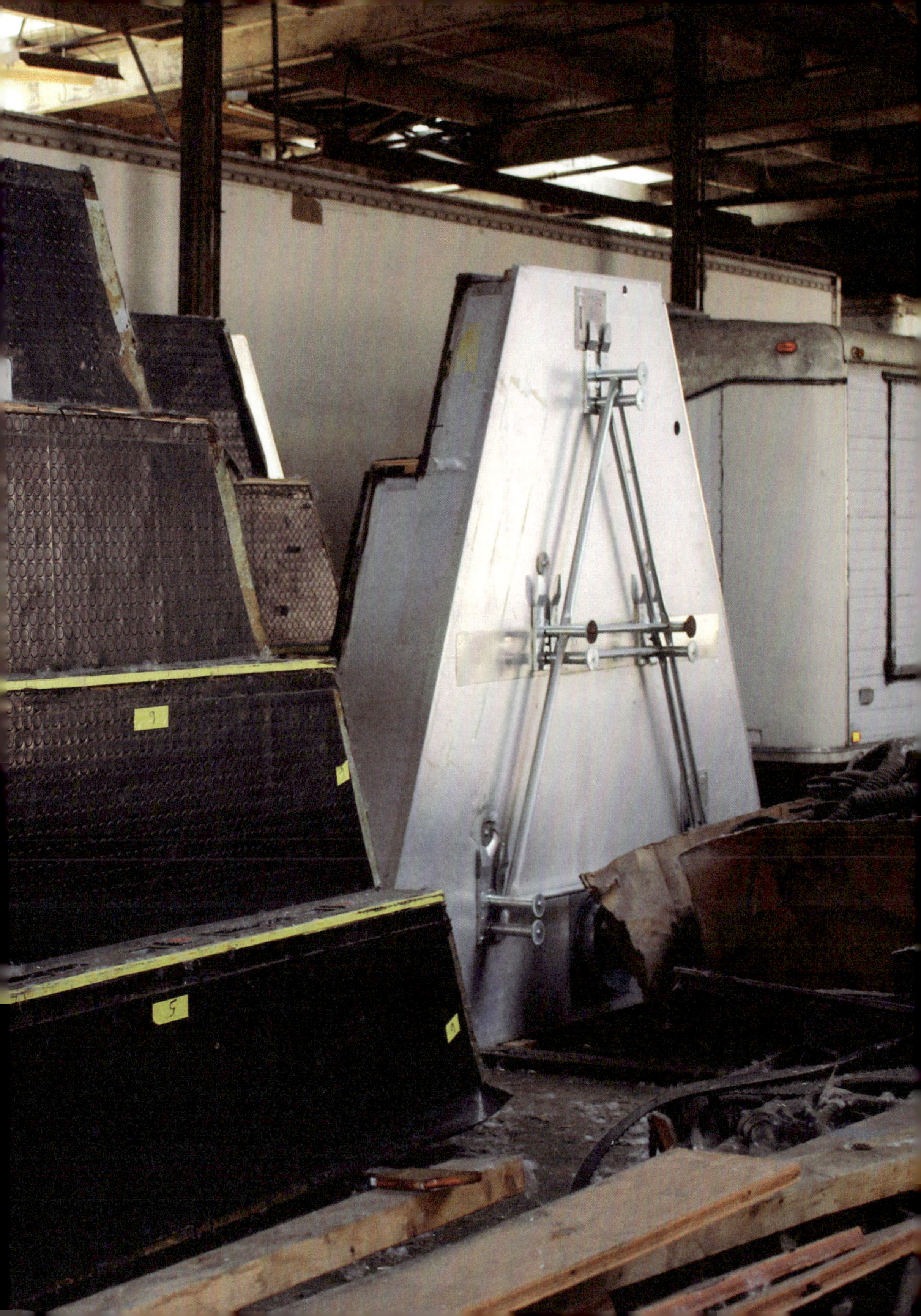

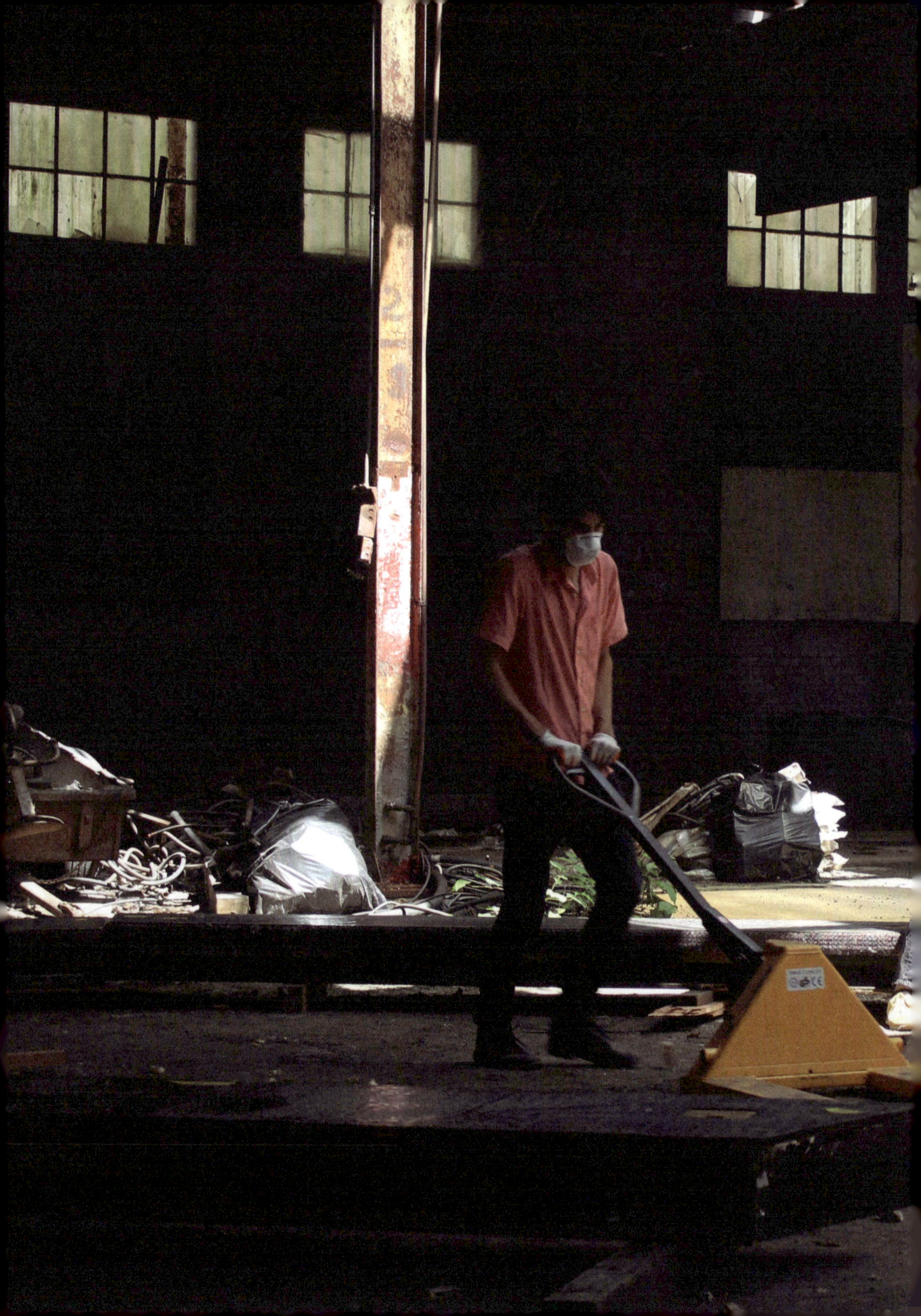

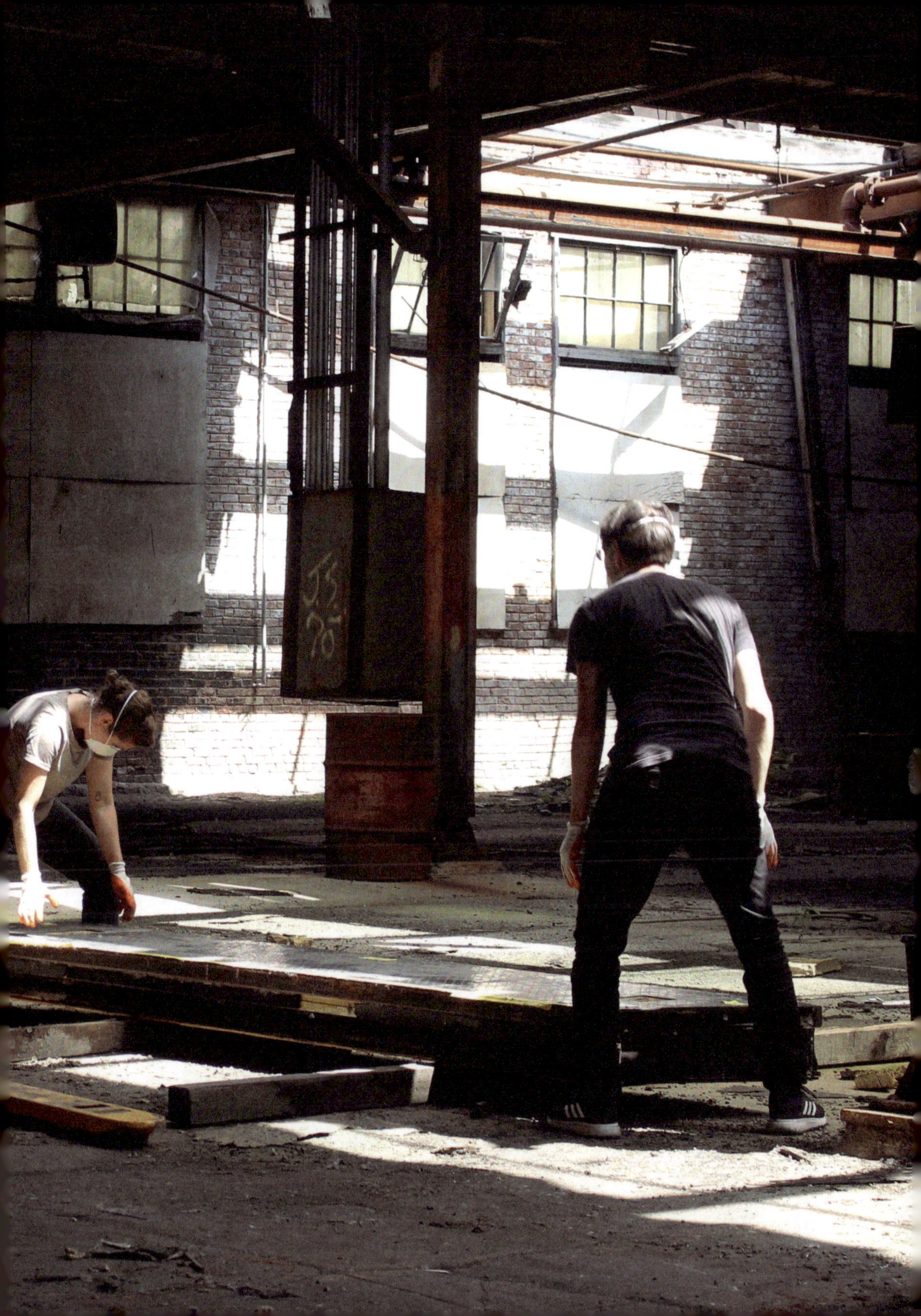

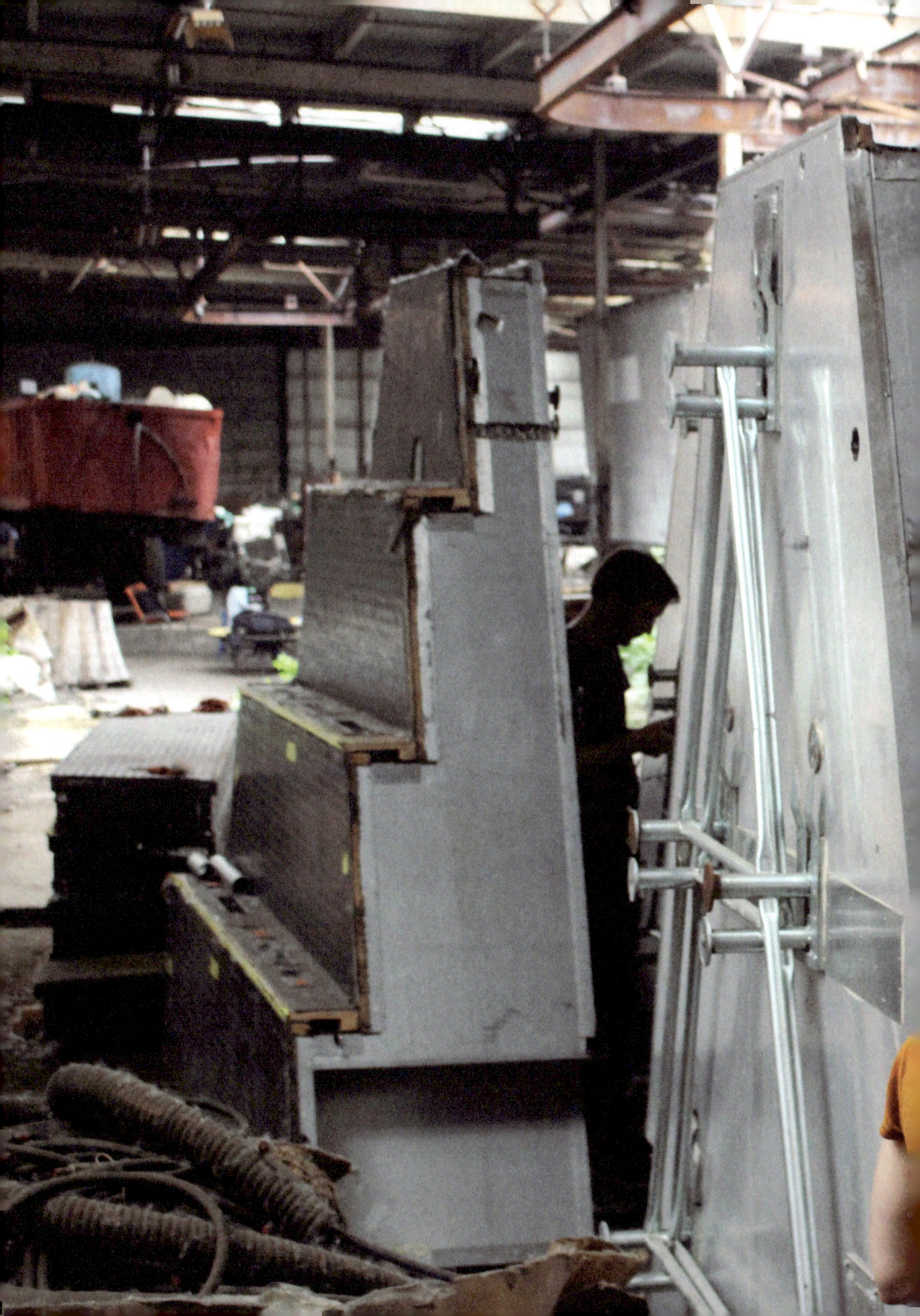

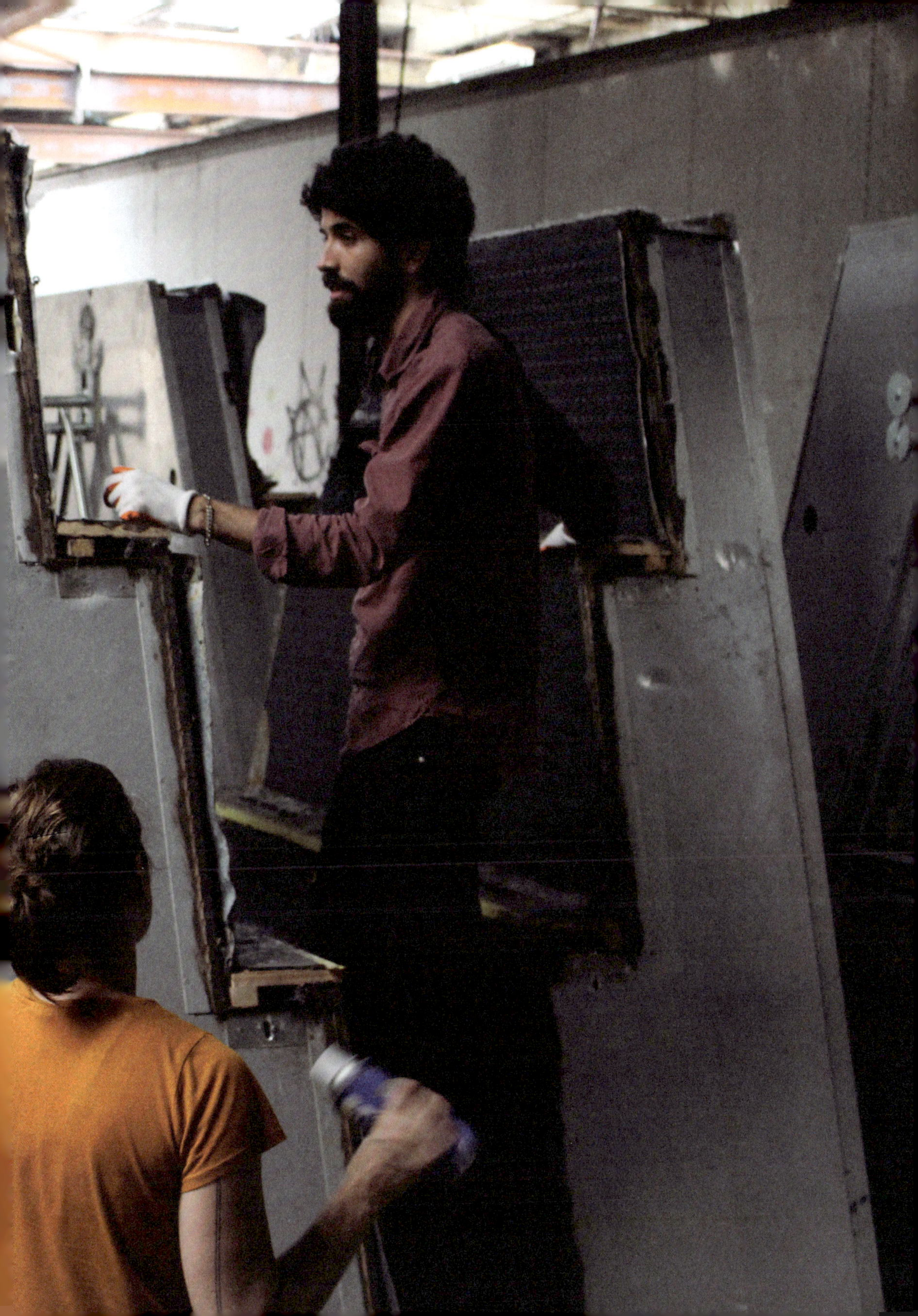

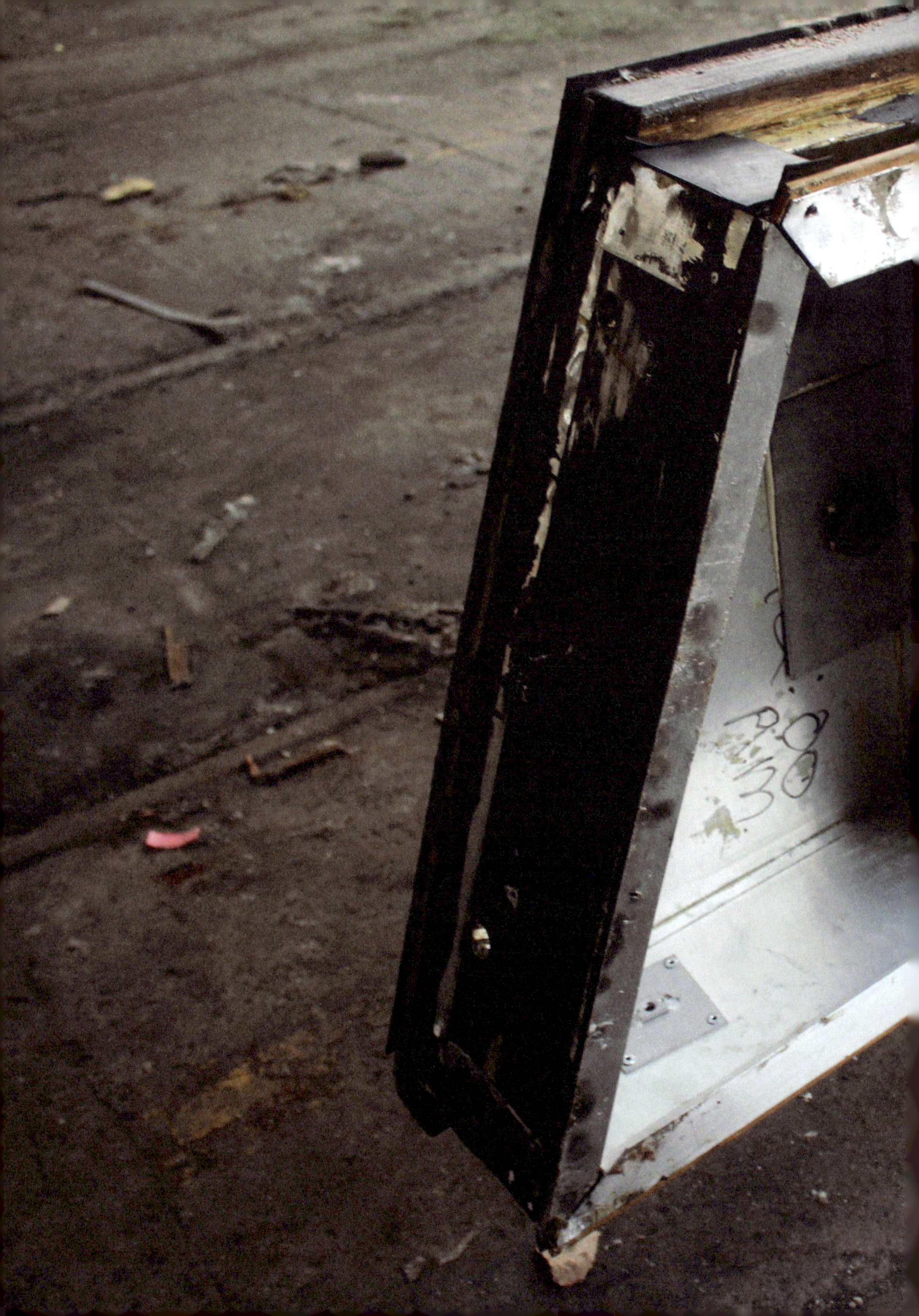

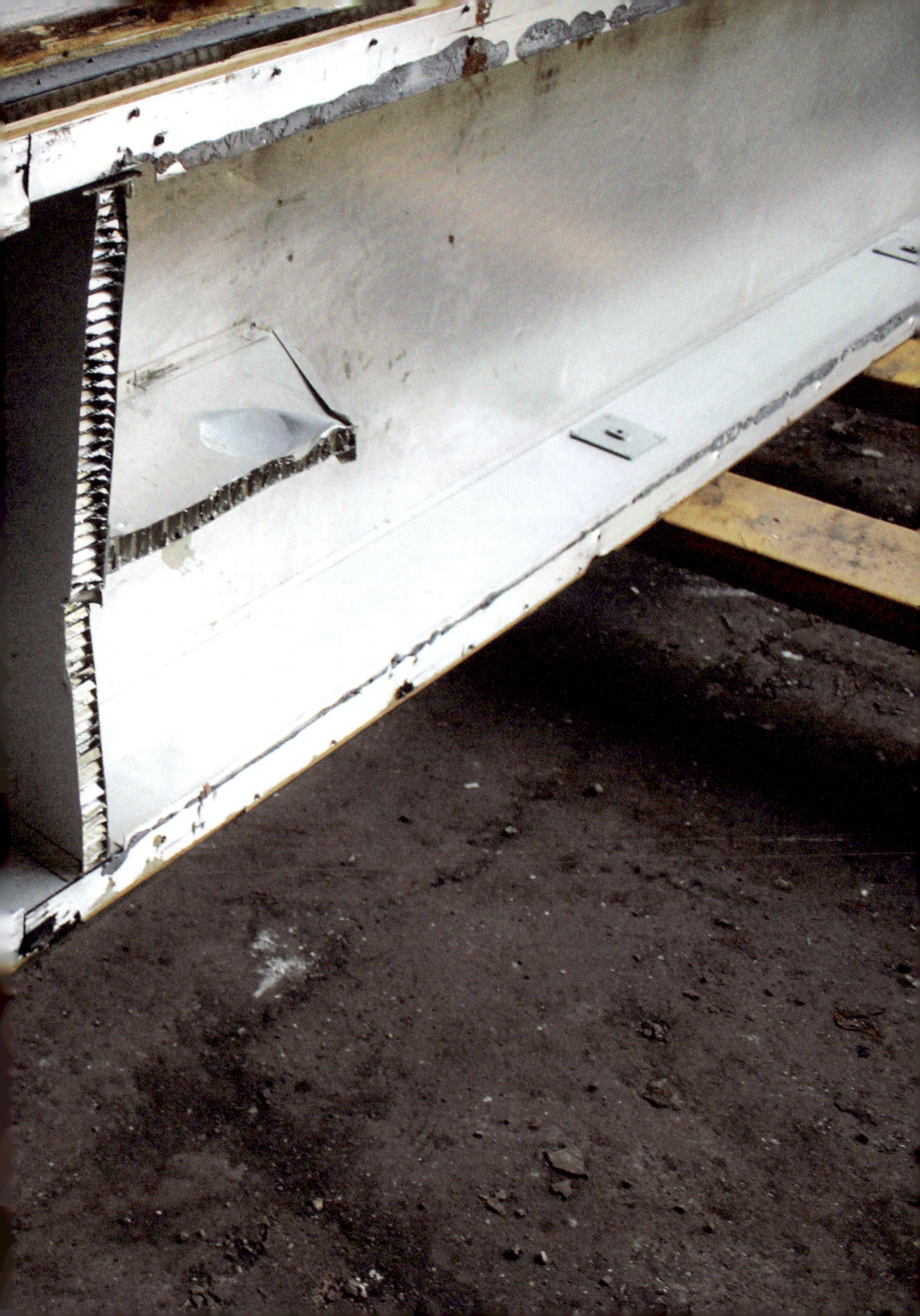

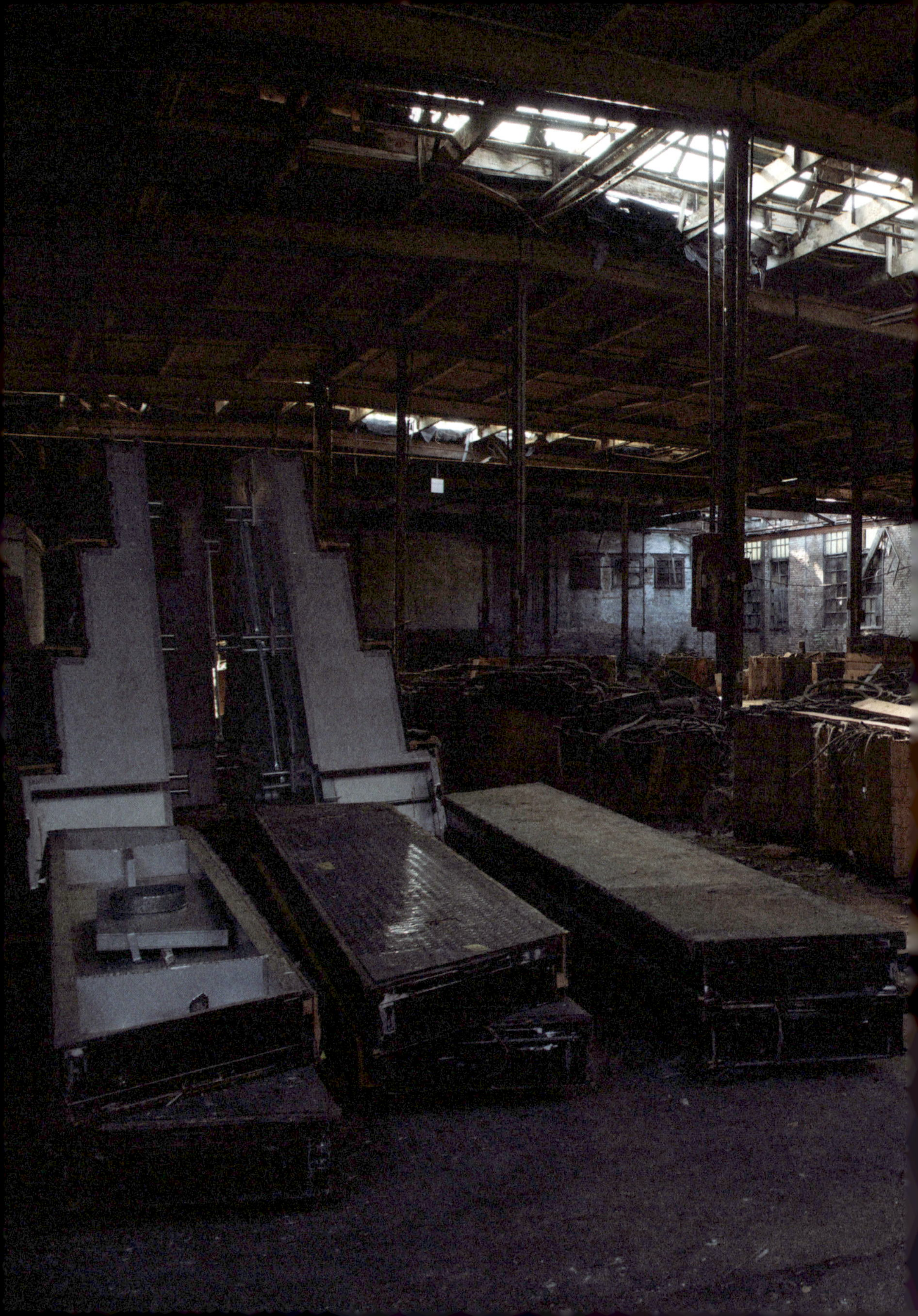

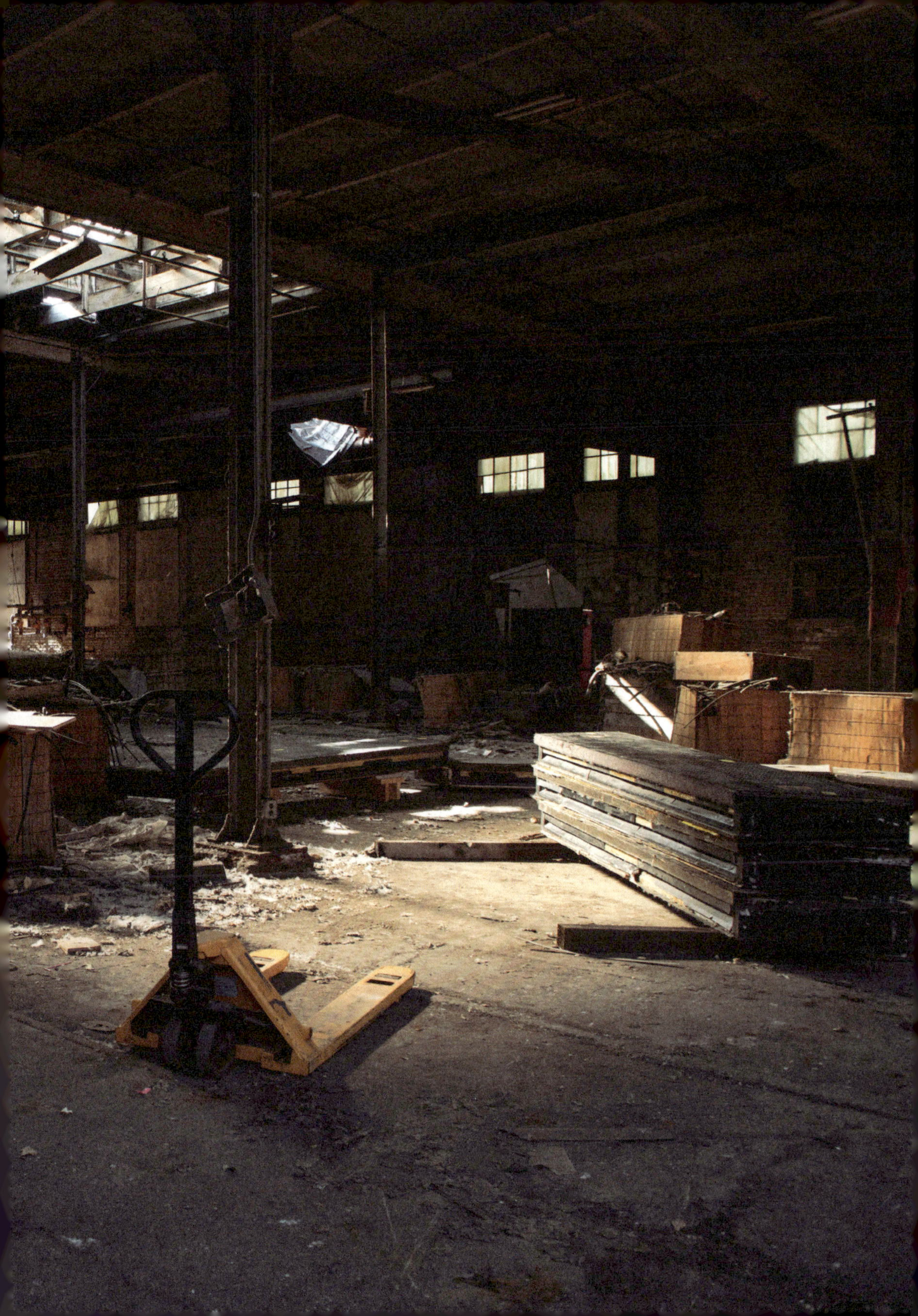

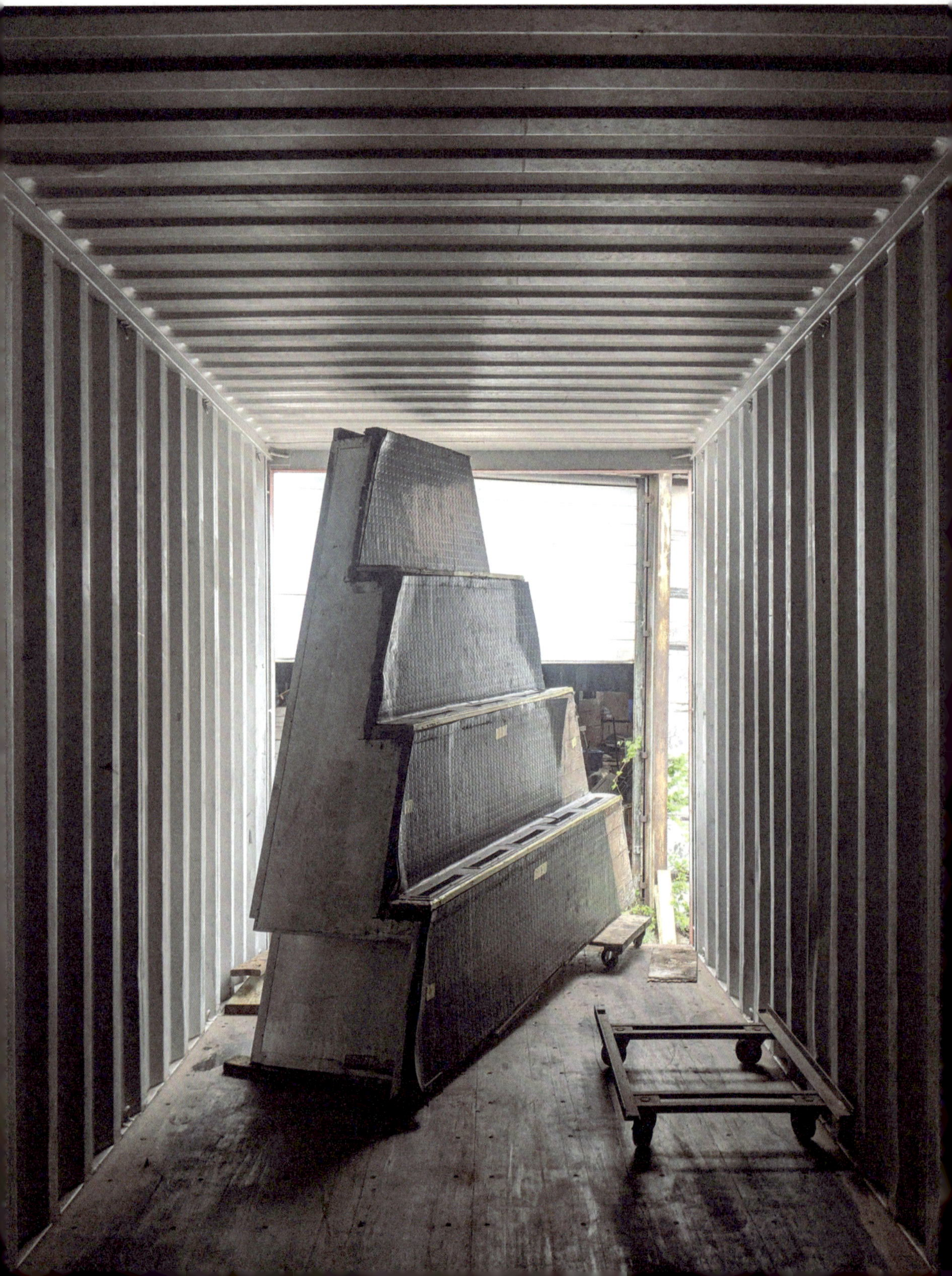

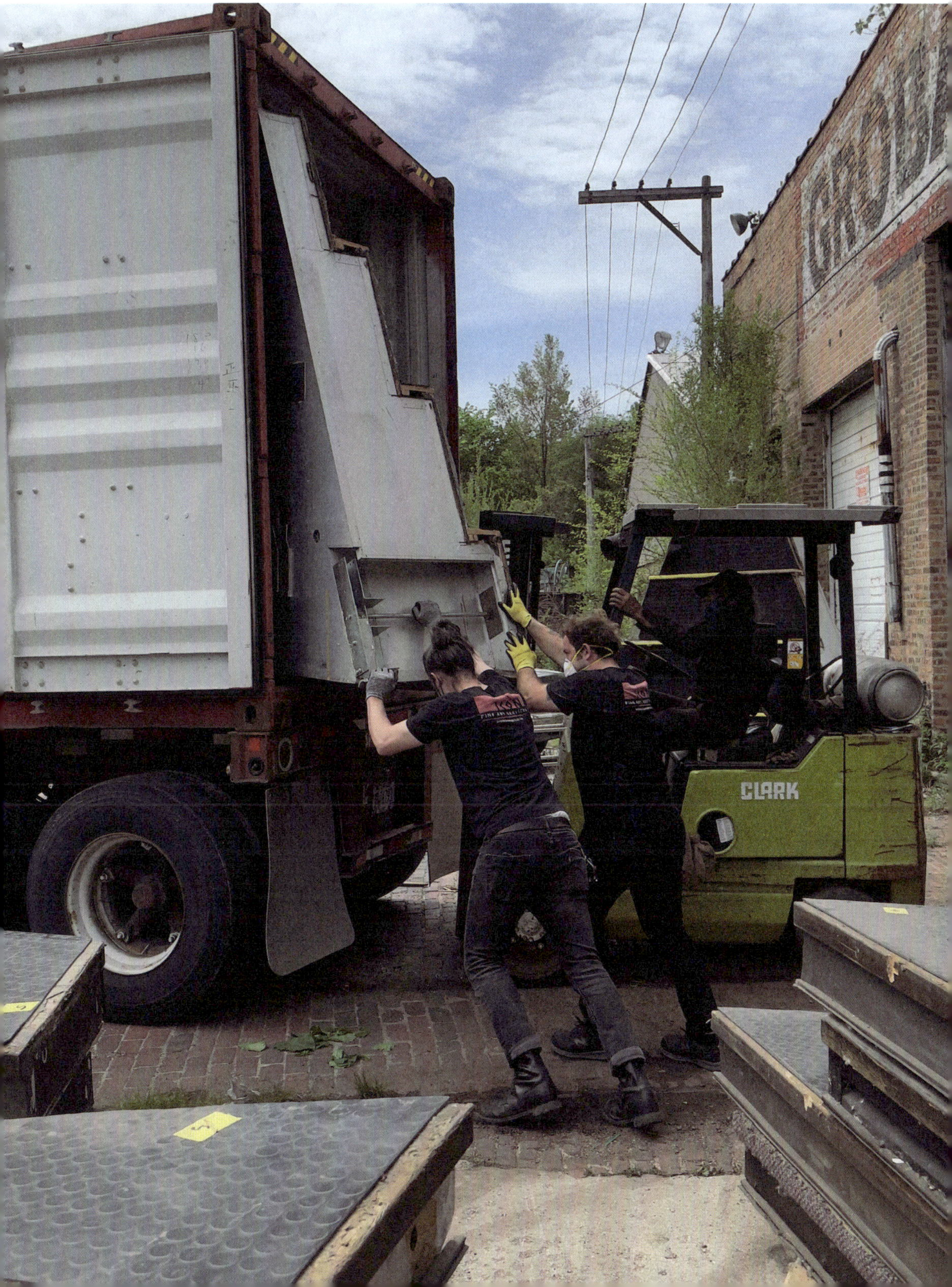
CLARK

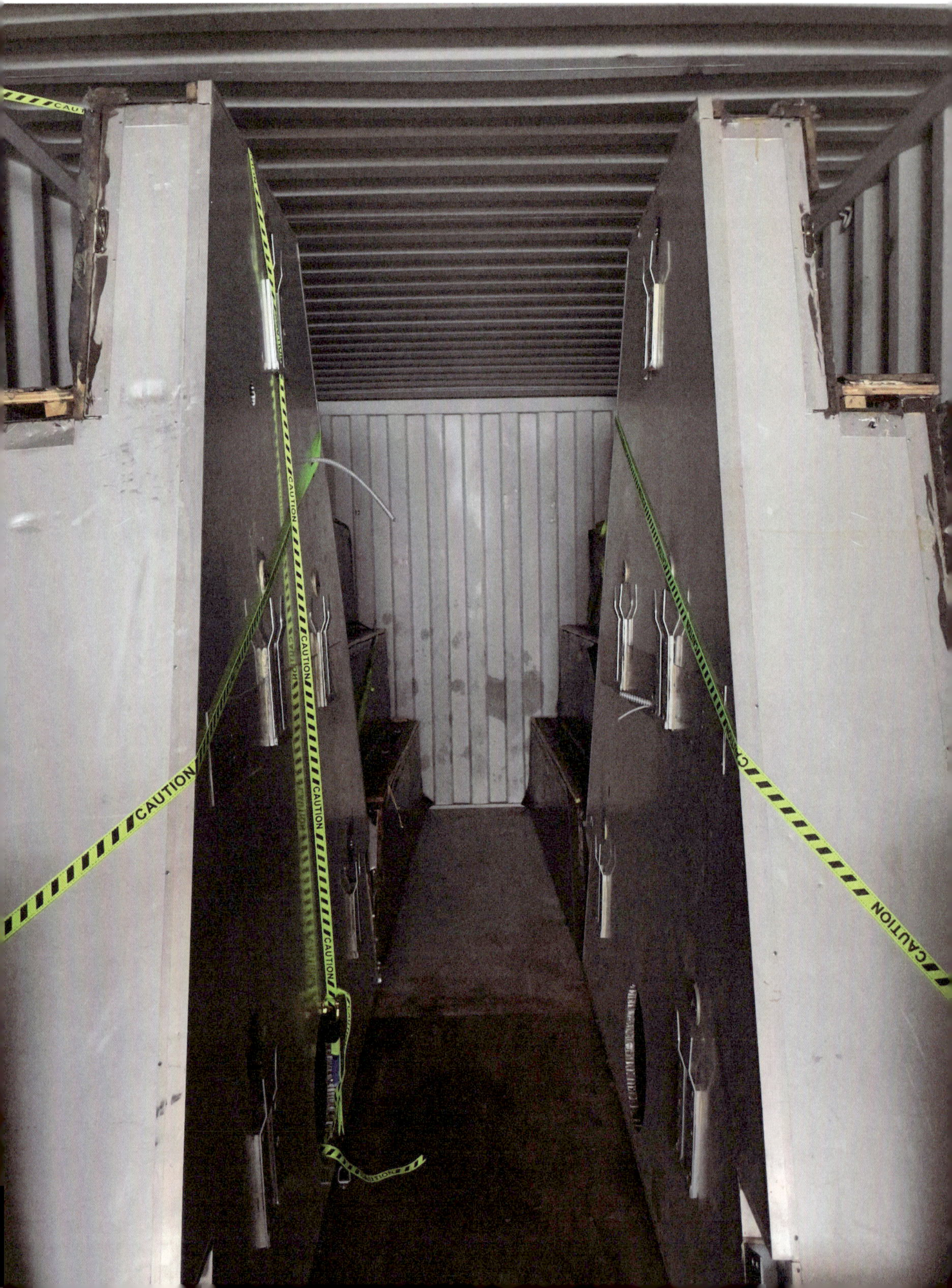
CAUTION
CAUTION
CAUTION

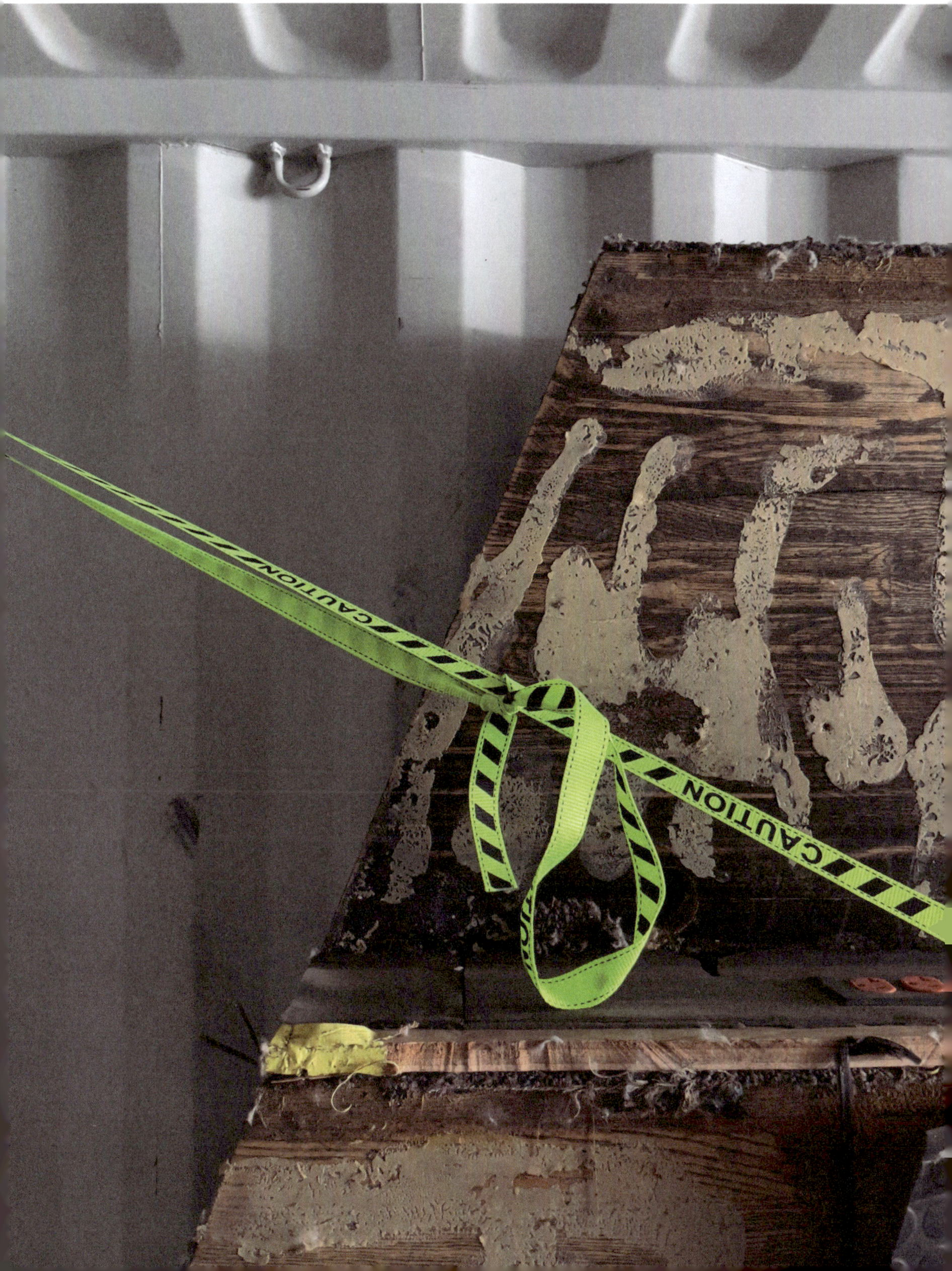
CAUTION
CAUTION

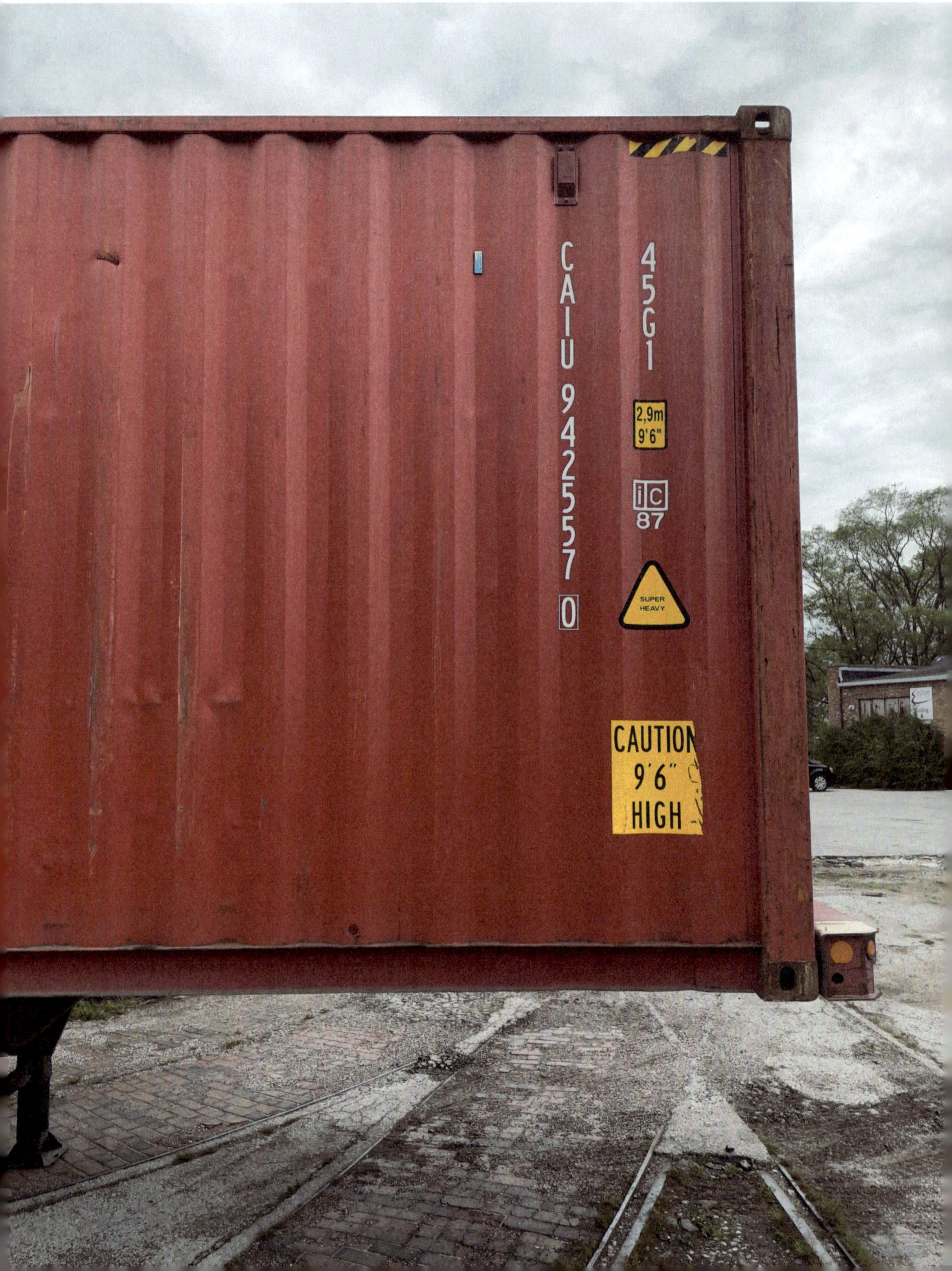
CAIU 942557 0
45G1
2,9m 9'6"
87
SUPER HEAVY
CAUTION 9'6" HIGH

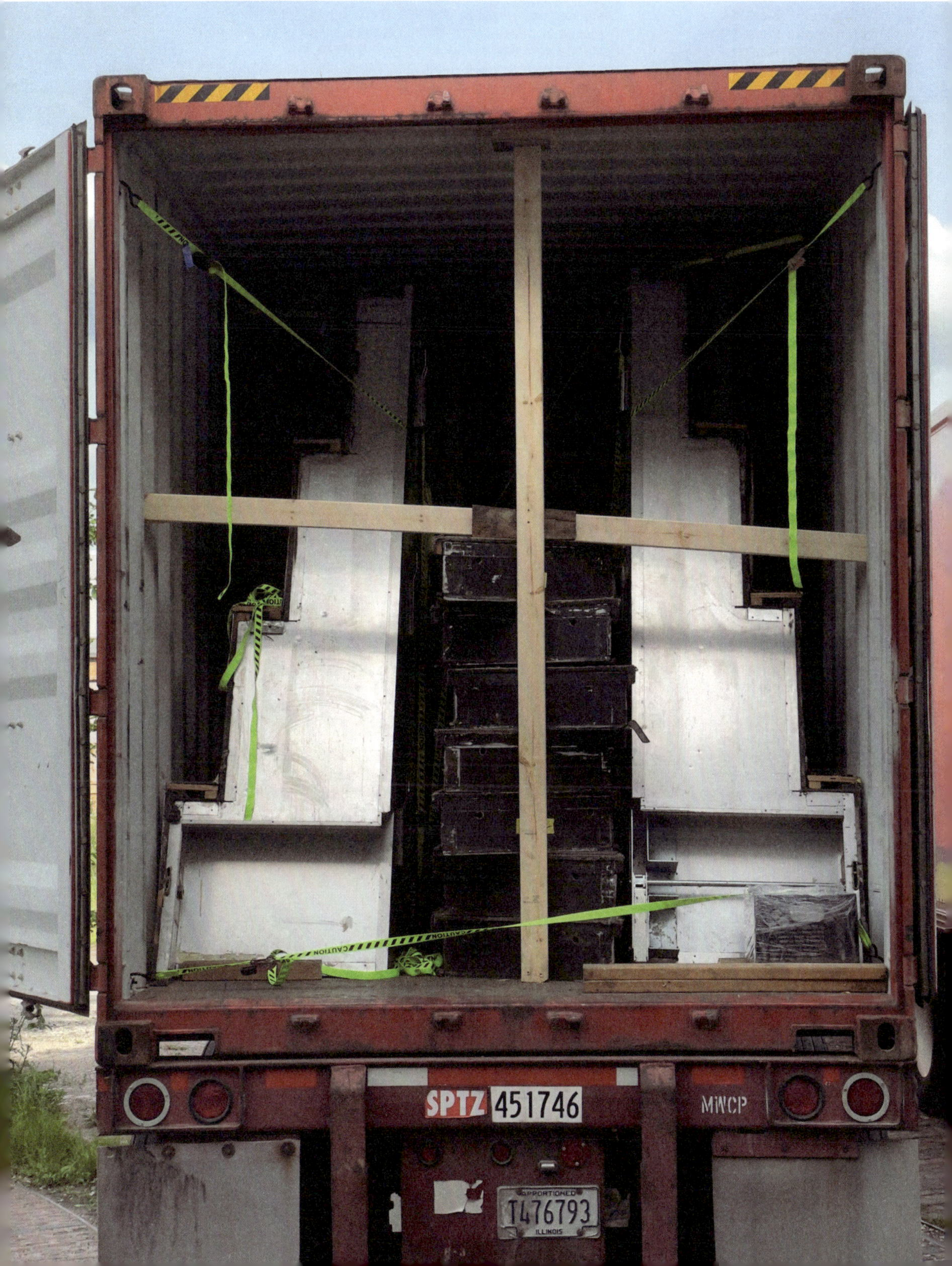
SPTZ 451746
MWCP
APPORTIONED
T476793
ILLINOIS

115	Entered Area of Interest	New York Approaches TSS SouthEast - Inbound
116	Left Area of Interest	Stayed within 'New York Approaches TSS SouthEast - Inbound' for 136 minutes
1	Midnight position	At N 40° 33' 49.20" - W 074° 01' 46.73"
100	Arrival	NEW YORK
38	Tug Operation started	Distance from vessel MARJORIE B.MCALLISTER is 10m
38	Tug Operation started	Distance from vessel CAPTAIN BRIAN A.MCALLISTER is 24m
38	Tug Operation started	Distance from vessel AVA M.MCALLISTER is 94m
38	Tug Operation started	Distance from vessel CHARLES D MCALLISTER is 52m
39	Tug Operation ended	Stayed close to vessel CHARLES D MCALLISTER for 19 minutes
107	Docked	Berth: Berth 96, Terminal: APM Terminals, Port: NEW YORK
39	Tug Operation ended	Stayed close to vessel AVA M.MCALLISTER for 93 minutes
39	Tug Operation ended	Stayed close to vessel CAPTAIN BRIAN A.MCALLISTER for 137 minutes
39	Tug Operation ended	Stayed close to vessel MARJORIE B.MCALLISTER for 152 minutes
16	AIS Status Changed	From Underway using Engine to Moored
2	Noon position	At N 40° 39' 39.36" - W 074° 09' 11.04"
15	AIS ETA Changed	From 2021-06-01 04:00:00 to 2021-06-03 17:00:00
14	AIS Draught Changed	From 14 m to 11.8 m
13	AIS Destination Changed	From USNWK to USPHL
1	Midnight position	At N 40° 39' 39.33" - W 074° 09' 11.01"
38	Tug Operation started	Distance from vessel AVA M.MCALLISTER is 10m
38	Tug Operation started	Distance from vessel CAPTAIN BRIAN A.MCALLISTER is 3m
15	AIS ETA Changed	From 2021-06-03 17:00:00 to 2021-06-03 18:00:00
16	AIS Status Changed	From Moored to Underway using Engine
38	Tug Operation started	Distance from vessel MARJORIE B.MCALLISTER is 0m
108	Undocked	Berth: Berth 96, Terminal: APM Terminals, Port: NEW YORK
39	Tug Operation ended	Stayed close to vessel MARJORIE B.MCALLISTER for 35 minutes
39	Tug Operation ended	Stayed close to vessel CAPTAIN BRIAN A.MCALLISTER for 83 minutes
39	Tug Operation ended	Stayed close to vessel AVA M.MCALLISTER for 99 minutes
101	Departure	NEW YORK
37	Pilot Event	Pilot vessel AMERICA is 24 m away
2	Noon position	At N 40° 26' 31.94" - W 073° 49' 27.32"
115	Entered Area of Interest	New York Approaches TSS South - Outbound
116	Left Area of Interest	Stayed within 'New York Approaches TSS South - Outbound' for 326 minutes
1	Midnight position	At N 39° 13' 42.76" - W 074° 05' 22.09"
3	In Terrestrial Range	At N 38° 41' 12.43" - W 074° 26' 45.40"
115	Entered Area of Interest	Delaware Bay Approaches TSS - South Inbound
2	Noon position	At N 38° 43' 39.66" - W 074° 55' 35.36"
116	Left Area of Interest	Stayed within 'Delaware Bay Approaches TSS - South Inbound' for 220 minutes
112	Crossed Strait or Passage	DELAWARE BAY
116	Left Area of Interest	Stayed within 'United States Exclusive Economic Zone (Atlantic)' for 4734 minutes
116	Left Area of Interest	Stayed within 'IV United States' for 12591 minutes
116	Left Area of Interest	Stayed within 'North America Winter Seasonal Area' for 4692 minutes
116	Left Area of Interest	Stayed within 'US East Coast' for 7543 minutes
116	Left Area of Interest	Stayed within 'US Atlantic ECA' for 4729 minutes
19	Start of proximity to another vessel	Distance from vessel CALUSA COAST is 167m
115	Entered Area of Interest	Inland, North America
34	End of proximity to another vessel	Stayed close to vessel CALUSA COAST for 87 minutes
38	Tug Operation started	Distance from vessel BEVERLY R.MCALLISTER is 0m
38	Tug Operation started	Distance from vessel ROBERT E.MCALLISTER is 0m
100	Arrival	GLOUCESTER
39	Tug Operation ended	Stayed close to vessel ROBERT E.MCALLISTER for 32 minutes
19	Start of proximity to another vessel	Distance from vessel ROBERT E.MCALLISTER is 0m
16	AIS Status Changed	From Underway using Engine to Moored
34	End of proximity to another vessel	Stayed close to vessel ROBERT E.MCALLISTER for 16 minutes
39	Tug Operation ended	Stayed close to vessel BEVERLY R.MCALLISTER for 88 minutes
16	AIS Status Changed	From Moored to At Anchor
16	AIS Status Changed	From At Anchor to Moored
16	AIS Status Changed	From Moored to At Anchor
16	AIS Status Changed	From At Anchor to Moored
2	Noon position	At N 39° 53' 59.05" - W 075° 08' 07.02"
16	AIS Status Changed	From Moored to At Anchor
38	Tug Operation started	Distance from vessel REID MCALLISTER is 0m
16	AIS Status Changed	From At Anchor to Underway using Engine
38	Tug Operation started	Distance from vessel BEVERLY R.MCALLISTER is 12m
14	AIS Draught Changed	From 11.7 m to 11.1 m
39	Tug Operation ended	Stayed close to vessel BEVERLY R.MCALLISTER for 24 minutes
39	Tug Operation ended	Stayed close to vessel REID MCALLISTER for 55 minutes
101	Departure	GLOUCESTER
116	Left Area of Interest	Stayed within 'Inland, North America' for 1601 minutes
115	Entered Area of Interest	US Atlantic ECA
115	Entered Area of Interest	United States Exclusive Economic Zone (Atlantic)
115	Entered Area of Interest	IV United States
115	Entered Area of Interest	North America Winter Seasonal Area
115	Entered Area of Interest	US East Coast

MAERSK KARACHI	USEC	US East Coast	308	40.14665,-73.2608	18.0	2021-06-01 01:20:00 -5
MAERSK KARACHI	USEC	US East Coast	304	40.40046,-73.71341	9.8	2021-06-01 03:31:00 -5
MAERSK KARACHI	USEC	US East Coast	348	40.56367,-74.02965	10.5	2021-06-01 05:13:00 -5
MAERSK KARACHI	USEC	Hudson River		null,null	null	2021-06-01 05:14:00 -4
MAERSK KARACHI	USEC	US East Coast	345	40.6178,-74.04903	6.4	2021-06-01 05:31:00 -5
MAERSK KARACHI	USEC	US East Coast	348	40.62377,-74.05085	6.5	2021-06-01 05:36:00 -5
MAERSK KARACHI	USEC	US East Coast	245	40.65023,-74.08741	5.8	2021-06-01 06:04:00 -5
MAERSK KARACHI	USEC	US East Coast	261	40.643,-74.13581	4.6	2021-06-01 06:28:00 -5
MAERSK KARACHI	USEC	US East Coast	22	40.65353,-74.14708	4.3	2021-06-01 06:48:00 -5
MAERSK KARACHI	USEC	Hudson River		null,null	null	2021-06-01 07:09:00 -4
MAERSK KARACHI	USEC	US East Coast	66	40.66092,-74.15304	0.0	2021-06-01 07:38:00 -5
MAERSK KARACHI	USEC	US East Coast	258	40.66092,-74.15305	0.0	2021-06-01 07:54:00 -5
MAERSK KARACHI	USEC	US East Coast	239	40.66093,-74.15308	0.0	2021-06-01 08:03:00 -5
MAERSK KARACHI	USEC	US East Coast	268	40.66093,-74.15305	0.0	2021-06-01 14:03:00 -4
MAERSK KARACHI	USEC	US East Coast	97	40.66093,-74.15307	0.0	2021-06-01 16:12:00 -4
MAERSK KARACHI	USEC	US East Coast	70	40.66092,-74.15305	0.0	2021-06-02 03:56:00 -4
MAERSK KARACHI	USEC	US East Coast	70	40.66092,-74.15305	0.0	2021-06-02 03:56:00 -4
MAERSK KARACHI	USEC	US East Coast	70	40.66092,-74.15305	0.0	2021-06-02 03:56:00 -4
MAERSK KARACHI	USEC	US East Coast	107	40.66093,-74.15306	0.0	2021-06-02 04:12:00 -4
MAERSK KARACHI	USEC	US East Coast	111	40.65896,-74.1502	2.2	2021-06-02 13:12:00 -5
MAERSK KARACHI	USEC	US East Coast	111	40.65896,-74.1502	2.2	2021-06-02 13:16:00 -5
MAERSK KARACHI	USEC	US East Coast	310	40.66093,-74.15307	0.0	2021-06-02 13:23:00 -4
MAERSK KARACHI	USEC	US East Coast	239	40.66092,-74.15307	0.0	2021-06-02 13:30:00 -4
MAERSK KARACHI	USEC	US East Coast	111	40.65896,-74.1502	2.2	2021-06-02 13:56:00 -5
MAERSK KARACHI	USEC	Hudson River		null,null	null	2021-06-02 14:02:00 -4
MAERSK KARACHI	USEC	US East Coast	208	40.65403,-74.14736	4.4	2021-06-02 14:32:00 -5
MAERSK KARACHI	USEC	US East Coast	138	40.64318,-74.15018	4.5	2021-06-02 14:39:00 -5
MAERSK KARACHI	USEC	US East Coast	75	40.64351,-74.12287	6.8	2021-06-02 14:51:00 -5
MAERSK KARACHI	USEC	Hudson River		null,null	null	2021-06-02 15:47:00 -4
MAERSK KARACHI	USEC	US East Coast	103	40.4622,-73.8456	8.8	2021-06-02 16:56:00 -5
MAERSK KARACHI	USEC	US East Coast	164	40.44221,-73.82426	5.2	2021-06-02 17:14:00 -5
MAERSK KARACHI	USEC	US East Coast	186	40.31771,-73.81772	6.4	2021-06-02 18:26:00 -5
MAERSK KARACHI	USEC	US East Coast	190	39.75708,-73.87373	6.1	2021-06-02 23:42:00 -5
MAERSK KARACHI	USEC	US East Coast	201	39.22855,-74.08947	6.0	2021-06-03 04:59:00 -5
MAERSK KARACHI	USEC	US East Coast	208	38.68679,-74.44595	6.2	2021-06-03 10:55:00 -5
MAERSK KARACHI	USEC	US East Coast	294	38.47613,-74.66129	5.9	2021-06-03 13:47:00 -5
MAERSK KARACHI	USEC	US East Coast	319	38.72768,-74.92649	5.9	2021-06-03 17:13:00 -5
MAERSK KARACHI	USEC	US East Coast	300	38.74566,-74.95379	6.3	2021-06-03 17:29:00 -5
MAERSK KARACHI	USEC	US East Coast	324	39.12243,-75.21886	15.7	2021-06-03 19:24:00 -5
MAERSK KARACHI	USEC	US East Coast	317	39.38929,-75.48299	16.1	2021-06-03 20:40:00 -5
MAERSK KARACHI	USEC	US East Coast	317	39.38929,-75.48299	16.1	2021-06-03 20:40:00 -5
MAERSK KARACHI	USEC	US East Coast	317	39.38929,-75.48299	16.1	2021-06-03 20:40:00 -5
MAERSK KARACHI	USEC	US East Coast	317	39.38929,-75.48299	16.1	2021-06-03 20:40:00 -5
MAERSK KARACHI	USEC	US East Coast	317	39.38929,-75.48299	16.1	2021-06-03 20:40:00 -5
MAERSK KARACHI	USEC	US East Coast	14	39.71434,-75.50754	7.8	2021-06-03 21:08:00 0
MAERSK KARACHI	USEC	US East Coast	334	39.60089,-75.56969	12.1	2021-06-03 21:37:00 -5
MAERSK KARACHI	USEC	US East Coast	16	39.73108,-75.50173	7.7	2021-06-03 22:35:00 -5
MAERSK KARACHI	USEC	US East Coast	73	39.88076,-75.19252	7.5	2021-06-04 00:35:00 -5
MAERSK KARACHI	USEC	US East Coast	91	39.88063,-75.15429	5.9	2021-06-04 00:55:00 -5
MAERSK KARACHI	USEC	US East Coast		null,null	null	2021-06-04 01:03:00 -4
MAERSK KARACHI	USEC	US East Coast	23	39.89771,-75.13493	1.3	2021-06-04 01:27:00 -5
MAERSK KARACHI	USEC	US East Coast	52	39.89971,-75.13528	0.0	2021-06-04 01:44:00 0
MAERSK KARACHI	USEC	US East Coast	330	39.89974,-75.13529	0.0	2021-06-04 01:49:00 -4
MAERSK KARACHI	USEC	US East Coast	333	39.89971,-75.13531	0.0	2021-06-04 02:00:00 -5
MAERSK KARACHI	USEC	US East Coast	333	39.89971,-75.13531	0.0	2021-06-04 02:04:00 -5
MAERSK KARACHI	USEC	US East Coast	313	39.89972,-75.13527	0.0	2021-06-04 02:10:00 -4
MAERSK KARACHI	USEC	US East Coast	275	39.89974,-75.13529	0.0	2021-06-04 02:15:00 -4
MAERSK KARACHI	USEC	US East Coast	279	39.89972,-75.13527	0.0	2021-06-04 02:37:00 -4
MAERSK KARACHI	USEC	US East Coast	327	39.89974,-75.13528	0.0	2021-06-04 16:13:00 -4
MAERSK KARACHI	USEC	US East Coast	327	39.89974,-75.13528	0.0	2021-06-04 16:13:00 -4
MAERSK KARACHI	USEC	US East Coast	330	39.89973,-75.13529	0.0	2021-06-04 16:23:00 -4
MAERSK KARACHI	USEC	US East Coast	133	39.89919,-75.13452	0.5	2021-06-04 18:00:00 -5
MAERSK KARACHI	USEC	US East Coast	6	39.89973,-75.13529	0.0	2021-06-04 18:23:00 -4
MAERSK KARACHI	USEC	US East Coast	133	39.89919,-75.13452	0.5	2021-06-04 18:27:00 -5
MAERSK KARACHI	USEC	US East Coast	152	39.89975,-75.13528	0.0	2021-06-04 18:41:00 -4
MAERSK KARACHI	USEC	US East Coast	194	39.89834,-75.13429	1.8	2021-06-04 18:52:00 -5
MAERSK KARACHI	USEC	US East Coast	200	39.89467,-75.13599	5.3	2021-06-04 18:56:00 -5
MAERSK KARACHI	USEC	US East Coast		null,null	null	2021-06-04 19:10:00 -4
MAERSK KARACHI	USEC	US East Coast	137	39.38021,-75.47287	14.8	2021-06-04 23:11:00 -5
MAERSK KARACHI	USEC	US East Coast	139	39.36301,-75.45306	14.8	2021-06-04 23:17:00 -5
MAERSK KARACHI	USEC	US East Coast	136	39.26373,-75.3382	15.7	2021-06-04 23:48:00 -5
MAERSK KARACHI	USEC	US East Coast	136	39.26373,-75.3382	15.7	2021-06-04 23:48:00 -5
MAERSK KARACHI	USEC	US East Coast	136	39.26373,-75.3382	15.7	2021-06-04 23:48:00 -5
MAERSK KARACHI	USEC	US East Coast	136	39.26373,-75.3382	15.7	2021-06-04 23:48:00 -5

112	Crossed Strait or Passage	DELAWARE BAY
37	Pilot Event	Pilot vessel PILOT LEWES is 0 m away
115	Entered Area of Interest	Delaware Bay Approaches TSS - South Outbound
116	Left Area of Interest	Stayed within 'Delaware Bay Approaches TSS - South Outbound' for 77 minutes
1	Midnight position	At N 38° 04' 09.36" - W 074° 33' 49.01"
115	Entered Area of Interest	Chesapeake Bay Approaches TSS - South Inbound
116	Left Area of Interest	Stayed within 'Chesapeake Bay Approaches TSS - South Inbound' for 39 minutes
112	Crossed Strait or Passage	CHESAPEAKE CHANNEL
100	Arrival	NORFOLK
38	Tug Operation started	Distance from vessel CLAYTON W MORAN is 0m
38	Tug Operation started	Distance from vessel WYATT MORAN is 7m
107	Docked	Berth: 3, Terminal: NIT South Container Terminal, Port: NORFOLK
16	AIS Status Changed	From Underway using Engine to Moored
39	Tug Operation ended	Stayed close to vessel WYATT MORAN for 72 minutes
39	Tug Operation ended	Stayed close to vessel CLAYTON W MORAN for 76 minutes
2	Noon position	At N 36° 54' 34.18" - W 076° 19' 37.78"
19	Start of proximity to another vessel	Distance from vessel MAXWELL PAUL MORAN is 18m
34	End of proximity to another vessel	Stayed close to vessel MAXWELL PAUL MORAN for 32 minutes
15	AIS ETA Changed	From 2021-06-05 13:00:00 to 2021-06-07 08:00:00
13	AIS Destination Changed	From USNFK to USCHS
14	AIS Draught Changed	From 11.1 m to 10.7 m
16	AIS Status Changed	From Moored to Underway using Engine
38	Tug Operation started	Distance from vessel MAXWELL PAUL MORAN is 0m
1	Midnight position	At N 36° 54' 34.22" - W 076° 19' 37.81"
19	Start of proximity to another vessel	Distance from vessel A.J.MCALLISTER is 14m
108	Undocked	Berth: 3, Terminal: NIT South Container Terminal, Port: NORFOLK
34	End of proximity to another vessel	Stayed close to vessel A.J.MCALLISTER for 47 minutes
39	Tug Operation ended	Stayed close to vessel MAXWELL PAUL MORAN for 64 minutes
101	Departure	NORFOLK
112	Crossed Strait or Passage	CHESAPEAKE CHANNEL
115	Entered Area of Interest	Chesapeake Bay Approaches TSS - South Outbound
116	Left Area of Interest	Stayed within 'Chesapeake Bay Approaches TSS - South Outbound' for 33 minutes
116	Left Area of Interest	Stayed within 'North America Winter Seasonal Area' for 2155 minutes
115	Entered Area of Interest	North Atlantic and Mediterranean Summer Zone
112	Crossed Strait or Passage	CAPE HATTERAS
2	Noon position	At N 34° 34' 32.13" - W 075° 55' 50.36"
15	AIS ETA Changed	From 2021-06-07 08:00:00 to 2021-06-07 20:00:00
1	Midnight position	At N 33° 31' 08.56" - W 077° 24' 20.02"
15	AIS ETA Changed	From 2021-06-07 20:00:00 to 2021-06-07 22:30:00
2	Noon position	At N 32° 39' 58.75" - W 079° 13' 28.12"
5	Stopped	At N 32° 39' 28.25" - W 079° 13' 50.84"
9	Drifting	From to
6	Underway	At N 32° 42' 25.18" - W 079° 15' 02.16"
7	Changed Course	New Course is 239°
100	Arrival	CHARLESTON
38	Tug Operation started	Distance from vessel ELIZABETH TURECAMO is 0m
38	Tug Operation started	Distance from vessel MARK MORAN is 7m
19	Start of proximity to another vessel	Distance from vessel CAPT. JIM MCALLISTER is 35m
107	Docked	Berth: 1, Terminal: Wando Welch Terminal, Port: CHARLESTON
16	AIS Status Changed	From Underway using Engine to Moored
39	Tug Operation ended	Stayed close to vessel ELIZABETH TURECAMO for 66 minutes
39	Tug Operation ended	Stayed close to vessel MARK MORAN for 54 minutes
34	End of proximity to another vessel	Stayed close to vessel CAPT. JIM MCALLISTER for 83 minutes
1	Midnight position	At N 32° 49' 46.79" - W 079° 53' 36.32"
2	Noon position	At N 32° 49' 46.79" - W 079° 53' 36.30"
19	Start of proximity to another vessel	Distance from vessel MARIE CLARE is 50m
34	End of proximity to another vessel	Stayed close to vessel MARIE CLARE for 19 minutes
19	Start of proximity to another vessel	Distance from vessel MOIRA MCALLISTER is 69m
19	Start of proximity to another vessel	Distance from vessel JAMES A.MORAN is 47m
34	End of proximity to another vessel	Stayed close to vessel JAMES A.MORAN for 20 minutes
34	End of proximity to another vessel	Stayed close to vessel MOIRA MCALLISTER for 72 minutes
16	AIS Status Changed	From Moored to Underway using Engine
15	AIS ETA Changed	From 2021-06-07 22:30:00 to 2021-06-09 14:00:00
14	AIS Draught Changed	From 10.7 m to 10.2 m
13	AIS Destination Changed	From USCHS to USJAX
38	Tug Operation started	Distance from vessel ELIZABETH TURECAMO is 4m
38	Tug Operation started	Distance from vessel JAMES A.MORAN is 0m
39	Tug Operation ended	Stayed close to vessel JAMES A.MORAN for 24 minutes
108	Undocked	Berth: 1, Terminal: Wando Welch Terminal, Port: CHARLESTON
39	Tug Operation ended	Stayed close to vessel ELIZABETH TURECAMO for 103 minutes
101	Departure	CHARLESTON
1	Midnight position	At N 32° 10' 38.90" - W 079° 44' 02.87"
100	Arrival	JACKSONVILLE
116	Left Area of Interest	Stayed within 'United States Exclusive Economic Zone (Atlantic)' for 6692 minutes

MAERSK KARACHI	USEC	US East Coast	156	39.08033,-75.18383	16.1	2021-06-05 00:38:00 -5
MAERSK KARACHI	USEC	US East Coast	134	38.83587,-75.07039	6.2	2021-06-05 01:44:00 -5
MAERSK KARACHI	USEC	US East Coast	144	38.69203,-74.95007	17.0	2021-06-05 02:24:00 -5
MAERSK KARACHI	USEC	US East Coast	145	38.43511,-74.7178	15.0	2021-06-05 03:37:00 -5
MAERSK KARACHI	USEC	US East Coast	195	38.06927,-74.56361	15.1	2021-06-05 05:13:00 -5
MAERSK KARACHI	USEC	US East Coast	305	36.85437,-75.81424	15.3	2021-06-05 12:13:00 -5
MAERSK KARACHI	USEC	US East Coast	317	36.92919,-75.92404	11.2	2021-06-05 12:43:00 -5
MAERSK KARACHI	USEC	US East Coast	281	36.95315,-76.01615	14.9	2021-06-05 13:06:00 -5
MAERSK KARACHI	USEC	US East Coast		null,null	null	2021-06-05 14:07:00 -4
MAERSK KARACHI	USEC	US East Coast	180	36.91959,-76.33854	3.9	2021-06-05 14:36:00 -5
MAERSK KARACHI	USEC	US East Coast	180	36.91959,-76.33854	3.9	2021-06-05 14:40:00 -5
MAERSK KARACHI	USEC	US East Coast		null,null	null	2021-06-05 15:22:00 -4
MAERSK KARACHI	USEC	US East Coast	26	36.9095,-76.32716	0.0	2021-06-05 15:40:00 -4
MAERSK KARACHI	USEC	US East Coast	107	36.9095,-76.32717	0.0	2021-06-05 15:52:00 -5
MAERSK KARACHI	USEC	US East Coast	107	36.9095,-76.32717	0.0	2021-06-05 15:52:00 -5
MAERSK KARACHI	USEC	US East Coast	356	36.9095,-76.32716	0.0	2021-06-05 16:13:00 -4
MAERSK KARACHI	USEC	US East Coast	306	36.90951,-76.32718	0.0	2021-06-05 22:35:00 0
MAERSK KARACHI	USEC	US East Coast	335	36.9095,-76.32717	0.0	2021-06-05 23:07:00 -5
MAERSK KARACHI	USEC	US East Coast	187	36.90951,-76.32717	0.0	2021-06-06 03:42:00 -4
MAERSK KARACHI	USEC	US East Coast	187	36.90951,-76.32717	0.0	2021-06-06 03:42:00 -4
MAERSK KARACHI	USEC	US East Coast	284	36.90951,-76.32717	0.0	2021-06-06 03:58:00 -4
MAERSK KARACHI	USEC	US East Coast	283	36.90951,-76.32716	0.0	2021-06-06 04:00:00 -4
MAERSK KARACHI	USEC	US East Coast	328	36.91026,-76.32916	1.6	2021-06-06 04:03:00 -5
MAERSK KARACHI	USEC	US East Coast	271	36.90951,-76.32717	0.0	2021-06-06 04:12:00 -4
MAERSK KARACHI	USEC	US East Coast	312	36.9095,-76.32716	0.0	2021-06-06 04:13:00 0
MAERSK KARACHI	USEC	US East Coast		null,null	null	2021-06-06 04:57:00 -4
MAERSK KARACHI	USEC	US East Coast	301	36.9146,-76.33484	3.5	2021-06-06 05:00:00 -5
MAERSK KARACHI	USEC	US East Coast	3	36.92155,-76.3382	4.1	2021-06-06 05:08:00 -5
MAERSK KARACHI	USEC	US East Coast		null,null	null	2021-06-06 05:42:00 -4
MAERSK KARACHI	USEC	US East Coast	133	36.92374,-75.95148	16.1	2021-06-06 06:50:00 -5
MAERSK KARACHI	USEC	US East Coast	134	36.88549,-75.90382	16.6	2021-06-06 07:02:00 -5
MAERSK KARACHI	USEC	US East Coast	125	36.81849,-75.77647	16.4	2021-06-06 07:29:00 -5
MAERSK KARACHI	USEC	US East Coast	162	35.97429,-75.23897	15.6	2021-06-06 11:05:00 -5
MAERSK KARACHI	USEC	US East Coast	162	35.83107,-75.18687	15.6	2021-06-06 11:40:00 -5
MAERSK KARACHI	USEC	US East Coast	199	35.0924,-75.21379	15.6	2021-06-06 14:24:00 -5
MAERSK KARACHI	USEC	US East Coast	228	34.57559,-75.93066	16.1	2021-06-06 17:13:00 -5
MAERSK KARACHI	USEC	US East Coast	229	34.49937,-76.03624	9.1	2021-06-06 17:54:00 -5
MAERSK KARACHI	USEC	US East Coast	229	33.51905,-77.40556	8.7	2021-06-07 05:12:00 -5
MAERSK KARACHI	USEC	US East Coast	242	32.69304,-79.1647	8.9	2021-06-07 16:47:00 -5
MAERSK KARACHI	USEC	US East Coast	227	32.66632,-79.22448	3.9	2021-06-07 17:13:00 -5
MAERSK KARACHI	USEC	US East Coast	199	32.65785,-79.23079	0.8	2021-06-07 17:31:00 -5
MAERSK KARACHI	USEC	US East Coast	331	32.6767,-79.24998	1.3	2021-06-07 19:08:00 -5
MAERSK KARACHI	USEC	US East Coast	112	32.707,-79.2506	4.1	2021-06-07 20:37:00 -5
MAERSK KARACHI	USEC	US East Coast	239	32.69554,-79.25809	10.0	2021-06-07 20:47:00 -5
MAERSK KARACHI	USEC	US East Coast		null,null	null	2021-06-07 23:19:00 -4
MAERSK KARACHI	USEC	US East Coast	40	32.81396,-79.91174	7.3	2021-06-07 23:32:00 -5
MAERSK KARACHI	USEC	US East Coast	44	32.81848,-79.90653	6.4	2021-06-07 23:44:00 -5
MAERSK KARACHI	USEC	US East Coast	275	32.82967,-79.89342	0.0	2021-06-08 00:00:00 0
MAERSK KARACHI	USEC	US East Coast		null,null	null	2021-06-08 00:12:00 -4
MAERSK KARACHI	USEC	US East Coast	312	32.82966,-79.89344	0.0	2021-06-08 00:38:00 -4
MAERSK KARACHI	USEC	US East Coast	312	32.82966,-79.89344	0.0	2021-06-08 00:38:00 -5
MAERSK KARACHI	USEC	US East Coast	312	32.82966,-79.89344	0.0	2021-06-08 00:39:00 -5
MAERSK KARACHI	USEC	US East Coast	307	32.82966,-79.89342	0.0	2021-06-08 01:23:00 -5
MAERSK KARACHI	USEC	US East Coast	298	32.82967,-79.89342	0.0	2021-06-08 04:11:00 -4
MAERSK KARACHI	USEC	US East Coast	316	32.82967,-79.89342	0.0	2021-06-08 16:12:00 -4
MAERSK KARACHI	USEC	US East Coast	125	32.82968,-79.89339	0.0	2021-06-08 16:56:00 0
MAERSK KARACHI	USEC	US East Coast	136	32.82967,-79.89342	0.0	2021-06-08 17:15:00 -5
MAERSK KARACHI	USEC	US East Coast	350	32.82967,-79.89342	0.0	2021-06-08 21:36:00 0
MAERSK KARACHI	USEC	US East Coast	4	32.82966,-79.89342	0.0	2021-06-08 22:24:00 0
MAERSK KARACHI	USEC	US East Coast	4	32.82966,-79.89342	0.0	2021-06-08 22:44:00 -5
MAERSK KARACHI	USEC	US East Coast	350	32.82967,-79.89342	0.0	2021-06-08 22:48:00 -5
MAERSK KARACHI	USEC	US East Coast	211	32.82965,-79.89344	0.0	2021-06-08 23:57:00 -4
MAERSK KARACHI	USEC	US East Coast	194	32.82966,-79.89342	0.0	2021-06-09 00:03:00 -4
MAERSK KARACHI	USEC	US East Coast	194	32.82966,-79.89342	0.0	2021-06-09 00:03:00 -4
MAERSK KARACHI	USEC	US East Coast	194	32.82966,-79.89342	0.0	2021-06-09 00:03:00 -4
MAERSK KARACHI	USEC	US East Coast	305	32.82983,-79.89429	0.6	2021-06-09 00:24:00 -5
MAERSK KARACHI	USEC	US East Coast	305	32.82983,-79.89429	0.6	2021-06-09 01:11:00 -5
MAERSK KARACHI	USEC	US East Coast	339	32.83208,-79.89437	1.1	2021-06-09 01:35:00 -5
MAERSK KARACHI	USEC	US East Coast		null,null	null	2021-06-09 01:44:00 -4
MAERSK KARACHI	USEC	US East Coast	193	32.79335,-79.91766	6.4	2021-06-09 02:07:00 -5
MAERSK KARACHI	USEC	US East Coast		null,null	null	2021-06-09 02:31:00 -4
MAERSK KARACHI	USEC	US East Coast	208	32.17747,-79.73413	17.8	2021-06-09 05:13:00 -5
MAERSK KARACHI	USEC	US East Coast		null,null	null	2021-06-09 14:24:00 -4
MAERSK KARACHI	USEC	US East Coast	259	30.38736,-81.53731	6.3	2021-06-09 15:02:00 -4

116	Left Area of Interest	Stayed within 'IV United States' for 6692 minutes
116	Left Area of Interest	Stayed within 'North Atlantic and Mediterranean Summer Zone' for 4536 minutes
116	Left Area of Interest	Stayed within 'US East Coast' for 6692 minutes
116	Left Area of Interest	Stayed within 'US Atlantic ECA' for 6689 minutes
101	Departure	JACKSONVILLE
16	AIS Status Changed	From Underway using Engine to Moored
116	Left Area of Interest	Stayed within 'United States Exclusive Economic Zone (Atlantic)'
116	Left Area of Interest	Stayed within 'IV United States'
116	Left Area of Interest	Stayed within 'North Atlantic and Mediterranean Summer Zone'
116	Left Area of Interest	Stayed within 'US East Coast'
116	Left Area of Interest	Stayed within 'US Atlantic ECA'
107	Docked	Berth: Berth 17, Terminal: Dames Point Terminal, Port: JACKSONVILLE
100	Arrival	JACKSONVILLE
115	Entered Area of Interest	Inland, North America
1	Midnight position	At N 30° 23' 35.03" - W 081° 33' 56.70"
15	AIS ETA Changed	From 2021-06-09 14:00:00 to 2021-06-11 08:00:00
13	AIS Destination Changed	From US JAX to US PEV
38	Tug Operation started	Distance from vessel SEWELLS POINT is 64m
38	Tug Operation started	Distance from vessel STACY MCALLISTER is 0m
16	AIS Status Changed	From Moored to Underway using Engine
39	Tug Operation ended	Stayed close to vessel STACY MCALLISTER for 36 minutes
39	Tug Operation ended	Stayed close to vessel SEWELLS POINT for 48 minutes
108	Undocked	Berth: Berth 17, Terminal: Dames Point Terminal, Port: JACKSONVILLE
116	Left Area of Interest	Stayed within 'Inland, North America' for 780 minutes
115	Entered Area of Interest	US Atlantic ECA
115	Entered Area of Interest	United States Exclusive Economic Zone (Atlantic)
115	Entered Area of Interest	IV United States
115	Entered Area of Interest	North Atlantic and Mediterranean Summer Zone
115	Entered Area of Interest	US East Coast
101	Departure	JACKSONVILLE
35	Pilot Event (off-board)	Pilot vessel PILOTBOAT2 is 4 m away
115	Entered Area of Interest	Caribbean - MARPOL Annex V
3	In Terrestrial Range	At N 29° 36' 29.68" - W 080° 26' 01.65"
2	Noon position	At N 28° 37' 57.56" - W 079° 59' 45.08"
5	Stopped	At N 26° 57' 48.73" - W 079° 53' 15.92"
6	Underway	At N 26° 57' 40.15" - W 079° 53' 17.02"
15	AIS ETA Changed	From 2021-06-11 08:00:00 to 2021-06-11 07:30:00
1	Midnight position	At N 26° 28' 44.62" - W 079° 53' 43.49"
37	Pilot Event	Pilot vessel PILOT NO 7 is 0 m away
100	Arrival	PORT EVERGLADES ANCH
38	Tug Operation started	Distance from vessel ST.JOHNS is 13m
38	Tug Operation started	Distance from vessel BROWARD is 47m
101	Departure	PORT EVERGLADES ANCH
19	Start of proximity to another vessel	Distance from vessel NELSON is 351m
19	Start of proximity to another vessel	Distance from vessel GO FREEDOM is 340m
38	Tug Operation started	Distance from vessel TRIDENT is 0m
38	Tug Operation started	Distance from vessel TATE MCALLISTER is 92m
19	Start of proximity to another vessel	Distance from vessel EILEEN MCALLISTER is 87m
39	Tug Operation ended	Stayed close to vessel TATE MCALLISTER for 5 minutes
34	End of proximity to another vessel	Stayed close to vessel NELSON for 16 minutes
34	End of proximity to another vessel	Stayed close to vessel GO FREEDOM for 16 minutes
39	Tug Operation ended	Stayed close to vessel TRIDENT for 36 minutes
100	Arrival	PORT EVERGLADES
107	Docked	Berth: 31, Terminal: Southport, Port: PORT EVERGLADES
16	AIS Status Changed	From Underway using Engine to Moored
39	Tug Operation ended	Stayed close to vessel ST.JOHNS for 76 minutes
39	Tug Operation ended	Stayed close to vessel BROWARD for 75 minutes
34	End of proximity to another vessel	Stayed close to vessel EILEEN MCALLISTER for 74 minutes
2	Noon position	At N 26° 04' 19.34" - W 080° 06' 54.89"
1	Midnight position	At N 26° 04' 19.35" - W 080° 06' 54.92"
19	Start of proximity to another vessel	Distance from vessel EILEEN MCALLISTER is 43m
34	End of proximity to another vessel	Stayed close to vessel EILEEN MCALLISTER for 22 minutes
15	AIS ETA Changed	From 2021-06-11 07:30:00 to 2021-06-22 05:00:00
14	AIS Draught Changed	From 10.4 m to 10.1 m
13	AIS Destination Changed	From USPEV to BR SSZ
16	AIS Status Changed	From Moored to Underway using Engine
38	Tug Operation started	Distance from vessel BROWARD is 8m
38	Tug Operation started	Distance from vessel TRIDENT is 21m
38	Tug Operation started	Distance from vessel ST.JOHNS is 0m
108	Undocked	Berth: 31, Terminal: Southport, Port: PORT EVERGLADES
39	Tug Operation ended	Stayed close to vessel TRIDENT for 43 minutes
38	Tug Operation started	Distance from vessel TATE MCALLISTER is 5m
39	Tug Operation ended	Stayed close to vessel ST.JOHNS for 55 minutes
39	Tug Operation ended	Stayed close to vessel BROWARD for 63 minutes

MAERSK KARACHI	USEC	US East Coast	259	30.38736,-81.53731	6.3	2021-06-09 15:02:00 -4
MAERSK KARACHI	USEC	US East Coast	259	30.38736,-81.53731	6.3	2021-06-09 15:02:00 -4
MAERSK KARACHI	USEC	US East Coast	259	30.38736,-81.53731	6.3	2021-06-09 15:02:00 -4
MAERSK KARACHI	USEC	US East Coast	259	30.38736,-81.53731	6.3	2021-06-09 15:02:00 -4
MAERSK KARACHI	USEC	US East Coast		null,null	null	2021-06-09 15:58:00 -4
MAERSK KARACHI	USEC	US East Coast	126	30.39307,-81.56576	0.0	2021-06-09 16:20:00 -4
MAERSK KARACHI	USEC	US East Coast	126	30.39307,-81.56576	0.0	2021-06-09 16:20:00 -4
MAERSK KARACHI	USEC	US East Coast	126	30.39307,-81.56576	0.0	2021-06-09 16:20:00 -4
MAERSK KARACHI	USEC	US East Coast	126	30.39307,-81.56576	0.0	2021-06-09 16:20:00 -4
MAERSK KARACHI	USEC	US East Coast	126	30.39307,-81.56576	0.0	2021-06-09 16:20:00 -4
MAERSK KARACHI	USEC	US East Coast	126	30.39307,-81.56576	0.0	2021-06-09 16:20:00 -4
MAERSK KARACHI	USEC	US East Coast		null,null	null	2021-06-09 16:20:00 -4
MAERSK KARACHI	USEC	US East Coast		null,null	null	2021-06-09 16:20:00 -4
MAERSK KARACHI	USEC	US East Coast	199	30.39306,-81.56575	0.0	2021-06-09 17:00:00 -4
MAERSK KARACHI	USEC	US East Coast	296	30.39307,-81.56575	0.0	2021-06-10 04:12:00 -4
MAERSK KARACHI	USEC	US East Coast	254	30.39307,-81.56575	0.0	2021-06-10 04:24:00 -4
MAERSK KARACHI	USEC	US East Coast	254	30.39307,-81.56575	0.0	2021-06-10 04:24:00 -4
MAERSK KARACHI	USEC	US East Coast	316	30.39367,-81.56725	0.5	2021-06-10 04:39:00 -5
MAERSK KARACHI	USEC	US East Coast	316	30.39367,-81.56725	0.5	2021-06-10 04:42:00 -5
MAERSK KARACHI	USEC	US East Coast	279	30.39312,-81.56618	0.4	2021-06-10 05:05:00 -4
MAERSK KARACHI	USEC	US East Coast	282	30.39411,-81.56805	0.5	2021-06-10 05:18:00 -5
MAERSK KARACHI	USEC	US East Coast	150	30.39038,-81.56637	5.0	2021-06-10 05:28:00 -5
MAERSK KARACHI	USEC	US East Coast		null,null	null	2021-06-10 05:30:00 -4
MAERSK KARACHI	USEC	US East Coast	69	30.39339,-81.48515	9.6	2021-06-10 06:02:00 -4
MAERSK KARACHI	USEC	US East Coast	69	30.39339,-81.48515	9.6	2021-06-10 06:02:00 -4
MAERSK KARACHI	USEC	US East Coast	93	30.39434,-81.47861	9.4	2021-06-10 06:04:00 -4
MAERSK KARACHI	USEC	US East Coast	93	30.39434,-81.47861	9.4	2021-06-10 06:04:00 -4
MAERSK KARACHI	USEC	US East Coast	93	30.39434,-81.47861	9.4	2021-06-10 06:04:00 -4
MAERSK KARACHI	USEC	US East Coast	93	30.39434,-81.47861	9.4	2021-06-10 06:04:00 -4
MAERSK KARACHI	USEC	US East Coast		null,null	null	2021-06-10 06:41:00 -4
MAERSK KARACHI	USEC	US East Coast	95	30.39692,-81.35743	12.4	2021-06-10 06:44:00 -5
MAERSK KARACHI	USEC	US East Coast	158	29.89847,-80.56532	14.0	2021-06-10 10:45:00 -5
MAERSK KARACHI	USEC	US East Coast	156	29.60825,-80.43379	13.7	2021-06-10 12:05:00 -5
MAERSK KARACHI	USEC	US East Coast	156	28.63266,-79.99586	10.9	2021-06-10 16:59:00 -5
MAERSK KARACHI	USEC	US East Coast	216	26.96354,-79.88776	0.2	2021-06-11 02:54:00 -5
MAERSK KARACHI	USEC	US East Coast	184	26.96115,-79.88806	4.8	2021-06-11 02:57:00 -5
MAERSK KARACHI	USEC	US East Coast	179	26.73347,-79.8952	12.8	2021-06-11 04:04:00 -5
MAERSK KARACHI	USEC	US East Coast	183	26.47906,-79.89542	13.0	2021-06-11 05:13:00 -5
MAERSK KARACHI	USEC	US East Coast	205	26.11417,-80.05051	2.9	2021-06-11 07:24:00 -5
MAERSK KARACHI	USEC	US East Coast		null,null	null	2021-06-11 07:31:00 -4
MAERSK KARACHI	USEC	US East Coast	269	26.0937,-80.10499	6.3	2021-06-11 07:55:00 -5
MAERSK KARACHI	USEC	US East Coast	269	26.0937,-80.10499	6.3	2021-06-11 07:56:00 -5
MAERSK KARACHI	USEC	US East Coast		null,null	null	2021-06-11 08:00:00 -4
MAERSK KARACHI	USEC	US East Coast	224	26.0928,-80.11489	1.7	2021-06-11 08:03:00 0
MAERSK KARACHI	USEC	US East Coast	224	26.0928,-80.11489	1.7	2021-06-11 08:03:00 0
MAERSK KARACHI	USEC	US East Coast	224	26.0928,-80.11489	1.7	2021-06-11 08:03:00 -5
MAERSK KARACHI	USEC	US East Coast	224	26.0928,-80.11489	1.7	2021-06-11 08:10:00 -5
MAERSK KARACHI	USEC	US East Coast	285	26.07204,-80.11527	0.0	2021-06-11 08:15:00 0
MAERSK KARACHI	USEC	US East Coast	224	26.0928,-80.11489	1.7	2021-06-11 08:15:00 -5
MAERSK KARACHI	USEC	US East Coast	157	26.09123,-80.11495	1.8	2021-06-11 08:19:00 -5
MAERSK KARACHI	USEC	US East Coast	157	26.09123,-80.11495	1.8	2021-06-11 08:19:00 -5
MAERSK KARACHI	USEC	US East Coast	181	26.07547,-80.11476	2.5	2021-06-11 08:39:00 -5
MAERSK KARACHI	USEC	US East Coast		null,null	null	2021-06-11 08:39:00 -4
MAERSK KARACHI	USEC	US East Coast		null,null	null	2021-06-11 08:48:00 -4
MAERSK KARACHI	USEC	US East Coast	280	26.07204,-80.11526	0.0	2021-06-11 09:02:00 -4
MAERSK KARACHI	USEC	US East Coast	345	26.07204,-80.11526	0.0	2021-06-11 09:11:00 -5
MAERSK KARACHI	USEC	US East Coast	345	26.07204,-80.11526	0.0	2021-06-11 09:12:00 -5
MAERSK KARACHI	USEC	US East Coast	17	26.07204,-80.11526	0.0	2021-06-11 09:29:00 -5
MAERSK KARACHI	USEC	US East Coast	92	26.07204,-80.11525	0.0	2021-06-11 16:09:00 -4
MAERSK KARACHI	USEC	US East Coast	260	26.07204,-80.11526	0.0	2021-06-12 04:12:00 -4
MAERSK KARACHI	USEC	US East Coast	177	26.07204,-80.11525	0.0	2021-06-12 05:48:00 0
MAERSK KARACHI	USEC	US East Coast	273	26.07204,-80.11526	0.0	2021-06-12 06:10:00 -5
MAERSK KARACHI	USEC	US East Coast	273	26.07204,-80.11526	0.0	2021-06-12 06:10:00 -4
MAERSK KARACHI	USEC	US East Coast	273	26.07204,-80.11526	0.0	2021-06-12 06:10:00 -4
MAERSK KARACHI	USEC	US East Coast	273	26.07204,-80.11526	0.0	2021-06-12 06:10:00 -4
MAERSK KARACHI	USEC	US East Coast	312	26.07209,-80.11527	0.0	2021-06-12 06:12:00 -4
MAERSK KARACHI	USEC	US East Coast	5	26.07344,-80.11471	1.7	2021-06-12 06:24:00 -5
MAERSK KARACHI	USEC	US East Coast	4	26.07755,-80.1144	2.6	2021-06-12 06:31:00 -5
MAERSK KARACHI	USEC	US East Coast	5	26.07344,-80.11471	1.7	2021-06-12 06:32:00 -5
MAERSK KARACHI	USEC	US East Coast		null,null	null	2021-06-12 06:58:00 -4
MAERSK KARACHI	USEC	US East Coast	351	26.08664,-80.11376	2.2	2021-06-12 07:15:00 -5
MAERSK KARACHI	USEC	US East Coast	90	26.09344,-80.09632	8.4	2021-06-12 07:27:00 -5
MAERSK KARACHI	USEC	US East Coast	99	26.09335,-80.11716	0.2	2021-06-12 07:27:00 -5
MAERSK KARACHI	USEC	US East Coast	99	26.09335,-80.11716	0.2	2021-06-12 07:27:00 -5

101	Departure	PORT EVERGLADES
39	Tug Operation ended	Stayed close to vessel TATE MCALLISTER for 16 minutes
116	Left Area of Interest	Stayed within 'United States Exclusive Economic Zone (Atlantic)' for 3069 minutes
116	Left Area of Interest	Stayed within 'US East Coast' for 3069 minutes
116	Left Area of Interest	Stayed within 'US Atlantic ECA' for 3071 minutes
115	Entered Area of Interest	Bahamas Exclusive Economic Zone
115	Entered Area of Interest	Caribbean Sea
112	Crossed Strait or Passage	PROVIDENCE CHANNEL
2	Noon position	At N 25° 40' 18.74" - W 076° 38' 43.00"
1	Midnight position	At N 23° 34' 03.99" - W 073° 04' 39.71"
116	Left Area of Interest	Stayed within 'Bahamas Exclusive Economic Zone' for 1440 minutes
115	Entered Area of Interest	Turks and Caicos Exclusive Economic Zone
116	Left Area of Interest	Stayed within 'Turks and Caicos Exclusive Economic Zone' for 319 minutes
115	Entered Area of Interest	Dominican Republic Exclusive Economic Zone
2	Noon position	At N 21° 30' 24.78" - W 069° 26' 53.67"
20	Vessel Changed Time Zone	From UTC -5 to UTC -4
116	Left Area of Interest	Stayed within 'Dominican Republic Exclusive Economic Zone' for 570 minutes
115	Entered Area of Interest	Overlapping claim: Puerto Rico / Dominican Republic
116	Left Area of Interest	Stayed within 'Overlapping claim: Puerto Rico / Dominican Republic' for 88 minutes
115	Entered Area of Interest	Puerto Rican Exclusive Economic Zone
116	Left Area of Interest	Stayed within 'North Atlantic and Mediterranean Summer Zone' for 5425 minutes
115	Entered Area of Interest	North Atlantic Seasonal Tropical Zone
1	Midnight position	At N 19° 48' 19.70" - W 066° 05' 18.43"
115	Entered Area of Interest	Puerto Rico ECA
116	Left Area of Interest	Stayed within 'Puerto Rican Exclusive Economic Zone' for 320 minutes
115	Entered Area of Interest	Virgin Islander Exclusive Economic Zone
116	Left Area of Interest	Stayed within 'Virgin Islander Exclusive Economic Zone' for 32 minutes
116	Left Area of Interest	Stayed within 'Puerto Rico ECA' for 51 minutes
115	Entered Area of Interest	British Virgin Islands Exclusive Economic Zone
3	In Terrestrial Range	At N 19° 06' 34.05" - W 064° 41' 54.13"
116	Left Area of Interest	Stayed within 'British Virgin Islands Exclusive Economic Zone' for 278 minutes
115	Entered Area of Interest	Anguilla Exclusive Economic Zone
3	In Terrestrial Range	At N 18° 29' 18.35" - W 063° 45' 49.31"
116	Left Area of Interest	Stayed within 'Anguilla Exclusive Economic Zone' for 127 minutes
115	Entered Area of Interest	Saint-Martin Exclusive Economic Zone
116	Left Area of Interest	Stayed within 'Saint-Martin Exclusive Economic Zone' for 32 minutes
115	Entered Area of Interest	Saint-Barthélemy Exclusive Economic Zone
116	Left Area of Interest	Stayed within 'Saint-Barthélemy Exclusive Economic Zone' for 44 minutes
115	Entered Area of Interest	Sint-Eustatius Exclusive Economic Zone
116	Left Area of Interest	Stayed within 'Sint-Eustatius Exclusive Economic Zone' for 25 minutes
2	Noon position	At N 17° 34' 47.85" - W 062° 44' 21.02"
115	Entered Area of Interest	Saint Kitts and Nevis Exclusive Economic Zone
116	Left Area of Interest	Stayed within 'Saint Kitts and Nevis Exclusive Economic Zone' for 98 minutes
115	Entered Area of Interest	Antigua and Barbuda Exclusive Economic Zone
112	Crossed Strait or Passage	GOUADELOUPE
116	Left Area of Interest	Stayed within 'Antigua and Barbuda Exclusive Economic Zone' for 178 minutes
115	Entered Area of Interest	Guadeloupean Exclusive Economic Zone
116	Left Area of Interest	Stayed within 'Guadeloupean Exclusive Economic Zone' for 356 minutes
115	Entered Area of Interest	Dominican Exclusive Economic Zone
116	Left Area of Interest	Stayed within 'Dominican Exclusive Economic Zone' for 76 minutes
115	Entered Area of Interest	Martinican Exclusive Economic Zone
1	Midnight position	At N 15° 36' 22.49" - W 059° 23' 28.13"
116	Left Area of Interest	Stayed within 'Martinican Exclusive Economic Zone' for 134 minutes
115	Entered Area of Interest	Barbados Exclusive Economic Zone
2	Noon position	At N 12° 35' 16.86" - W 056° 26' 25.20"
116	Left Area of Interest	Stayed within 'Barbados Exclusive Economic Zone' for 683 minutes
1	Midnight position	At N 10° 21' 33.69" - W 053° 06' 19.56"
116	Left Area of Interest	Stayed within 'Caribbean Sea' for 5270 minutes
115	Entered Area of Interest	North Coast South America
116	Left Area of Interest	Stayed within 'North Atlantic Seasonal Tropical Zone' for 3024 minutes
20	Vessel Changed Time Zone	From UTC -4 to UTC -3
115	Entered Area of Interest	Tropical Zone
116	Left Area of Interest	Stayed within 'Caribbean - MARPOL Annex V' for 8626 minutes
2	Noon position	At N 08° 11' 03.04" - W 049° 48' 10.00"
116	Left Area of Interest	Stayed within 'IV United States' for 9504 minutes
115	Entered Area of Interest	V Brazil
1	Midnight position	At N 05° 29' 14.47" - W 046° 24' 32.42"
2	Noon position	At N 02° 53' 39.19" - W 042° 49' 23.63"
116	Left Area of Interest	Stayed within 'North Coast South America' for 2161 minutes
115	Entered Area of Interest	East Coast South America
1	Midnight position	At N 00° 36' 34.32" - W 039° 48' 52.67"
115	Entered Area of Interest	Brazilian Exclusive Economic Zone
20	Vessel Changed Time Zone	From UTC -3 to UTC -2

MAERSK KARACHI	USEC	US East Coast		null,null	null	2021-06-12 07:33:00 -4
MAERSK KARACHI	USEC	US East Coast	85	26.09323,-80.08678	8.8	2021-06-12 07:44:00 -5
MAERSK KARACHI			82	26.17092,-79.59033	21.2	2021-06-12 09:10:00 -5
MAERSK KARACHI			82	26.17092,-79.59033	21.2	2021-06-12 09:10:00 -5
MAERSK KARACHI			82	26.17266,-79.57469	21.2	2021-06-12 09:13:00 -5
MAERSK KARACHI	CARIBS	Caribbean Sea	8	26.20678,-79.27943	21.0	2021-06-12 09:58:00 -5
MAERSK KARACHI	CARIBS	Caribbean Sea	8	26.20678,-79.27943	21.0	2021-06-12 09:58:00 -5
MAERSK KARACHI	CARIBS	Caribbean Sea	100	25.7352,-77.06116	21.2	2021-06-12 15:59:00 -5
MAERSK KARACHI	CARIBS	Caribbean Sea	110	25.67187,-76.64528	21.0	2021-06-12 17:03:00 -5
MAERSK KARACHI	CARIBS	Caribbean Sea	132	23.56778,-73.0777	19.2	2021-06-13 05:04:00 -5
MAERSK KARACHI	CARIBS	Caribbean Sea	122	22.88721,-71.85445	19.6	2021-06-13 09:07:00 -5
MAERSK KARACHI	CARIBS	Caribbean Sea	123	22.80076,-71.70871	19.2	2021-06-13 09:37:00 -5
MAERSK KARACHI	CARIBS	Caribbean Sea	121	21.97156,-70.31093	19.9	2021-06-13 14:23:00 -5
MAERSK KARACHI	CARIBS	Caribbean Sea	121	21.85993,-70.11272	19.9	2021-06-13 15:02:00 -5
MAERSK KARACHI	CARIBS	Caribbean Sea	118	21.50688,-69.44824	19.6	2021-06-13 16:54:00 -5
MAERSK KARACHI	CARIBS	Caribbean Sea	117	20.46735,-67.38755	19.4	2021-06-13 23:53:00 -5
MAERSK KARACHI	CARIBS	Caribbean Sea	117	20.46735,-67.38755	19.4	2021-06-13 23:53:00 -5
MAERSK KARACHI	CARIBS	Caribbean Sea	117	20.46735,-67.38755	19.4	2021-06-13 23:53:00 -5
MAERSK KARACHI	CARIBS	Caribbean Sea	118	20.22161,-66.90971	18.8	2021-06-14 01:29:00 -4
MAERSK KARACHI	CARIBS	Caribbean Sea	118	20.16533,-66.79604	18.7	2021-06-14 01:52:00 -4
MAERSK KARACHI	CARIBS	Caribbean Sea	118	19.97363,-66.41479	19.4	2021-06-14 03:09:00 -4
MAERSK KARACHI	CARIBS	Caribbean Sea	118	19.85866,-66.19127	19.6	2021-06-14 03:53:00 -4
MAERSK KARACHI	CARIBS	Caribbean Sea	118	19.80547,-66.08846	19.7	2021-06-14 04:13:00 -4
MAERSK KARACHI	CARIBS	Caribbean Sea	118	19.47598,-65.43707	19.4	2021-06-14 06:21:00 -4
MAERSK KARACHI	CARIBS	Caribbean Sea	117	19.42745,-65.33963	19.4	2021-06-14 06:41:00 -4
MAERSK KARACHI	CARIBS	Caribbean Sea	117	19.38081,-65.24745	19.4	2021-06-14 06:59:00 -4
MAERSK KARACHI	CARIBS	Caribbean Sea	116	19.34791,-65.17864	19.7	2021-06-14 07:12:00 -4
MAERSK KARACHI	CARIBS	Caribbean Sea	116	19.34791,-65.17864	19.7	2021-06-14 07:12:00 -4
MAERSK KARACHI	CARIBS	Caribbean Sea	117	19.23214,-64.93559	19.2	2021-06-14 08:00:00 -4
MAERSK KARACHI	CARIBS	Caribbean Sea	118	19.10946,-64.69837	19.6	2021-06-14 08:47:00 -4
MAERSK KARACHI	CARIBS	Caribbean Sea	138	18.57345,-63.84115	19.9	2021-06-14 11:49:00 -4
MAERSK KARACHI	CARIBS	Caribbean Sea	139	18.52115,-63.79318	19.9	2021-06-14 12:02:00 -4
MAERSK KARACHI	CARIBS	Caribbean Sea	139	18.48843,-63.7637	19.9	2021-06-14 12:09:00 -4
MAERSK KARACHI	CARIBS	Caribbean Sea	138	18.0501,-63.35044	19.7	2021-06-14 13:56:00 -4
MAERSK KARACHI	CARIBS	Caribbean Sea	137	18.02871,-63.33009	19.7	2021-06-14 14:01:00 -4
MAERSK KARACHI	CARIBS	Caribbean Sea	126	17.93685,-63.22197	19.7	2021-06-14 14:26:00 -4
MAERSK KARACHI	CARIBS	Caribbean Sea	125	17.81553,-63.07708	19.7	2021-06-14 15:00:00 -4
MAERSK KARACHI	CARIBS	Caribbean Sea	125	17.67833,-62.87616	19.7	2021-06-14 15:43:00 -4
MAERSK KARACHI	CARIBS	Caribbean Sea	126	17.62385,-62.79717	19.6	2021-06-14 16:00:00 -4
MAERSK KARACHI	CARIBS	Caribbean Sea	126	17.61053,-62.77837	19.7	2021-06-14 16:04:00 -4
MAERSK KARACHI	CARIBS	Caribbean Sea	131	17.57996,-62.73917	19.9	2021-06-14 16:12:00 -4
MAERSK KARACHI	CARIBS	Caribbean Sea	134	17.394,-62.5464	20.0	2021-06-14 16:59:00 -4
MAERSK KARACHI	CARIBS	Caribbean Sea	137	17.21741,-62.36723	20.1	2021-06-14 17:43:00 -4
MAERSK KARACHI	CARIBS	Caribbean Sea	137	17.15248,-62.30541	20.6	2021-06-14 17:58:00 -4
MAERSK KARACHI	CARIBS	Caribbean Sea	103	16.84924,-61.61047	20.0	2021-06-14 20:14:00 -4
MAERSK KARACHI	CARIBS	Caribbean Sea	103	16.81068,-61.45771	19.7	2021-06-14 20:41:00 -4
MAERSK KARACHI	CARIBS	Caribbean Sea	105	16.78669,-61.36119	19.6	2021-06-14 20:58:00 -4
MAERSK KARACHI	CARIBS	Caribbean Sea	142	15.98623,-59.70841	19.3	2021-06-15 02:38:00 -4
MAERSK KARACHI	CARIBS	Caribbean Sea	141	15.88933,-59.62989	19.1	2021-06-15 03:00:00 -4
MAERSK KARACHI	CARIBS	Caribbean Sea	140	15.66401,-59.44013	19.6	2021-06-15 03:55:00 -4
MAERSK KARACHI	CARIBS	Caribbean Sea	140	15.63583,-59.41616	19.6	2021-06-15 04:01:00 -4
MAERSK KARACHI	CARIBS	Caribbean Sea	140	15.60625,-59.39115	19.5	2021-06-15 04:04:00 -4
MAERSK KARACHI	CARIBS	Caribbean Sea	141	15.07488,-58.95358	20.5	2021-06-15 06:11:00 -4
MAERSK KARACHI	CARIBS	Caribbean Sea	136	14.82764,-58.73677	20.9	2021-06-15 07:07:00 -4
MAERSK KARACHI	CARIBS	Caribbean Sea	134	12.58802,-56.44033	20.5	2021-06-15 16:14:00 -4
MAERSK KARACHI	CARIBS	Caribbean Sea	134	12.26396,-56.10585	20.4	2021-06-15 17:34:00 -4
MAERSK KARACHI	NCSA	North Coast South America	122	10.35936,-53.10543	19.9	2021-06-16 04:05:00 -4
MAERSK KARACHI	NCSA	North Coast South America	121	10.31895,-53.0397	20.1	2021-06-16 04:26:00 -4
MAERSK KARACHI	NCSA	North Coast South America	120	10.1529,-52.75925	20.4	2021-06-16 05:23:00 -4
MAERSK KARACHI	NCSA	North Coast South America	122	9.992302,-52.49758	20.7	2021-06-16 06:17:00 -4
MAERSK KARACHI	NCSA	North Coast South America	122	9.971144,-52.46441	20.7	2021-06-16 06:23:00 -4
MAERSK KARACHI	NCSA	North Coast South America	122	9.971144,-52.46441	20.7	2021-06-16 06:23:00 -4
MAERSK KARACHI	NCSA	North Coast South America	122	9.290243,-51.3718	21.6	2021-06-16 10:01:00 -3
MAERSK KARACHI	NCSA	North Coast South America	127	8.18418,-49.80278	22.1	2021-06-16 15:11:00 -3
MAERSK KARACHI	NCSA	North Coast South America	131	6.990308,-48.33102	21.1	2021-06-16 20:26:00 -3
MAERSK KARACHI	NCSA	North Coast South America	131	6.967868,-48.30553	21.1	2021-06-16 20:32:00 -3
MAERSK KARACHI	NCSA	North Coast South America	127	5.487355,-46.40901	22.5	2021-06-17 03:10:00 -3
MAERSK KARACHI	NCSA	North Coast South America	125	2.894222,-42.82323	19.7	2021-06-17 15:08:00 -3
MAERSK KARACHI	ECSA	East Coast South America	125	2.56716,-42.36942	19.0	2021-06-17 16:57:00 -3
MAERSK KARACHI	ECSA	East Coast South America	125	2.476275,-42.24216	18.6	2021-06-17 17:27:00 -3
MAERSK KARACHI	ECSA	East Coast South America	134	0.609535,-39.81463	18.6	2021-06-18 03:04:00 -3
MAERSK KARACHI	ECSA	East Coast South America	134	0.2919317,-39.50229	18.4	2021-06-18 04:34:00 -3
MAERSK KARACHI	ECSA	East Coast South America	139	-1.824848,-37.40397	17.5	2021-06-18 14:34:00 -3

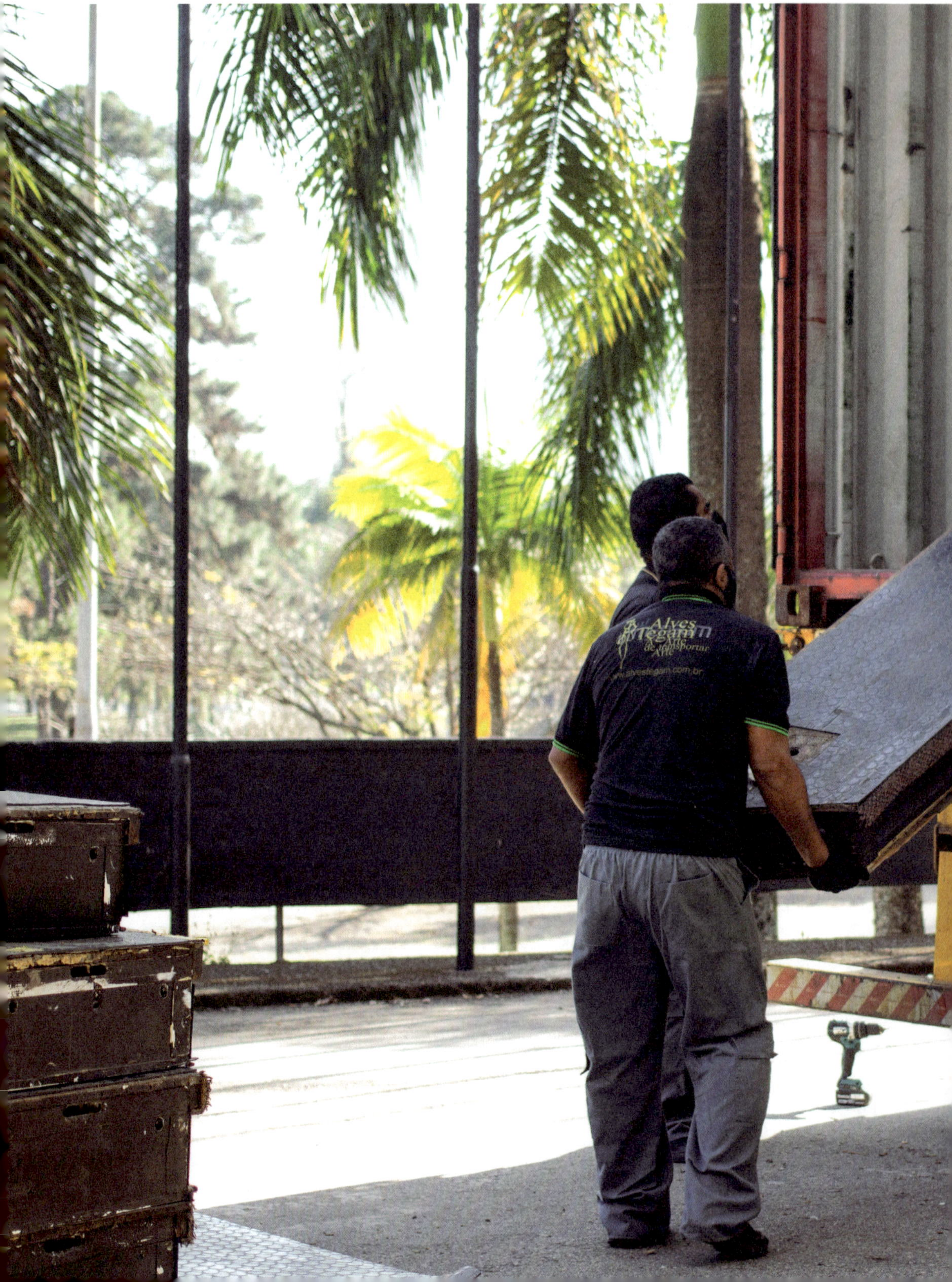
Alves
Tegam

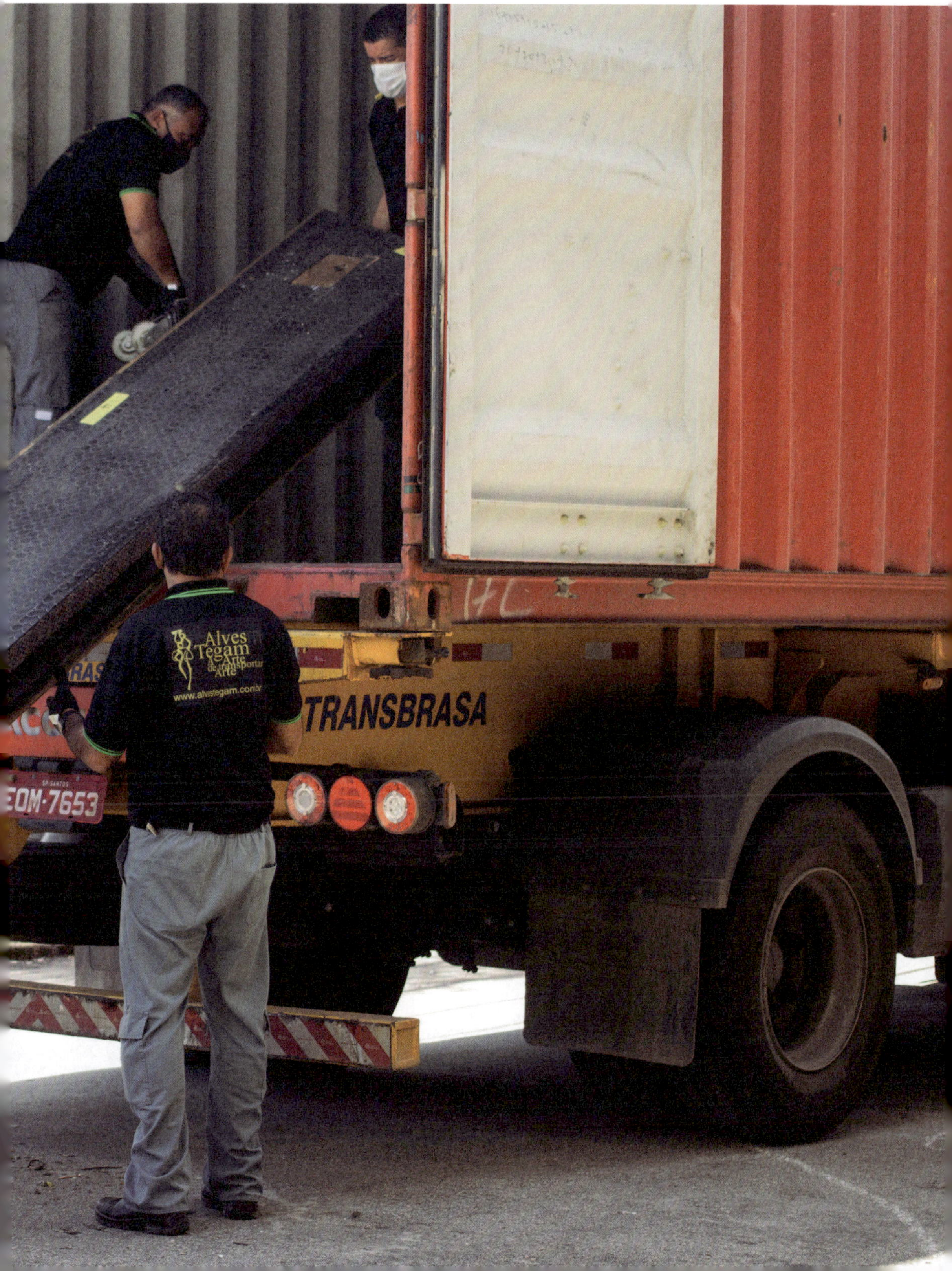
Alves
Tegam
TRANSBRASA
EOM-7653

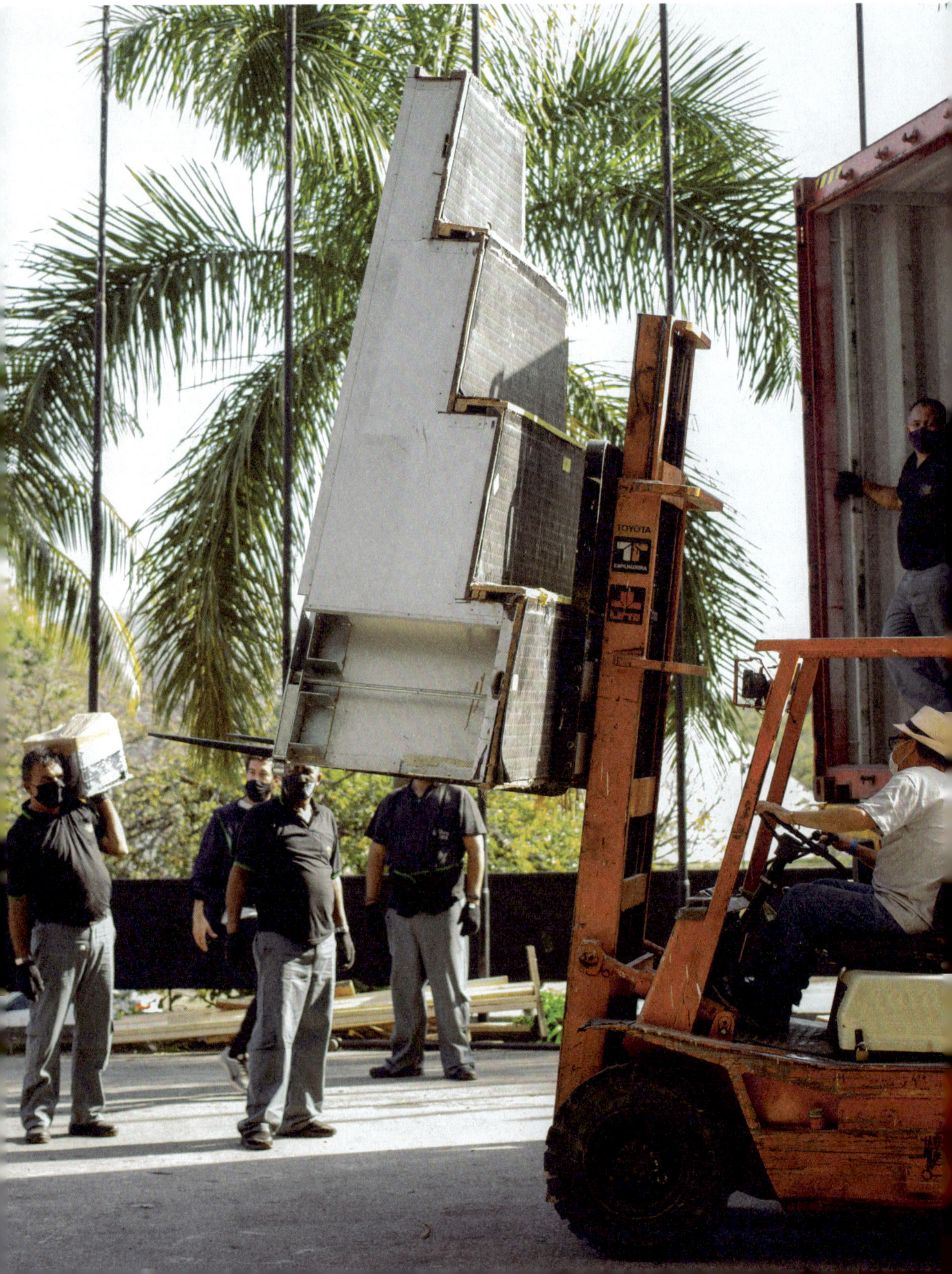
TOYOTA

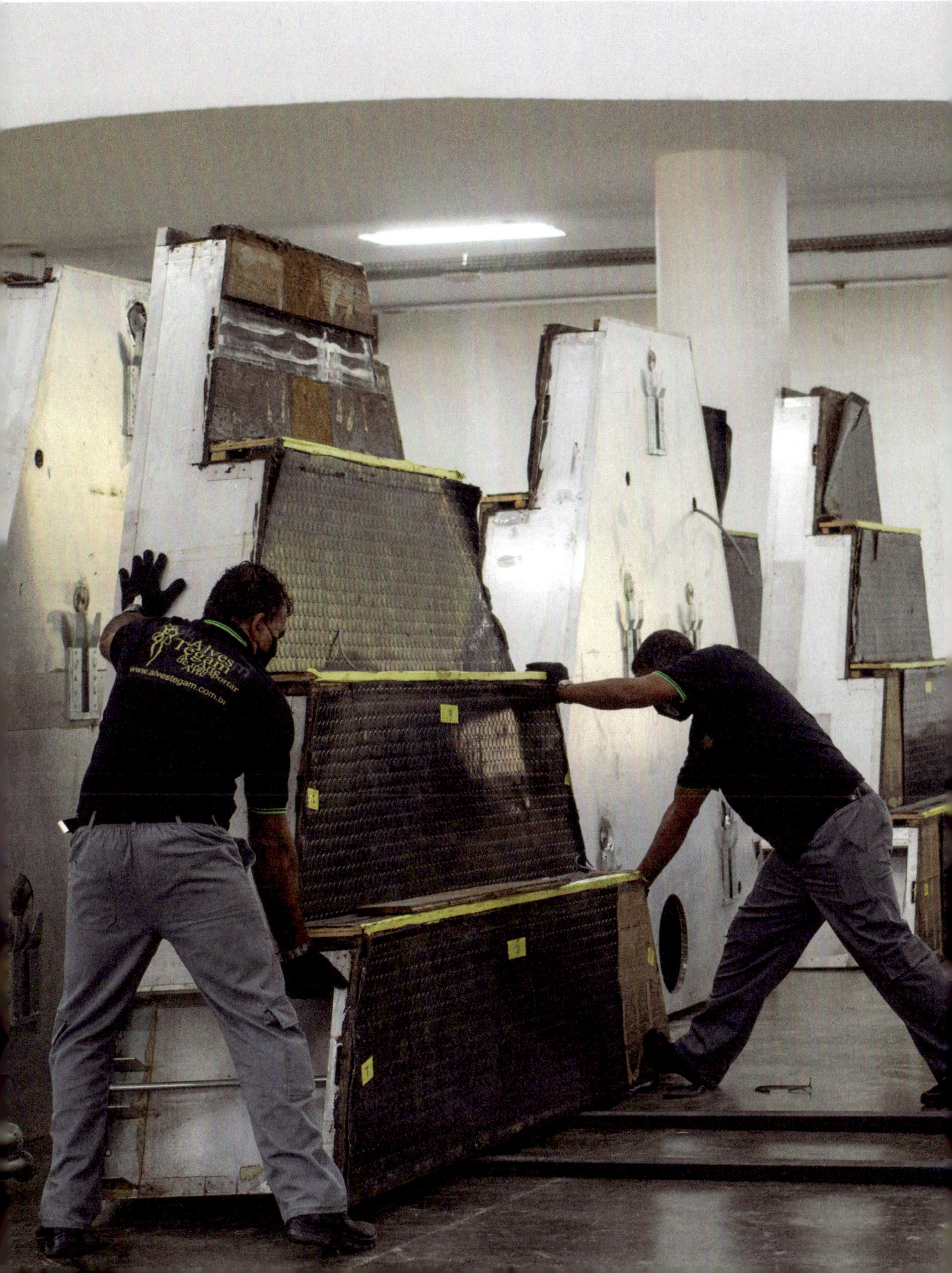
Alves
Tegam
www.alvestegam.com.br

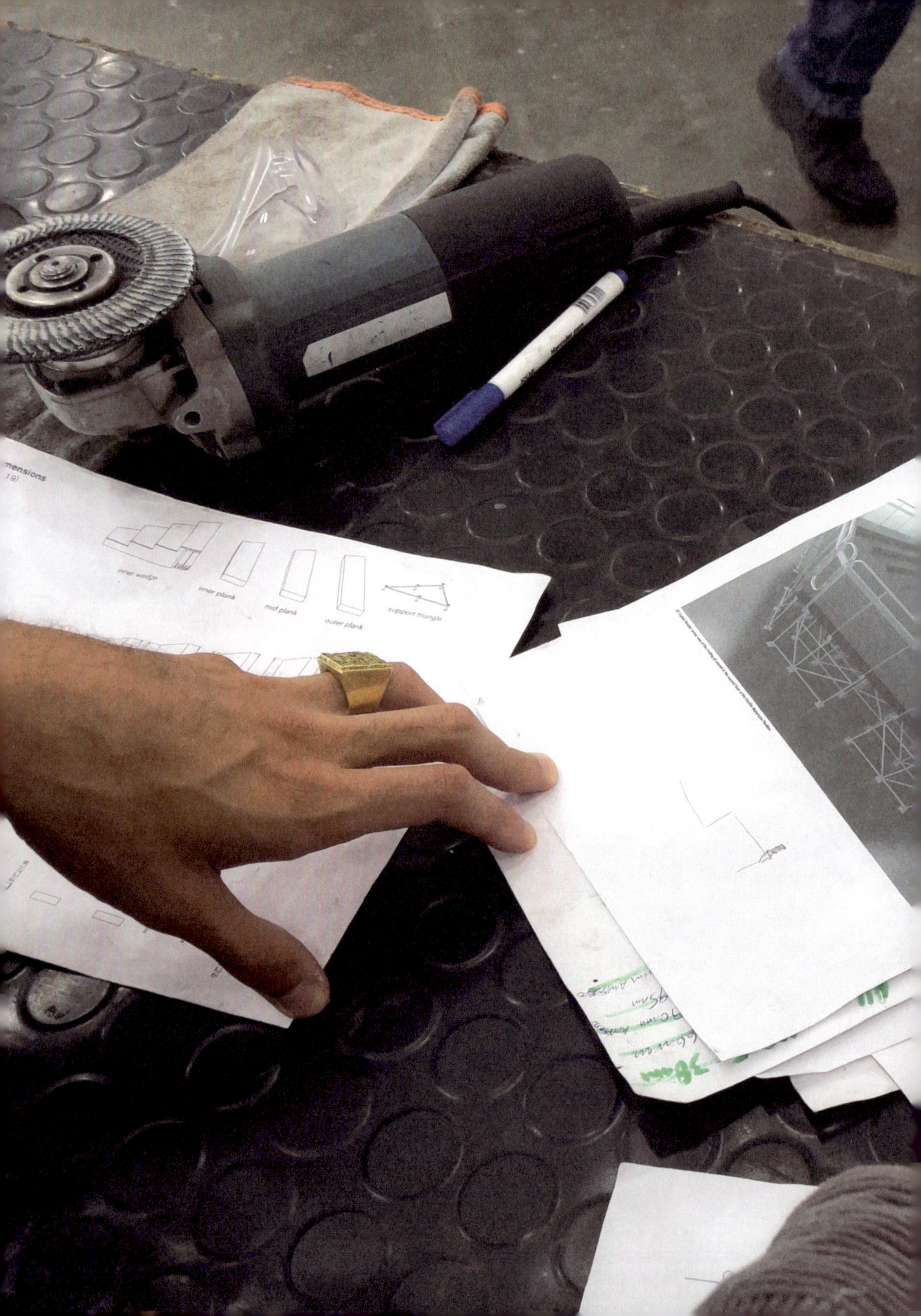

inner wedge
inner plank
mid plank
outer plank
support triangle

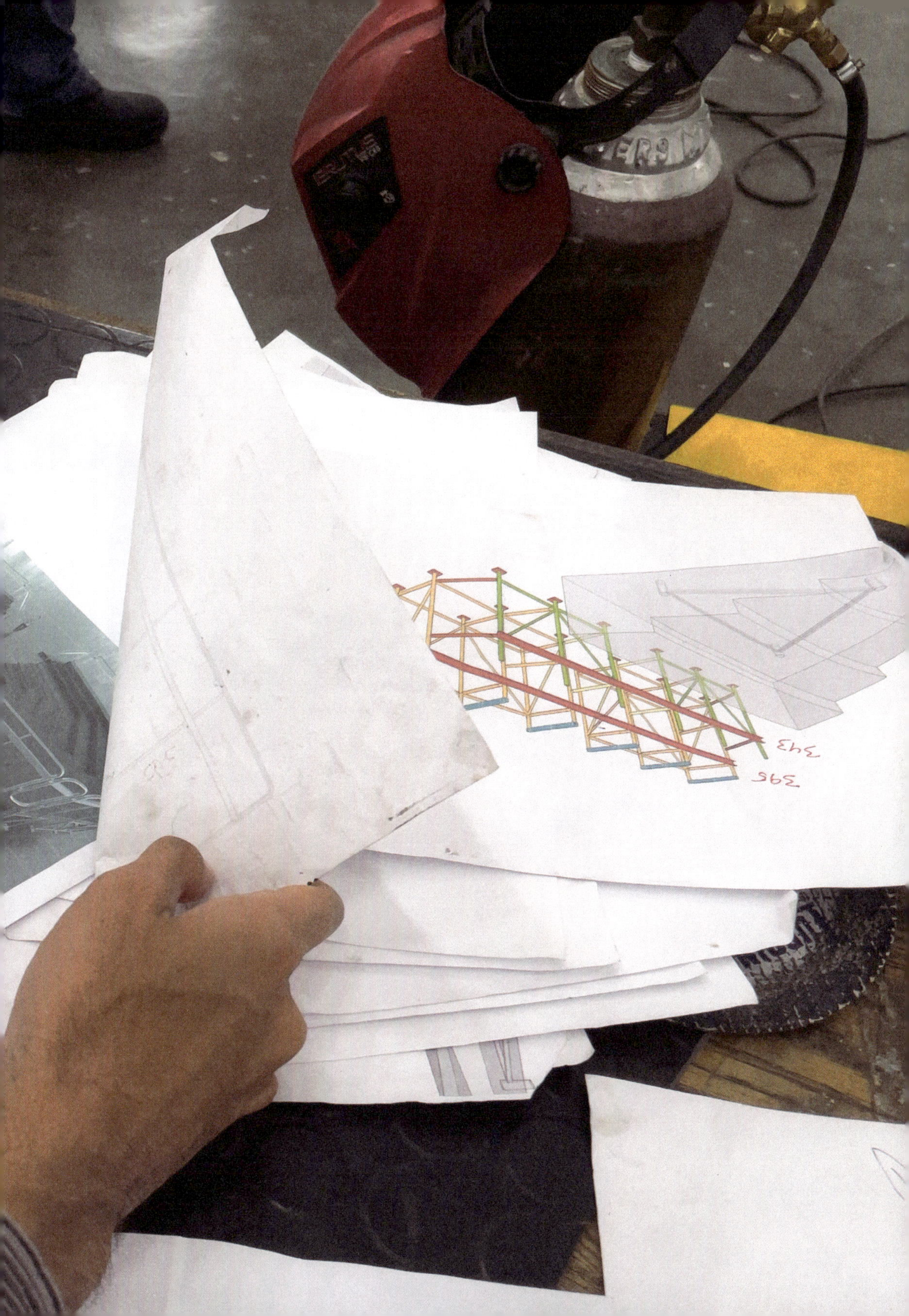

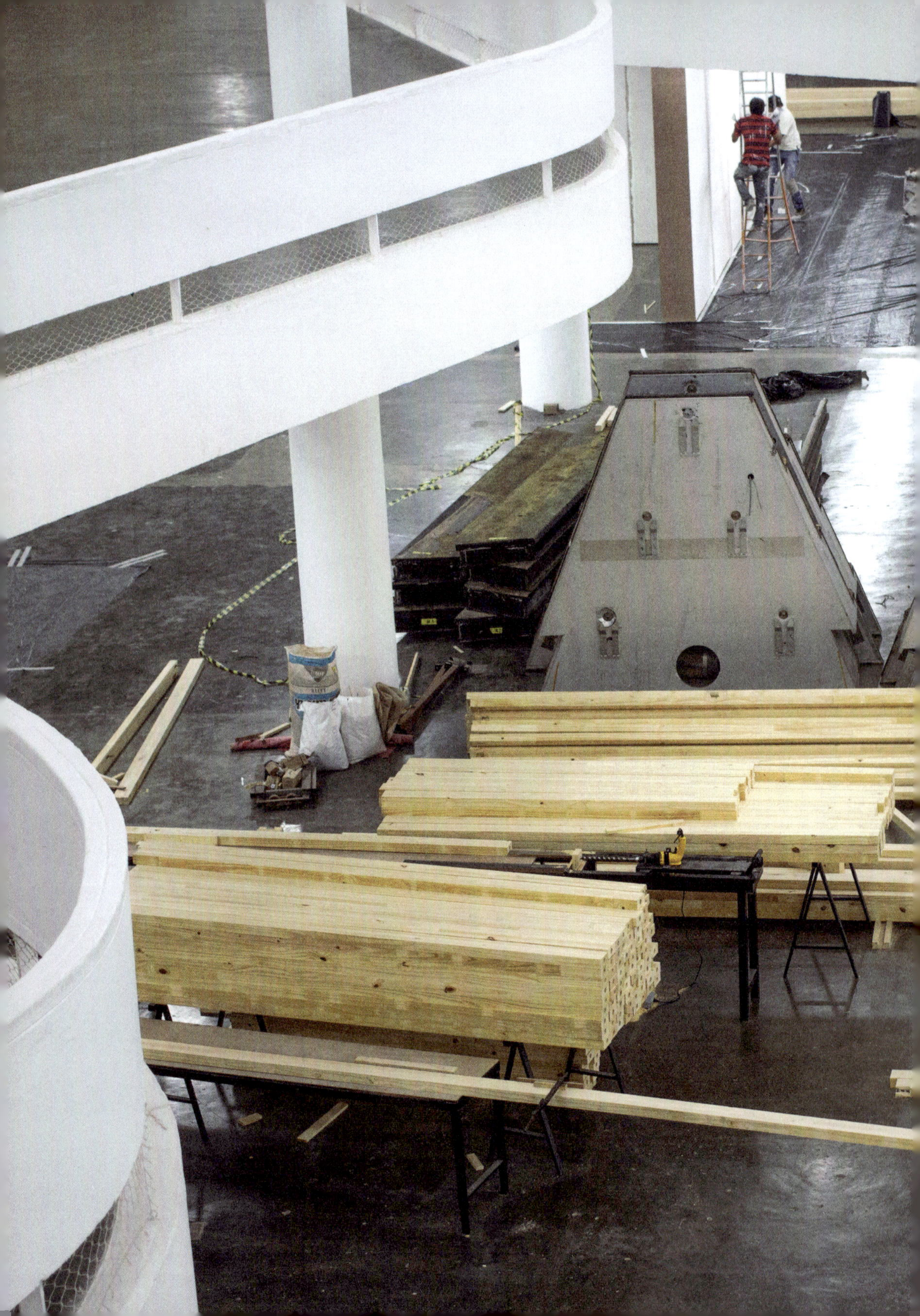

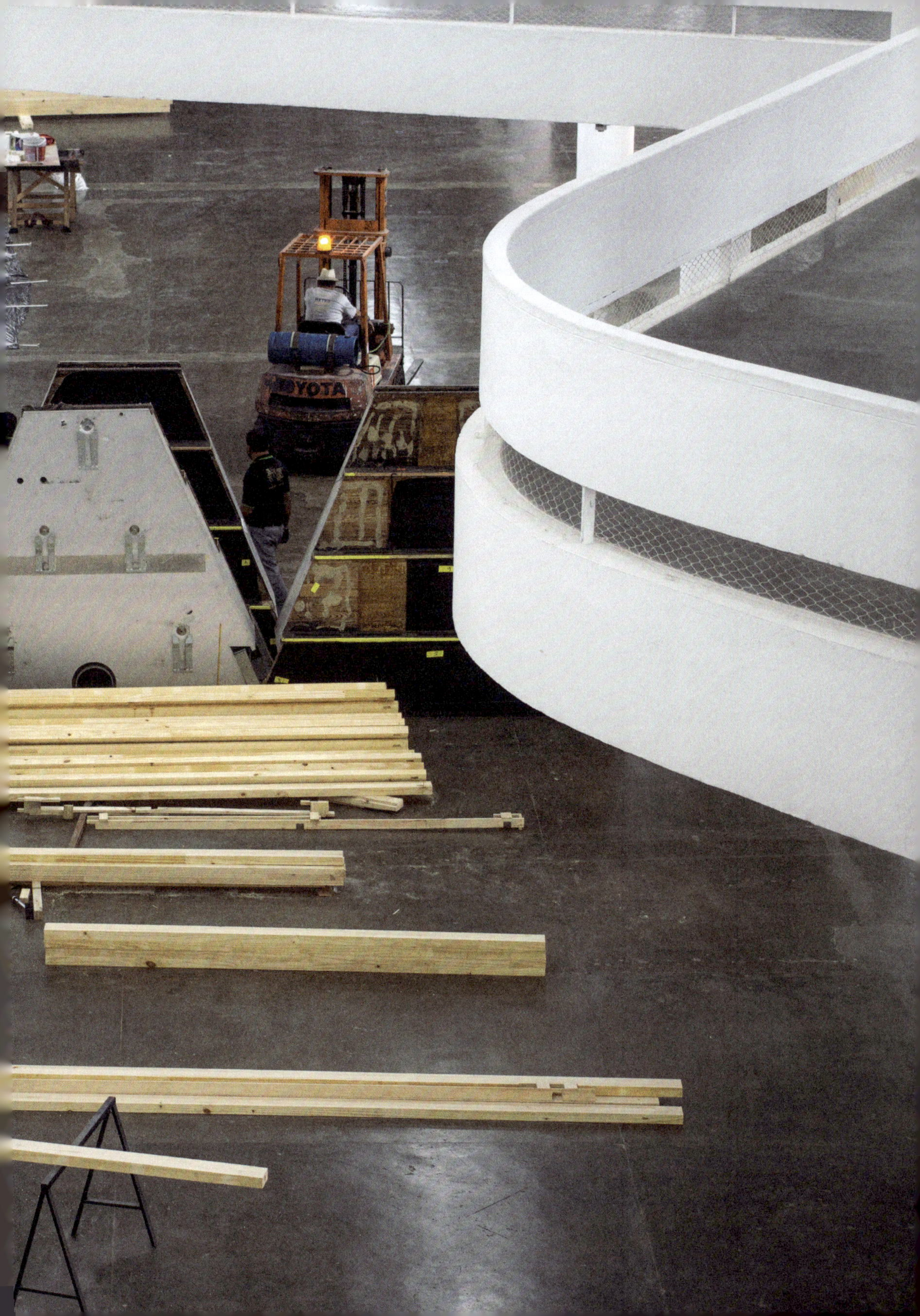
YOTA

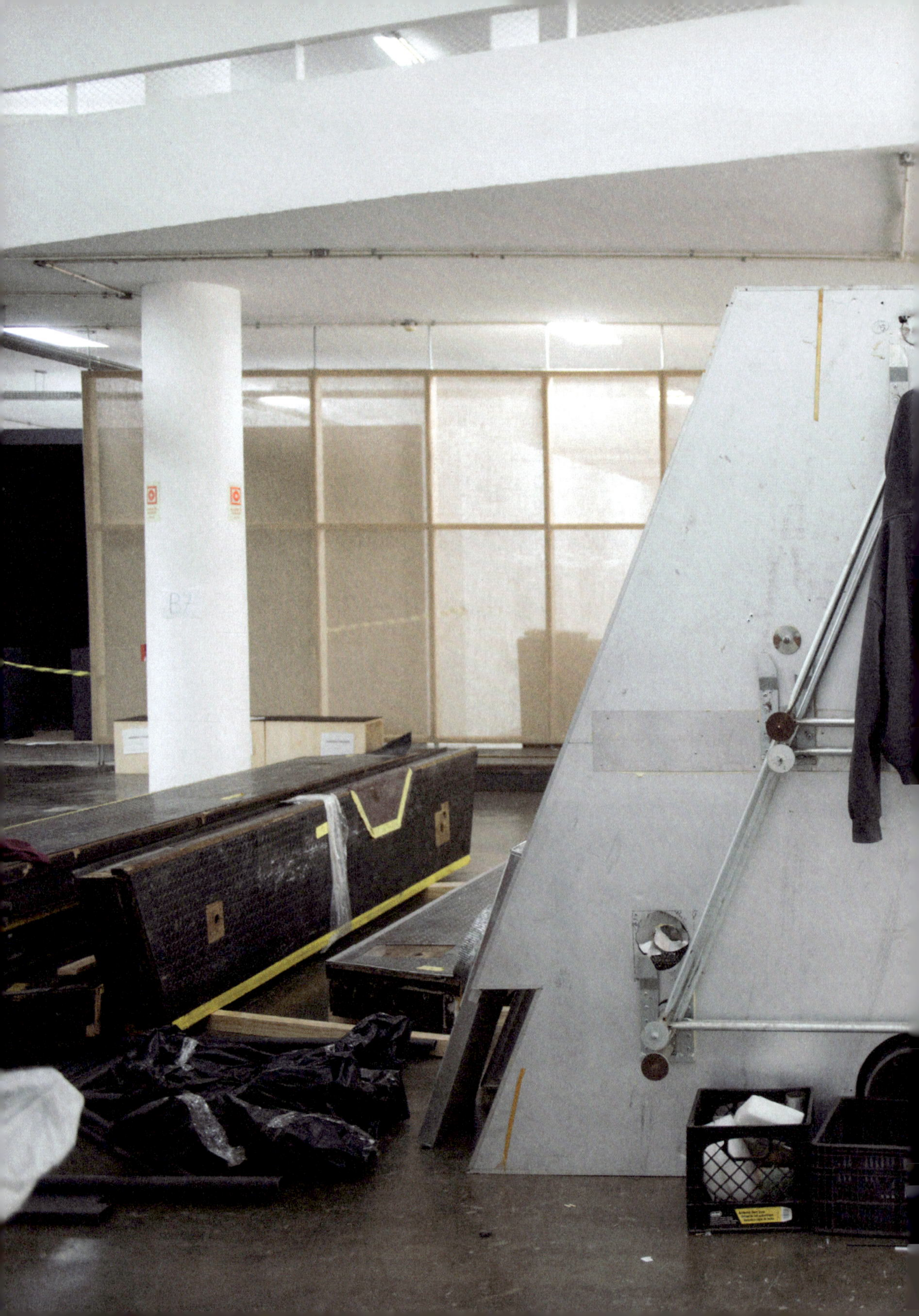

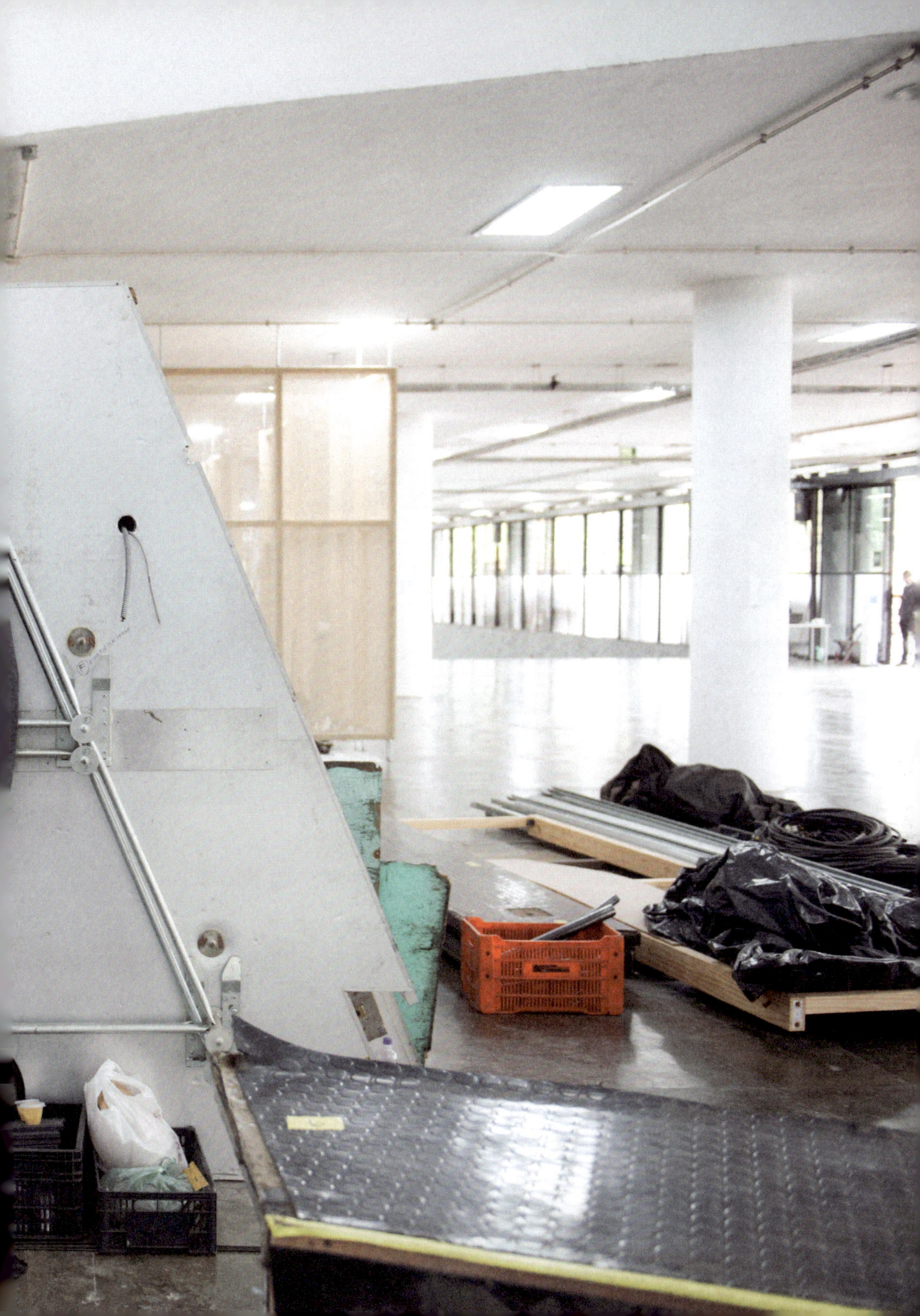

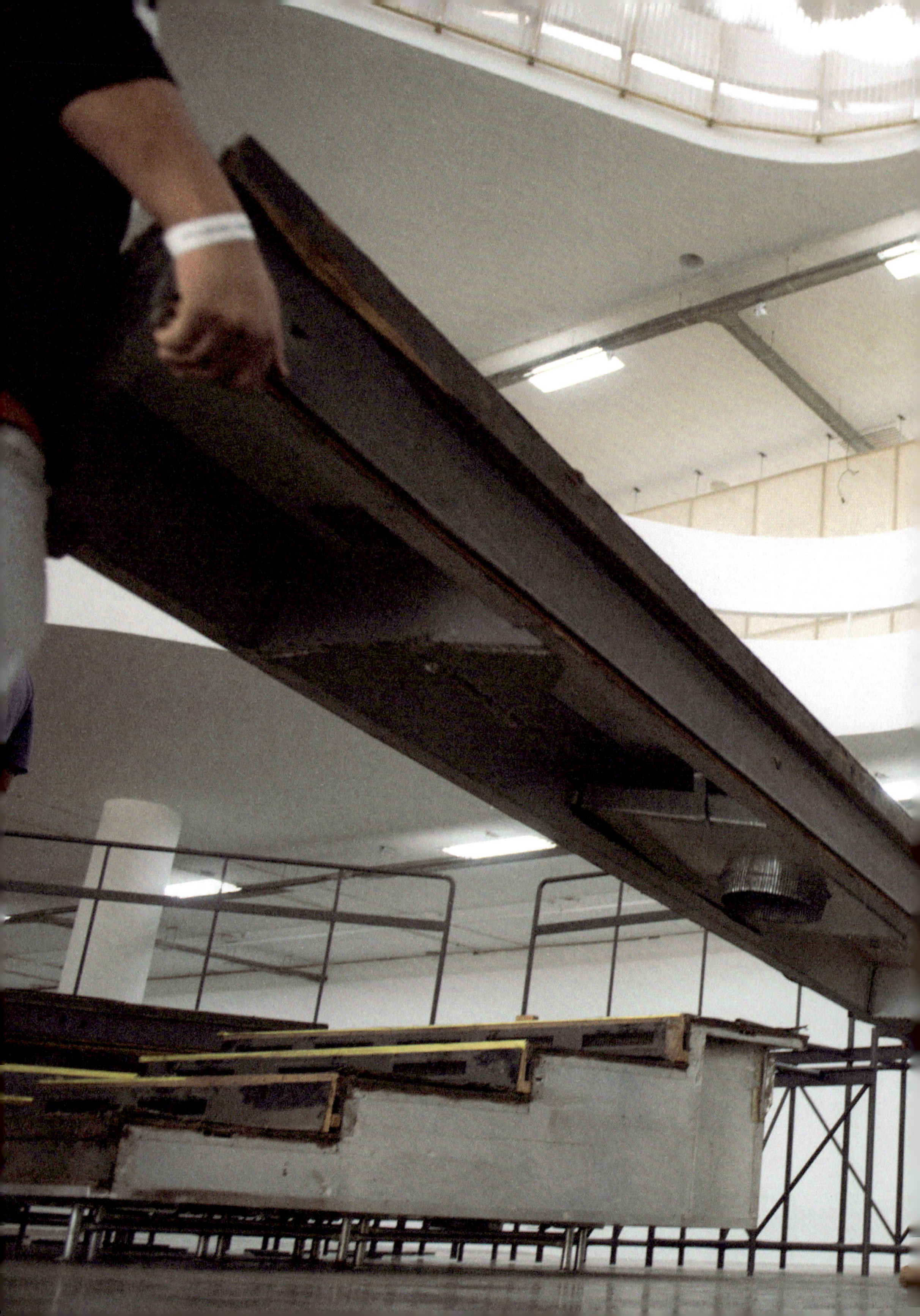

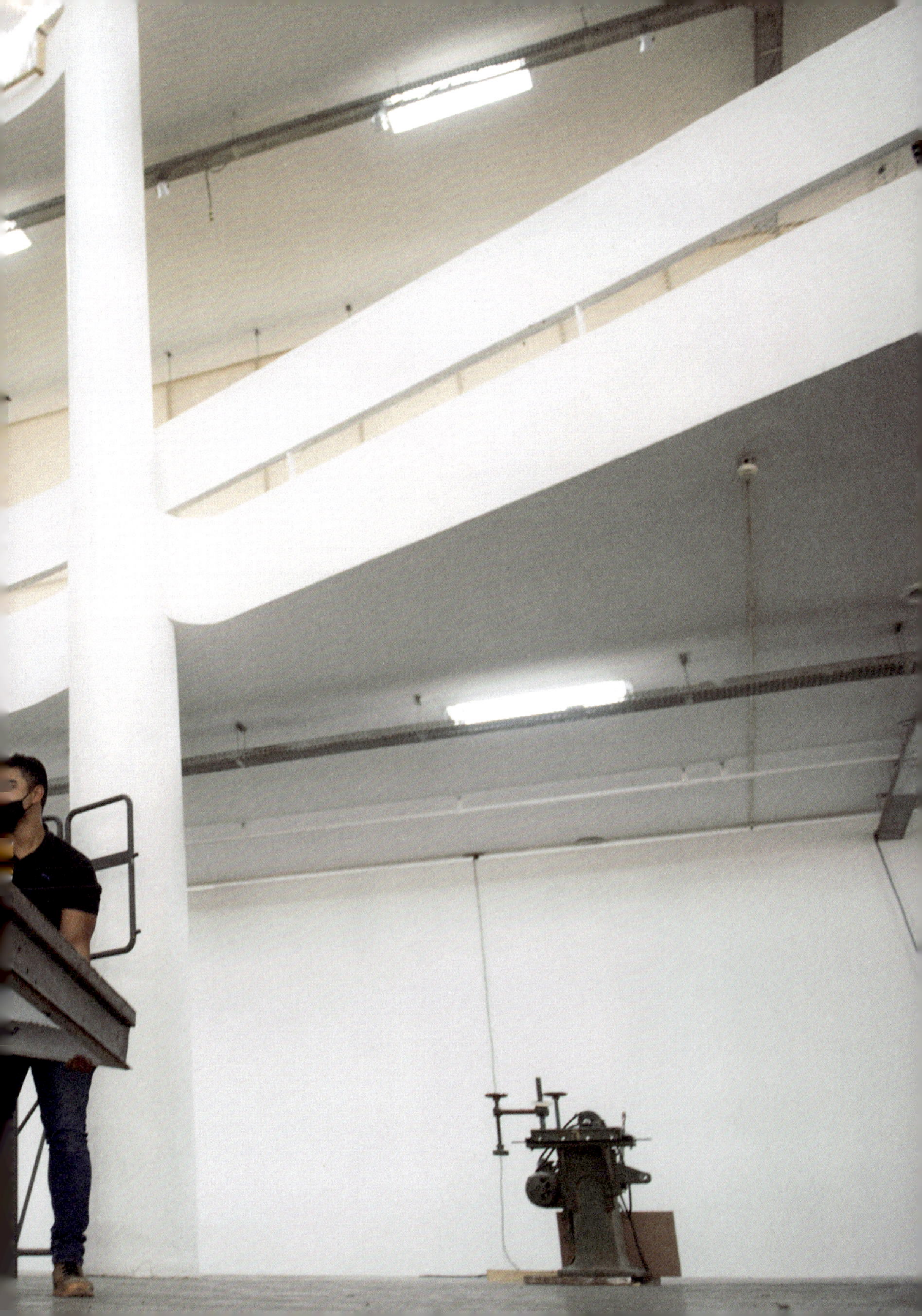

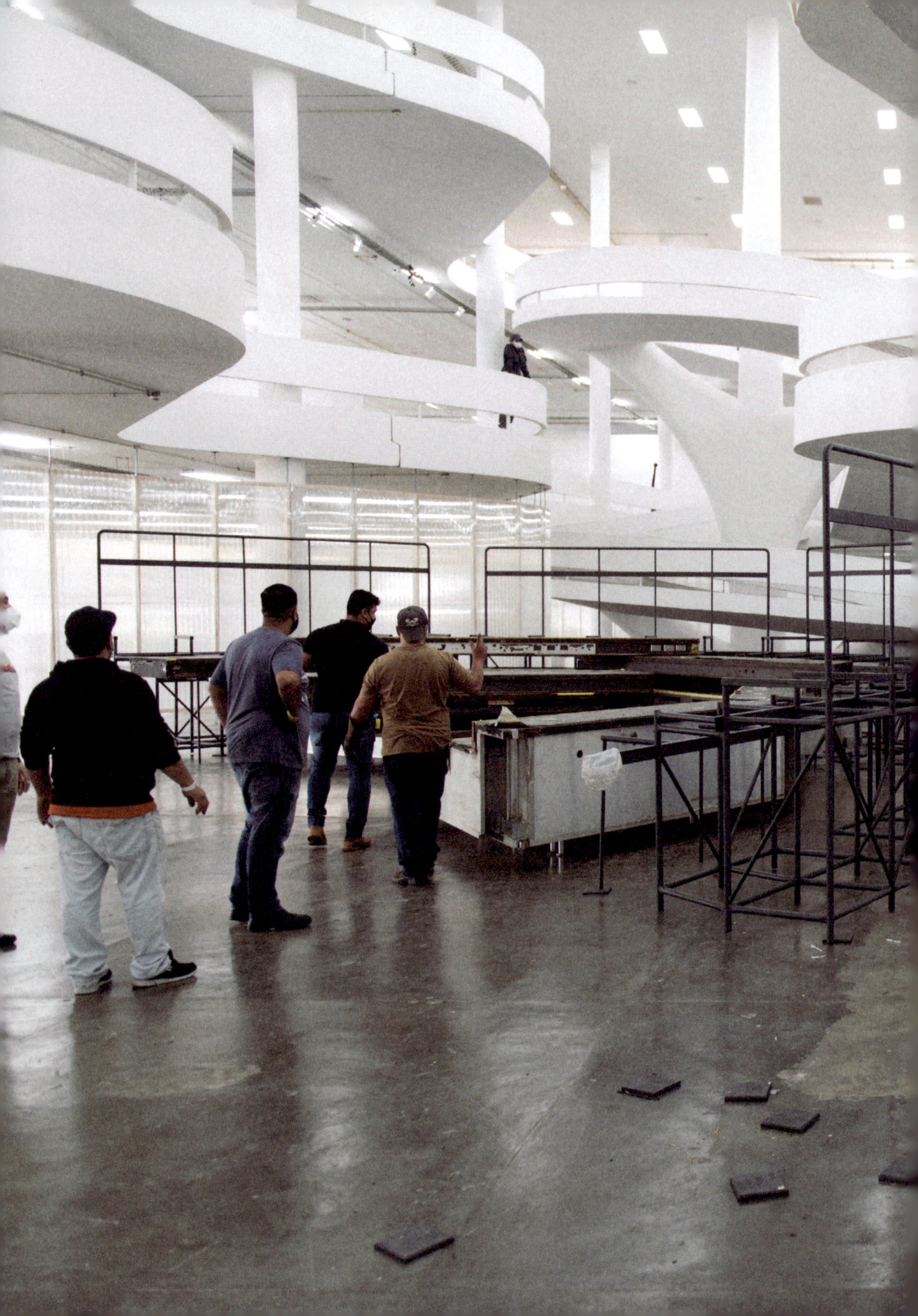

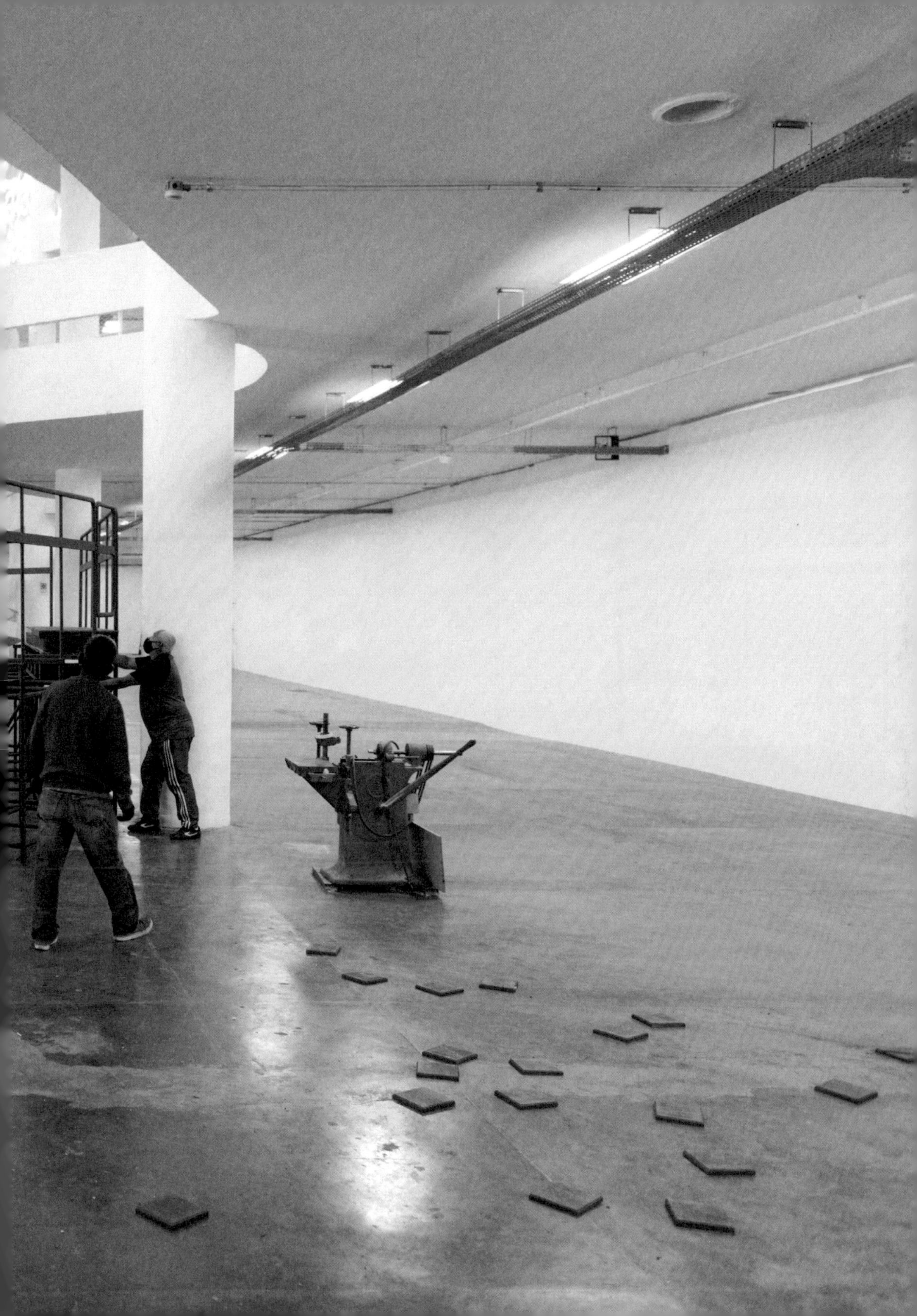

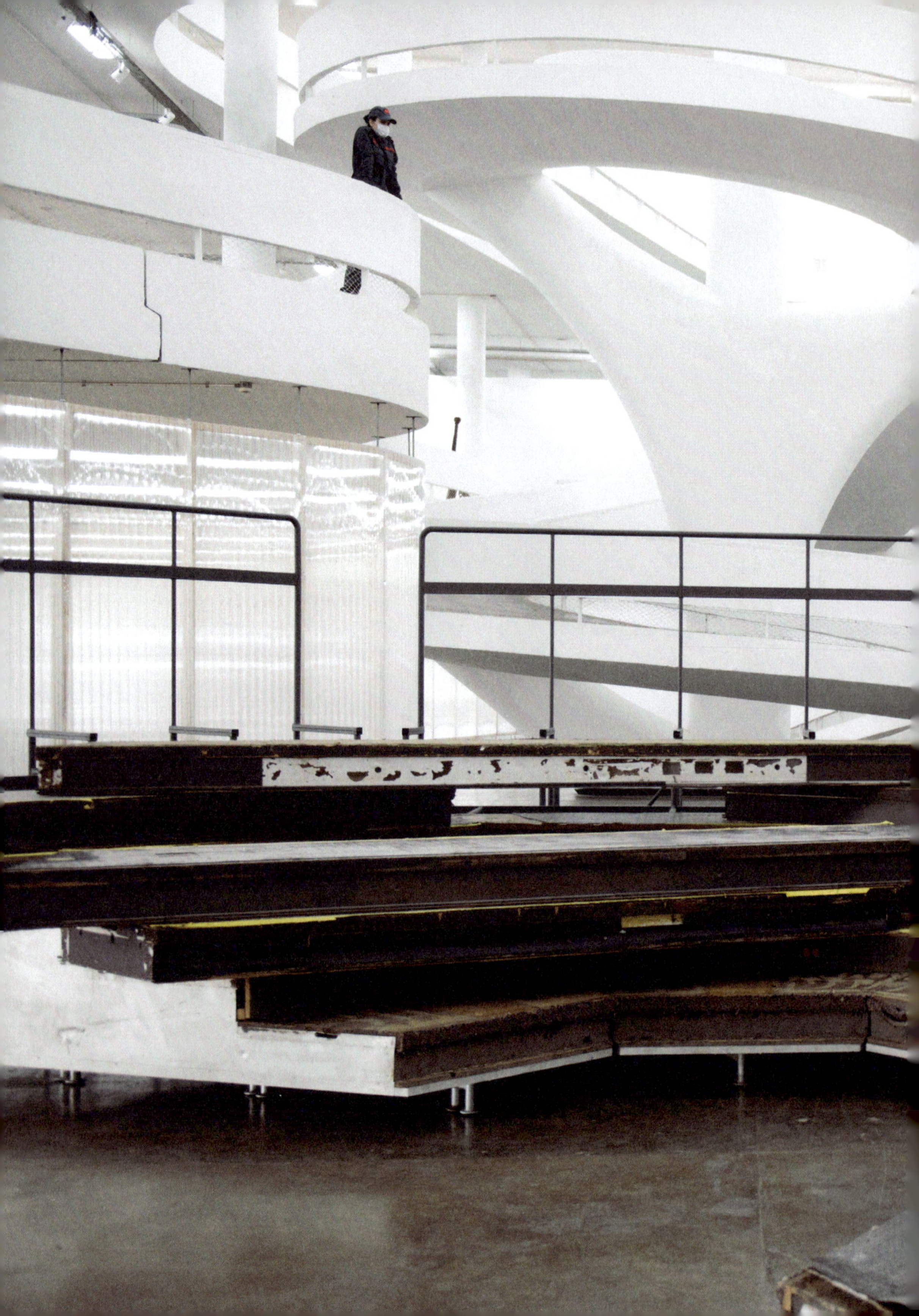

Banco Itaú - Comprovante de Pagamento
TED C – outra titularidade

Identificação no extrato: SISPAG FORNECEDORES

Dados da conta debitada:

Nome: FUNDACAO BIENAL DE SAO PAULO

Agência: 2923 Conta corrente: 22769 - 4

Dados da TED:

Nome do favorecido: DANIEL DE PAULA

CPF/CNPJ: 00C

Número do banco, nome e ISPB: 237 - BCO BRADESCO S A - ISPB 60746948

Agência: 2976RUA PADRE JOAO MANUEL-USP

Conta corrente: 00003155013

Valor da TED: R$ 8,76

Finalidade: CREDITO EM CONTA

Informações fornecidas pelo pagador: DANIEL DE PAULA

Controle: 994876209000117

TED solicitada em 03/12/2021 às 14:52:59 via Sispag.

Autenticação:

F38A7D1CB470F004FE60A05EA4454A07EA943768

INSTALLATION 160
PROPERTY LEASE AGREEMENT (TEMPLATE) 172
CONTRATO DE LOCAÇÃO DE BEM (EXECUTADO) 173
AN OBJECT DISPLACED, A PLACE TO GATHER DIFFERENT BODIES 206

DEPO SITION VI

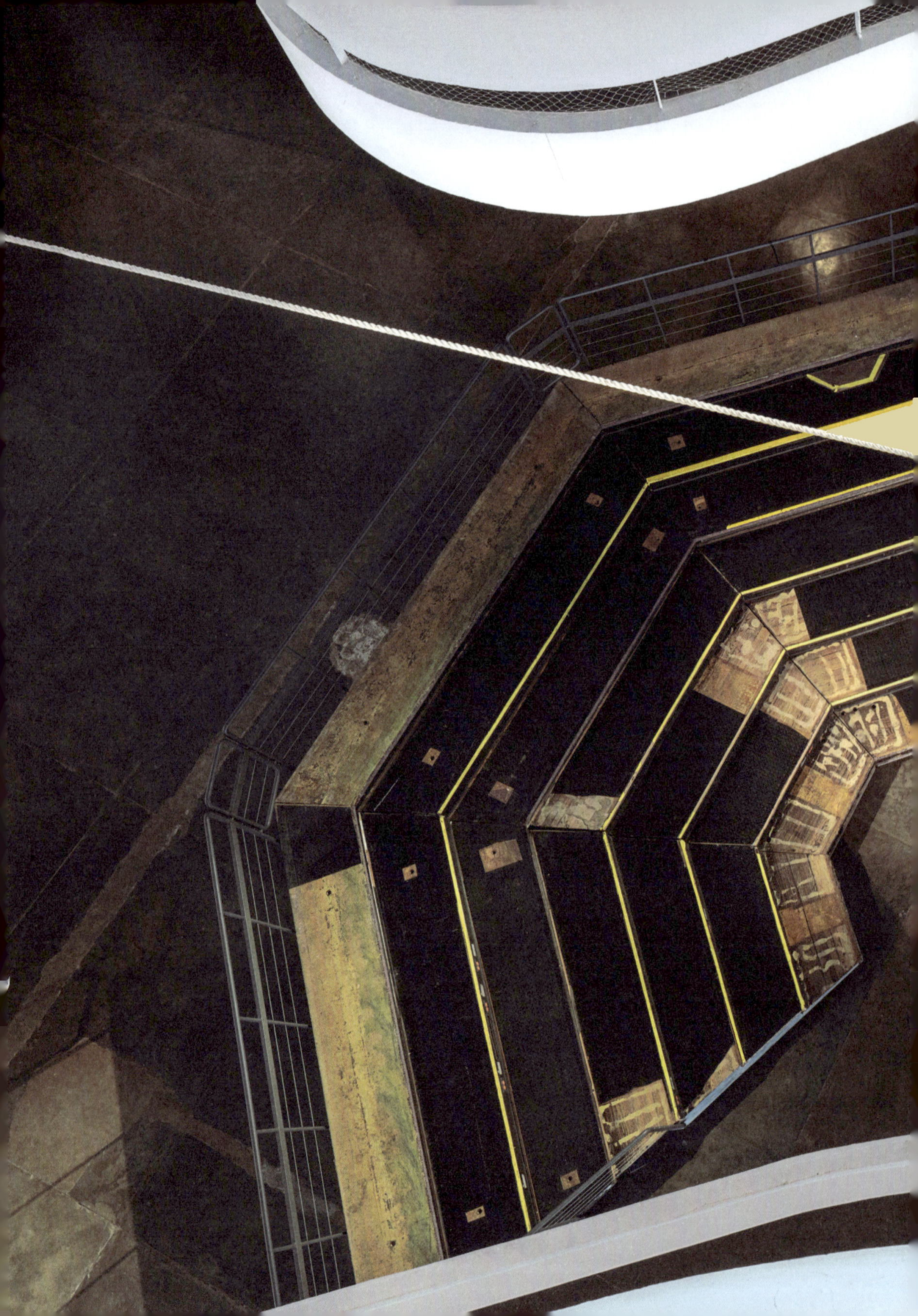

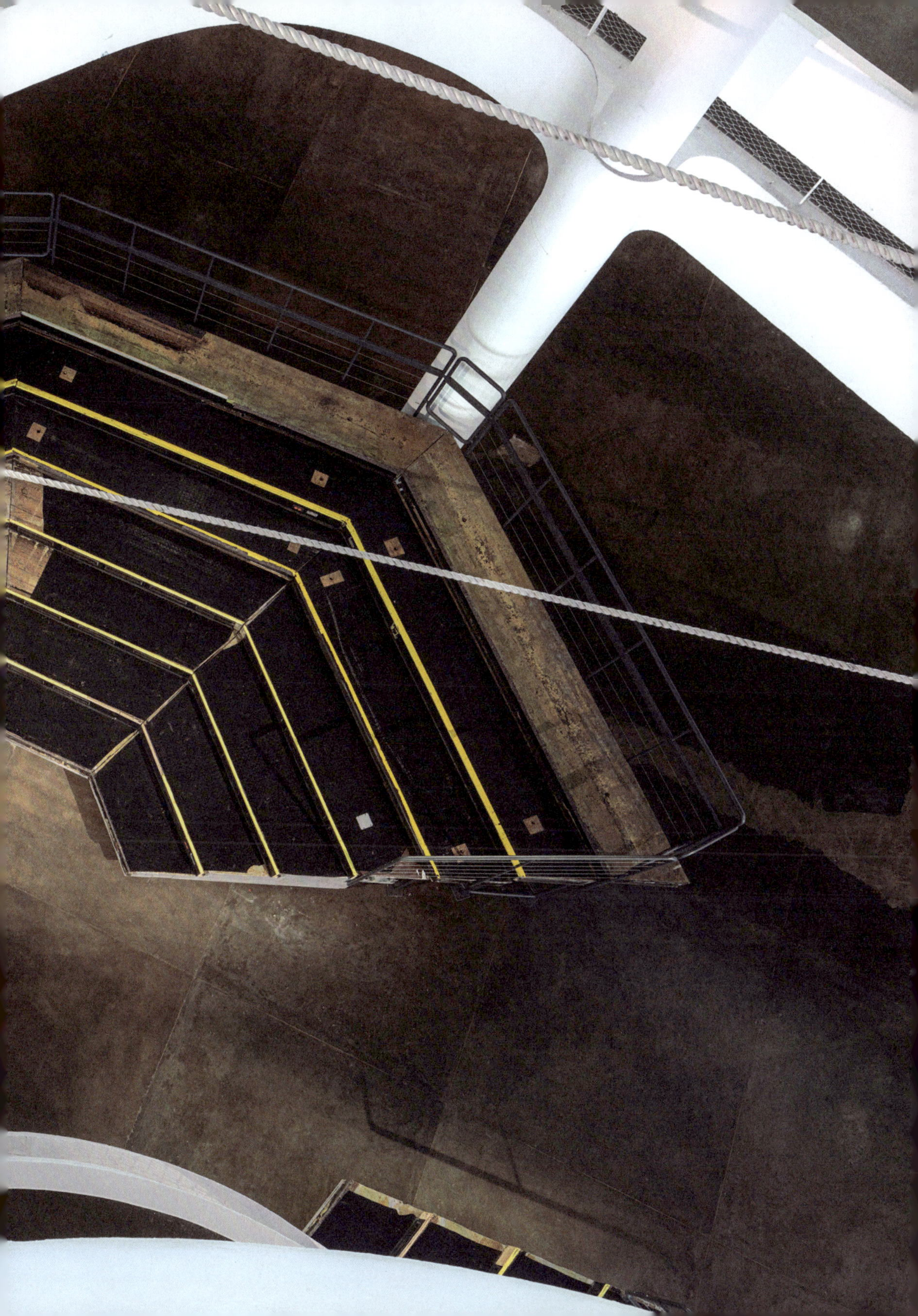

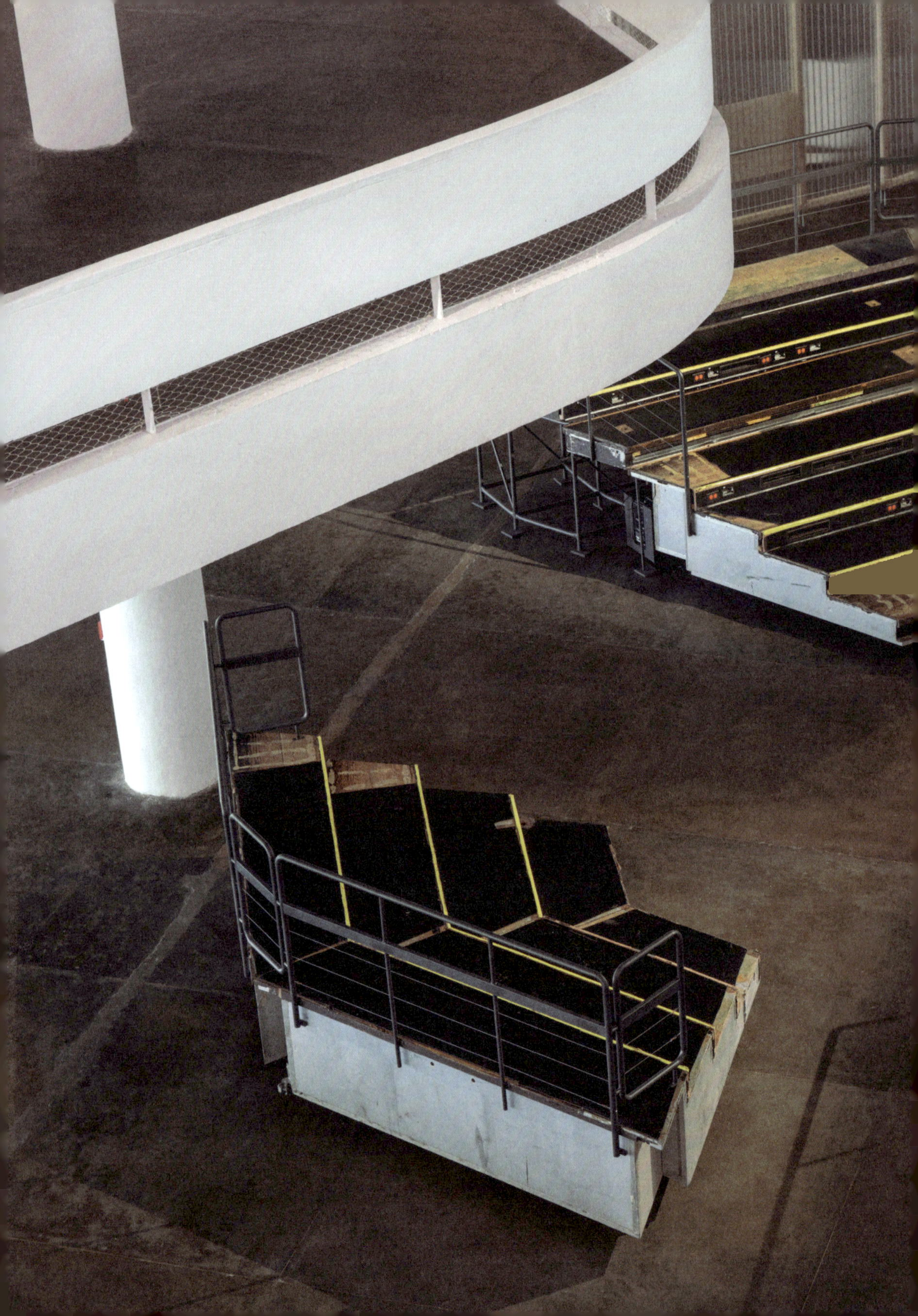

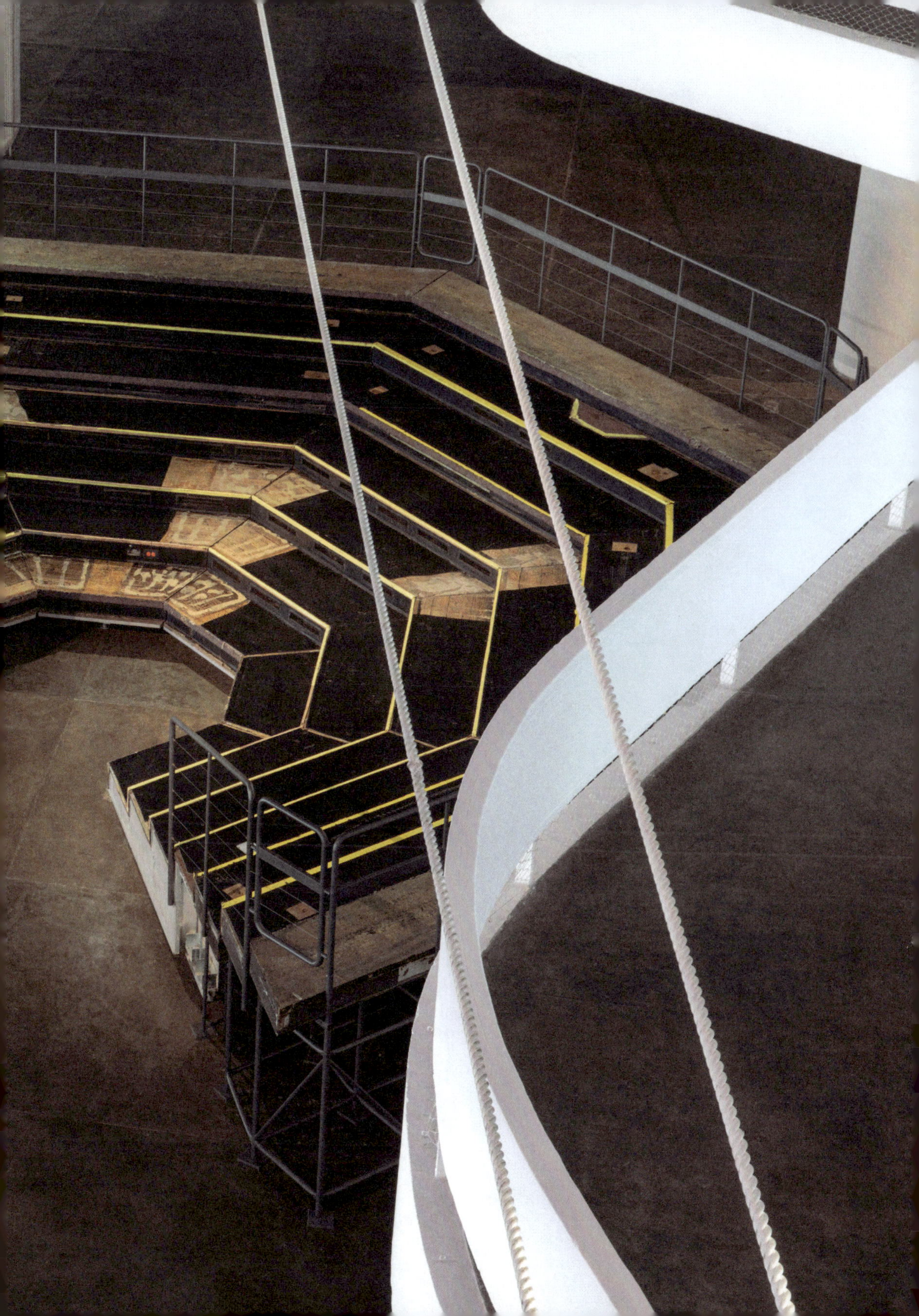

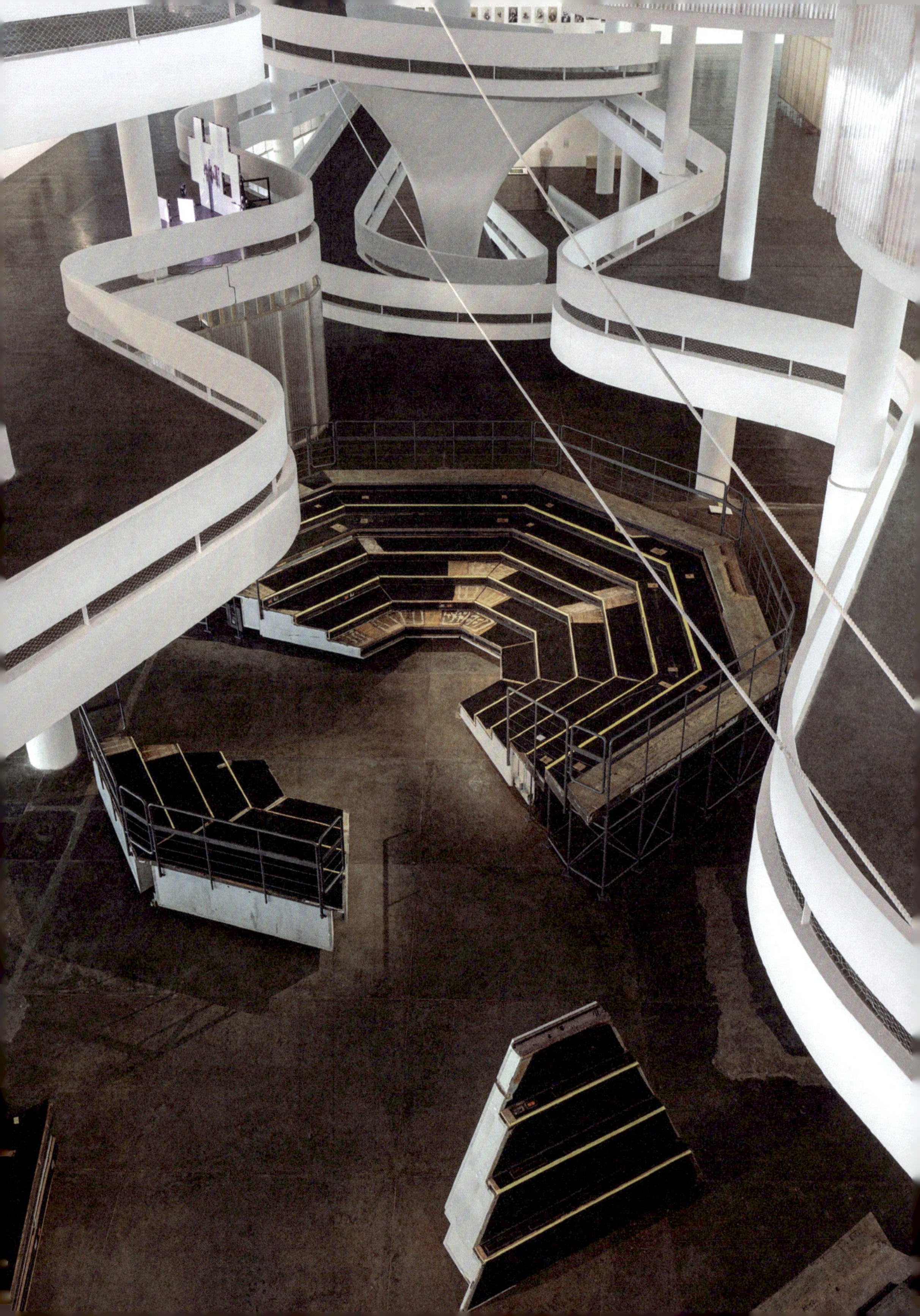

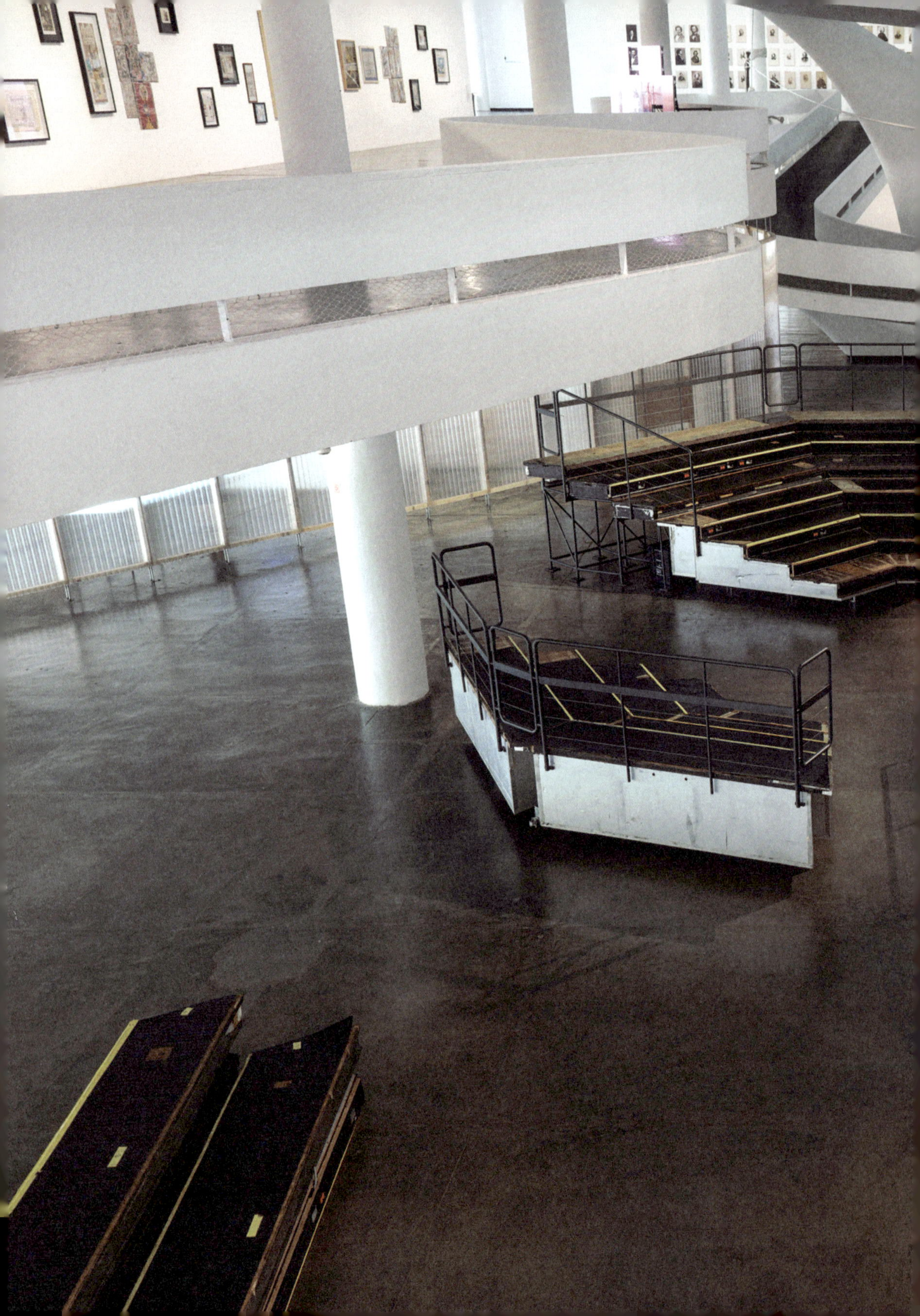

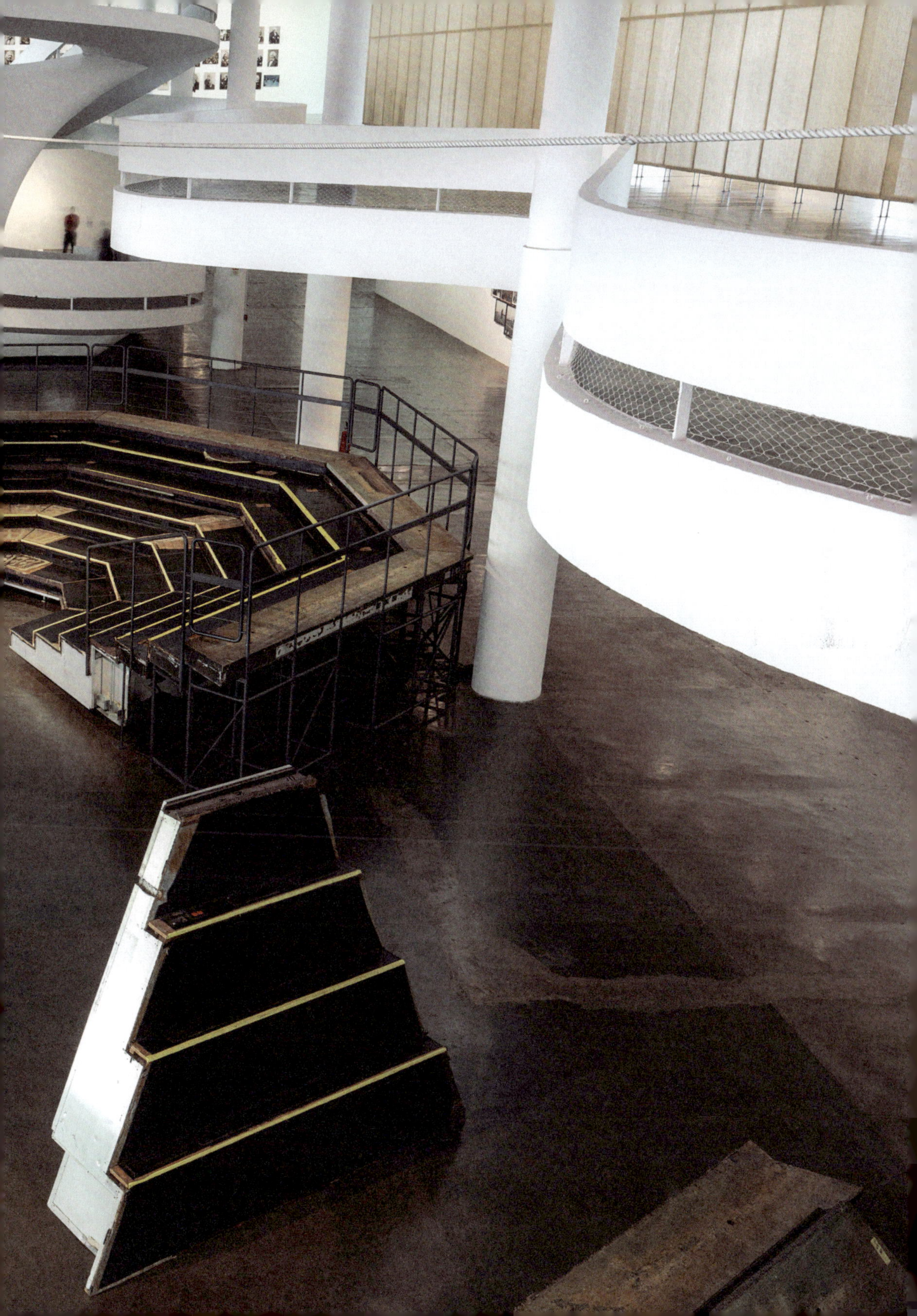

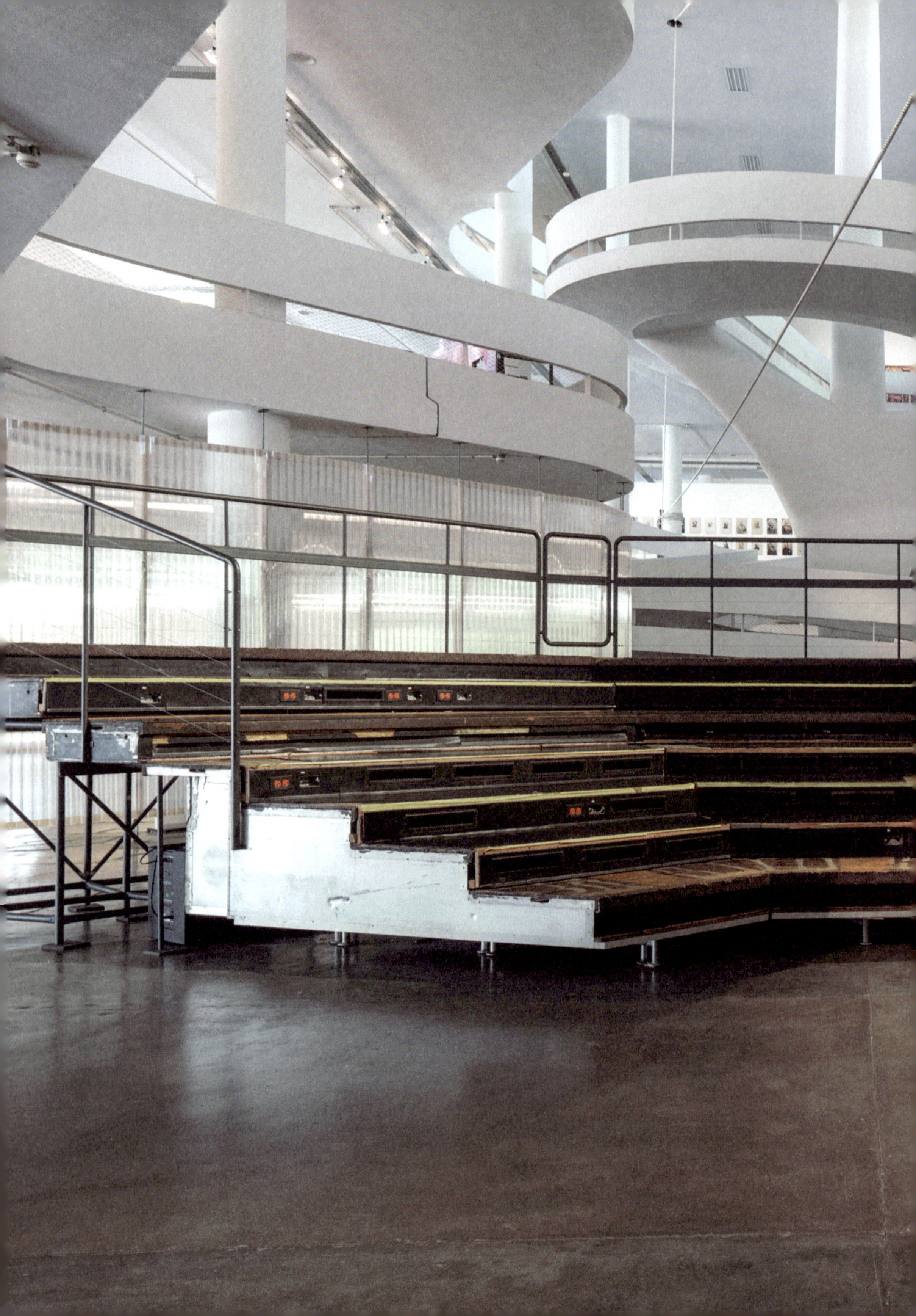

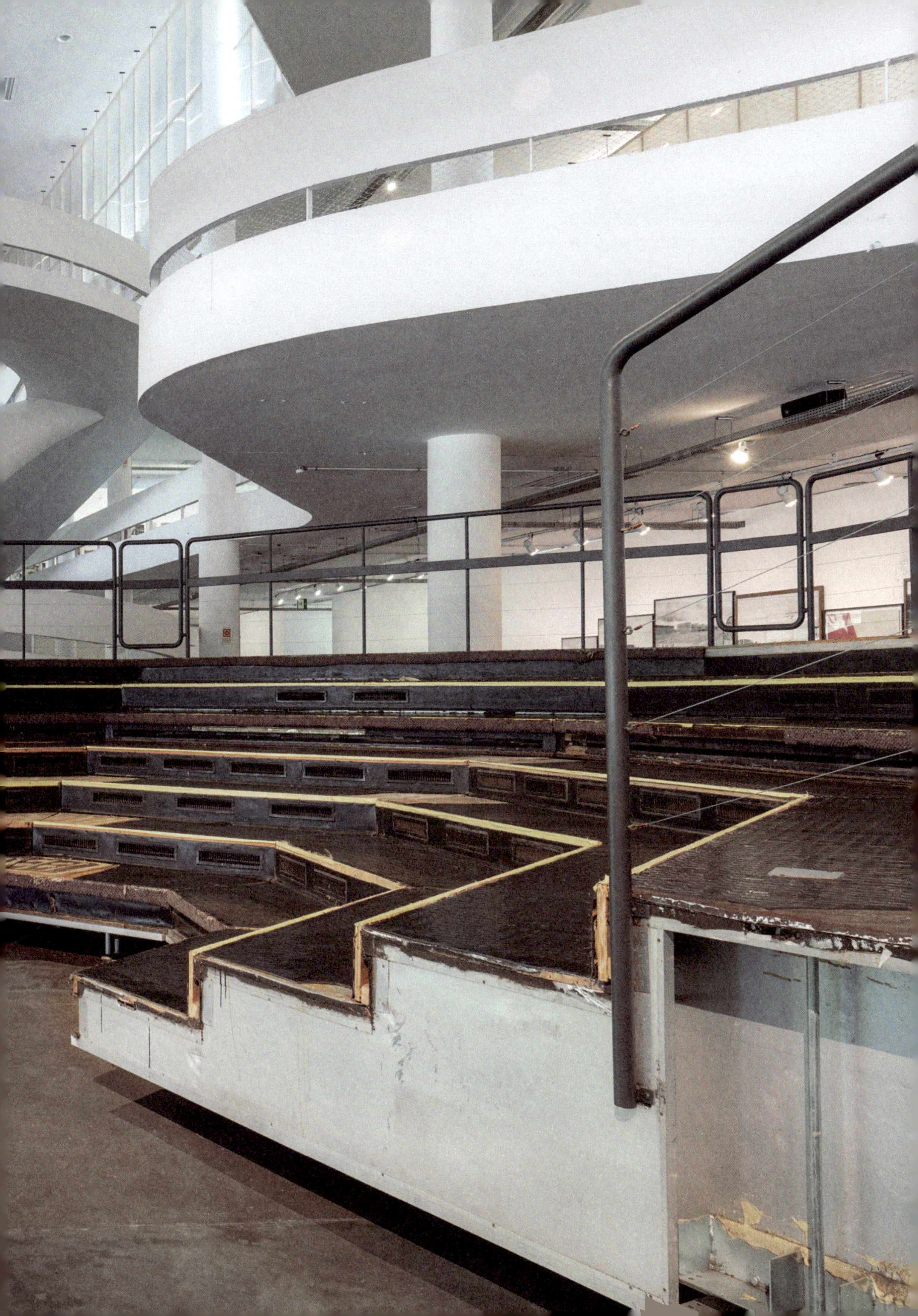

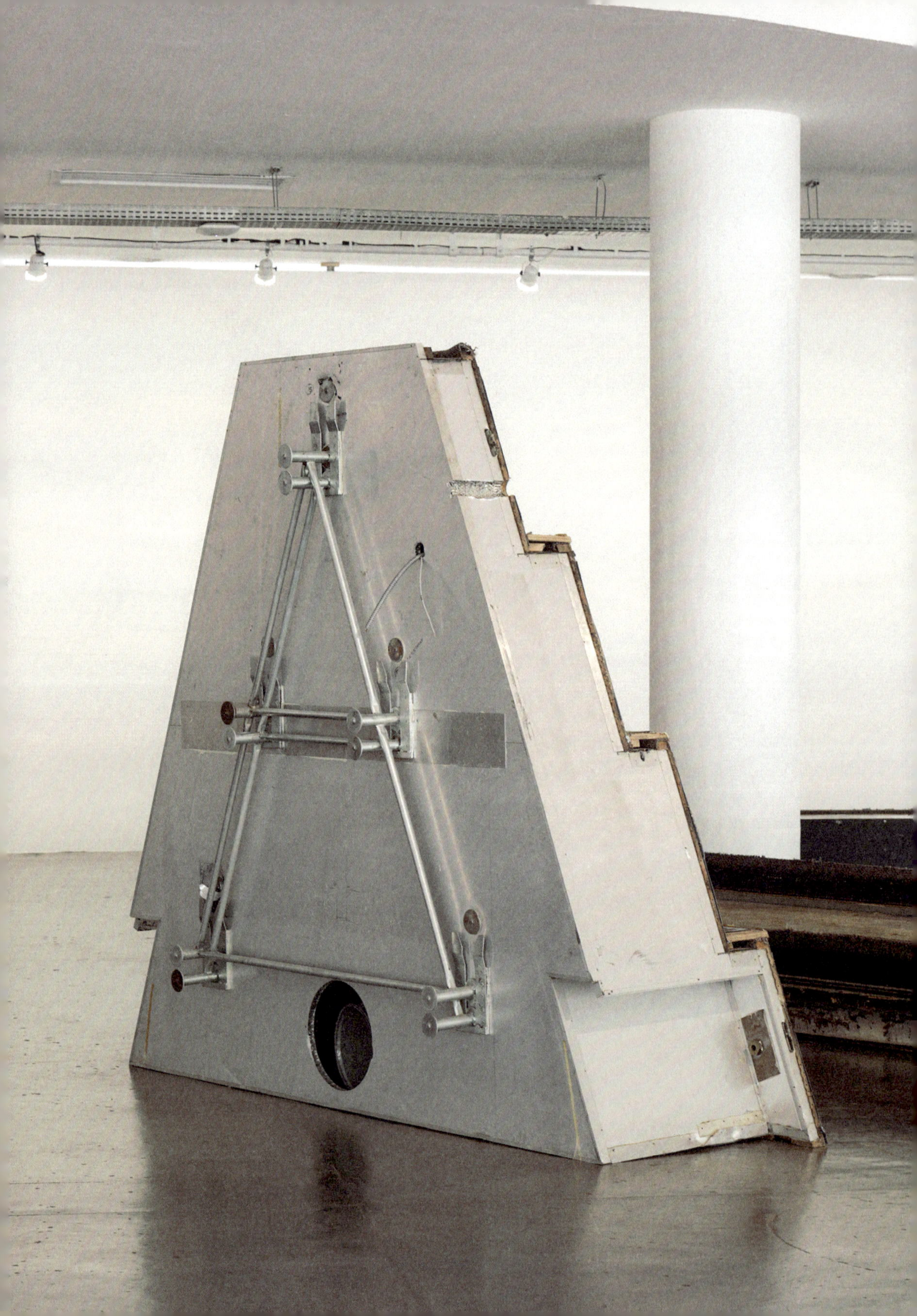

PROPERTY LEASE AGREEMENT

This PROPERTY LEASE AGREEMENT (this "**Agreement**"), dated as of ____________________(the "**Effective Date**"), is entered into by and among:

DANIEL DE PAULA, MARISSA LEE BENEDICT and DAVID RUETER,

individual artists, as lessors (collectively, the "**Artists**") and:

(the "**Lessee**").

SECTION 1. INTRODUCTORY PROVISIONS

1.1 Basic Lease Provisions. Each reference in this Agreement to any of the following subjects shall be construed to incorporate the data stated for that subject in this Section 1.1.

(a) Trading Pit. A salvaged Chicago Mercantile Exchange (CME) / Chicago Board of Trade (CBOT) Corn Trading Pit Floor, comprising 32 pieces, including 24 single steps and 8 four-step sections, as detailed in Exhibit "A" and Exhibit "B" attached hereto and made a part hereof.

(b) Commencement Date.

(c) Expiration Date.

(d) Rent. $0.26 per month, corresponding to, and determined by, the 0.023 acres of surface area of the Trading Pit, indexed to the United States Department of Agriculture's National Agricultural Statistics Service survey of the 2020 national cropland cash rent average of $139.00 per acre, as detailed in Exhibit "B" attached hereto and made a part hereof.

CONTRATO DE LOCAÇÃO DE BEM

Este CONTRATO DE LOCAÇÃO DE BEM (o "**Contrato**"), datado de 1 de julho de 2021 (a "**Data de Entrada em Vigor**"), é celebrado entre:

DANIEL DE PAULA, MARISSA LEE BENEDICT e DAVID RUETER,

artistas individuais, como locadores (em conjunto, os "**Artistas**") e:

FUNDAÇÃO BIENAL DE SÃO PAULO,

instituição brasileira sem fins lucrativos (a "**Locatária**").

CLÁUSULA 1. DISPOSIÇÕES INTRODUTÓRIAS

1.1 **Disposições Básicas da Locação**. Cada referência neste Contrato a qualquer um dos seguintes assuntos deve ser interpretada para incluir os dados referidos para esse assunto nesta Seção 1.1.

(a) *Roda de Negociação [Trading Pit]*. — *Roda de Negociação [Trading Pit]* de Milho da *Bolsa Mercantil de Chicago [CME - Chicago Mercantile Exchange] / Registro do Comércio de Chicago [CBOT – Chicago Board of Trade]* apropriado, compreendendo 32 peças, incluindo 24 degraus simples e 8 seções de quatro degraus, conforme detalhado no Anexo "A" e Anexo "B" deste documento.

(b) Data de Início. — 1 de julho de 2021.

(c) Data de Vencimento. — 31 de janeiro de 2022.

(d) Aluguel. — US$ 0,26 por mês, correspondente a, e determinado por, 0,023 acres de área de superfície da Roda de Negociação, indexado à pesquisa do *Serviço Nacional de Estatísticas Agrícolas do Departamento de Agricultura dos Estados Unidos [United States Department of Agriculture's National Agricultural Statistics Service]* da média nacional do arrendamento de terras agrícolas de 2020 de US$ 139,00 por acre, conforme detalhado no Anexo "B" deste documento.

(e) Uso Permitido. — *Consulte*, Seção 5.1.

(e) Permitted Use. *See,* Section 5.1.

SECTION 2. LEASE AND LEASE TERM

2.1 Property. The Artists hereby lease to the Lessee, to install, set up, use, rent and document, for cultural purposes only, according to the Lessee's obligations as provided herein, in the context of the ____________________ , the following property: a salvaged Chicago Mercantile Exchange (CME) / Chicago Board of Trade (CBOT) Corn Trading Pit Floor, comprising 32 pieces, including 24 single steps and 8 four-step sections, consisting of approximately 0.023 acres of surface area, as detailed in Exhibit "A" and Exhibit "B" attached hereto and made a part hereof (such property, the "**Trading Pit**", and such lease, the "**Lease**"), currently kept in the warehouse located in ____________________ ("**Storage Facility**").

2.2 Term. The term of the Lease shall be from ____________________ , to ____________________(the "**Initial Term**" and, as extended, the "**Term**"). Lessee shall return the Trading Pit to the Storage Facility and surrender its possession to the Artists at the end of the Initial Term or of any extension thereof. Requests for extensions of the Term must be presented by one party to another not less than five (5) days prior to the end of the Initial Term or applicable extension period thereafter. Extensions must be agreed by both parties, upon the same terms and conditions of this Agreement (with the exception of the Rent), by writing and attached to, and refer to, this Agreement.

SECTION 3. RENT

3.1 Rent. Lessee agrees to pay the Artists, in advance, beginning on the Commencement Date, and on the first day of each succeeding month throughout the Term, the Rent. Rent for any period during the Term which is less than a full month shall be a prorated based upon the number of days in such month. Lessee shall pay to the Artists the rent in cash by wire transfer of immediately available funds to an account to be determined by the Artists.

3.2 Payment. All dollar amounts in this Agreement refer to U.S. dollars, and all payments required to be paid under this Agreement will be paid in U.S. dollars unless Artists and Lessee otherwise agree in writing.

SECTION 4. EXPENSES OF LESSEE

4.1 Lessee will be responsible for and shall pay any and all expenses related to the following:

(a) Transportation and Insurance:

(i) To arrange the packing of the Trading Pit, as well as the transportation and delivery thereof from the Storage Facility to the Lessee's address by no later than the start of the Term and for the packing, transportation, and delivery of the

CLÁUSULA 2. LOCAÇÃO E PRAZO DO LOCAÇÃO

2.1 **Bem**. Os Artistas, por este ato, alugam para a Locatária instalar, montar, utilizar, alugar e documentar, apenas para fins culturais, de acordo com as obrigações da Locatária previstas neste documento, no âmbito da 34ª EDIÇÃO DA BIENAL DE SÃO PAULO, o seguinte Bem: *Roda de Negociação* [*Trading Pit*] de Milho da *Bolsa Mercantil de Chicago* [*CME - Chicago Mercantile Exchange*] / *Registro do Comércio de Chicago* [*CBOT – Chicago Board of Trade*] apropriado, compreendendo 32 peças, incluindo 24 degraus simples e 8 seções de quatro degraus, consistindo de aproximadamente 0,023 acres de área de superfície, conforme detalhado no Anexo "A" e Anexo "B" deste documento (tal Bem, a "***Roda de Negociação [Trading Pit]***", e tal locação, a "**Locação**"), atualmente mantido no armazém localizado em 9300 South Drexel Ave, Chicago, IL 60619, EUA ("**Local de Armazenamento**").

2.2 **Prazo**. O prazo da Locação será de 1 de julho de 2021 a 31 de janeiro de 2022 (o "**Prazo Inicial**" e, conforme prorrogado, o "**Prazo**"). A Locatária deve devolver a *Roda de Negociação* [*Trading Pit*] para o Local de Armazenamento e restituir sua posse para os Artistas no final do Prazo Inicial ou de qualquer prorrogação do mesmo. Os pedidos de prorrogação do Prazo devem ser apresentados por uma parte à outra, pelo menos 5 (cinco) dias antes do final do Prazo Inicial ou do período de prorrogação aplicável seguinte. As prorrogações devem ser acordadas por ambas as partes, nos mesmos termos e condições deste Contrato (com exceção do Aluguel), por escrito e anexadas a, e se referirem a, este Contrato.

CLÁUSULA 3. ALUGUEL

3.1 **Aluguel**. A Locatária concorda em pagar aos Artistas, antecipadamente, começando na Data de Início e no primeiro dia de cada mês subsequente ao longo do Prazo, o Aluguel. O aluguel para qualquer período durante o Prazo que seja inferior a um mês inteiro será proporcional com base no número de dias em tal mês. A Locatária pagará o aluguel em dinheiro para os Artistas através de transferência bancária dos fundos imediatamente disponíveis para uma conta a ser determinada pelos Artistas.

3.2 **Pagamento**. Todos os montantes em dólares neste Contrato referem-se a dólares americanos, e todos os pagamentos exigidos nos termos deste Contrato serão pagos em dólares americanos, a menos que os Artistas e a Locatária concordem por escrito de outra forma.

CLÁUSULA 4. DESPESAS DA LOCATÁRIA

4.1 A Locatária será responsável por, e deverá pagar, todas e quaisquer despesas relacionadas com o seguinte:

(a) Transporte e Seguro:

(i) Providenciar o acondicionamento da *Roda de Negociação* [*Trading Pit*], bem como o transporte e entrega da mesma do Local de Armazenamento para o endereço da Locatária até o início do Prazo, e o acondicionamento, transporte e entrega do *Roda de Negociação* [*Trading Pit*], no final do Prazo, do endereço da Locatária para o

Trading Pit, at the end of the Term, from the Lessee's address to the Storage Facility or any other location the Artists may determine in their sole discretion;

(ii) To adhere to all instructions for packaging and transportation which are supplied in a timely manner by or on behalf of the Artists;

(iii) To ensure that a count of the 32 pieces of the Trading Pit is carried out as soon as practicable after the Lessee comes into possession of the Trading Pit and prior to return to the Artists; and

(iv) To insure the Trading Pit for its price[1] and "nail to nail" under an "all risks" insurance policy at Lessee's own cost from the date that the Trading Pit is picked up by the Lessee at the Storage Facility and until (inclusively) the date the Trading Pit is returned to the Artists.

(b) Handling of the Trading Pit:

(i) To ensure all due care and diligence in the transportation, handling, installation, set up, use, and documentation of the Trading Pit;

(ii) To use reasonable endeavors to ensure that third parties exercise all due care and diligence in the transportation, handling, installation, set up, use, and documentation of the Trading Pit; and

(iii) To inform the Artists of any loss of or damage to the Trading Pit as soon as reasonably practicable.

(c) Installation and Setup:

(i) To arrange for all installation services, equipment, materials, and power necessary for the proper setup of the Trading Pit;

(ii) To install the Trading Pit in accordance to all health and safety protocols required by law;

(iii) To determine, by means of consultation with the appropriate engineering and safety professionals and regulations, the maximum occupancy limit of the Trading Pit;

[1] For insurance purposes only, the price of the Trading Pit is $50,000, corresponding to the sum of the Artists' initial costs of $5,000.00 for salvaging the Trading Pit, the Artists' storage costs to date, costs of the labor of the artists, and $94.00, determined by, the 0.023 acres of surface area of the Trading Pit, indexed to the United States Department of Agriculture's National Agricultural Statistics Service survey of the 2020 national cropland real estate price average of $4,100 per acre. *See* Section 5.1 (q) for Lessee's rights and obligations concerning sale of the Trading Pit.

Local de Armazenamento, ou qualquer outro local acordado por ambas as partes, nos mesmos termos e condições deste Contrato, por escrito e anexadas a, e se referirem a, este Contrato;

(ii) Cumprir todas as instruções de acondicionamento e transporte fornecidas em tempo hábil pelos ou em nome dos Artistas;

(iii) Garantir que a contagem das 32 peças da *Roda de Negociação* [*Trading Pit*] seja realizada o mais rápido possível após a Locatária imitir-se na posse da *Roda de Negociação* [*Trading Pit*] e antes da devolução para os Artistas; e

(iv) Assegurar a *Roda de Negociação* [*Trading Pit*] pelo seu preço[1] e "prego a prego" sob uma apólice de seguro contra "todos os riscos" às custas da própria Locatária, a partir da data em que a *Roda de Negociação* [*Trading Pit*] for retirada pela Locatária do Local de Armazenamento e até (inclusive) a data em que a *Roda de Negociação* [*Trading Pit*] for devolvido para os Artistas.

(b) Manuseio do *Roda de Negociação* [*Trading Pit*]:

(i) Garantir todo o cuidado e diligência no transporte, manuseio, instalação, montagem, uso e documentação da *Roda de Negociação* [*Trading Pit*];

(ii) Envidar todos os esforços razoáveis para garantir que terceiros envidem todo o cuidado e diligência no transporte, manuseio, instalação, montagem, uso e documentação da *Roda de Negociação* [*Trading Pit*]; e

(iii) Informar os Artistas de qualquer prejuízo ou dano à *Roda de Negociação* [*Trading Pit*] assim que razoavelmente possível.

(c) Instalação e Montagem:

(i) Providenciar todos os serviços de instalação, equipamentos, materiais e energia necessários para a correta montagem da *Roda de Negociação* [*Trading Pit*];

(ii) Instalar a *Roda de Negociação* [*Trading Pit*] de acordo com todos os protocolos de saúde e segurança exigidos por lei;

---

[1] Apenas para fins de seguro, o preço da *Roda de Negociação* [*Trading Pit*] é de US$ 50.000,00, correspondente à soma dos custos iniciais dos Artistas de US$ 5.000,00 para apropriaram-se da *Roda de Negociação* [*Trading Pit*], os custos de armazenamento dos Artistas até à data, custos de mão de obra dos Artistas e US$ 94,00, determinado por 0,023 hectares de área de superfície da *Roda de Negociação* [*Trading Pit*], indexado à pesquisa do *Serviço Nacional de Estatísticas Agrícolas do Departamento de Agricultura dos Estados Unidos* [*United States Department of Agriculture's National Agricultural Statistics Service*] da média nacional de preços de imóveis agrícolas em 2020 de US$ 4.100,00 por acre. Consulte a Seção 5.1(q) para os direitos e obrigações da Locatária relativos à venda da *Roda de Negociação* [*Trading Pit*].

(d) Audio and Visual Documentation: To arrange for all audio and visual documentation of the Trading Pit that the Artists may reasonably require during the Term.

(e) Documentation: To meet the cost of preparing and delivering any and all documents, certificates, forms or other documentation which the Artists reasonably may require for the purposes of transportation, delivery and handling of the Trading Pit during the Term.

(f) Artists' Fee: To pay the Artists the designated fee in the context of their participation in the 34th edition of the Bienal de São Paulo and the commissioning of the lease of the Trading Pit.

(g) Workers Compensation: To, without exception, appropriately compensate the Lessee's employees and contractors, and any and all other persons, for all services and labor directed towards the transportation, handling, storage, occupation, use, exhibit, and documentation of the Trading Pit.

(h) Utility Charges: Lessee shall pay, directly to the appropriate supplier, the cost of all light, power, natural gas, sewer service, water, telephone, refuse disposal and other utilities and services supplied to the Trading Pit, if any.

SECTION 5. LESSEE'S RIGHTS AND OBLIGATIONS

5.1 Permitted Use. Lessee shall use the Trading Pit in accordance with the terms set forth in this Section 5.1(a) – (t)and for no other purposes except as are otherwise approved by all of the Artists, in their sole discretion (each, a "**Permitted Use**"). Lessee agrees to, and it shall:

(a) use the Trading Pit for cultural purposes only, by means of its public exhibition and as a platform for ____________________ .

(b) ensure that the public exhibition and use of the Trading Pit as a platform for ____________________ is contextualized by an awareness, which is implicitly critical, of the embedded roles of the Artists and the Lessee in the reproduction of violent social and economic relations inscribed in the notions of land, labor, and capital. The parties hereby acknowledge and agree that the Lessee shall be deemed to have complied with this provision 5.1(b) by performing a public proclamation of the enunciation in Exhibit "C" attached hereto and made a part hereof, in accordance with the instructions set forth in Section 5.1(c) below.

(c) perform the public enunciation, as detailed in Exhibit "C" attached hereto and made a part hereof, prior to the start of any activity of a public program to be held in the Trading Pit, in accordance with the following conditions:

(i) The public enunciation must be performed each time by varying voluntary representatives of the ____________________ .

(iii) Determinar, mediante consulta aos profissionais e regulamentos apropriados de engenharia e segurança, o limite máximo de ocupação da *Roda de Negociação* [*Trading Pit*];

(d) Documentação: Cobrir os custos de elaboração e entrega de todos e quaisquer documentos, certificados, formulários ou outra documentação que os Artistas possam razoavelmente exigir para fins de transporte, entrega e manuseio da *Roda de Negociação* [*Trading Pit*] durante o Prazo.

(e) Honorários dos Artistas: Pagar aos Artistas os honorários designados no âmbito de sua participação na 34ª EDIÇÃO DA BIENAL DE SÃO PAULO, e o comissionamento da locação da *Roda de Negociação* [*Trading Pit*].

(f) Remuneração dos Trabalhadores: Remunerar adequadamente, sem exceção, os funcionários e contratados da Locatária, e todas e quaisquer outras pessoas, por todos os serviços e mão de obra direcionados ao transporte, manuseio, armazenamento, ocupação, uso, exibição e documentação da *Roda de Negociação* [*Trading Pit*].

(g) Despesas de Serviços Públicos: A Locatária pagará, diretamente ao fornecedor apropriado, o custo de toda luz, energia, gás natural, serviço de esgoto, água, telefone, eliminação de resíduos e demais serviços públicos fornecidos à *Roda de Negociação* [*Trading Pit*], se houver.

CLÁUSULA 5. DIREITOS E OBRIGAÇÕES DA LOCATÁRIA

5.1 Uso Permitido. A Locatária deverá usar a *Roda de Negociação* [*Trading Pit*] de acordo com os termos estabelecidos nesta Seção 5.1(a) – (t) e para nenhum outro propósito, exceto conforme aprovado por todos os Artistas, a seu exclusivo critério (cada, o "**Uso Permitido**"). A Locatária concorda e deverá:

(a) usar a *Roda de Negociação* [*Trading Pit*] apenas para fins culturais, por meio de sua exposição pública e, possivelmente, mas não exclusivamente, como plataforma para a programação pública no âmbito da 34ª EDIÇÃO DA BIENAL DE SÃO PAULO.

(b) assegurar que a exposição pública e a possível utilização da *Roda de Negociação* [*Trading Pit*] como plataforma para a programação pública no âmbito da 34ª EDIÇÃO DA BIENAL DE SÃO PAULO sejam contextualizadas por uma consciência, implicitamente crítica, dos papéis integrados dos Artistas e da Locatária na reprodução das violentas relações sociais e econômicas inseridas nas noções de terra, trabalho e capital, evidenciada e efetivada pela enunciação pública a ser realizada pela Locatária conforme detalhado na Seção 5.1(c) e no Anexo "C" deste documento. As partes reconhecem e concordam que a Locatária cumprirá com as obrigações descritas nesta cláusula 5.1(b) ao realizar a proclamação pública da enunciação descrita no Anexo "C" em anexo e feito parte deste contrato, conforme necessário com base na cláusula 5.1(c) abaixo.

(ii) All employees, regardless of department within the ___________________, must be briefed by the Lessee about the possibility of performing the public enunciation.

(iii) All representatives must have freely volunteered to perform the enunciation. No mandates are to be made of employees to perform the enunciation.

(iv) A select representative can only perform the enunciation once, unless no other voluntary representative comes forth.

(v) In the case no voluntary representative comes forth, or is present, to perform the public enunciation, the scheduled activity of the public program of the ___________________ that is to be held in the Trading Pit must be postponed indefinitely, or until a voluntary representative is made available.

(vi) The enunciation must be performed in the official language of the Lessee's country.

(d) acknowledge in decisions regarding the public exhibition and use of the Trading Pit as a platform for the public program of the ___________________ that the Trading Pit is a historical and contextual object that carries latent functions and relations.

(e) abide by the following installation requirement: *"the Trading Pit will never go back together the way it was before"*, meaning, the Trading Pit cannot be installed in the same configuration or form as it was at the Chicago Board of Trade (CBOT).

(f) Subject to Section 5.6 of this Agreement, repair or cause any of its agents to repair, any existing damage, wear or tear to the Trading Pit.

(g) ensure the Trading Pit is installed without its absent central piece of flooring, such that the floor of the exhibition space of the ___________________ itself serves as the center of the Trading Pit at all times.

(h) neither treat the Trading Pit as a monument, nor allow the Trading Pit to be monumentalized, including, but not limited to, by means of the historical reenactment or restaging in the Trading Pit through the activities of the public program of the ___________________ .

(i) treat the Trading Pit at all times as an image: *"a representation of capital"*, and shall not exhibit any historical images contextualizing the Trading Pit adjacent to the Trading Pit.

(j) allow for free access to the Trading Pit by the visiting public during opening hours of the ___________________ . Access may be restrained only in consideration

(c) realizar a enunciação pública, conforme detalhado no Anexo "C" deste documento, previamente ao início de qualquer possível atividade da programação pública no âmbito da 34ª EDIÇÃO DA BIENAL DE SÃO PAULO a ser realizada dentro da *Roda de Negociação* [*Trading Pit*], de acordo com as seguintes condições:

(i) A enunciação pública deve ser realizada cada vez por diferentes representantes voluntários no âmbito da 34ª EDIÇÃO DA BIENAL DE SÃO PAULO.

(ii) Todos os funcionários, independentemente do departamento, no âmbito da 34ª EDIÇÃO DA BIENAL DE SÃO PAULO, devem ser informados pela Locatária sobre a possibilidade de realização da enunciação pública.

(iii) Todos os representantes devem ter se voluntariado livremente para realizar a enunciação. Nenhuma determinação deve ser feita aos funcionários para realização da enunciação.

(iv) O respectivo representante só pode fazer a enunciação uma vez, a menos que nenhum outro representante voluntário se apresente.

(v) Se nenhum representante voluntário se apresentar, ou estiver presente, para fazer a enunciação pública, a atividade prevista na programação pública da 34ª edição da Bienal de São Paulo que seria realizada na *Roda de Negociação* [*Trading Pit*] deverá ser adiada indefinidamente, ou até que um representante voluntário seja disponibilizado.

(vi) A enunciação deve ser realizada no idioma oficial do país da Locatária.

(d) reconhecer nas decisões relacionadas à exposição pública e ao uso da *Roda de Negociação* [*Trading Pit*] como possível plataforma da programação pública no âmbito da 34ª EDIÇÃO DA BIENAL DE SÃO PAULO que a *Roda de Negociação* [*Trading Pit*] é um objeto histórico e contextual que carrega consigo funções e relações latentes.

(e) cumprir o seguinte requisito de instalação: "*A Roda de Negociação* [*Trading Pit*] *nunca mais voltará a ser como era antes*", ou seja, a *Roda de Negociação* [*Trading Pit*] não pode ser instalado na mesma configuração ou forma em que estava no *Registro do Comércio de Chicago* [*CBOT – Chicago Board of Trade*].

(f) Sujeito à Seção 5.6 deste Contrato, consertar, ou fazer com que qualquer um de seus agentes conserte, qualquer dano à *Roda de Negociação* [*Trading Pit*], com exceção ao desgaste natural como resultado de seu Uso Permitido.

(g) garantir que a *Roda de Negociação* [*Trading Pit*] seja instalado sem seu piso central, de modo que o próprio piso do espaço expositivo no âmbito da 34ª EDIÇÃO DA BIENAL DE SÃO PAULO sirva o tempo todo como centro da *Roda de Negociação* [*Trading Pit*].

of the maximum occupancy limit of the Trading Pit or on occasion of scheduled activities of the public program of the ___________________ .

(k) elaborate and employ strategies to avoid conflicting usage of the Trading Pit by the visiting public and the public program of the ___________________ .

(l) disallow hate speech, harassment, or non-consensual violent acts in the Trading Pit, whether such acts should occur through its use by the visiting public, or through the scheduled activities of the public program of the ___________________ .

(m) forbid use of institutional or state force in the mediation of conflicts within, or in proximity to, the Trading Pit.

(n) ensure that the Trading Pit is not a podium or a platform for individual discourse or agency by requiring that all activities of the public program of the ___________________ be structured around two or more discrete, ideally agonistic, agents.

(o) require all agents related to, or participating in, the public program of the ___________________ , to be informed of, and comply with, the regulations pertaining to the Permitted Use of the Trading Pit.

(p) not require the Artists to perform within the Trading Pit as agents or hosts for the scheduled activities of the public program of the ___________________ .

(q) prohibit the sale, consignment, or loan of the Trading Pit, and/or this Agreement, in written or digital form, to a third party. The Trading Pit and this Agreement are not for sale and cannot be collected.

(r) reasonably document and register, via audio and visual documentation, all public programs proposed by the Lessee. The Artists have the rights to reproduce all documentation material for future purposes, such as, but not limited to: publications, websites, and presentations. Lessee shall grant, and shall cause to be granted, any written permissions, if necessary, for the Artists to document and register the Lease, this Agreement, and the rights and obligations set forth in this Agreement.

(s) reproduce and use audio and visual documentation of the Trading Pit, in connection with the Lessee's rights and obligations, for promotional and marketing purposes, in connection with the exhibition and use of the Trading Pit as a platform for the public program of the ___________________ .

(t) use reasonable efforts to give credit to (or to procure to give credit to), both the Artists and the Lessee, on any promotional or other material that incorporates any image of the Trading Pit, and where the Trading Pit is displayed publicly, in a form similar to the following: "Courtesy of the Artists (Daniel de Paula, Marissa Lee Benedict, and David Rueter) and ___________________ ("Lessee")".

(h) não tratar a *Roda de Negociação* [*Trading Pit*] como um monumento, tampouco permitir que a *Roda de Negociação* [*Trading Pit*] seja monumentalizado, incluindo, mas não se limitando a, meios de reconstituição histórica ou reencenação dentro da *Roda de Negociação* [*Trading Pit*] por meio das atividades na programação pública no âmbito da 34ª EDIÇÃO DA BIENAL DE SÃO PAULO.

(i) tratar a *Roda de Negociação* [*Trading Pit*] sempre como uma imagem: "*uma representação do capital*", e não deverá exibir quaisquer imagens históricas contextualizando a *Roda de Negociação* [*Trading Pit*] adjacente à própria *Roda de Negociação* [*Trading Pit*].

(j) permitir o livre acesso à *Roda de Negociação* [*Trading Pit*] para o público visitante durante o horário de funcionamento no âmbito da 34ª EDIÇÃO DA BIENAL DE SÃO PAULO. O acesso poderá ser restrito apenas em virtude do limite máximo de ocupação da *Roda de Negociação* [*Trading Pit*] ou por ocasião das atividades previstas na possível programação pública no âmbito da 34ª EDIÇÃO DA BIENAL DE SÃO PAULO, ou em função de restrições sanitárias relacionadas à pandemia de COVID-19.

(k) elaborar e aplicar estratégias para evitar o uso conflitante da *Roda de Negociação* [*Trading Pit*] pelo público visitante e a possível programação pública no âmbito da 34ª EDIÇÃO DA BIENAL DE SÃO PAULO.

(l) proibir discurso de ódio, assédio ou atos violentos não consensuais dentro da *Roda de Negociação* [*Trading Pit*], quer tais atos ocorram por meio de seu uso pelo público visitante, ou por meio das possíveis atividades previstas na programação pública no âmbito da 34ª EDIÇÃO DA BIENAL DE SÃO PAULO.

(m) proibir o uso de força institucional ou estatal na mediação de conflitos dentro ou nas proximidades da *Roda de Negociação* [*Trading Pit*].

(n) garantir que a *Roda de Negociação* [*Trading Pit*] não seja um pódio ou uma plataforma de discurso ou agência individual, exigindo que todas as atividades da possível programação pública no âmbito da 34ª EDIÇÃO DA BIENAL DE SÃO PAULO sejam estruturadas em torno de dois ou mais agentes distintos e idealmente agonistas.

(o) exigir que todos os agentes vinculados ou participantes da possível programação pública no âmbito da 34ª EDIÇÃO DA BIENAL DE SÃO PAULO sejam informados e cumpram os regulamentos relativos ao Uso Permitido da *Roda de Negociação* [*Trading Pit*].

(p) não obrigar os Artistas a performarem dentro da *Roda de Negociação* [*Trading Pit*] como agentes ou anfitriões das atividades previstas na possível programação pública no âmbito da 34ª EDIÇÃO DA BIENAL DE SÃO PAULO.

5.2 **Compliance with Laws.** Lessee shall use the Trading Pit in compliance with all applicable laws, statutes, rules, and regulations of any applicable federal, state or local governmental authority pertaining to Lessee's particular use of the Trading Pit.

5.3 **Lessee's Maintenance**. Subject to Artists' obligations hereunder, Lessee shall maintain the Trading Pit in a safe condition and ensure that, at all times during the ____________________, the Lessee will prevent loss of, or unnecessary additional damage to, the Trading Pit (with exception to ordinary wear and tear as a result of its Permitted Use).

5.4 **Access to Trading Pit**. Artists shall have access to the Trading Pit to inspect the Trading Pit.

5.5 **No Alterations**. Lessee may not make any permanent changes or additions to the Trading Pit without Artists' prior written consent.

5.6 **Lessee's Fixtures and Equipment**. Lessee shall have the right to install trade fixtures required by Lessee or used by it in its business and, if installed by Lessee, to remove any or all such trade fixtures from time to time during the Term, and Lessee shall remove all such trade fixtures prior to the expiration or earlier termination of this Agreement; provided, however, that Lessee shall not remove any such trade fixture, without the prior written consent of Artists, if the removal of such trade fixtures will impair the structure of the Trading Pit. Lessee shall repair and restore any damage or injury to the Trading Pit caused by the installation and/or removal of any such trade fixtures, *provided, that* Lessee shall request the prior consent of Artists before conducting any repairs on the Trading Pit. The term "trade fixtures" means any personal property placed or attached to the Trading Pit by Lessee which Lessee uses to conduct the trade or business for which Lessee occupies the Trading Pit.

5.7 **Condition Upon Surrender**. At the expiration or earlier termination of the Lease, Lessee shall surrender the Trading Pit in good order and condition (with exception to ordinary wear and tear as a result of its Permitted Use).

5.8 **Quiet Enjoyment**. Artists agree that Lessee, while paying the rental and performing its other covenants and agreements contained in this Agreement, shall peaceably and quietly have, hold and enjoy the Trading Pit for the Term without hindrance or molestation.

SECTION 6. DEFAULT; REMEDIES

6.1 **Events Of Default**. It shall be considered an "**Event of Default**" if any one or more of the following events shall occur:

(a) Payment Default. If Lessee shall fail to make payment of the Rent or other amounts payable by Lessee under this Agreement when the same becomes due and payable and such failure is not cured within ten (10) days after any of the Artists' written notice thereof, or

(q) proibir a venda, consignação ou empréstimo a *Roda de Negociação* [*Trading Pit*] e/ou este Contrato, por escrito ou digitalmente, a terceiros. A *Roda de Negociação* [*Trading Pit*] e este Contrato não estão à venda e não podem ser colecionados.

(r) envidar todos os esforços razoáveis para dar crédito (ou procurar dar crédito) aos Artistas e à Locatária, em qualquer material promocional ou outro que inclua qualquer imagem da *Roda de Negociação* [*Trading Pit*], e onde a *Roda de Negociação* [*Trading Pit*] for exibido publicamente, de forma semelhante ao seguinte: "Cortesia dos Artistas DANIEL DE PAULA, MARISSA LEE BENEDICT e DAVID RUETER e FUNDAÇÃO BIENAL DE SÃO PAULO".

5.2 **Conformidade com as Leis.** A Locatária deve usar a *Roda de Negociação* [*Trading Pit*] em conformidade com todas as leis, estatutos, normas e regulamentos de qualquer autoridade pública federal, estadual ou local relativa ao uso específico da a *Roda de Negociação* [*Trading Pit*] pela Locatária.

5.3 **Manutenção da Locatária**. Sujeito às obrigações dos Artistas nos termos deste instrumento, a Locatária deverá manter a *Roda de Negociação* [*Trading Pit*] em condições seguras e garantir que, em todos os momentos no âmbito da 34ª EDIÇÃO DA BIENAL DE SÃO PAULO, a Locatária evitará prejuízos ou danos adicionais desnecessários à *Roda de Negociação* [*Trading Pit*] (com exceção do desgaste natural como resultado de seu Uso Permitido).

5.4 **Acesso à *Roda de Negociação* [*Trading Pit*].** Os Artistas devem ter acesso à *Roda de Negociação* [*Trading Pit*] para inspecioná-lo.

5.5 **Inexistência de Alterações**. A Locatária não pode fazer quaisquer mudanças ou acréscimos permanentes à *Roda de Negociação* [*Trading Pit*] sem o consentimento prévio por escrito dos Artistas.

5.6 **Acessórios e Equipamentos da Locatária**. A Locatária terá o direito de instalar acessórios comerciais exigidos pela Locatária ou usados por ela em seus negócios e, se instalado pela Locatária, remover todos ou quaisquer acessórios comerciais de tempos em tempos durante o Prazo, e a Locatária deverá remover todos os acessórios comerciais antes do vencimento ou rescisão antecipada deste Contrato; ressalvado, no entanto, que a Locatária não remova qualquer acessório comercial sem o consentimento prévio por escrito dos Artistas, se a remoção de tais acessórios comerciais prejudicar a estrutura da *Roda de Negociação* [*Trading Pit*]. A Locatária deverá reparar e restaurar qualquer dano ou prejuízo à *Roda de Negociação* [*Trading Pit*] causado pela instalação e/ou remoção de tais acessórios comerciais, *ressalvado que* a Locatária deve solicitar o consentimento prévio dos Artistas antes de conduzir quaisquer reparos à *Roda de Negociação* [*Trading Pit*]. O termo "acessórios comerciais" significa qualquer Bem colocada ou anexada à *Roda de Negociação* [*Trading Pit*] pela Locatária que a Locatária usa para conduzir o comércio ou negócio para o qual a Locatária ocupa a *Roda de Negociação* [*Trading Pit*].

(b) Non-Payment Default. If Lessee shall fail to observe or perform any other term, covenant or condition of this Agreement and such failure is not cured by Lessee within ten (10) days after any of the Artists' written notice thereof, unless such failure cannot with due diligence be cured within such 10-day period, in which case such failure shall not be deemed to continue if Lessee proceeds promptly and with due diligence to cure the failure.

6.2 Remedies Available. If an Event of Default shall have occurred and is then continuing, in addition to any other rights or remedies the Artists may have, the Artists shall have the options to exercise any one or more of the following remedies:

(a) Request for a conflict resolution emergency meeting with the Lessee, or representatives of the Lessee;

(b) Terminate the Lease and/or this Agreement by written notice to Lessee, in which event Lessee shall immediately surrender possession of the Trading Pit to Artists and Artists may repossess the Trading Pit; or

(c) With or without terminating this Agreement, and without notice to Lessee, Artists, at their option, exercisable in their sole discretion, may initiate negotiations to attempt to re-let the Trading Pit, without advertisement, by private conversations and for any term and rental rate, which Artists in their sole discretion may determine. Lessee shall not be liable to Artists for the deficiency, if any, between all Rent and other amounts due hereunder for the entire Term and the rent paid by the new lessee applicable to the remaining Term.

6.3 Additional Damages. In the event of any termination of this Agreement or repossession of the Trading Pit or any part thereof because of an Event of Default, Artists shall be entitled to recover from Lessee the Rent and other sums required to be paid by Lessee to and including the date of such expiration, termination or repossession; and, thereafter, Lessee shall, until the end of what would have been the expiration of the Term in the absence of such expiration, termination or repossession, and whether or not the Trading Pit or any part thereof shall have been re-let, be liable to Artists for, and shall pay to Artists, as liquidated and agreed current damages, the Rent and other charges which would be payable under this Agreement by Lessee in the absence of such expiration, termination or repossession, less the proceeds, if any, of any re-letting, after deducting from such proceeds all of Artists' reasonable expenses in connection with such re-letting. Lessee shall pay such current damages on the days on which the Rent would have been payable under this Agreement in the absence of such expiration, termination or repossession, and Artists shall be entitled to recover the same from Lessee on each such day.

6.4 Cumulative Rights. Each right and remedy provided for in this Agreement shall be cumulative and shall be in addition to every other right or remedy provided for in this Agreement or now or hereafter existing at law or in equity or by statute or otherwise, and the exercise or beginning of the exercise by Artists of any one or more of the rights or remedies provided for in this Agreement or now or hereafter existing at law or in equity or by statute or otherwise shall not preclude the simultaneous or later exercise by Artists of any and all other

5.7 **Condição Após a Entrega**. No vencimento ou rescisão antecipada da Locação, a Locatária deverá entregar a *Roda de Negociação* [*Trading Pit*] em boas condições (com exceção do desgaste natural como resultado de seu Uso Permitido).

5.8 **Uso Pacífico**. Os Artistas concordam que a Locatária, ao pagar o aluguel e cumprir suas outras avenças e acordos previstos neste Contrato, deverá de forma tranquila e pacífica ter, manter e gozar da *Roda de Negociação* [*Trading Pit*] durante o Prazo, sem impedimento ou abuso.

CLÁUSULA 6. INADIMPLEMENTO; TUTELA

6.1 **Eventos de Inadimplemento**. Será considerado um "**Evento de Inadimplemento**" se um ou mais dos seguintes eventos ocorrerem:

(a) Falta de Pagamento. Se a Locatária deixar de realizar o pagamento do Aluguel ou outros montantes devidos pela Locatária nos termos deste Contrato quando o mesmo vencer e tal falha não for sanada no prazo de 10 (dez) dias após qualquer notificação por escrito dos Artistas, ou

(b) Falta de Não Pagamento. Se a Locatária deixar de observar ou cumprir qualquer outro termo, obrigação ou condição deste Contrato, e tal falha não for sanada pela Locatária no prazo de 10 (dez) dias após qualquer notificação por escrito dos Artistas, a menos que tal falha não possa ser com o devido cuidado sanada dentro de tal período de 10 dias, caso em que tal falha não será considerada permanente se a Locatária proceder imediatamente com o devido cuidado para sanar a falha.

6.2 **Tutelas Disponíveis**. Se um Evento de Inadimplemento tiver ocorrido e continuar, além de quaisquer outros direitos ou tutelas que os Artistas possam ter, os Artistas terão a opção de exercer qualquer uma ou mais das seguintes tutelas:

(a) Solicitação de reunião de emergência para resolução de conflitos com a Locatária ou representantes da Locatária;

(b) Rescindir a Locação e/ou este Contrato por notificação por escrito à Locatária, caso em que a Locatária deve imediatamente entregar a posse do Trading Pit aos Artistas e os Artistas podem retomar a posse da *Roda de Negociação* [*Trading Pit*]; ou

(c) Com ou sem rescisão deste Contrato, e sem notificação para a Locatária, os Artistas, a sua opção, exercíveis a seu exclusivo critério, podem iniciar negociações para alugar, após o fim do prazo, a *Roda de Negociação* [*Trading Pit*], sem publicidade, através de conversas privadas e por qualquer prazo e aluguel que os Artistas, a seu exclusivo critério, podem determinar.

6.3 **Indenizações Adicionais**. Em caso de rescisão deste Contrato ou reintegração de posse da *Roda de Negociação* [*Trading Pit*], ou de qualquer parte da mesma devido a um Evento de Inadimplemento, os Artistas terão o direito de ser indenizados pela Locatária a respeito do Aluguel e outras quantias exigidas pela Locatária, e incluindo a data de tal vencimento, rescisão ou reintegração de posse; e, posteriormente, a Locatária deverá, até o final do que teria sido o

rights and remedies provided for in this Agreement or now or hereafter existing at law or in equity or by statute or otherwise. Notwithstanding anything to the contrary provided herein, if an Event of Default occurs, Artists agrees to use reasonable efforts to mitigate its damages.

6.5 **Holdover.** If Lessee retains possession of the Trading Pit upon expiration of the Term by lapse of time or otherwise, Lessee shall be deemed to be holding over on a month-to-month basis and, in such event, Lessee shall pay Artists for each day of such holdover at the rate which shall be (a) for the first three (3) months of such holdover, One Hundred Percent (100%) of the amount of the Rent for the last period prior to the date of such termination and (b) for any period thereafter, One Hundred Twenty-Five Percent (125%) of the amount of the Rent for the last period prior to the date of such termination, plus all additional amounts payable under this Agreement, prorated on a daily basis. In the event of a holdover, Lessee shall be liable to Artists for any and all costs, expenses, losses, damages, or claims that Artists may incur arising from the holdover.

SECTION 7. MISCELLANEOUS

7.1 **Notices.** All notices required or permitted hereunder shall be in writing and shall be deemed to be delivered (a) when actually received if personally delivered, (b) on the first business day following deposit of such notice with a nationally recognized overnight courier service for next business day delivery, or (c) three (3) business days after deposit in the United States Mail, postage prepaid, certified mail, return receipt requested, addressed to Artists or Lessee, as the case may be, as follows:

If to Artists:

Attn: Daniel de Paula, Marissa Lee Benedict, and David Rueter

If to Lessee:

Attn:

vencimento do Prazo na ausência de tal vencimento, rescisão ou reintegração de posse, e se a *Roda de Negociação* [*Trading Pit*] ou qualquer parte do mesmo tiver sido alugado novamente ou não, ser responsável em relação aos Artistas por, e pagar aos Artistas, conforme liquidado e acordado por indenização atual, o Aluguel e outros encargos que seriam devidos nos termos deste Contrato pela Locatária na ausência de tal vencimento, rescisão ou reintegração de posse, menos os rendimentos, se houver, de qualquer nova locação, após deduzir de tais rendimentos todas as despesas razoáveis dos Artistas em relação a tal nova locação. A Locatária deverá pagar tais indenizações atuais nos dias em que o Aluguel teria sido devido nos termos deste Contrato na ausência de tal vencimento, rescisão ou reintegração de posse, e os Artistas terão o direito de ser indenizados pelo mesmo da Locatária em cada um desses dias.

6.4 Direitos Cumulativos. Cada direito e tutela previsto neste Contrato será cumulativo e será adicionado a todos os outros direitos ou tutelas previstos neste Contrato, existentes agora ou no futuro pela lei ou por equidade, ou por estatuto ou de outra forma, e o exercício ou início do exercício pelos Artistas de qualquer um ou mais dos direitos ou tutelas previstos neste Contrato, existentes agora ou no futuro pela lei ou por equidade, ou por estatuto ou de outra forma, não deve impedir o exercício simultâneo ou posterior pelos Artistas de todos e quaisquer outros direitos e tutelas previstos neste Contrato, existentes agora ou no futuro pela lei ou por equidade, ou por estatuto ou de outra forma. Não obstante qualquer disposição em contrário prevista neste documento, se ocorrer um Evento de Inadimplemento, os Artistas concordam em envidar esforços razoáveis para mitigar seus danos.

6.5 Continuação na Posse. Se a Locatária preservar a posse do Trading Pit após o vencimento do Prazo por decurso de tempo ou de outra forma, a Locatária será considerado como detendo em uma base mês a mês e, em tal caso, a Locatária deverá pagar aos Artistas por cada dia de tal continuação na posse a taxa que será (a) durante os primeiros 3 (três) meses de tal continuação na posse, 100% (cem por cento) do montante do Aluguel para o último período anterior à data de tal rescisão e (b) para qualquer período posterior, 125% (cento e vinte e cinco por cento) do montante do aluguel para o último período antes da data de rescisão, mais todos os montantes adicionais devidos nos termos deste Contrato, proporcionais em uma base diária. No caso de continuação na posse, a Locatária será responsável perante os Artistas por todos e quaisquer custos, despesas, prejuízos, danos ou reivindicações que os Artistas possam incorrer decorrentes da continuação na posse.

CLÁUSULA 7. DISPOSIÇÕES GERAIS

7.1 Notificações. Todas as notificações exigidas ou permitidas neste documento devem ser por escrito e devem ser consideradas entregues (a) quando efetivamente recebidas, se entregues pessoalmente, (b) no primeiro dia útil após o depósito de tal notificação em um serviço de correio expresso reconhecido nacionalmente para o próximo dia útil de entrega, ou (c) 3 (três) dias úteis após o depósito no correio dos Estados Unidos, com postagem pré-paga, carta registrada, aviso de recebimento solicitado, endereçado aos Artistas ou à Locatária, conforme o caso, da seguinte forma:

Either party hereto may change the address for notice specified above by giving the other party written notice of such change of address.

7.2 **Severability**. If any provision of this Agreement is found by a court of competent jurisdiction to be illegal, invalid or unenforceable, the remainder of this Agreement will not be affected, and in lieu of each provision which is found to be illegal, invalid, or unenforceable, there will be added as a part of this Agreement a provision as similar to such illegal, invalid, or unenforceable provision as may be possible and be legal, valid, and enforceable.

7.3 **Entire Agreement**. This Agreement constitutes the full and entire understanding and agreement between the parties with respect to the subject matter hereof, and any other written or oral agreement relating to the subject matter hereof existing between the parties is expressly superseded by this Agreement. Lessee acknowledges that it has read the manifesto attached hereto as Exhibit D and that such acknowledgment is a material inducement for the Artists to enter into this Agreement.

7.4 **Headings**. The headings preceding the text of the paragraphs and subparagraphs hereof are inserted solely for convenience of reference and shall not constitute a part of this Agreement, nor shall they affect its meaning, construction or effect.

7.5 **Confidentiality**. Lessee and its directors, employees, representatives and agents agree to keep and cause to keep the terms of this Agreement and all documentary or verbal information concerning the circumstances leading to or surrounding this Agreement absolutely confidential and will not publicize or disclose such confidential information to anyone without the Artists' prior written consent.

7.6 **Governing Law**. This Agreement shall be governed by the internal law of the State of Illinois, without regard to conflict of law principles that would result in the application of any law other than the law of the State of Illinois.

7.7 **Counterparts**. This Agreement may be executed in a number of identical counterparts, each of which shall be deemed an original, but all of which together shall constitute one and the same instrument. Counterparts may be delivered via electronic mail (including pdf or any electronic signature complying with the U.S. federal ESIGN Act of 2000, *e.g.*, www.docusign.com) or other transmission method and any counterpart so delivered shall be deemed to have been duly and validly delivered and be valid and effective for all purposes.

7.8 **Force Majeure**. Neither party will be liable in damages or have the right to terminate this Agreement for any delay of default in performance if such delay or default is caused by conditions beyond its control including, but not limited to, Acts of God, governmental restrictions unrelated to the COVID-19 pandemic, wars, insurrections, natural disasters, such as

Se para os Artistas:

DANIEL DE PAULA, MARISSA LEE BENEDICT e DAVID RUETER
Rua Alves Guimarães, 265, apto. 10,
São Paulo/SP, 05410-000, Brasil

Se para a Locatária:

FUNDAÇÃO BIENAL DE SÃO PAULO
Parque Ibirapuera, Portão 03,
Pavilhão Ciccillio Matarazzo,
São Paulo/SP, 04094-050, Brasil

Qualquer uma das partes pode mudar o endereço para notificação especificada acima, dando à outra parte notificação por escrito de tal mudança de endereço.

7.2 **Autonomia das Disposições**. Se qualquer disposição deste Contrato for considerada por um tribunal de jurisdição competente como ilegal, inválida ou inexequível, o restante deste Contrato não será afetado, e em vez de cada disposição considerada ilegal, inválida ou inexequível, será adicionada como parte deste Contrato uma cláusula semelhante a tal cláusula ilegal, inválida ou inexequível conforme possível e legal, válida e exequível.

7.3 **Acordo Integral**. Este Contrato constitui o entendimento e acordo total e integral entre as partes com relação ao objeto tratado neste documento, e qualquer outro contrato escrito ou verbal relacionado ao objeto existente entre as partes está expressamente cancelado e substituído por este Contrato. A Locatária reconhece que leu o manifesto anexo a este documento como Anexo "D" e que tal reconhecimento e um incentivo material para os Artistas celebrarem este Contrato.

7.4 **Títulos**. Os títulos que precedem o texto dos parágrafos e subparágrafos deste documento são inseridos apenas para conveniência de referência e não devem constituir uma parte deste Contrato, nem devem afetar seu significado, interpretação ou efeito.

7.5 **Lei Aplicável**. Este Contrato será regido pela lei interna do Estado de Illinois, sem levar em consideração as normas de conflitos de lei que resultariam na aplicação de qualquer lei, exceto a lei do Estado de Illinois.

7.6 **Vias**. Este Contrato pode ser celebrado em várias vias idênticas, cada uma das quais deve ser considerada um original, mas todas juntas devem constituir um e o mesmo instrumento. As vias podem ser entregues por correio eletrônico (incluindo pdf ou qualquer assinatura eletrônica em conformidade com a Lei Federal ESIGN dos EUA de 2000, por exemplo, www.docusign.com), ou outro método de transmissão, e qualquer via assim entregue será considerada devidamente e validamente entregue, e válida e em vigor para todos os fins.

earthquakes, hurricanes or floods and/or any other cause beyond reasonable control of the party whose performance is affected.

7.9 **WAIVER OF JURY TRIAL**. EACH PARTY HERETO HEREBY IRREVOCABLY WAIVES, TO THE FULLEST EXTENT PERMITTED BY APPLICABLE LAW, ANY RIGHT IT MAY HAVE TO A TRIAL BY JURY IN ANY LEGAL PROCEEDING DIRECTLY OR INDIRECTLY ARISING OUT OF OR RELATING TO THIS AGREEMENT OR ANY OTHER LOAN DOCUMENT OR THE TRANSACTIONS CONTEMPLATED HEREBY OR THEREBY (WHETHER BASED ON CONTRACT, TORT OR ANY OTHER THEORY). EACH PARTY HERETO (A) CERTIFIES THAT NO REPRESENTATIVE, AGENT OR ATTORNEY OF ANY OTHER PERSON HAS REPRESENTED, EXPRESSLY OR OTHERWISE, THAT SUCH OTHER PERSON WOULD NOT, IN THE EVENT OF LITIGATION, SEEK TO ENFORCE THE FOREGOING WAIVER AND (B) ACKNOWLEDGES THAT IT AND THE OTHER PARTIES HERETO HAVE BEEN INDUCED TO ENTER INTO THIS AGREEMENT AND THE OTHER LOAN DOCUMENTS BY, AMONG OTHER THINGS, THE MUTUAL WAIVERS AND CERTIFICATIONS IN THIS SECTION.

[***Remainder of Page Left Intentionally Blank***]

7.7 **Força Maior**. Nenhuma das partes será responsabilizada por danos ou terá o direito de rescindir este Contrato por qualquer atraso em descumprimento do desempenho se tal atraso ou descumprimento for causado por condições além de seu controle, incluindo, mas não se limitando a, caso fortuito, restrições governamentais não relacionadas à pandemia de COVID-19, guerras, insurreições, desastres naturais, como terremotos, furacões ou inundações e/ou qualquer outra causa além do controle razoável da parte cujo desempenho é afetado.

7.8 **RENÚNCIA A JULGAMENTO POR JÚRI**. CADA UMA DAS PARTES RENUNCIA IRREVOGAVELMENTE, DENTRO DOS LIMITES PERMITIDOS PELA LEI APLICÁVEL, A QUALQUER DIREITO QUE POSSA TER A UM JULGAMENTO POR JÚRI EM QUALQUER PROCESSO JUDICIAL DIRETA OU INDIRETAMENTE DECORRENTE DE, OU RELACIONADO A ESTE CONTRATO OU QUALQUER OUTRO DOCUMENTO DE EMPRÉSTIMO, OU AS OPERAÇÕES PREVISTAS NESTE OU POR ESTE DOCUMENTO (SEJA COM BASE EM CONTRATO, ATO ILÍCITO OU QUALQUER OUTRA TEORIA). CADA UMA DAS PARTES (A) CERTIFICA QUE NENHUM REPRESENTANTE, AGENTE OU ADVOGADO DE QUALQUER OUTRA PESSOA REPRESENTOU, EXPRESSAMENTE OU DE OUTRA FORMA, QUE ESSA OUTRA PESSOA NÃO IRIA, EM CASO DE LITÍGIO, PROCURAR FAZER CUMPRIR A RENÚNCIA ANTERIOR E (B) RECONHECE QUE ELE E AS OUTRAS PARTES DESTE INSTRUMENTO FORAM INDUZIDAS A CELEBRAR ESTE CONTRATO E OS OUTROS DOCUMENTOS DE EMPRÉSTIMO POR, ENTRE OUTRAS COISAS, RENÚNCIAS MÚTUAS E CERTIFICAÇÕES NESTA SEÇÃO.

[*Restante da Página Deixada Intencionalmente em Branco*]

IN WITNESS WHEREOF, Artists and Lessee have executed this Agreement as of the day and year first written above.

ARTISTS:

____
Daniel de Paula

____
Marissa Lee Benedict

____
David Rueter

LESSEE:

By: ______________________________
Name:
Title:

EM TESTEMUNHO DO QUE, os Artistas e a Locatária assinaram este Contrato a partir do dia e ano escritos acima.

ARTISTAS:

DANIEL DE PAULA

MARISSA LEE BENEDICT

DAVID RUETER

LOCATÁRIA:

FUNDAÇÃO BIENAL DE SÃO PAULO

NOME: Antônio Thomaz Lessa Garcia Júnior

CARGO: superintendente executivo

EXHIBIT A

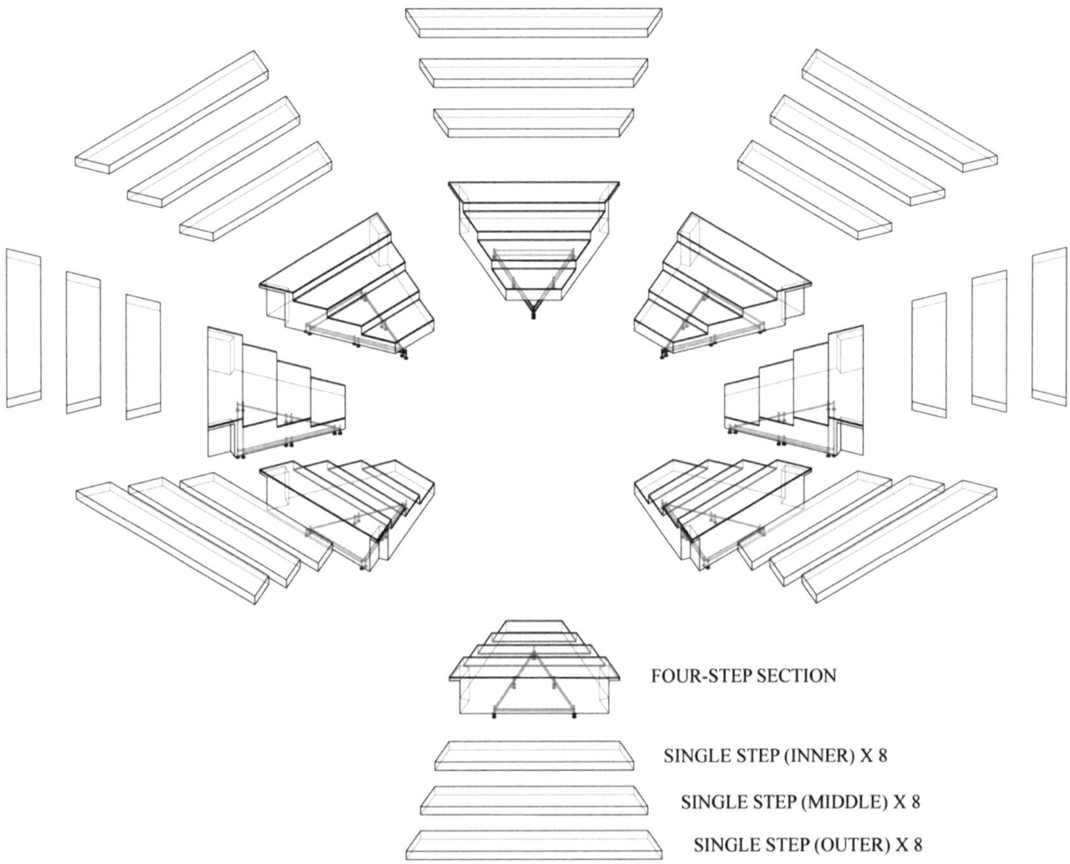
FOUR-STEP SECTION
SINGLE STEP (INNER) X 8
SINGLE STEP (MIDDLE) X 8
SINGLE STEP (OUTER) X 8

ANEXO A

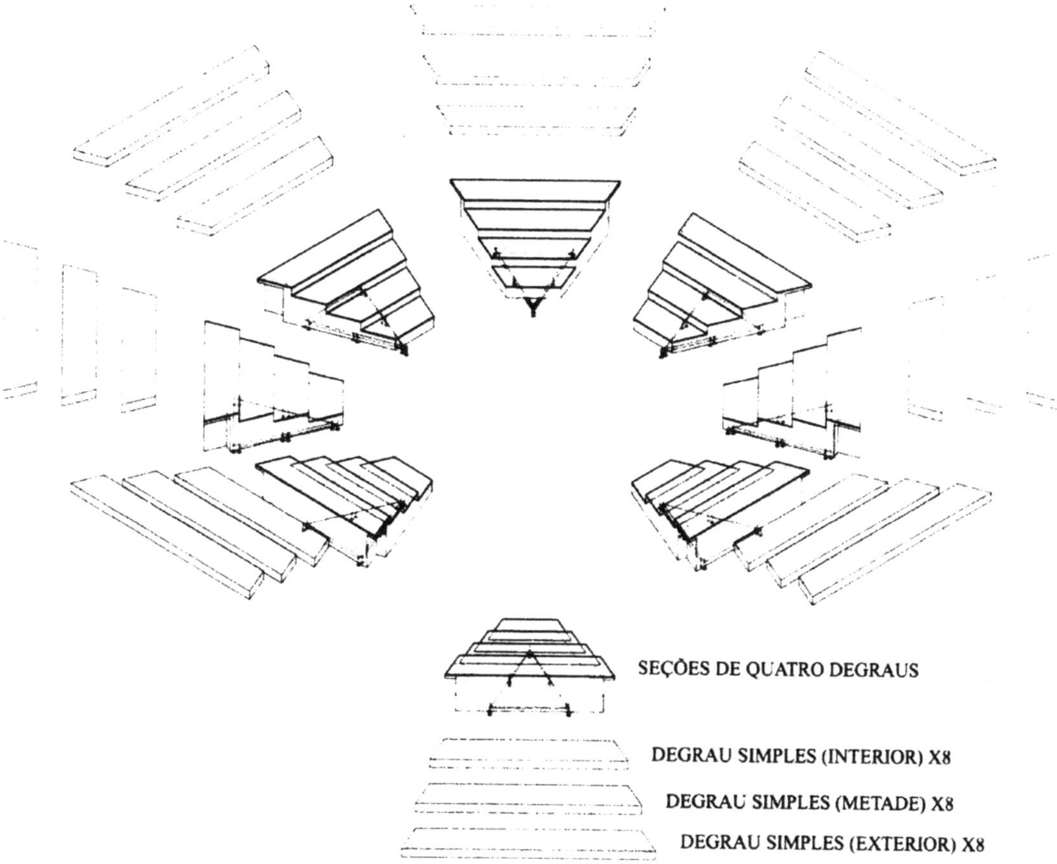
SEÇÕES DE QUATRO DEGRAUS
DEGRAU SIMPLES (INTERIOR) X8
DEGRAU SIMPLES (METADE) X8
DEGRAU SIMPLES (EXTERIOR) X8

EXHIBIT B

TOP VIEW

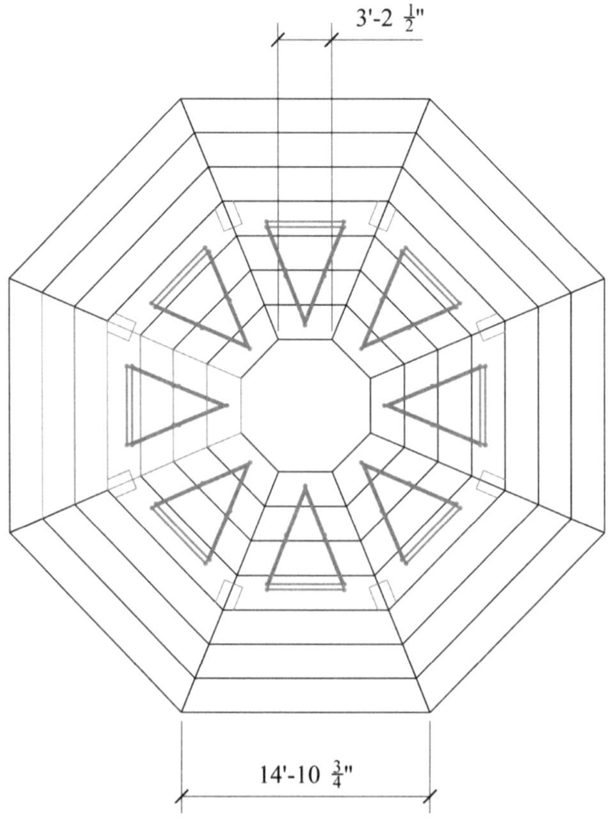

TOTAL AREA

$$Atotal = Aouter - Ainner$$

$$Aoctagon = 2(1+\sqrt{2})a^2$$

$$Aouter = 2(1+\sqrt{2})(14.854ft)^2 = 1065ft^2$$
$$Ainner = 2(1+\sqrt{2})(3.208ft)^2 = 49.69ft^2$$

$$Atotal = 1065ft^2 - 49.69ft^2 = 1015.31ft^2$$

$$Atotal = 0.0233ac$$

ANEXO B

VISTA AÉREA

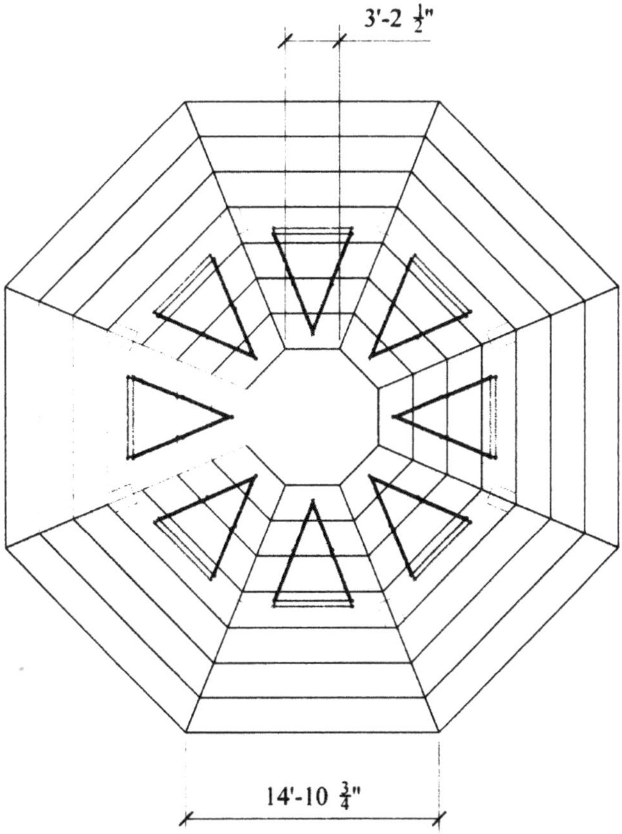

ÁREA TOTAL (unidade: pés)

$$Atotal = Aouter - Ainner$$

$$Aoctagon = 2(1 + \sqrt{2})a^2$$

$$Aouter = 2(1 + \sqrt{2})(14.854ft)^2 = 1065ft^2$$
$$Ainner = 2(1 + \sqrt{2})(3.208ft)^2 = 49.69ft^2$$

$$Atotal = 1065ft^2 - 49.69ft^2 = 1015.31ft^2$$

$$Atotal = 0.0233ac$$

EXHIBIT C

ENUNCIATION:

This is a trading pit.

It is an instrument of finance built in Chicago.

It was used in the 19th, 20th, and 21st centuries, but computer technology made it obsolete.

It was designed to optimize communication between people as they bought and sold agricultural commodities, and their futures.

It determined prices of grains such as corn, soya, and wheat for the global markets.

Many bodies, mostly white and mostly male, fought and yelled at each other in the pit.

It holds the weight of land, labor, and capital.

It is part of complex stories of violence and exploitation.

It is too heavy for only us.

It is never going back together the way it was before.

The trading pit cannot be sold.

This is a temporary installation.

ANEXO C

ENUNCIADO:

Isto é uma roda de negociação.

Um dispositivo financeiro construído em Chicago.

A roda de negociação foi utilizada nos séculos XIX, XX e XXI, mas tecnologias computacionais a tornaram obsoleta.

A roda de negociação foi projetada para otimizar a comunicação entre pessoas enquanto compravam e vendiam commodities agrícolas e seus futuros.

A roda de negociação era determinante para a precificação de grãos como milho, soja e trigo para mercados globais.

Corpos, majoritariamente brancos e masculinos, enfrentaram-se aos gritos e empurrões dentro da roda de negociação.

A roda de negociação contém o peso da terra, do trabalho e do capital.

A roda de negociação faz parte de complexas histórias de violência e exploração.

A roda de negociação é pesada demais para nós.

A roda de negociação nunca voltará a ser o que era antes.

A roda de negociação não pode ser vendida.

Trata-se de uma instalação temporária.

EXHIBIT D

UNITED STATES PATENT OFFICE.

DANIEL DE PAULA OF BRAZIL
MARISSA LEE BENEDICT AND DAVID RUETER OF THE USA

IMPROVEMENT IN TRADING-PITS.

Specification forming part of Letters Patent No. **203,837,** dated May 21, 1878; application filed December 19, 1877.

To all whom it may concern:

WE[1] HAVE A TRADING PIT.[2]

IT IS SIGNIFICANT BECAUSE IT WAS USED IN THE 19TH, 20TH & 21ST CENTURIES,[3] BUT NOW IT IS OBSOLETE. IT IS OBSOLETE BECAUSE COMPUTER TECHNOLOGY AUTOMATED THE PRACTICES IT WAS DESIGNED FOR.[4]

WE GOT IT FOR FREE WHEN THEY THREW IT AWAY.[5] IT IS VERY HEAVY AND VERY BIG. IT IS BOTH MATERIAL AND IMAGE. IT HOLDS THE WEIGHT OF LAND, LABOR, AND CAPITAL.[6]

MANY BODIES, MOSTLY WHITE AND MOSTLY MALE, FOUGHT AND YELLED AT EACH OTHER IN THE PIT.[7]

WE WANT TO PUT THE PIT IN A GALLERY. OR A PUBLIC SQUARE. OR A WAREHOUSE OR STORAGE FACILITY. OR A UNIVERSITY. FIRST IN PIECES. THEN AS A WHOLE THING AGAIN. WE ARE AWARE IT IS NEVER GOING BACK TOGETHER THE WAY IT WAS BEFORE.

WE WANT TO TALK ABOUT IT, WE WANT TO LISTEN TO IT, WE WANT TO TALK TO IT. WE WANT TO DISSECT IT, TEAR IT APART, WEAR IT DOWN.

WE WANT IT TO HOST CONTEXTUAL PUBLIC PROGRAMS.[8] IT IS TOO HEAVY FOR JUST US. IT CONTAINS THE POSSIBILITY OF A PUBLIC. THIS PUBLIC MIGHT NOT GET ALONG WELL BUT WE THINK IT NEEDS TO GET TOGETHER AND FIGURE SOME THINGS OUT.

WE WANT TO MOVE IT AROUND. IT MAY KEEP MOVING, MAYBE FOR YEARS. WE THINK IT SHOULD MOVE SOUTH. ITS WEIGHT WILL GOUGE HOLES AS IT IS DRAGGED. IT WILL GENERATE FRICTION.

WE WANT IT TO SIT WITH PEOPLE AND PLACES WHO HAVE BEEN AFFECTED BY IT. IT IS PART OF COMPLEX STORIES OF VIOLENCE AND EXPLOITATION.[9]

WE WANT IT TO HOUSE A DEBATE ABOUT WHAT IT DISPLACES, AND WHAT DISPLACES IT. WE WANT TO EXTRADITE IT. WE WANT TO EXPOSE IT TO POTENTIAL EXPULSION.

THE PIT CANNOT BE SOLD. THIS IS A TEMPORARY INSTALLATION.[10]

Fig. 1.

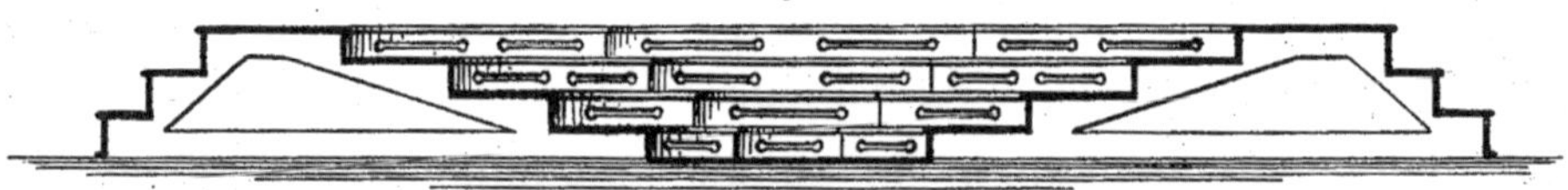

Fig. 2.

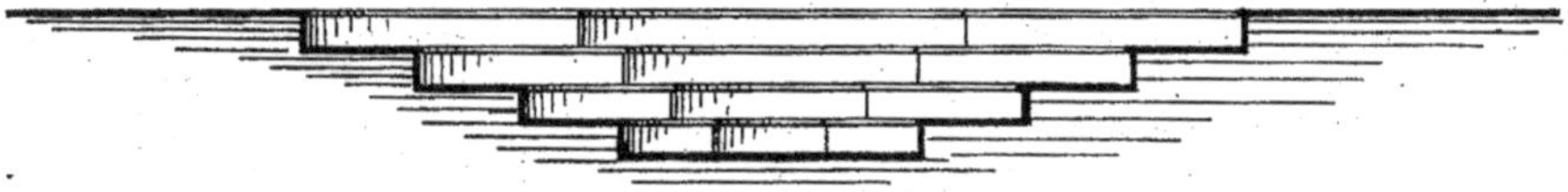

N. PETERS, PHOTO-LITHOGRAPHER, WASHINGTON, D. C.

ANEXO D

ESCRITÓRIO DE PATENTES DOS ESTADOS UNIDOS.

DANIEL DE PAULA DO BRASIL
MARISSA LEE BENEDICT E DAVID RUETER DOS EUA.

INOVAÇÃO DA RODA DE NEGOCIAÇÃO (TRADING-PIT).

Parte constituinte de especificação da Carta da Patente nº 203,937, de 21 de Maio de 1878; requerimento de 19 de Dezembro de 1877.

A todos que possam interessar:

NÓS[1] TEMOS UMA RODA DE NEGOCIAÇÃO *(TRADING PIT)*.[2]

TRATA-SE DE UMA ESTRUTURA EMBLEMÁTICA DEVIDO A SEU USO NOS SÉCULOS XIX, XX & XXI,[3] MAS QUE SE TORNOU OBSOLETA DEVIDO ÀS TECNOLOGIAS QUE SUBSTITUÍRAM AS PRÁTICAS PARA AS QUAIS HAVIA SIDO PROJETADA.[4]

NÓS A CONSEGUIMOS DE FORMA GRATUITA EM SEU MOMENTO DE DESCARTE.[5] TRATA-SE DE ALGO MUITO PESADO E MUITO GRANDE. É SIMULTANEAMENTE MATERIALIDADE E IMAGEM, E CONTÉM O PESO DA TERRA, DO TRABALHO E DO CAPITAL.[6]

MUITOS CORPOS, MAJORITARIAMENTE BRANCOS E MASCULINOS, ENFRENTARAM-SE AOS GRITOS E EMPURRÕES DENTRO DESTA ESTRUTURA.[7]

NÓS QUEREMOS COLOCAR A ESTRUTURA EM UMA GALERIA, UMA PRAÇA PÚBLICA, UM GALPÃO, OU UMA UNIVERSIDADE, PRIMEIRO EM PEDAÇOS E DEPOIS INTEGRALMENTE. NÓS SABEMOS QUE ELA NUNCA VOLTARÁ A SER O QUE ERA ANTES.

NÓS QUEREMOS CONVERSAR SOBRE A ESTRUTURA, ESCUTÁ-LA, FALAR COM ELA. QUEREMOS DISSECÁ-LA, RASGÁ-LA E DESGASTÁ-LA.

NÓS QUEREMOS QUE A ESTRUTURA ABRIGUE PROGRAMAÇÕES PÚBLICAS E CONTEXTUAIS.[8] A ESTRUTURA É PESADA DEMAIS APENAS PARA NÓS. ELA CONTÉM EM SI A POTENCIALIDADE DE UM PÚBLICO. ESTE PÚBLICO PODE NÃO SE DAR BEM ENTRE SI, MAS ACREDITAMOS QUE ESSAS PESSOAS PRECISAM SE ENCONTRAR PARA RESOLVER CERTAS QUESTÕES.

NÓS QUEREMOS DESLOCÁ-LA E DEIXÁ-LA EM MOVIMENTO, POSSIVELMENTE POR VÁRIOS ANOS. QUEREMOS LEVÁ-LA PARA O SUL. AO SER ARRASTADA, SEU PESO IRÁ GERAR ATRITO E PRODUZIR BURACOS.

NÓS QUEREMOS QUE A ESTRUTURA SENTE COM AS PESSOAS E LUGARES QUE AFETOU. ELA FAZ PARTE DE COMPLEXAS HISTÓRIAS DE VIOLÊNCIA E EXPLORAÇÃO.[9]

NÓS QUEREMOS ABRIGAR UM DEBATE DENTRO DA ESTRUTURA. UM DEBATE SOBRE O QUE ELA MOVE E O QUE A MOVE. QUEREMOS EXTRADITÁ-LA. QUEREMOS EXPÔ-LA À EXPULSÃO.

A ESTRUTURA NÃO PODE SER VENDIDA. TRATA-SE DE UMA INSTALAÇÃO TEMPORÁRIA.[10]

Fig. 1.

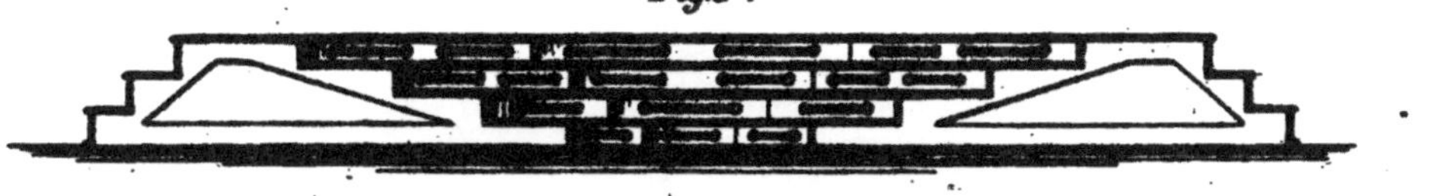

Fig. 2.

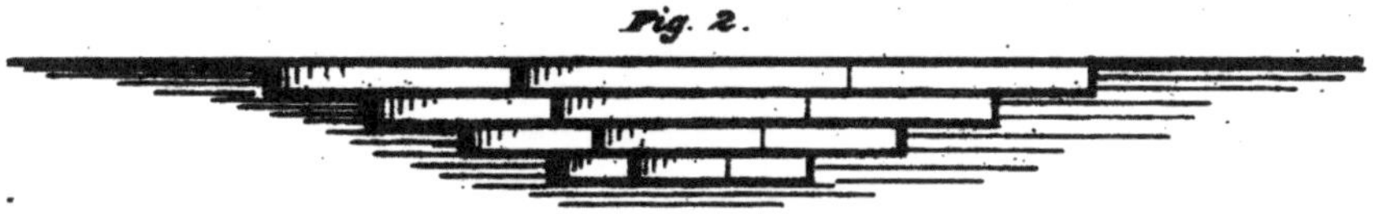

N. PETERS, FOTO-LITOGRAVURISTA, WASHINGTON, D. C.

D. DE PAULA. M. BENEDICT. D. RUETER.
Trading-Pit

N°. 203,837 Patented May 21, 1878.

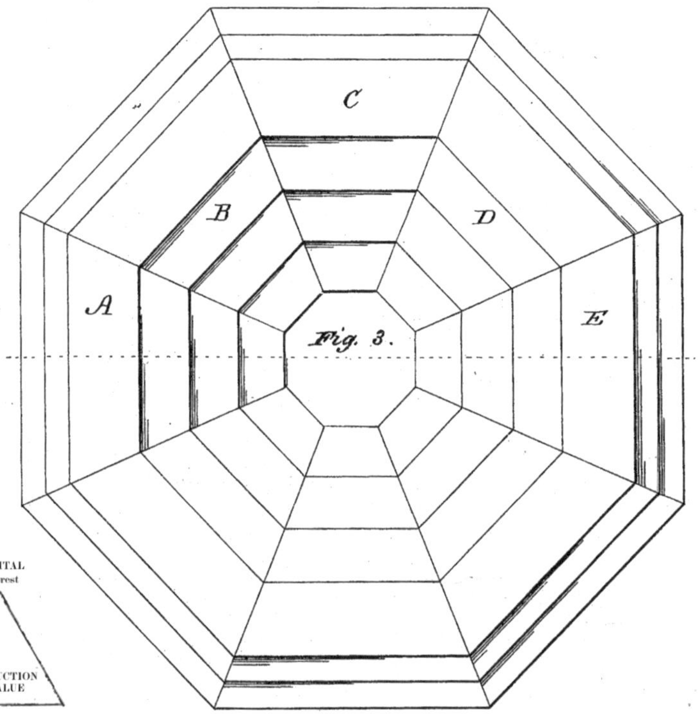

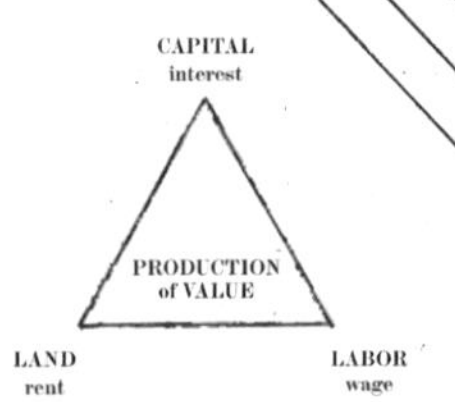

1. We, henceforth, refers to the three artists involved in the project: Daniel de Paula, Marissa Lee Benedict, and David Rueter.
2. The project began with the last-minute salvage of a 12-meter in diameter octagonal trading pit from the grain room trading floor of the Chicago Board of Trade (CBOT). Consisting of a series of stepped platforms, facing each other, and descending to a center space, the structure was designed to optimize peer-to-peer communication for commodities trading. Verbal signals and hand gestures were used by trading professionals in the pit to buy and sell a particular asset: in this case corn futures contracts legal agreements or obligations to deliver a quantity of a particular grade of corn at a specified future date.
3. In 1878, Ruben S. Jennings of Chicago attempted but failed to enforce a patent for "a new and Improved Trading Pit or Platform." In active use at the CBOT since 1870, the trading pit design borrows from classical Western architectures of social representation, exchange, and spectacle: from the agora of Greece and the Roman Forum, to amphitheaters and parliaments across the globe. Similarly designed trading floors were later replicated throughout financial markets worldwide due to their capacity to optimize trade.
4. The CBOT's grain trading room, responsible for determining prices of grains such as corn, soya, and wheat for the global markets, ceased operation in 2015 after years of decreasing physical use driven by the proliferation of electronic trading. The once tangible and visible architecture of the trading pit is sinking into the obscurity of the black box server racks of the contemporary world interior of capital.
5. On August 6th 2018, artist Daniel de Paula contacted K.L., real estate manager at the Chicago Mercantile Exchange Group (CME, owner of the CBOT), to request, for research purposes, detailed plans or 3D architectural models of the grain room trading floor. In their exchanges, K.L. informed de Paula that the CME Group was currently in the process of disposing of the corn pit. All of the other grain trading pits had already been dismantled and removed from the commodities trading floor. Realizing there was a short time window for possible salvage, de Paula began a series of email exchanges and negotiations. In the process, a collaboration with artists David Rueter and Marissa Lee Benedict was initiated. de Paula, Rueter and Benedict jointly financed the salvage through personal loans and revolving credit, and, finally, with on-site assistance and in-kind contributions from artist Dan Peterman and contractor G. Lane, the corn pit was brought in six dump truck loads to a warehouse managed by Ken Dunn's Resource Center located on the South Side of Chicago.
6. The pit bears a double weight: the weight of its thick layers of rubber, wood, and honeycomb aluminum, and the weight of the millions of transactions transporting masses of corn from one piece of land to another, enriching certain bodies and territories, and extracting from others.
7. A visit to a trading pit in action would yield a bodily metaphor for the gendered and racial violence endemic to the financial system, while electronic price feeds appear more innocent of such implications.
8. Any exhibiting institution will agree to enter into negotiations with the artists (de Paula, Rueter, and Benedict) to generate a contract specifying a framework for contextual programming that activates the pit and its history by staging various forms of adversarial investigation and exchange. The contract will provide guidelines for positioning the pit and the bodies that occupy it.
9. The expansion of the global production of grain commodities, especially soya and corn, conceals an interest in rural real estate as a financial asset. Consequently, in countries such as Brazil, the accelerated territorial occupation of agribusiness, stimulated by financial agents, electronic trading, and international investment and pension funds, leads to recurring violent practices such as land grabbing and deforestation, along with violence committed towards local peasant and indigenous communities, revealing inextricable colonial-era holdovers that continually organize space.
10. The pit is not to be owned by any single institution or individual, although a multitude of institutions may play a key role in its logistical transportation, maintenance, rental, installation, programming, and public exhibition. The continued displacement of the pit will necessarily wear it down, rendering it finite and unmonumental.

D. DE PAULA. M. BENEDICT. D. RUETER.

Roda de Negociação (Trading-Pit)

N°. 203,837 Patenteado em 21 de Maio de 1878.

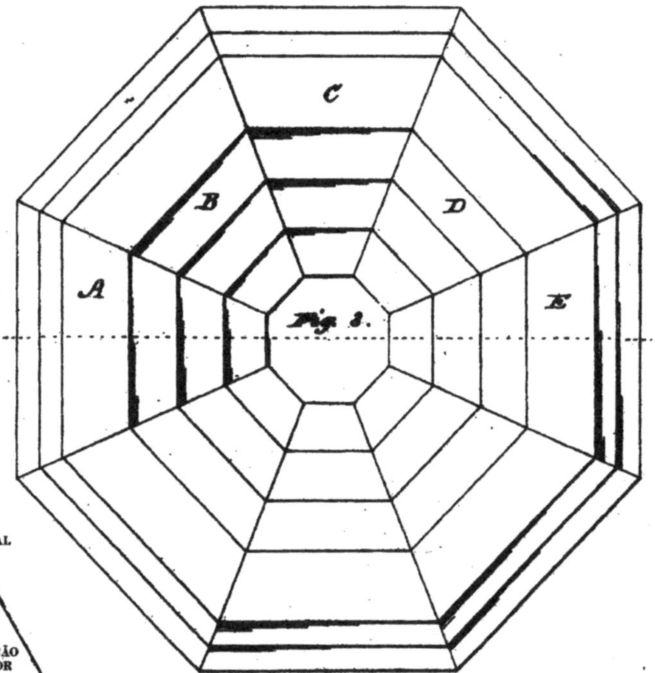

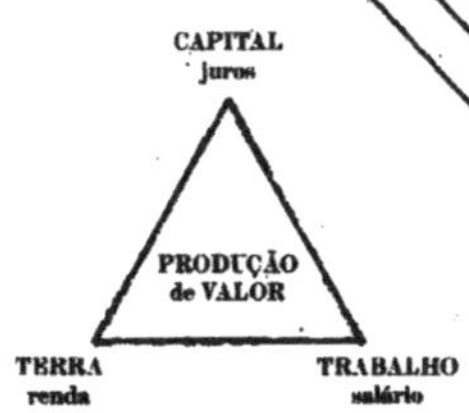

1. Nós, a partir de agora, designa os três artistas proponentes do projeto: Daniel de Paula, Marissa Lee Benedict e David Rueter.
2. O projeto teve início em meio à apropriação de última hora de uma roda de negociação (*trading pit*) octogonal de 12 metros de diâmetro, previamente utilizada no pregão de grãos da junta comercial de Chicago, o Chicago Board of Trade (CBOT). Consistindo de uma série de plataformas escalonadas, frente a frente e descendo para um espaço central, a estrutura da roda de negociação foi projetada para otimizar a comunicação entre operadores financeiros para o comércio de *commodities*. Sinais verbais e gestos feitos com as mãos eram empregados pelos operadores dentro da roda de negociação para comprar e vender um ativo específico: nesse caso, contratos futuros de milho - acordos ou obrigações legais para pagamento e entrega de uma quantidade e qualidade determinada de milho em uma data futura especificada.
3. Em 1878, Ruben S. Jennings, de Chicago, fracassou ao tentar patentear "uma nova e aprimorada roda de negociação". Em uso ativo na junta comercial de Chicago (CBOT) desde 1870, a configuração da roda de negociação foi influenciada por clássicas arquiteturas ocidentais de representação social, troca e espetáculo: da ágora Grega e do Fórum Romano a anfiteatros e parlamentos em todo o mundo. Rodas e estruturas semelhantes foram posteriormente replicadas em mercados financeiros e pregões de todo o mundo devido à sua capacidade de otimizar o comércio.
4. O pregão viva voz de grãos da junta comercial de Chicago (CBOT), determinante para a precificação de grãos como milho, soja e trigo para os mercados globais, interrompeu suas operações em 2015, após anos de diminuição do uso físico impulsionada pela proliferação do comércio eletrônico. A arquitetura outrora tangível e visível da roda de negociação está agora afundando-se em meio à obscuridade das prateleiras dos servidores de caixa preta do interior do capital do mundo contemporâneo.
5. Em 6 de agosto de 2018, o artista Daniel de Paula entrou em contato com K.L., gerente imobiliário do Chicago Mercantile Exchange Group (CME, grupo proprietário do CBOT), solicitando, para fins de pesquisa, plantas e modelos arquitetônicos detalhados do pregão de grãos da junta comercial. Em suas trocas e conversas, K.L. informou de Paula que o grupo CME estava em processo de remoção e descarte da roda de negociação de contratos futuros de milho. Todos as outras rodas ou *trading pits* de grãos que negociavam soja, trigo, arroz etc. já haviam sido desmontadas e removidas do pregão de *commodities*. Percebendo que havia um curto espaço de tempo para uma possível apropriação, de Paula iniciou uma série de trocas e negociações por email. No processo, foi iniciada uma colaboração com os artistas David Rueter e Marissa Lee Benedict. Assim, de Paula, Rueter e Benedict financiaram conjuntamente a remoção da estrutura através de empréstimos pessoais e crédito rotativo e, finalmente, com assistência *in loco* e contribuições em espécie do artista Dan Peterman e do empreiteiro G. Lane, a roda de negociação de contratos futuros de milho foi transposta, por meio de seis caminhões basculantes, para um armazém gerenciado pelo Resource Center de Ken Dunn, localizado na zona sul de Chicago.
6. A roda de negociação tem um peso duplo: o peso de suas camadas espessas de borracha, madeira e alumínio alveolado, e o peso de milhões de transações e negociações que acarretaram no deslocamento de massas de milho de um pedaço de terra para outro, enriquecendo certos corpos e territórios, e extraindo recursos de outros.
7. Uma visita a um pregão viva voz em ação produziria uma metáfora corporal para a violência racial e de gênero endêmica ao sistema financeiro, enquanto os *feeds* e atualizações de preços eletrônicos parecem mais inocentados de tais implicações.
8. Toda e qualquer instituição expositora concorda em entrar em negociações com os artistas (de Paula, Rueter e Benedict) para gerar um contrato especificando uma estrutura para a programação contextual que ative a roda de negociação e sua respectiva história por meio de variadas formas de investigação e trocas antagônicas. O contrato fornecerá diretrizes para o posicionamento da roda de negociação e dos corpos que a ocupam.
9. A expansão da produção global de *commodities* de grãos, especialmente soja e milho, oculta o interesse sobre a terra e propriedade rural como ativo financeiro. Consequentemente, em países como o Brasil, a ocupação territorial acelerada do agronegócio, estimulada por agentes financeiros, o comércio eletrônico e fundos internacionais de investimento e pensão, leva a recorrentes práticas violentas, como a grilagem de terras e desmatamentos, além de violência cometida contra camponeses e comunidades indígenas, revelando assim heranças coloniais que organizam continuamente o espaço.
10. A roda de negociação não deve ser de propriedade de nenhuma instituição ou indivíduo, embora várias instituições possam desempenhar um papel fundamental em seu transporte logístico, manutenção, aluguel, instalação, programação e exibição pública. O deslocamento contínuo da roda de negociação necessariamente a desgastará, tornando-a finita e não-monumental.

AN OBJECT DISPLACED, A PLACE TO GATHER DIFFERENT BODIES

iii.

Paulo Miyada and Jacopo Crivelli Visconti with Marissa Lee Benedict, Daniel de Paula, and David Rueter

São Paulo (BR)
Amsterdam (NL)

Daniel de Paula What were some of the underlying factors that were determinant for the selection of the work *deposition* for the 34th Bienal de São Paulo?

Jacopo Crivelli Visconti I think there are a few central ideas of the work, *deposition*, that are in line with our curatorial thinking for the Bienal. The first is that, from a curatorial and institutional point of view, the Bienal was conceived as a dialogue. We were a team of curators in dialogue[1]—understanding that dialogue involves tension, and friction, and different views and opinions on things—which is something that I think is very central to the work *deposition*. This idea that nobody is talking by themself; there is always some kind of negotiation going on—this is very central to the exhibition, and, I think, very central to the piece.

It started, then, to make sense for us to have *deposition* in such an important place in the Bienal. We began to understand that it also made sense from an architectural point of view. Historically, it has often been the case that works in that space, the *vão* or central atrium,[2] are somehow trying to compete with the architecture in a phallic way. Very vertical, very male, white pieces are often positioned there. In the history of the Bienal exhibitions you can find several examples of towers, let's say, done in various ways.[3] We liked the idea of having something that is, in theory, aligned with, and not competing with, the architecture. We had a clear sense of this when we started moving the pieces of the trading floor around. They visually highlighted the architecture.

However, in another sense, the trading floor did compete with the building as it was a magnet for people to sit together, talk together, be together. This happened, of course, through all the programmed activities, but also in a very natural way. Often, you would go there and you would see people just sitting there. That was a very strong statement. I think this addressing of the space between things is related to the way this Bienal was conceived from the start. Curatorially, we made quite a few decisions that were not so typical for a biennial: like choosing not to work with a theme,[4] expanding the Bienal across time and place, and even presenting the same works more than once during different points of the exhibition.[5] These are things that are not so common for a biennial exhibition. We did this, I think, in a very quiet way. Our interest was not in presenting these as bold, revolutionary curatorial strategies. We did what we thought was meaningful, without shouting about it. I see this way of working as very much in line with your work *deposition*. It was a very strong piece, enormous in scale, but you could walk by it and not see it. I'm sure that a lot of people walked by it and didn't see it—and this I see as a compliment, not as a negative point.

David Rueter This makes me think of an official photo of the Bienal exhibition I came across where a number of the works in the main area were named in the article, but not *deposition*.[6] I was actually happy about that omission.

Marissa Lee Benedict It was so integrated into the architecture of the building, of the institution, and of the exhibition.

Paulo Miyada And I would add that, on another level, the curatorial statements that were positioned throughout the exhibition were a way that we found to strongly address both a historical moment and a present one,[7] and the struggles that are in place in the present that determine whether we have a future or not. Each curatorial statement was an object or a document or an image: something that was really charged with a history that we could refer to in order to tell a story, and to see how that story would resonate with what was around it. We saw the displacement of these objects as a curatorial gesture that put the history of these objects back into play in the present. In a way, *deposition* also addressed this kind of possibility of displacement: of bringing a piece of history to bear, of summoning facts—not purely in a documentary mode, but rather as a way of evoking some kind of memory. It evoked the struggles that are built around memory, built *from* and *by* a narration of the historical and social processes that surround memory.[8] We were putting memory back into play in the present, in the future, and, in doing so, promoting a new process of remembering that might develop into something else that goes beyond the original history that's been told—forming a kind of resonance. Of course, this strong relationship between *deposition* and the curatorial statements of the Bienal is not a mandatory curatorial concern. Otherwise we would have a curatorship that was always trying to find itself mimetically in the works, which would be quite bizarre. But in this case, the resonance of methodologies and referents was also meaningful. Because, in a way, the curatorial statements that the audience would find throughout the Bienal, before getting to *deposition*, could provide an approach that might help them relate to the work, or vice versa. If they hadn't noticed the statements before encountering *deposition,* but they had a powerful experience on the trading pit floor, they might go back and look again at the statements and see them in a more meaningful light.

MLB As you're speaking, I'm curious to hear more from each of you about your experience of the displacement of the corn trading pit. I think it's fascinating the way this object, the trading pit floor, was situated in the Bienal, as it was activated and occupied. But, as you say Paulo, it carries this latent history of this other space or place: the Chicago Board of Trade (CBOT). I'm curious if, for you, there was a sense that the corn trading pit had shed its history upon arriving at the Bienal? Or was it still freighted? Or perhaps, to put it another way: was there a particular sense of historical displacement, or relation, created by the placement of the floor in Oscar Niemeyer's modernist pavilion?

JCV I mean, putting together Édouard Glissant's ideas of relationality and modern architecture, as a way of seeing the work, was present from the start. There was this inherent relationship with the architecture.[9] It was also very fascinating to see how precisely the thirty-two pieces of the corn trading pit actually fit into the container. That was something very stunning. And, curiously enough, I don't know if you've ever noticed this and I don't know why—maybe Paulo, who has studied more architecture than all of us here, might know—but the 6 or 12 meter size is often recurrent in modern architecture. In this case, 12 meters is the distance between the columns in the Bienal building, the original diameter of the corn trading pit, and the length of a shipping container. I was doing a proposal recently for the UNESCO Headquarters, Paris, because there was an idea of bringing part of the Bienal exhibition there, which is not going to happen, but the columns in the building are also 6 meters apart, so it's a weird series of coincidences, or repetitions.

But anyway, that said, I think for us, in building the exhibition, we referenced this concept of displacement through the idea of circulation, which was taken up on the second floor. Circulation can be of commodities, of ideas, or of movements of a cultural kind, let's say. It can be an idea, like Négritude, or it could be a specific style, such as the modern International Style in architecture. So all these kinds of circulation—which on the second floor were more directly linked with ideas of building an image of oneself—were intertwined. And I think it was also, again, curatorially, very subtle and probably almost unnoticeable. But if you did notice, it became a very beautiful thing. As Paulo was saying, *deposition* also worked in a way as part of this statement. It was, to some extent, the statement of the second floor and not the first floor. I find this idea—that *deposition* is a work that is physically low, but that conceptually occupies the whole of the Bienal—quite powerful.

PM I guess the thing that I've read that could relate to the 12 meters that you were mentioning before, Jacopo, is this book that is quoted and referred to, but very few people have actually read, which is *Le Modulor* by Le Corbusier.[10] The text reflects on why we build things the size that we build them, and how this relates, or not, with a mind, with a problem of composition, with a mental organization of space, or with the body and the movements and the anatomy of human existence. I remember it begins by describing Roman roads, which were defined by the size of a tree trunk, or a certain log, which made the Romans build their roads a certain size for the horses and the chariots. And then those chariots defined the train, and the train defined the railways, and the railways defined the scale of the building materials they moved, and that defined the scale of consumption in industries, and so on and so forth. And maybe this eventually led to this 6 and 12 meter dimension. Le Corbusier was very critical of casuistic reasoning, pointing out that there was never a moment that we, humanity, collectively said, “You know, let’s stop and think about this. Let’s choose what really makes sense, and not just continue with this given size and that size,” and so on.

But yes, Jacopo was emphasizing circulation. What I find that the object of the trading pit does—and what was very meaningful to the Bienal—is that it was an object that itself had been displaced yet remained a place to gather different bodies. So it was a place of people arriving to meet and to negotiate. And, both in the context of the Bienal and in its previous life as a trading pit in Chicago, it was a place where different notions, ideas, and values could be brought, exchanged, and transformed. This would have effects, practical and physical effects, elsewhere. Symbolically, now, and in terms of culture, but in terms of materiality, production, accumulation, and appropriation then.[11] So, in experiencing *deposition*, you would be thinking or relating to ideas of movement, displacement, and circulation in a number of ways, all of them intertwined in both the past and the present, and, as it seems, also in the future. This is something interesting, because at a certain point, when we build a discussion about displacement or the tools of appropriation in modern and contemporary arts theory and history, a thing could be referred to as having once been here and then brought there. As in: it belonged here, and then an artist or an institution, a museum, re-placed it in another semantic and physical and visual field. But this work, *deposition*, allows us to think about displacement as a condition, rather than as a situation of adjustment.

DR What were some of the curatorial and contextual risks implicated in presenting the work *deposition* within the Bienal?

PM I saw two big sets of risks. The first set, the most tangible one when we opened the Bienal, was that we were dealing with the pandemic,[12] and occupying the center of the most visible, photographable, memorable part of the pavilion with a work that required—or at least invited—human gathering, occupation, and exchange amidst this moment in our global history in which we were very much concerned with the outcomes of human gatherings, exchanges, and meetings. So there was a real risk that the work would be there and we—meaning the curators, the curators plus the artists, the institution, a few different kinds of “we”—might end up not advising anyone to actually use it, which is always a little bit of a failure—in that you initiate a gesture and you don’t get to go all the way through with it. This is not ideal: not in art, nor politics, nor anywhere. Throughout the pandemic the health security situation was changing all the time, day after day, week after week. It made the whole planet cope with the idea of failure on a quotidian basis. So we decided it was best to at least attempt the gesture, and if it failed it would be because things were failing. The other set of risks involved in inviting people together was that people do not only carry the virus and antivirus: people carry ideas, and hate, and conflicting ideologies, and a number of misalignments in this moment. This Bienal was conceived, and happened, in a moment when dialogue was not our strongest set of skills as a society. So things could have gone out of control, so to say. In the events that we organized as an institution, the people we invited could come face to face with an audience that was unexpected, or the debate between people could go sideways—because the idea was always that we wouldn't be inviting only people who belong to a certain field, or set of ideas, or a certain profession, or a certain political alignment. The idea was that we would want to have different perspectives colliding in the pit, *in* the work. And we also understood the possibilities of spontaneous occupation of the work, which was always an aspect of *deposition*, as stated in the contract.[13] This was a part of the proposition that stood apart from the things that the institution could officially organize. People were always welcome to sit on the trading floor and do whatever. I think this is the kind of risk that a large-scale art institution of public interest should be willing to take, every day. Otherwise we could just operate as other parts of the art system do and not make such efforts to present and organize at such a large scale and in a space of such public interest and access.

JCV I agree with what Paulo said. I think, to go back to the question: it's also more than just risks. When you do a show of this size, you have to choose your battles. I think we were dedicated to choosing a lot of battles and pursuing them until the end, and in this sense, *deposition* was not an easy piece from an institutional point of view, for some of the reasons that I have mentioned before. It was not visible, you know, and not attractive on a conventional level. Embedded in the risks that Paulo mentioned, I think there was also a certain degree of courage, on our side, to say, "No, we want this piece to be there, and we stand by it, even if conversations cannot take place on the trading floor, even if people cannot gather here, even if we don't have the funds to do an amazing program with the most well-known participants who will bring a larger audience to the Bienal—we believe that this project is important, and we stand by it." It is very significant and relevant that we had to defend these choices at first. I would never say there was a strong opposition to the work—that wouldn't be true—we did have to defend it, but in the end, everybody was very happy with the piece, and everybody was very engaged. When I say everybody, I mean the institution, not just the curators or the artists, of course, or the other people who are involved in the program, you know, with Vânia Medeiros and Beatriz Cruz,[14] and so on. The whole institution was, in the end, very convinced that this was a very good piece.

I think from one point of view we have what Paulo said—the whole pandemic situation made everything harder—but, in another way, it also made it even more necessary than any of us could have imagined before. When people—the audience, but also ourselves, and yourselves, David and Marissa and Daniel—could actually sit and talk and see music or whatever was happening there, it was a very, very strong feeling that we all had. And I think, just as I always say this for the Bienal—and I think this is also true for *deposition*—we, as curators, made a very good biennial. You, as artists, made a very good piece. But the way people reacted transcended what we could have done. It was really about the moment that we were all living through; we could not control that, and we cannot take credit for that. But nevertheless, I think this was really a very strong sense for us all.

DdP A question that maybe follows that line of thought, Jacopo, is to think about the significance of a collaborative work occupying the *vão*, the center, or let's say the heart, of the exhibition in this current sociopolitical landscape.[15] Could you both develop a bit further this idea of collaboration, both in terms of your curatorial input—which was a collaborative process—but also in terms of a more general sociopolitical context as well?

JCV We've discussed the curatorial point of view of the Bienal already. However, I think there is another aspect of your collaborative practice—especially brought forth by Daniel—that is exemplified by *deposition*. I know that your work, Daniel, always carries a degree of negotiation, and particularly institutional negotiation, which I think is quite fascinating. This is probably true for all of you; it is something very central to *deposition*. I think this word, "negotiation," is interesting to bring up in answering your question about collaboration, because in the art world we have this very easy approach to an idea of collaboration: that collaboration is nice, flawless, and paved with good intentions. But when you bring the idea of negotiation, especially negotiating with institutions, this is not always so easy—but I think this, as well, is a form of collaboration. It's not the conventional idea of a collaboration, where two people meet and do something together with the same goals and the same vision from the start, but that is exactly why it's a very meaningful mode of collaboration. I know with this project, specifically through the contract, you really make a point of tensioning some of the ways that an institution normally works. You do it in a very straightforward, apparently naive way, let's say, but it's very direct and clear. What you encountered while negotiating with the Fundação Bienal de São Paulo, I wouldn't say it was the most difficult situation that you could have possibly faced because, in the end, the Bienal responded quite well. Still it took six months or more to translate the contract, and to have it signed, but I think that is normal. This is exactly why you proposed the contract in the first place, because you want to tension that gray area, of the collaboration and negotiation between the artists' way of thinking and the institutional way of thinking.[16] I find this a very important aspect of the work. And again, I see a correspondence here with the way the Bienal was more generally organized. Backstage, we—Paulo and I, especially—had to do a huge amount of negotiating with all of the institutions that were invited to be part of the Bienal. All of these negotiations and conversations with other institutions, ones very different from the Bienal, were important in making us think about the show that we wanted to do. And, like in your case, this is something that the audience just doesn't see—and it's okay that they don't see—but it's there, somewhere. I think that's important for us. In your case, 99.9 percent of the audience didn't see the contract and didn't really think about that element of the work, which is an essential part of the project. So it's a different way of thinking about the forms of collaboration that we usually engage in, especially in the art scene. And, I think, a very fascinating part of the project.

PM ______ In the case of *deposition*, the public programming added new layers of negotiation because we ended up deciding to invite Beatriz and Vânia to put together programming, and then they invited many other speakers and subjects and voices to occupy the space—but not in a monolithic way, because their program would go back and forth and alternate with things that the Bienal organization itself came up with, like the musical shows at the very end of the exhibition, and things that the curatorial team had developed beforehand or kept developing during the Bienal, like the ending with composer Neo Muyanga,[17] or other kinds of events, such as the book launches and other presentations that emerged during the process. So the programming expanded to incorporate other editors, curators, and organizers who then invited other people onto the floor, who also managed to bring with them different sources of programming and thinking. And now, looking back with perspective, I have been thinking about how in collaboration, and also possibly in negotiation, there is this naive understanding that success is when everyone rapidly agrees and no one has to give anything up. But that is not really a negotiation; that is a convergence of interests. If you agree quickly it's because you didn't have to negotiate much in the first place. It's a simple exchange. The real negotiation starts when you recognize at a certain point that there is something that is untranslatable, or unnegotiable, or that's really unfair, and yet you keep working to go beyond this acknowledgment. You see there is a problem, but then what? Then everyone has to move around and rethink where they come through, where they came from, and how they deal with it. In the end, the result is not necessarily a resolution of the sources of discontent that might arise during the process. In many cases, these discontents go back too far: they have historical depth and structural meaning. They're not something that the people sitting at the table can really solve or erase, but they can find ways to compensate, or to turn around, or to at least acknowledge the thing and then move on. This piece, *deposition*, from the beginning to the end demanded that the artists, and the curators, and the institution, and the participants, and the audience to do this *real* version of negotiation. And the thing is that it never really stopped; every now and then we had to deal with discomfort.

MLB Maybe this refers back to the residual history or the contractual elements of the work?

JCV Right. Like when the floor of *deposition* was a trading pit, and you had people negotiating something that they didn't really control at all. They couldn't see it. They couldn't smell it. They maybe didn't even fully know what it was they were participating in. I think it was very clear that you, the artists, wanted certain factors of the work to be beyond your control as a way of highlighting how this is a work; that this is a point where forces that come from great distances, and that are way bigger than this actual small point—this 12-meter-wide section of floor—converge. So I see it as a very poetic approach, let's say, to the piece, which is very much within the institutional critique of the work, but is also part of a conceptual way of thinking about art. Now you're just—for a very tiny fraction of time—in the life of this object, and you're sort of doing something with it, but in the end, it's directly connected by thousands of threads to huge things that we don't really control. I think that also became very visible through the *Conversações* programming, and through the unprogrammed things that took place in the work. In the last large events that we had—Muyanga's closing event, or the event that marked one month since the death of Jaider Esbell,[18] or the popular music shows put on by the Bienal—the trading floor really became something that people were using, and that was it. Even though we had the statement, or enunciation,[19] always read at the beginning of each event, it was something that people didn't fully process, you know, especially when we had the shows. I think that sense of being present was beautiful—the fact that it worked very well as just a platform—which I think was part of what you, the artists, had envisioned from the beginning. It all relates to this idea of the work being something that goes way beyond what you, as artists, we, as curators, or the institution alone can do, or control.

PM And that's a nice part of the work: you have negotiation and you have contracts, but you also have conversation and hearsay. So you have these very structured things that you can really condense in the telling of the work—or you can put in a book, let's say—because they're factual or documentary, but then there's everything else around the work. So when the contract lays out that this thing is the responsibility of that party, or this thing is delegated to the institution or to the artists or to the curators, etc., it's good. It's settled in the contract. But this doesn't solve how the conversations around and before and through the work might take place, and this introduces doubts, which I also like—doubts that make me ask: is this really the best way? For example, you decided not to have any documents, or the contract for the work, or original historic photos available to the public in the space. In the end you decided not to exhibit any set of documents that would contextualize the work besides the piece itself, and this was a debatable choice. I mean, you could always justify it the other way around, but in the end, I like this choice because there's so much about this work that is very factual and structured, but when you do not have documents present in the space describing this, you demand a certain level of hearsay and conversation to take place. So, the conceptual framing of the work is very structured, however if someone is standing in front of the work they will have to make an effort to speak to someone, or to overhear someone talking about it. As in: "Hmm, what was that again? What is this about?" And this activates this more ungraspable layer of the work.

DdP I think maybe this last answer could be a good transition for us to talk about the programming a bit, and maybe some of your core curatorial concerns. How were these revealed through the programming hosted within the trading pit? And, I think you touched upon this a little bit already, but were there any specific program activities that were special for both of you?

JCV Well, I think the program that Vânia and Beatriz did was very challenging from a number of points of view, and very inspiring. They were very careful in the way they selected the people who took part in their programs. And of course, some programs were more appealing to me, and some others probably to other people, which was part of their intentions. I think one fascinating thing is that most people participating in the *Conversações* events—not everybody, but most people—were actually representing other people: they were talking on behalf, either directly or indirectly, of specific communities or identities. This was a way of going beyond the immediate conversation taking place. On the other hand, I have to say, I think that I would have liked to have more conversations that felt like debates. I think the program they created was amazing, and I wouldn't change a thing, but I would have loved to have other people talking. Like you, Marissa, Daniel, and David, said from the beginning, you wanted the trading platform to be, to some extent, a confrontational space. We also wanted this, even though we were very concerned, as Paulo said, with the specific times that we live in—you know, the very aggressive social media reactions that can happen to everything now. I think we missed a level of debate that could have happened. If I have to say—this is probably the first criticism that I have of our realization of *deposition*, and it's because I really love the work and everything that happened—but I think we missed this. I think we should have had more people invited onto the platform who think differently from the way we think. I think 99 percent of the people who stepped on the pit to speak publicly were people we agreed with on most things that might be said. Of course, we were more taken by the way some said it and less by the way others said it, but in the end, we agreed with all the fights and the visions of the world that those people had. I missed, personally, somebody who I didn't agree with. However, I think this is something that probably was impossible to do at that time. Again, I think we chose our battles, and we stood by them. And this battle—to produce a more challenging series of debates—was something that we wanted, but we didn't really manage, for various reasons. But I'm saying this because I think this is something that's still very much a potential in, and of, the work, and is something the work really needs at some point. This is something that we could have done, I wouldn't say better, but more of. Which is good. I mean, you will probably not find a better architectural environment in which to install the work, so you need to have something to look forward to in the next versions of the piece. And I think this sense of greater friction is something you will probably look for as well.

DR I agree wholeheartedly with that sentiment. I think that a desire for debate was a core concern from the beginning in thinking about this potential for conversational speech and its difficulties; the fact that it didn't happen is also reflective of something. Finding this work to have some potential that remains unexhausted by even the tremendous space that it was afforded is fantastic.

MLB I agree, and I think there was also something in the moment that we're a bit past now. But in that moment, in that pandemic-inflected moment, I felt such gratitude to just be together. And I agree that, from a distance, from our perspectives now, I'm again thinking about the qualities of friction and debate. But back then, I remember feeling very fragile, and I thought it was so interesting that many of the reviews and the writing about the Bienal reflected this question of dealing with the ashes of—or processing the grief of—being together after being apart for so long.

JCV So that's why I said that it was not possible to do it as we originally intended, let's say. I think that's why I also said that Vânia and Beatriz's program was perfect, because everybody whom they invited and who stepped onto the platform was actually talking about this fragility, in a very personal way and from a historical perspective that goes far beyond the pandemic. So, I think it was exactly what we needed to talk about.

MLB ______ And I agree that hopefully there will be more fights hosted on the floor. I also had this moment during the installation, when the platform was starting to be rebuilt in the Bienal pavilion, and the pit was starting to come together almost as an arena, that I suddenly felt the floor to be a much more aggressive, more violent structure. And I thought that it was very interesting—architecturally as well—this decision to position the trading pit such that it was more open, and fractured, and allowed for a different energy to potentially occupy it. An energy entered it that was different from the originating one I felt from the material itself. In that moment—when the thing was becoming a full octagon again, approaching its original formation—I thought it had a really different fighting energy; that energy didn't feel right for the time of the Bienal. But I remember that feeling, and perhaps it is something to explore in future.

DdP ______ I agree as well. I think there's this capacity of the work, also, in a more self-critical posture that makes it somehow capable of mirroring certain desires that are projected onto it—by the institution itself, by the artists, by the people involved in the program. In this sense, *deposition* has the potential of revealing some of the incapacities, or the impossibilities, that these desires might have when they're named. And I think the work has this capacity, this level of institutional critique, that it is able to point to these impossibilities. It's an interesting aspect of the work, *deposition*, that it doesn't necessarily intend to have resolutions that are—like you've mentioned before, Jacopo—seamless and flawless, or even able to host or speak to everything it might call forth. So I think it's interesting for the work to describe what it couldn't do, as much as what it could do.

PM ______ I think this has to do not only with the moment, but with the scale of the Bienal—both physically in regards to the size of audience, but also virtually and through media representations—because it's a kind of operation on a scale that has allowed, historically, for things to escalate very abruptly. This will probably not be the case every other time the work appears. There might be exhibitions or institutions that are more mid-scale and where, as a result, these elements of conflict and agonism can be enacted live, and the situation will not blow out as it could have, and has done, throughout the past few years.

And it's not that we're just speculating about this. What I feel is that, through the public use of *deposition*, there manifested some extreme modes of discourse that the Bienal exhibition itself chose not to engage in due to the nature of the space, the nature of the program, and the fact that life was already happening in and around it. Independently, some groups used the trading pit floor to vocalize some political extremes, pushing the array of possibilities for addressing debate. They expanded this array in ways the Bienal itself did not anticipate. For instance, in one of these extreme instances, we curated a theater play that unexpectedly escalated to a demonstration with MST flags, and so on.[20] That was a level of direct political speech, and an act of demonstration, that many of the works in the show related to, in the sense that they shared a similar political critique and level of concern regarding the logics of financial capital, the dynamics of unregulated speculation, the abuse of the earth, the abuse of the idea of progress, and the expropriation of the earth, and so on. These critiques were present throughout the Bienal in many works, but the directness of these concerns being put onto flags was something you wouldn't find elsewhere, in any other moment, in the exhibition.

There was also the musical performance with Maria Gadú, who is a pop singer with a large audience that has some aesthetic and political concerns,[21] along with a reading of Brazilian music history. She usually occupies a social and cultural arena that doesn't often overlap with that of the Bienal. So her performance is an example of another kind of extreme that was on the platform, and which brought a completely new audience—a different audience—and a different, populist atmosphere into the heart of the exhibition.

And then, not in opposition to, but at some other extreme of scale, there were some really, really quiet moments in which there were only three or four people talking on the trading floor, having a conversation surrounded by the audience of the Bienal. These conversations were almost just for themselves, almost like private round tables on a public stage, with mostly Vânia, Beatriz, Jacopo, two or three invited people, and maybe two other attendees. These conversations took place at such a small scale that they were at odds with the scale of the Bienal—the building, the institution, the exhibition.

So, *deposition* was a place to reach some extremes, and when you look at it as a whole it really made the whole Bienal more complicated, or more nuanced, even if there wasn't so much conflict in the individual program sessions themselves.[22]

DdP I think, as a last question, in respect to the deteriorating and kind of lifeless object that was salvaged—the corn commodities trading floor—I want to ask you both, Paulo and Jacopo, if you feel that somehow the materiality of the trading pit, the object, was in some way transformed through its exhibition. At least on a personal note, in some of the musical performances and the programming proposed by Cultura Artística and also by Novas Frequências[23] that had this deep bass reverberating through the whole object, I sometimes felt as if the floor was almost going through an exorcism of sorts. Do you feel that this object has changed, from the moment of its arrival to the moment it left?

JCV I think we discussed that at some point, Daniel, when we were probably in the last month of the exhibition. Rather than being just one or another specific thing—even though some of the presentations were very strong or very touching—I think *deposition* was the layering of all these things happening. There was something very beautiful that Vânia and Beatriz brought: this ritual of grounding the audience in the building, in relation to the floor and each other that happened before each of their *Conversações* programs. I think this idea of a ritual that happened there, on the trading pit, in the *vão*, on a regular basis, became something very strong for me. And that's why I said that more than any one specific thing, I think it was the combination of all those things that really changed the way the pit was. Like Marissa said earlier, the trading floor was very aggressive when she looked at it as the temporarily closed-in octagon. But I would say, even beyond the change in its shape, between the way it arrived and the way it left, to us at least it had become a different object. That's why I think this relation to ritual makes sense, because it was like we were adding other layers on top of something that was previously business and exploitation and destruction and capitalism. You know when you have to go from a black wall to a white one, and you have to put on layer after layer of paint, because it will take time until it really changes color: it was like this, like something we were putting coat after coat on top of. With each of those presentations and happenings and discussions there was another coat. If you asked the pit 100 years ago what it thought would happen in its future, it could never have expected this would happen, right? Because it was something completely far beyond the pit's mind, for sure. I really hope it travels to other cultural institutions in completely different cultural contexts and is exposed to completely different kinds of discussions, performances, and presentations. And I think this will be the ritual: of layering one thing on top of another, and another, and so it will go on. And this will eventually maybe change the structure and the material so much that everybody will notice. And then, if you look at it—I'm already talking metaphorically—but if you look at it even more metaphorically, this is a very beautiful idea of how culture and art can, in a way, change things. How this object was taken—this object which epitomizes the ideas of capitalism—and was turned into a platform for other things. That this could actually change the molecular structure of the material to some extent—I think it's very beautiful to think about. I felt it; and I think if it goes on traveling for the next ten years to different places, this will be something that will be perceivable. I think it's not so complicated to think that objects also have a life. A material change in the structure of the trading pit is probably too small to be perceived by anybody yet, but maybe, as I was saying, if it travels for another decade, and these coatings go on and on, then maybe these changes become more accessible and perceivable. That would be the most amazing thing.

PM ——— It's our job, then, to make sure to believe that the object is never the same again.

1. Jacopo Crivelli Visconti, Paulo Miyada, Carla Zaccagnini, Francesco Stocchi, and Ruth Estévez formed the curatorial team of the 34th Bienal de São Paulo.
2. *deposition* was installed in the *vão,* the nickname for the central atrium of the Pavilhão Ciccillo Matarazzo, São Paulo. The atrium is a vast opening in the architecture of the pavilion, framed on all sides by undulating balconies that converge at one end of the atrium into an iconic helical ramp, which rises through all three stories of the building.
3. Works such as Lais Myrrha, *Dois pesos, duas medidas (Double Standards)* (2016) for the 32nd Bienal de São Paulo; Choi Jeonghwa's sculpture *Encore, Encore, Encore* (1997) installed for the 24th Bienal de São Paulo; or Tunga's installation *Enquanto Flora a Borda . . .* (1987) for the 19th Bienal de São Paulo.
4. ". . . rather than . . . a theme, the title of the 34th Bienal de São Paulo, *Faz escuro mas eu canto* (*Though it's dark, still I sing*), is a line from a poem by Amazonian poet Thiago de Mello, published in 1965. Through this poetic phrase, we recognize the urgency of the problems that challenge life in the current world, while underscoring the need for art as a field of resistance, rupture and transformation." Excerpt from a curatorial statement for *Though it's dark, still I sing*, http://34.bienal.org.br/en/post/7511.
5. "The starting point of the curatorial project for the 34th Bienal de São Paulo, originally planned for 2020, was the desire to unfold the show in time and space, extending its duration over several months and expanding the presence of participating artists through an unprecedented partnerships with more than twenty cultural institutions in the city. Due to the COVID-19 pandemic, various aspects of the initially imagined choreography were modified and the collective exhibition was postponed. These changes reinforced the relevance of a show in constant transformation and adaptation, which seeks to reflect on itself publicly, as in a great open rehearsal. Preliminary events, both digital and in-person, preceded the opening of the exhibition *Though it's dark, still I sing* in September 2021 simultaneously to dozens of exhibitions in partner institutions in the city of São Paulo, marking the high point of this Bienal" See: 34.bienal.org.br/en/sobrea34.
6. This may have been in reference to a review of the 34th Bienal de São Paulo by Ela Bittencourt published in *Hyperallergic* that led with a photo featuring *deposition,* but in the photo caption did not name the work or the artists involved. See: https://hyperallergic.com/683942/the-sao-paulo-biennial-captures-a-perpetually-discontinuous-world.
7. "Searching for a language to delineate the force fields created by the combined presence of artworks from very different places and times, we proposed some objects [and ephemera and actions, 14 in total], coupled with their stories, as *statements*: a bell that was rung at different moments of a story that is repeated [the "bell of Tiradentes" from the Capella de Nossa Senhora do Rosário dos Homens Brancos in Ouro Preto, Minas Gerais]; the images of the most portrayed man [Frederick Douglass] at a time when almost no one was portrayed . . . a set of objects that survived the same fire in different ways [including the meteorite of Bendegó that survived the fire that destroyed the Museu Nacional in Rio de Janeiro in September 2018] . . . These statements are scattered around the exhibition, suggesting a tone for the artworks around them to be read in, conveying the curatorship's concerns and reflections, making them tangible. In this sense, they operate like the tuning fork that helps to tune a musical instrument, or the beginning of a song." Excerpt from a curatorial statement for *Though it's dark, still I sing*, http://34.bienal.org.br/en/post/7511. Also see: http://34.bienal.org.br/en/enunciados.
8. The curatorial team further expands on these concepts in open letters to the public that think through the complexities of historical, present, and future conditions. The letters are shared under the title "Correspondence" and published on the official Bienal de São Paulo website. See: http://34.bienal.org.br/en/publicacoes.
9. "The first Bienal Internacional de São Paulo took place in 1951 . . . It is not only the first international biennial to succeed the archetype of Venice, but also the first modern (and modernist) biennial and the first to be realized in a geopolitical location outside the Northern hemisphere and the canonical United States–Western European axis. The inauguration of the Bienal Internacional de São Paulo was motivated by the combined cultural, economic, and political forces that shaped the post-war period within Brazil and internationally. It was founded by Francisco "Ciccillo" Matarazzo Sobrinho, an Italian-Brazilian industrialist . . . Matarazzo's aim was 'a festival in the mould of Venice,' and the twin aspirations of the Bienal Internacional were, in the words of its first artistic director, Lourival Gomes Machado, 'to put modern art of Brazil not simply in proximity but in living contact with the art of the rest of the world' and 'for São Paulo to conquer the position of international artistic centre.' . . . The Bienal Internacional de São Paulo moved into its present-day permanent home, the Oscar Niemeyer-designed Ciccillo Matarazzo pavilion (originally named the Palace of Industries [and designed to house agro-industrial world fairs]) . . . in 1957." Isobel Whitelegg, "The Bienal Internacional de São Paulo: a concise history, 1951–2014," *Perspective* 2 (2013), 380–386.
10. Le Corbusier published *Le Modulor* in 1948, followed by *Modulor 2* in 1955; both books detail an anthropometric, universalizing system of scaling and relating proportions developed by Le Corbusier.
11. "The changes in Chicago's markets suddenly made it possible for people to buy and sell grain not as the physical product of human labor on a particular tract of prairie earth but as an abstract claim on the golden stream flowing through the city's elevators . . . The entire transaction could be completed—and repeated dozens of times—without a single kernel of wheat or corn moving so much as an inch . . . Elevator receipts, as traded on the floor of 'Change, accomplished the transmutation of one of humanity's oldest foods,

obscuring its physical identity and displacing it into the symbolic world of capital. The elevator helped turn grain into capital by obscuring and distancing its link with physical nature, while another new technology extended that process by weakening its link with geography. In 1848, the same year that Chicago merchants founded the Board of Trade, the first telegraph lines reached the city . . . The result was a new market geography that had less to do with the soils or climate of a given locality than with the prices and information flows of the economy as a whole . . . When the Board of Trade adopted a standard grading system, it made grain interchangeable not just between elevator bins but between cities and continents as well . . . Telegraphic orders of this sort encouraged a sharp rise in what traders called 'to arrive' contracts for grain. Under these contracts, a seller promised to deliver grain to its buyer by some specified date in the future. . . . 'To arrive' contracts in combination with standardized elevator receipts made possible Chicago's greatest innovation in the grain trade: the futures market . . . Grain elevators and grading systems had helped transmute wheat and corn into monetary abstractions, but the futures contract extended the abstraction by liberating the grain trade itself from the very process which had once defined it: the exchange of physical grain." William Cronon, *Nature's Metropolis: Chicago and the Great West* (New York: W. W. Norton & Company, 1991), 120–126.

12. In reference to the COVID-19 pandemic, which was declared by the World Health Organization (WHO) on 11 March 2020.

13. "SECTION 5. LESSEE'S RIGHTS AND OBLIGATIONS, Section 5.1 (j)." See pages 180–183.

14. Vânia Medeiros and Beatriz Cruz were commissioned by the curatorial team of the 34th Bienal de São Paulo to propose a series of programs to be convened atop *deposition*. Medeiros and Cruz titled their programming series *Conversações*. An interview with them, conducted by Daniel de Paula, can be found on pages 256–267 (English) and 332–337 (Portuguese).

15. International English- language articles, such as Ariel Goldstein's "Brazil leads the third wave of the Latin American far right," published 1 March 2021 for the University of Oslo's Center for Research on Extremism, outline the rise of Brazilian president Jair Bolsonaro as part of a "third wave" of Latin American far right politics that has capitalized on interlocked crises in Brazil and is built on a coalition of evangelical pastors, the military, financial markets, and the agribusiness sector. This is one in many such descriptions of Bolsonaro's presidency, which began 1 January 2019, and the related historical conditions in South American and Latin American politics that speak to the sociopolitical landscape in which the 34th Bienal de São Paulo took place. Other writing on the topic includes *New York Times* opinion pieces by Gaspard Estrada ("Brasil y el autoritarismo de Bolsonaro," 7 April 2021) and Vanessa Barbara ("Bolsonaro Said His 'Specialty Is Killing.' He's Been True to His Word," 31 March 2022); reports such as Oliver Stuenkel's "Brazil's Polarization and Democratic Risks," published for the Carnegie Endowment for International Peace (17 February 2021); and reporting by Simone Preissler Iglesias and Andrew Rosati for Bloomberg, "Bolsonaro Wages Trumpian Campaign to Sow Doubts About Voting" (12 July 2021), and for Reuters, "Human Rights Watch says Bolsonaro a threat to democracy in Brazil" (13 January 2022).

16. This act of tensioning Visconti refers to could be as much in reference to the social, linguistic aspects of the work as to the physical elements. The permitted uses of the trading pit are determined in accordance with the terms set by the artists' contract and realized through a process of contextual negotiation conducted with the curatorial team and any other necessary institutional representatives. See the "PROPERTY LEASE AGREEMENT" for *deposition* on pages 172–205.

17. The group exhibition of the 34th Bienal ended on 5 December 2021 with Neo Muyanga's *A Grace Note* (2021), part of the larger project *A Maze in Grace* (2020), a large-scale collective performance created in collaboration with the Legítima Defesa collective and artist Bianca Turner. Images documenting the performance can be found on pages 310–315.

18. Jaider Esbell (1979–2021) was an artist, organizer, educator, and curator of Macuxi descent whose significant work was included in the 34th Bienal de São Paulo.

19. As a stipulation of the artist contract of the work *deposition*, a written enunciation is required to be read by a voluntary representative of the exhibiting institution at the initiation of each official organized exhibition program, as detailed in "SECTION 5. LESSEE'S RIGHTS AND OBLIGATIONS, Section 5.1 (b) and (c) i-vi." See pages 178–181.

20. On 23 September 2021 a group called Movimento dos Trabalhadores Sem Teto (MTST) occupied the São Paulo stock exchange. Their protest highlighted food insecurity, the effects of inflation, and the precarity of workers in a space where billions of Brazilian reais in securities are traded daily, as documented in photos published by *O Globo* on 23 September 2021. A little more than a month later, on 11 November 2021, in a similar act of organization, a number of theater groups and popular movements, including the collective Dolores Boca Aberta, Brava Companhia, Companhia Antropofágica, Estudo De Cena, Cia Canina, the Levante Popular da Juventude, the Movimento dos Trabalhadores pelos Direitos (MTD), and the Movimento dos Trabalhadores Rurais Sem Terra (MST) staged an occupation on *deposition* calling for an end to hunger and food insecurity while standing on the steps of the former CBOT corn commodities trading pit in the midst of the 34th Bienal de São Paulo. Images of this manifestation and performance can be found on pages 294–299. MST documented this action and their intentions in an article published on their website on 12 November 2021 titled "MST faz intervenção contra o agronegócio em espaço nobre da 34° Bienal de São Paulo," https://mst.org.br/2021/11/12/

mst-faz-intervencao-contra-o-agronegocio-em-espaco-nobre-da-34-bienal-de-sao-paulo.

21. Gadú has publicly expressed her concerns about the deforestation and destruction of the Amazon, along with critiques of Bolsonaro's government, and the need for indigenous rights in articles such as the 9 March 2022 piece by Michelle Portela for *Correio* Braziliense titled "Cenário de continuidade de Bolsonaro é inaceitável, diz Maria Gadú," https://www.correiobraziliense.com.br/politica/2022/03/4991663-cenario-de-continuidade-de-bolsonaro-e-inaceitavel-diz-maria-gadu.html. Images of her performance on *deposition* can be found on pages 300–301.

22. This question of the friction and distinction between voices on the floor is part of a stipulation of the "Permitted Uses" section of Benedict, de Paula, and Rueter's contract for *deposition*, which states that no singular voice is to be invited or allowed to speak on the trading pit ("Section 5.1 (n), ensure that the Trading Pit is not a podium or a platform for individual discourse or agency by requiring that all activities of the public program of the 34th edition of the Bienal de São Paulo be structured around two or more discrete, ideally agonistic, agents").

23. Novas Frequências, founded in 2011, is a Brazilian experimental music and sound art festival. The curators of the Bienal de São Paulo invited general director and curator of Novas Frequências, Chico Dub, to curate a series of experimental music programs on *deposition* that took place over the course of the Bienal exhibition.

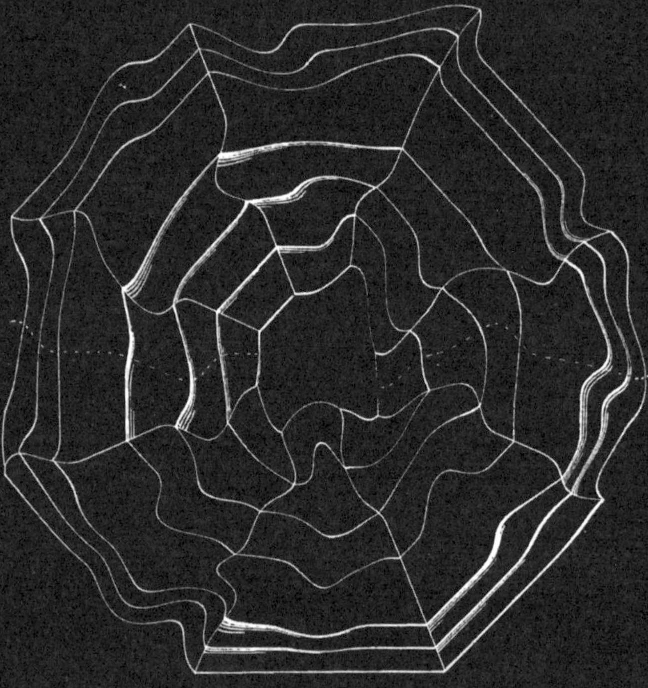

LEVITATORS 226
ABOUT WHEELS, MILLS, GEARS, AND THE CIRCLE OF LIFE 238
TAKING STOCK 246

CIR CUM SCRIP TION VII

LEVITATORS

iv. Cameron Hu — Vienna (AT)

ONE

Scanning family albums, I come across a photograph of several people I don't recognize. They crowd around the spinet piano in my childhood home in Danbury, Connecticut, where the Union Carbide Corporation directed a worldwide chemical empire from a glass-and-steel spaceship hidden in the woods. These strangers are dark-haired, in early-middle age. One woman holds a violin. The men wear beards. They look like they are enjoying themselves. A second photograph displays the same strangers stretched out on couches and folding cots. And then I remember: these were "our Russians." For a handful of days in 1991 or 1992, my parents played hosts in a cultural exchange. Sponsored by some US service club, maybe the Rotarians, groups from the former USSR toured the United States in the first years of the End of History. The idea was to make contact with some of these post-Soviets, no longer adversaries, and introduce them to the way of life that had prevailed—for good, it was thought—over their own.

Our Russians, schoolteachers and musicians, had already spent a week exploring small-town life in South Carolina. Now their visit culminated in a long weekend in the North. At the suggestion of their sponsors, my father, a recent émigré from the Philippines, arranged for the group to take a long breakfast with his boss. The petrochemicals executive delivered a prepared lecture on the workings of the free market. Coffee from an electric urn, cold bagels, individual cups of cream cheese, transparencies passed over the hot surface of an overhead projector. And then—I think this was meant to be the climax of their tour, toward which the entire trip built—my parents drove our Russians to see the New York Stock Exchange. They had journeyed through the land of the market and now they would see a market being made.

It is reported that our Russians looked politely around the exchange but found nothing to hold their interest. By all accounts they were confused to have been delivered to this, of all possible New York vistas—men sweating through their suits in a fluorescent-lit room strewn with wastepaper. Our Russians were impatient to go shopping. They wanted souvenirs, solid objects they could bring home. What were they supposed to see, what were they supposed to understand, as they looked out onto the trading floor?

TWO

In 2018, Marissa Lee Benedict, Daniel de Paula, and David Rueter bought one of the last trading pits of the Chicago Board of Trade. It was inside these octagonal pits, set into the floor of a few buildings downtown, that traders bought and sold the world's wheat, soy, corn, livestock, and much else from the later nineteenth century onward. In the same decades that global politics and economy were remade by Europe's new imperialism and US westward expansion, the pits assumed a central position in the geography of an increasingly worldwide capitalism. Men crowding into the octagons would trade whatever on the earth could be commodified; in the course of trading it they continuously set and reset—or as traders say, "discovered"—the cash value of the earth and of the lives that worked it. Long-distance vectors of gain and loss, accumulation and dispossession, came to flow through a few hundred (usually male, mostly white) bodies packing themselves into the rigid shape of an octagon in downtown Chicago. Brokers and speculators at the intersection of LaSalle Street and Jackson Boulevard came to stand between Argentine farmers and the working classes of urban Europe. Filling the pits, the new intermediaries grew powerful to enrich or impoverish either, or both.

By the end of the 2010s, electronic transactions had shouldered the sweat and noise of in-person commodity trading from the center of capitalism's concentric circles of profit and ruin. The architecture of that hustle, the octagonal trading pit, arena and icon of commodity trading across the so-called American Century, was bound for the landfill. The pit itself became an object lesson in that merciless invention of obsolescence some economists celebrate as "creative destruction." Our artists paid $5,000 to divert one pit to a damp warehouse on 93rd Street, a facility it shared with thousands of moldering naval uniforms. They have since dismantled the pit, mapped its dimensions, made rubbings of its surfaces, prepared analytical drawings by hand and machine, lifted and turned this heavy, awkward structure at precarious angles, and placed it and its traces on public display—first at the Arts Club of Chicago, shouting distance from the Board of Trade, later at the Pavilhão Ciccillo Matarazzo in São Paulo. What, if anything, can the pit show us when it is mapped, turned, and transported throughout a planet whose value it determined, often to catastrophic effect? What are we supposed to see, what are we supposed to understand, when we look into the pit?

THREE

Looking at photographs of the pit's arrival in São Paulo from my computer in Vienna, I can see it is jet black, eight equal sides if you bother to count them up, complete unto itself in the way of all regular geometry, its monolithic *thereness* overwhelming whatever it might index beyond itself. Tony Smith might as well have sculpted the pit. And Smith might have said of the trading pits, like he pronounced of his own sculptures, like US think tanks would pronounce of the laws of the market at the close of the Cold War: "they just exist," they are "just present."[1]

It was the thereness of Tony Smith's sculptures that most vexed Michael Fried in his epochal critique of Minimalism, the 1967 essay, "Art and Objecthood."[2] From Smith's geometries, Fried augured the coming degeneration of Western art. Fried worried that Smith's sculptures, works that "just exist" like everything else, works that function as still more objects in a world already reduced to so many objects, would only suck their viewers deeper into the encompassing whirlpool of spectacle and commodity. Looking at Smith's black masses, Fried forecast a crash in the value of the modernists he loved best. Smith's objects suggested the declining currency of artists like Frank Stella and Anthony Caro, whose paintings and sculptures, Fried believed, could now and then add up to more than mere objects that "just exist." Stella and Caro, he argued, endeavored not only to furnish the world but to suspend its power, to lift viewers out of the vortex of life corrupted by capital and onto some other, more contemplative, plane. Modernism, Fried insisted, could deliver us to "grace"; Smith's minimalism, Fried worried, amounted to stupid, cheerful participation in the general debasement of the post-WWII system.

Fifty-odd years out from "Art and Objecthood," I have a few doubts about the distinction it draws. The argument depends on the most exhausted premise of North Atlantic culture, one that underlies both the languages of capitalism and the languages of the critique of capitalism, showing their continuity: that we are only ever either transcending our present circumstances or trapped in their muck, emancipating ourselves from our situation or unfreely confined to it. That everything we do either repudiates or flatters a corrupted life. This is the monomaniacal premise of a historicist way of life, the common substance of its affirmative and radical variations, of both the incessant trade in commodities and the incessant trade in critical essays. Still, I like to imagine Fried stationed in the viewer's gallery of the Board of Trade, staring out onto the trading floor, observing so many men pressing themselves into octagonal shapes that look rather like Smith's dark volumes. Fried would surely have noticed how closely the stage-setting of the market resembled the sculptures that he claimed turned art into one more spectacle of the market society.

FOUR

Electronic trading, faster and cheaper, and powering a previously unthinkable frequency and automaticity of transaction, made the pits obsolete. Now that the pits are ruins it is easy to forget that, just like algorithms, they once proposed a brand new way for human beings to encounter one another. The pit is Chicago's contribution to those nineteenth-century architectures that organized desire and power by organizing proximity and vision. It is the crude American relation of Bentham's panopticon, Benjamin's arcades, Paxton's Crystal Palace. The pit's concentric platforms are staggered vertically, each several inches taller than the next, and in this way the octagonal risers establish not a hierarchy but a democracy of vision. From any point in the pit, one trader can meet eyes with any other. The pit embodies the extravagant commitment to equality peculiar to the spaces of high-throughput financial transaction. Online, I watch clips from *The Trading Game*, a news special shot on the floor of the Board of Trade in the late 1980s—picture it broadcast between reports on the demise of organized labor, Reaganomics and the upward redistribution of US wealth, the scandal of the "welfare queen" that turned one woman from the South Side into an argument for hollowing out American social protections. The narrator marvels that a membership to the trading floor, a place among equals in the octagon, costs $300,000.

FIVE

After the Cold War, US development strategists and political engineers would argue that capitalism not only secured an abundant life but also prepared individuals for democratic citizenship. They proposed that the formal equality of waged labor and market encounter would encourage post-Socialist peoples to embrace the formal equality of participants in a liberal democracy. This was a common premise of arguments for the denationalization of the Soviet Union's economic machinery. Privatization *was* democratization—the pit was training for the agora. Yet this particular idea about capitalism has been reliably haunted by so much evidence for a rival consideration: that the market does not, in fact, create freely associating reflective individuals but rather presses them into a homogenous mass, so many automata in thrall to the shifting mood of the market. On this possibility one can read Marx's *Capital*, but one can also skim Frank Norris's 1903 novel *The Pit: A Story of Chicago*, among the most widely read American fictions of its era.[3] (D. W. Griffith turned *The Pit* into a film, released in 1909, and the success of this first populist feature launched him toward the racist mythmaking of 1915's *Birth of a Nation*.) *The Pit* plots the rise and fall of a Chicago broker increasingly possessed by a fever for speculation in wheat. As he moves to corner the global market, putting the world's growers and eaters of wheat at his mercy, his own thoughts are gradually replaced by those of an alien intelligence, the autonomous intelligence of the pits themselves. “Wheat-wheat-wheat, wheat-wheat-wheat” goes the pit’s stream of consciousness, and then the protagonist’s too. Norris likens the churn of the pit-brain to an “ungovernable torrent.” Ultimately he assigns to the octagons all the dubious liberation of a “whirlpool,” a “vortex.” Packed into their eight-sided arena, Chicago’s speculators did not so much discover their voices as they “. . . lost their individualities, they became a conglomerate—a mass, slow-moving, black.”

Lately the obsolescence of the pits and the rise of automated electronic trading has induced anxiety about the radical abstraction of economic life in the twenty-first century, an anxiety that is the obverse of so much enthusiasm for “decentralization.” Informatics, we have learned to worry, stand to shoulder human temporalities, human sensoria, and human judgment out from the very systems that distribute pain and pleasure throughout the human world. But one might equally consider that from the moment human lives were first drawn into the pit—as, in the end, almost all lives were in the twentieth century, whether they crowded the octagon or rotated its vortex at some greater physical distance—this process was already well underway.

SIX

In the slim entry for “Octagon” that appears halfway through *A Dictionary of Symbols*, the Spanish poet Juan Eduardo Cirlot declares that the octagon is an intermediary between two more common shapes: the circle and the square.[4] The possibility of a regular, eight-sided polygon suggests itself as soon as you circumscribe a square with pencil and paper. In consequence, Cirlot detects something like aspiration in the form of an octagon. It is a square attempting to become a circle, a circle straightening itself into a rectangle. I flip forward in the *Dictionary* to Cirlot’s lengthier entry for “Square.” The square, I read, symbolizes nature and the mundane: “four elements, the four seasons, stages of Man’s life.” I flip backward to the entry for “Circle.” The circle means “heaven and perfection,” it means “eternity.” If the octagon is the intermediary between the square and the circle, then it might be said that the worth of grain, lumber, cattle, and indeed most of the substance of the world has received its value in a sort of nonplace between earthly and ethereal planes—an intermediate region between the physical and metaphysical, the temporal and the eternal, corruption and grace. This is appropriately esoteric given the undisguised theology that suffuses the modern financial industries. In the opening minutes of *The Trading Game*, one broker describes his very best days on the floor. They are, he says, those days when the market so packs the pit with human flesh that, "we could pick our feet off the ground and not fall." The traders press themselves into the shape of the octagon, finance fulminates against gravity and planet, capital accumulates in downtown Chicago through a marvelous feat of collective levitation.

When he applied to patent an "Improved Trading Pit or Platform," the businessman Reuben S. Jennings was noncommittal about the shape of the octagon. "The pit or series of platforms," reads his 1877 application, "is represented as octagonal, but it may be any form or shape desired, so that it be a series of steps or platforms around a center space."[5] The patent was soon invalidated; I suspect the courts found it too vague to enforce. Even in America, and even in its cathedrals of property and trade, one cannot own the idea of concentric risers in every possible shape. Still, the multiple generations of trading pits seem to have only ever been octagonal, never hexagons or decagons, never odd-sided. It is as if, in the proportions of an eight-sided polygon, human bodies discovered their most extreme capacities to speculate, to distribute loss and enjoy risk, the way a baseball diamond measures their furthest powers to throw, catch, run.

How few things come in eights. I read about the emergence of crabs, how they seem to evolve from an astonishingly wide range of crustaceans, as if organic life is destined to be eight-legged. I look up an old flatmate who consulted the eight trigrams of the *Book of Changes* every morning during the summer doctors declared him a schizophrenic. And then I try to remember if an octagonal *ba gua* mirror hung among the many ornaments in my grandmother's Chinatown apartment, reflecting Jim Cramer's *Mad Money* program off the TV screen while she traded options on the phone from her monumental La-Z-Boy. Arriving from Manila to San Francisco in the 1970s, her taste for speculative investment had already developed in that country's small stock exchange. She found herself admitted to a financial system more vast and complex and less and less regulated, and suddenly proliferating novel financial instruments, so many new possibilities for profit, so many new possibilities for loss, each possibility requiring the other, each profoundly exciting. Drawn by the imperial vortex from colony to metropole, "periphery" to "center," she had arrived to the land where speculation often amounted to a way of life. Always syncretic in her religious practices—we placed a pearl into my grandfather's mouth at his otherwise Christian funeral—my grandmother might have deployed the octagonal mirror's protection like a further hedge against the secular contingencies of the market. Hunting wild octagons by search engine, I have also learned that mixed martial artists (MMA) pummel one another in an octagonal cage. This calls to mind another businessman interviewed on *The Trading Game*, who declares that inside the pit, "all the gladiators get together and do battle every day." Within the MMA octagon, where every angle is gentle and obtuse, fighters are not so easily trapped in corners, are not so quickly corralled in a tight spot that destines them for a bloodying. This has been explained to me as merciful design-thinking. But it may also be considered that the octagon stretches out the duration of every fight, so that each unfolds in time as a captivating drama of toughness and cruelty, justifying the price of admission.

SEVEN

Being trapped in place, being corralled in a position without exit, being available in consequence to a bloodying: this is the condition grasped in the language of finance as "exposure." A market in commodity futures exists at all because moderns believe the future is indeterminate, and exposure names the continuous possibility that the future might organize itself against you, that when the future arrives as fact it comes closed like a fist. For example: in the flatlands that extend south from Chicago for hundreds of miles, exposure is the possibility that traders will determine a price for soybeans less than what you spent to grow them. And when that "discovery" is made, it will be too late. Because you are already cornered (some corner the market and some are cornered within it), you are long since *exposed*. There is no exit to the commitments made months, years, centuries prior, to farm these things and not others, to be a farmer at all, to be born into a life where that option presents itself as an obvious one, a life where the value of each and every thing on earth is made to oscillate wildly, now by the men in the pit, now by the competition of algorithms.

The pit was supposed to take the edge off the agony of exposure. The gladiators fighting, levitating, above the octagons at the Board of Trade would soften the sharp angles of modern economic time by way of a particular device, a futures contract. The futures contract was an agreement that at some future date one of the gladiators would buy or sell a commodity at a predetermined price, no matter what happened in the meantime. The pit offered itself as a means to stabilize an unstable world. But almost immediately the pit would itself become a new engine of instability. It would elaborate a new possibility for pain. Traders would quickly learn, if it was not already there *a priori*, that there could be no final determination of the future value of any object save what someone might pay for it in the pit. And this implied that by buying and selling contracts in bulk they might not only "discover" but indeed also manipulate the value of any object; and it entailed in turn that indeed "discovery" and "manipulation," finding and making, nature and artifice would become harder and harder to distinguish. Thus did the men levitating above the octagon come to set the terms of life and death for a whole world swirling about its center. A minor character in *The Pit* spells this out. On the earth live people who grow things and people who eat them and "right between these two comes the speculator, who raises or lowers the price out of all reason." The trader, supposed to soften the market's blow, now delivers it. "If we send the price of wheat down too far, the farmer suffers, the fellow who raises it if we send it up too far, the poor man in Europe suffers, the fellow who eats it, the fellow who eats bread."

But for all their mastery of the wheat trade, the traders feared wheat—feared its thereness—too. The traders would never take physical possession of any of those objects they bought. They were middlemen, their participation in any commodity was temporary; if all went as it should, the traders would never in their lives lay hands on the wheat, soy, cattle, etc., they would never crash back down into the stuff of the earth. Any trader who exited the octagon as the terminal owner of 50,000 bushels of wheat would likely have ruined himself. On *The Trading Game* TV special, a trader insists, unprovoked, that although he may sometimes "own" so many tons of wheat or soy or corn, no truck will ever dump it on his front lawn. Our levitators envision catastrophe as a dune of carbohydrates piled in the Chicago suburbs.

EIGHT

Bertolt Brecht once failed to finish a play about the global wheat trade. In an autobiographical sketch, translated by Patty Lee Parmalee in her study *Brecht's America*, Brecht recalls traveling "from Berlin to Vienna after a broker who had worked all his life at the Chicago exchange." But this broker could make no sense for Brecht of what went on in and through the trading pits. Indeed, no one, Brecht later wrote,

neither well-known writers on economics nor business people could explain the processes of the wheat exchange to me adequately. I won the impression that these processes were simply inexplicable, i.e. not to be grasped by reason, i.e. unreasonable. The way the world's wheat was distributed was simply incomprehensible.[6]

Now the pit has gone silent and the trading goes online; now the pit, eight-sided-architecture-against-thereness, is itself demoted to brute thereness, dumped first on the Chicago exurbs and then São Paulo's Parque do Ibirapuera, onto the high-visibility front yard of the highly leveraged global art industry; now our artists have made themselves its terminal owners, lightly ruining themselves with possession of the pit; now the traders value and devalue the world from home computers; now the End of History is over (if it ever began); now almost all of what we call our life comes at us like an "ungovernable torrent," is "simply inexplicable, i.e., not to be grasped by reason, i.e., unreasonable"; and now we are asked what we see, what we understand, if we corral ourselves within the inoperative pit; but even there we may find no moral to the story, no determination of the true and final value of things; still no conclusion brings this object lesson to a comprehensible end; still we have no measure of transcendence or History but simply confront one thing after another, one object after another, one transaction and then the next transaction and then the next after that; now we idle inside the octagon and levitation eludes us.

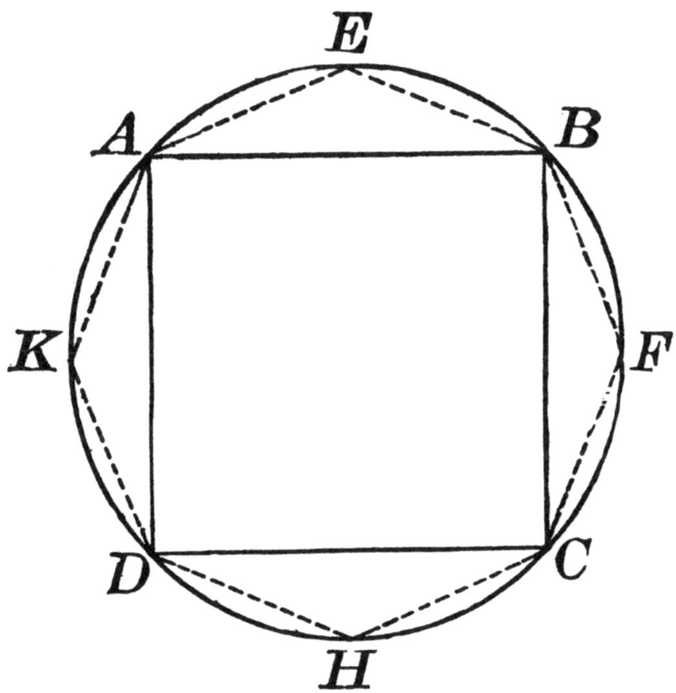

1. Cited in Charlene Spretnak, *The Spiritual Dynamic in Modern Art* (New York: Palgrave, 2014), 144.
2. Michael Fried, "Art and Objecthood," *Artforum* (June 1967).
3. Frank Norris, *The Pit* (New York: Doubleday, 1903).
4. Juan Eduardo Cirlot, *A Dictionary of Symbols* (New York: NYRB, 2020).
5. Reuben Jennings, US letters patent for " Improvement in Trading-Pits," (1876).
6. From Patty Lee Parmalee, *Brecht's America* (Miami: Ohio University, 1981), 139.

ABOUT WHEELS, MILLS, GEARS, AND THE CIRCLE OF LIFE

v. Yamila Goldfarb São Paulo (BR)

A gente vai contra a corrente
Até não poder resistir
Na volta do barco é que sente
O quanto deixou de cumprir
Faz tempo que a gente cultiva
A mais linda roseira que há
Mas eis que chega a roda-viva
E carrega a roseira pra lá

Chico Buarque, "Roda Viva" (1967)

The *wheel** turns, turns, turns, and yet nothing seems to move. Negotiations that circle around crops and livestock take on new dimensions and new scales as new technologies and necropolitical instruments are made available. Notable in this is the perpetuation, or the re-edition, of a colonial project in which people sell cheap and pay a high price, at the expense of life—especially people's lives—as well as the environment, our natural resources, our territories, and the planet.

Examining how the *wheel* used to physically function, circularly, we can observe that much hasn't changed. The old Bancada Ruralista (Ruralist Caucus), disguised as the Frente Parlamentar da Agropecuária (FPA, Parliamentary Agricultural and Livestock Front), constituted itself as the most enduring and effective political force in Brazilian parliament. The *latifúndio*, so called until the 1970s, was termed "agribusiness" in the 1980s, establishing a modern appearance. Later, between the 1990s and 2016, it gained new guises and came to be called *agronegócio*. Now, it transmutes into Agro and reproduces itself via links to an immense cultural strategy that tries to convince everyone, or at least almost everyone, that Agro is what we, Brazil, need to be a great nation capable of feeding the world—even though a considerable portion of the population dies of hunger every day.[1]

Today's *wheels of negotiation* are no longer round, nor are they made of wood, nor do they place people face to face. They are digital and connect producers, traders, and investors across the world. These digitized and globalized *wheels of negotiation* determine how people insert themselves into global chains of value—and, as such, continue to be through subordination. It continues to despoil; it continues to exhaust our territories and peoples. In the Global South, the

* Translator's note: In Portuguese, the phrase "trading pit" translates to *roda de negociação*, or "wheel of negotiation." Much of this essay relies on the metaphor of a trading pit as a wheel.

cursed logic that imposes itself determines that we must sell produce cheap and pay for it at increased prices. In the Global North, the *wheel* turns the other way around, as it has always been: they buy cheap and charge us a high price. It is the re-edition of the colonial subordination project in which hunger is one more structuring element. In a country where hunger has been naturalized for decades, it is necessary to understand it as a political project.

A raiva dá pra parar, pra interromper
A fome não dá pra interromper
A raiva e a fome é coisas dos home
A fome tem que ter raiva pra interromper
A raiva é a fome de interromper
A fome e a raiva é coisas dos home

Aldir Blanc and João Bosco,
"O ronco da cuíca" (1976)

But doesn't Brazil feed the world with its Agro Pop and Agro Tech?** Isn't it the world's farm? Doesn't it export tons of grains? We feed the world, but not our population. Today 58.7 percent of Brazilians are in a condition of food insecurity. That is, they do not know if they will eat their three meals a day. There are 125.2 million people in Brazil; 33 million of them have already known hunger.

How did the *wheel* turn and reach this point? It has turned by taking the negotiations around the buying and selling of grains to the level of buying and selling natural resources, territories, and life itself. Let's make a brief historical review to comprehend this long process.

In the post–World War II period, the world entered a period where there was a strong state presence in the economies of the Global North, and the flows of capital were regulated. It is the period when Keynesian policies dominated, as did the so-called Bretton Woods institutions (World Bank, Washington, D.C.; International Monetary Fund, Washington, D.C.; and World Trade Organization, Geneva). The world, particularly the so-called Western European world, lived then its thirty golden years of capitalism that were accompanied by wealth redistribution and the construction of the welfare state. It was a period marked by strong state regulation of the private sector. The Chicago Board of Trade's (CBOT) *wheel of negotiation* had been operating

** Translator's note: A popular idea of agricultural progress marketed widely by media giant Rede Globo in Brazil from 2017 onward, built on the slogan "Agro is Tech. Agro is Pop. Agro is everything."

since the previous century, playing an important role in determining the price of grain. Yet this *wheel*, too, would enter the new cycle of capital accumulation that was to come.

In the 1970s, the world plunged into a deep recession. With the crisis of the Bretton Woods system, great masses of capital that could not obtain profitability, given their over-accumulation, were directed to the financial sector in search of better returns. The availability of capital from the center of capitalism, particularly from the United States and Europe, came to finance, through debt, the industrialization of agriculture in Brazil, as well as of other countries of the Global South. The over-accumulation of capital at the center of capitalism at that time contributed to the formation of agro-industrial complexes—chains that connected input and machinery industries with agriculture. This conservative modernization, coined the "Green Revolution," resulted in the elimination of manual labor jobs in agriculture and provoked a great migratory wave to large urban centers.

Thus, financialization and the indebtedness of the peripheral countries were the mechanisms that drove the new economic cycle. The accumulated, devalued capital of the central countries was sent as loans to the peripheral countries, on the condition that they carried out structural adjustment reforms. This process of recuperating profit margins was supported ideologically, politically, and economically by neoliberalism, which made possible this deregulation of capital. This meant that capital was loosening from its moorings—its regulation and state control—and enormously expanding the possibilities of valorization, from the moment a whole normative and legal apparatus was created for this purpose. This process was particularly visible in the field of agriculture. If before, exchanges such as the CBOT only negotiated the price of grain futures and options, they now began to negotiate the future prices of a huge variety of other products. At this point, the wheel began to gyrate even more uncontrollably, to the tune of the interests of the capitalists in the central countries and not to the interests of the people.

This deregulation allowed the international financial system to undergo profound changes in the late 1980s and early 1990s that would generate a greater capacity to create and value money. Several mechanisms were created as a way to make the invested money appreciate in value. An infinite number of securities and negotiable papers on the stock, commodities, and futures exchanges appeared. Investments became, more and more, a great speculative betting game.

Beginning in the 1990s, these financial assets rose in value. The inflation of technology company stocks on the NASDAQ exchange was one of the most emblematic cases of US capitalist accumulation in the 1990s.[2] Starting in 2001, the stock prices of these companies plummeted, creating the need for now-idle financial capital to appreciate in new markets that could quickly inflate their assets. This capital was then directed to the US and European real estate market as well as to the commodities market.[3] Yet in 2007 and 2008, the bursting of the US real estate bubble caused new waves of searches for commodities and farmland investments.

Pension funds, mutual funds, and so-called hedge funds are like massive savings accounts that require high rates of return for their deposits. One option was to finance agricultural production, now that the so-called third world states had been pushed to withdraw from regulatory and financing roles in order to access IMF loans. Large input suppliers, processors, and traders did the same. These were the new players that started to command the wheel of negotiation on which world agriculture turned. The world witnessed agriculture evolve from a market for financing production to a market for speculation and the transformation of food into commodities.

In the 2000s, with the creation of increasingly complex financial mechanisms mediated by the commodities and futures exchanges, this process intensified. The increase in commodity prices and, mainly, the increase in oil prices from 2004 onward, initiated a process of falling global profit rates. The increase in the value of raw materials and grains has increased the value of food, putting upward pressure on wages. What would be the way out for those masters of the *wheel of negotiation*? They continued to atrophy the productive sphere in order to increase their income. Financial capital imposed upon the world a contraction of production and deflation through fiscal austerity policies, as we have witnessed in Portugal, Greece, Spain, and Ireland.

In short, this new financial accumulation crisis of the 2000s increased the demand for environmental inputs, raw materials, and food, thus increasing the scale of the search for land by private investors, speculative funds, and foreign governments in a process that has been called *acaparamiento de tierras* (land grabbing) or land foreignization. Such investments are a way to anticipate crises—like the 2008 financial crisis—by transforming this fictitious capital—bonds, papers, and shares—into real wealth, from farms, soy, eucalyptus, and palm oil, etc. This process heated up the land market in Brazil; the search for new farms led to a true process of expropriation of traditional territories, expulsion of communities, environmental devastation, and threats to food sovereignty.

Not by chance, as of mid-2008 and 2009, several transnational commodity-producing companies, such as Cosan S/A and SLC Agrícola S/A, started to invest in land as the main financial asset of their business. Some examples of these real estate companies are Radar Propriedades Agrícolas S/A and SLC LandCo., owned respectively by Cosan and Cargill, which have joined in partnership with pension funds or international investment funds.[4]

Other examples of companies that have partnered with funds to invest in land are: BrasilAgro and TibaAgro, through the Vision Brazil Gestão de Investimentos e Participações Ltda Fund; Sollus Capital, related to Ceagro (with capital from Mitsubishi in Japan and Grupo Los Grobo in Argentina); Xingú Agri (which deals with Multigrain in the US, Mitsui in Japan, and SLC Agrícola in Brazil); Adecoagro (with capital from financial mega-investor George Soros); Agrinvest (with capital from funds from Ridgefield in the US and Touradji in Brazil); Calyx Agro (linked to Louis Dreyfus Commodities Group in the Netherlands and PineBridge investment fund from the US); Colorado Group (with capital from the funds Global Opportunity and BlackRock); Insolo AgroIndustrial (with capital from Harvard University, Cambridge); and trading companies such as Bunge and Cargill.[5]

In this context, financial capital is also spreading to other sectors related to agriculture, such as mining, water resources, and the land market itself. This is reflected in the commodification of nature's goods and the internationalization of these goods, which has increased the overexploitation of land, soil, and water. The evidence of overexploitation is dramatic: dam bursts, water supply crises, worsening of greenhouse gas emission rates, increased contamination by agrochemicals, soil degradation, burning and devastation of biomes, and the pollution of the oceans. This overexploitation is, in short, a pact with death. The wealth generated by these sectors is highly concentrated and internationalized, which is reflected in the impoverishment of the Brazilian population and an increase of contagious and non-contagious diseases, hunger, and death.

The masters of the *wheel of negotiation* don't seem to be concerned about this, since the numbers negotiated through the wheel conceal its impacts. It is important to produce what is most interesting to capital—that which makes the wheel turn. This fictitious and speculative capital has no commitment to the development of countries. Today they are here, tomorrow they are somewhere else. They are accompanied by tax exemptions and exonerations that function as a veritable plunder of resources—both monetary and natural.

Added to this is the abandonment of policies to support small and medium-sized agricultural producers. The production of food—the food itself that goes to the workers' tables—is abandoned. This abandonment is supported by the discourse of market freedom and of noninterference by the state. Without support, food production falls, prices rise, and the state has no more instruments for the control of prices. The price is paid by the population through their hunger.

How is it possible to exit this fatal circle? It is necessary to impose limits on financial capital. It is necessary to strengthen the role of the state in controlling regulatory stocks, in planning and financing food production, and in controlling the land market. It is necessary to protect national production systems and our agrobiodiversity. Family agriculture and that of traditional peoples and communities must be strengthened, and the right to territories for these populations must be guaranteed. The principle of food sovereignty must be implemented so that what is produced, how it is produced, and how it is marketed and consumed respects the interests of the Brazilian population and not those of capital. The logic of state action should be that of food, environmental, energy, and territorial sovereignty and security. The spaces for participation in this by larger society, such as the Conselho Nacional de Segurança Alimentar e Nutricional (National Council for Food and Nutritional Security), must be resumed and fortified. This global wheel of negotiation has to be replaced by small participative circles, which build and support short commercialization circuits, popular supply spaces, and spaces for the exchange of social technologies. There is an urgent need to return to the democratization of access to land. A concentrated landholding structure like Brazil's only generates inequality, poverty, environmental devastation, and hunger. The global wheel of negotiation turns in the direction of wealth concentration. We urgently need to make it turn around, or it will pass over everything and everyone. We need to leave the *wheel* that turns from a pact with death; we need the *mandala* of a pact with life.

1. Yamila Goldfarb and Marco Antonio Mitidiero Jr. elaborate this argument in their publication “O Agro Não É Tech, O Agro Não É Pop E Muito Menos Tudo” (São Paulo: Abra and Friederich Ebert Stftung, 2021). See: https://library.fes.de/pdf-files/bueros/brasilien/18319-20211027.pdf.
2. Cássio Arruda Boechat, Maria Luisa Mendonça, and Fábio Teixeira Pitta, “A produção do espaço na região do MATOPIBA: violência, transnacionais imobiliárias agrícolas e capital fictício,” *Internacionais: Revista De relações Internacionais Da PUC Minas* 5, no. 2 (2018), 155–179.
3. Boechat, Mendonça, and Pitta, “A produção do espaço na região do MATOPIBA.”
4. Boechat, Mendonça, and and Pitta, “A produção do espaço na região do MATOPIBA.”
5. Boechat, Mendonça, Pitta, “A produção do espaço na região do MATOPIBA.

CIRCUMSCRIPTION

TAKING STOCK

vi. Ana Teixeira Pinto Berlin (DE)

The term "capitalism," Jean-Joseph Goux argues, names the divorce of economic practices from their symbolic valences, and the dominance of the "depersonalized, disaffected and asignificant" relations that undergird a market economy.[1] But these relations need manufacturing. As a great many authors have argued, capital takes on a totalizing role in modernity.[2] It "wants to reproduce itself everywhere" and thus needs to "subsume all other modes of production into itself."[3] Though there is little consensus among scholars as to when corporate stock was first traded, the first modern stock exchange was created in Amsterdam in 1611, with the Dutch East India Company as its first publicly traded company. Soon thereafter, trade in various derivatives emerged on the Amsterdam market.

Capitalization, Jonathan Nitzan and Shimshon Bichler detail, "not only predates 'industrialization' by a few hundred years, but also that it is far more encompassing than is typically assumed—so encompassing, in fact, that in our own day and age it has penetrated every corner of society and absorbed many of its power processes. Production, narrowly defined, has become merely one of the many faces of capitalization."[4]

Financial apparatuses, however abstract, are not autonomous but rather work in tandem with, and under the aegis of, sovereign power. In the early modern period, the feedback loop between sovereign power and military commerce will become the driving force behind the global economy: the logic of war shapes the pursuit of hegemonic power, but the military costs of such pursuit tend to exhaust state revenues, creating in turn an ever-greater compulsion for imperial expansion. If we believe modern states "to be essentially capitalist," as Siraj Ahmed argues, "the responsibility lies not with 'the market' in some abstract sense but rather with these two deeply interwoven credit mechanisms, national debts and stock exchanges."[5] In the eighteenth century, European states were so militarized that they bankrupted the Commonwealth, with the English state creating the Bank of England to finance its war debt.

In yet another defining moment, enslaved bodies will become "a portable, convertible, and exchangeable source of capital," which could thus "take the place of money, or indeed signify the underwriting material, in a number of transactions." Prior to financialization, as Amy Bride argues, the value of enslaved bodies was a function of their laboring capacities. This "exchangeability between the commodity and the labourer further cements the connection between slave value and slave labour" up to the point where "slaves forced to labour in the cultivation of cotton were later sold or exchanged for bales of cotton cloth." A further transition occurs when enslaved bodies cease to be just producers of material value to become instead valuable in themselves, to the point where they can be collateralized.[6]

> Whilst this monetization of the slave body is still connected with its ability to produce material goods, it indicates a step away from the direct equivalency between slave value and commodity production into a more abstracted form of capitalism . . . the implication is that the slave is valuable because it has the capacity to perform labour, but when the slave body is used in place of cash, this labour is yet to take place. The valuation of the slave body is then based on something that has not yet happened and may not happen in the future, and is therefore entirely intangible at the time of valuation. *The transition from value based on materiality to value based on possibility is also the transition from economic capitalism to finance capitalism.*[7]

The history of money as a general equivalent is also "marked by a progression toward abstraction and convention" but, crucially, this shift also entails a shift away from the concreteness of material value to the arbitrariness of a sign.[8] The abstraction realized in the system of monetary value reduces socioeconomic activity to its financial surface. Capital, however, as Nitzan and Bichler note, is not a narrow economic entity, but a symbolic quantification of power. Hence the difficulties surrounding its basic nature and properties:[9]

> Note that this is not "economic power." Neither is it "political power" that somehow distorts the economy. Instead, what we deal with here is organized power at large. Numerous

> power institutions and processes—from ideology, through culture, to organized violence, religion and law, ethnicity, gender, international conflict, labor relations, manufacturing and accounting innovations—all bear on the differential level and volatility of earnings. When these earnings and their volatility are discounted into capital values, the power institutions and processes that underlie them become part of capital. And since capital is a vendible commodity, available for purchase and sale on the stock and bond markets, its relative value represents the commodification of power. From this viewpoint, we can no longer speak of "economic efficiency" versus "political power," or distinguish "economic exploitation" from "political oppression." Instead, there is a single process of capital accumulation/state formation, a process of restructuring by which *power is accumulated as capital*.[10]

Processes of conversion—between different types of assets or between assets and money—and the anxiety they elicit, will also find expression at multiple levels, not simply at an economic one. Ahmed's *The Stillbirth of Capital* (2011) details the entanglement and attrition between patriarchal values and exchange value by looking at the eighteenth-century novel, in which the theme of conversion takes center stage. In *The King of Pirates*, first published in 1720, Daniel Defoe describes the tribulations of Captain Avery, a pirate who seizes the dowry of a Mughal princess. At first euphoric at the sight of the immense wealth he has captured, Captain Avery will soon be bitterly disappointed: the goods he has seized cannot be converted to monetary value in European markets. The pirate's bounty is, as Ahmed observes, "caught between the diverse economies of the premodern world." The impossibility to estimate its value marks the limit of European modernity, by pointing to "other worlds."[11] Whereas capitalism demands these other worlds be subsumed into the world of international trade monopolies, the conversion of all forms of value into monetary value threatens to entail the breakdown of age-honored patriarchal values at the heart of imperial centers. Hence the paradox at the heart of modernity: asignificant market relations are hard to reconcile with patriarchal hierarchies. To borrow from Sylvia Wynter, a ceremony must be found in order to reconcile former and latter.[12] This is also the reason why, I would argue, the "salient conversion that accompanies capitalism" does not simply "take place at points of exchange like the stock market where illicit wealth reappears as legitimate property,"[13] but also crops up inside the walls of literary salons or universities.

In the gothic novel, the anxiety about conversion is figured as a deformation or transmogrification, and all economic and geopolitical flows, however mobile, are fixed within an imperial frame. In the same manner, any conversion that runs counter to the colonial norm is figured as an unnatural inversion. The gothic representations of monstrosity in Bram Stoker's *Dracula* (1897), and Robert Louis Stevenson's *Dr. Jekyll and Mr. Hyde* (1886), show how monstrosity is mobilized to connote value conversions via their embellishment with racialized inscriptions of difference, in order to strengthen colonial categories of Self and Other.

It is also interesting to me that *geist*—as in the Hegelian *weltgeist*—would mistranslate into ghost. As literary theorist Sladja Blažan noted at a recent conference, the sighting of a ghost always exposes the entanglements of horror and history.[14] The university is here a point of conversion where the friction between values and value is elevated into a metaphysical scheme.

Reconciling spiritual value with monetary value, G. W. F. Hegel conceptualizes processes of conversion along a chronopolitical axis, whereby nature is converted onto culture: to be human, for Hegel, is to negate the given, to free oneself from nature.[15] Nature is an alienation in which spirit does not find itself; nature negates the idea. The spirit must negate this negation. The function of culture is to undo nature, in order to create a (man-made) second world: "Man appears on the scene as the antithesis of nature; he is the being who raises himself up."[16] The failure to free oneself from nature is thus conceptualized as a cultural failure, which Hegel attributes to conceptual inadequacy. From Hegel's perspective, race is an index of failure and inadequacy; "whiteness" is thus not a race, but the absence thereof. By playing race "against a falsely transparent humanity," Hegel makes the notion of openness to history "into the measure of authentic development," which he then uses to generate racist images of those who are defined by its "lack."[17] Patriarchal ideology can thus be sublated into a metapolitical plot and reappear under the guise of universal history.

To quote Susan Buck-Morss by way of conclusion, "The economy, when it was discovered, was already capitalist."[18] When the exchange of goods, "rather than denoting the edge of community, is capable of functioning as the fundament of collective life,"[19] the community becomes an effect of the economy. Miranda Joseph argues, in *Debt to Society* (2014), that community is thus not opposed to capitalism—"that it's [not] prior to, destroyed, or damaged by capitalism and, as a result, a force of resistance to it"—but is instead shaped by it: "Financialized capitalism is the way we interact and are in relation with one another. It depends on and shapes racialization and class, gender, familial structures, kinship, sexuality."[20] To study the accumulation or conversions of capital is to study the social formations—financial, legal, epistemological, racial, social—that are constituted by financial capitalism.

1. Jean-Joseph Goux, *Symbolic Economies: After Marx and Freud* (Ithaca, NY: Cornell University Press, 1990), 123.
2. Siraj Ahmed, *The Stillbirth of Capital: Enlightenment Writing and Colonial India* (Palo Alto, CA: Stanford University Press, 2011), 4. The author is here referring to the *Grundrisse* and its critical reception.
3. Ahmed, 4.
4. Jonathan Nitzan and Shimshon Bichler, *Capital as Power: A Study of Order and Creorder* (London: Routledge, 2009), 13.
5. Ahmed, 84.
6. Amy Bride, "Dead or Alive: Racial Finance and the Corpse-Value of the African American Slave Body," *Journal of Historical Sociology* 33, no. 1 (2020): 99–115.
7. Bride, "Dead or Alive." Emphasis added.
8. Goux, 49.
9. Nitzan and Bichler, 9–13.
10. Nitzan and Bichler, 9. Emphasis added.
11. Ahmed, 20.
12. In her two essays, "The Ceremony Must be Found: After Humanism" (1984) and "The Ceremony Found: Towards the Autopoetic Turn/Overturn, its Autonomy of Human Agency and Extraterritoriality of (Self-)Cognition" (2015), Sylvia Wynter describes the difficulty of reconciling the emancipatory processes and the subjugating processes that together define modernity as an *aporia* or "endemic contradiction." See Wynter, "The Ceremony Found: Towards the Autopoetic Turn/Overturn, its Autonomy of Human Agency and Extraterritoriality of (Self-)Cognition," in *Black Knowledges/Black Struggles: Essays in Critical Epistemology*, (Liverpool, UK: Liverpool University Press, 2015), 184–245.
13. Wynter, "The Ceremony Found," 189.
14. Sladja Blažan, "Whose Imaginary? The Question of World-Making," presented at *WHOSE UNIVERSAL?*, 2 July 2022, Akademie der Künste, Hanseatenweg. Organized by Haus der Kulturen der Welt (HKW) in collaboration with the 12th Berlin Biennale for Contemporary Art. See: https://12.berlinbiennale.de/media/lecture-sladja-blazan-whose-imaginary-the-question-of-world-making/.
15. Teshale Tibebu, *Hegel and the Third World: The Making of Eurocentrism in World History* (Syracuse, NY: Syracuse University Press, 2011), 28.
16. G. W. F. Hegel, "B: The Realisation of Spirit in History," in *Lectures on the Philosophy of World History,* 44. As cited in Tibebu, *Hegel and the Third World,* 190.
17. Rei Terada, "Hegel's Racism for Radicals," *Radical Philosophy* 2, no. 5 (Autumn 2019): 11–22.
18. Susan Buck-Morss, "Envisioning Capital: Political Economy on Display," *Critical Inquiry* 21, no. 2 (Winter 1995), 439.
19. Buck-Morss, "Envisioning Capital."
20. Quoted in Miranda Trimmier, "Called to Account," *The New Inquiry*, 22 February 2016, https://thenewinquiry.com/called-to-account/.

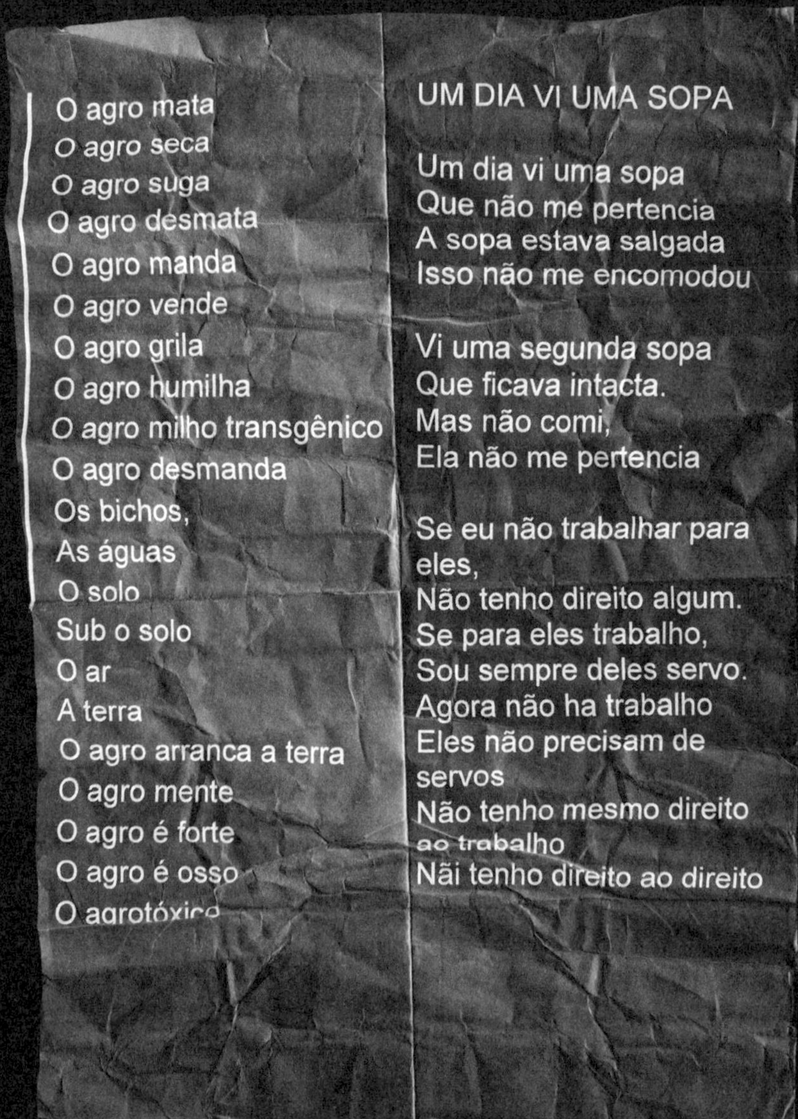

O agro mata
O agro seca
O agro suga
O agro desmata
O agro manda
O agro vende
O agro grila
O agro humilha
O agro milho transgênico
O agro desmanda
Os bichos,
As águas
O solo
Sub o solo
O ar
A terra
O agro arranca a terra
O agro mente
O agro é forte
O agro é osso
O agrotóxico

UM DIA VI UMA SOPA

Um dia vi uma sopa
Que não me pertencia
A sopa estava salgada
Isso não me encomodou

Vi uma segunda sopa
Que ficava intacta.
Mas não comi,
Ela não me pertencia

Se eu não trabalhar para
eles,
Não tenho direito algum.
Se para eles trabalho,
Sou sempre deles servo.
Agora não ha trabalho
Eles não precisam de
servos
Não tenho mesmo direito
ao trabalho
Nãi tenho direito ao direito

256
268

REAC TI VA TION VIII

DIMENSION OF ART, DIMENSION OF LIFE

vii. Beatriz Cruz and Vânia Medeiros with Daniel de Paula São Paulo (BR)

Daniel de Paula By way of introduction, I'd like to ask each of you about how you understand your respective artistic practices. Could you highlight some investigative processes and procedures that are dear to you?

Beatriz Cruz I come from a background in scenic arts and, over the years—especially through encounters on the street, working in the city—I have been in dialogue with the field of visual arts. The street has always been the engine behind my practice—and when I say "street," I mean the city and the urban environment as a potential site of encounter. Sensorial encounters permeate my work—from the body in the city—and these encounters propose interactions with otherness. This is always part of the work I do. The work is physical and practical: it is, at once, an entangling of my body with the foundation of the city and its architecture, while also being a commitment to the creation of shared spaces of experience—spaces for exchanging looks, exchanging clothes, exchanging stories, and seeking to be contaminated by other subjectivities. Since 2009 I have been working with the Coletivo Teatro Dodecafônico,[1] which is where I first met Vânia. The collective works through performative theater, through urban interventions, and through practicing walking as an aesthetic and political practice. More recently, Vânia and I have been jointly developing a body of artistic research that is based on the oneiric universe. That has been very inspiring to me, and I hope it will have a sustained life.

Vânia Medeiros I am a visual artist, but my background and training is in communication, so my path in the arts began with a long-standing interest in publishing, and related forms of graphic design. Illustration, as a medium of representation, has also been part of my research trajectory, and text has always been very present in my work. The idea of publishing books and fanzines out of the diverse proposals that get made by collective situations—that is, by the kinds of shared spaces in which groups are formed—has always been part of my creative process. Some encounters along the way taught me lessons that guide my practice today—as Beatriz mentioned, meeting Coletivo Teatro Dodecafônico is one of them. In the context of working collectively in urban space, a specific interest emerged for me in finding ways to document such experiences. How can ephemeral, experiential, or corporeal situations take on a format that allows them to persist? I am very interested in researching how one might make ephemeral encounters sustain over time. Overall, my artistic research and practice is very much in this vein; it has strong connections with graphic design and participatory design. Drawing manifests as an important element in my work, both as personal expression and as a device for creating groups and recording situations. I am very interested in drawing that is not virtuosic or specialist: a kind of drawing that is a trace, or is incidental to a process. Beatriz and I have a project called *Mulheres Possíveis*

(2016–ongoing),[2] which has been a great space for us to learn in relation to these questions. Our project was developed with two other artists, Sandra Ximenez and Letícia Olivares, and took place in the Women's Penitentiary of São Paulo. That work unites our personal research—Beatriz's with the body, mine with drawing, and our partners' with performance. Everything came together in the way we worked with those incarcerated women.

To synopsize: I am interested in processes that situate the formation of groups. In the creative process, we are really invested in this kind of work, aren't we? An initial project becomes something else as it is realized—it becomes a *work-experience*, a *work-contamination*—and I think that this has a lot to do with the work of *deposition* as well. I believe it is very much related to our practices in general—to the extent that Beatriz and I are interested in spaces where collectivity becomes possible, whether in the street or in an institutional setting. We are always looking for those places from which collective processes can emerge.

DdP Great to hear you two speak about your work in this way. In a gesture of generosity to the reader, could you tell us a bit about the invitation you received from the curators of the 34th Bienal de São Paulo for your contribution to the work *deposition*, and how this came about? Maybe you could speculate a bit on why you were chosen as interlocutors charged with producing one of the main axes of the public program of the 34th Bienal de São Paulo.

VM I think I can start, as I was the first person contacted. Paulo Miyada reached out to me, in a very informal way, telling me a bit about what *deposition* proposed—about where you were all coming from. He left it completely open—that is, we could propose whatever we wanted within the existing frameworks. The curators had some sense of the people they would like to present on the trading floor—especially some artists participating in the Bienal—thinking that the pit could be a platform for participating artists to speak to the public. But, in general, the curatorial team didn't have a thematic angle. It was from your text, from that "manifesto" or statement that you shared with us,[3] that the political framing of the work revealed itself as fundamental. For me, it was very clear, then, that this was a kind of work that I couldn't do alone. And I think that calling Beatriz—for us to do this work together—was very natural, since we have had a long-term exchange and share deep trust, so I thought this would be a process that we could share in a very fluid and powerful manner. From the moment you proposed that the trading pit articulates issues of land, labor, and capital, we felt the need to tie our programming around very urgent issues in Brazil, and, at the same time, to bring a poetic dimension to the program that, for us, is also very political. And, well, that is where you come in, Beatriz.

BC The dimension of the work we were going to do, for me, was gradually amplifying. You know when you throw a stone into water, and it creates a series of ripples? Little by little we could see the power of the encounters that could be generated in that space. The day I went there and saw *deposition* for the first time, installed in the middle of the Bienal pavilion, it was very striking. We were in that significant space, the *vão* of the Bienal, and we were at the same time processing what it meant to temporarily come out of a pandemic in which people were totally isolated in their private spheres—for so long we were only seeing each other as squares on screens.

DdP I find it somewhat revealing, Vânia, that you had this impulse to immediately respond to the invitation from the Bienal with a collaborative proposal—and not collaborative in the sense of simply inviting people to occupy that space within the program, rather by inviting a collaborator to think through this program with you. It's remarkable that in all instances of this work, collaboration has been a core element: whether between us—the proposing artists, Marissa, David, and myself—or in our exchanges with the curators, yourselves, or the other programmers. Perhaps this is a more personal question, Vânia, but I wondered whether you could, if possible, share your first reactions from when you encountered the trading floor in that Bienal. Beatriz just mentioned a little bit about this sense of the magnitude of the space—about its spatial location—and it would be interesting to know more about your initial reactions as well, and how they informed the strategies you collaboratively devised to frame your programming, which you named *Conversações*.[4]

VM Yes, I think it is funny because the object, the trading floor, has a history of violence—it is structurally part of a process of dispossession, which is evident in your investigations—but in dislocating the trading pit from its original context, it presents itself as a broken circular structure, which is conducive to interactions that are nonhierarchical and allows for potential equal or less asymmetric relationships. Within the structure, it was very natural for the audience, guests, and artists to mix; it was all very dispersed on the floor. This is a quality of the object that calls attention to itself right away. Of course we could have quickly turned it into a space for lectures, which would have promoted hierarchical stratifications, but this didn't happen. As for documentation—recording the events—we chose not to take pictures of the conversations that took place on the trading floor.[5] Even if we had taken photos, I believe that it wouldn't have been possible, on most occasions, to see who was supposed to be leading the conversations, right? So, having an object of this nature to hold conversations on is quite unique.

BC For me, the first impulse I had upon encountering the trading floor was to want to walk around it, to go up and down it. But I remember we arrived and someone was already sitting there, so we sat down too. Then I went on another day to the Bienal, and I just kept walking around the trading floor, positioning myself in different parts of the wheel-shape[6]—nothing more than this. And I said to myself: we have to do something physical with our bodies, walking in this space, experiencing the object, learning from it in another way. The trading pit allowed us to see the exhibition space of the Bienal from different perspectives. I thought we should take advantage of this object by locating our bodies within it, inviting those who participated in the *Conversações* to walk around the work: to circulate, to go up and down, to choose different perspectives from which to see the space and to see each other. There is an immediate reading that the trading floor looks like a theater in the round. It is a circular space that makes reference to a wheel and makes a reference to a space without hierarchy. And then it is very wild to think—very terrible, in fact—that capital appropriated this form to facilitate a kind of visuality that drove speculative practices. It is, after all, an architectural dynamic that allows for those occupying it to have an overview of the space, and the people in it—that's how it worked, and how it worked was appropriated.

VM I also think that this bodily dynamic, which Beatriz mentioned now, was super important for each conversation that took place. We didn't arrive and simply start up a conversation out of nowhere. I think that this initial moment that we proposed to the public—of circulating around the trading pit and having different perspectives on the space—built a kind of communion between those who were present. People saw each other from head to toe—we didn't sit in our own corners. This was something that brought a sense of belonging, in the moment, to the conversation. Another important point was the fact that the trading pit was formally opened up, because you all decided to position it this way. I believe this also diluted what could have been, hierarchically, the concentration of power within the structure. Perhaps—with this structure opened—the middle broke down, promoting a kind of fragmentation: the center lost strength.

DdP It is nice that you mention this, because in the contract, which mediates the work with the institution, there are only two clauses that deal with the configuration of the trading pit in the exhibition space. One of them stipulates that the object, the floor, can never, again, be what it was before. The contract doesn't say how this should be, just that it can't be. So in formal terms—in terms of configuration—that means that the trading floor can no longer be installed as a closed octagon—as it was in the context of the financial market. It's something else now. The decision of that particular, open configuration, as you said, was the decision of the curators. They could have chosen a different configuration. Everything could have been stacked, scattered, dispersed in space. But they opted for that semicircle—that "open wheel" form. The other clause or condition that is in the contract is that the central piece of the trading pit—which would be an octagonal wooden board, below the first set of steps in the center, on the floor—is not included in the work. The floor of the institution must always serve as this missing central piece, which suggests that the institution is a foundational context for this transposed object. When you, Beatriz and Vânia, come to this, you bring to it this dimension of the body—of the bodies, and of a communion that is, in my view, a precise answer or critical counterpoint articulated by you both that arises from perceiving the latent grammars of the object itself and its original function.

Vânia, you brought up the word "belonging" just now. The trading pit, in its previous life, was a private space which only certain people had access to. In what you said earlier, you brought up this dimension of a public—a public by way of the street—and I wanted to ask you about this friction between public and private, and whether you understand there to be a kind of friction within the institutional space of the Bienal—between the concept of a public body and a private institution. Do you think it was possible to transform this private, more restricted, space of the Bienal, let's say, into a more public one? Or do you all find that the work has failed in this sense? Or maybe, was this not its intended function, or role, from the outset?

VM Look, I don't know if we transformed the Bienal into a public space—I don't think so. It was still a very hierarchical space, and this was mentioned in the *Conversações*, especially by artists from the institutional world of contemporary art. Egos are wild in contemporary art, and there are certain artistic practices that only exist, in short, as an institutional critique of the art world. In our conversations series, we felt that the people who were asked onto the trading pit—activists, creators from diverse areas, and artists who work in their communities and in communities that are mostly peripheral, not only in museums and galleries—were interested in the field of art with a great freshness. We saw in these talks the notion of artistic practice as something powerful and free, and not the professionalism of a certain institutional criticism that seems, to me, to bring a certain bitterness. So, the people speaking on the trading pit floor were speaking about claiming the space of art as an exercise in democracy. They spoke about the importance of being invited to be part of that roundtable format in the middle of the Bienal. We saw in the conversation with Carmen Silva, from the Movimento Sem Teto do Centro (MSTC),[7] for example, the importance she placed on the movement's interactions with artists, and the power these interactions have at MSTC's sites of occupation within politically contested spaces. The institutional critique of more established contemporary artists, like Roger Bernat, appeared more forcefully precise, which was also important to have present. But in general, it was very gratifying to invite people into the Bienal context: people who have experiences that are far outside the sphere of the commercialized art world—a professionalization which brings with it, to a great extent, a certain affectation. In *Conversações,* a dimension of art was affirmed as a dimension of life and not, necessarily, as a dimension of formalism. Thinking this way, maybe this has brought a more public dimension to the work, but I don't know.

DdP I think I found something there—a kind of necessary self-criticism, both of the position of the institution itself and of us, the artists who participate in these processes. I remember a line from a dear professor who said, "Without self-criticism, everything is self-promotion." So, in this sense, I think it is also important to elaborate upon the differences between a public space and an institutional space—its limitations *and* its reach. Maybe this is a possible place of intersection that your work brings to bear.

BC When you brought up this question—whether the work failed in that sense or not—for me, the first thing that came to my mind was that maybe failure could have been a great merit. For me it would have been no different than succeeding. The space of the Bienal already poses these institutional questions—it is a private space, and we know the role that it occupies, and how its hierarchies are exercised, and the forms of decision-making power present within these institutionalized spaces. I don't know if any work would be able to transform this kind of private space into a public space, nor should it, really. The point is maybe to show that there are limits, and that they are here, and maybe that a possibility for the dilution of these entities is something else, somewhere else.

VM The Bienal holds an important position within the field of art, and generates, like it or not, an institutionalized environment. For us, with *Conversações* it became clear that the Bienal needs the people we invited and what they contributed, and not the other way around. I think that the people who participated don't need the Bienal to legitimize any of their practices—their work is art-life. People situate their practices between the social, the political, and the artistic in an organic way. The Bienal, if it is interested in a wider social resonance, will have to realize that it needs more and more spaces that bring these kinds of voices to the front, rather than just continue to endorse practices that are already legitimized by galleries, museums, curators, etc. I think our work on the trading pit floor brought this to the table.

DdP I remember in those first moments, when we had our first meeting—Marissa, David, you both, and I—and we were explaining the importance of *deposition*'s contract, how it frames the work conceptually and legally, and I remember you brought to that discussion the impossibility of translation presented by this object, the trading pit floor. You were thinking of the object as a contextual object, already foreseeing the arduous mission of what it would be to translate it to another context—in this case a local context. Thinking about this idea of translating an object from one particular context to another, how do you see this aspect of translation operating in your proposed programs?

VM Oh yes, that's super interesting. I was just reading Júlio Plaza's book, *Tradução Intersemiótica* (1987), and I have been thinking a lot about this issue of translation. What is it to translate one thing into another—to translate one practice into another? I think that, actually, the work of translation is, in some way, the work of *deposition*. Recounting Plaza's words, translation is a crossing out and writing over, an amendment, an extrojection, or a transformation. He goes on to say that "the creative project of the translator defines itself through the conflicts, frictions, and ambiguous routes of its interpreters."[8] I think *deposition*, as a work, really promotes this: it is a process of creative translation, and will act precisely on any gaps. It will look for forms of conflict that are intrinsic to it—that are *of* it or *in* it. These conflicts are not something that we created. The conflicts were born with this object—this trading floor—and it is on top of these conflicts that you all will work, and where you will all find a kind of creative transposition. It is not a case of erasing the trading pit's archival history, or saying, "No, now we are one big circular community"—it is not the same as wanting to do what Rui Barbosa did with the slavery files, that is, burn them.[9] The work is saying and remembering what it was and what it is, and from there on it will operate within the contradictions of its past and present—within the breach that it itself produces.

DdP I was wondering at what point you chose the title *Conversações* for your trading pit programming series, with this suffix of *ações* (actions)?[10] I think this is very revealing of the potential of gestures, actions, and happenings that are informed by, or are transforming, the space—both in the sense of the space physically produced by the transposition of the trading floor, and the other intersecting more ephemeral spaces circumscribed by the institution, the audience, etc. Adding to this, I'm wondering how you understand, comprehend, or perceive the trading pit—in its object-ness, its materiality, its physicality—and whether you think it comes out transformed by this exhibition experience?[11] Is there a difference in the object, from the initial moment of the Bienal's opening until now? How is it changed as it returns to the circuit of global logistics—flowing in the same routes as commodities inside its container—after the Bienal? Or does the object remain the same, and the actions performed upon it remain circumscribed in a more ephemeral, temporal, and spatial dimension?

BC I don't know if I'm being too utopian, but I think that the trading pit will leave the Bienal modified, yes. I can't think of it being any other way. I think the object is transformed practically, as well, from the moment of its arrival at the Bienal and especially for the duration of the exhibition when the guard-railing had to be added to it,[12] or while people sat there and kept peeling bits of the rubber off the trading pit floor. In short, I think that this describes some physical modifications, but I think the modifications are vibrational as well, in the intention that we put into it and that we all put into these exchanges. So I would say yes.

DdP At a certain moment—I think in one of the presentations from the Novas Frequências program,[13] and also in Kaká Werá's talk[14]—I felt that the object was being exorcized or excommunicated in some way. But there is still a lot of work ahead of us.

BC And maybe the work will be complete if the trading pit really leaves institutionalized art spaces. Maybe then it will complete its exorcism.

VM That's true.

BC Well, there are thousands of spatial possibilities, right? Maybe the trading pit has to go to a camp of the Movimento dos Trabalhadores Rurais Sem Terra (MST),[15] where it could be filled with land too.

VM It's just that the art field is a protective one—and it maintains this aspect of preserving the structure.

BC Yes, the trading pit is part of this other kind of speculation—this institutionalized art world one.

DdP We are in conversation, perhaps for a future iteration about installing the trading pit in the context of a public university. But this is still another form of institution, let's say. I think, with this, you are also revealing a desire of ours, a desire that the object circulates to other places. And a question I have with this work is, in an abstract dimension, how might one measure the violence produced by this object? What might be the total amount of the transactions facilitated by the floor? What might be the amount of square meters of land that—due to this object—were speculated, grabbed, and deforested? How many communities were decimated by these speculative processes? This gets into an abstract and conceptual place, asking questions about what is possible to measure and record and to what end, but I think that your proposal—to use drawing as the main documentation of the conversations during *Conversações*—is somehow related to this question of registering or measuring. Could you talk a little about the publication you produced from these drawings?

VM The way in which we conceived of the publication is very much based on our collaborative process. Having the public actively participate in and produce a record of the programs interested us—especially as an alternative to a documentary gesture produced by a specialist, who alone decides how to frame a narrative. So I think bringing the public in to participate in this framing—deciding what survives from *Conversações*—is important. Also in relation to the current state of image production, this seems delicate—there is a kind of incessant documentary and photographic impulse in contemporary life. Our publication expresses our desire to not make photography the protagonist of record keeping. Photographs end up creating a very asymmetric instance of documentation: whoever has the camera makes the decisions about an image—about who is going to be seen and who is going to be cut—and for us, this discourse didn't express what we were after. It is also important to note that the programs happened directly after the COVID-19 pandemic, in which the force of virtualization was brutal, constant, and excessive. The production of video recordings was very intense. So, on the trading pit floor, the conversations were neither virtually recorded nor live transmitted. There were almost no photos taken: the documentation was mostly corporeal, and corporeal presence was what allowed these conversations to happen in the first place. Drawing has a very corporeal dimension, and it felt coherent as a continuum with the choices we made throughout the process. People, both audience members and invited participants, didn't sign their drawings and writings—and neither was this of interest to us. People were very generous in their documentation. The publication of our book of these anonymous drawings, on the Bienal's free online public platform,[16] gives the drawings back to the participants in some manner, right? I think that the online publication is a mesh of connective lines: a non-hierarchical fabric produced without much editing.

BC For me this manner of documentation takes on the form of a counternarrative. In the artistic actions that we—in our collective practices—do together in the street, in our actions in the city, we always look for this dimension of storytelling because the records of cities are usually very hegemonic accounts of history. We think it is fundamental to create other forms of record keeping. Incorporating notes, doodles, and drawings, created by everyone that participated in the conversation, was an active way for people to be involved. They were responsible for defining what remains and what will remain. I also see these drawings as accounts; as a historical record created with and by the bodies that participated in that moment. To see space as a trace left by your hand—as a presence, as a horizontality—I think that there is a very important potential in this act of documentation.

1. Coletivo Teatro Dodecafônico, founded in 2008, creates provocations and transdisciplinary stimuli. The collective is formed by artists from a diverse range of backgrounds, including performance, theater, dance, visual arts, sound, and music. Since 2014, the collective has been researching walking as an aesthetic and political practice, focusing its investigations on the space of the street, and on the unfolding of bodily actions as reflected within the city. See: https://coletivoteatrododecafonico.com.
2. *Mulheres Possíveis* is a multidisciplinary artist project by Beatriz Cruz, Letícia Olivares, Sandra Ximenez, and Vânia Medeiros built around the subjects of body, gender, and incarceration, and developed in collaboration with women imprisoned at the Penitenciária Feminina da Capital (PFC), São Paulo, since 2016. The project's propositions take place in various languages, and the body is always at the center of the experience. The project is composed of actions taken inside the PFC and in public.
3. See pages 29–30.
4. *Conversações* was a public program designed by Cruz and Medeiros and convened on the floor of *deposition* during the three-month-long public exhibition of the 34th Bienal de São Paulo in the Pavilhão Ciccillo Matarazzo. The program invited speakers from social movements, organizations, communities, researchers, artists, and educators to be in conversation with one another. Audience members were openly invited to join the conversation during various portions of the program. Each program began with a reading of an *Enunciation* (written by Benedict, de Paula, and Rueter; see page 200–201; followed by a "corporeal activation of space," and then the conversation of "counter-narratives." Beatriz Cruz and Vânia Medeiros, *Arquivo gráfico do programação de ativação da obra "deposição"* (2021), https://issuu.com/bienal/docs/arquivo_grafico_bienal.
5. At the start of each program Medeiros and Cruz provided attendees with free paper and pens. The resulting spontaneous drawings, which were collected at the end of each program, are documented in the previously mentioned online publication by Cruz and Medeiros, *Arquivo gráfico do programação de ativação da obra "deposição"* (2021), https://issuu.com/bienal/docs/arquivo_grafico_bienal.
6. In Portuguese the technical term for "trading pit" is *roda de negociação* (wheel of negotiation).
7. The Movimento Sem Teto do Centro (MSTC) is a movement fighting for the fundamental right to housing in the center of São Paulo, and is made up of more than two thousand people, including adults, children, and youth. See: https://www.atados.com.br/ong/mstc.
8. Júlio Plaza, "Tradução intersemiótica," *Coleção Estudos* 93 (1987).
9. Rui Barbosa was the finance minister of Brazil who, on 14 December 1890, issued a proclamation that ordered the destruction of all government records officially documenting Brazil's ties to slavery, including slave registers, claiming that this was a necessary erasure of the "stain" left by this history. Lamonte Aidoo, "The Racial and Sexual Paradoxes of Brazilian Slavery and National Identity." *Slavery Unseen: Sex, Power, and Violence in Brazilian History*, Duke University Press (2018), 11–28. See: http://www.jstor.org/stable/j.ctv11314xj.5.
10. In Portuguese, the words *conversa* and *conversação* are both nouns meaning "conversation," however *conversação* implies an idea of conversation as a form of action through its suffix, as referenced here by de Paula.
11. A similar question is posed in "An Interview: Jacopo Crivelli Visconti and Paulo Miyada." See pages 218–219.
12. A powder-coated steel guard railing was custom built for *deposition* as required by Brazilian architectural code. In the original grain trading room, commodities pits were accessed from the top by interstitial raised flooring that served as the ground floor of the room. Without this, in its installation at the Bienal, the former trading pit was accessed from what was the center, or bottom, steps; and the outer, or top, ring of floor boards—supported by a scaffolding substructure—dropped off steeply (by approximately 2 meters or 6 feet). This required a safety railing be installed along the outer edges of the floor. The railing was designed by the artists, in discussion with the curatorial team of the Bienal, and visually referenced a standard railing design for modern commodities trading floors in Chicago and elsewhere. The custom guard railings, and the reconstructed scaffolding for the floor, built by the Bienal are elements that do not travel with *deposition*; rather, these supporting elements, or necessary architectural adaptations, are contextually renegotiated with each exhibiting institution.
13. Novas Frequências, founded in 2011, is a Brazilian experimental music and sound art festival. The curatorial team of the 34th Bienal de São Paulo invited general director and curator of Novas Frequências, Chico Dub, to curate a series of experimental music programs on *deposition* that took place over the course of the Bienal exhibition.
14. Kaká Werá, a Brazilian Kayapo writer, activist, and teacher, led a participatory conversation on the trading pit floor, with Medeiros and Cruz, about the political and poetic power of dreams in indigenous traditions for a *Conversações* program that took place on 4 December 2021. His work, over twenty-five years, has involved disseminating indigenous ancestral knowledge and values. See: http://34.bienal.org.br/agenda/9560.
15. "Brazil's Landless Workers

Movement, Movimento dos Trabalhadores Rurais Sem Terra (MST) in Portuguese, is a mass social movement, formed by rural workers and by all those who want to fight for land reform and against injustice and social inequality in rural areas. The MST was born through a process of occupying latifundios (large landed estates) and become [sic] a national movement in 1984. Over more than two decades, the movement has led more than 2,500 land occupations, with about 370,000 families—families that today settled on 7.5 million hectares of land that they won as a result of the occupations." See: https://www.mstbrazil.org/content/what-mst.

16. Cruz and Medeiros, *Arquivo gráfico do programação de ativação da obra "deposição"* (2021), https://issuu.com/bienal/docs/arquivo_grafico_bienal.

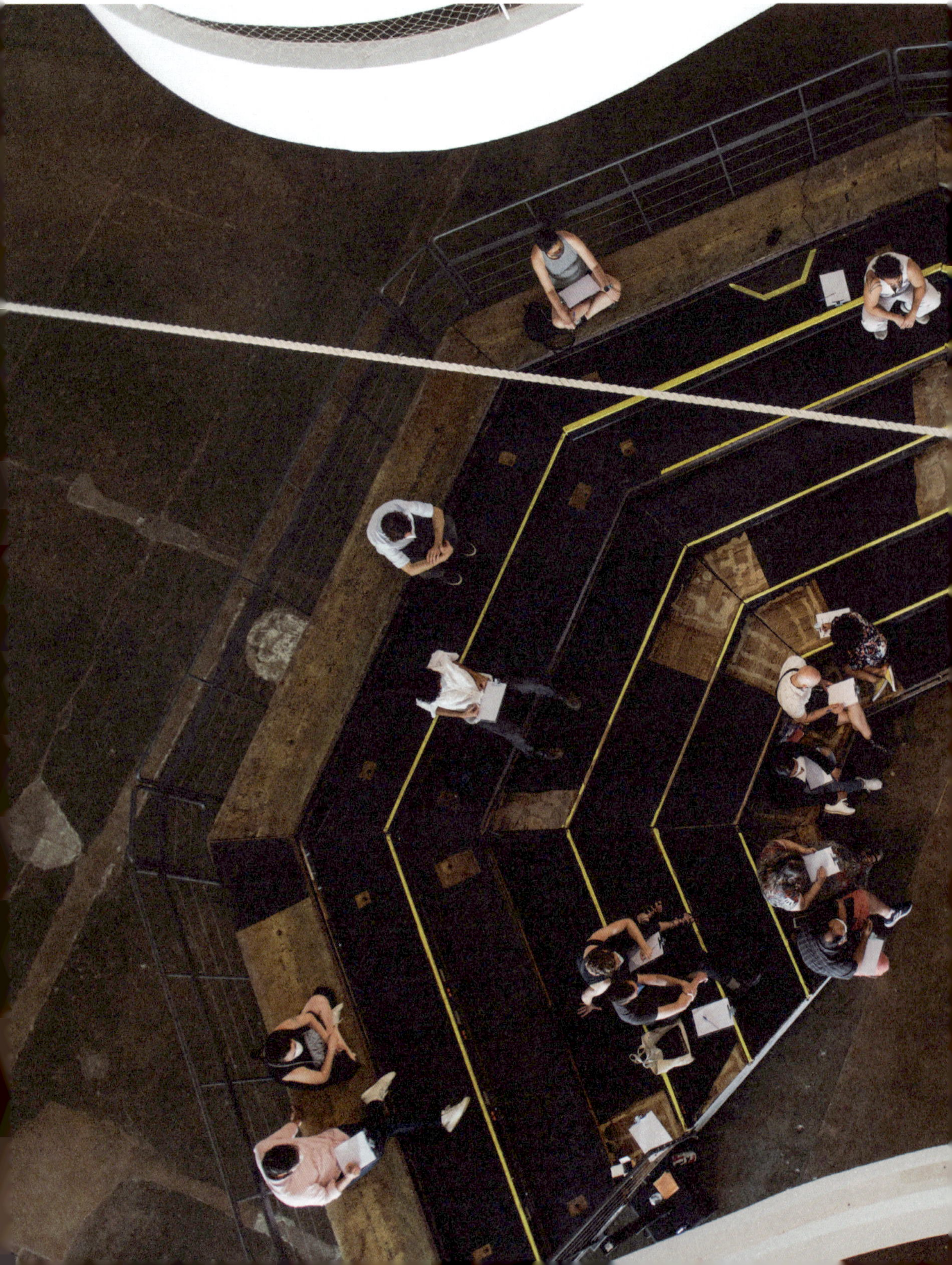

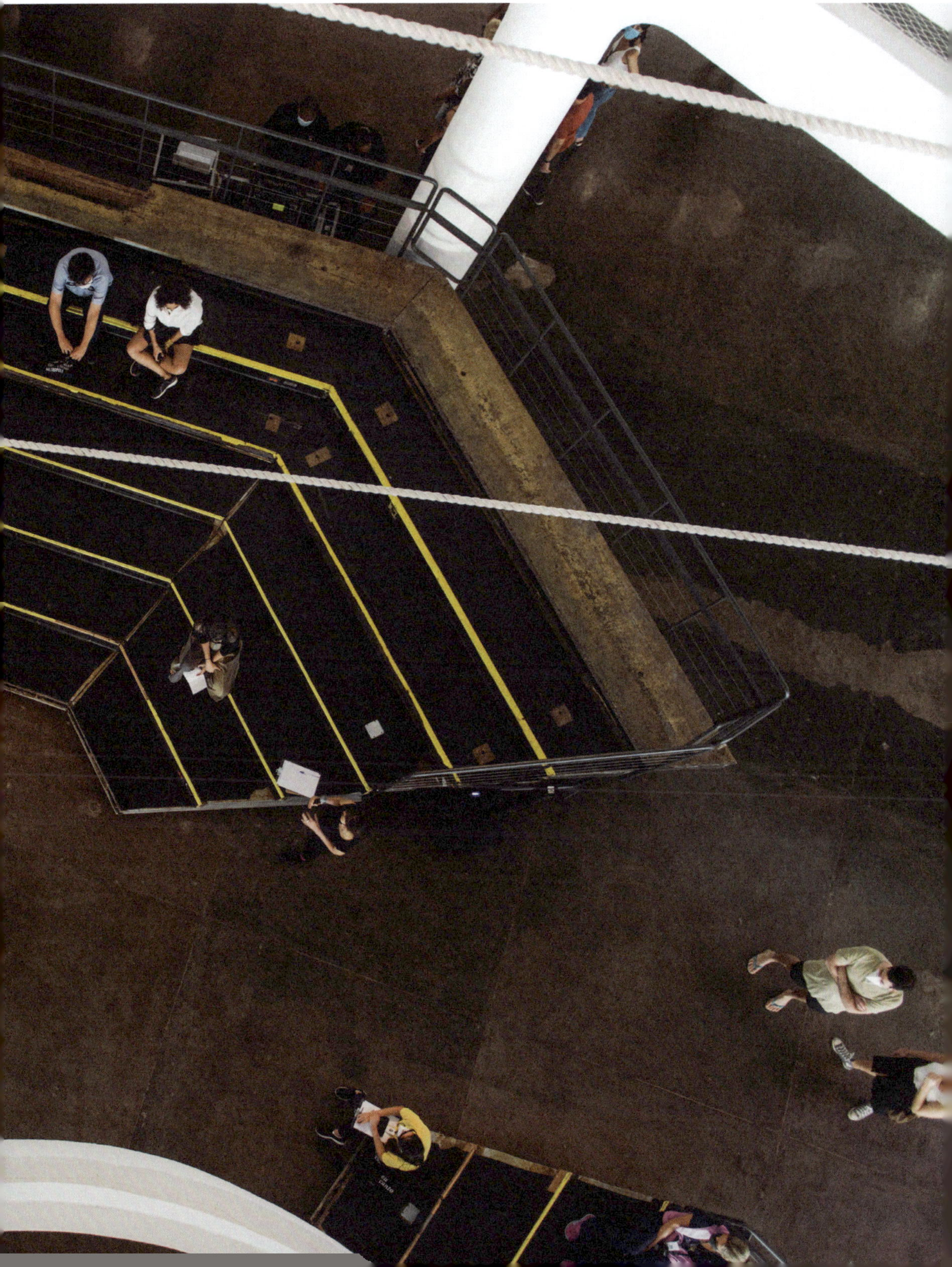

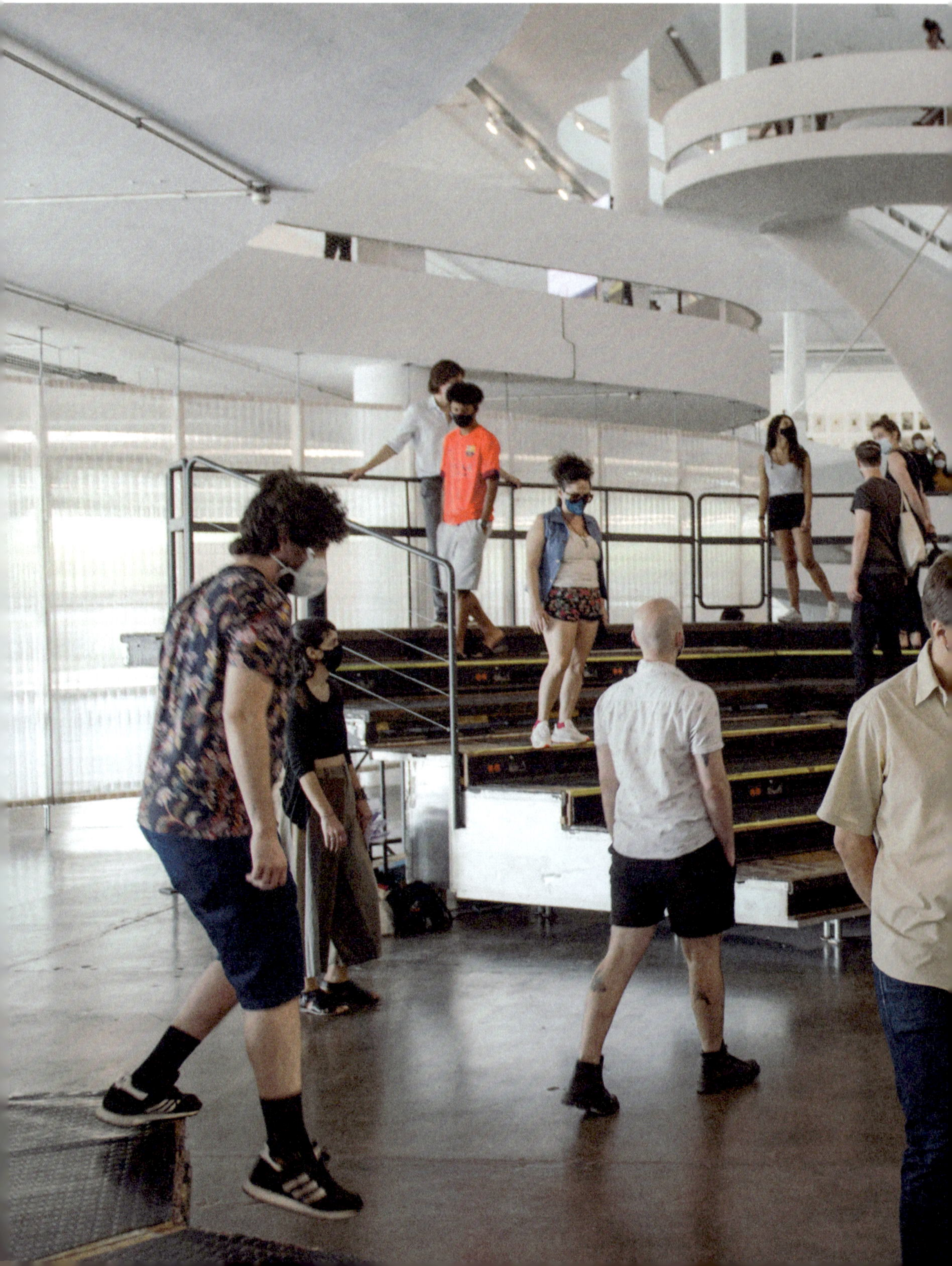

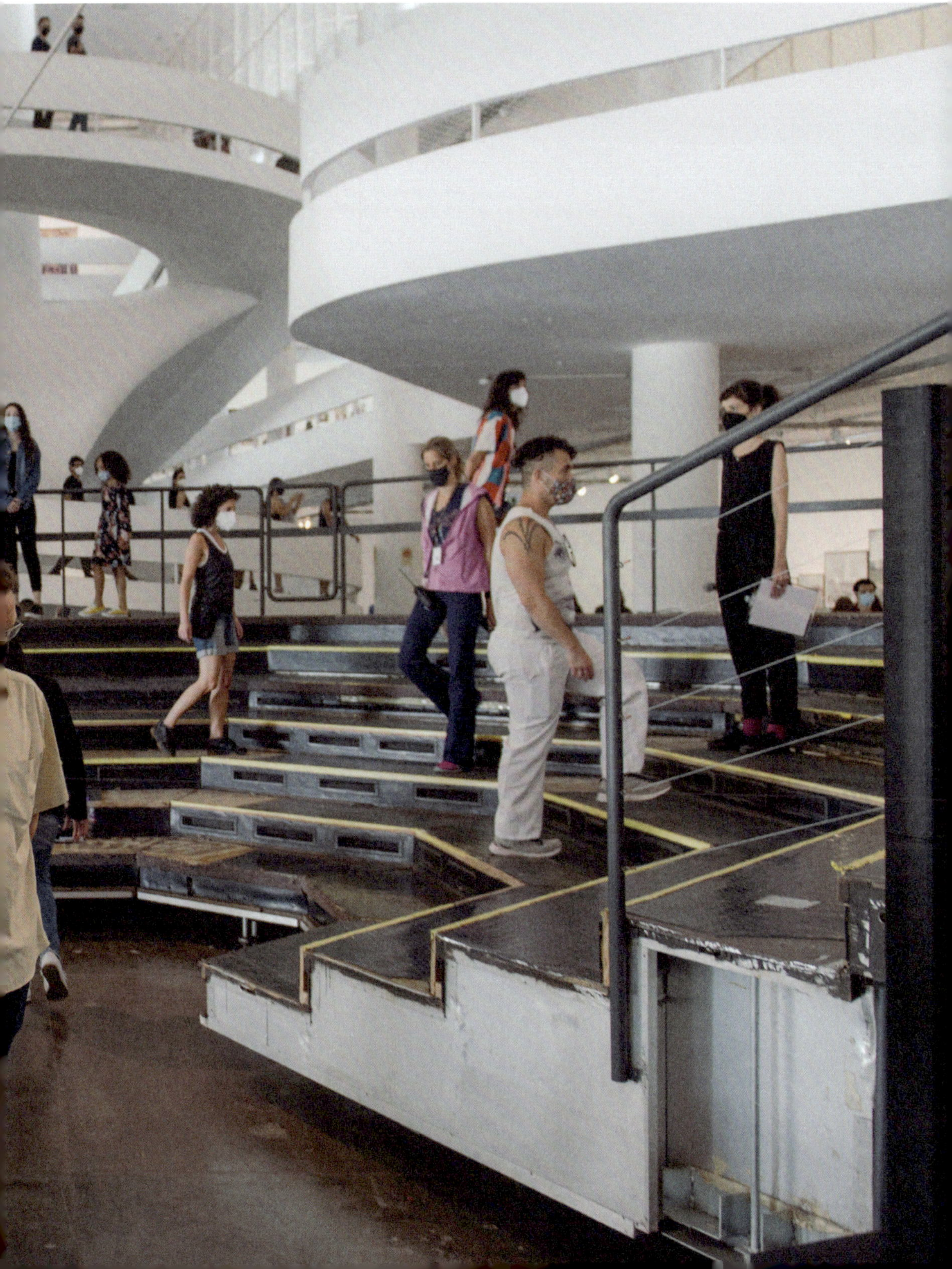

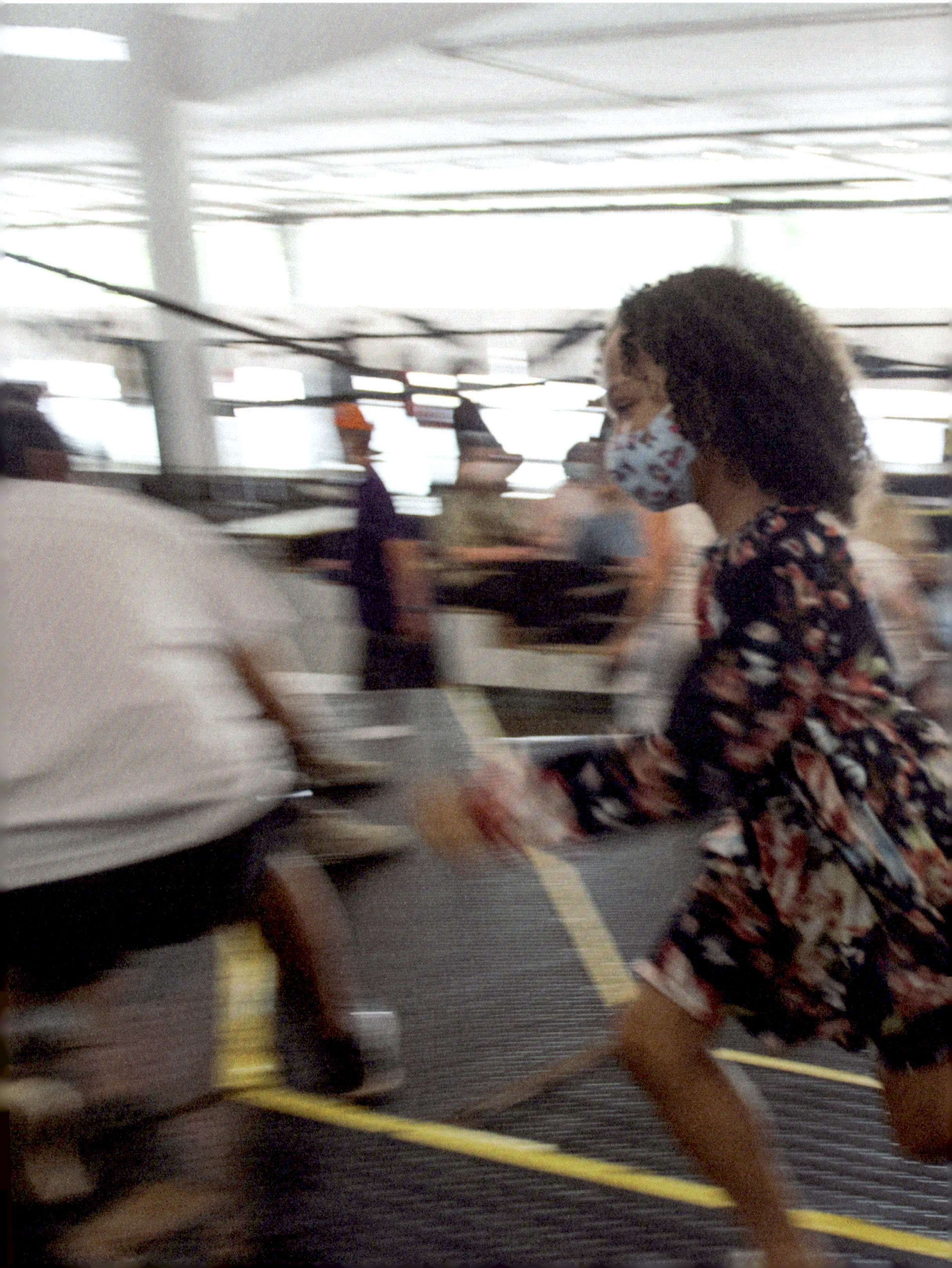

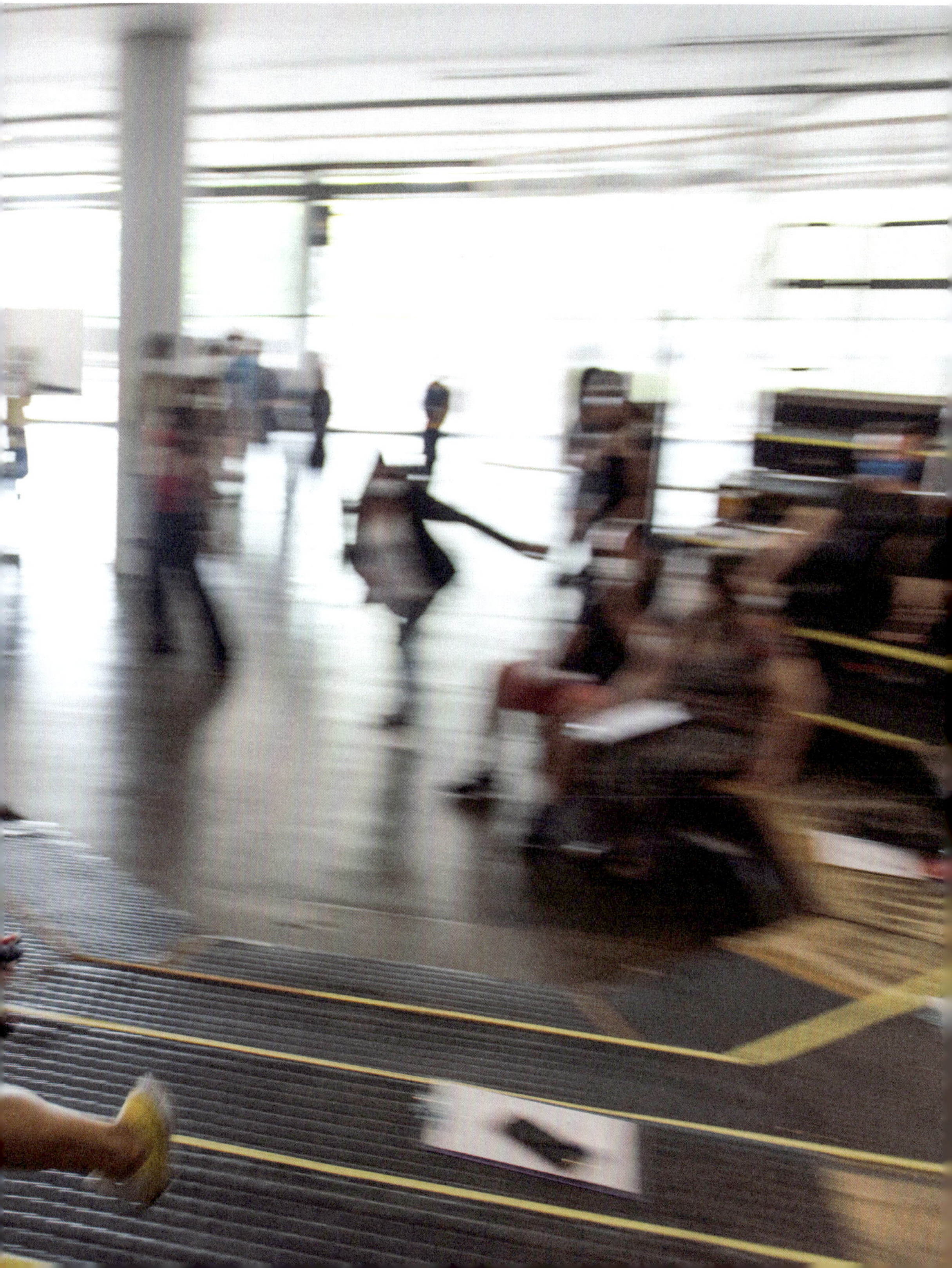

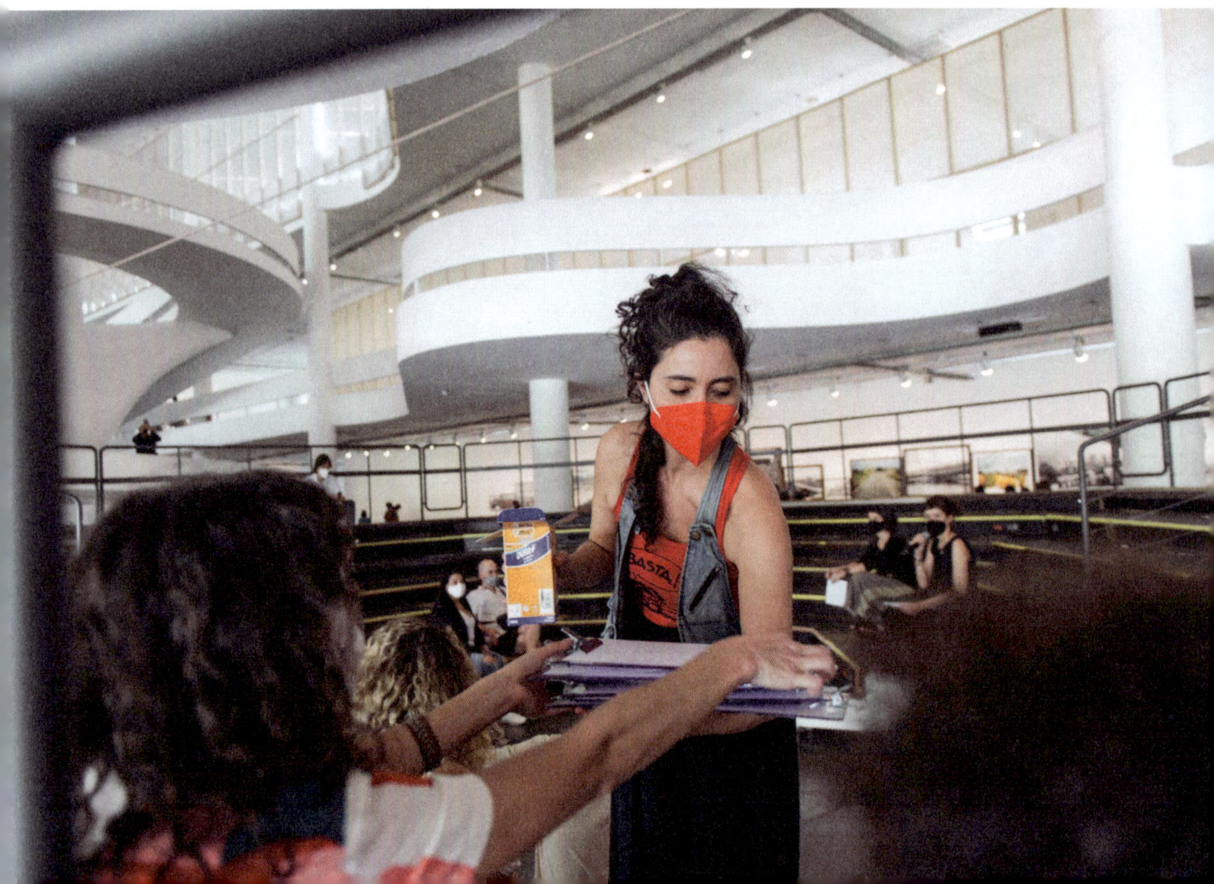
BASTA!

BIENAL PROGRAMMING (SEPTEMBER)

07 Sept 2021	*Conversações* with Roger Bernat, Verônica Veloso, and Murilo Gaulês
09 Sept 2021	Performance by Orquestra Errante
11 Sept 2021	*Conversações* with Carmen Silva, Dedê Ferreira, and Rafael Ferro
16 Sept 2021	Performance by MIHNA
18 Sept 2021	*Conversações* with Raphael Escobar and Matuzza Sankofa
25 Sept2021	*Conversações* with Gabriela de Matos and Guilherme Soares Dias
25 Sept 2021	Book launch for the translation of *Poética da Relação* by Édouard Glissant (Bazar do Tempo)
30 Sept 2021	*Conversações* with Gih Trajano, João Inecco, and Miriam Baião

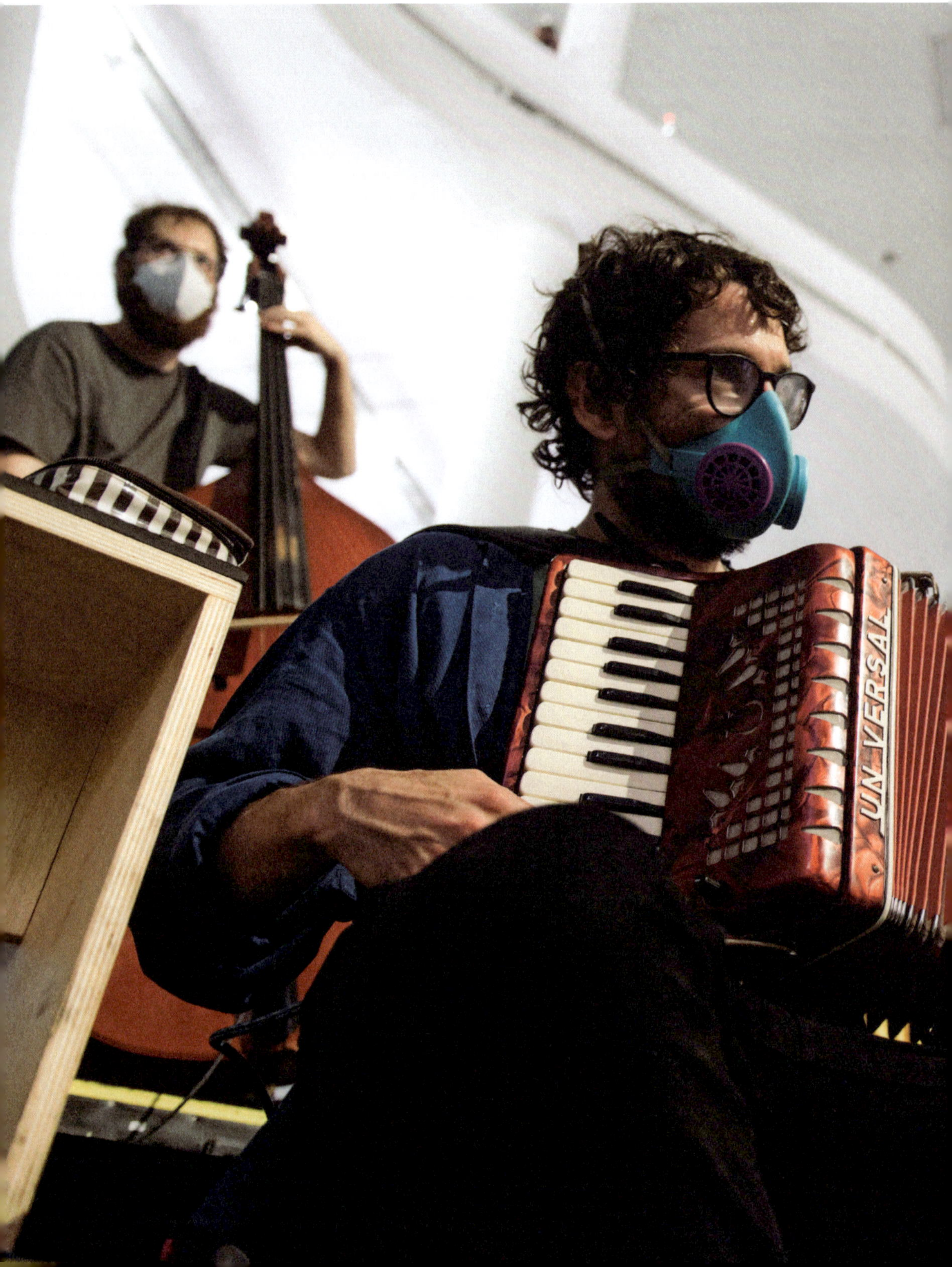
UNIVERSAL

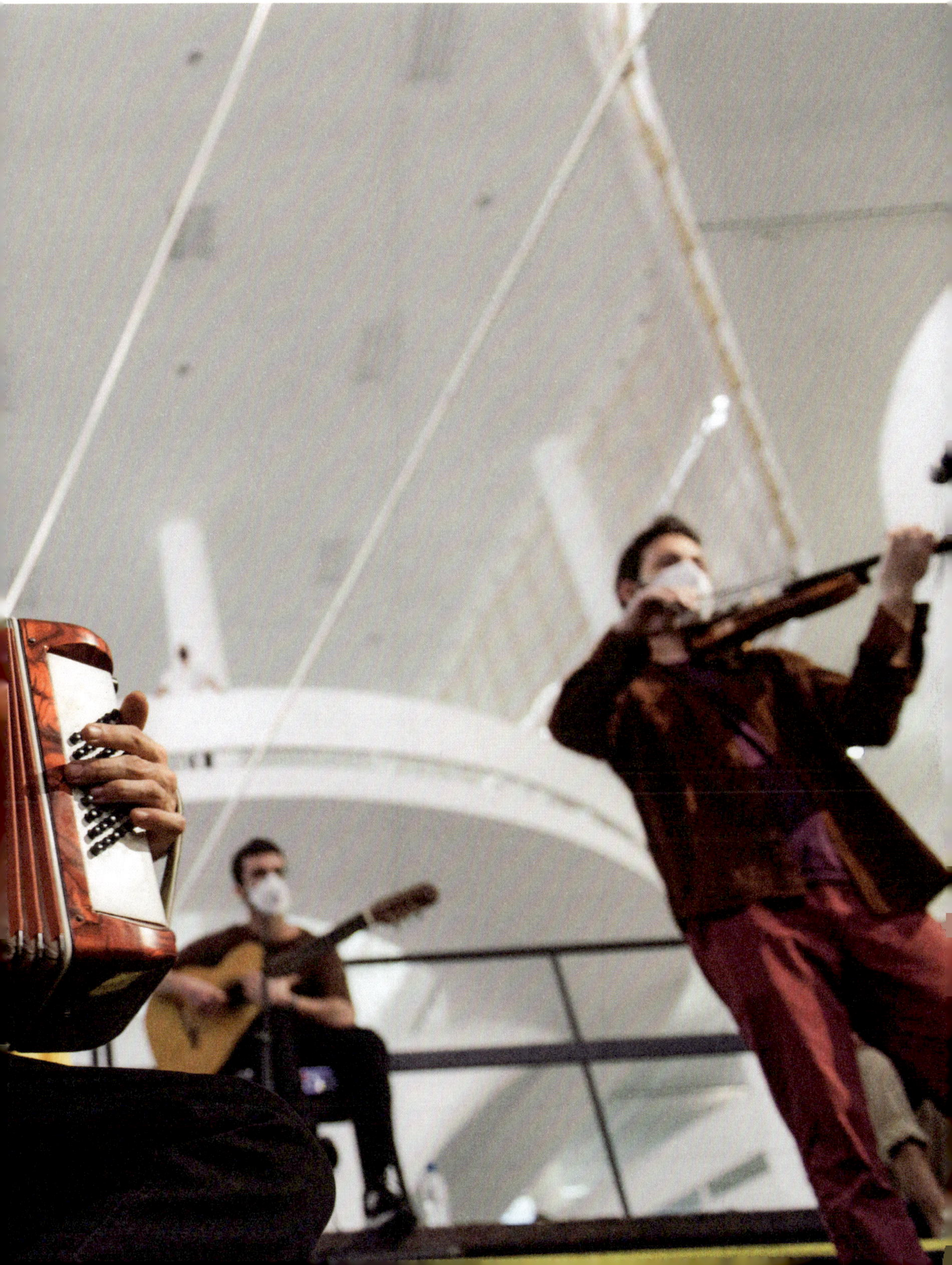

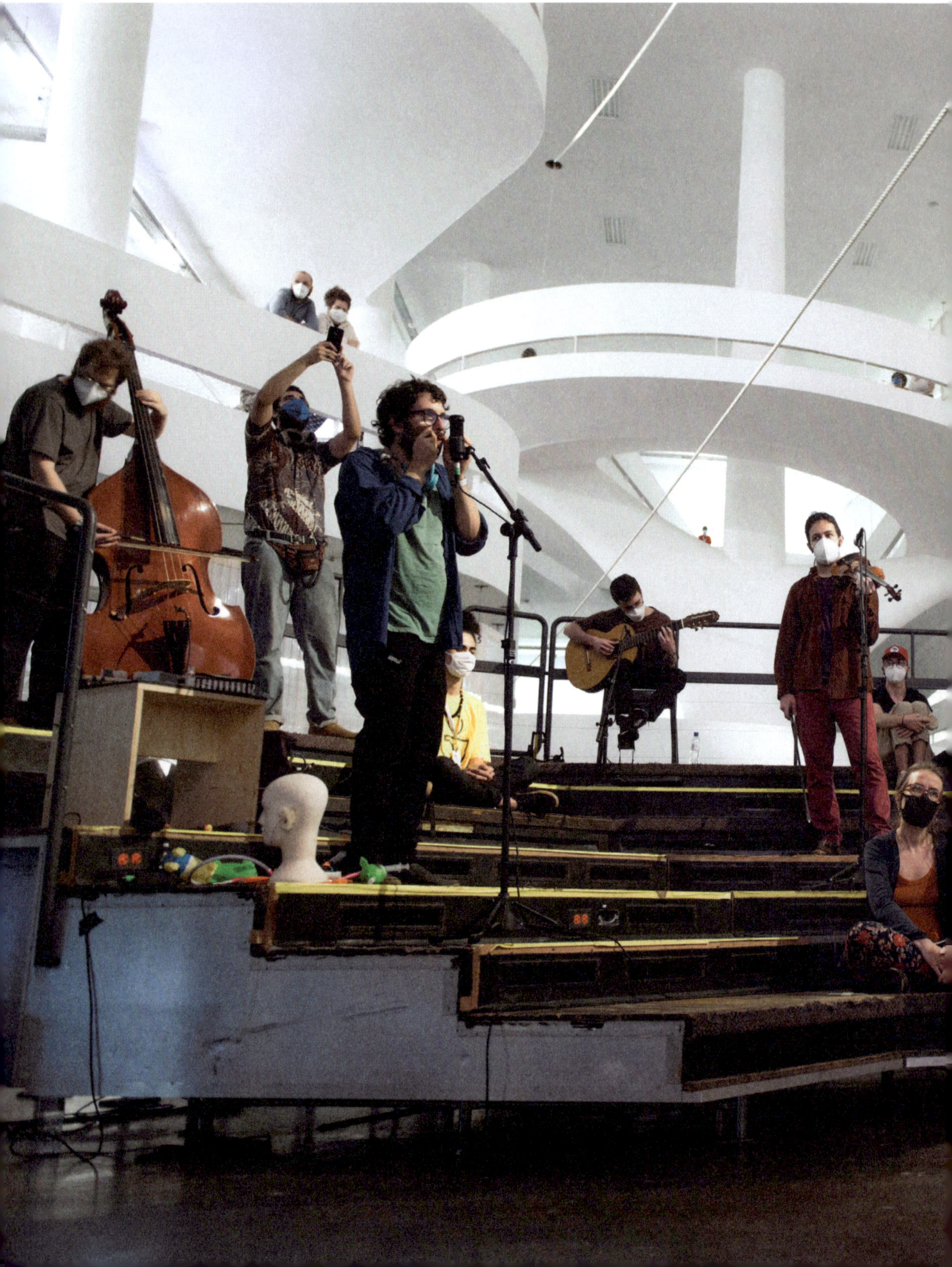

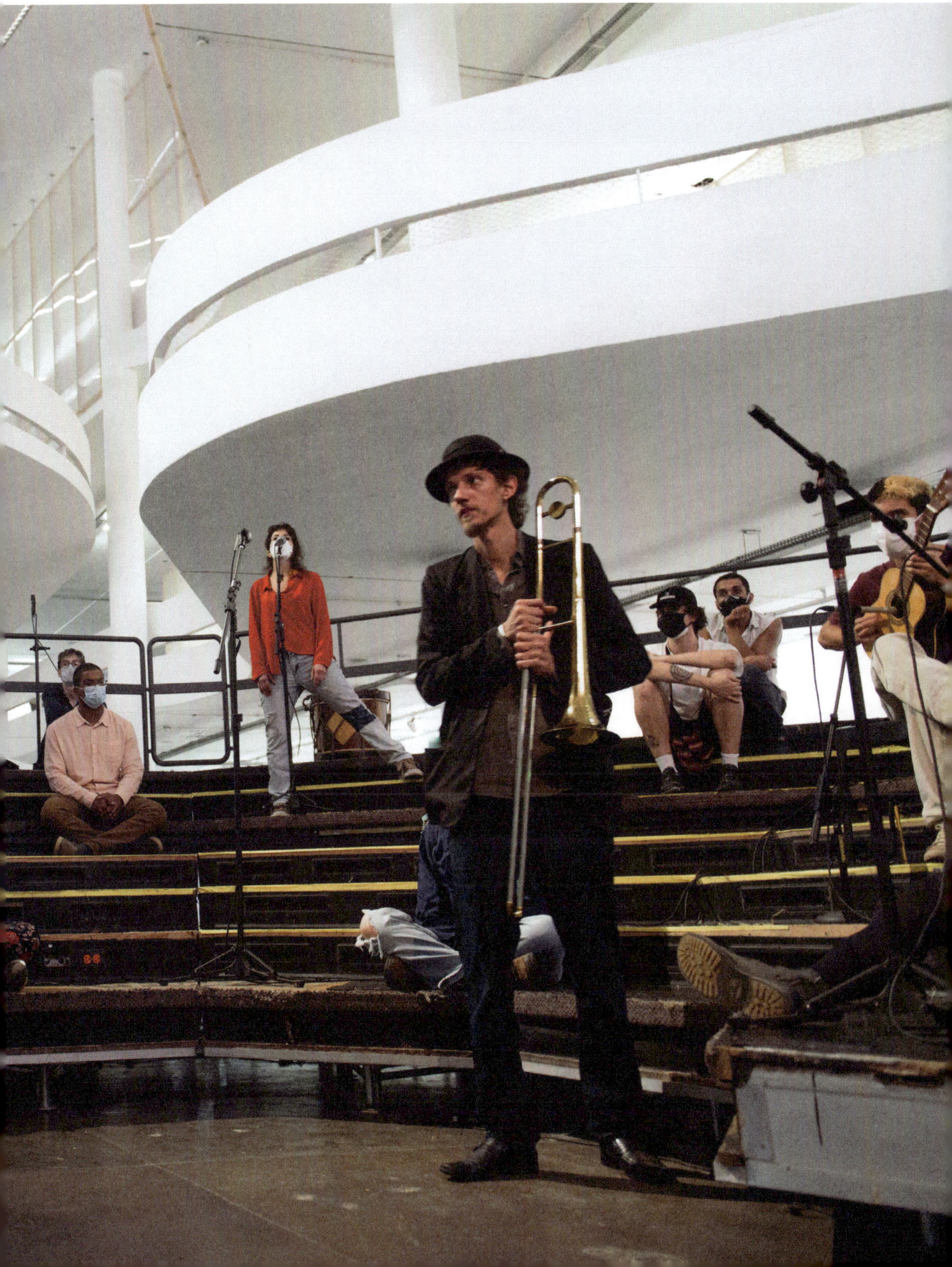

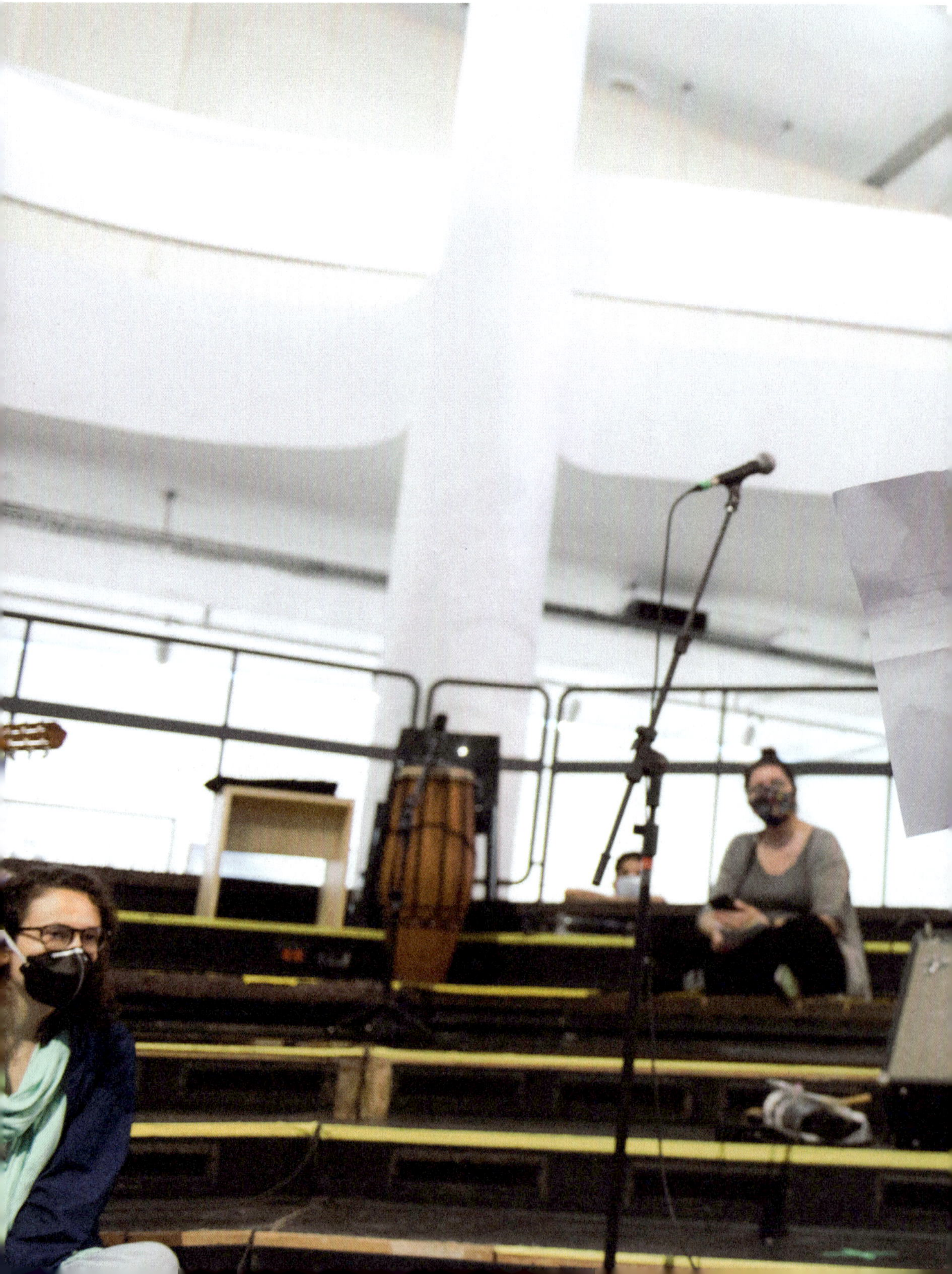

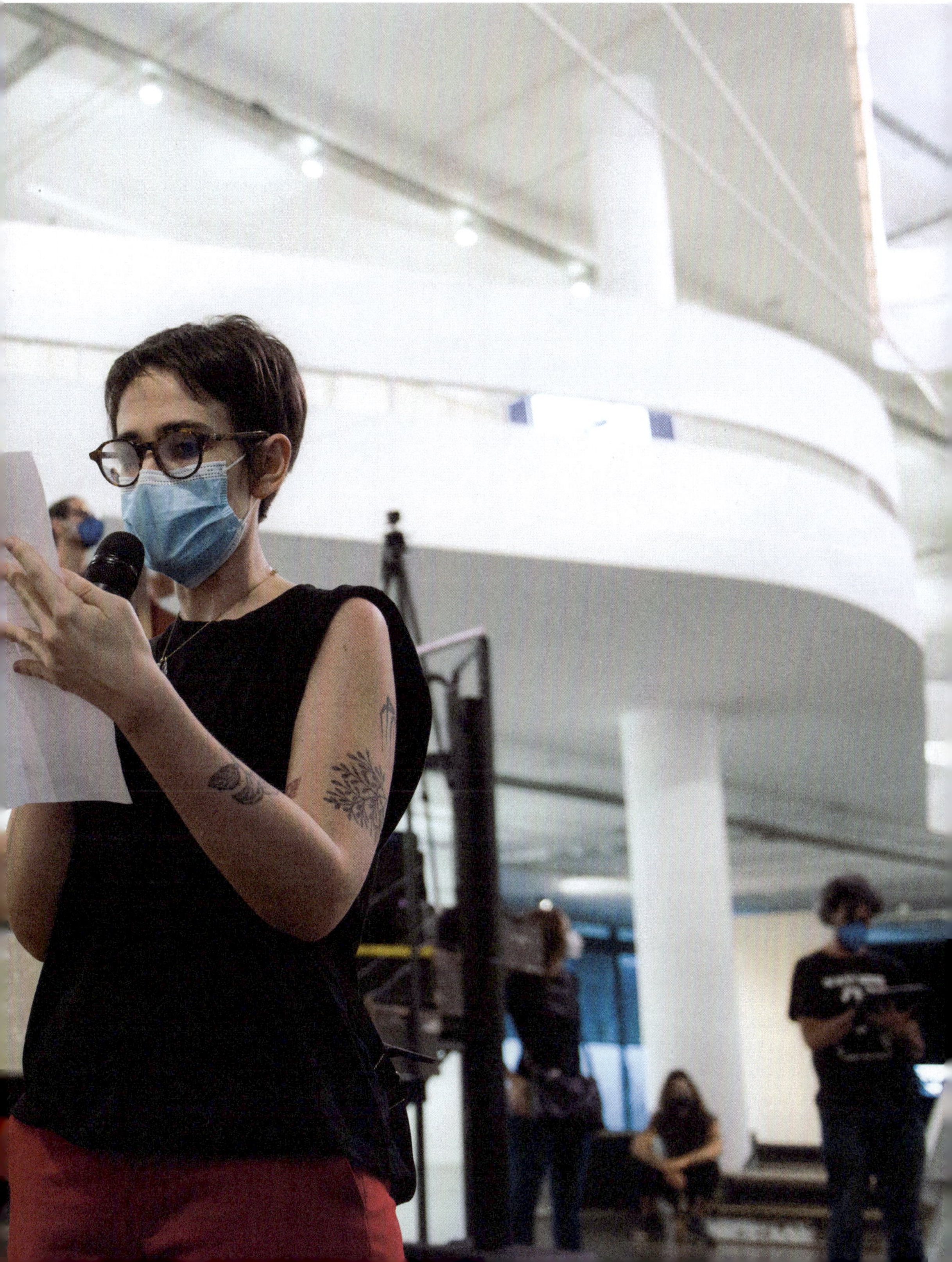

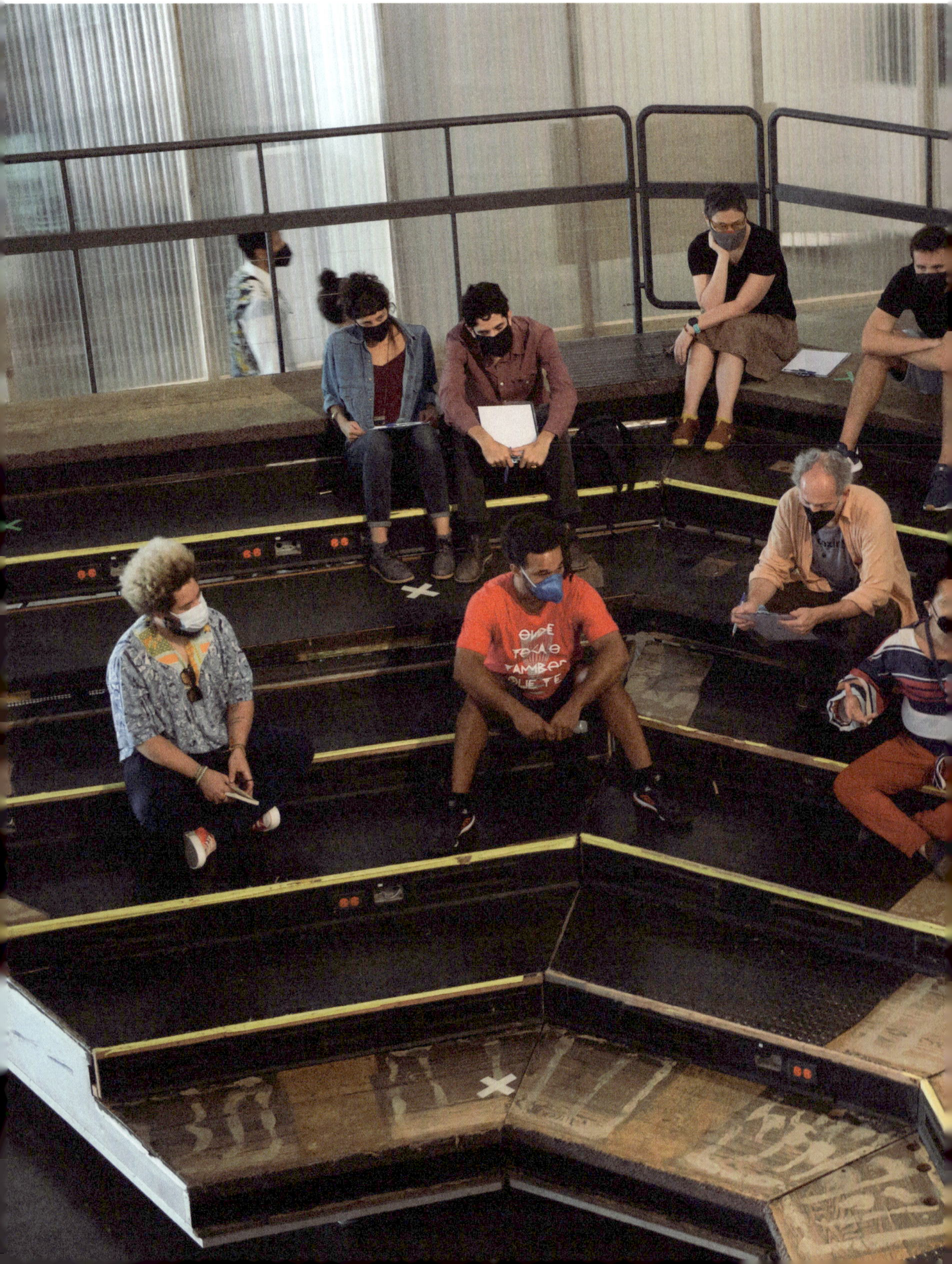

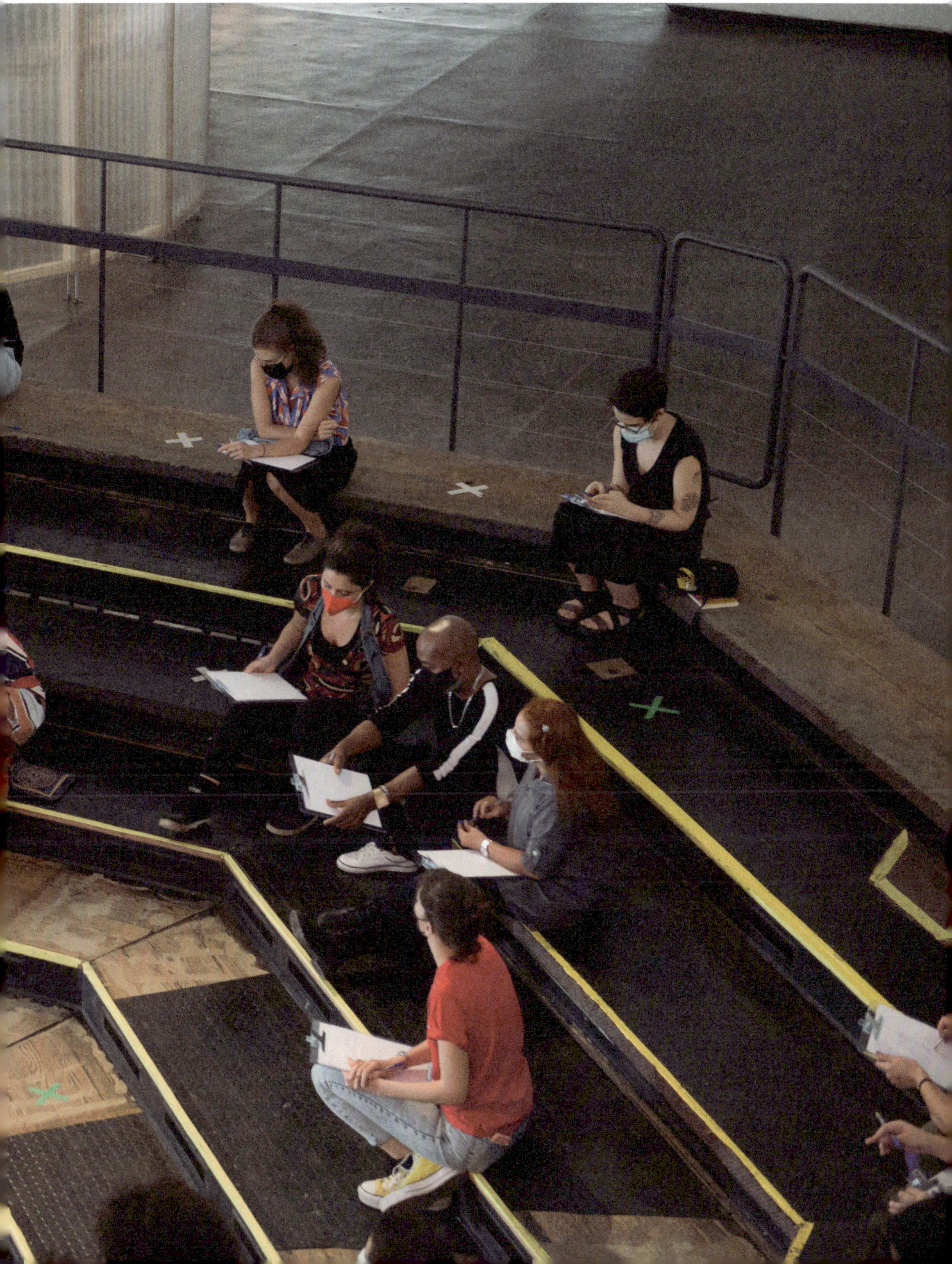

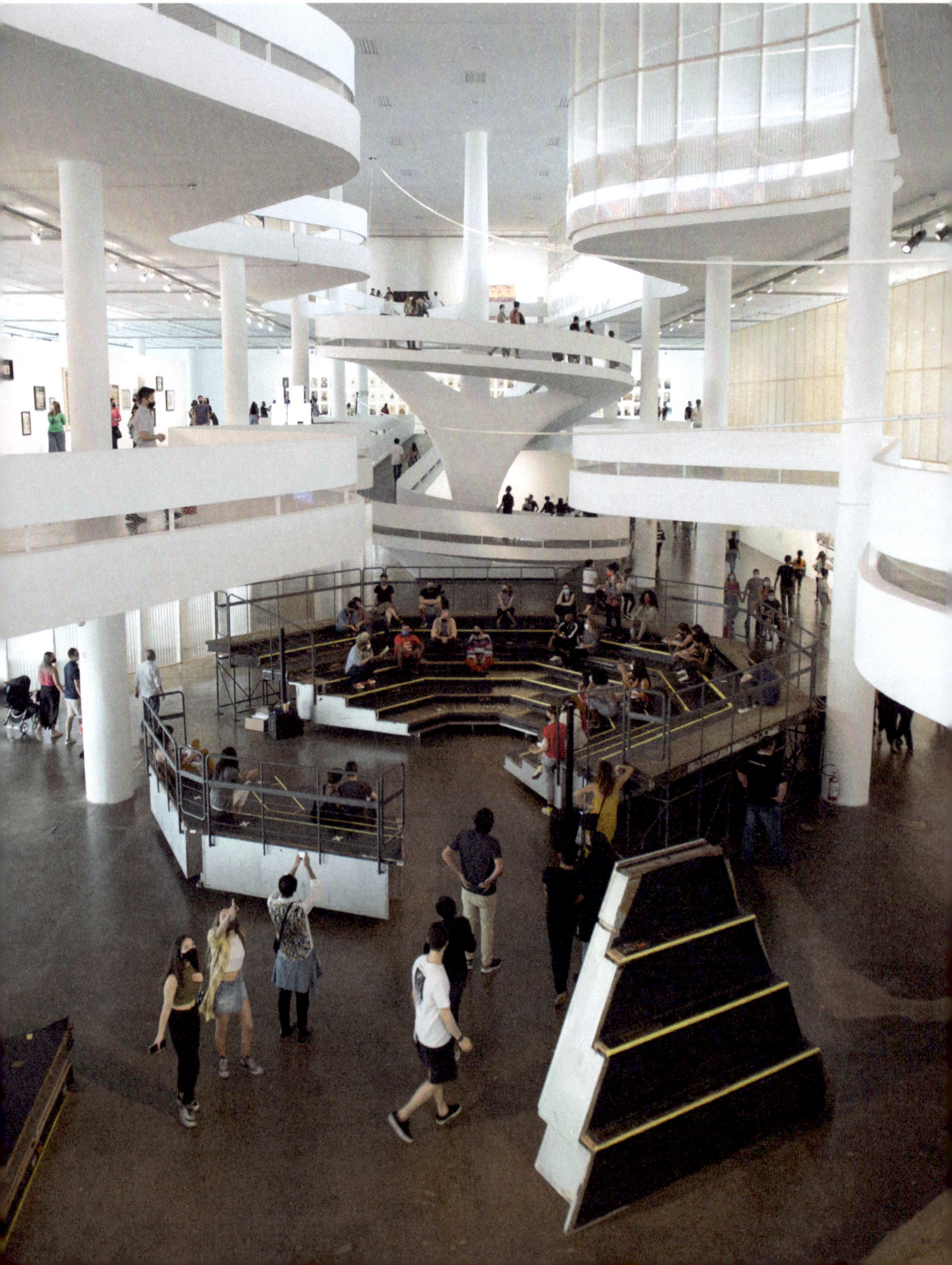

BIENAL PROGRAMMING (OCTOBER)

07 Oct 2021	Performance by Irmãs Brasil
02 Oct 2021	*Conversações* with Amara Moira and Lino Arruda
09 Oct 2021	*Conversações* with Luciano Carvalho, Yamila Goldfarb, and Adélia Rodrigues
14 Oct 2021	*Conversações* with Luz Ribeiro, Jô Freitas, and Luiza Romão
16 Oct 2021	*Conversações* with Sanara Santos and Bruno Mendonça
21 Oct 2021	Performance by Trio Girassol
23 Oct 2021	*Conversações* with Alice Shintani and Brígida Campbell
28 Oct 2021	*Conversações* with Juraci Dórea and Luciana Lyra
30 Oct 2021	*Conversações* with Paulo Galo and Flavio VM Costa

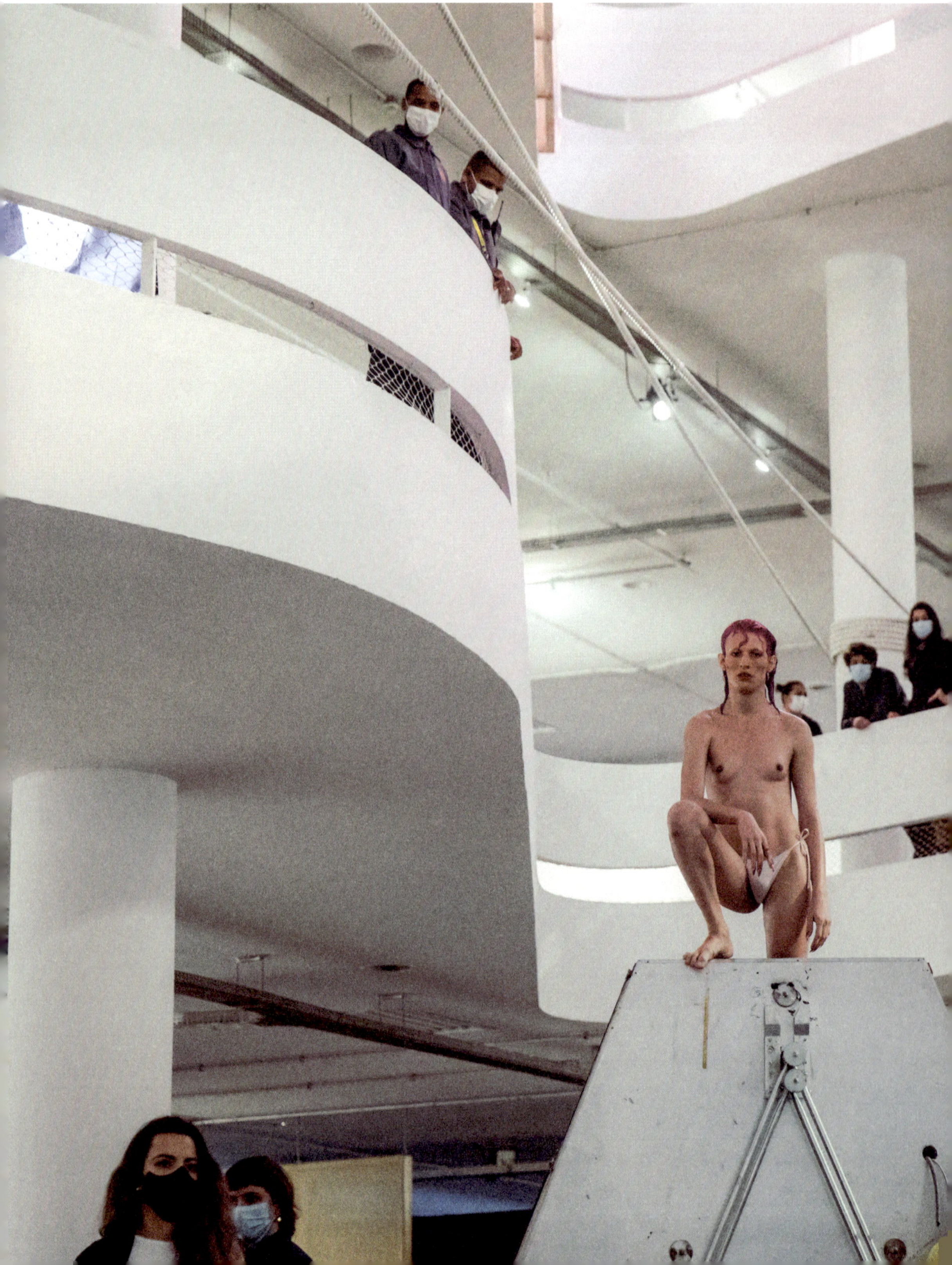

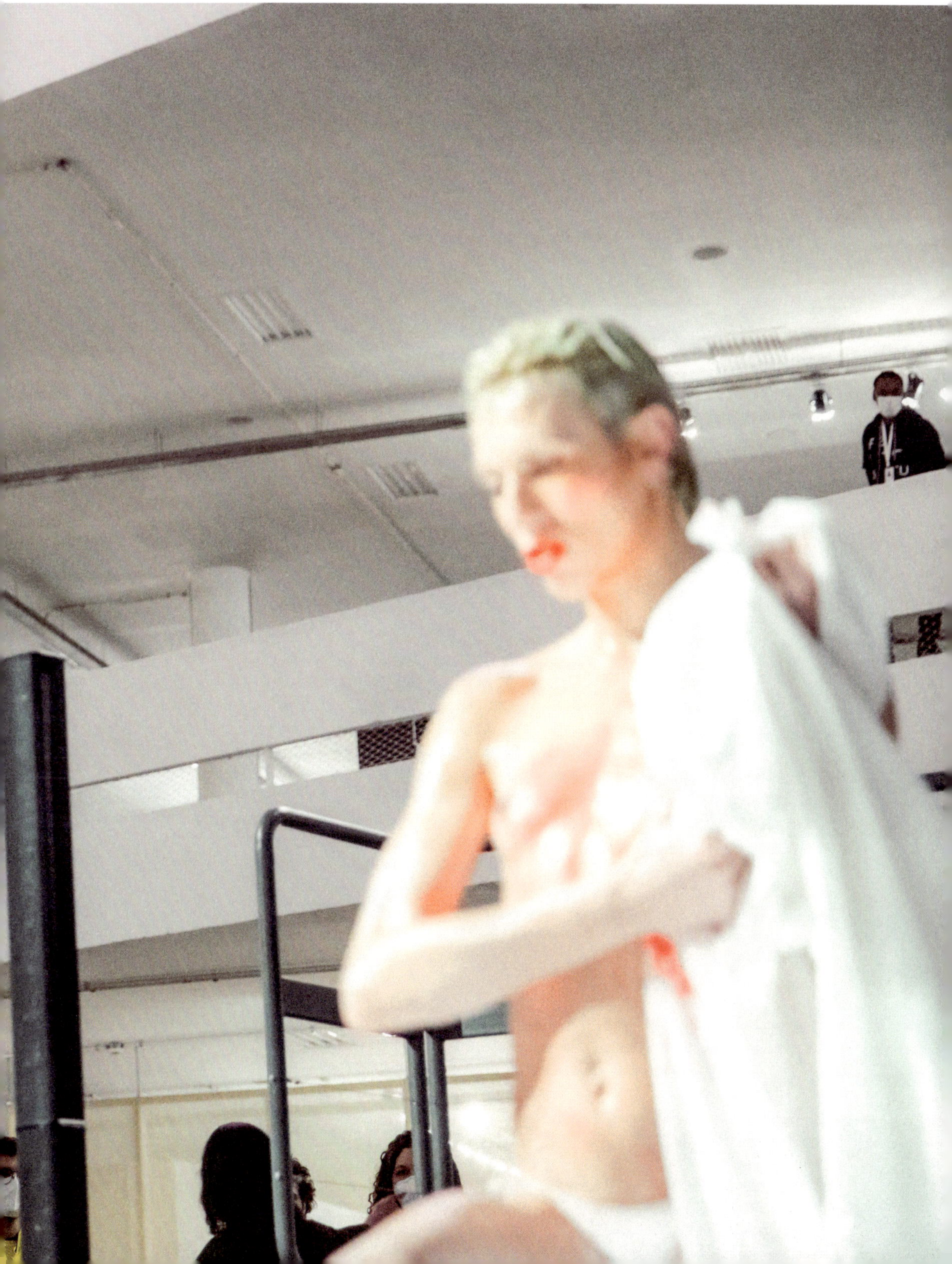

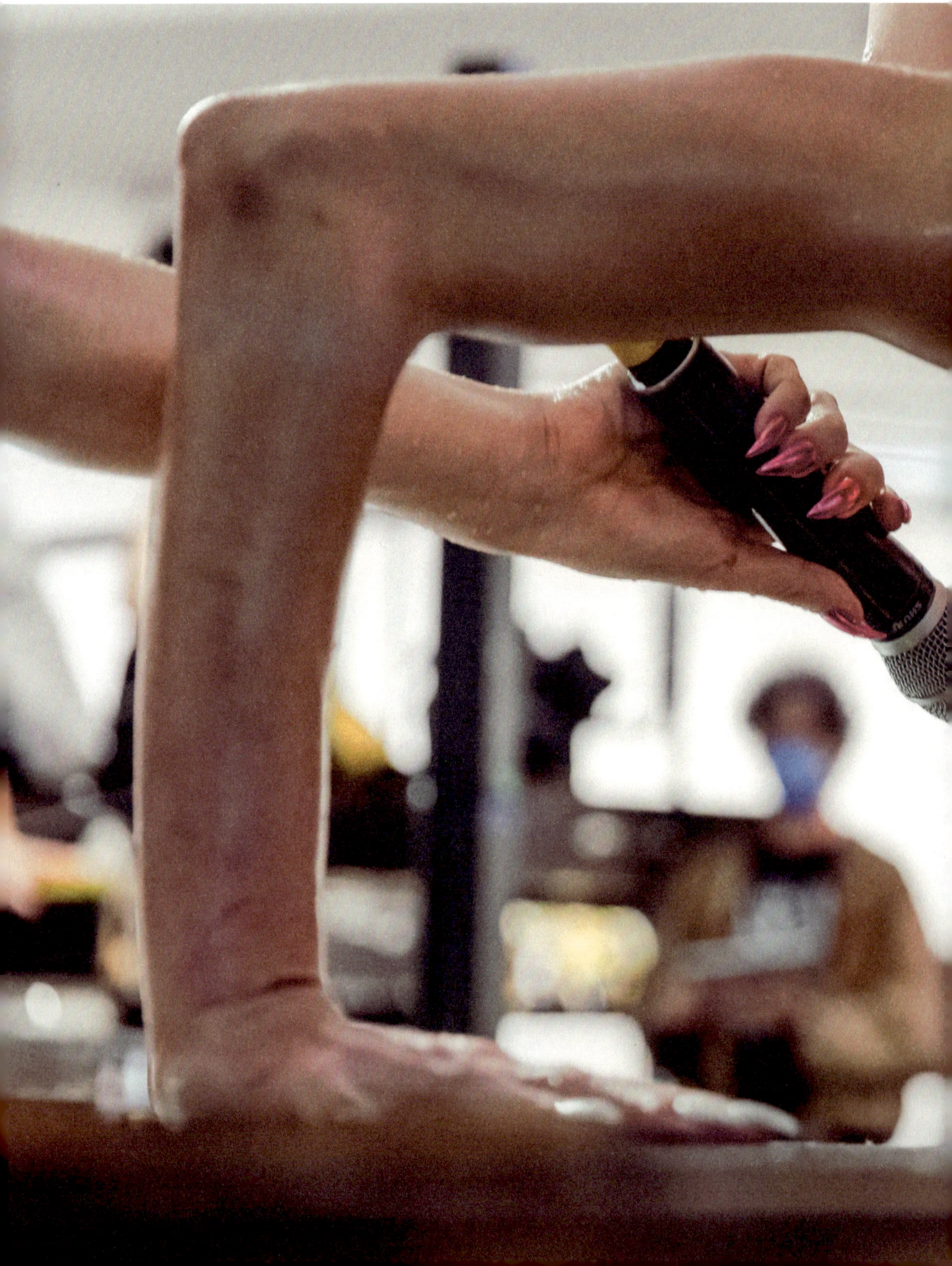

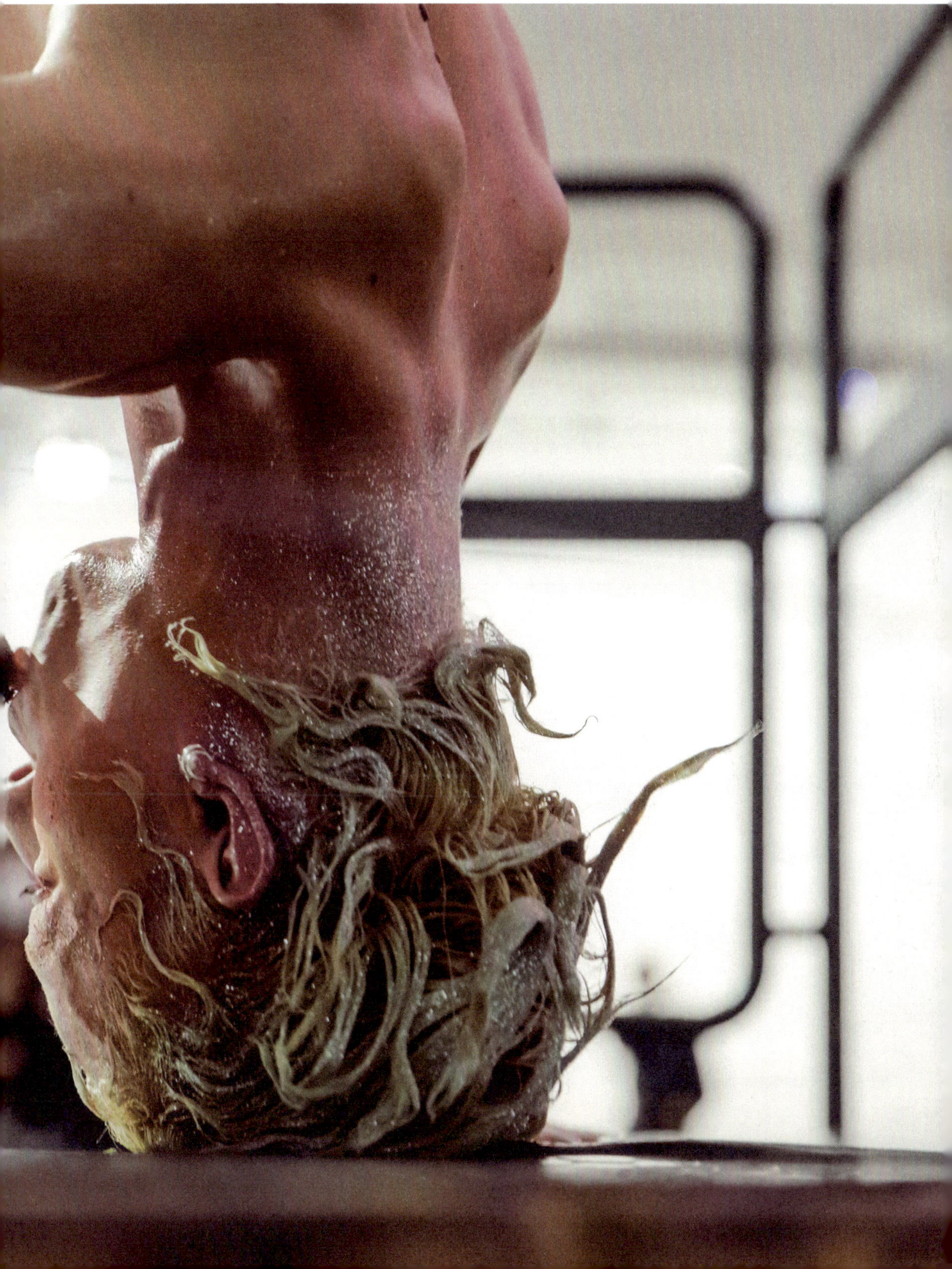

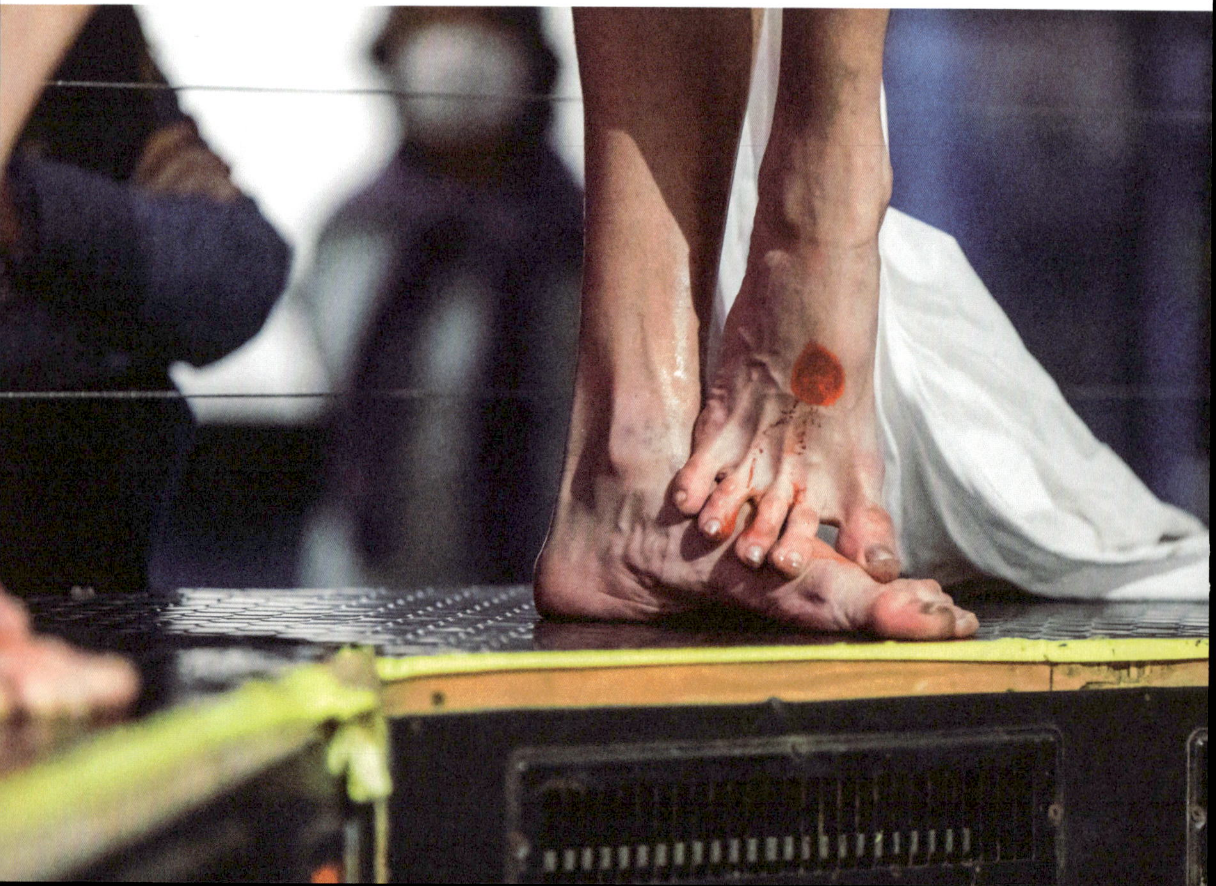

BIENAL PROGRAMMING (NOVEMBER)

04 Nov 2021	Performance by Novíssimo Edgar
11 Nov 2021	*Conversações* with the collective Dolores Boca Aberta, Brava Companhia, and Companhia Antropofágica with Estudo De Cena, Cia Canina, the Levante Popular da Juventude, the Movimento dos Trabalhadores pelos Direitos (MTD), and the Movimento dos Trabalhadores Rurais Sem Terra (MST)
13 Nov 2021	*Conversações* with Renato Lopes, Tai Nascimento, and Uila
13 Nov 2021	Performance by Maria Gadú
18 Nov 2021	Performance by Paola Ribeiro and Inés Terra
20 Nov 2021	Performance by BNegão, Paulão King, Pedro Selector, Gilber T, Sandro Lustosa, and DJ Castro
21 Nov 2021	*Conversações* with Haris Epaminonda, Manthia Diawara, and Olivia Plender
25 Nov 2021	Performance by Mbé and Marco Scarassatti
27 Nov 2021	*Conversações* about meteorites with Miriam Della Posta de Azevedo and João Eduardo Fonseca
27 Nov 2021	Book launch for *Roda Gigante* by Carmela Gross

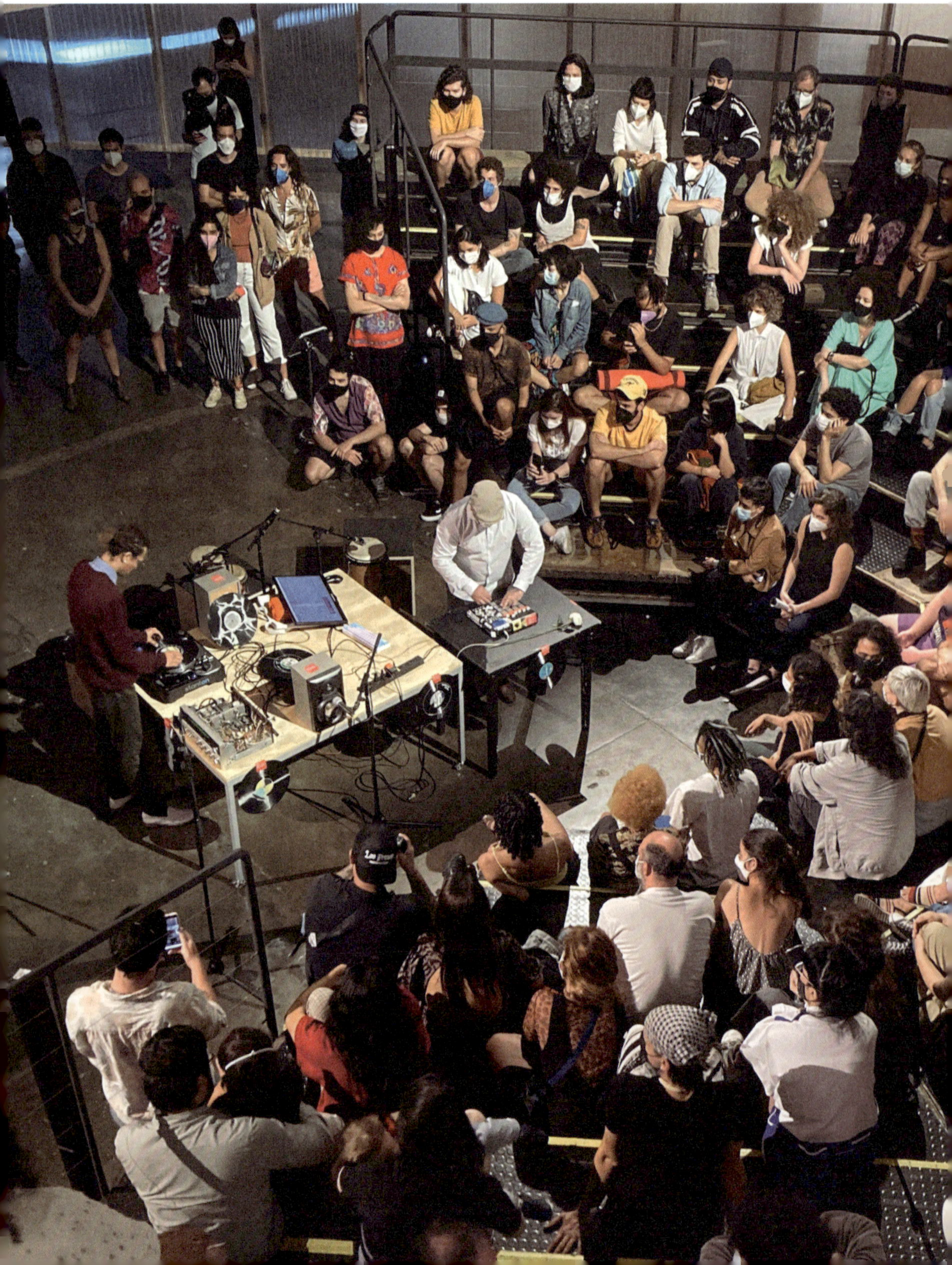

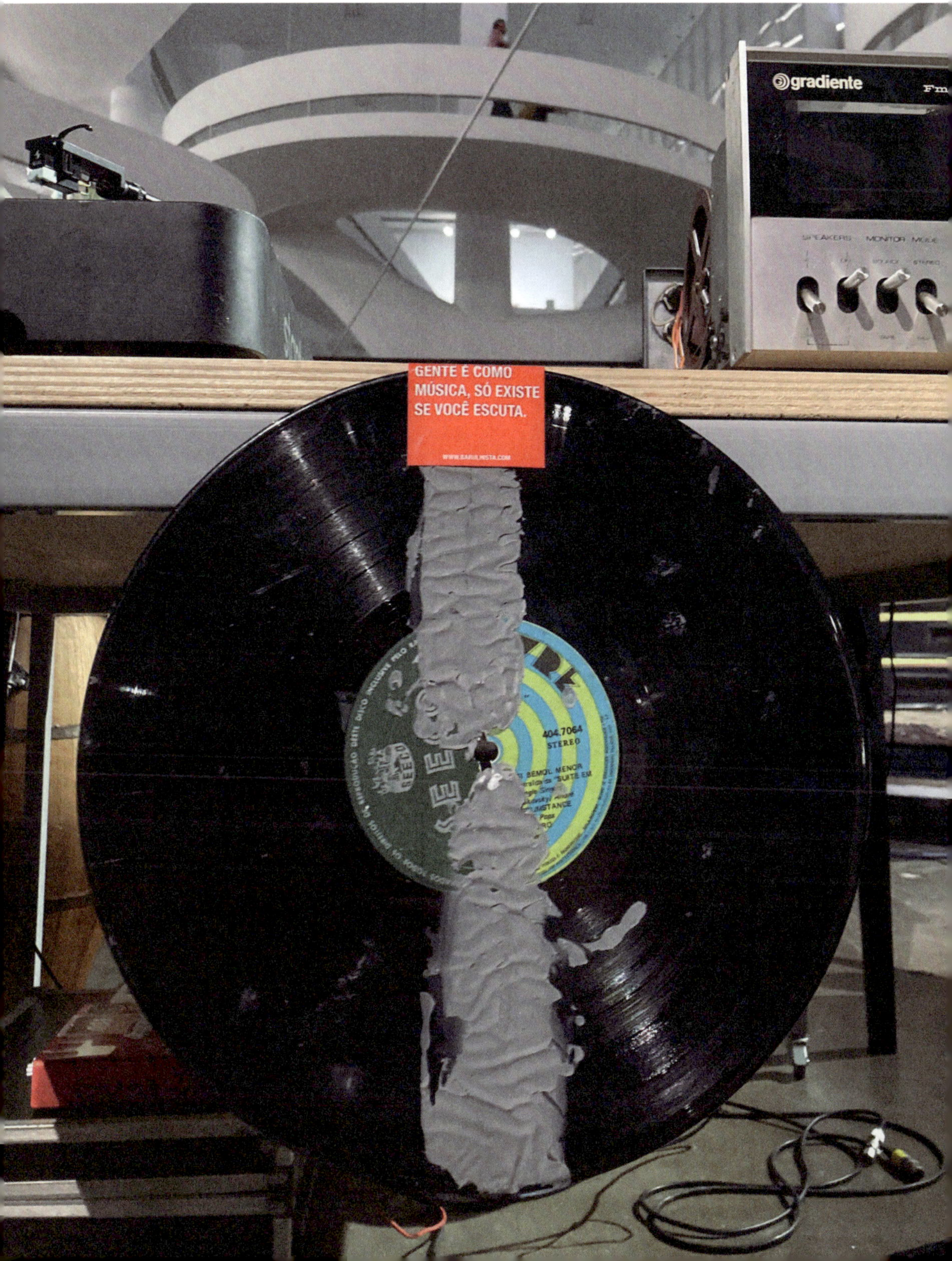
gradiente
GENTE É COMO MÚSICA, SÓ EXISTE SE VOCÊ ESCUTA.
404.7064
STEREO

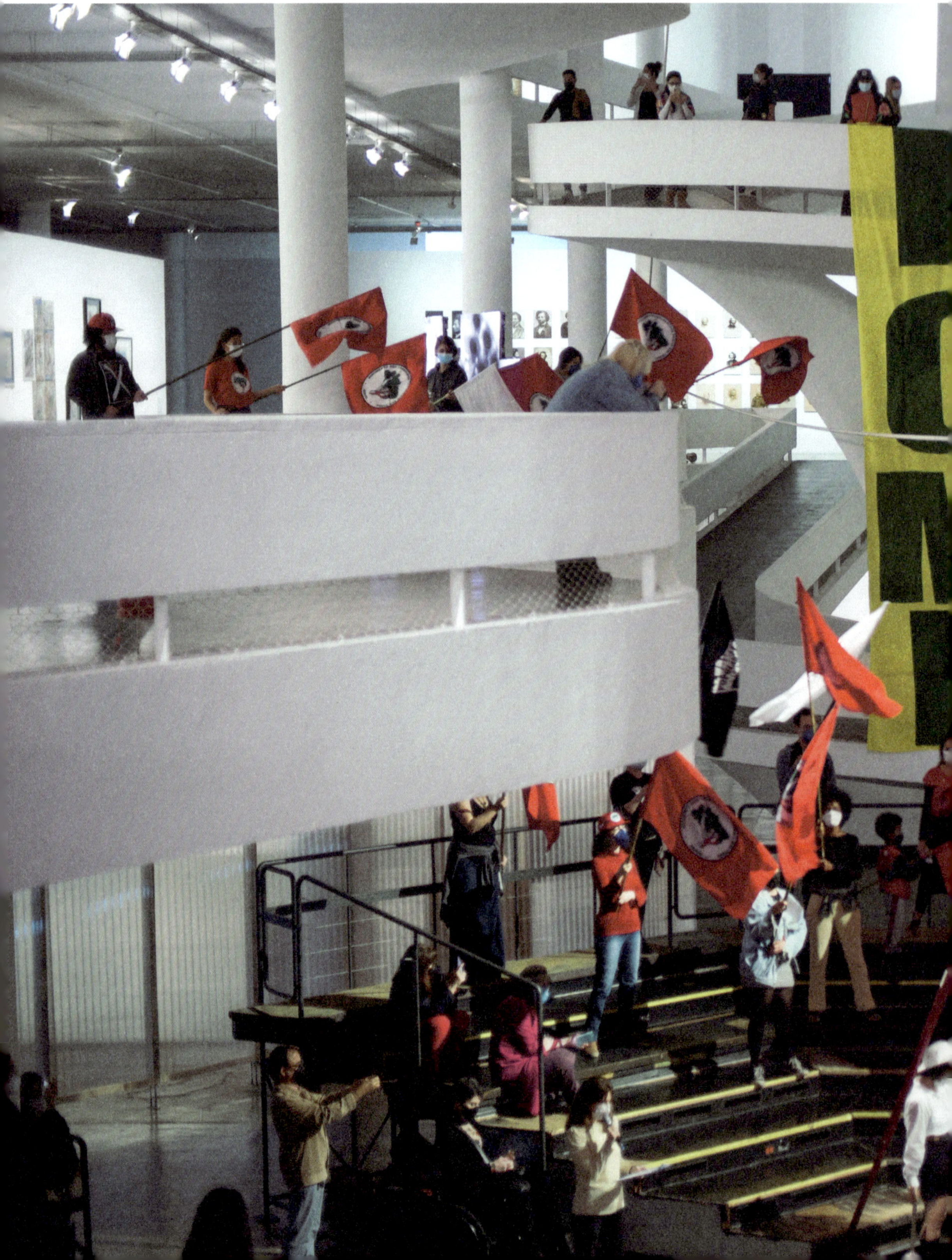

Conversações with the collective Dolores Boca Aberta, Brava Companhia, and Companhia Antropofágica with Estudo De Cena, Cia Canina, the Levante Popular da Juventude, the Movimento dos Trabalhadores pelos Direitos (MTD), and the Movimento dos Trabalhadores Rurais Sem Terra (MST)

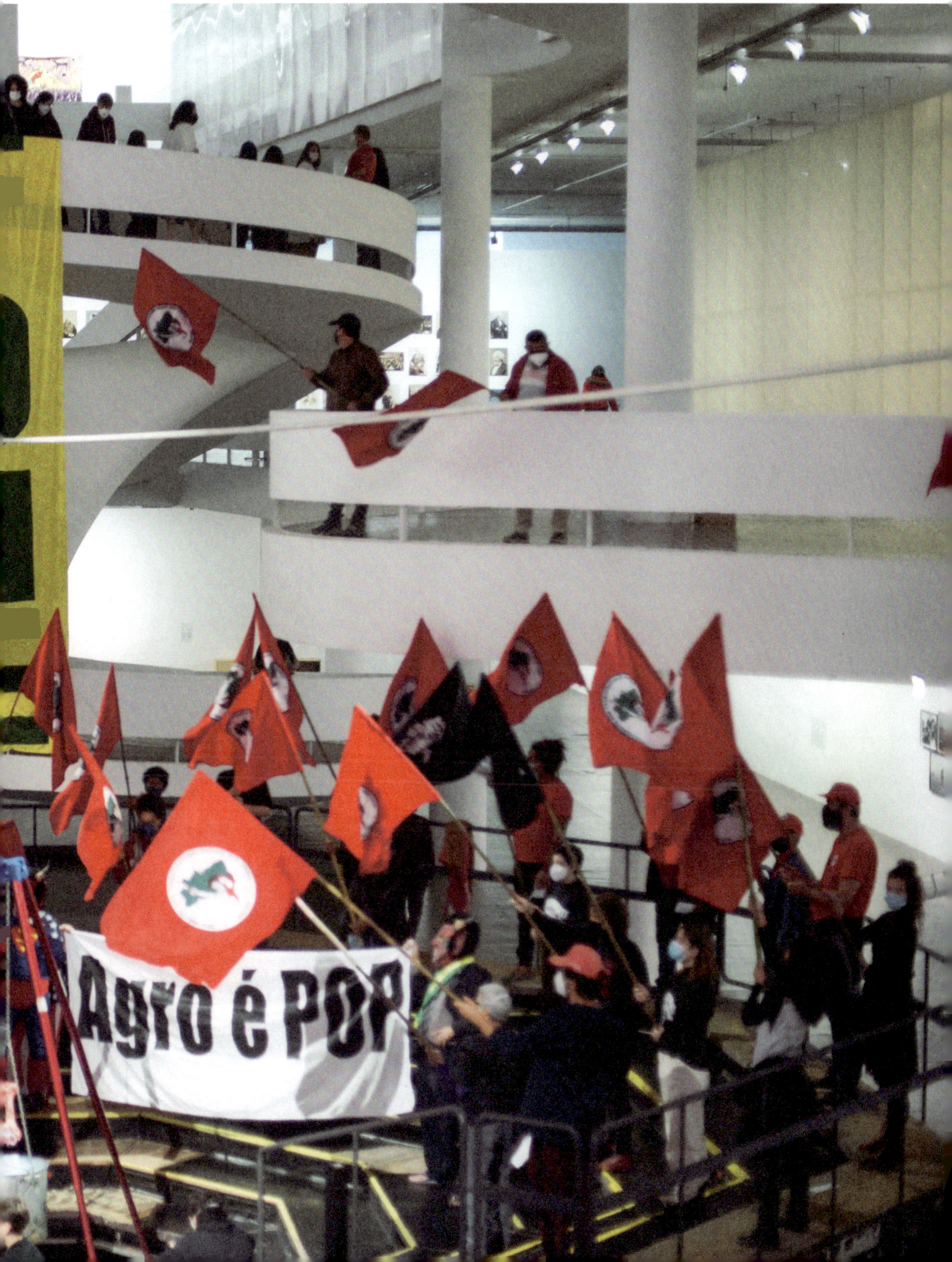

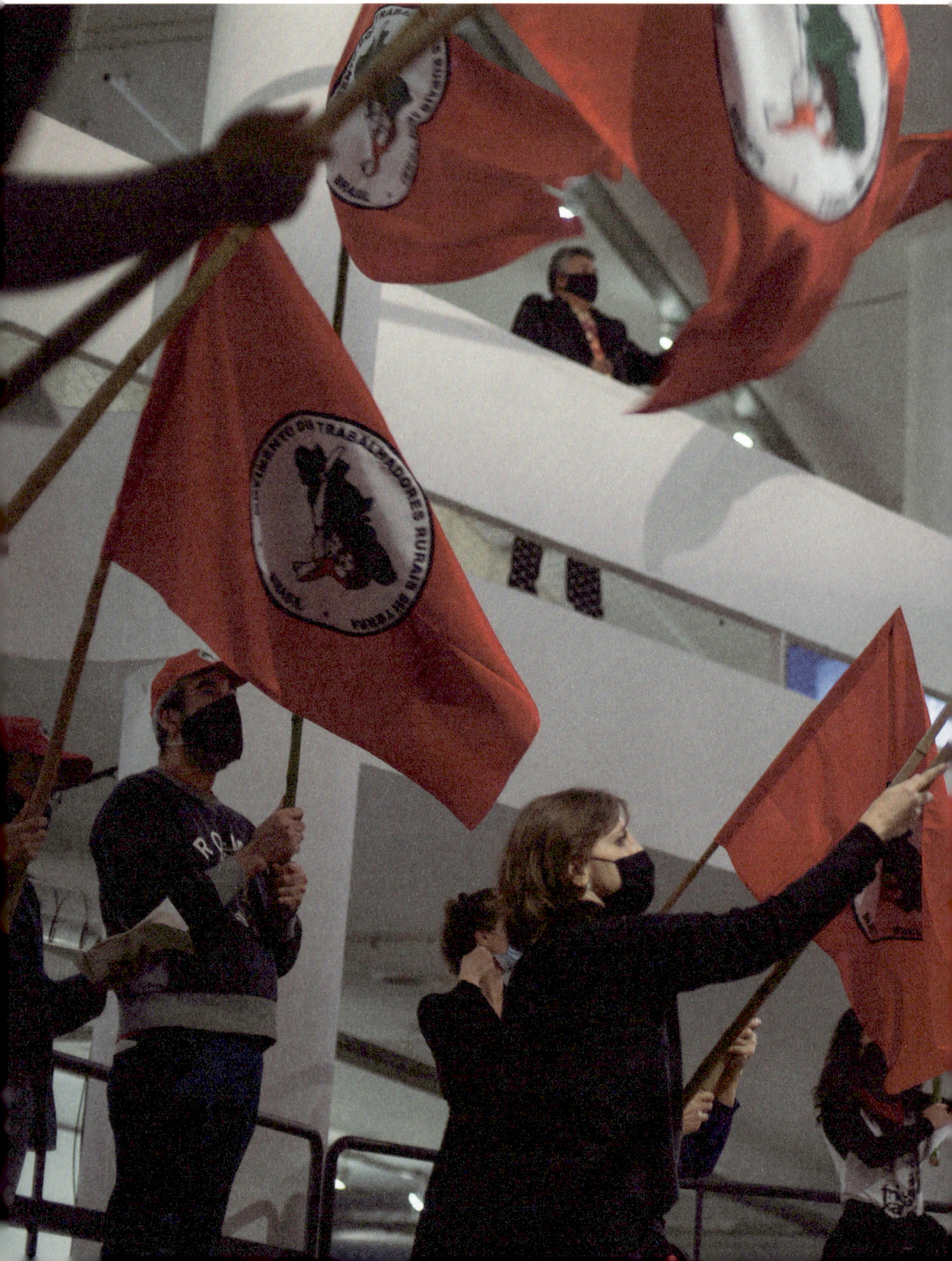

11 Nov 2021

Conversações with the collective Dolores Boca Aberta, Brava Companhia, and Companhia Antropofágica with Estudo De Cena, Cia Canina, the Levante Popular da Juventude, the Movimento dos Trabalhadores pelos Direitos (MTD), and the Movimento dos Trabalhadores Rurais Sem Terra (MST)

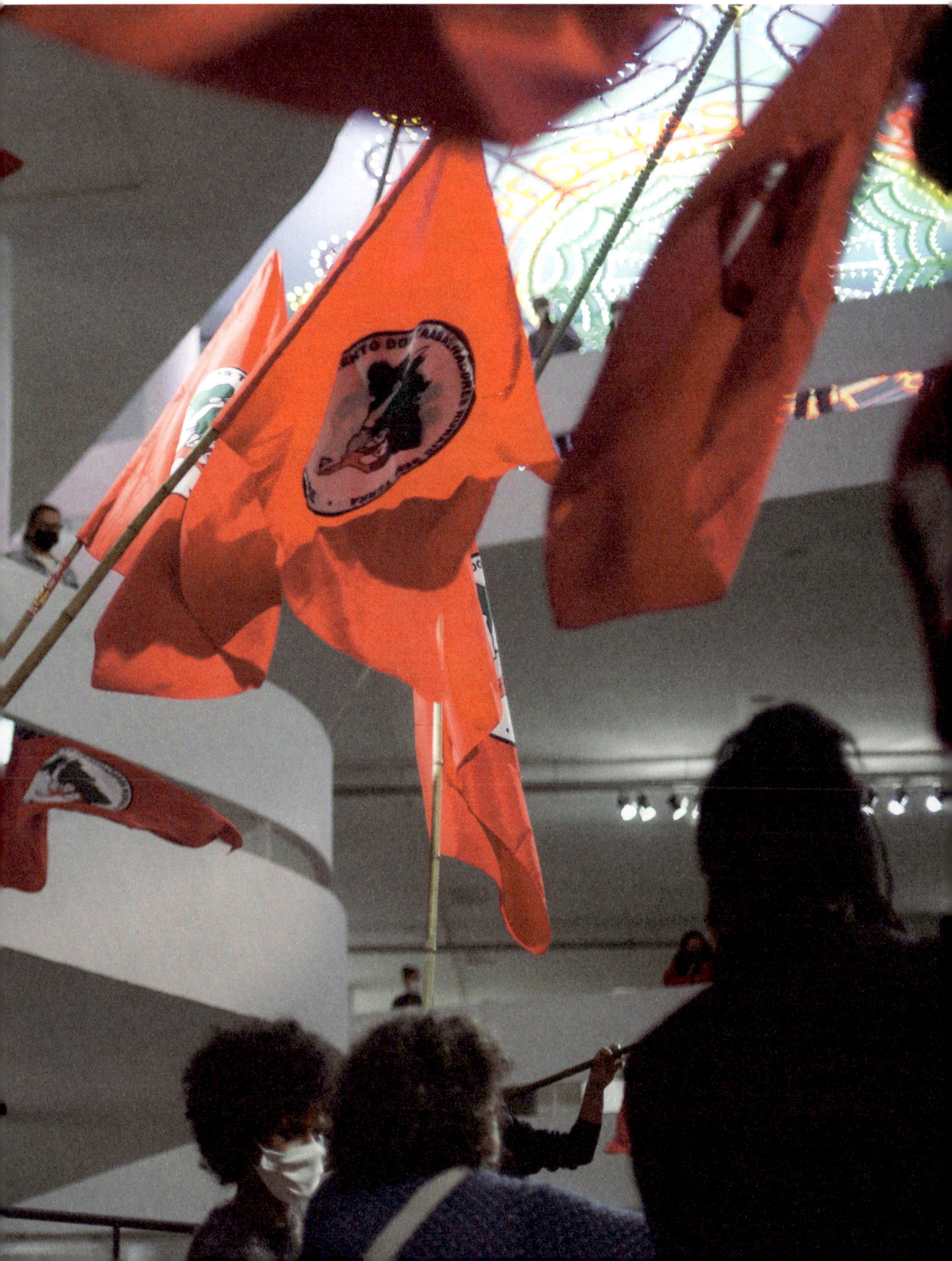

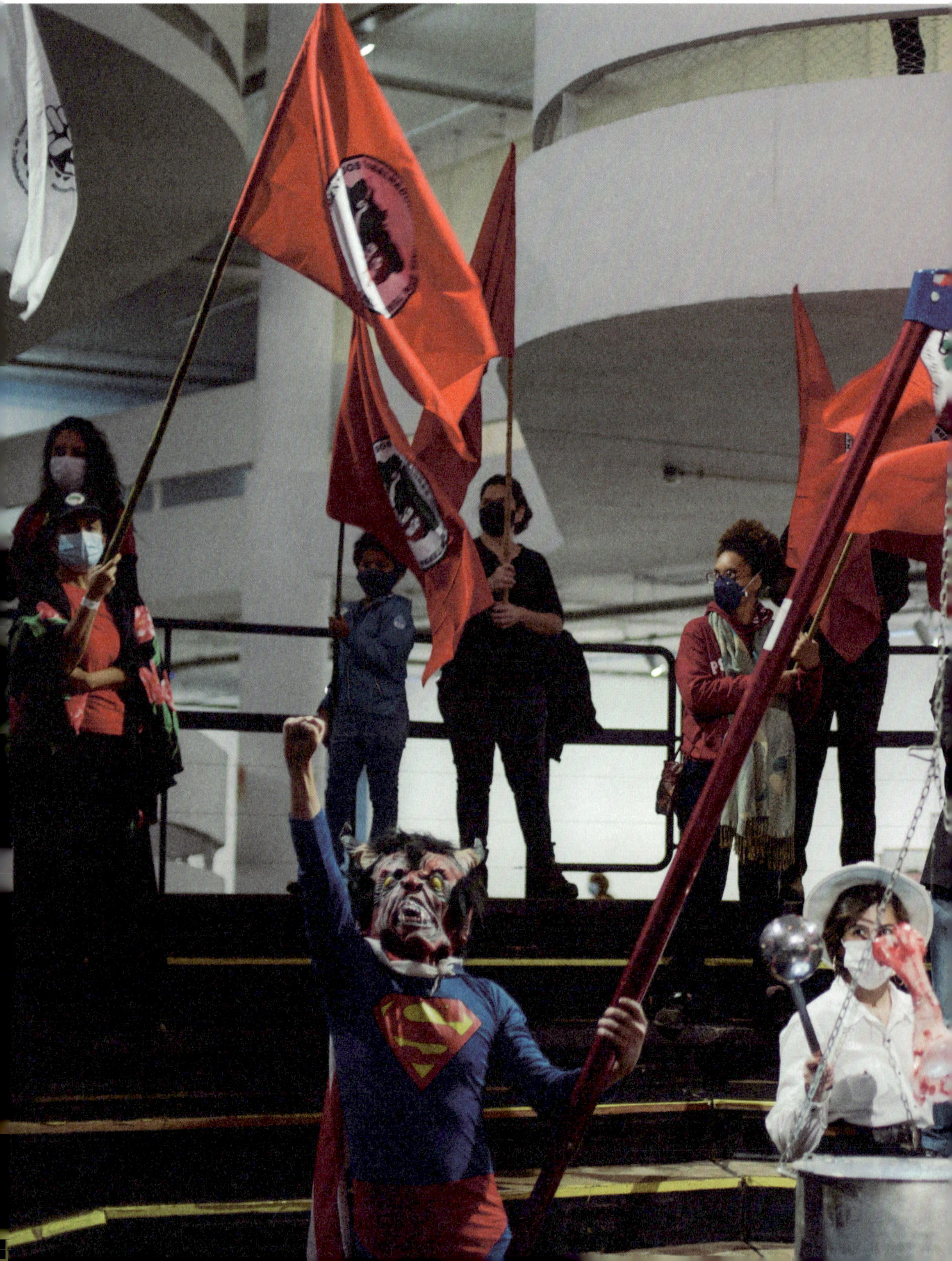

11 Nov 2021

Conversações with the collective Dolores Boca Aberta, Brava Companhia, and Companhia Antropofágica with Estudo De Cena, Cia Canina, the Levante Popular da Juventude, the Movimento dos Trabalhadores pelos Direitos (MTD), and the Movimento dos Trabalhadores Rurais Sem Terra (MST)

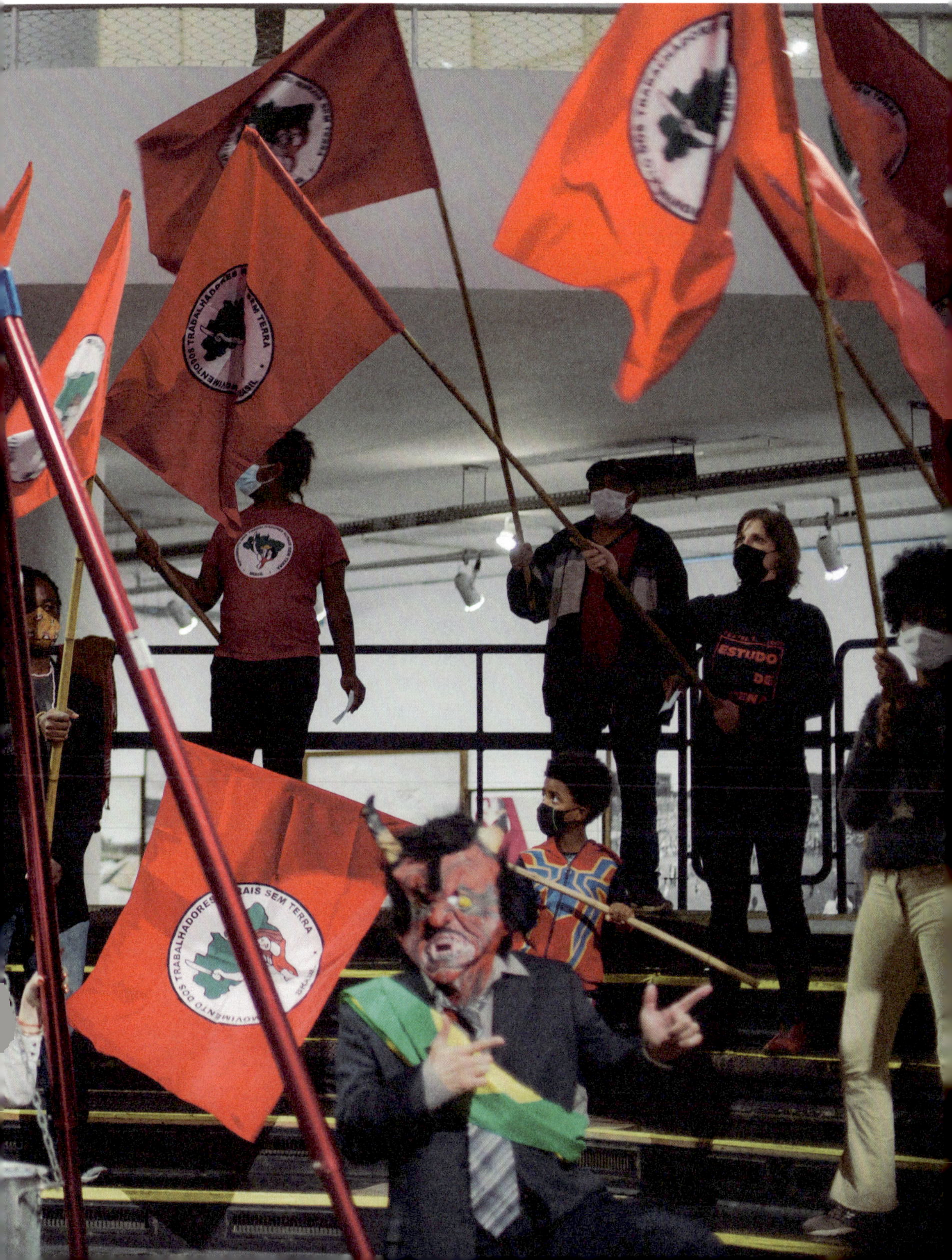

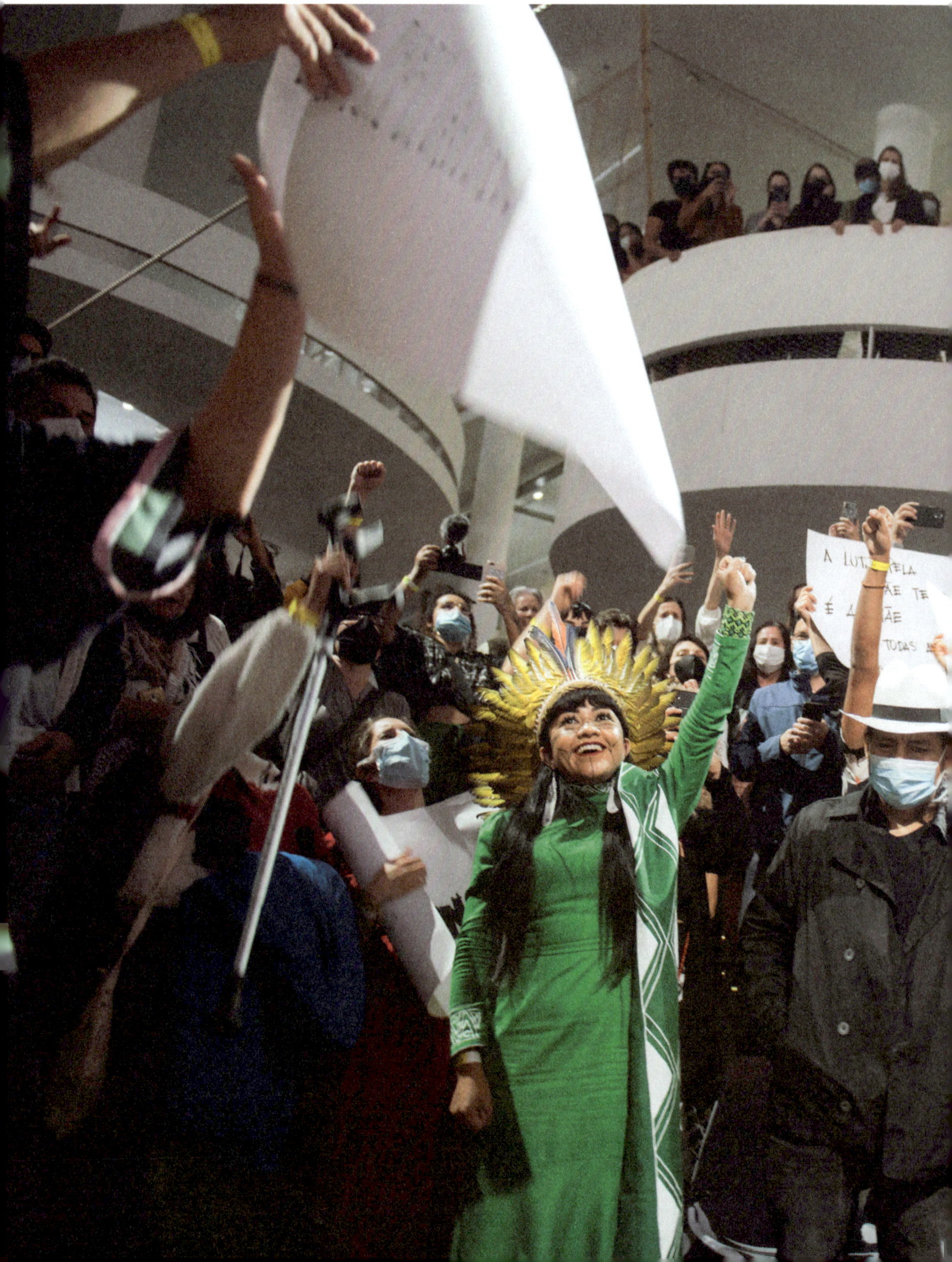

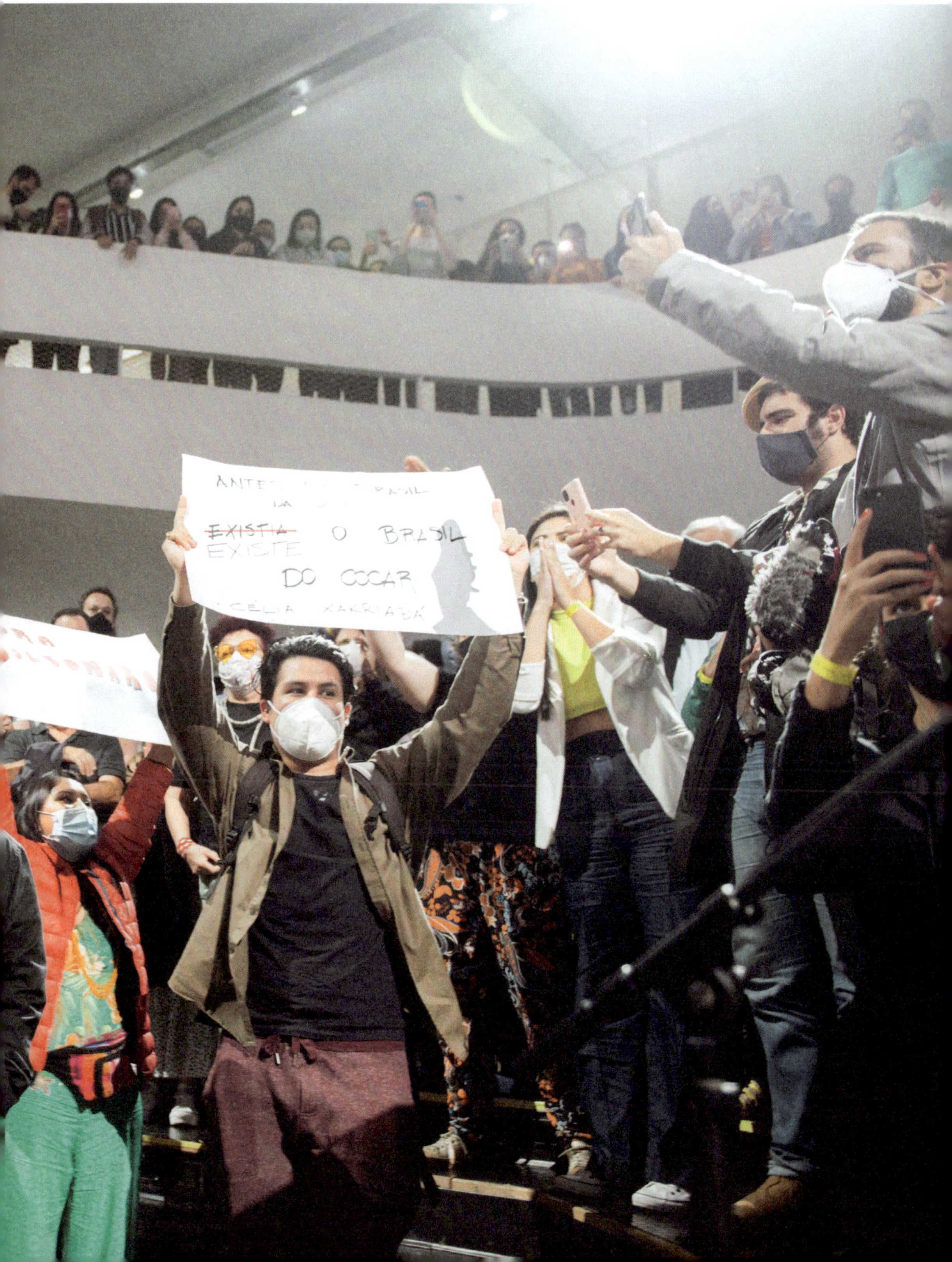
EXISTIA
EXISTE O BRASIL
DO COCAR
XAKRIABÁ

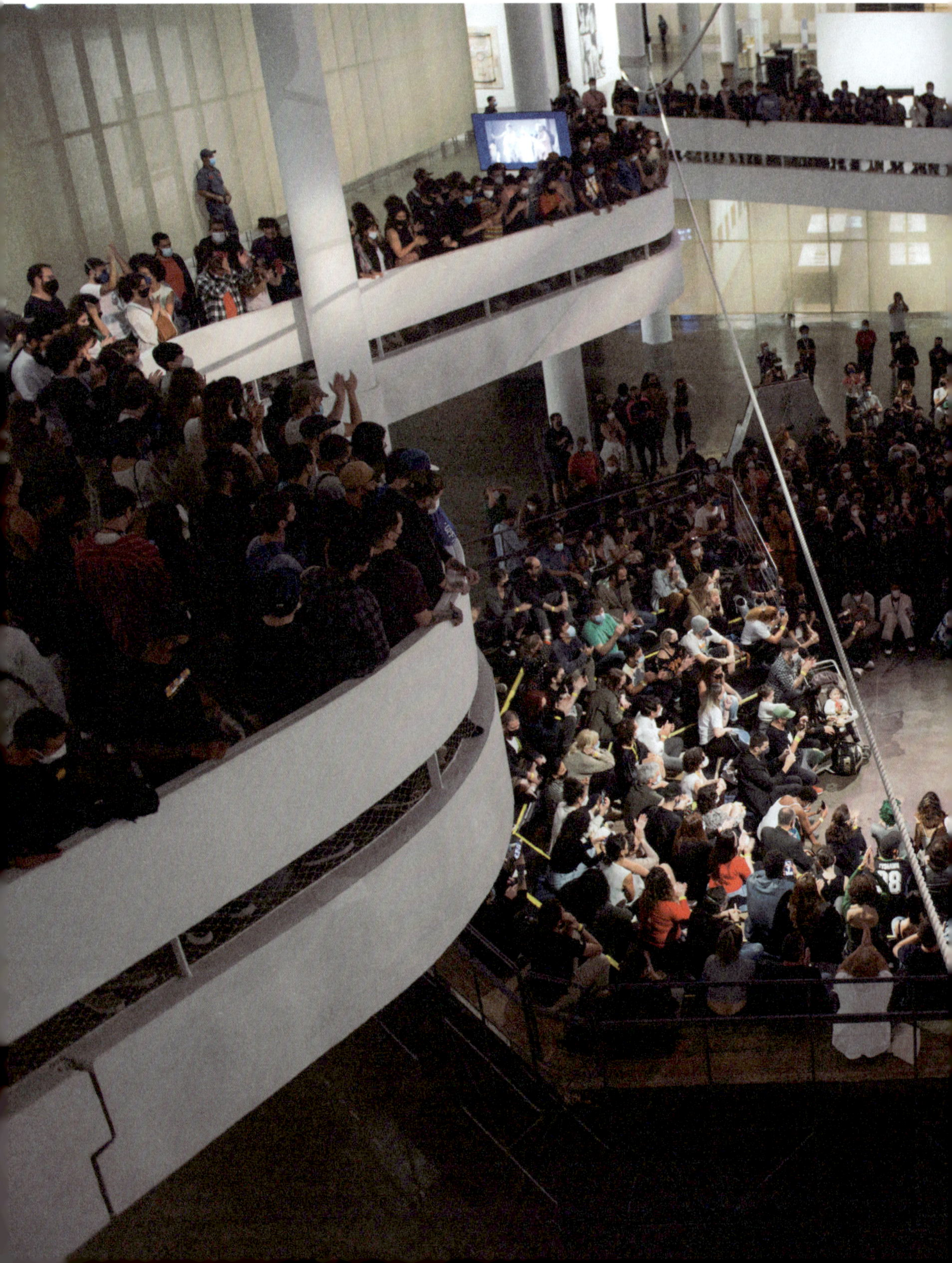

Performance by BNegão, Paulão King, Pedro Selector, Gilber T, Sandro Lustosa, and DJ Castro

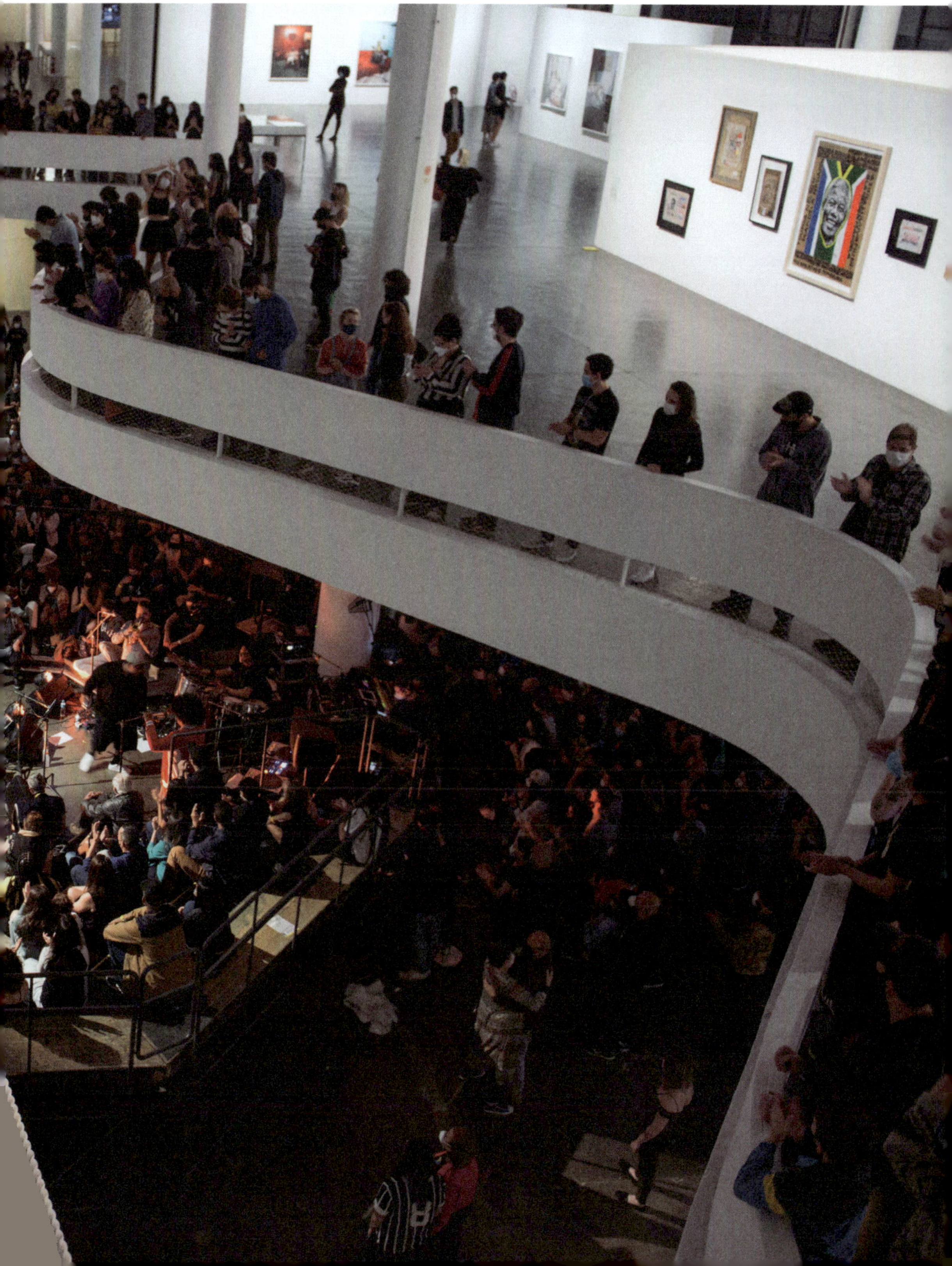

20 Nov 2021 Performance by BNegão, Paulão King, Pedro Selector, Gilber T, Sandro Lustosa, and DJ Castro

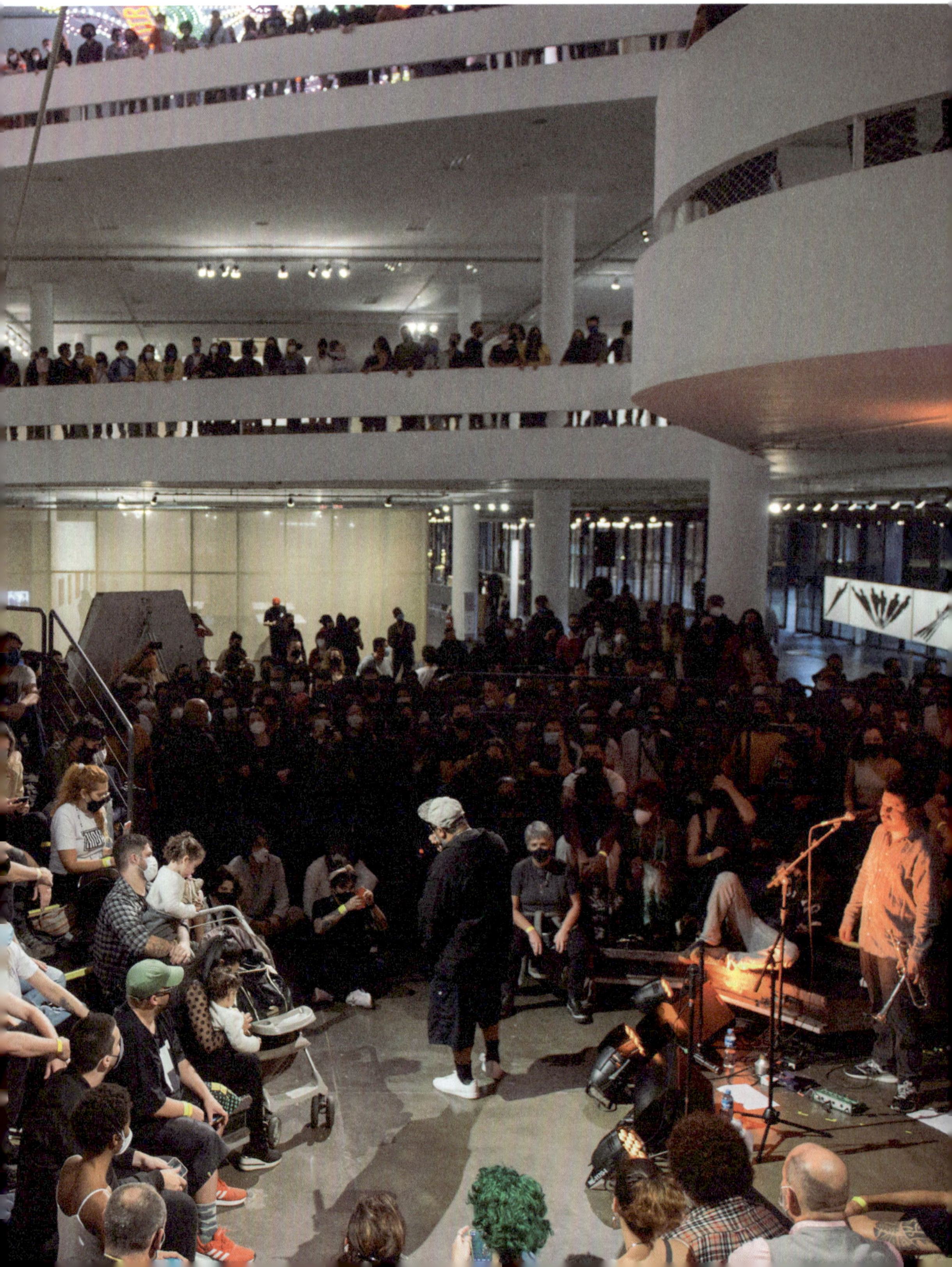

BIENAL PROGRAMMING (DECEMBER)

02 Dec 2021	*Ciclo Bienal dos índios*: performance by Xondaro Kuery Kaguy Ijá [Guerreiros Guardiões da Floresta], tribute to Jaider Esbell (1979–2021)
03 Dec 2021	Jacopo Crivelli Visconti and Pedro França
04 Dec 2021	*Conversações* with Kaká Werá
05 Dec 2021	*A Grace Note* by Neo Muyanga with Coletivo Legítima Defesa

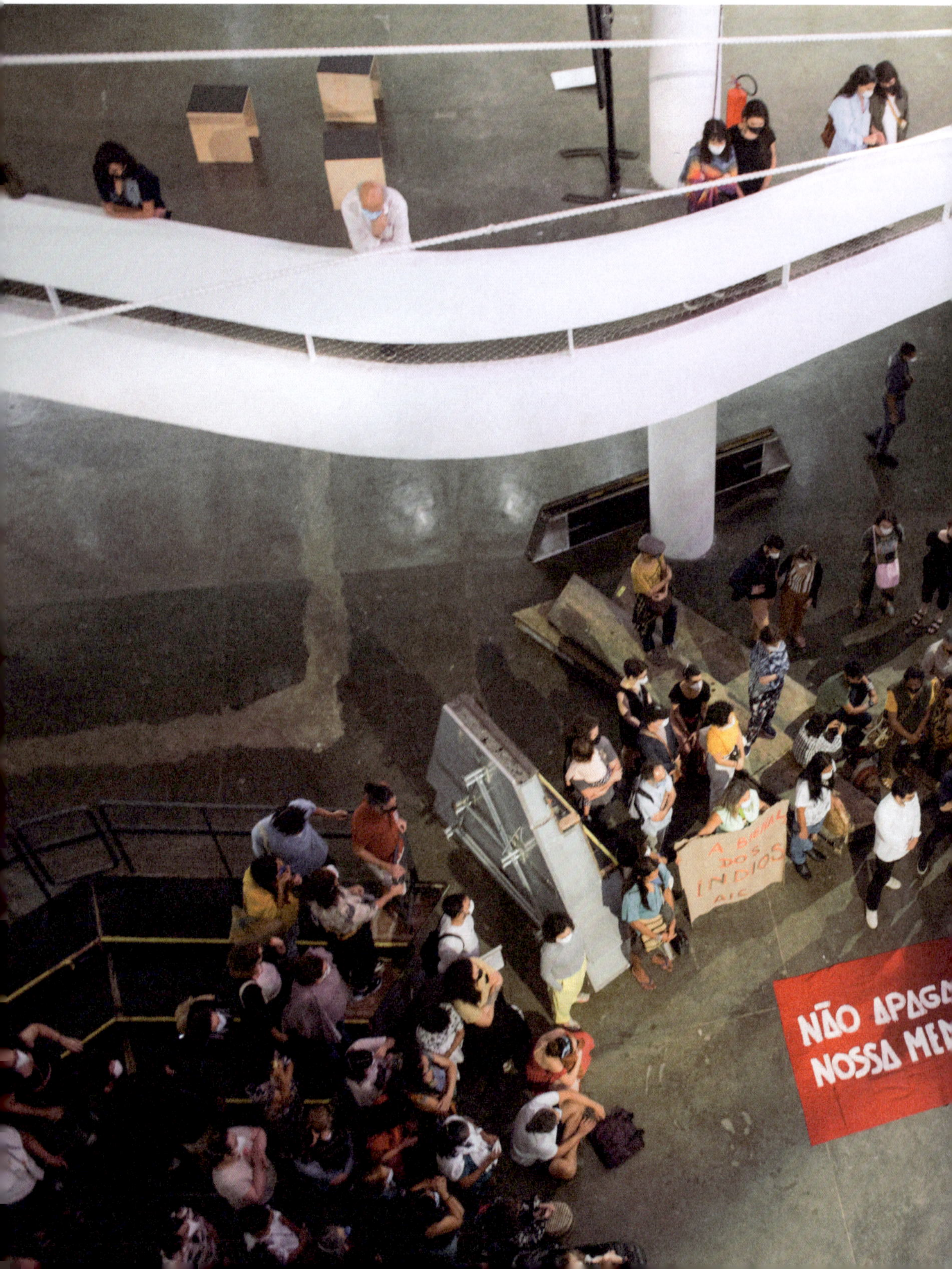
A BIENAL
DOS
INDIOS
NÃO APAGA
NOSSA

02 Dec 2021 *Ciclo Bienal dos índios*: performance by Xondaro Kuery Kaguy Ijá [Guerreiros Guardiões da Floresta], tribute to Jaider Esbell (1979–2021)

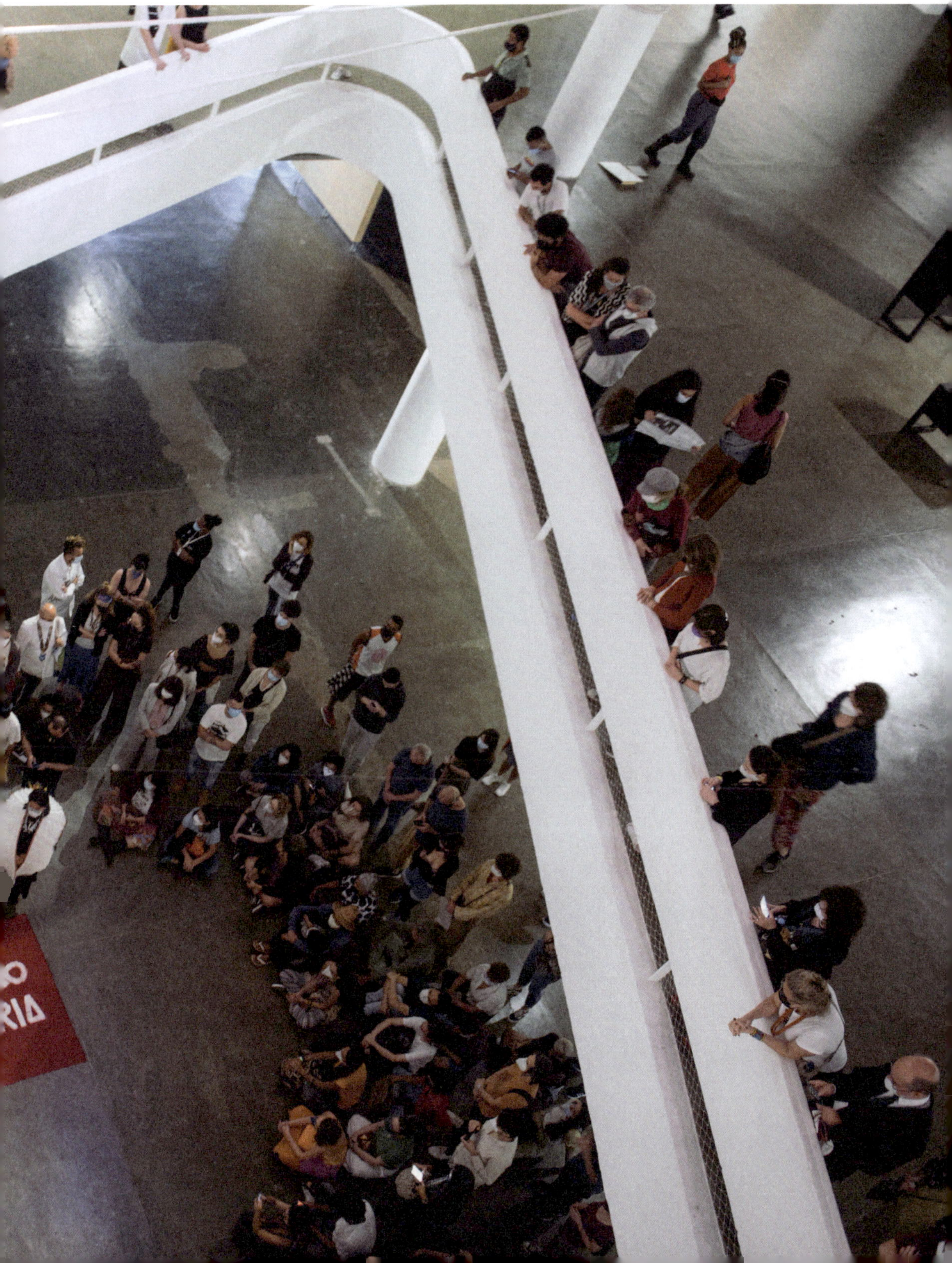

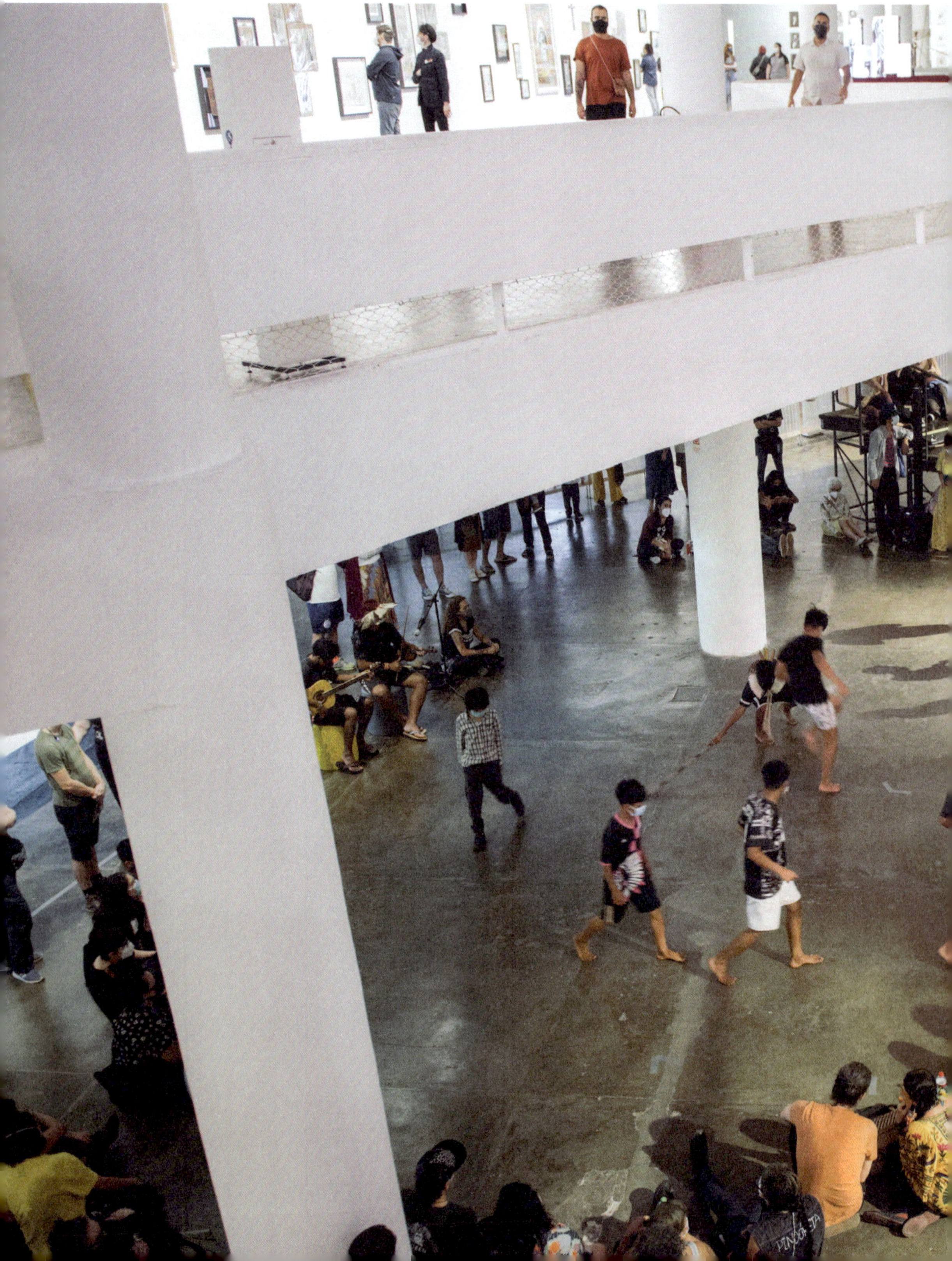

02 Dec 2021

Ciclo Bienal dos índios: performance by Xondaro Kuery Kaguy Ijá [Guerreiros Guardiões da Floresta], tribute to Jaider Esbell (1979–2021)

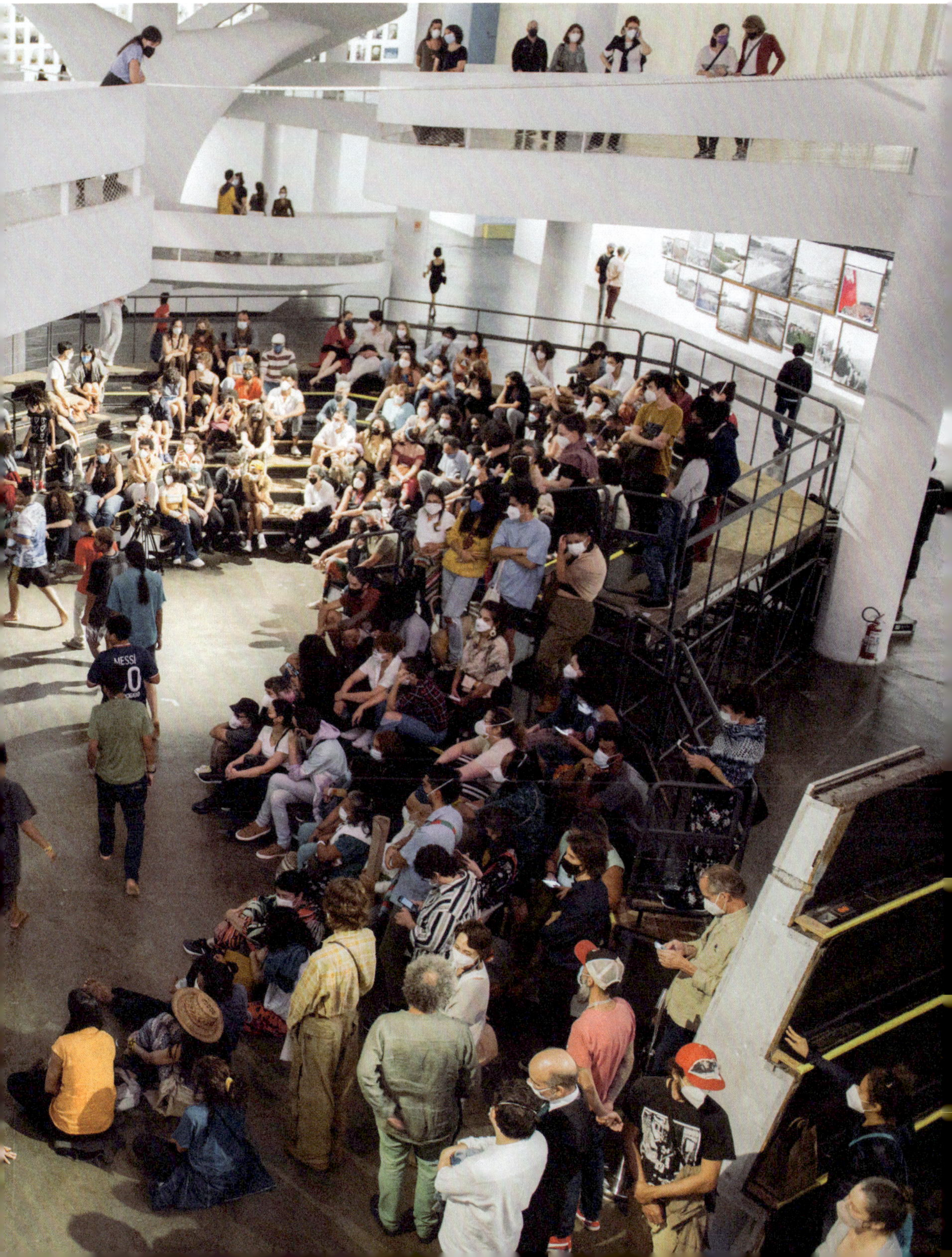

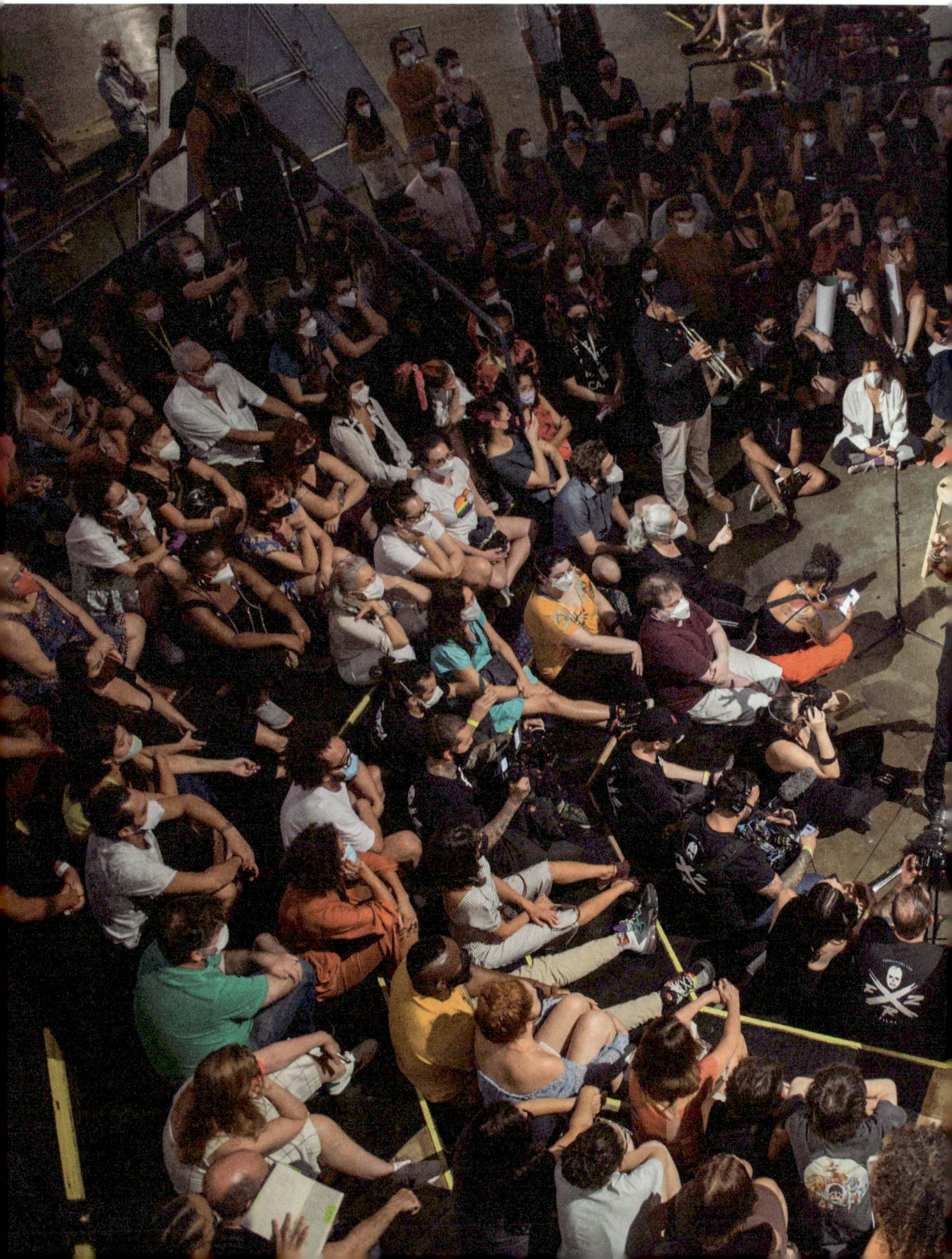

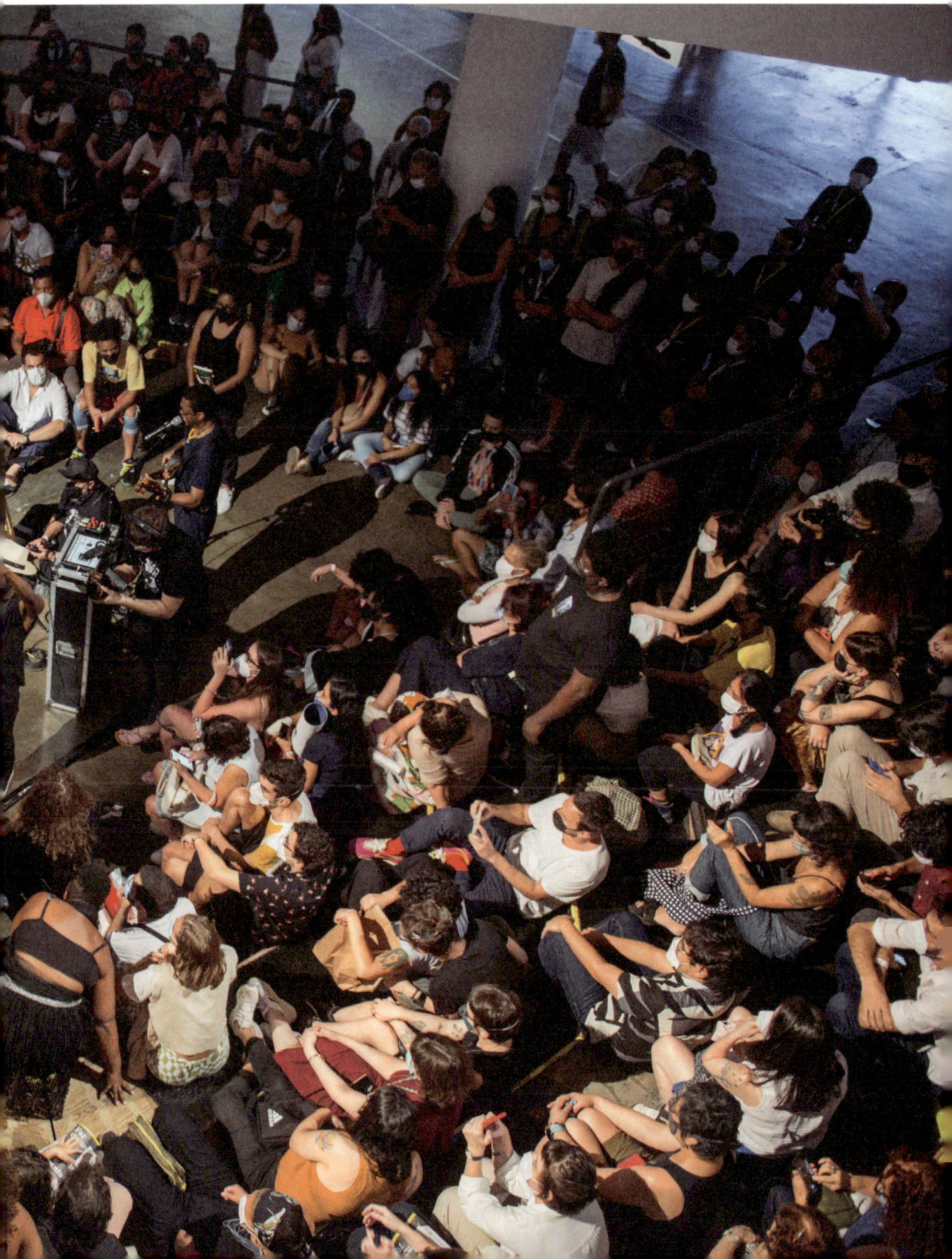

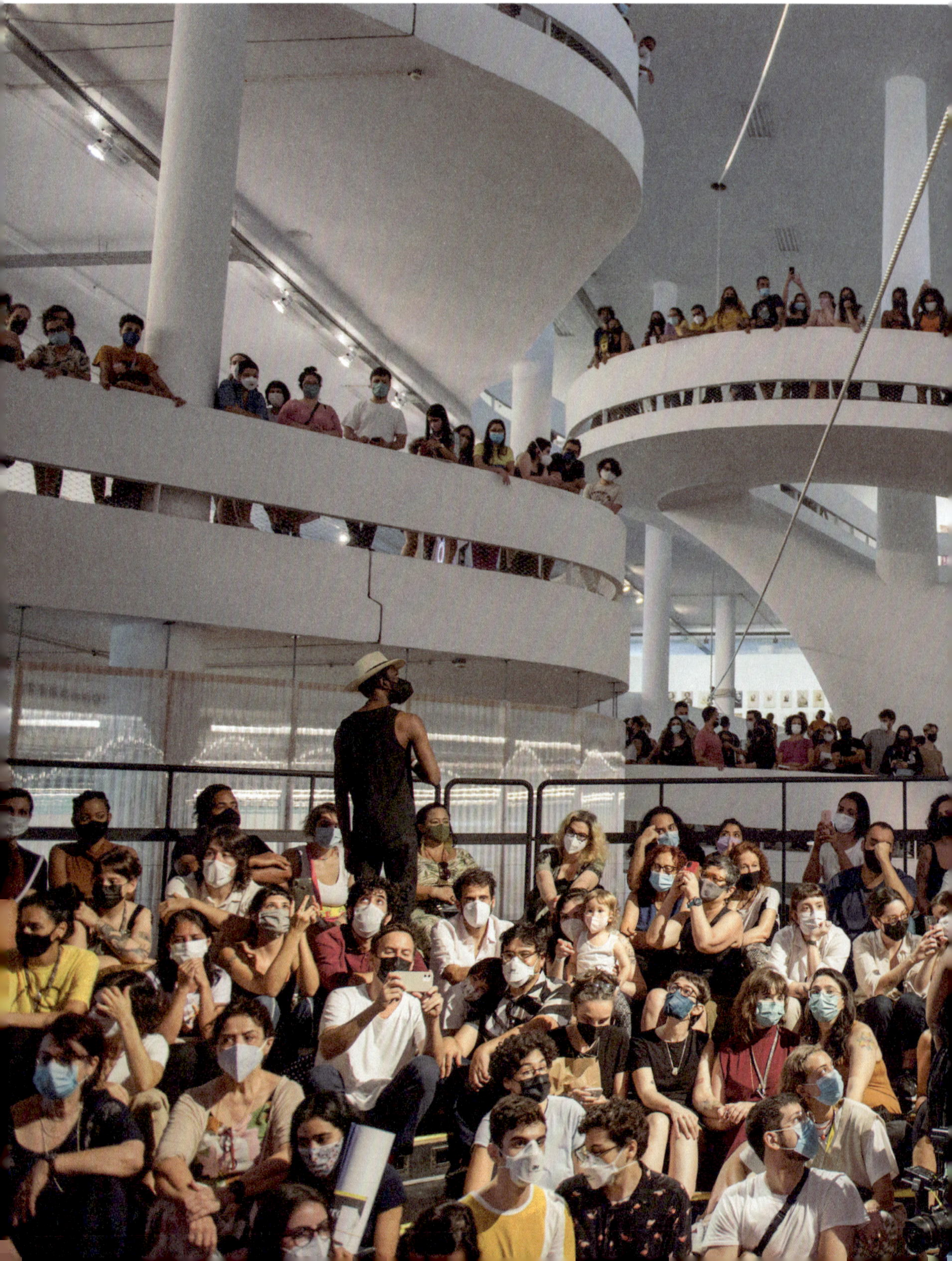

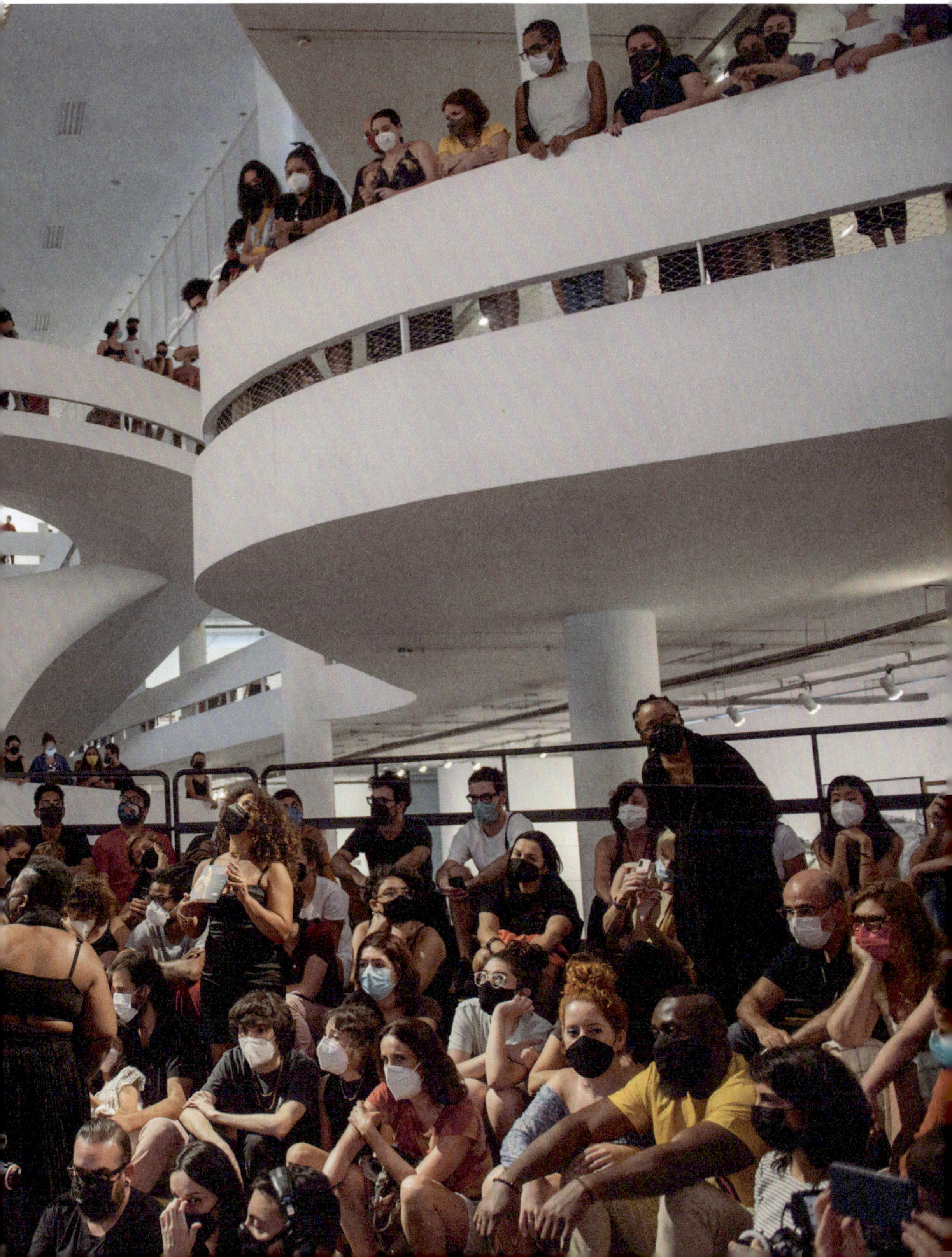

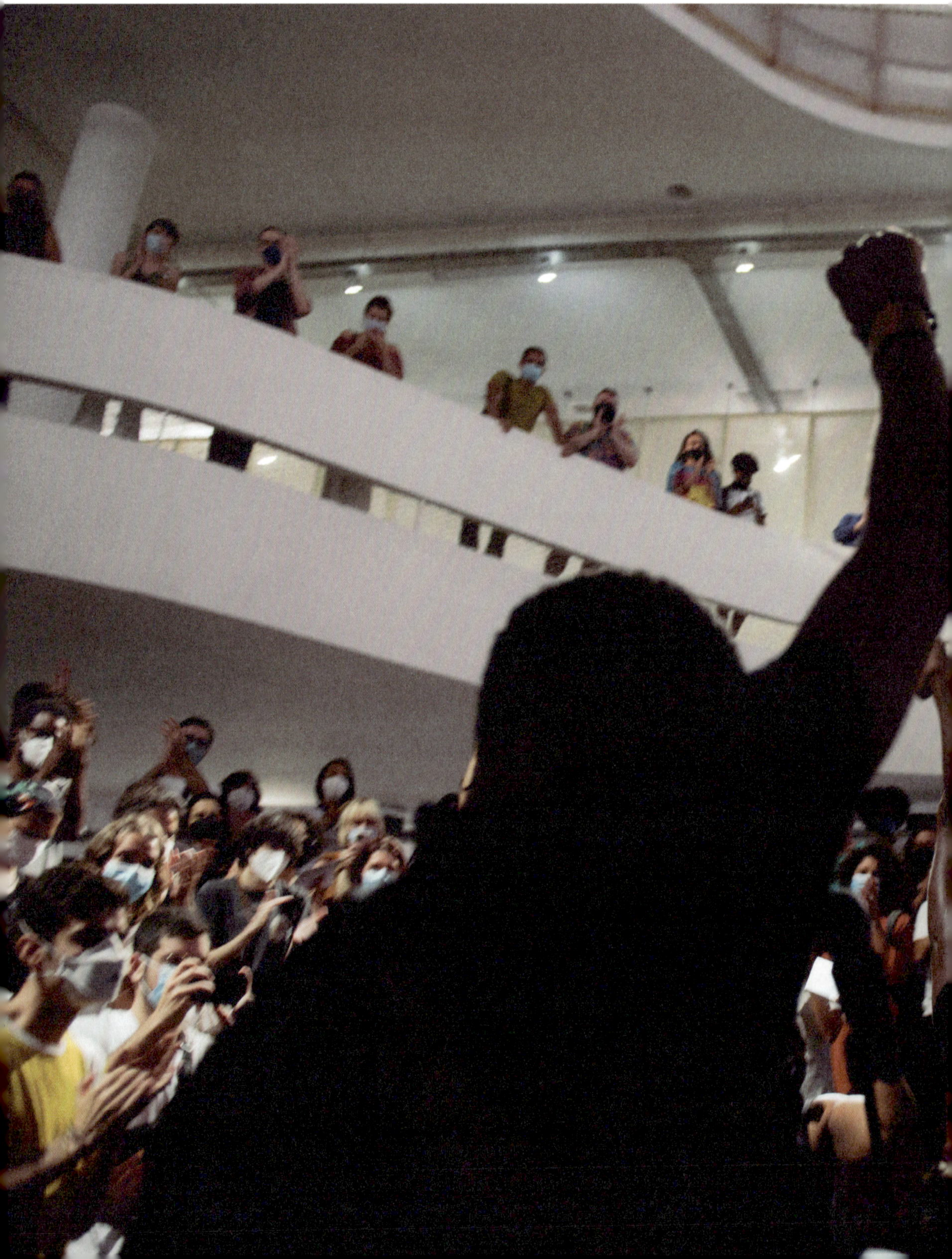

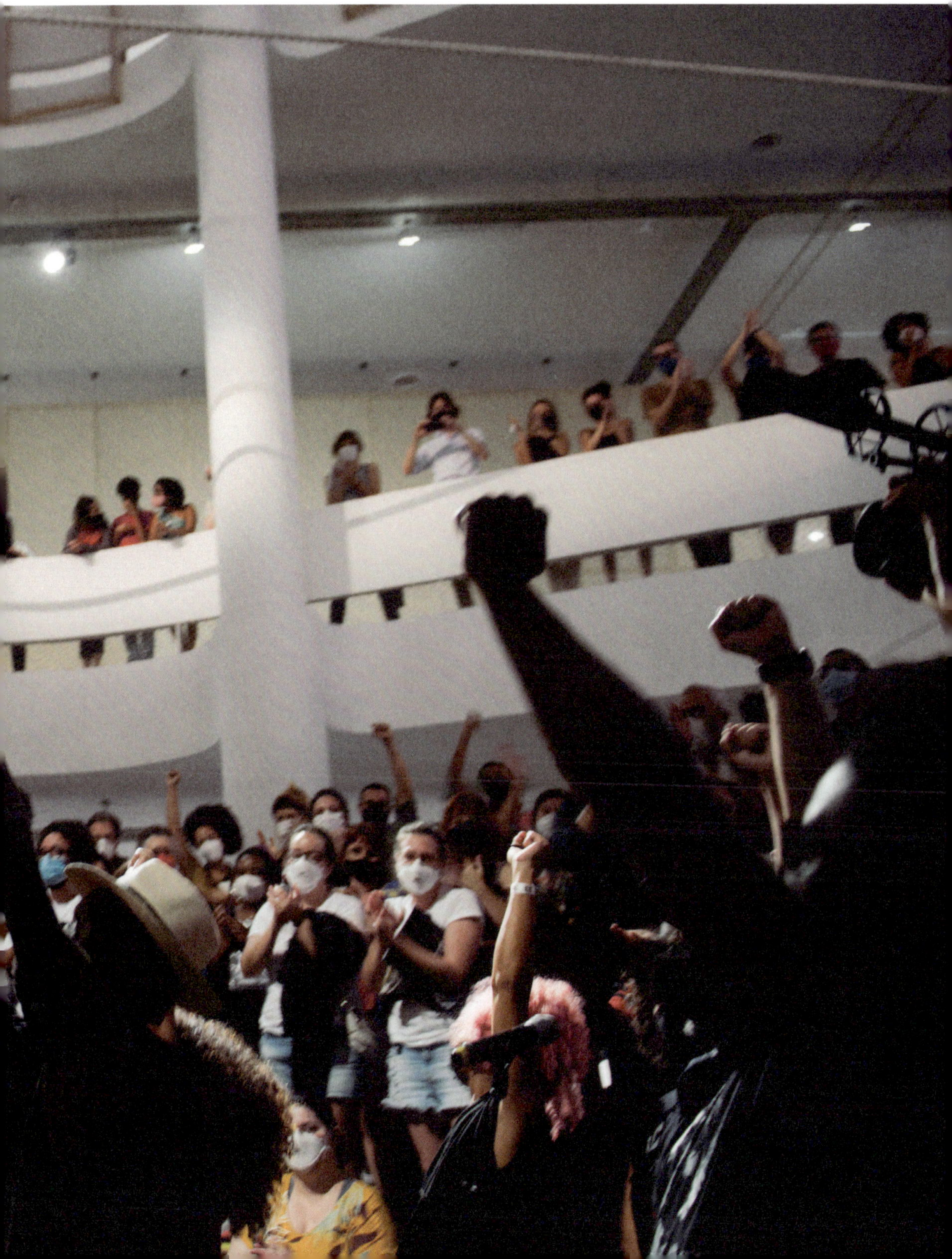

UM OBJETO DESLOCADO, UM LUGAR PARA REUNIR DIFERENTES CORPOS

Daniel de Paula —
Quais foram alguns dos fatores determinantes para a seleção do trabalho *deposição* para a 34ª Bienal de São Paulo?

Jacopo Crivelli Visconti —
Vou começar, então. Embora estejamos um pouco enferrujados agora, já fomos melhores nisso, Paulo e eu. Já fomos muito precisos, mas agora temos de voltar atrás. Penso que há algumas ideias centrais do trabalho, *deposição*, que estão alinhadas com o nosso pensamento curatorial para a Bienal. A primeira é que, de um ponto de vista curatorial e institucional, a Bienal foi concebida como um diálogo.[1] Eramos uma equipe de curadores em diálogo–compreendendo que o diálogo envolve tensão e atrito, diferentes pontos de vista e opiniões sobre as coisas–o que penso ser um fator central para o trabalho *deposição*,[2] a ideia de que ninguém está falando sozinho, que há sempre algum tipo de negociação em curso. Isso foi muito central para a exposição e, penso eu, muito central para a obra.

Começou, então, a fazer sentido para nós ter *deposição* num lugar de destaque na Bienal, e assim, começamos a compreender que também fazia sentido do ponto de vista arquitetônico.[3] Tem sido frequente, historicamente, o caso de obras nesse espaço, de o vão ou átrio central da Bienal estarem, de alguma forma, tentando competir com a arquitetura de uma maneira fálica. Peças muito verticais, muito masculinas, brancas, são frequentemente posicionadas ali. Na história das exposições da Bienal, podemos encontrar vários exemplos de torres, digamos, feitas de várias maneiras.[4] Nos interessou a ideia de ter algo que, em teoria, estivesse alinhado e não competisse com a arquitetura. Tivemos uma noção clara disso quando começamos a mover as peças do piso da roda de negociação, pois elas realçavam visualmente a arquitetura.

Contudo, num outro sentido, a roda de negociação competia com o edifício, pois era um ímã para que as pessoas se sentassem juntas, falassem juntas, estivessem juntas. Isso aconteceu, claro, através de todas as atividades programadas, mas também de uma forma muito natural. Muitas vezes, ia-se lá e viam-se pessoas apenas sentadas ali. Essa era uma afirmação muito forte. Penso que esse discurso sobre o espaço entre as coisas está relacionado com a forma como esta Bienal foi concebida desde o início. Curatorialmente, tomamos algumas decisões que não eram tão típicas para uma bienal, como escolher não trabalhar com um tema,[5] expandir a Bienal através do tempo e do espaço,[6] e mesmo apresentar as mesmas obras mais do que uma vez em diferentes pontos da exposição.[7] Estas são coisas que não são tão comuns para uma exposição bienal. Fizemos, penso eu, algo significativo, mas de uma forma muito silenciosa. O nosso interesse não era apresentar tais estratégias curatoriais como ousadas e/ou revolucionárias. Fizemos o que achamos relevante, sem alarde. Vejo essa forma de trabalhar muito alinhada ao seu trabalho, *deposição*. Era uma obra muito marcante, enorme em escala, mas também era possível passar por ela e não vê-la. Tenho a convicção de que muitas pessoas passaram por ela e não a viram - e vejo isso como um elogio, não como um ponto negativo.

David Rueter —
Isso me faz pensar numa foto oficial da exposição da Bienal com que me deparei em um artigo, em que várias das obras da área principal, do vão, foram mencionadas, com exceção da obra *deposição*.[8] Lembro que fiquei contente com essa omissão.

Marissa Lee Benedict —
Ficou tão integrada à arquitetura do edifício, da instituição e da exposição.

Paulo Miyada —
E acrescentaria que, em outro nível, os enunciados curatoriais posicionados ao longo da exposição foram uma maneira que encontramos para abordar fortemente tanto um momento histórico quanto um presente,[9] e as lutas que estão em curso no presente que determinam se teremos, ou não, um futuro. Cada enunciado curatorial era ou um objeto, ou um documento, ou uma imagem–algo que era realmente carregado com uma história da qual pudéssemos nos referir para contar uma narrativa, e para ver como essa história ressoaria com o que estava à sua volta. Vimos o deslocamento desses objetos como um gesto curatorial que punha as suas histórias de novo em jogo, mas no presente. De certa forma, o trabalho *deposição* também abordou esse tipo de possibilidade de deslocamento, o de trazer um pedaço da história à tona, de convocar os fatos, não apenas de modo documental, mas antes, como uma forma de evocar algum tipo de memória, evocando as lutas que se constroem em torno da memória, construídas a partir de e por uma narração dos processos históricos e sociais que envolvem a memória.[10] Estávamos colocando

a memória de novo em jogo no presente, no futuro e, ao fazê-lo, promovendo um novo processo de memória que poderia evoluir para algo mais, que vai além da história original que foi contada, formando uma espécie de ressonância. Evidentemente, esta forte relação entre o trabalho *deposição* e os enunciados curatoriais da Bienal não é uma preocupação curatorial obrigatória. Caso contrário, teríamos uma curadoria que estaria sempre na tentativa de se encontrar mimeticamente nas obras, o que seria bastante bizarro. Mas, neste caso, a ressonância das metodologias e referências também foi significativa. Porque, de certa forma, os enunciados curatoriais que o público encontrava ao longo da Bienal, antes de chegar ao trabalho *deposição*, poderiam proporcionar uma abordagem que, talvez, o ajudasse a se relacionar com a obra, ou vice-versa. Caso o público não tivesse reparado nos enunciados antes de se deparar com *deposição*, mas tivesse tido uma experiência poderosa na roda de negociação, poderia voltar atrás e olhar novamente para os enunciados e vê-los sob uma luz mais significativa.

MLB

Fico curiosa em ouvir mais de cada um de vocês sobre as suas respectivas experiências em relação ao deslocamento da roda de negociação de milho. A meu ver, é fascinante a forma como esse objeto, esse piso do pregão, esteve situado na Bienal, sua ativação e ocupação. Mas, como vocês disseram, ele carrega a história latente desse outro espaço ou lugar: o *Registro do Comércio de Chicago* [CBOT - Chicago Board of Trade]. Fico curiosa em saber se, para vocês, havia a sensação de que a roda de negociação de milho tinha derramado sua história sobre a Bienal. Ou será que a roda de negociação ainda estava sobrecarregada? Ou talvez, para dizer de outra forma: houve uma forma particular desse deslocamento histórico, ou relação, produzida pela colocação do piso do pregão no pavilhão modernista projetado por Oscar Niemeyer?

JCV

A meu ver, a junção das ideias de Édouard Glissant sobre a poética da relação e a arquitetura moderna, como forma de ver a obra de arte, esteve presente desde o início. Havia essa relação inerente com a arquitetura.[11] Era também muito fascinante ver como as 32 peças da roda de negociação de milho couberam de fato dentro do contêiner. Isso foi algo muito impressionante. E, curiosamente, não sei se já repararam nisso e não sei exatamente o porquê–talvez o Paulo, que estudou mais arquitetura do que todos nós aqui, possa saber–mas, o tamanho de 6 ou 12 metros é frequentemente recorrente na arquitetura moderna. Neste caso, 12 metros é a distância entre as colunas do edifício da Bienal, o diâmetro original da roda de negociação de milho e o comprimento de um contêiner de transporte. Fiz, recentemente, uma proposta para a sede da UNESCO, Paris, porque havia a ideia de trazer para lá parte da exposição da Bienal, o que não vai acontecer, mas as colunas do edifício estão a seis metros de distância, sendo assim uma estranha série de coincidências, ou repetições.

Mas, dito isso, penso que nós, na construção da exposição, fizemos referência a esse conceito do deslocamento através da ideia de circulação, que foi retomada no segundo andar, a circulação de mercadorias, de ideias, ou de movimentos culturais, digamos assim. Pode ser um conceito, como Negritude, ou pode ser um estilo específico, como o Estilo Internacional na arquitetura moderna. Assim, todos esses tipos de circulação–que no segundo andar estavam mais diretamente ligados às ideias de construção de uma imagem de si próprio–estavam entrelaçados. E penso que foi também, mais uma vez, curatorialmente muito sutil e provavelmente quase imperceptível. Mas, se repararmos, tornou-se algo bonito. Como dizia Paulo, a obra *deposição* também funcionou, de certa forma, como parte dessa afirmação. Era, até certo ponto, o enunciado referente ao segundo andar e não ao primeiro andar. Acho essa ideia–que *deposição* é uma obra que é fisicamente baixa, mas que conceitualmente ocupa todo o poder da Bienal–um tanto potente.

PM

Acredito que a literatura que já acessei e que poderia se relacionar com a recorrência do uso dos 12 metros na arquitetura, mencionado pelo Jacopo, é um livro que é citado e referido habitualmente, mas que de fato poucas pessoas leram, que é o *Le Modulor,* de Le Corbusier.[12] O texto reflete sobre o porquê de construirmos as coisas do tamanho que as construímos, e como isso se relaciona, ou não, com uma mente, com um problema de composição, com uma organização mental do espaço, ou com o corpo, os movimentos e a anatomia da existência humana. Lembro-me que o livro começa por descrever estradas Romanas, que eram definidas pelo tamanho de um tronco de árvore ou de um certo tronco, o que fez com que os Romanos construíssem as suas estradas com um certo tamanho para os cavalos e para as carruagens. E, depois, essas carruagens definiriam os vagões de trem, os vagões de trem definiriam as ferrovias, as ferrovias definiriam a escala dos materiais de construção que movimentavam, definindo a escala de consumo nas indústrias e assim sucessivamente. E talvez, isso tenha eventualmente levado a essa dimensão de 6 e 12 metros. Le Corbusier foi muito crítico ao raciocínio casuístico, salientando que nunca houve um momento em que nós, humanidade, disséssemos coletivamente: "Sabe, vamos parar e pensar sobre isto. Vamos escolher o que realmente faz sentido, e não apenas continuar com este tamanho dado e aquele tamanho," e assim por diante.

Mas sim, Jacopo estava enfatizando o conceito de circulação e, nesse sentido, o que acho que a estrutura da roda de negociação traz–e que foi muito significativo para a Bienal–é que era um objeto que, por si só, já tinha sido deslocado, mas que, ainda assim, continuava sendo um lugar para reunir diferentes corpos. Portanto, foi, para as pessoas que chegavam, um lugar para se encontrarem e negociarem. E, tanto no contexto da Bienal como na sua vida anterior, como roda de negociação no pregão em Chicago, foi um lugar onde diferentes noções, ideias e valores puderam ser trazidos, trocados e transformados. Isso teve efeitos, efeitos práticos e físicos, noutros locais. Simbolicamente agora, e em termos de cultura, mas também em termos materiais, de produção, de acumulação e de apropriação naquele outro momento.[13] Assim, ao vivenciar a obra *deposição*, você estaria pensando ou se relacionando com ideias de movimento, deslocamento e circulação de várias maneiras, todas elas entrelaçadas tanto no passado como no presente e, como parece, também no futuro. Isso é algo interessante, porque a certa altura, quando construímos uma discussão sobre o deslocamento ou os instrumentos de apropriação na teoria e história das artes modernas e contemporâneas, uma coisa poderia ser citada como tendo estado aqui uma vez e depois trazida para lá. Como em: pertenceu aqui, e depois um artista ou uma instituição, um museu, recolocou-o noutro campo semântico, físico e visual. Mas este trabalho, *deposição*, permite-nos pensar no deslocamento como uma condição, e não como uma situação de ajuste.

DR

Quais foram alguns dos riscos curatoriais e contextuais implicados na apresentação da obra *deposição* no âmbito da Bienal?

PM

Eu vi dois grandes conjuntos de riscos. O primeiro conjunto, o mais tangível quando abrimos a Bienal, era que estávamos lidando com a pandemia[14] e, ocupando o centro da parte mais visível, fotografável e memorável do pavilhão com uma obra que exigia—ou pelo menos convidava—o encontro, a ocupação e a troca humana no meio de um momento da nossa história global em que estivemos muito preocupados com as consequências dos encontros, intercâmbios e reuniões sociais. Assim, havia um risco real de que o trabalho estivesse lá e que os curadores, os curadores mais os artistas, a instituição—alguns tipos diferentes de "nós"—acabaríamos por não aconselhar ninguém a ativar o trabalho de fato, o que é sempre um pequeno fracasso, na medida em que se inicia um gesto e não se consegue ir até o fim com ele. Isso não é o ideal: nem na arte, nem na política, nem em lado nenhum. Durante toda a pandemia, a situação de segurança sanitária estava sempre mudando, dia após dia, semana após semana. Fez com que todo o planeta lidasse com a ideia de fracasso numa base *quotidiana*. Assim, decidimos que era melhor, pelo menos, tentar o gesto e, se ele falhasse, seria porque as coisas estavam sujeitas a falhar. O outro conjunto de riscos envolvidos em convidar as pessoas em conjunto é que as pessoas não transportam apenas o vírus e o antivírus: as pessoas transportam ideias, ódio, ideologias conflituosas e uma série de desalinhamentos do momento presente. Essa Bienal foi concebida, e aconteceu, num momento em que o diálogo não é o nosso conjunto mais forte de competências como sociedade. Por isso, as coisas poderiam ter ficado fora de controle, por assim dizer. Nos eventos que organizamos como instituição, as pessoas que convidamos poderiam estar frente a frente com uma audiência inesperada, ou o debate entre as pessoas poderia ir para um campo perigoso–porque a ideia era sempre a de que não convidaríamos apenas pessoas que pertencessem a uma determinada área, ou a um conjunto de ideias, ou a uma determinada profissão, ou a um determinado alinhamento político. A ideia era ter perspectivas diferentes colidindo na roda de negociação, no trabalho. E também compreender as possibilidades de ocupação espontânea da obra, o que foi sempre um de seus aspectos, tal como constava do contrato.[15] Esta era uma parte da proposta que se destacava das coisas que a instituição podia organizar oficialmente. As pessoas eram sempre bem-vindas a se sentarem na roda de negociação e fazerem o que quer que fosse. Penso que este é o tipo de risco que uma grande instituição de arte de interesse público deveria estar disposta a correr, todos os dias. Caso contrário, poderíamos simplesmente operar como outras partes do sistema artístico e não fazer tais esforços para apresentar e organizar em tão grande escala, e num espaço de tão grande interesse público e de acesso.

JCV

Concordo com a colocação do Paulo. Penso, para voltar à questão, que é também mais do que apenas correr riscos. Quando se faz uma exposição deste tamanho, é preciso escolher as batalhas. Penso que nos dedicamos a escolher muitas batalhas e a persegui-las até o fim e, nesse sentido, *deposição* não foi uma obra fácil do ponto de vista institucional, por algumas das razões que mencionei anteriormente. Não era visível, sabe, e não era atraente a um nível convencional. Incorporando os riscos que o Paulo mencionou, penso que houve também um certo grau de coragem, do nosso lado, para dizer: "Não, queremos que esta obra esteja lá, e a apoiamos, mesmo que as conversas talvez não possam ter lugar na roda de negociação, mesmo que as pessoas não possam se reunir aqui, mesmo que não tenhamos fundos para fazer um programa espantoso com os participantes mais conhecidos e que trariam uma audiência maior à Bienal—acreditamos que este projeto é importante, e o apoiamos". É muito significativo e relevante que tenhamos tido que defender essas escolhas no início. Eu nunca diria que houve uma forte oposição ao trabalho—já que não seria verdade. Tivemos de o defender, mas, no final, todos ficaram muito satisfeitos com o trabalho, todos ficaram muito empenhados. Quando digo todos, refiro-me à instituição, não apenas aos curadores ou aos artistas, claro, ou às outras pessoas envolvidas no programa, sabe, como a Vânia Medeiros e a Beatriz Cruz,[16] e assim por diante. Toda a instituição estava, no final, muito convencida de que se tratava de um trabalho muito relevante.

Penso que, de um ponto de vista, temos o que Paulo disse–a situação pandêmica tornou tudo mais difícil–mas, de outra forma, tornou o trabalho ainda mais necessário do que qualquer um de nós poderia ter imaginado antes. Quando as pessoas–o público, mas também nós mesmos, e vocês, Marissa, David e Daniel–puderam realmente sentar e conversar e ouvir música, ou o que quer que ali estivesse acontecendo, foi um sentimento muito, muito forte sentido por todos nós. E penso, tal como digo sempre para a Bienal–e penso que isto também é verdade para o trabalho *deposição*–nós, como curadores, fizemos uma exposição muito boa. Vocês, como artistas, fizeram uma obra muito boa. Mas, a forma como as pessoas reagiram, transcendeu o que poderíamos ter feito. Tratava-se realmente do momento que todos nós estávamos vivendo. Não pudemos controlar isso, e não podemos ficar com os louros por isso. Mas, ainda assim, penso que fez realmente sentido para todos nós.

DdP

Uma questão que talvez siga essa linha de pensamento, Jacopo, é pensar no significado de um trabalho colaborativo ocupando o vão, o centro ou, digamos, o coração da exposição nesta atual paisagem sociopolítica.[17] Poderiam ambos desenvolver um pouco mais essa ideia de colaboração, tanto em termos do ponto de vista curatorial–que foi um processo colaborativo–como também em termos de um contexto sociopolítico mais amplo?

JCV

Já discutimos o ponto de vista curatorial da Bienal. No entanto, penso que há outro aspecto da sua prática colaborativa - especialmente trazido por você, Daniel - que é exemplificado no trabalho *deposição*. Entendo que a sua prática, Daniel, implica sempre um grau de negociação e, particularmente, de negociação institucional, o que me parece bastante fascinante. Isto é, provavelmente, verdade para todos vocês, e é algo muito central para a obra *deposição*. Penso que essa palavra, "negociação," é interessante de ser trazida à tona, respondendo à sua pergunta sobre colaboração, porque no mundo da arte temos essa abordagem muito fácil incorrendo sobre o conceito de colaboração, que é essa colaboração agradável, sem falhas e pavimentada com boas intenções. Mas, quando se traz a ideia de negociação, especialmente negociar com instituições, isso nem sempre é tão fácil–mas, penso que isso, também, é uma forma de colaboração. Não é o conceito convencional de colaboração, em que duas pessoas se encontram e fazem algo em conjunto com os mesmos objetivos e a mesma visão desde o início. Mas, é exatamente por isso que é um modo de colaboração muito significativo. Sei que com esse projeto, especificamente através do contrato, faz-se realmente questão de tensionar algumas das formas como uma instituição normalmente funciona. Faz isso de uma forma muito simples, aparentemente ingênua, digamos, mas é muito direta e clara. O que vocês encontraram durante as negociações com a Fundação Bienal de São Paulo, não diria que foi a situação mais difícil que poderiam ter enfrentado porque, no final, a Bienal respondeu bem. Mesmo assim, levou seis meses ou mais para traduzir o contrato e para tê-lo assinado, mas penso que isso é normal. Foi exatamente por isso que vocês propuseram o contrato em primeiro lugar, porque queriam tensionar essa área cinzenta da colaboração e negociação entre o modo de pensar dos artistas e o modo de pensar institucional.[18] Considero isso um aspecto muito importante do trabalho. E, mais uma vez, vejo aqui uma correspondência com a forma como a Bienal foi organizada de uma forma mais geral. Nos bastidores, nós–Paulo e eu, especialmente–tivemos que fazer uma enorme quantidade de negociações com todas as instituições que foram convidadas a fazer parte da Bienal. Todas essas negociações e conversas com outras instituições, muito diferentes da Bienal, foram importantes para nos fazer refletir sobre a exposição que queríamos fazer. E, como neste seu caso, isso é algo que o público simplesmente não vê–e não faz mal que não veja–mas está lá, em algum lugar. Penso que isso é importante para nós. Neste caso, 99,9% da audiência não viu o contrato e não pensou realmente nesse elemento da obra, que é uma parte essencial do projeto. Portanto, é uma forma diferente de pensar sobre as formas de colaboração em que normalmente nos envolvemos, especialmente na cena artística. E, penso eu, uma parte muito fascinante do projeto.

PM

No caso do trabalho *deposição*, a programação pública acrescentou novas camadas de negociação, porque decidimos convidar Beatriz e Vânia para montar a programação, que depois convidaram muitos outros convidados e temas e vozes para ocupar o espaço–mas, não de uma forma monolítica, porque a programação sobre a roda de negociação andou para trás e para a frente, em alternância com proposições que a própria organização da Bienal sugeriu, como as performances musicais logo no final da exposição e coisas que a equipe curatorial tinha desenvolvido antes, ou que continuou desenvolvendo durante a Bienal, como a apresentação final com o compositor Neo Muyanga,[19] ou outros tipos de eventos, tais como os lançamentos de livros e outras apresentações que surgiram durante o processo. Assim, a programação expandiu-se para incorporar outros editores, curadores e organizadores, que depois convidaram outras pessoas para entrar na roda, que também conseguiram trazer consigo diferentes fontes de programação e pensamento. E agora, olhando para trás com perspectiva, tenho pensado em como, na colaboração, e também possivelmente na negociação, existe esse entendimento ingênuo de que o sucesso é quando todos concordam rapidamente e ninguém tem que abdicar de nada. Mas isso não é realmente uma negociação; isso é uma convergência de interesses. Quando se concorda rapidamente, é porque não se teve que negociar muito, em primeiro lugar. É uma troca simples. A verdadeira negociação começa quando se reconhece, a certa altura, que há algo que é intraduzível ou não negociável, ou que é realmente injusto e, mesmo assim, continua-se trabalhando para ir além desse entendimento. Vê-se que há um problema, mas e depois? Depois todos têm de se deslocar e repensar por onde passaram, de onde vieram e como lidam com isso. No final, o resultado não é necessariamente uma resolução das causas de descontentamento que possam surgir durante o processo. Em muitos casos, esses descontentamentos estão fundados demasiado longe: têm profundidade histórica e significado estrutural. Não é algo que as pessoas sentadas à mesa possam realmente resolver ou apagar, mas podem encontrar formas de compensar, de dar a volta, ou pelo menos reconhecer a coisa e depois seguir em frente. Essa obra, *deposição*, do princípio ao fim, exigiu que os artistas, os curadores, a instituição, os participantes e a audiência fizessem essa versão real da negociação. E a questão é que nunca parou realmente; de vez em quando tínhamos de lidar com o desconforto.

MLB

Isto se refere, novamente, à história residual ou aos elementos contratuais da obra?

JCV

Certo. Como quando o piso da roda de negociação estava no pregão, e haviam pessoas negociando algo que elas não controlavam totalmente. Não conseguiam ver. Não conseguiam cheirar o que estava sendo negociado. Talvez nem sequer soubessem em que é que estavam participando. Penso que era muito claro que vocês, os artistas, queriam que certos fatores do trabalho estivessem fora do controle de vocês, como uma forma de destacar a obra; que este é um ponto nos quais forças que vêm de grandes distâncias, e que são muito maiores do que esse pequeno ponto rea–essa seção de 12 metros de chão do pregão–convergem. Por isso, vejo-a como uma abordagem muito poética, digamos, à obra, que está muito dentro da crítica institucional, mas também faz parte de uma forma conceitual de se pensar sobre arte. Agora é apenas por uma fração muito pequena de tempo na vida desse objeto, e está se fazendo algo com ele, mas, no final, está diretamente ligado por milhares de fios a coisas enormes que não controlamos realmente. Penso que isso também se tornou muito visível através da programação *Conversações*, e através das coisas não-programadas que tiveram lugar no trabalho. Nos últimos grandes eventos que tivemos–o evento de encerramento do Muyanga, o evento que marcou um mês desde a morte de Jaider Esbell,[20] as apresentações de música popular propostas pela própria Bienal–a roda de negociação tornou-se realmente algo que as pessoas estavam usando, e só isso. Apesar de termos a declaração (ou o enunciado),[21] sempre lido no início de cada evento, era algo que as pessoas não processavam completamente, sabe, especialmente quando tínhamos as apresentações musicais. Penso que a sensação de estar presente foi bela–o fato de ter funcionado muito bem como apenas uma plataforma–o que penso que fazia parte daquilo que vocês, os artistas, tinham imaginado desde o início. Tudo se relaciona com essa ideia de que o trabalho é algo que vai muito além daquilo que vocês enquanto artistas, nós enquanto curadores, ou só a instituição pode fazer, ou controlar.

PM

E essa é uma boa parte do trabalho: tem negociações e tem contratos, mas também conversas e boatos. Portanto, tem essas coisas muito estruturadas que podem realmente se condensar no relatar do trabalho—ou podem ser colocadas num livro, digamos–porque são factuais ou documentais, mas depois há todo o resto em volta do trabalho. Portanto, quando o contrato estabelece que esta coisa é de responsabilidade daquela parte, ou esta coisa é delegada à instituição ou aos artistas ou aos curadores, etc., é bom. Está estabelecido no contrato. Mas, isso não resolve como é que as conversas em volta e antes e através do trabalho podem ter lugar, e isso introduz dúvidas, dúvidas que gosto e que me levam a perguntar: será que esta é realmente a melhor maneira? Por exemplo, decidiu-se não ter quaisquer documentos–o contrato da obra, fotos históricas originais–à disposição do público no espaço. No final, decidiu-se por não exibir qualquer conjunto de documentos que contextualizassem a obra para além da própria peça, e esta foi uma escolha discutível. Quer dizer, poderia sempre justificá-la ao contrário, mas, no final, gosto dessa escolha porque há tanto sobre essa obra que é muito factual e estruturado mas, quando não se tem documentos presentes no espaço que a descrevem, exige-se um certo nível de rumores e conversas a ter lugar. Assim, o enquadramento conceitual do trabalho é muito estruturado, no entanto, se alguém estiver diante do trabalho, terá de fazer um esforço para falar com alguém ou para ouvir alguém falar sobre ele, algo como: "Hmm, o que foi isso? Do que se trata isto?" Ativando essa camada mais ingrata do trabalho.

DdP

Penso que, talvez, esta última resposta possa ser uma boa transição para falarmos um pouco sobre a programação, e talvez algumas das principais preocupações curatoriais. Como é que estas foram reveladas através da programação alojada dentro da roda de negociação? E, penso que já tocamos um pouco nisso, mas existiu alguma atividade específica da programação que foi especial para ambos?

JCV

Bem, penso que o programa que a Vânia e a Beatriz fizeram foi muito desafiante de vários pontos de vista, e muito inspirador. Foram muito cuidadosas na forma como selecionaram as pessoas que participaram dos seus programas. E claro, alguns programas foram mais atraentes para mim, e outros provavelmente para outras pessoas, o que fazia parte das intenções da programação. Uma coisa fascinante, penso, é que a maioria das pessoas participantes nos eventos *Conversações* - não todas, mas a maioria das pessoas–representaram, efetivamente, outras pessoas–falaram em seu nome, direta ou indiretamente, de comunidades ou identidades específicas. Essa foi uma forma de ir para além da conversa imediata que estava naquele lugar. Por outro lado, devo dizer, penso que teria gostado de ter mais conversas que se assemelhassem a debates. Penso que o programa que criaram foi espetacular, e eu não mudaria nada, mas teria adorado ter outras pessoas falando. Como vocês, Marissa, Daniel e David, disseram desde o início, que queriam que a roda de negociação, até certo ponto, fosse um espaço de confronto. Também queríamos isso, embora estivéssemos muito preocupados, como disse Paulo, com os tempos específicos que vivemos, com as reações muito agressivas dos meios de comunicação social que podem acontecer em qualquer momento. Penso que nos escapou um nível de debate que poderia ter acontecido. Se tenho que dizer–e esta é, provavelmente, a primeira crítica que tenho à nossa realização da obra *deposição*, e é porque adoro realmente o trabalho e tudo o que aconteceu–penso que perdemos isso. Penso que deveríamos ter tido mais pessoas convidadas para a plataforma que pensassem de forma diferente da nossa. Penso que 99% das pessoas que pisaram sobre a roda para falar publicamente foram pessoas com quem concordamos na maioria das coisas que poderiam ser ditas. Claro que fomos mais levados pela forma como alguns o disseram e menos pela forma como outros o disseram, mas, no final, concordamos com todas as lutas e visões de mundo que essas pessoas reivindicaram. Senti falta, pessoalmente, de alguém com quem não estava de acordo. No entanto, penso que isso seria algo provavelmente impossível de se fazer naquele momento. Mais uma vez, penso que escolhemos as nossas batalhas, e as apoiamos. E essa batalha–produzir uma série de debates mais desafiadores–era algo que queríamos, mas não conseguimos, por várias razões. Mas, digo isto porque penso que isso é algo que ainda é potencial no e do trabalho, e é algo que o trabalho realmente precisará em algum momento. Isso é algo que poderíamos ter feito, não diria melhor, mas mais do que foi. O que é bom. Quer dizer, provavelmente não se encontrará um melhor ambiente arquitetônico para instalar a obra, por isso precisa haver algo pelo que almejar nas próximas versões da obra. E penso que essa sensação de maior fricção é algo que provavelmente vocês também irão procurar.

DR

Concordo plenamente com esse sentimento. Penso que o desejo de debate foi uma preocupação central desde o início, ao pensarmos nesse potencial do discurso e nas suas dificuldades. O fato de não ter acontecido é também reflexo de algo. Encontrar esse trabalho tendo algum potencial que permanece inexaurível, mesmo pelo enorme espaço que lhe foi concedido, é fantástico.

MLB

Concordo, e penso que também houve algo daquele momento, algo que agora já se passou. Mas, naquele momento, no momento da pandemia, senti tamanha gratidão por estarmos apenas juntos. E concordo que, à distância, das nossas perspectivas de agora, estou de novo contemplando as qualidades do atrito e do debate. Mas, naquele momento, lembro-me de me sentir muito frágil e de pensar o quão interessante era que muitas das críticas e dos escritos sobre a Bienal refletissem essa questão de lidar com as cinzas do–ou o processar do luto de–estarmos juntos depois de tanto tempo separados.

JCV

Foi por isso que eu disse que não era possível fazê-lo como pretendíamos inicialmente, digamos. Penso que foi por isso que também disse que o programa da Vânia e da Beatriz foi perfeito, porque todas as pessoas que foram convidadas e que entraram na roda realmente falaram dessa fragilidade de uma forma muito pessoal e de uma perspectiva histórica que vai muito além da pandemia. Portanto, penso que era exatamente isso que precisávamos colocar.

MLB

E concordo que, assim o espero, haverá mais lutas sobre esse piso. Também recordo desse momento que tive durante a instalação da obra, quando a roda de negociação estava começando a ser reconstruída no pavilhão da Bienal, começando a juntar-se, quase como uma arena, no qual senti, de repente, que a roda era uma estrutura muito mais agressiva, mais violenta. E pensei o quão interessante–arquitetonicamente também–foi essa decisão de posicionar e configurar a roda de negociação de modo mais aberto–partido - e que permitisse uma energia potencialmente diferente para a sua ocupação. Entrava nela uma energia distinta da originária, daquela que sentia com o próprio material. Naquele momento–quando a coisa estava se tornando novamente um octógono completo, aproximando-se da sua formação original–pensei que havia uma energia de combate realmente diferente. Essa energia não parecia ser a correta para aquele momento da Bienal. Mas lembro-me dessa sensação. Talvez seja algo a se explorar no futuro.

DdP

Também concordo. Penso que há essa capacidade da obra, também, numa postura mais autocrítica, que a torna de alguma forma capaz de espelhar certos desejos que lhe são projetados–pela própria instituição, pelos artistas, pelas pessoas envolvidas no programa. Nesse sentido, *deposição* tem o potencial de revelar algumas das incapacidades, ou as impossibilidades, que estes desejos podem ter quando são nomeados. E penso que o trabalho tem essa capacidade, esse nível de crítica institucional que é capaz de apontar para essas impossibilidades. É um aspecto interessante do trabalho, que não pretende necessariamente ter resoluções que são, como as que você já mencionou anteriormente, Jacopo, sem fraturas e sem falhas, ou mesmo capaz de acolher ou falar com tudo o que possa suscitar. Por isso, penso que é interessante para o trabalho descrever o que ele não poderia fazer, tanto quanto o que poderia fazer.

PM

Penso que isso tem a ver não só com o momento, mas também com a escala da Bienal–tanto fisicamente e quanto ao tamanho do público, mas também virtualmente e através de representações midiáticas–porque é um tipo de operação sobre uma escala que tem permitido, historicamente, que as coisas escalem de forma muito abrupta. Este, provavelmente, não será o caso em toda apresentação do trabalho. Podem haver exposições ou instituições que sejam mais de média escala onde, como resultado, esses elementos de conflito e agonismo podem ser decretados ao vivo, e a situação não vai explodir como poderia ter acontecido, e tem acontecido, ao longo dos últimos anos.

E não é que estejamos apenas especulando sobre isso. O que eu sinto é que, através do uso público do trabalho *deposição*, manifestaram-se alguns modos extremos de discurso que a própria exposição da Bienal optou por não se envolver, devido à natureza do espaço, à natureza do programa, e ao fato de que a vida já estava acontecendo dentro e em volta da obra. Independentemente, alguns grupos utilizaram o chão da roda de negociação para vocalizar alguns extremos políticos, empurrando o leque de possibilidades para abordar o debate. Expandiram esse leque de formas que a própria Bienal não antecipou. Por exemplo, numa dessas instâncias extremas, tivemos uma peça teatral que, de forma não programada, se transformou numa demonstração com as bandeiras do MST, e assim por diante. Foi um nível de discurso político direto e um ato de demonstração que muitas das obras da exposição faziam referência, no sentido em que partilhavam uma crítica política semelhante e um certo nível de preocupação à lógica do capital financeiro, à dinâmica da especulação não regulada, ao abuso da Terra, ao abuso da ideia de progresso, à expropriação da Terra e assim por diante. Estas críticas estiveram presentes ao longo da Bienal em muitas obras, mas, o fato destas preocupações serem colocadas diretamente nas bandeiras era algo que não se encontraria em nenhum outro momento na exposição.

Houve também a apresentação musical com Maria Gadú, que é uma cantora pop com um grande público, que tem algumas preocupações estéticas e políticas somadas a uma compreensão da história da música brasileira. Ela ocupa, normalmente, uma arena social e cultural que não se sobrepõe muitas vezes à da Bienal. Assim, a sua atuação é um exemplo de outro tipo de extremo que esteve na plataforma, e que trouxe um público completamente novo - um público diferente - e uma atmosfera diferente, cotidiana, para o coração da exposição.

E depois, não em oposição, mas em qualquer outro extremo de escala, houve alguns momentos muito, muito calmos, em que apenas três ou quatro pessoas falaram sobre a roda de negociação, tendo uma conversa rodeada pela audiência da Bienal. Estas conversas foram quase só para si, quase como mesas redondas privadas num palco público, com a maioria delas compostas por Vânia, Beatriz, Jacopo, duas ou três pessoas convidadas, e talvez outros dois participantes. Estas conversas tiveram lugar e uma escala tão pequena que contrariavam a escala da Bienal - o edifício, a instituição, a exposição.

Assim, *deposição* foi um local para alcançar alguns extremos e, quando se olha para ele como um todo, realmente tornou toda a Bienal mais complicada, com nuances, mesmo que não houvesse tanto conflito nas próprias sessões individuais do programa.

DdP

Penso como última pergunta, a respeito da deterioração deste objeto quase sem vida que foi apropriado–a roda de negociação de milho–e quero perguntar a ambos, Paulo e Jacopo, se sentem que, de alguma forma, a materialidade da roda, o objeto em si, foi de alguma forma transformada através de sua exposição. Pelo menos a título pessoal, em algumas das apresentações musicais e na programação proposta pela Cultura Artística e também pelo festival Novas Frequências–o qual ecoava um grave profundo, reverberando através de todo o objeto–senti por vezes como se a roda estivesse passando por um processo de transformação. Vocês sentem que este objeto mudou, desde o momento de sua chegada até ao momento de sua partida?

JCV

Penso que discutimos isso a dada altura, Daniel, quando estávamos provavelmente no último mês da exposição. Em vez de ser apenas uma ou outra coisa específica–embora algumas das apresentações fossem muito fortes ou muito comoventes–penso que o trabalho *deposição* foi a sedimentação de todas essas camadas e de coisas que aconteceram. Houve algo muito belo que a Vânia e a Beatriz trouxeram: esse ritual de aterrar o público no edifício - em relação ao piso e um ao outro - que aconteceu antes de cada um dos respectivos eventos do programa *Conversações*. Penso que essa ideia de um ritual que acontecia ali, na roda de negociação, no vão, numa frequência regular, se tornou algo muito forte para mim. E foi por isso que eu disse que mais do que qualquer coisa específica, penso que foi a combinação de todas essas coisas que realmente transformou a roda de negociação. Como Marissa disse anteriormente, a roda parecia muito agressiva quando ela a olhou como o octógono temporariamente fechado. Mas eu diria que, para além da mudança da sua configuração, entre como chegou e como partiu, pelo menos para nós, ela se tornou um objeto diferente. É por isso que penso que essa relação com o ritual faz sentido, porque era como se estivéssemos acrescentando outras camadas em cima de algo que antes era negócios e exploração; destruição e capitalismo. Sabe quando se tem de passar de uma parede preta para uma branca, e tem de se colocar camada após camada de tinta, porque levará tempo até mudar realmente de cor? Foi assim, como se estivéssemos colocando camada após camada em cima de algo. Com cada uma dessas apresentações e acontecimentos e discussões, havia outra demão. Se perguntassem para a roda, há 100 anos atrás, o que ela pensava que iria acontecer no seu futuro, nunca se poderia esperar que isso acontecesse, certo? Porque era algo que estava completamente para além da mente da roda, com certeza. Espero realmente que ela viaje para outras instituições culturais e para contextos culturais completamente diferentes, e que esteja exposta a tipos completamente diferentes de discussões, atuações e apresentações. E penso que esse será o ritual: de colocar uma coisa em cima da outra, e de outra, e assim continuar. E isso irá, eventualmente, mudar a estrutura e o material de tal forma que todos irão reparar. E depois, se olharmos para isso—já estou falando metaforicamente—mas se olharmos ainda mais metaforicamente, essa é uma ideia muito bonita de como a cultura e a arte podem, de certa forma, transformar as coisas. Como esse objeto que foi apropriado—esse objeto que resume as ideias do capitalismo—foi transformado numa plataforma para outras coisas, de tal modo que poderia realmente mudar, até certo ponto, a estrutura molecular de seu material. Penso que é muito bonito pensar sobre isso. Sinto e penso que se continuar viajando durante os próximos 10 anos para lugares diferentes, isso será algo que será perceptível. Penso que não é tão complicado pensar que os objetos também têm uma vida. Uma mudança material na estrutura da roda de negociação é provavelmente demasiadamente pequena para ser percebida por alguém ainda, mas, talvez, como eu estava dizendo, se viajar por mais uma década, e essa sedimentação de camadas continuar e continuar, talvez essas mudanças se tornassem mais acessíveis e perceptíveis. Isso seria a coisa mais incrível.

PM

É o nosso trabalho, então, é assegurarmo-nos de que o objeto nunca mais será o mesmo.

1 A equipe curatorial da 34ª Bienal de São Paulo foi composta por Jacopo Crivelli Visconti, Paulo Miyada, Carla Zaccagnini, Francesco Stocchi e Ruth Estévez.

2 A discussão colaborativa dos artistas enquanto desenvolviam o trabalho, *deposição*, fez referência a escritos sobre estética relacional, agonismo, fricção e a delegação de performances, particularmente como teorizado pela historiadora e crítica de arte Claire Bishop em artigos como "Art of the Encounter: Antagonism and Relational Aesthetics" (*Circa* 114, 2005).

3 A obra *deposição* foi instalada no vão, denominação do átrio central do Pavilhão Ciccillo Matarazzo, São Paulo - Brasil. O edifício recebeu o nome do industrial ítalo-brasileiro (1898-1977), e foi projetado por uma equipe liderada pelos arquitetos Oscar Niemeyer e Hélio Uchôa. O átrio é uma vasta abertura na arquitetura do pavilhão, enquadrada por varandas onduladas que convergem numa extremidade do átrio para uma rampa helicoidal icônica, que se eleva ao longo dos três andares do edifício.

4 Obras tais como Lais Myrrha, *Dois pesos, duas medidas [Double Standards]* (2016) durante a 32ª Bienal de São Paulo; a escultura de Choi Jeonghwa *Encore, Encore, Encore* (1997) para a 24ª Bienal de São Paulo; ou a instalação de Tunga *Enquanto Flora a Borda . . .* (1987) no contexto da 19ª Bienal de São Paulo.

5 "Funcionando como o primeiro [desses enunciados curatoriais], mais que como um tema, o título da 34ª Bienal de São Paulo, *Faz escuro mas eu canto*, é um verso do poeta amazonense Thiago de Mello, publicado em 1965. Por meio desse verso, reconhecemos a urgência dos problemas que desafiam a vida no mundo atual, enquanto reivindicamos a necessidade da arte como um campo de resistência, ruptura e transformação." Trecho de uma declaração da equipe curatorial para *Faz escuro mas eu canto*, por Jacopo Crivelli Visconti, Paulo Miyada, Carla Zaccagnini, Francesco Stocchi, e Ruth Estévez, http://34.bienal.org.br/post/7510.

6 "O ponto de partida do projeto curatorial da 34ª Bienal de São Paulo, originalmente planejada para 2020, foi o desejo de ampliar a mostra no tempo e no espaço, estendendo sua duração ao longo de vários meses e expandindo a presença dos artistas participantes por meio de uma inédita parceria com mais de vinte instituições na cidade. A pandemia de Covid-19 trouxe mudanças na coreografia imaginada inicialmente e o adiamento para 2021 da grande exposição coletiva, mas também reforçou a pertinência de uma mostra em constante transformação e afinação, que busca refletir sobre si mesma publicamente, como num grande ensaio aberto. Eventos preliminares, presenciais e virtuais, culminaram na inauguração da exposição *Faz escuro mas eu canto*, em setembro de 2021, concomitante a dezenas de exposições em instituições parceiras na cidade de São Paulo, marcando o momento de maior intensidade desta Bienal." http://34.bienal.org.br/sobrea34.

7 "A maneira como a 34ª Bienal de São Paulo foi concebida ecoa uma premissa análoga: o desejo de apresentar as obras dos artistas, mas também o processo de construção da própria exposição. Por isso o esforço, constante e constantemente reformulado, de pensar e repensar a exposição publicamente, de não deixar de falar do que havíamos planejado, do que seguiu conforme o plano e do que se transformou, do que se *tornou* outra coisa. Para que possa ficar ainda mais claro que ela não é separada do mundo, mas é parte dele." Jacopo Crivelli Visconti, "Correspondência #21," 9 de Setembro de 2021, http://www.bienal.org.br/post/9133.

8 Isto pode ter sido em referência a uma crítica sobre a 34ª Bienal de São Paulo escrita por Ela Bittencourt e publicada no dia 18 de Outubro de 2021, no veículo de imprensa *Hyperallergic,* intitulada "The São Paulo Biennial Captures a Perpetually Discontinuous World", https://hyperallergic.com/683942/the-sao-paulo-biennial-captures-a-perpetually-discontinuous-world. O artigo se apresenta com uma foto contendo o trabalho *deposição,* mas não menciona a obra ou os artistas envolvidos, trazendo apenas a legenda "Vista da 34ª Bienal de São Paulo (© Levi Fanan/Fundação Bienal de São Paulo)".

9 "Na busca por uma linguagem para delinear os campos de força criados pelo encontro de obras produzidas em lugares e momentos distintos, propusemos alguns objetos e suas histórias, como *enunciados*: um sino que soou em momentos diversos de uma história que se repete; as imagens do homem mais retratado num tempo em que quase não havia retratos; os bordados que outro homem não teria feito se não fosse às escondidas; cartas que, para chegar a uma criança, tiveram que atravessar as grades da cadeia e os olhos da censura; um conjunto de objetos que sobreviveram de maneiras diferentes ao mesmo incêndio... Esses enunciados pontuam a exposição, sugerem o tom no qual podem vibrar as obras ao seu redor, aglutinando e tornando tangíveis as preocupações e as reflexões da curadoria. Funcionam, nesse sentido, como o diapasão que ajuda a afinar um instrumento musical ou a começar um canto. Na curadoria de uma exposição também é almejado algo parecido com uma afinação, um ajuste não isento de erros, acidentes e desvios, que o tempo expandido da 34ª Bienal nos permitiu." Trecho de uma declaração da equipe curatorial para *Faz escuro mas eu canto*, por Jacopo Crivelli Visconti, Paulo Miyada, Carla Zaccagnini, Francesco Stocchi, e Ruth Estévez, http://34.bienal.org.br/post/7510.

10 A equipe curatorial da 34ª Bienal de São Paulo aborda e amplia estas questões através do pensamento sobre as relações complexas entre condições históricas, presentes e futuras, em cartas abertas ao público, partilhadas sob o título "Correspondência" e publicadas no site oficial da Bienal de São Paulo. Em particular, "Correspondência #1" (Carla Zaccagnini), "Correspondência #6" (Paulo Miyada), "Correspondência #10" (Carla Zaccagnini), e "Correspondência #16" (Francesco Stocchi).

11 "A primeira Bienal Internacional de São Paulo teve lugar em 1951... Não é apenas a primeira bienal internacional a suceder ao arquétipo de Veneza, mas é também a primeira bienal moderna (e modernista) e a primeira a ser realizada em uma localização geopolítica fora do hemisfério Norte e do eixo canônico Estados Unidos-Europa Ocidental. A inauguração da Bienal Internacional de São Paulo foi motivada pela combinação de forças culturais, econômicas e políticas que moldaram o período pós-guerra no Brasil e a nível internacional. Foi fundada por Francisco "Ciccillo" Matarazzo Sobrinho, um industrial ítalo-brasileiro... Seu objetivo era criar "um festival no molde de Veneza", e as aspirações gêmeas da Bienal Internacional eram, nas palavras do seu primeiro diretor artístico, Lourival Gomes Machado, 'colocar a arte moderna do Brasil não simplesmente em proximidade, mas em contato vivo com a arte do resto do mundo,' e 'para que São Paulo conquistasse a posição de centro artístico internacional'... A Bienal Internacional de São Paulo mudou-se para a sua atual casa permanente, o pavilhão Ciccillo Matarazzo, concebido por Oscar Niemeyer (originalmente designado Palácio das Indústrias [e concebido para acolher feiras mundiais agro-industriais]), em 1957." Isobel Whitelegg, "The Bienal Internacional de São Paulo: a concise history, 1951–2014," Perspective 2 (2013), pp. 380–386.

12 Le Corbusier publicou *Le Modulor*, em 1948, seguido de *Modulor 2*, em 1955; ambos os livros detalham uma série de sistemas antropométricos e universais de escalas e proporções desenvolvidos pelo autor.

13 "As mudanças nos mercados de Chicago tornaram subitamente possível às pessoas comprar e vender cereais, não como produto físico do trabalho humano numa determinada área de terra de pradaria, mas como uma reivindicação abstrata sobre a corrente dourada que flui através dos elevadores

da cidade... Toda a transação poderia ser concluída — e repetida dezenas de vezes — sem que um único grão de trigo ou milho se movesse um centímetro sequer . . . As receitas dos elevadores, tal como negociadas no piso do pregão, conseguiram a transmutação de um dos alimentos mais antigos da humanidade, obscurecendo a sua identidade física e deslocando-a para o mundo simbólico do capital. O elevador ajudou a transformar cereais em capital, obscurecendo e distanciando a sua ligação com a natureza física, enquanto outra nova tecnologia ampliou esse processo, enfraquecendo a sua ligação com a geografia. Em 1848, no mesmo ano em que os comerciantes de Chicago fundaram o Registro do Comércio, as primeiras linhas telegráficas chegaram à cidade ... O resultado foi uma nova geografia de mercado que tinha menos a ver com os solos ou clima de uma determinada localidade do que com os preços e fluxos de informação da economia como um todo . . . Quando o Registro do Comércio de Chicago adotou um sistema de classificação padrão, tornou os cereais intercambiáveis não só entre caixas de elevadores, mas também entre cidades e continentes ... Os pedidos telegráficos deste tipo encorajaram um forte aumento daquilo que os comerciantes chamavam contratos "a chegar" para os cereais. Por meio destes contratos, um vendedor prometia entregar os cereais ao seu comprador até uma data específica no futuro. . . Contratos "a chegar", em combinação com recibos de elevadores padronizados, tornaram possível a maior inovação de Chicago no comércio de cereais: o mercado de futuros... Elevadores de grãos e sistemas de classificação tinham ajudado a transmutar o trigo e milho em abstrações monetárias, mas o contrato de futuros estendeu a abstração, libertando o próprio comércio de cereais do processo que outrora o tinha definido: a troca de cereais físicos". William Cronon, Nature's Metropolis: Chicago and the Great West (Nova Iorque: W.W. Norton & Company, 1991), pp. 120-126.

14 Referente ao contexto da pandemia de COVID-19, anunciada pela Organização Mundial de Saúde no dia 11 de março de 2020.

15 "CLÁUSULA 5. DIREITOS E OBRIGAÇÕES DA LOCATÁRIA, Cláusula 5.1 (j)". Veja páginas 180–183.

16 Vânia Medeiros e Beatriz Cruz foram comissionadas pela equipe curatorial da 34ª Bienal de São Paulo para propor uma série de programas a serem convocados e realizados sobre a obra deposição. Medeiros e Cruz intitularam a sua série de programas como *Conversações*. Uma entrevista com elas, conduzida por Daniel de Paula, pode ser encontrada nas páginas 256–267 (inglês) e 332–337 (português)..

17 Artigos internacionais em língua inglesa, como o de Ariel Goldstein "Brazil leads the third wave of the Latin American far right," publicado em 1º de Março de 2021 para o Centro de Pesquisa sobre Extremismo da Universidade de Oslo, esboçam a ascensão do presidente brasileiro Jair Bolsonaro como parte de uma "terceira onda" da política da extrema-direita latino-americana que capitalizou numa crise interligada no Brasil, e é construída sobre uma coligação de pastores evangélicos, militares, o mercado financeiro, e o setor do agronegócio. Esta é uma de muitas descrições da presidência de Bolsonaro, que teve início no dia 1º de Janeiro de 2019, e das condições históricas relacionadas dentro da política sul-americana e latino-americana que abordam o panorama sociopolítico em que ocorreu a 34ª Bienal de São Paulo. Outros escritos sobre o tema incluem artigos de colunistas do New York Times como Gaspard Estrada ("Brasil y el autoritarismo de Bolsonaro," 7 de Abril de 2021) e Vanessa Barbara ("Bolsonaro Said His 'Specialty Is Killing.' He's Been True to His Word," 31 de Março de 2022); artigos como o de Oliver Stunekel "Brazil's Polarization and Democratic Risks," publicado para o Carnegie Endowment for International Peace (17 de Fevereiro de 2021); a reportagem de Simone Preissler Iglesias e Andrew Rosati para a Bloomberg, "Bolsonaro Wages Trumpian Campaign to Sow Doubts About Voting" (12 de Julho de 2021); e para a Reuters "Human Rights Watch says Bolsonaro a threat to democracy in Brazil" (13 de Janeiro de 2022).

18 Este modo de tensionar, mencionado por Visconti, pode ser tanto em referência aos aspectos sociais e linguísticos, como também aos elementos físicos do trabalho. O uso permitido da roda de negociação é determinado pelo contrato produzido pelos artistas e realizado através de um processo de negociação contextual, conduzido pela equipe curatorial e quaisquer outros representantes institucionais necessários.

19 A exposição coletiva da 34ª Bienal de São Paulo foi encerrada no dia 5 de dezembro de 2021, com uma performance coletiva de Neo Muyanga, intitulada *A Grace Note* (2021), parte do projeto *A Maze in Grace* (2020), junto ao Coletivo Legítima Defesa e a artista Bianca Turner. Imagens documentando a performance podem ser encontradas nas seguintes páginas 310–315.

20 Jaider Esbell (1979-2021) foi artista, organizador, educador e curador de origem Macuxi e cuja significativa obra fez parte da 34ª Bienal de São Paulo.

21 Como estipulado no contrato proposto pelos artistas como parte da obra deposição, um enunciado escrito e presente no contrato é obrigatoriamente lido por um representante voluntário da instituição, no início de cada evento da programação oficial da exposição que acontece sobre a roda de negociação, tal como detalhado na "CLÁUSULA 5. DIREITOS E OBRIGAÇÕES DA LOCATÁRIA (Seção 5.1 (b) e (c) i-vi)," ver páginas 178–181.

SOBRE RODAS, MOENDAS, ENGRENAGENS E MANDALAS

Yamila Goldfarb

"...A gente vai contra a corrente
Até não poder resistir
Na volta do barco é que sente
O quanto deixou de cumprir
Faz tempo que a gente cultiva
A mais linda roseira que há
Mas eis que chega a roda-viva
E carrega a roseira pra lá..."

Chico Buarque, "Roda Viva" (1967)

A RODA gira, gira, gira e nada parece sair do lugar As negociações em torno dos frutos da agricultura e da pecuária tomam novas dimensões, novas escalas, se utilizam de novas tecnologias e instrumentos da necropolítica, e o que se nota é a perpetuação ou a reedição de um projeto colonial no qual se vende barato e se compra caro às custas da vida, especialmente da vida das pessoas, do meio ambiente, dos nossos recursos naturais, dos territórios, do planeta.

Observando como a RODA DE NEGOCIAÇÃO funcionava fisicamente, em um semicírculo, e os dias atuais, veremos que muita coisa mudou. A velha Bancada Ruralista, travestida de Frente Parlamentar da Agropecuária (FPA), constitui-se como a mais duradoura e efetiva força política no parlamento. O latifúndio, assim denominado até a década de 1970, passou a ser chamado de *agrobusiness* na década de 1980, ganhando um caráter moderno. Mais tarde, entre as décadas de 1990 e 2016, ganhou novas roupagens e passou a ser chamado de agronegócio. Agora, transmuta-se em "Agro" e se reproduz atrelado a uma imensa estratégia cultural que tenta convencer a todos, ou quase todos, de que o AGRO é o que precisamos para sermos a grande Nação capaz de alimentar o mundo, ainda que uma parcela considerável da população morra diariamente de fome.[1]

As RODAS DE NEGOCIAÇÃO de hoje não são mais redondas, não são de madeira, não colocam as pessoas frente a frente. São digitais e conectam produtores, comerciantes (os chamados *traders*) e investidores do mundo todo.

Essas RODAS DE NEGOCIAÇÃO digitalizadas e mundializadas determinam como vamos nos inserir nas cadeias globais de valor. E essa forma continua sendo subordinada. Continua sendo espoliativa. Continua exaurindo nossos territórios e povos. No Sul Global, a lógica maldita que se impõe determina que devemos vender barato e comprar caro. No Norte global a RODA gira ao contrário, como sempre foi: compram barato e nos vendem caro. É a reedição do projeto de subordinação colonial no qual a fome é mais um elemento estruturante. Num país onde, por décadas, se naturalizou a fome, é preciso entender que ela é um projeto político.

"... A raiva dá pra parar, pra interromper
A fome não dá pra interromper
A raiva e a fome é coisas dos home
A fome tem que ter raiva pra interromper
A raiva é a fome de interromper
A fome e a raiva é coisas dos home..."

Aldir Blanc e João Bosco, "O ronco da cuíca" (1976)

Mas o Brasil não alimenta o mundo com seu agro pop e *tech*? Não é a fazenda do mundo? Não exporta toneladas de grãos? Alimentamos o mundo, mas não a nossa população? Hoje, 58,7% dos brasileiros se encontram em Situação de Insegurança Alimentar, isto é, não sabem se comerão as três refeições do dia, ou do dia seguinte. São 125,2 milhões de pessoas sendo que, destas, 33 milhões já passam fome.

Como a RODA girou até chegar neste ponto? Ela girou levando as negociações em torno da compra e venda de grãos até o patamar da compra e venda dos recursos naturais, dos territórios e da própria vida. Façamos uma breve retomada histórica para compreender esse longo processo.

Após a Segunda Grande Guerra, o mundo entrou num período de regulação dos fluxos de capitais e de forte presença do Estado nas economias. Foi o período em que predominaram as políticas keynesianas e as chamadas instituições de Bretton Woods (Banco Mundial, Fundo Monetário Internacional e Organização Mundial do Comércio). O mundo, particularmente o chamado mundo ocidental europeu, viveu então seus trinta anos de ouro do capitalismo, que foram acompanhados de distribuição de riquezas e da construção do estado de bem estar social nas economias centrais. Foi um período marcado pela forte regulação dos Estados nas economias. A Roda de Negociação da *Chicago Board of Trade* já se fazia presente, desde o século anterior, tendo importante papel na determinação do preço dos grãos, e essa roda também entraria no novo ciclo de acumulação do capital que estava por vir.

Por volta dos anos 1970, o mundo mergulhou em uma profunda recessão. Com a crise do sistema de Bretton Woods, grandes massas de capitais que não podiam obter rentabilidade, dada a sua sobreacumulação, foram destinadas ao setor financeiro em busca de melhores rendimentos. A disponibilidade de capitais do centro do capitalismo, particularmente dos Estados Unidos e da Europa, financiaram, por meio do endividamento, a industrialização da agricultura no Brasil, assim como em outros países do Sul Global. É correto afirmar que a sobreacumulação de capital, no centro do capitalismo daquele momento, contribuiu para a formação dos Complexos Agroindustriais, cadeias que conectavam indústrias de insumos e maquinários com a agricultura. Como bem se sabe, essa modernização conservadora, cunhada de "Revolução Verde", resultou na redução da mão-de-obra empregada na agricultura e provocou uma grande onda migratória para os grandes centros urbanos.

Assim, a financeirização e o endividamento dos países periféricos foram os mecanismos que impulsionaram o novo ciclo econômico. Ou seja, o dinheiro que sobrava e, portanto, se desvalorizava nos países centrais, era enviado como empréstimo para os países periféricos que, por sua vez, se endividaram - não sem antes realizar as reformas do ajuste estrutural que lhes era exigido. Esse processo de recuperação das margens de ganho foi sustentado ideologicamente, politicamente e economicamente pelo neoliberalismo, que possibilitou justamente a desregulação do capital. Isso significa que este foi soltando suas amarras (sua regulação e controle estatal) e ampliando enormemente as possibilidades de valorização a partir do momento em que foi se criando todo um aparato normativo e legal para tal, sendo esse processo particularmente visível no campo da agricultura. Se antes, por exemplo, em bolsas de mercadorias e futuros, ou mercadorias e opções, como a *Chicago Board of Trade*, se negociavam os preços dos grãos, elas agora passaram a negociar os valores futuros de uma variedade enorme de outros produtos, girando a RODA de forma ainda mais sem controle ao som dos interesses capitalistas dos países centrais, e não do interesse da população.

Essa desregulamentação foi permitindo que, ao final dos anos 1980 e início dos anos de 1990, o sistema financeiro internacional passasse por profundas mudanças que gerariam uma maior capacidade de criação e valorização do dinheiro. Diversos mecanismos foram criados como forma de fazer o dinheiro investido se valorizar. Surgiram uma infinidade de títulos, papéis negociáveis nas bolsas de valores e de mercadorias e futuro. Os investimentos foram se tornando, cada vez mais, um grande jogo de apostas especulativas.

A partir da década de 1990, esses ativos financeiros tiveram grande valorização. A inflação das ações de empresas de tecnologia na bolsa de NASDAQ foi um dos casos mais emblemáticos e fomentou a acumulação capitalista dos EUA na década de 1990.[2] A partir de 2001, os preços das ações dessas empresas despencaram e capitais financeiros, agora ociosos, precisaram se valorizar em novos mercados que pudessem, rapidamente, inflacionar seus ativos. Esse capital foi então direcionado para o mercado imobiliário dos EUA e da Europa, bem como para o mercado de commodities.[3] Mas em 2007/2008, o estouro da bolha do mercado imobiliário estadunidense fez com que houvesse uma nova onda de busca por investimentos em commodities e terras agrícolas.

Fundos de pensão, fundos mútuos e os chamados *hedge funds* eram como enormes poupanças que precisavam valorizar o dinheiro ali depositado.[4] Uma alternativa foi financiar a produção agrícola, já que os Estados do chamado terceiro mundo haviam sido impelidos a se retirarem do papel regulador e financiador para poder acessar os empréstimos do FMI. Grandes empresas fornecedoras de insumos, processadoras, *trades* (grandes comercializadoras) fizeram o mesmo. Esses foram os novos atores que passaram a comandar a RODA DE NEGOCIAÇÃO da agricultura mundial. O que o mundo viu ocorrer foi a evolução de um mercado de financiamento de produção para um mercado de especulação e a transformação do alimento em commoditiy.

Nos anos 2000, com a criação de mecanismos financeiros cada vez mais complexos, mediados pela bolsa de Mercadorias e Futuro, esse processo se intensifica. O aumento dos preços das commodities e, principalmente, o aumento do petróleo a partir de 2004, fez o mundo entrar num processo de queda das taxas de lucro. O aumento dos valores das matérias primas e dos grãos aumentou o valor dos alimentos pressionando para cima os salários. Qual foi a saída para aqueles senhores da RODA DE NEGOCIAÇÃO? Continuar atrofiando a esfera produtiva para aumentar seus rendimentos. O capital financeiro impôs ao mundo a contração da produção e a deflação por meio de políticas de austeridade fiscal, como vimos ocorrer em Portugal, Grécia, Espanha e Irlanda.

Em suma, o ocorrido foi que essa nova crise de acumulação financeira dos anos 2000 fez ampliar a demanda por insumos ambientais, matérias-primas e alimentos, aumentando a escala de busca por terras por parte de investidores privados, fundos especulativos e governos de outros países num processo que tem sido chamado de *land grabbing*, *acaparamiento de tierras* ou estrangeirização de terras. Tais investimentos são uma forma de se antecipar às crises (como a de 2008), transformando esse capital fictício (títulos, papéis, ações) em riqueza real (fazendas, soja, eucalipto, óleo de palma, etc.). Esse processo aqueceu o mercado de terras no Brasil e, a busca por novas fazendas, levou a um verdadeiro processo de expropriação de territórios tradicionais, expulsão de comunidades, devastação ambiental e ameaças à soberania alimentar.

Não por acaso, diversas transnacionais produtoras de commodities, como a Cosan S/A, a SLC Agrícola S/A, passaram, a partir de meados de 2008/2009, a investir na terra como principal ativo financeiro de seus negócios. Em alguns casos, como as duas citadas acima, as empresas criaram ou se uniram às imobiliárias agrícolas, verdadeiros "braços" transnacionais, a fim de negociarem a terra como negócio. Exemplos dessas imobiliárias são a Radar Propriedades Agrícolas S/A e a SLC LandCo., de propriedade, respectivamente, da Cosan e da Cargill, que se uniram em sociedade aos fundos de pensão e de investimentos internacionais.[5]

Outros exemplos de empresas que se associaram aos fundos de pensão para investirem em terras são: BrasilAgro; a TibaAgro (por meio do Fundo VisionBrazil Gestão de Investimentos e Participações Ltda); a Sollus Capital, relacionada com a Ceagro (com capital da Mitsubishi-Japão e do Grupo Los Grobo-Argentina); a XingúAgri (com negócios com a Multigrain-EUA/Mitsui-Japão e com a SLC Agrícola-Brasil); Adecoagro (com capital do megainvestidor financeiro George Soros); a Agrinvest (com capital dos fundos Ridgefield-EUA e Touradji-Brasil); a CalyxAgro (vinculada ao Grupo Louis Dreyfus Commodities-Holanda e ao fundo PineBridge Investment); o Grupo Colorado (com capital dos fundos Global Oportunity e Black Rock); a Insolo AgroIndustrial (com capital da Universidade de Harvard), ainda sem mencionar com maior profundidade as *tradings* como a Bunge e a Cargill.[6]

Nesse contexto, o capital financeiro vai também se espraiando para outros setores conexos à agricultura, como a mineração, os recursos hídricos, além do próprio mercado de terras, como já dissemos. Isso se reflete na mercantilização de bens da natureza e na internacionalização destes bens. Isso aumentou a superexploração da terra, do solo e das águas. As evidências de que há uma superexploração são dramáticas: rompimento de barragens; crises de abastecimento de água; piora nas taxas de emissão de gases do efeito estufa; aumento da contaminação por agrotóxico; degradação do solo; queimadas e devastação de biomas, poluição dos oceanos. A geração de riquezas por meio desses segmentos é altamente concentrada e internacionalizada, o que se reflete no empobrecimento da população, aumento de doenças transmissíveis e não transmissíveis e a fome. Em resumo, é um pacto com a morte.

Mas veja, os senhores da RODA DE NEGOCIAÇÃO não parecem preocupados com isso. Porque os números ali negociados escondem os impactos nos territórios. Importa produzir o que é mais interessante ao capital, o que faz essa RODA girar. Esse capital fictício, especulativo, não tem compromisso com o desenvolvimento dos países. Hoje estão aqui, amanhã estão em outro lugar. Eles vêm acompanhados de isenções fiscais e desonerações que funcionam como uma verdadeira pilhagem de recursos, tanto monetários como naturais.

Soma-se a isso o abandono das políticas de subsídio aos pequenos e médios produtores, a chamada agricultura familiar ou camponesa. Deixa-se de produzir alimentos, a comida propriamente dita, aquela que vai para a mesa dos trabalhadores e trabalhadoras, tendo como apoio o discurso da liberdade de mercado, da não interferência do Estado. Sem subsídio a produção de alimentos cai, os preços sobem e o Estado não tem mais instrumentos de controle dos preços. Quem paga o preço é a população, com a fome.

Para sair dessa RODA fatal é preciso impor limites ao capital financeiro. É preciso fortalecer o papel do Estado no controle de estoques reguladores, no planejamento e financiamento da produção de alimentos e no controle sobre o mercado de terras. É preciso proteger os sistemas produtivos nacionais e a nossa agrobiodiversidade. Fortalecer a agricultura familiar e dos povos e comunidades tradicionais, garantindo o direito sobre os territórios por parte dessas populações. Implementar o princípio de soberania alimentar para que, aquilo que se produz, a forma como se produz, e como é comercializado e consumido, respeite os interesses da população brasileira, e não o do Capital. A lógica da ação estatal deve ser a de soberania e segurança alimentar, ambiental, energética e territorial. Os espaços de participação da sociedade, tais como o Conselho Nacional de Segurança Alimentar e Nutricional, devem ser retomados e fortalecidos. Essa GRANDE RODA DE NEGOCIAÇÃO global tem que ser substituída por pequenas rodas participativas, que criem e fortaleçam circuitos curtos de comercialização, espaços de abastecimento popular de trocas e de tecnologias sociais. É preciso urgentemente voltar a se falar na democratização do acesso à terra pois, uma estrutura fundiária concentrada, como a brasileira, só gera desigualdade, pobreza, devastação ambiental e fome. A GRANDE RODA DE NEGOCIAÇÃO global gira no sentido da concentração de riquezas. Precisamos fazê-la girar ao contrário urgentemente, ou passará por cima de tudo e de todos. Precisamos sair da Roda do pacto com a morte, para a mandala do pacto com a vida.

1 Yamila Goldfarb e Marco Antonio Mitidiero Jr., "O Agro Não É Tech, O Agro Não É Pop E Muito Menos Tudo" (São Paulo: Abra and Friederich Ebert Stftung, 2021). Veja: https://library.fes.de/pdf-files/bueros/brasilien/18319-20211027.pdf.

2 Cássio Arruda Boechat, Maria Luisa Mendonça, e Fábio Teixeira Pitta, "A produção do espaço na região do MATOPIBA: violência, transnacionais imobiliárias agrícolas e capital fictício," *Estudos Internacionais: Revista de Relações Internacionais Da PUC Minas,* v. 5, no. 2 (2017), pp .155–179.

3 Boechat, Mendonça, Pitta, "A produção do espaço na região do MATOPIBA."

4 Boechat, Mendonça, Pitta, "A produção do espaço na região do MATOPIBA."

5 Boechat, Mendonça, Pitta, "A produção do espaço na região do MATOPIBA."

6 Boechat, Mendonça, Pitta, "A produção do espaço na região do MATOPIBA."

DIMENSÃO DA ARTE, DIMENSÃO DA VIDA

Beatriz Cruz e Vânia Medeiros
com Daniel de Paula

Daniel de Paula A título de introdução, talvez fosse interessante perguntar como vocês compreendem suas respectivas práticas artísticas e, se possível, vocês poderiam destacar alguns processos e procedimentos investigativos que são caros a vocês?

Beatriz Cruz Eu venho das artes cênicas e, com o passar dos anos, principalmente por meio do encontro com a rua e do trabalho na cidade, venho criando diálogos com o campo das artes visuais. A rua sempre foi o motor da minha criação e, quando eu falo rua, falo da cidade e do ambiente urbano como espaço potencial de encontro. Isso permeia muito do meu trabalho, o encontro sensorial do corpo com a cidade e o encontro que propõe interações com alteridades. Isso sempre está nos trabalhos que faço. É físico e prático. É, ao mesmo tempo, um emaranhado do meu corpo com o chão da cidade, com a arquitetura, mas também com uma aposta na criação de espaços de experiência partilhada—de troca de olhares, troca de roupas, troca de histórias—na busca de se deixar ser contaminada por outras subjetividades.

Desde 2009, tenho um trabalho junto com o Coletivo Teatro Dodecafônico[1] que é, enfim, onde meu encontro com a Vânia se deu, num primeiro momento. O coletivo trabalha com teatro performativo, intervenção urbana e com o caminhar como prática estética e política. Mais recentemente, Vânia e eu temos desenvolvido um outro trabalho juntas de pesquisa artística, a partir do universo onírico. Tem sido algo muito inspirador e que, espero, tenha vida longa.

Vânia Medeiros Poxa. Sou sua fã, Beatriz Cruz.

DdP Obrigado, Beatriz. Acho que essa resposta informa algumas das outras perguntas que virão mais adiante.

VM Eu sou artista visual, mas a minha formação é em comunicação, então, meu percurso nas artes parte de uma história que começa com o interesse editorial, em publicações e na visualidade gráfica da apresentação das coisas. A ilustração também já passou pela minha trajetória como um lugar de pesquisa e o texto sempre esteve muito presente. A ideia de publicar livros e fanzines a partir da proposição de situações diversas de coletividade, ou seja, espaços compartilhados nos quais se formam grupos, sempre acompanhou meus processos criativos. Alguns dos encontros desse percurso me trouxeram aprendizados que hoje orientam minhas práticas. O encontro com o *Coletivo Teatro Dodecafônico* é um deles, como a Beatriz falou. Foi no contexto do trabalho coletivo no espaço urbano que surgiu um interesse muito particular meu nas maneiras de registrar a experiência. Como é que situações que são efêmeras, vivenciais, corporais, podem ganhar um formato que as faz sobreviver? Me interessa muito pesquisar modos de fazer encontros efêmeros sobreviverem no tempo.

Minha pesquisa artística vai muito nesse sentido. Existe uma ponte com o design gráfico e com o design participativo muito forte. O desenho se manifesta como um elemento importante, tanto como expressão pessoal quanto como dispositivo de criação de grupos e de registro de situações. Sou muito interessada no desenho que não é virtuoso, que é não especialista, o desenho que é rastro, que é incidental nos processos.

Nós duas, Beatriz e eu, temos um projeto chamado *Mulheres Possíveis*,[2] que é um espaço de aprendizado muito grande pra nós em relação a todas essas questões. Ele é desenvolvido com outras duas artistas, Sandra Ximenez e Letícia Olivares, na Penitenciária Feminina da Capital, em São Paulo. Esse trabalho junta muito das nossas pesquisas pessoais, a da Beatriz com o corpo, a minha com o desenho, e as das nossas parceiras com suas práticas performativas de maneira geral. Entra tudo muito junto nesse trabalho com mulheres encarceradas.

Então, resumindo, existe um interesse na situação de processos de produção de grupos. E, no processo criativo, a gente realmente é muito tomado pela obra, né? O projeto inicial vira outra coisa, vira obra-experiência, obra-contaminação, e aí acho que isso tem muito a ver com o trabalho *deposição,* também. Acredito que ele se relaciona muito com nossas práticas de maneira geral, na medida em que a gente está sempre interessada em espaços nos quais a coletividade se faça possível, seja ela na rua, seja ela em âmbitos institucionais. Estamos sempre buscando lugares onde o processo coletivo de produção possa se dar.

DdP Muito bom ouvir vocês. Agora, num gesto de generosidade com um público leitor, vocês poderiam narrar, minimamente, como se deu o convite por parte da curadoria da Bienal de São Paulo para a participação de vocês na obra *deposição*? Especular o porquê vocês foram escolhidas como interlocutoras naquela instância, encarregadas da função de produzir um dos eixos principais da programação pública da 34ª Bienal de São Paulo?

VM Acho que posso começar, já que fui a primeira pessoa contactada. Paulo Miyada entrou em contato comigo, de maneira bastante informal, contando um pouquinho da proposta da obra *deposição* e um pouco da trajetória de vocês. Ele deixou completamente em aberto, ou seja, a gente poderia propor o que desejássemos dentro daquilo. Os curadores tinham algumas indicações de pessoas que gostariam que estivessem presentes, especialmente alguns artistas participantes da Bienal, de maneira que a roda de negociação fosse uma plataforma onde os artistas pudessem conversar com o público. Mas, de maneira geral, não tinha um recorte temático.

Foi a partir do texto de vocês, daquele "manifesto" ou *statement* que vocês trouxeram,[3] que o desenho de um quadro mais político se mostrou fundamental. Para mim, ficou muito claro, então, que era um trabalho que não cabia fazer sozinha. E acho que ter chamado a Beatriz para a gente fazer isso junto foi muito automático, já que temos uma troca de muito tempo e de muita confiança. Então, eu achei que poderia ser um processo que a gente ia dividir de forma muito fluida e muito potente.

A partir do momento em que vocês propõem que a roda articule as questões de terra, trabalho e... Qual era o terceiro eixo?

DdP Capital.

VM Isso, capital. Terra, trabalho e capital. Veio muito para a gente a necessidade de amarrar essa programação em torno de pautas muito urgentes no Brasil e, ao mesmo tempo, trazer uma dimensão poética que, para a gente, é muito política também. E, bom... contribui aí, Beatriz.

BC A dimensão do trabalho que iríamos realizar ali foi, para mim, se ampliando aos poucos. Sabe quando você joga uma pedra na água e ela cria uma série de círculos? Aos poucos, dava pra ver a potência dos encontros que poderiam ser gerados naquele espaço. O dia em que eu fui lá e vi a obra pela primeira vez, instalada no meio do pavilhão da Bienal, foi bem marcante. Você está naquele lugar, naquele espaço que tem um significado, no vão da Bienal, e você está, ao mesmo tempo, saindo, saindo de um processo de volta de uma pandemia em que as pessoas estavam totalmente nas suas esferas particulares, a gente só se vendo por quadradinhos nas telas. Então você volta para esse lugar.

DdP Eu acho um tanto revelador, Vânia, você ter esse impulso de, imediatamente, responder ao convite com uma proposta colaborativa, e não colaborativa no sentido de simplesmente convidar pessoas para ocuparem aquele espaço dentro da programação, mas sim, de convidar alguém para pensar contigo essa própria programação. É notável que, em todas as instâncias desse trabalho, a colaboração tem sido um cerne, seja entre nós, os artistas propositores—Marissa, David e eu—ou em nossas trocas com os curadores, ou com vocês e outros agentes.

Mas agora, talvez uma questão de ordem mais sensível. Queria que, se possível, vocês tentassem recordar as primeiras reações que vocês tiveram ao encontrar o objeto naquele espaço, encontrar a roda de negociação. A Beatriz acabou de mencionar um pouco sobre essa magnitude do espaço, sobre a localização, mas, talvez, fosse interessante saber mais das reações iniciais de vocês e como elas informaram as estratégias que vocês elaboraram para emoldurar a programação, denominada por vocês de *Conversações*.[4] Então é isso: vocês poderiam falar do primeiro encontro com o objeto e como isso informou o trabalho de vocês?

VM É, eu acho que é engraçado porque, o objeto tem uma história de violência e é um grande pilar de um processo de expropriação, o que fica evidente com a investigação de vocês. Mas, na medida em que a roda de negociação foi deslocada de seu contexto original, ela se apresentou como uma estrutura circular, muito propícia para interações que não são hierarquizadas, permitindo relações menos assimétricas. Dentro da estrutura, era muito natural uma mistura entre público, convidados e artistas, ficava tudo muito diluído ali dentro. Essa é uma qualidade do objeto que chamou atenção logo de cara. Claro, poderíamos ter feito ele virar rapidamente um espaço de palestra, promover separações hierárquicas, mas isso não aconteceu.

Como documentação, registro das rodas, a gente escolheu não tirar fotos dos encontros.[5] Mas, talvez, se fossem tiradas por nós, acredito que não ia dar nem para perceber muito bem quem seria o suposto agente principal ali, naqueles encontros, né? Assim, ter um objeto dessa natureza para realizar *Conversações* é muito, muito interessante.

BC Para mim, o primeiro impulso que tive foi o de querer andar por ali, subir e descer. Mas eu lembro que a gente chegou e alguém já estava ali sentadinho, e a gente sentou também. Mas depois, eu fui outro dia para a Bienal, aí eu fiquei andando ali, me posicionando em diferentes locais da roda, nada além disso. E eu falei, a gente tem que fazer alguma coisa física com os corpos caminhando nesse espaço, vivenciar o objeto, aprender de uma outra forma com ele. A roda de negociação também permitia que se visse o espaço expositivo da Bienal de diferentes perspectivas. Então, eu também achava que a gente deveria se aproveitar desse objeto colocando nosso corpo ali e convidando quem participasse das *Conversações* para andar na obra. Circular, subir e descer, escolher diferentes perspectivas para ver o espaço e para ver uns aos outros. Acho que a leitura de que isso parece um teatro de arena é imediata. Um lugar circular que remete à roda, que remete a um espaço sem hierarquia. E aí é muito louco pensar, é muito terrível, na verdade, pensar que o capital se apropria disso para facilitar a visualidade, para gerar um processo especulativo em cima. Mas, enfim, é uma relação arquitetônica que funciona para você ter uma visão geral de um espaço e das pessoas que estão nele. E então assim funciona. E o que funciona será apropriado.

VM Acho também que essa dinâmica de corpo, que a Beatriz mencionou agora, foi super importante em cada conversação. A gente não chegou e simplesmente começou uma conversa do nada. Acho que esse momento inicial que propusemos para o público, de circular pela roda de negociação e ter diferentes perspectivas do espaço, gerou uma pequena comunhão entre quem estava ali. As pessoas se viram de corpo inteiro, todo mundo se viu, né? A gente não sentou cada um no seu cantinho. Isso foi algo que trouxe um pertencimento ao momento da conversa. Outro ponto importante foi o fato da roda de negociação estar aberta, por uma decisão de vocês de posicioná-la dessa forma. Acredito que isso também diluiu o lugar que hierarquicamente seria o centro do seu poder. Ali, talvez, e com essa abertura da estrutura, esse meio se quebrou e promoveu essa fragmentação, também. O Centro perdeu força.

DdP É bonito você falar isso porque, no contrato, que de alguma forma media o trabalho com a instituição, existem apenas duas cláusulas que lidam com a configuração da roda de negociação no espaço expositivo. Uma delas estipula que o objeto nunca mais poderá ser o que era antes. Então, em termos formais, de configuração, isso significa que não pode mais ser um octógono fechado, tal como era no contexto do pregão, no contexto do mercado financeiro. Agora é outra coisa. Assim sendo, a decisão daquela configuração específica, aberta, tal qual você disse, foi dos curadores que poderiam ter optado, ainda, por uma outra configuração. Poderia estar tudo empilhado, espalhado, disperso no espaço. Mas eles optaram por aquele semicírculo, digamos, aquela roda aberta. E a outra cláusula, ou condição, que a gente colocou, é que o piso central da roda de negociação, que seria uma tábua octogonal de madeira que ficava no centro, nunca será apresentado ou exibido. Então, é sempre o chão da instituição que está implicado como fundação para aquele objeto transposto. E agora, Beatriz e Vânia, quando vocês tocam nisso, vocês trazem essa dimensão do corpo, dos corpos, da comunhão que, a meu ver, é uma resposta precisa, ou um contraponto crítico articulado por vocês, que surge da compreensão de uma gramática latente do próprio objeto e da sua função original. E nesse sentido, talvez a minha próxima pergunta vá um pouco por esse caminho. Vânia, você trouxe também a palavra pertencimento. A roda de negociação, no seu uso antecedente, era um espaço privado, no qual apenas certas pessoas tinham acesso e, na fala de vocês, vocês trazem a dimensão do público, do público por meio da rua. Então, eu queria entender um pouco e perguntar para vocês sobre isso, sobre esse atrito entre público e privado, e se vocês entendem que, talvez, tenha ocorrido uma espécie de fricção dentro do espaço institucional da Bienal, entre uma ideia de um corpo público e a própria instituição? Vocês acham que foi possível transformar aquele espaço privado, restrito, digamos, em um espaço um pouco mais público? Ou até mesmo entendem se a obra fracassou nesse sentido, ou se era ou não era sua função ou papel desde o princípio?

VM Olha, eu não sei. Eu acho que transformar a Bienal em um espaço público, me parece que não. Ainda é um espaço muito hierarquizado, isso inclusive foi falado nas conversas, trazido especialmente por artistas do campo institucional. O EGO é louco nesse lugar da arte, e tem certas práticas—vou derivar um pouco—certas práticas artísticas que só existem a partir de uma crítica institucional ao próprio campo da arte, enfim. No contexto das *Conversações*, a gente sentiu que as pessoas que estavam lá, ativistas, criadores de diversas áreas, artistas que atuam em suas comunidades—em sua maioria periféricas, não apenas em museus e galerias—estavam interessadas no campo da arte com um grande frescor. Vimos nessas falas a noção da prática artística como algo potente e livre, e não a de certa crítica institucional que, me parece, traz certo amargor. Assim, as falas das pessoas eram muito sobre reivindicar o espaço da arte para exercer a democracia e sobre estarem felizes por poder colocar isso naquela situação de circularidade na Bienal. A gente viu na fala de Carmem Silva, do Movimento Sem-Teto do Centro (MSTC),[6] por exemplo, a importância, para ela do movimento estar interagindo com os artistas, da potência dessa interação para o espaço das ocupações, para o espaço político. A crítica institucional apareceu de forma mais contundente justamente em artistas mais institucionalizados, como Roger Bernat, o que também foi importante. De maneira geral, foi muito gratificante, através da roda de negociação, trazer para a Bienal pessoas que têm uma vivência fora do âmbito mercantilizado que traz, em grande medida, certa afetação. Foi afirmada a dimensão da arte como uma dimensão da vida e não uma dimensão de um trabalho formal, necessariamente. Pensando dessa forma, talvez isso tenha trazido uma dimensão mais pública mesmo, não sei.

DdP Eu acho que tem algo aí, uma espécie de autocrítica necessária também, tanto da posição da própria instituição quanto de nós, artistas, que participamos desses processos. Lembro-me de uma fala de um querido professor que dizia que sem autocrítica é tudo autopromoção. Então, nesse sentido, acho importante também explicitar as diferenças entre um espaço público e um espaço institucional, as suas limitações, o seu alcance. E, talvez, qual é esse lugar de uma intersecção possível que você traz.

BC Era essa a questão. Assim, quando você falou na pergunta—será que a obra fracassou nesse sentido— para mim, a primeira coisa que me veio à cabeça é que, talvez, ela ter fracassado tenha sido um grande mérito. Sim, porque, para mim, não seria diferente. O espaço da Bienal já coloca essas questões institucionais por ser um espaço privado, e a gente sabe o papel que ele tem, que ele exerce e onde estão as hierarquias e as formas de poder de decisão desses espaços institucionalizados. Acho que colocar isso em uma obra, sei lá... nenhuma obra conseguiria fazer isso, transformar o espaço privado em público, e nem deveria, na verdade. A questão é, talvez, mostrar que existem fronteiras e que elas estão aqui—e que talvez a diluição seja outra coisa, em outro lugar.

VM A Bienal é uma instância super importante dentro do campo institucionalizado da arte, o que gera, querendo ou não, um ambiente extremamente formal. Para nós, com as *Conversações* e o que elas aportaram, ficou claro que a Bienal precisa dessas pessoas, e não o contrário. Sim, eu acho que as pessoas que participaram não precisam da Bienal para legitimar nada, nenhuma das práticas delas, que são de arte-vida. As pessoas desenvolvem suas práticas entre o social, o político e o artístico de forma orgânica. A Bienal, se tiver interesse em uma ressonância social mais ampla, vai precisar perceber que precisa cada vez mais de espaços que tragam esses agentes, e não que os que endossam o tempo todo apenas o que já está legitimado pelas galerias, pelos museus, pelos curadores, etc. Então, eu acho que a roda trouxe também isso.

DdP Recordo, em um primeiro momento, quando tivemos uma primeira reunião entre nós artistas, Marissa, David e eu, e vocês. Estávamos explicitando a importância do contrato e como ele emoldura o trabalho— conceitualmente e legalmente. Me recordo de vocês trazerem ao debate a impossibilidade de tradução deste objeto, da roda de negociação, pensando o objeto como um objeto contextual e já antevendo a árdua missão de traduzi-lo para um contexto outro, nesse caso um contexto local. Assim, pensando sobre o conceito de tradução de um objeto de um contexto particular para outro contexto específico, para além da questão do idioma, como vocês enxergam isso? Como veem a tradução desta obra na programação proposta por vocês?

VM Menino. Que interessante. Acabei de ler o livro de Júlio Plaza, "Tradução Intersemiótica", e eu tenho pensado muito nessa questão da tradução. O que é traduzir uma coisa em outra, traduzir uma prática em outra, e acho que, de fato, há um trabalho de tradução mesmo, de alguma forma, na obra *deposição*. Ele, Júlio Plaza, traz as palavras "tradução como rasura, tradução como emenda, tradução como extrojeção, tradução como transformação". Então, ele diz que "o projeto tradutor criativo define-se assim pelos conflitos, atritos e roteiros ambíguos dos seus interpretantes".[7] Eu acho que o trabalho *deposição*, ele próprio, realmente promove isso. É um processo de tradução criativa que vai justamente atuar nessas brechas. Ele vai procurar o conflito intrínseco daquele objeto, o que é dele, o conflito que está nele. Não é uma coisa que foi criada, o conflito nasce com aquele objeto e é em cima dele que vocês vão trabalhar, vão justamente encontrar essa transposição criativa. Não é o caso de esquecer os arquivos da roda de negociação e dizer não, agora a gente é uma grande comunidade circular, tal... querer fazer o que Rui Barbosa fez com os arquivos da escravidão, ou seja, queima-los.[8] É dizer o que ele é e, a partir daí, ir operando dentro da contradição, dentro da brecha que ele mesmo promove. Sim, acho que é um pouco isso.

DdP Sim, isso é ótimo. Agora, mais uma outra pergunta que eu estava pensando aqui. Em que momento vocês escolhem o título de *Conversações* para a programação da roda de negociação, com esse sufixo de "ção"? Acho que isso é muito revelador da potencialidade dos gestos, das ações e dos acontecimentos, de informarem ou transformarem aquele espaço, espaço tanto no sentido do objeto em si, como também num espaço mais amplo, institucional, e de um público, etc. E aí, talvez uma pergunta para você primeiro, Beatriz, você compreende, entende ou percebe que a roda de negociação, aquele objeto, aquela materialidade, aquela fisicalidade, se ela sai transformada dessa experiência?[9] Há uma diferença no objeto, do momento inicial da Bienal, da abertura, para agora? Como que ele volta para o circuito logístico global, fluindo nas mesmas rotas das commodities, dentro de um contêiner, após a Bienal? Ou, se o objeto segue sendo o mesmo e as ações estavam circunscritas em um contexto temporal e espacial mais efêmero? Então, queria que pensássemos um pouco nisso e, depois disso, eu acho que talvez a gente pudesse encerrar falando um pouco dos registros que vocês propuseram.

BC Eu não sei se eu estou sendo muito utópica, mas eu acho que a roda de negociação sai modificada sim. Eu não consigo pensar diferente. Eu acho que sai diferente praticamente desde o momento em que ela chega na Bienal e tem que se agregar a ela um guarda corpo durante a exposição.[10] E até mesmo as pessoas que, enquanto estiveram lá, sentadas, ficaram descascando a borracha da roda de negociação. Enfim, acho que isso produz uma modificação física, mas acho que vibracional também. É sobre a intenção que a gente coloca, que todos nós colocamos nessas trocas. Então eu diria que sim.

DdP De um certo momento, acho que em uma das apresentações do programa Novas Frequências,[11] e também na conversação do Kaká Werá,[12] ali eu senti que o objeto estava sendo exorcizado ou excomungado de alguma forma. Mas, ainda tem muito trabalho pela frente.

BC E talvez o trabalho vá ser completo se a roda de negociação realmente sair dos espaços institucionais da arte. Talvez aí ele complete a sua exorcização.

VM Verdade.

BC Enfim, tem milhares de possibilidades de espaços, não?

DdP Sim, sim.

BC Mas talvez, a roda de negociação tenha que ir para um acampamento do Movimento Sem-Terra (MST),[13] onde vai se encher de terra também.

DdP Quem sabe.

VM É que o campo da arte ainda é protegido, né, ainda tem a dimensão de proteção daquela estrutura.

BC *Sim, e* agora a roda de negociação faz parte de uma outra especulação, institucionalizada.

DdP A gente está em conversa, talvez para uma futura itinerância, com o contexto de uma universidade pública. Mas, ainda assim, é uma outra forma de instituição, digamos. Mas, acho que vocês, aí, revelaram também um pouco de um desejo nosso, um desejo de que o objeto também circule em outros lugares. Agora, talvez finalizando, eu fiquei pensando, em uma dimensão abstrata, de como mensurar a violência produzida por esse objeto, sobre qual é o montante dos valores que por ali passaram? O montante de metros quadrados de terra que, devido a esse objeto, foram especulados, grilados, desmatados? Quantas comunidades foram dizimadas pelo processo especulativo disso tudo? Entra em um lugar abstrato em termos da possibilidade de mensurar. E aí, nesse sentido, eu acho que a proposição de vocês, dos registros, acho que é algo que vale a pena tocar, que é como registrar o que ocorreu nas *Conversações*. Se vocês pudessem falar um pouco da publicação, acho que talvez fosse uma boa nota, sim, pra tentar fechar aqui essa entrevista.

VM Essa maneira com a qual propusemos a publicação parte muito dos nossos processos colaborativos. Uma participação ativa do público nos registros nos interessa, uma vez que promove uma alternativa ao gesto de um suposto especialista decidir sozinho quais os recortes que aquilo vai ter enquanto narrativa. Então, acho que a ideia de trazer o público como participante desse recorte, do que sobrevive dessas *Conversações*, é importante. Tem uma relação com a fotografia, hoje, que também nos parece delicada, que é a necessidade de fotografar o tempo inteiro nos processos contemporâneos. A publicação também expressa o nosso desejo de não fazer com que a fotografia seja a protagonista do registro. As fotografias acabam criando uma instância de documentação muito assimétrica. Quem tem a câmera toma as decisões da imagem, de quem vai estar ali, do recorte, e, para nós, esse discurso não expressa o que desejamos. É curioso, porque aconteceu justamente depois de uma pandemia na qual a virtualização foi brutal, foi constante, foi excessiva. O processo de gravação de vídeos foi muito intenso. Então, na roda de negociação, as conversas não tiveram nem gravação nem transmissão ao vivo. Quase não houve fotos, então o registro foi também corporal, né? A presença corporal foi o que fez com que essas conversações acontecessem. O desenho é uma dimensão muito corporal, então ele é um contínuo coerente com as escolhas do processo todo. Eu acredito assim. As pessoas não assinaram seus desenhos e escritas, e também nem houve esse interesse. As pessoas foram muito generosas nos seus registros. A publicação disso na plataforma pública da Bienal online devolve um pouco isso para os participantes, né? Essa malha de linhas que são nossa documentação. Acho que a publicação é uma grande malha, um grande tecido, sem muita hierarquia, sem muita edição do que aconteceu.[14]

BC Para mim, essa forma de registro tem a dimensão de uma contranarrativa. Nas ações artísticas que realizamos juntas, na rua, nas ações na cidade, sempre buscamos essa dimensão do relato. Porque normalmente o relato das cidades é bastante hegemônico, é um relato hegemônico da história. Então, achamos fundamental criar outras formas de registro. A possibilidade de incorporar anotações, rabiscos, desenhos criados por todos que participavam da roda, era também uma forma ativa das pessoas estarem envolvidas. Elas são responsáveis por definir o que daquilo fica, o que daquilo permanecerá. Também vejo esses relatos como o registro histórico criado com e pelos corpos que participaram daquele momento. O traçar, o olhar o espaço com o traço que sai da mão. Acho que tem uma potencialidade muito, muito importante neste ato de registro, como presença, como horizontalidade.

DdP Incrível. Me parece que é algo que foi atingido com os registros que vocês propuseram, algo menos hierárquico e mais plural como documentação.

Eu acho que a gente já está encerrando a entrevista, já foi cerca de uma hora de uma troca muito potente. Superou as minhas expectativas em muitos sentidos. Vocês vão agregar uma dimensão muito relevante e necessária para o livro. Obrigado.

VM Que maravilha a gente! A gente está super feliz. Foi lindo, né? A gente gostou muito de fazer essa história e a gente viveu muito aquele espaço da Bienal. Para a gente foi muito, muito prazeroso ter a oportunidade de conhecer essas pessoas e de dialogar com elas de uma forma tão presente.

DIMENSÃO DA ARTE, DIMENSÃO DA VIDA

1 O Coletivo Teatro Dodecafônico, fundado em 2008, cria provocações e estímulos transdisciplinares. O coletivo é formado por artistas de diversas formações, incluindo performance, teatro, dança, artes visuais, som e música. Desde 2014, o coletivo vem pesquisando o caminhar como prática estética e política, centrando suas investigações no espaço da rua e na reflexão sobre os desdobramentos das ações do corpo na cidade. Veja: https://coletivoteatrododecafonico.com.

2 *Mulheres Possíveis* é um projeto artístico multidisciplinar de Beatriz Cruz, Leticia Olivares, Sandra Ximenez e Vânia Medeiros, construído em torno dos temas corpo, gênero e encarceramento, e desenvolvido em colaboração com mulheres presas na Penitenciária Feminina da Capital (PFC) em São Paulo, desde 2016. As propostas do projeto ocorrem em vários idiomas, e o corpo está sempre no centro da experiência. O projeto é composto de ações realizadas dentro da PFC e em público.

3 Ver páginas 29–30.

4 *Conversações* foi um programa público projetado por Cruz e Medeiros e convocado sobre o piso da roda de negociação durante os três meses de exposição pública da 34ª Bienal de São Paulo no Pavilhão Ciccillo Matarazzo. O programa convidou palestrantes de movimentos sociais, organizações, comunidades, pesquisadores, artistas e educadores para conversar uns com os outros. O público visitante também foi convidado a participar da conversa durante várias partes do programa. Cada programa começou com a leitura de um *Enunciado* (escrito por Benedict, de Paula e Rueter; ver página 200–201); seguido por uma "ativação corpórea do espaço", e depois uma conversa de "contra-narrativas". Beatriz Cruz e Vânia Medeiros, *Arquivo gráfico da programação de ativação da obra "deposição"* (2021), https://issuu.com/bienal/docs/arquivo_grafico_bienal.

5 No início de cada programa, Medeiros e Cruz disponibilizaram aos participantes papel e caneta gratuitamente. Os desenhos espontâneos resultantes, que foram coletados no final de cada programa, estão documentados na publicação online mencionada anteriormente por Cruz e Medeiros: *Arquivo gráfico do programa de ativação da obra "deposição"* (2021), https://issuu.com/bienal/docs/arquivo_grafico_bienal.

6 O Movimento Sem-Teto do Centro (MSTC) é um movimento que luta pelo direito fundamental à moradia no centro de São Paulo, e é formado por mais de duas mil pessoas, entre adultos, crianças e jovens. No site, o MSTC afirma que "A moradia não é apenas uma propriedade física. 'Casa' significa muito mais e inclui a vida familiar, segurança, saúde, educação, acesso ao transporte e vida comunitária". Veja: https://www.movimentosemtetodocentro.com.br.

7 Júlio Plaza, "Tradução intersemiótica", *Coleção Estudos* 93 (1987).

8 Rui Barbosa foi o ministro da Fazenda do Brasil que, em 14 de dezembro de 1890, emitiu uma proclamação que ordenou a destruição de todos os registros governamentais que documentavam oficialmente os vínculos do Brasil com a escravidão, incluindo os registros de escravos, alegando que esta era uma rasura necessária da "mancha" deixada por esta história. Lamonte Aidoo, "The Racial and Sexual Paradoxes of Brazilian Slavery and National Identity." *Slavery Unseen: Sex, Power, and Violence in Brazilian History*, Duke University Press (2018), pp. 11–28. Ver: http://www.jstor.org/stable/j.ctv11314xj.5.

9 Uma pergunta semelhante é colocada na entrevista com Jacopo Crivelli Visconti e Paulo Miyada. Ver página 325.

10 Um guarda-corpo de aço foi construído sob medida para *deposição*, conforme exigido pelo código arquitetônico brasileiro. Anteriormente, em seu uso original na sala de comércio de grãos, as rodas de negociações de commodities agrícolas eram espaços negativos, acessados pelo topo por meio de um piso elevado intersticial que servia como piso térreo da própria sala. Sem isso, em sua instalação na Bienal, a antiga roda de negociação era acessada pelo centro, ou nível inferior dos degraus; e o anel externo, ou superior e último, das tábuas da roda de negociação, estava apoiado sobre uma subestrutura de andaimes como uma elevação de aproximadamente 2 metros. Isto exigiu a instalação de guarda-corpo ao longo das bordas externas da roda de negociação. O corrimão foi projetado pelos artistas, em discussão com a equipe curatorial da Bienal, e visualmente faz referência a um projeto padrão de corrimão para as rodas de negociações modernas de comércio de commodities em Chicago e em outros lugares. O guarda-corpo personalizado e o andaime reconstruído para sustentar os níveis superiores da roda de negociação, construídos pela Bienal, são elementos que não viajam com o trabalho *deposição*; ao contrário, estes elementos de suporte, ou adaptações arquitetônicas necessárias, são contextualmente renegociados com cada instituição expositora.

11 Novas Freqüências, fundado em 2011, é um festival brasileiro de música experimental e arte sonora. A equipe curatorial da 34ª Bienal de São Paulo convidou o diretor geral e curador do Novas Freqüências, Chico Dub, para curar uma série de programas de música experimental no contexto da obra *deposição*, realizado ao longo da exposição da Bienal.

12 Kaka Werá, um escritor, ativista e professor brasileiro Kayapó, conduziu uma conversa participativa no piso da roda de negociação, com Medeiros e Cruz, sobre o poder político e poético dos sonhos nas tradições indígenas, para um dos programas *Conversações* , realizado no dia 4 de dezembro de 2021. Seu trabalho, ao longo de 25 anos, envolveu a disseminação de conhecimentos e valores ancestrais indígenas. Veja: http://34.bienal.org.br/agenda/9560.

13 "O Movimento dos Trabalhadores Rurais Sem Terra (MST) é um movimento social de massa, formado por trabalhadores rurais e por todos aqueles que querem lutar pela reforma agrária e contra a injustiça e a desigualdade social no meio rural. O MST nasceu através de um processo de ocupação de latifúndios e tornou-se um movimento nacional em 1984. Ao longo de mais de duas décadas, o movimento liderou mais de 2.500 ocupações de terras, com cerca de 370.000 famílias—famílias que hoje se estabeleceram em 7,5 milhões de hectares de terra, conquistados como resultado das ocupações". Veja: https://www.mstbrazil.org/content/what-mst.

14 Beatriz Cruz e Vânia Medeiros, *Arquivo gráfico da programação de ativação da obra "deposição"* (2021), https://issuu.com/bienal/docs/arquivo_grafico_bienal.

Daniel de Paula (BR/NL) is a Brazilian visual artist and researcher. de Paula has been awarded the Mondriaan Funds Proven Talent Award and has exhibited widely at institutions such as MASP, São Paulo; The Renaissance Society, Chicago; Padiglione d'Arte Contemporanea, Milan; Kunsthal Gent; The Arts Club of Chicago; Estação Pinacoteca, São Paulo; and the 2022 Lyon Biennale. His work is represented by Galeria Jaqueline Martins, Francesca Minini Gallery and Lumen Travo Gallery, and has been reviewed in Artforum, Texte zur Kunst, Flash Art, Mousse Magazine, Folha de São Paulo, and Het Parool. He has participated in several international artistic residencies such as the Jan van Eyck Academie, FLACC, and KIOSKO.

Marissa Lee Benedict (US/NL) and David Rueter (US/NL) are visual artists, writers, and researchers working in collaboration since 2014. Benedict and Rueter have exhibited works at The US Pavilion for the 2018 Venice Architecture Biennale; The Arts Club of Chicago; The Museum of Contemporary Photography, Chicago; The Renaissance Society at the University of Chicago; and Contemporary Art Brussels, amongst others. They have received major grants from institutions such as the National Endowment for the Arts and the Joan Mitchell Foundation. Their work has been reviewed by publications such as *Artforum*, *Revista, Agenda Magazine,* and *Hyperallergic*. They have collaboratively participated in numerous international artistic residencies including Rupert, the Banff Centre, and the Jan van Eyck Academie.

It was at the Jan van Eyck Academie in 2018 that Benedict, de Paula and Rueter began their collaborative work *deposition* (2018–ongoing) with the salvage of the last remaining commodities trading pit from the Chicago Board of Trade. Their work has been awarded individual grant support from The Graham Foundation for Advanced Studies in the Fine Arts, and and has been exhibited at the 34th Bienal de São Paulo, The Arts Club of Chicago, and The Renaissance Society.

Karsten Lund (US) is Curator at the Renaissance Society at the University of Chicago, where he organizes exhibitions, edit publications, and oversees public programs. His most recent exhibitions include new commissions by Haig Aivazian (2021), Jill Magid (2021), Matthew Metzger (2021), and LaToya Ruby Frazier (2019, co-curated with Solveig Øvstebø), as well as group shows such as *Nine Lives* (2020, with Caroline Picard) and *Unthought Environments* (2018). His latest group exhibition, *Fear of Property* (2022), features new work by Benedict, de Paula and Rueter, an off-shoot of *deposition*. As an editor, Lund works on three to four books every year at the Renaissance Society, including recent titles by Kevin Beasley and Jill Magid. He has also independently edited volumes such as *Spells* by Irena Haiduk (2015, Sternberg Press).

Beatriz Cruz (BR) is a performer and educator. Her creations move between the scenic and visual arts as she seeks the crossings between art and life; body-city; and art-activism. A specialist in body studies, she researches walking as an artistic and political practice. In collaboration with Vânia Medeiros (BR), a visual artist and educator, Cruz curated and organized the *Conversações* programming series convened on the work *deposition* for the 34th Bienal de São Paulo.

Yamila Goldfarb (BR) holds a PhD in human sciences from the University of São Paulo. Her research develops and deepens studies in Latin-American geopolitics, geoeconomic, social movements, and development of rural territories and food security with an emphasis on the financialization of agriculture, territorial impacts and the corporatization of the agricultural sector in Brazil and Argentina.

Cameron Hu (US/DE) studies emerging formations of liberal imperialism and technoscientific capitalism. He received a BA in Arabic and Islamic Studies from the University of Pennsylvania and a PhD in Anthropology from the University of Chicago, where his dissertation, *Knowing Destroying*, received the Daniel F. Nugent Prize in historical anthropology. He has published widely in social theory and art criticism. As a member of collective LiCo he makes fictions, films, and installations that contemplate emerging choreographies of the mental and the environmental (most recently for Het Nieuwe Instituut, Rotterdam, and Haus der Kulturen der Welt, Berlin). Currently living in Berlin, he is at work on a book about a Texas oil field and a series of essays about necessity.

Vânia Medeiros (BR) is a visual artist, designer, and professor. She is completing a Masters and PhD in Architecture and Urbanism from the University of São Paulo (FAU-USP), where she is researching transdisciplinary practices and collaborative structures. She has programmed, performed, and exhibited at institutions such as the Museum of Modern Art, São Paulo; Institutio Tomie Ohtake, São Paulo; and Sesc, São Paulo. She coordinates an independent publishing platform called Conspire Edições. Medeiros, in collaboration with Beatriz Cruz (BR), a performer and educator, curated and organized the *Conversações* programming series convened on the work *deposition* for the 34th Bienal de São Paulo.

Paulo Miyada (BR) is a curator and researcher of contemporary art. He holds a Master's Degree in History of Architecture and Urbanism from FAU - USP, for which he is also a graduate. He was the adjunct curator of the 34th Bienal de São Paulo (2020-21) and is the chief curator of the Tomie Ohtake Institute, where he coordinates the Research and Curation Center and where he curated, amongst other exhibitions, *AI-5 50 Years - It is Still Not Over Yet* (2018), and *Anna Maria Maiolino - PSSSIIIUUU . . .* (2022). He is currently the Adjunct Curator at large for Centre Pompidou, Paris, with focus on Latin American art.

Dan Peterman (US) is an internationally recognized visual artist and Chicago-based organizer. He is the Founder of Blackstone Bicycle Works (now an ongoing youth education program of Experimental Station), and Founder of Monk Parakeet, a flexible experimental art project and curatorial platform co-located with Peterman Studio and Experimental Station. Peterman is Professor in the College of Architecture and the Arts at the University of Illinois at Chicago. His works have been exhibited at Documenta 14 in Athens and Kassel; Museum of Contemporary Art, Chicago; Venice Biennial; Van Abbe Museum, Eindhoven; Kunsthalle Basel; Smart Museum of Art, Chicago; University of Chicago; among other venues.

Ana Teixeira Pinto (PR/DE) is a writer and cultural theorist based in Berlin. She is a guest professor at the Academy of Fine Arts Nuremberg (AdBK) and a theory tutor at the Dutch Art Institute. Her writings have appeared in publications such as *Third Text*, *Afterall*, *e-flux journal*, *Manifesta Journal*, and *Texte zur Kunst*. She is the editor of a forthcoming book series on the anti-political turn to be published by Sternberg Press. Together with Kader Attia and Anselm Franke, she is organizing the conference and podcast series *The White West: Whose Universal*, taking place at HKW Berlin, and she is a member of the 2022 Berlin Biennial artistic team.

Jacopo Crivelli Visconti (BR) is an independent critic and curator. Born in Naples, Italy, and a resident of São Paulo, he holds a PhD in architecture from the Universidade de São Paulo (USP) and is the author of the book *Novas derivas* (WMF Martins Fontes, São Paulo, Brazil, 2014; Ediciones Metales Pesados, Santiago, Chile, 2016). He was chief curator of the 34th Bienal de São Paulo (2020-21). Other recent curation includes the Brazilian pavilion for the 59th Venice Biennale (2022); *Untimely, Again*, Pavilion of the Republic of Chipre at the 58th Venice Biennale (2019); *Brasile – Il coltello nella carne*, Padiglione d'arte contemporanea (PAC), Milan (2018), among other exhibitions. He regularly collaborates with publications on contemporary art, architecture and design, contributes to exhibition catalogs, and writes monographs on artists.

IMAGE CREDITS

All images of artworks, renderings, drawings, video stills, and documents produced by and copyright of the artists (Benedict, de Paula, and Rueter) unless otherwise noted.

13: Diagram (2018, 2022), de Paula, Rueter, Benedict.

14–27: Renderings of trading pit pieces (2018–2022), David Rueter.

29–30: Manifesto (2018–2020), Rueter, Benedict, de Paula.

32: Surveillance camera diagram from US Patent.

34–44: Remotely captured surveillance of the trading pit in storage, 2020–2021. Camera installation assistance by Alexander DeGraaf.

46: “A Flurry of Wheat” printed in Harper’s New Monthly Magazine, Volume 61, June-November 1880. Artist unknown.

48–76: All historic image sources and credits included in chapter captioning (77–78).

80: Receipt for the issue of Reuben S. Jenning’s patent for “Improvement in Trading-Pits” (Letters Patent No. 203,837; dated 21 May 1878, application filed 19 December 1877). Record Group 241; United States Patent and Trademark Office; Patent Case Files, 1836-1978; National Archives Identifier 302050; National Archives at Kansas City.

82–97: Photos by Renata de Bonis.

108: Photo by Dan Peterman.

109: (Top) photo by Renata de Bonis, (bottom) photo by Dan Peterman.

110: Photo by Dan Peterman.

112: Scan of shipping container receipt, 2021.

116–125: Photos by Renata de Bonis.

126–133: Photos by David Rueter.

134–141: Ship tracking data collected by David Rueter, 2021.

142–156: © Fundação Bienal de São Paulo, photos by Levi Fanan.

157: Receipt of transfer of R$ 8,76 to the artists by the Fundação Bienal de São Paulo, executing the artists’ Property Lease Agreement (2021–2021).

160–170: Photos by Everton Ballardin.

172–205: Property Lease Agreement (2021–2021) by the artists, produced with the generous legal expertise of Rodrigo Sadi, Esq., Partner of McLaughlin & Stern LLP.

224: Liquified pit patent diagram (2018), Benedict, de Paula, Rueter.

237: G.A. Wentworth and David Eugene Smith, Plane And Solid Geometry (Boston: Ginn and Company, 1899) 94. See: https://archive.org/details/planeandsolidge04wentgoog/page/n109/mode/2up.

254: A script from the 11 November 2021 manifestation by the collective Dolores Boca Aberta, Brava Companhia, Companhia Antropofágica, Estudo De Cena, Cia Canina, the Levante Popular da Juventude, the Movimento dos Trabalhadores pelos Direitos (MTD), and the Movimento dos Trabalhadores Rurais Sem Terra (MST). Poem in the right column by Luciano Carvalho.

268–280: © Fundação Bienal de São Paulo, photos by Levi Fanan.

282–284: Photos by José Antonio Pelegrini Jr.

286–290: Photos by Miguel Salvatore.

292–293: Photos by Chico Dub.

294–299: Photos by José Antonio Pelegrini Jr.

300–315: © Fundação Bienal de São Paulo, photos by Levi Fanan.

348–352: Renderings of trading pit pieces (2018–2022), David Rueter.

ARTIST ACKNOWLEDGMENTS

Daniel de Paula

Com amor para Renata, pelo afeto telúrico; para Christopher, pela potência transgressora; para Edson, pelo clarão compartilhado; e para Ana, espírito perpétuo, pelo alimento copioso.

David Rueter

With immense gratitude and affection for my family: Marissa, Marc, Anne, Joan, and Dylan — for their endless love and their inquisitive spirit.

Marissa Lee Benedict

With deep gratitude, to the extended community of Chicago artists; to the many hands and voices sharing the weight of this work; to Patricia and John, for all they have gifted; to Anne, for the morning light; to Harry, Allyson, and Alex, for all I have learned in love; to Daniel, para o coração aberto e a visão crítica; and to David, for the continuously unfolding joy of life with you.

BIENAL ACKNOWLEDGMENTS

Jacopo Crivelli Visconti
Paulo Miyada
Carla Zaccagnini
Francesco Stocchi
Ruth Estévez
Ana Roman
Divina Prado
Elvira Dyangani Ose
José Olympio da Veiga Pereira
Dora Silveira Corrêa
Antonio Lessa Garcia
Felipe Isola
Joaquim Millan
Dorinha Santos
Felipe Melo Franco
Maurizio Zelada
Cenotécnica
Deborah Moreira
Caroline Carrion
Giovanna Querido
Levi Fanan
Luciana Alves
Vânia Medeiros
Beatriz Cruz
Chico Dub
Festival Novas Frequências
Simone Lira
Teatro Cultura Artística
Fernanda Carvalho
Educational Team

The exhibition of *deposition* (2018–ongoing) in 2021 at the 34th Bienal de São Paulo—*Though it's dark, still I sing* received generous support from the Graham Foundation for Advanced Studies in the Fine Arts, Resource Center (Chicago, IL), University of Oregon, Oregon Arts Commission, and the Ford Family Foundation.

bienal são paulo

Graham Foundation

ACKNOWLEDGMENTS

The publication received generous institutional support from the Graham Foundation for Advanced Studies in the Fine Arts, Francesca Minini, and Lumen Travo Gallery.

The publication received generous individual support from Greg and Margo Plaunt, Naomi Sabel, Collin Canright and Lillian Canright, Sarah Finlay and Patrick Murcia, Janine Mileaf, A. Laurie Palmer, Teresa Silva, Dan Sullivan and Edra Soto, Laura Vandenburgh, Anne Wilson.

Copies of the book are included in the collections of: the Museum of Contemporary Photography at Columbia College Chicago (US); the Flaxman Library at the School of the Art Institute of Chicago (US); the Jan van Eyck Academie Library (Netherlands); and the Fleet Library at Rhode Island School of Design (US).

Graham Foundation

FRANCESCA MININI

LUMEN TRAVO

COLOPHON

Editor: Karsten Lund
Design: Carolina Aboarrage, Studio Kader
Publication producer: Marissa Lee Benedict
Copyediting (English): Sarah Kramer, Aidan Wall, Jayne Wilkinson
Translations (Portuguese / English): Daniel de Paula, Marissa Lee Benedict
Copyediting (Portuguese): Paloma Durante

Published and distributed by
Mousse Publishing
Contrappunto s.r.l.
Via Pier Candido Decembrio 28,
20137, Milan–Italy

First edition: 2023
Printed in Belgium by die Keure
ISBN: 978-88-6749-546-7

Available through:
Mousse Publishing, Milan
moussemagazine.it
DAP | Distributed Art Publishers, New York
artbook.com
Les presses du réel, Dijon
lespressesdureel.com
Antenne Books, London
antennebooks.com

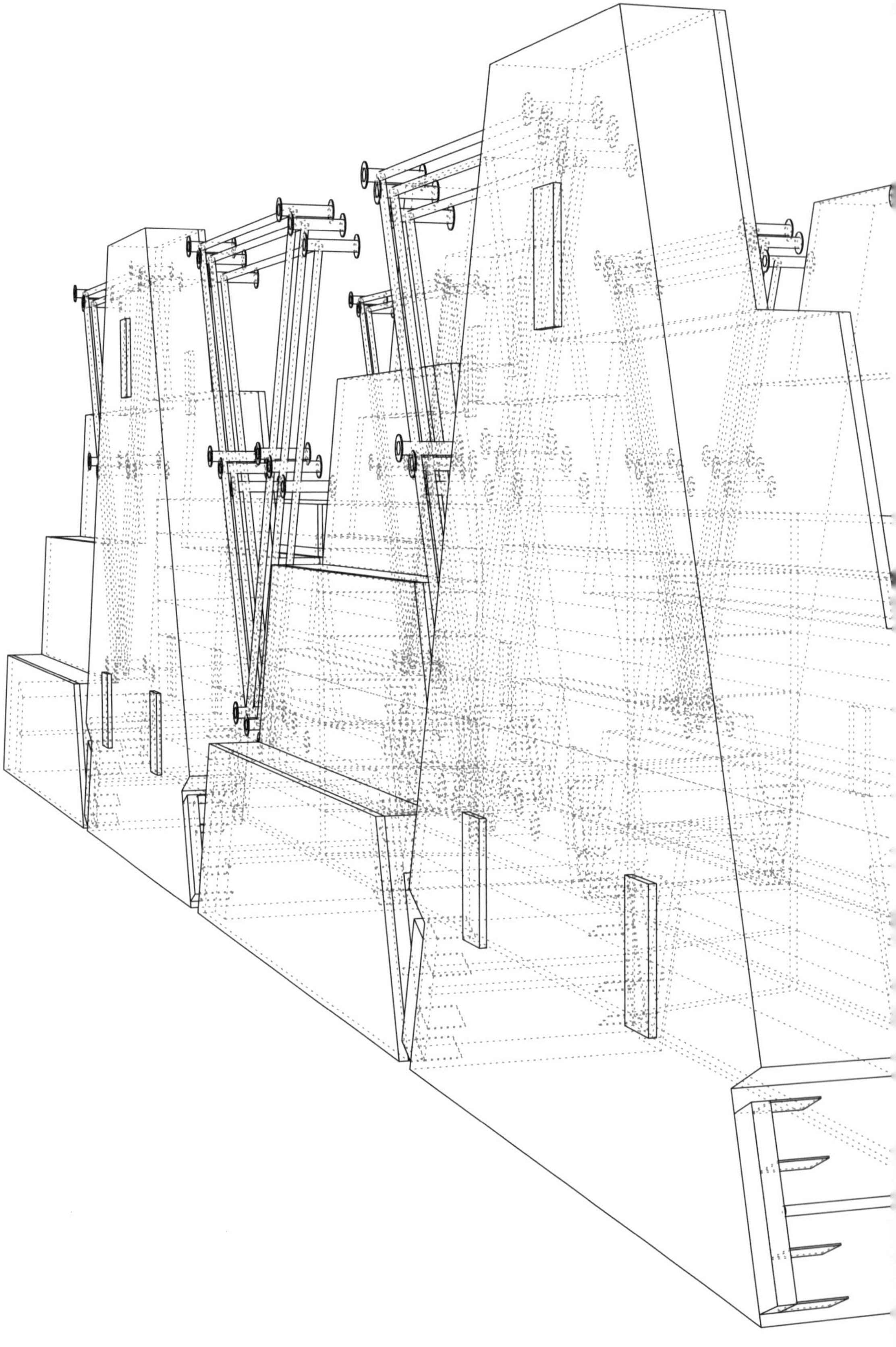

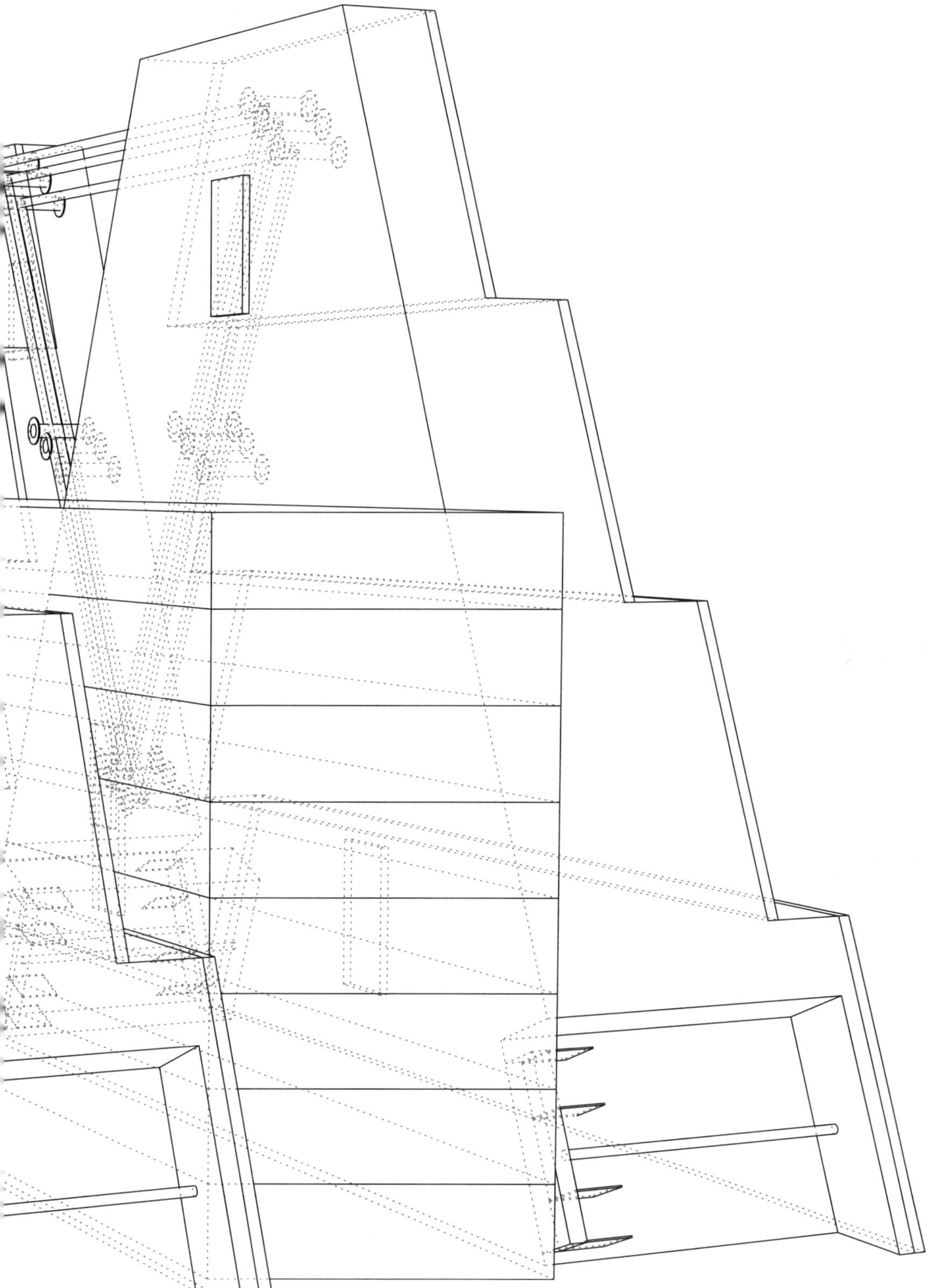

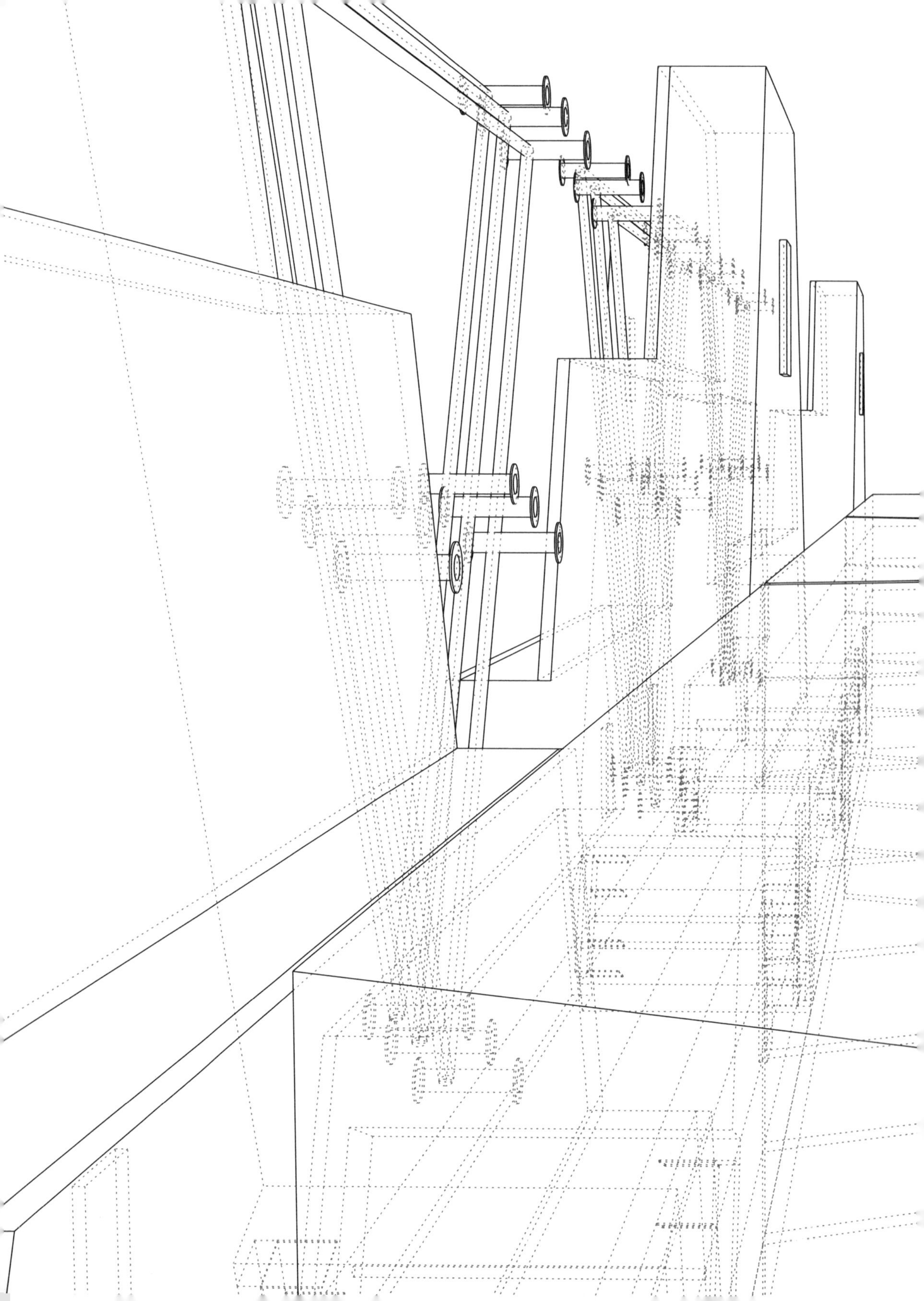

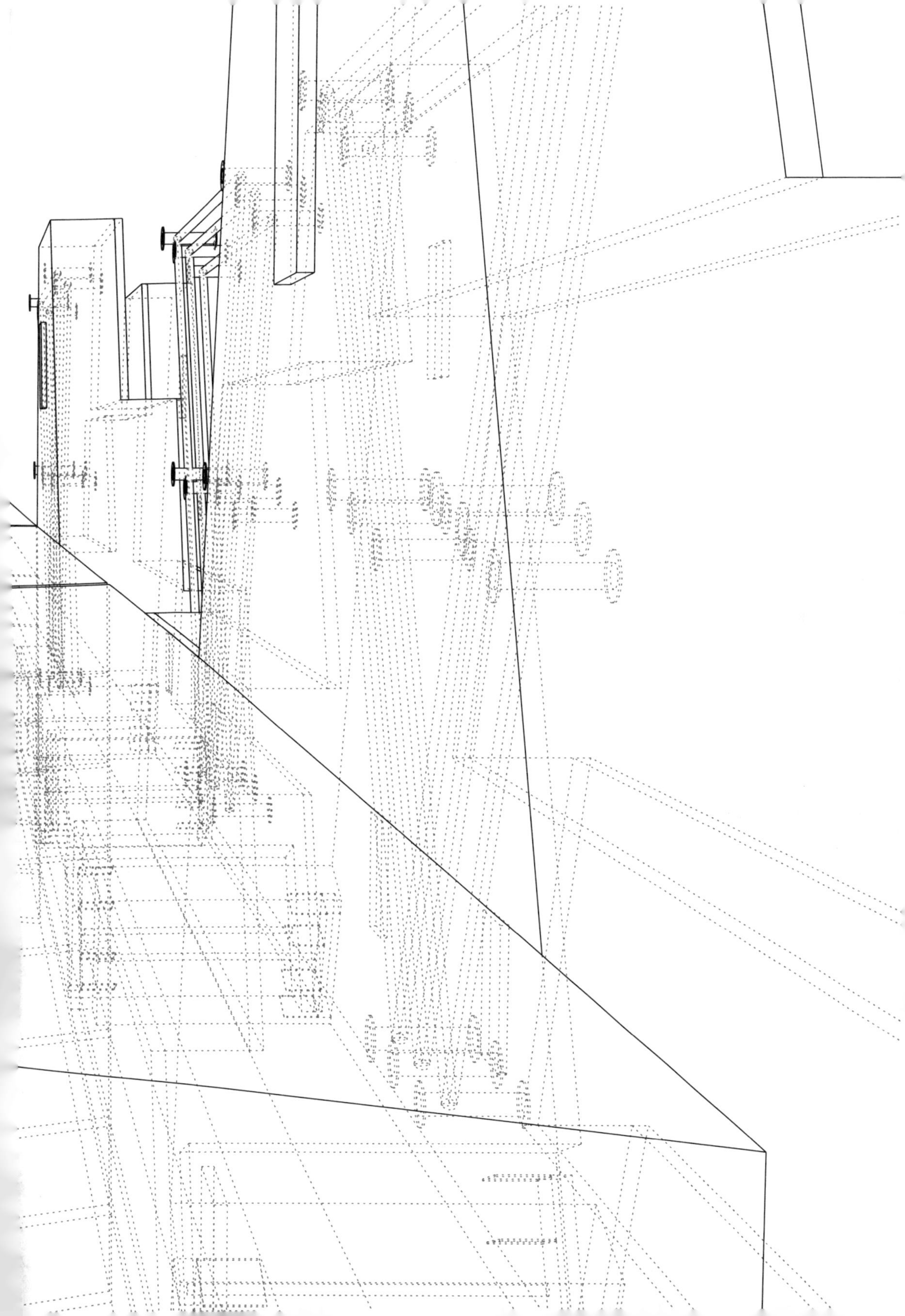

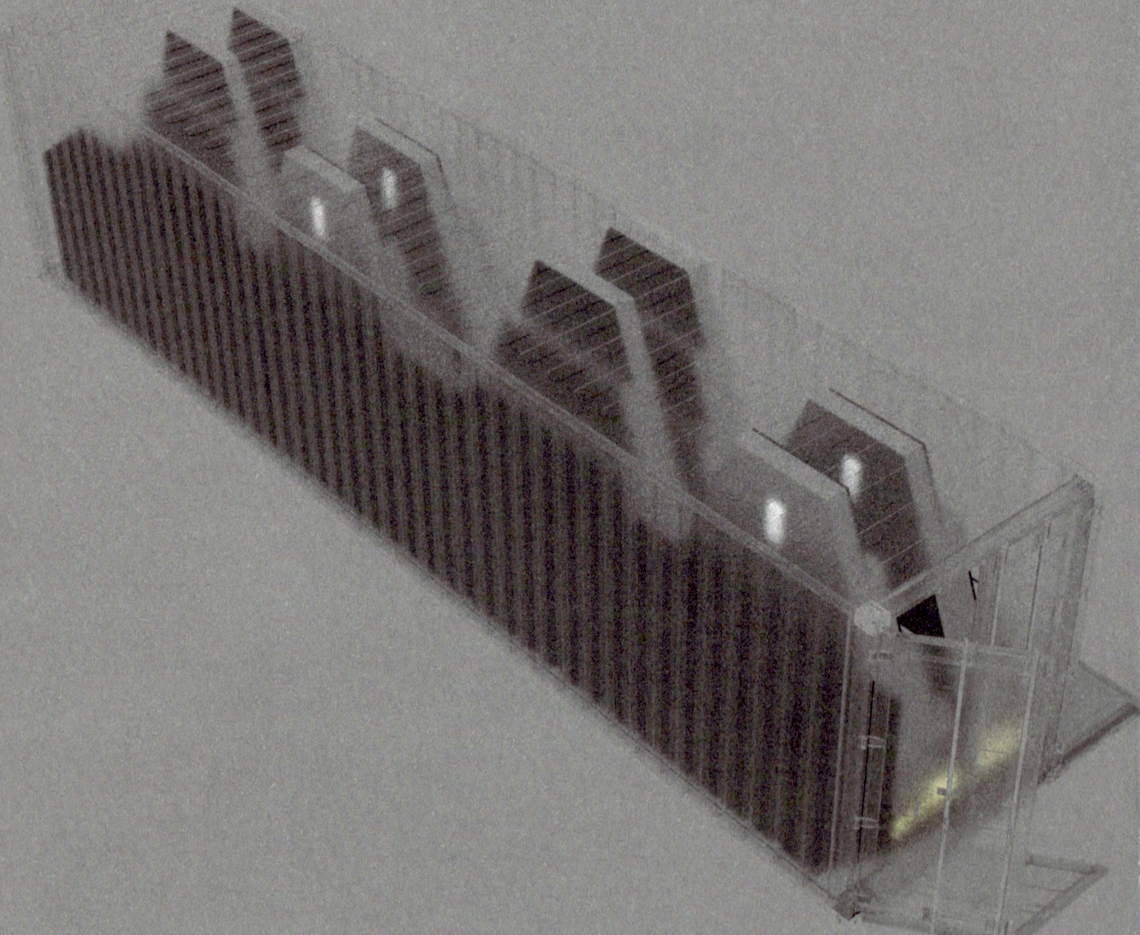